FROMMER'S
HAWAII
ON $50 A DAY

by Faye Hammel
and Sylvan Levey

1988–89 Edition

Published by Prentice Hall Press
A Division of Simon & Schuster, Inc.
Gulf + Western Building
One Gulf + Western Plaza
New York, NY 10023

ISBN 013-384538-9

Manufactured in the United States of America

CONTENTS

MAPS

HAWAII ON $50 A DAY

The $25-A-Day Travel Club—How to Save Money on All Your Travels

THIS BOOK WAS WRITTEN for the express purpose of disposing of a couple of myths. The first is that a South Seas idyll—that longed-for journey to enchanted islands that everyone dreams of at one time or another—is beyond the means of the budget traveler. We're here to tell you that all that is ancient history. Less than five jet hours and as little as $169 away from the West Coast lie the islands of Hawaii, a name to conjure dreams, a place to explore on a shoestring budget.

People will tell you, of course, that the 50th American state is one of the most expensive areas on earth to visit. It is—and it isn't—depending on which Hawaii you care to see. If you choose prepackaged and preconceived Hawaii, you'll undoubtedly stay at plush hotels, dine at expensive restaurants, be herded around in sightseeing limousines with people just like the folks you left back home—and pay a pretty penny for it. But if you agree with us that travel is a do-it-yourself activity, if you'd rather leave the plush and nonsense to others and strike out on your own to find out how the islanders really live, you'll find that a vacation in Hawaii is one of the best travel bargains anywhere. For, contrary to legend, Hawaii has dozens of comfortable, clean, and reasonable hotels; scores of restaurants where the food is exotic and inexpensive; and most important, an almost endless list of free and low-cost entertainment—from beaches to bon dances, from museum browsing to mountain climbing, from hiking to dancing the hula. Add to that an incredibly cheap air fare, and you've got the ideal place for a budget vacation—even in these inflationary times.

WHAT $50 A DAY MEANS: As in most of the other books in this series, our aim is to show you how to keep your basic living costs—*room and three meals only*—down to somewhere around $50 a day. There's nothing fantastic or gimmicky about that goal. Since the costs of transportation, shopping, sightseeing, and entertainment are all in addition to that figure, our book prescribes reasonable methods of vacationing on a budget.

We think you'll agree that by keeping these room-and-meal expenses low, you can make a substantial dent in the overall cost of your trip. But more important, we believe you'll have more fun—and enjoy a more meaningful vacation—by relying on your brains rather than your pocketbook. Hawaii is one of the few places where you can still live comfortably on a limited budget, even in the face of tremendous inflation that is raising prices everywhere. In fact, many people who used to travel abroad for their holidays are finding Hawaii one of the best bargain areas anywhere. And considering that this is an enormously popular resort area, $50 a day is very little to pay. We'll give you specific tips on how to do it elsewhere in this chapter. But first, back to our debunking.

MYTHS AND PARADOXES: The second myth was neatly put by a friend of ours, a sophisticated woman who travels regularly to Europe. "Why go all the way to Hawaii," she asks, "just to find yourself at a beach?" Now no one in his or her right mind would dispute the glory of Hawaii's beaches, some of the best in the world. But anyone who looks on Hawaii as merely a seaside resort is missing some of the most profound, exciting, and exotic travel experiences available anywhere.

The essence of Hawaii, its special mystery, lies in its startling and subtle paradoxes. Take its people, as fascinating a mixture of humanity as you'll find on this planet. The children and grandchildren of Stone Age warriors, New England missionaries, and Oriental plantation workers mingled and intermarried to create nothing less than a new race. Scratch an islander and you'll find a Hawaiian-Chinese-Portuguese, a Japanese-American-Tahitian or perhaps an English-Filipino-Korean. The typical islander—if such a creature exists—long ago gave up counting the racial strains in his or her background; it got too complicated. Hawaii's people, American in ideals, optimism, and drive, still retain the serenity of Polynesia and the Orient. They avidly follow the scores of baseball games played by fellow citizens 6,000 miles away in Boston or Philadelphia, yet many of them dream of going to visit "the old country"—Japan, China, the Philippines. And as if in answer to the bigots who cringe at "mongrelization," the interracial democracy of Hawaii has produced the most attractive Americans anywhere. Hawaii's children are unbelievably exquisite, a mixture of the best the races can give to each other.

But the paradoxes don't stop here. They are even more astonishing on a sheer topographical level; Hawaii has the kind of scenery that all but overwhelms the senses. Steep cliffs tumbling down to coral beaches, tropical rain forests and woods that run a hundred shades of green, black sand beaches and pounding blue surf, scores of tropical blossoms, vying for attention at every turn —this is the landscape. Even more awe-inspiring, the volcanoes that created these islands from the vast nothingness of ocean are still alive. The land is still being born. Drive mile after mile on the Big Island of Hawaii and see where the lava flows have scalded their way to the sea and how slowly life renews itself over the years. Then go to Kauai and see what the centuries and the forces of erosion have done to a much older and extinct volcano. You will have a sense of the youth—and age—of the earth that you can get nowhere else.

The paradox that is Hawaii continues on a third level as well. In less than 200 years it has gone from Stone Age to Space Age, from a primitive island kingdom ruled by stern gods of nature to the fastest-growing state in the U.S., ruled by booming laws of economics. Industry soars, hotel and apartment construction grows apace, population and tourism increase astronomically, Space Age science and education become established, and wherever one looks, something new is being built, planned, developed. "Full speed ahead" are the words on every front. Still, despite the aggressive energy of the times, Hawaii somehow manages to retain its gentleness, its warmth, its relaxed nature. The spirit of aloha remains untouched, a calm center in the eye of the hurricane of progress. Which is perhaps why so many people who've been everywhere and back can't seem to get enough of Hawaii.

LIVING ON $50 A DAY: The trick in Honolulu is to stay at a small apartment-hotel or condominium complex, complete with a built-in money-saving device: a kitchenette. This doesn't mean, however, that you'll spend your vacation slaving away at a hot stove. It means only that you'll fix breakfast, maybe pack a sandwich or some marvelous fresh fruit for a picnic or a light supper, and dine out once a day (preferably at lunchtime, when prices are always low and values best). Many of Hawaii's visitors live just this way—but they live in expensive apartment-hotels. We've scoured the state looking for *budget* apartment-hotels and have come up with a surprisingly large number of them.

To stay within the boundaries of a $50-a-day budget, you should be part of a twosome, which means that you will have a total of $100 per day to spend on room and meals. To stay on the low side of this budget, you will want to choose a room between $25 and $45 a day double. If you wish to live a little higher, then choose a room that goes between $45 to $55 or more a day. Whatever will be left over from your planned $100-a-day-for-two living expenses can be used for your meals; in our chapter on restaurants, we'll show you how to eat inexpensively and well, figuring about $12 to $14 for dinner, about $5 or $6 for lunch, roughly $3 to $4 for breakfast. Of course, whatever you save by eating in means so much more in the kitty for other pleasures.

THE SEASON, THE COMPETITION, AND THE PRICE: You should bear in mind another important fact about hotels in Hawaii: their rates usually vary according to season and business. The hotel industry is highly competitive, and room prices go up or down as conditions dictate.

In general, you'll get a much better bargain if you avoid the winter season —mid-December to mid-April. That's when *everybody* seems to want to go to Hawaii, and many visitors—especially those from cold areas like western Canada and Alaska—often stay for a few months at the budget apartment-hotels. Many hotels routinely impose a surcharge of at least $5 to $10 per room during that period. The summer months of June, July, and August are also busy, but many hotels maintain "low-season" rates in those months, and during the months of October, November, and May all kinds of choice rooms are yours for the picking. If you think you'd like to spend the Christmas–New Year's season in the islands, make reservations as far in advance as you possibly can; many hotels accept reservations as much as six months to a year in advance for this insanely popular period. Reservations are a good idea, in fact, any time of the year. Budget accommodations do exist, but they are much sought after even now that the supply of hotel rooms has overshot the demand—few of the new hotels that have been built in Waikiki in the past few years have been in the economy category.

The high-season markup also extends to car rentals and other visitors' services as well. The motto seems to be, alas: "Get what the traffic will bear."

The Hawaiian "season," incidentally, has little to do with the weather, except the weather back home. In the islands the weather is usually good year round. Hawaii's climate is subtropical, with spring-like temperatures averaging about 75° Fahrenheit and seldom going more than six or seven degrees above or below this point. In midwinter you can occasionally get some "raw" days in the low- to mid-60s and in midsummer some humid ones in the 80s. (August is probably the most humid month of the year; if your room does not have cross-ventilation to allow the trade winds to come through, air conditioning is essential at that time.) Cool waters drifting down from the Bering Sea make the islands ten degrees cooler than other places in the same latitude—and the trade winds provide balmy breezes. As for rain, we must admit that we have experienced some dreary, rainy days here, especially in the winter—anytime from November to March. But most of the time showers are brief and seldom heavy enough to spoil the pleasures of a vacation.

A BIT OF GEOGRAPHY: Most people think of Hawaii as synonymous with Honolulu and Waikiki Beach (they probably know they're on the island of Oahu), but they're a bit vague about the names of the other islands. Actually, there are 122 islands in the Hawaiian chain, a great volcanic mountain range spreading 1,500 miles across the floor of the Pacific, from Hawaii on the southeast to Midway and Kure islands in the northwest. Many of these are just jagged rocks or sand shoals, however, and the term "Hawaiian Islands" usually refers only to eight: Oahu (on which you find Honolulu), Hawaii or the Big Island, Maui, Kauai, Molokai, Lanai, Kahoolawe, and Niihau. The first five are the ones of greatest interest to the visitor, and the ones we'll describe in this book. Of the last three, Lanai is a pineapple plantation island, almost completely owned by Castle & Cooke, the parent company of the Dole Pineapple Company, with some possible resort development in the near future; Kahoolawe, uninhabited, is a target range for American planes and ships; and Niihau, where an ancient Hawaiian community survives, is private property not open to the public.

ISLANDER ORIGINS: The Hawaiian Islands were settled about a thousand years ago by Polynesians who came most likely from Tahiti, crossing the Pacific in outrigger canoes and performing feats of navigation undreamed of by their European contemporaries. They were Stone Age people, blissfully unaware of the modern world until Captain Cook inadvertently discovered the islands in 1778 (he was seeking the Northwest Passage) and received a god's welcome. He named them the Sandwich Islands, in honor of the Earl of Sandwich. Then came fur traders, merchants, whalers, adventurers from all over, to the crossroads of the Pacific and its languorous pleasure ports. In 1820, from Boston, arrived other travelers, those who would settle the islands and, more than any others, determine Hawaii's pattern of civilization. These were the missionaries, earnest men and women intent on converting the "childlike" heathen to the nononsense Calvinism of New England. The missionaries never went home; their children stayed to inherit the islands and their riches, to create the great business empires that still rule Hawaii. The Polynesians sickened and dwindled and refused to work the white man's sugar and pineapple plantations. But the poor of the Orient came, tens of thousands of them—contract labor pursuing the dream of a better life. (In the great mainland cities at the same time, the dispossessed of Europe were finding their America.) Somehow the welcoming aloha of the islands found a way to absorb them all. Now the era of settling the land is over, and today's "immigrants" are Japanese, Filipinos, and many, many mainland *haoles* (whites or foreigners): Westchester businessmen, California schoolteachers, tourists from all over who fall in love with the islands and forget to go home.

REQUIRED READING: Don't—this is a must—get on the plane without having read James Michener's great epic novel of the islands, *Hawaii;* not to do so would be as bad as forgetting your bathing suit. Michener has taken a leading figure from each of the groups who settled in the islands—the Polynesians, American missionaries, Chinese, Japanese—and through their stories, told the story of the islands. The book, which is available in paperback, will illuminate your trip as nothing else will. According to Michener, Francine du Plessix Gray's *Hawaii: The Sugar-Coated Fortress,* published by Random House, picks up where his book left off, and we agree with that judgment. It is not a novel, but an insightful, uncompromising look at what is really happening in modern Hawaii. (This one is no longer available in the bookstores, but you should be able to get it at the public library.) A newer book, *Hawaii: An Uncommon History*, by Edward Koesting, published by W. W. Norton & Co., has received high critical praise and is well worth your time. So, too, certainly, is Gavan Daws's *A Shoal of Time*, a history of Hawaii from 1778 (Captain Cook) until statehood (1959), published by the University of Hawaii Press. For more about Hawaii's background, read Ben Adams's *Hawaii, The Aloha State*, a beautifully lucid history of the islands, published by Hill and Wang and available in any library, as is Lawrence Fuch's *Hawaii Pono*, published by Harcourt Brace Jovanovich, a masterful sociological study. Scores of photographers were given one day assignments in Hawaii and the result was a fascinating tome that may cause you to exceed your airline baggage weight limit: *A Day in the Life of Hawaii*, Workman Publishing. *A Hawaiian Reader*, a delightful anthology of pieces on Hawaii past and present written by, among others, Jack London, Robert Louis Stevenson, and W. Somerset Maugham, also makes absorbing reading before, during, or after a stay in the islands. This one's in paperback too.

KNOWING SOME HAWAIIAN: You don't have to learn the language, since everyone speaks English. But the islanders do pepper their vocabulary with lots of Hawaiian words, and almost all place names are Hawaiian. So it's a good idea to bone up on a few pronunciation rules and learn a few words. The original Hawaiians spoke a Polynesian dialect but they had no written language; the missionaries transcribed it in order to teach them to read the Bible, and they made it as easy as possible. There are only 12 letters in the alphabet: the five vowels and seven consonants: *h, k, l, m, n, p, w*. Every syllable ends in a vowel; every vowel is pronounced no matter how many there are in the word (these have a frightening way of piling up one after another); and the accent is almost always on the penultimate syllable (the next to the last), as it is in Spanish. Consonants receive their English sounds, but vowels get the Latin pronunciation: *a* as in farm, *e* as in they, *i* as in machine, *o* as in cold, and *u* as in tutor.

Lists of Hawaiian words can be obtained in most tourist offices, but check out our Appendix—"A Hawaiian Vocabulary"—first. Do bear in mind that the name of the state is pronounced Ha-wye-ee (it does not rhyme with how-are-yuh). You are a newcomer, a malihini (mah-lee-hee-nee), and longtime residents of the islands are kamaainas (kama-eye-nahs). The haoles (properly pronounced ha-o-lays, but more commonly how-lays) are the whites, originally foreigners.

The mysterious lanai (lah-neye) that landlords are always boasting about is nothing but a balcony or porch. Kau kau (cow-cow) means food; you'll go to a lot of luaus (loo-ows) Hawaiian feasts; and people will say thank you—rather, mahalo (mah-hah-low)—for your kokua (ko-koo-ah), your help. It's kanes (kah-nays) for men, wahines (wah-hee-nays) for women. You may already know that a lei (lay) is a necklace of flowers. And just as you expected, everyone says aloha (ah-low-hah)—one of the most beautiful words in any language—meaning hello, good-bye, good luck, and salud! It also means love, as in "I send you my aloha."

THE ALOHA SPIRIT: The warm, welcoming hospitality of the islanders is perhaps the thing that most impresses the visitor, who usually goes back home and reports to friends: "I couldn't get over the people—they're the nicest I've met anywhere." One celebrated visitor expressed it very well. Mrs. Jacqueline Kennedy Onassis, returning home after a visit to Hawaii with her family some years back, wrote to the editors of the *Honolulu Advertiser and Star Bulletin* (who had asked the public to give the Kennedys privacy and assigned no reporters or photographers to follow them around): ". . . In this strange land everyone constantly goes out of his way to be kind to the other. From Governor Burns, who so kindly watched over us and asked people to help make our visit private, to the driver of a vegetable truck who went out of his way to lead us several miles, when we merely asked for directions, everyone in Hawaii has been the same. Now I know what the Aloha spirit means. I hope it is contagious—for it could change the world."

A FEW MATTERS OF USAGE: It's preferable to refer to the residents of the 50th state as "islanders," rather than as natives or Hawaiians—unless they happen to be of Hawaiian descent. You are from the mainland, not the States; islanders are very sensitive about this. And don't make the dreadful mistake of calling Americans of Japanese ancestry "Japs." They're as proud of being Americans as any descendants of the *Mayflower* passengers. During World War II, in fact, the Nisei volunteers so distinguished themselves in the bloody battles of southern Europe that their unit—the 442nd Regimental Combat Team—was designated "probably the most decorated unit in United States military history." One of its veterans is Daniel K. Inouye (of Watergate and "Irangate" investigation fame), chosen as Hawaii's first representative in Congress, now its senior senator. Spark M. Matsunaga, now its junior senator, is also a veteran of the 442nd. Both Matsunaga, 70, and Inouye, 62, started their careers in the Territorial House in the 1954 elections. In 1987, state leaders of Japanese ancestry included the Superintendent of Schools, the House Leader, the Chairman of the Senate's powerful Ways and Means Committee, and a number of judges. Remember, too, that although statehood was achieved only in 1959, residents of Hawaii have been American citizens since 1898, when, five years after the Hawaiian monarchy was overthrown in a bloodless revolution with U.S. Marines standing by (a triumph for the haole sugar and other commercial interests), the Republic of Hawaii was annexed by the government of President McKinley.

INCIDENTAL INTELLIGENCE: One of the nicest things about going to Hawaii is that you don't have to get one single shot, you don't have to fiddle with passports or visas, or have the slightest worry about unsanitary food or polluted drinking water. Standards of sanitation are very high, and the islands have an excellent supply of pure water. As far as health goes, Hawaii is way ahead of the rest of the United States: a male child has a life expectancy of 74 years compared to 66.5 on the mainland; a female child has a life expectancy of 78.1 years compared to 73 for women in the 49 other states.

TELEPHONE AREA CODE: All of the Hawaiian islands share one area code number: it's 808. The only area code numbers we list in the text are the 800, toll-free numbers.

A WORD FROM OUR READERS: As the years have gone by (this book is now in its 23rd edition), we have printed hundreds of Readers' Selections and Readers' Suggestions. If you come across any particularly appealing hotel, restaurant, beach, shop, bargain—please don't keep it to yourself. Let us hear about it. And we also welcome any comments you may have about the existing listings: the fact that a hotel or restaurant is recommended in this edition doesn't mean that it will necessarily appear in future editions if readers report that its service has slipped, that bugs have gotten out of hand (something which, alas, happens now and then in this climate), or that prices have risen unreasonably. Send your comments to us, Faye Hammel and Sylvan Levey, c/o Frommer Books, One Gulf + Western Plaza, New York, NY 10023. We regret that we cannot personally answer the many hundreds of letters we receive each year. You can, however, be sure that your letter is carefully read and that we are grateful for your comments. Please note that we reserve the right to make minor editorial changes for the sake of brevity and clarity.

To those of our readers who follow the Readers' Selections listed at the end of most chapters, we should also add a word of caution: we cannot personally vouch for these selections, since we have not seen and tried most of them for ourselves. Our general experience, however, has been that 90% of them are excellent. We also try to give a cross-section of opinion on various establishments that we do cover, knowing that somebody's great little discovery may be somebody else's great little disaster. But that's all part of the fun of traveling and discovering.

INFLATION: We don't have to tell you that inflation has hit Hawaii as it has everywhere else. For that reason it is quite possible that prices may be slightly higher at a given establishment when you read this book than they were at the time this information was collected in mid-1987. This may be especially true of restaurant prices. Be that as it may, we feel sure these selections will still represent the best travel bargains in the islands.

And please don't be one of those nonunderstanding types (we understand there are some!) who become furious with proprietors whose current rates have gone up above the prices mentioned here. Remember that the prices we give here are the most specific the proprietors could project as we went to press. Remember too that this book is revised each year to keep prices as accurate as possible; always be sure you are reading the very latest copy available.

SAFETY: Yes, it's true; there is crime and violence in Hawaii, as there is everywhere else in the world. Only, because Hawaii was indeed a trouble-free paradise for so many years, people tend to ignore basic safety precautions. Our advice is: *Don't.* Don't go hiking on deserted trails except in a group; don't go wandering on isolated beaches alone; and don't go jogging in the canefields alone at the crack of dawn, as one recent crime victim did. (There are many marijuana farms in secluded areas, and the owners do not take kindly to strangers.) Stay in well-lighted areas at night, travel with a friend if possible, lock your car and remove valuables from your trunk, and use your common sense—just as you would at home. Follow these precautions, and you should find a visit to Hawaii no more dangerous than one to your own hometown.

The $25-A-Day Travel Club—How to Save Money on All Your Travels

In this book we'll be looking at how to get your money's worth in Hawaii, but there is a "device" for saving money and determining value on *all* your trips. It's the popular, international $25-A-Day Travel Club, now in its 25th successful year of operation. The Club was formed at the urging of numerous readers of the $$$-A-Day and Dollarwise Guides, who felt that such an organization could provide continuing travel information and a sense of community to value-minded travelers in all parts of the world. And so it does!

In keeping with the budget concept, the annual membership fee is low and is immediately exceeded by the value of your benefits. Upon receipt of $18 (U.S. residents), or $20 U.S. by check drawn on a U.S. bank or via international postal money order in U.S. funds (Canadian, Mexican, and other foreign residents) to cover one year's membership, we will send all new members the following items.

(1) *Any two* of the following books
Please designate in your letter which two you wish to receive:

Frommer's $-A-Day Guides
    Europe on $30 a Day
    Australia on $25 a Day
    Eastern Europe on $25 a Day
    England on $40 a Day
    Greece including Istanbul and Turkey's Aegean Coast on $25 a Day
    Hawaii on $50 a Day
    India on $15 & $25 a Day
    Ireland on $30 a Day
    Israel on $30 & $35 a Day
    Mexico on $20 a Day (plus Belize and Guatemala)
    New York on $45 a Day
    New Zealand on $25 a Day
    Scandinavia on $50 a Day
    Scotland and Wales on $40 a Day
    South America on $30 a Day
    Spain and Morocco (plus the Canary Is.) on $40 a Day
    Turkey on $25 a Day
    Washington, D.C., on $40 a Day

Frommer's Dollarwise Guides
    Dollarwise Guide to Austria and Hungary
    Dollarwise Guide to Belgium, Holland, & Luxembourg
    Dollarwise Guide to Bermuda and The Bahamas
    Dollarwise Guide to Canada
    Dollarwise Guide to the Caribbean
    Dollarwise Guide to Egypt
    Dollarwise Guide to England and Scotland
    Dollarwise Guide to France
    Dollarwise Guide to Germany
    Dollarwise Guide to Italy
    Dollarwise Guide to Japan and Hong Kong
    Dollarwise Guide to Portugal, Madeira, and the Azores
    Dollarwise Guide to the South Pacific
    Dollarwise Guide to Switzerland and Liechtenstein
    Dollarwise Guide to Alaska
    Dollarwise Guide to California and Las Vegas
    Dollarwise Guide to Florida
    Dollarwise Guide to the Mid-Atlantic States
    Dollarwise Guide to New England
    Dollarwise Guide to New York State
    Dollarwise Guide to the Northwest
    Dollarwise Guide to Skiing USA—East
    Dollarwise Guide to Skiing USA—West
    Dollarwise Guide to the Southeast and New Orleans
    Dollarwise Guide to the Southwest

Dollarwise Guide to Texas
(Dollarwise Guides discuss accommodations and facilities in all price ranges, with emphasis on the medium-priced.)

Frommer's Touring Guides
    Egypt
    Florence
    London
    Paris
    Venice
(These new, color illustrated guides include walking tours, cultural and historic sites, and other vital travel information.)

A Shopper's Guide to Best Buys in England, Scotland, and Wales
(Describes in detail hundreds of places to shop—department stores, factory outlets, street markets, and craft centers—for great quality British bargains.)

A Shopper's Guide to the Caribbean
(Two experienced Caribbean hands guide you through this shopper's paradise, offering witty insights and helpful tips on the wares and emporia of more than 25 islands.)

Bed & Breakfast—North America
(This guide contains a directory of over 150 organizations that offer bed & breakfast referrals and reservations throughout North America. The scenic attractions, and major schools and universities near the homes of each are also listed.)

Dollarwise Guide to Cruises
(This complete guide covers all the basics of cruising—ports of call, costs, fly-cruise package bargains, cabin selection booking, embarkation and debarkation, and describes in detail over 60 or so ships cruising the waters of Alaska, the Caribbean, Mexico, Hawaii, Panama, Canada, and the United States.)

Dollarwise Guide to Skiing Europe
(Describes top ski resorts in Austria, France, Italy, and Switzerland. Illustrated with maps of each resort area plus full-color trail maps.)

Fast 'n' Easy Phrase Book
(French, German, Spanish, and Italian—all in one convenient, easy-to-use phrase guide.)

Guide to Honeymoons
(A special guide for that most romantic trip of your life, with full details on planning and choosing the destination that will be just right in the U.S. [California, New England, Hawaii, Florida, New York, South Carolina, etc.], Canada, Mexico, and the Caribbean.)

How to Beat the High Cost of Travel
(This practical guide details how to save money on absolutely all travel items—accommodations, transportation, dining, sightseeing, shopping, taxes, and more. Includes special budget information for seniors, students, singles, and families.)

Marilyn Wood's Wonderful Weekends
(This very selective guide covers the best mini-vacation destinations within a 175-mile radius of New York City. It describes special country inns and other accommodations, restaurants, picnic spots, sights, and activities—all the information needed for a two- or three-day stay.)

Motorist's Phrase Book
(A practical phrase book in French, German, and Spanish designed specifically for the English-speaking motorist touring abroad.)

Swap and Go—Home Exchanging Made Easy
(Two veteran home exchangers explain in detail all the money-saving benefits of a home exchange, and then describe precisely how to do it. Also includes information on home rentals and many tips on low-cost travel.)

The Candy Apple: New York for Kids
(A spirited guide to the wonders of the Big Apple by a savvy New York grandmother with a kid's eye view to fun. Indispensable for visitors and residents alike.)

Travel Diary and Record Book
(A 96-page diary for personal travel notes plus a section for such vital data as passport and traveler's check numbers, itinerary, postcard list, special people and places to visit, and a reference section with temperature and conversion charts, and world maps with distance zones.)

Where to Stay USA
(By the Council on International Educational Exchange, this extraordinary guide is the first to list accommodations in all 50 states that cost anywhere from $3 to $30 per night.)

(2) A one-year subscription to *The Wonderful World of Budget Travel*

This quarterly eight-page tabloid newspaper keeps you up to date on fast-breaking developments in low-cost travel in all parts of the world, bringing you the latest money-saving information—the kind of information you'd have to pay $25 a year to obtain elsewhere. This consumer-conscious publication also features columns of special interest to readers: **Hospitality Exchange** (members all over the world who are willing to provide hospitality to other members as they pass through their home cities); **Share-a-Trip** (offers and requests from members for travel companions who can share costs and help avoid the burdensome single supplement); and **Readers Ask . . . Readers Reply** (travel questions from members to which other members reply with authentic firsthand information).

(3) A copy of *Arthur Frommer's Guide to New York*

This is a pocket-size guide to hotels, restaurants, nightspots, and sightseeing attractions in all price ranges throughout the New York area.

(4) Your personal membership card

Membership entitles you to purchase through the Club all Arthur Frommer publications for a third to a half off their regular retail prices during the term of your membership.

So why not join this hardy band of international budgeteers and participate in its exchange of travel information and hospitality? Simply send your name and address, together with your annual membership fee of $18 (U.S. residents) or $20 U.S. (Canadian, Mexican, and other foreign residents), by check drawn on a U.S. bank or via international postal money order in U.S. funds to: $25-A-Day Travel Club, Inc., Frommer Books, Gulf + Western Building, One Gulf + Western Plaza, New York, NY 10023. And please remember to specify which *two* of the books in section (1) above you wish to receive in your initial package of members' benefits. Or, if you prefer, use the last page of this book, simply checking off the two books you select and enclosing $18 or $20 in U.S. currency.

Once you are a member, there is no obligation to buy additional books. No books will be mailed to you without your specific order.

ABOUT THIS BOOK: And now, here's how to plan to handle the details of low-cost Hawaiian living.

Chapter I describes the easiest and the cheapest ways to get to the islands and gives you information on packing to save money.

Chapter II gets you off the plane, onto the island of Oahu and into the city of Honolulu, and outlines the best hotel bargains in Honolulu, especially in the heart of the tourist scene, Waikiki Beach.

Chapter III takes you to Honolulu restaurants, on and off the beaten tourist path, where an appetizing meal costs less than you would expect—and to the inexpensive nightspots all over town.

Chapter IV discusses the pros and cons of guided tours, taxis, bus trips, and auto rentals, and delves into the cheapest way of getting around the fabulous city of Honolulu.

Chapter V is devoted to shopping in Hawaii—where to buy items ranging from muumuus to orchids to macadamia nuts, concentrating on bargains, of course.

Chapter VI tells you about the enormous range of activities and entertainment available in Honolulu at little or no cost—with a rundown on beaches, sports, free classes, concerts, films, folk festivals, art galleries, and learning the hula, to mention just a few.

Chapter VII provides an alternative to the expensive guided tour: seven do-it-yourself bus and walking trips in Honolulu, only one of which should cost you more than $1.20 for transportation.

Chapter VIII takes you out of Honolulu, for a low-cost, never-to-be-forgotten drive around the island of Oahu.

Chapter IX outlines the ABCs of Honolulu living.

Chapter X gives you the basic orientation on traveling in the neighbor islands: Kauai, Hawaii, Maui, and Molokai.

Chapter XI introduces you to the Garden Isle of Kauai and gives you the essentials on hotels, restaurants, car rentals, and the night scene.

Chapter XII takes you sightseeing in Kauai.

Chapter XIII describes the biggest island in the 50th state—Hawaii. Essentials again: hotels, restaurants, car rentals, nightlife.

Chapter XIV takes you sightseeing on the Big Island.

Chapter XV provides all the basics about the island of Maui.

Chapter XVI shows you the sights on Maui.

Chapter XVII takes you to Hawaii's newest tourist destination: Molokai.

The *Appendix* offers a Hawaiian vocabulary.

ADDITIONAL SOURCES: For further information on traveling and living in Hawaii, you can contact the **Hawaii Visitors Bureau (HVB),** which has offices in the following cities:

Los Angeles—Room 502, Central Plaza, 3440 Wilshire Blvd., Los Angeles, CA 90010 (tel. 213/385-5301).

San Francisco—Suite 450, 50 California St., San Francisco, CA 94111 (tel. 415/392-8173). (*Note:* The California offices request that you write to the main office in Honolulu—see below—instead of contacting them.)

Chicago—Suite 1031, 180 N. Michigan Ave., Chicago, IL 60601 (tel. 312/236-0632).

New York—Room 1407, 441 Lexington Ave., New York, NY 10017 (tel. 212/986-9203).

Vancouver, B.C.—4915 Cedar Crescent, Delta, BCV4M1J9 (tel. 604/945-8555).

In Hawaii, the **HVB** offices are as follows:

Oahu—Suite 801, Waikiki Business Plaza, 2270 Kalakaua Ave., Honolulu, HI 96815; or P.O. Box 8527, Honolulu, HI 96815 (tel. 808/923-1811).

Hawaii—75–5719 W. Alii Dr., Kailua-Kona, HI 96740 (tel. 808/329-7787); or Suite 104, Hilo Plaza, 180 Kinoole St., Hilo, HI 96720 (tel. 808/961-5797).

Maui—Maui Visitors Bureau, Suite 100, 172 Alamaha St., Kahului, Maui, HI 96732 (tel. 808/871-8691).

Kauai—Suite 207, Lihue Plaza Bldg., 3016 Umi St. (or Kauai P.O. Box 507), Lihue, Kauai, HI 96766 (tel. 808/245-3971).

READERS' TIPS ON BOOKS AND MAPS: "Your reading list should include *Plants of Hawaii National Parks* by Otto Degener, $4.50, paperback, available in most of the larger bookstores and in the National Park Service visitor centers. Far more than a botanical guide, it contains fascinating essays on Polynesian and modern uses of various plants. One can learn to make poi, tapa cloth, and many other things. It also goes into the history and religious practices of the Hawaiians. We used it every day. It is a gold mine" (David and Marilynn Rowland, Oakland, Calif.). . . . "The best, most comprehensive, and altogether most fascinating work on Hawaii is Frederick Simpich, Jr.'s *Anatomy of Hawaii* (Coward-McCann Geoghegan, Inc., 1971. Mr. Simpich's discussion of early Hawaii, modern Hawaii, the land, the military influence, the social scene, tourism, politics, and island psychology and sociology is the most concise and interesting I have read anywhere" (Hobbs A. Brown, Mesa, Ariz.) . . . "As an addition to your recommended reading on Hawaii, I would suggest that 'on the spot' account by Lucien Young, U.S.N., in *The Real Hawaii, Its History and Present Condition, Including the True Story of the Revolution (American Imperialism—Viewpoints of U.S. Foreign Policy, 1898–1941),* reprint edition published by Arno Press, N.Y., 1970, covering the author's personal observations of the political situation in 1892 and 1893 and later years. It provides another perspective (and background) to Michener's *Hawaii* and du Plessix Gray's *Hawaii: The Sugar-Coated Fortress*" (Donna Inguerson, Calgary, Alberta, Canada) . . . "For those who like books about the islands, might we suggest *Above Hawaii* by Cameron, with pictures from the satellite and then present-day and 50-year-ago pictures of the same site—really gorgeous photography" (Mr. and Mrs. B. D. Riley, Rockford, Ill.) . . . "For a background to the islands, we recommend Insight Guides' *Hawaii* by APA Productions, 1980, 413 pages, $15.95 in paperback. Hundreds of color photos. Sensitive and accurate text. A combination guide and history" (Larry Sprecher, Beaverton, Ore.).

"For northerners like me, a trip to Hawaii means a chance to see southern stars. You don't even need pitch-black skies: I got my first view of Alpha Centauri (Earth's nearest stellar neighbor) and the Southern Cross from the beach at Kaanapali. For identification, I used the star map in *Sky and Telescope* magazine, which is published monthly and is available in newsstands. Each issue carries a sky map for that month . . . Much of the bird life on the islands is different from what we have on the mainland. Some are native, like the apapene, which we saw many of in Volcanoes National Park. Some have been introduced, such as the Indian mynah, Hawaii's answer to the starling. *Peterson's Guide to Western Birds* has a short, convenient section on Hawaii. I also recommend a short book on Hawaiian birds published by the Hawaii chapter of the Audubon Society, available in book shops and souvenir stands throughout the islands" (Brent Warner, Charleston, W. Va.). . . . "I enjoyed reading *Aloha, The Magazine of Hawaii and the Pacific* when I was in the islands and decided to take a subscription. I think other readers might also enjoy it. It is published every other month. Write to them at P.O. Box 3260, Honolulu, HI 96801." (Mrs. Beatrice Solomon, Philadelphia, Pa.).

"I would hope that you could include Euell Gibbons's *Beachcombers' Guide* and *The Rising Sun* by John Toland, or Gordon Prange's *At Dawn We Slept,* as further enlightenment. These last two are essentially historical rather than political and give quite a challenge and stimulus to some of the historical and geographical highlights to one's interest" (Bob Thompson, Stockton, Calif.).

"For those who really want to get the feel of the history of Hawaii, but who have already read Michener and don't want to get into history books, there is no better source than the three beautifully written novels by O.A. Bushnell, which begin with Captain Cook and carry through until the end of the monarchy. They are exciting, enjoyable, and tremendously informative in a painless way. They are: *The Return of Lono* ($4.95, paper); *Kaawa* ($10, hardback only); and *Molokai* ($5.95, paper). Many public libraries carry all three volumes, but for those who would like to buy them, they are available from the Book Department of *Aloha, The Magazine of Hawaii,* P.O. Box 3260, Honolulu, HI 96801" (William S. McDonald, Houston, Tex.). . . . "Thor Heyerdahl's book *Early Man and the Ocean* has an excellent section on Hawaii, pages 164 to 184. Reading these will make visits to the Bishop Museum and the Academy of Arts much more enlightening" (Mrs. Lydia Marie Matz, Lehigh Acres, Fla.).

"I would like to recommend the five beautiful pictorial books by Robert Wenkam; his photography is superb and his thoughts about the people and the environment are really excellent. *Honolulu Is an Island* is surely a book to reminisce with. *Hawaii* has 150 full-color photographs of Kauai, Oahu, Maui, Molokai, Hawaii, and Lanai. *Maui: The Last Hawaiian Place, Kauai and the Park Country of Hawaii,* and *The Big Island Hawaii* are the other three. These books cost about $25 each, but they are available in libraries and it's enjoyable to read them and look at the photographic beauty of Hawaii" (Margaret Niezgoda, Calumet City, Ill.). [*Authors' Note:* Agreed: these are books to treasure.] . . . "I picked up a most interesting historical novel of Hawaii, covering the period from approximately 1820 to 1850, called *To Raise a Nation,* by Mary Cooke, at the airport on the way home. I wish I had read it on the way to Hawaii instead" (Carole McIvor, Calgary, Alberta, Canada). . . . "The best **maps** of Oahu island are now available from the State of Hawaii, Department of Transportation, Highway Planning Branch, Honolulu. These maps are available to the public at nominal cost. There are also maps available from the Map Information Center, Denver, Colo., prepared by the U.S. Geological Survey" (David C. Moore, Phoenix, Ariz.). . . . "A worthwhile purchase was the full color *Topographic Map of Hawaii* published by the University Press of Hawaii for $2.50. It is a very detailed map showing all the points of interest" (Linda Fox, Soldotna, Alaska).

Chapter I

GETTING THERE

1. The Fares
2. Inter-Island Travel
3. Packing to Save Money

WHAT WILL IT COST you to travel to Hawaii? We wish we could tell you precisely, but our crystal ball is cloudy. Ever since the federal government reduced its tight regulation of the airline industry, competition—and massive confusion—have set in. Fares can vary from airline to airline, and even within one airline, depending on when you're going, how long you're staying, whether you make land arrangements through the airlines, and how long in advance you book your ticket. Or fares can vary depending on what new, low-cost gimmick one airline might introduce to beat the competition. But you can rely on this: the airlines want your business, and the 2,400-mile route from California to the Hawaiian Islands is a highly competitive one. A little smart shopping on your part and that of your trusted travel agent will usually turn up a good deal.

1. The Fares

In case you're wondering about flying on one of the new airlines that seem to crop up every six months or so with bargain fares to the islands, we can only repeat to you what a very wise person in the travel industry has stated: "To be perfectly sure that the airline doesn't go out of business and leave you holding your tickets, fly only on reputable carriers that you know have been in business for at least five years." Sounds like good advice to us.

The major air carriers flying into Honolulu are United, American, Northwest Orient, Delta, Western, Canadian Pacific, Hawaiian Air and TWA (which offers direct service from New York to Honolulu weekday mornings; on weekends, connecting service is available from St. Louis to Honolulu). All occasionally offer special bargain flights, promotion deals, and excursions. United offers the most flights to Hawaii, with nonstop service not only from the West Coast, but also from interior cities such as Denver and Chicago. With United the only airline to serve all 50 states, connections to Hawaii are frequent and convenient. Given the recent volatility in the airline industry, air fares change constantly, and it is virtually impossible at this writing to know what kind of "bargains" might be available. Generally speaking, United offers fares that are lower the further in advance they are booked. Keep in mind that it's usually cheaper to fly in the middle of the week than on weekends, and in the fall or at off-peak times rather than during holidays or peak vacation months. United Vacations, the airline's tour operators, offers a wide variety of Hawaiian packages and prices.

DIRECT TO THE NEIGHBOR ISLANDS: Here's good news for repeat visitors who may wish to drop Honolulu from their itinerary and go directly to Maui, Kauai, or the Big Island (or route their trips to start on the neighbor islands and end in Honolulu). United is the only carrier to service all four major islands from the mainland. Currently, United offers daily nonstop service to the island of Maui from Los Angeles, San Francisco, and Chicago. In addition, United has daily nonstop departures from San Francisco and Los Angeles to Kona on the Big Island. One-stop service is also available from Los Angeles to Lihue on Kauai. Trips to the outer islands may or may not require an additional charge, depending on the time of year and the original city.

EN ROUTE TO THE PACIFIC: An exciting new option for Hawaii travelers has been introduced as a result of United's new service to the Pacific. Travelers can now stop over in Hawaii on their way to exotic destinations in both the North and South Pacific. At this writing, United offers flights through Honolulu to Auckland and Sydney, as well as to Narita, Japan, and the Orient. Keep watching as more new and exciting Pacific destinations become available to the Hawaii traveler.

GROUP TOURS: Some excellent values are available on group tours, for short periods of one or two weeks. Many package options are available, including condominium vacations and multi-island packages. We usually prefer the do-it-yourself brand of travel, but if you do want a group trip, consult your travel agent or airline for a variety of choices.

THE ROYAL TREATMENT: We gave up a long time ago counting how many trips we've taken to Hawaii in the past 23 years or so, but we remember very well the especially delightful one we made via United Airlines last summer. Still caught up in the big-city atmosphere of Los Angeles, it came as a pleasant shock to find ourselves surrounded at the gate by Kahili poles, tiki gods, tapa cloth, birds of paradise, and anthuriums, all part of United's Royal Hawaiian Service. Culture shock continued as we were welcomed aboard the widebodied 747 jet (United offers mostly widebody service) Hawaiian style, with island music, and greeted by flight attendants in aloha shirts and tapa-patterned dresses. Mainland tension disappeared quickly as we relaxed with island music, sipped a mai-tai, and studied the attractive menu describing the Polynesian dishes that had been prepared for us. By the time dinner was served, home could have been at least a million miles away. First came our pupus (that's Hawaiian for appetizers), shrimp and fresh Hawaiian pineapple. The salad of fresh garden greens was presented on a tray garnished with—shades of the islands!—an orchid. Our entree was an island favorite—chicken teriyaki served with Oriental vegetables —but it might have been strip sirloin of beef or Rocky Mountain trout. Dessert was a freshly baked macadamia-nut/carrot cake. We watched a movie, noticed that the hours were skimming away, and by the time we were approaching the islands we knew again what aloha was all about.

JET LAG: If you're going all the way through from the East Coast to Honolulu or the neighbor islands in one stretch—about ten air hours—you'll be crossing at least six time zones, and your normal body rhythms are going to be thrown out of sync. Here are some tips from the experts in avoiding jet lag. First, they advise that several days before your departure, you gradually accommodate your eating and sleeping times to be closer to those of your destination. You'll be heading west, so go to bed a little later each night and sleep a little later in the morning. When you come home, reverse that pattern. Second, avoid smoking, drinking, and heavy eating in flight—another reason to bring your own picnic lunch! You may have heard of the Argonne Anti-Jet-Lag Diet, which alternates feasting and fasting for several days before departure, and is effective for many people. (We're told that President and Mrs. Reagan have been using it when they travel abroad.) To get a free copy of the program (over 200,000 cards have been sent out to date), send a stamped, self-addressed envelope to Office of Public Affairs, Argonne National Laboratory, 9700 South Cass Ave., Argonne, IL 60439. Our personal prescription for avoiding jet lag is to stop off at one of the airport hotels in either Los Angeles or San Francisco en route. For years, we've enjoyed staying at the Los Angeles Airport Marriott, which has a pool set in a magnificent garden and a variety of restaurants, including the very reasonable Fairfield. If you call far enough in advance (tel. toll free 800/228-9290), you may be able to get a Family Plan rate (for at least two people) during the week; weekend rates are always available, and both of these are approximately $69, about half the regular price. After a swim in the pool (or a workout in the exercise room), and a good night's sleep, we board our plane the next morning and arrive in Hawaii refreshed.

THE TRIP BY SHIP: Forget about it. There is no crossing to Hawaii that costs less than the lowest air fares. Only luxury ships now call at Honolulu Harbor.

ANOTHER TIP: Try not to arrive in Hawaii on a weekend, when Honolulu is crowded with visitors from the outer islands. Everything is easier and less crowded on weekdays, especially checking into hotels, and air fares are lower during the week as well.

TIME TRICKS: Don't forget that you'll be flying into yesterday when you head for Hawaii from mainland U.S. You pick up an extra five hours in flight (six during daylight saving time) if you're starting from the East Coast, three hours if you begin on the West Coast. Going home, of course, you lose the hours and can find yourself leaving this afternoon and arriving tomorrow morning.

2. Inter-Island Travel

THE FARES: Hawaii has three major inter-island carriers: **Hawaiian Airlines, Aloha Airlines,** and **Mid Pacific Air.** All have excellent safety records, superfrequent service, and friendly crews. Hawaiian and Aloha have been around for many years and run mostly jet equipment; Mid Pacific Air came in a few years ago with 60-passenger turbo-props, dropped the fares, and the price wars began. Now, all three of these airlines have basically the same fares give or take a few dollars; if one of them drops prices, the others will quickly follow suit. Then United started flying planes directly from the mainland to the neighbor islands, and the competition for the inter-island traveler's dollar became fiercer than ever; and that's where we budget travelers can benefit. Because fares change so often and because all three inter-island carriers offer periodic promotion fare and tie-ins with hotel and car packages, it pays to do some personal research on this, either by calling the airlines direct, or with your travel agent, before you book. Expect fares to be their highest during peak winter and summer travel periods.

Mid Pacific bills itself as "The Little Guy," an image made popular by their cute little yellow chick most often seen and heard saying "Cheep." They operate a fleet of 60-passenger, YS-11 aircraft with two-by-two seating, as well as new Rolls Royce-powered, 80-passenger Fokker F28 jets (we can attest to the comfort of seats on the latter for anyone with a temperamental back). Full coach fare is $46.95; capacity-controlled fare (basically, first-come, first-served on a limited number of seats) is $36.95. First-class fare is $69. Mid Pacific offers service to all the major islands (it is flying smaller Reeves Aircraft to the new Kapalua-West Maui Airport) with the exception of Molokai. The first flight in the morning and the last flight at night are cheaper, and so are flights for senior citizens, the military, and children. Passengers flying Continental from the mainland can receive mileage credits on Mid Pacific.

When you're already in Honolulu, check out Mid Pacific's air-room-car packages to the nieghbor islands. They are not allowed to advertise these outside of Hawaii, but there are many good deals.

Hawaiian Airlines also keeps the budget traveler in mind with a variety of price-savers. It has two price structures: $46.95 to the major islands on jet equipment, $38.95 on DeHavilland Dash 7, 70-seat turbo-props. Reduced fares (first-come, first-served) are $44.95 on the jets, $36.95 on the turbo-props. Sunrise and sunset flights are $36.95. If you're going direct to one of the neighbor islands and bypassing Honolulu, you can save money by flying from the West Coast on Hawaiian, which has recently inaugurated service from Los Angeles, San Francisco, Seattle, Las Vegas, and Portland, as well as Anchorage, American Samoa, Western Samoan, and the Kingdom of Tonga. The first flight to a neighbor island is free; you can change planes in Honolulu. If you wish to stop in Honolulu first, the fee is $20. Hawaiian is the only major airline to stop at Molokai. Special fares are available for senior citizens, children, and the military. Hawaiian's mileage program, known as "Gold Plus," offers passengers mileage credits which are good for free inter-island transportation, transportation on Hawaiian to the mainland, and also transportation on Alaska Airlines and other cooperating airlines from mainland United States.

On Aloha Airlines, the regular fare on its all-jet fleet is $48.95; reduced fare (first-come, first-served), is $44.95. Thrift fare—sunrise and sunset flights—is $36.95. Special fares are offered for senior citizens, the military, and children. Aloha also offers first-class service; the fare for this is $65.95. And your Aloha mileage counts toward mileage plus (250 miles per flight) when you fly with United or American Airlines.

There are no longer standby flights on any of these airlines.

Should you wish to call the airlines, here are their **toll-free numbers:** Hawaiian Airlines, 800/367-5320; Aloha Airlines, 800/367-5250; Mid Pacific Airlines, 800/367-7010.

SCHEDULING SECRETS: Now that United is running its big jets directly into Maui, Kauai, Kona, and Lihue, it's not necessary to both arrive at and depart from Honolulu; you can be more flexible with your itinerary. You might, for example, start in Honolulu, travel from there to Kauai, then to Maui, from there to Molokai, and on to Kona, where you pick up your plane for your return flight to Los Angeles or San Francisco. Another routing that we have found very pleasant is to fly directly to Kona from the West Coast, then on to Maui, Molokai, and Kauai, making the last stop Honolulu, and departing from there to home. (Plan it this way if you want peace and quiet first, excitement later.)

3. Packing to Save Money

Another important way to save money on your Hawaiian trip is to give careful thought to the clothes you take and the way you pack. First rule is *not* to go on a big shopping spree in advance. If you need to fill out your wardrobe, do it in Hawaii, where the stores are packed with colorful island resort clothes at prices cheaper than those you'll probably pay at home (see Chapter V).

Second important rule: Pack a light suitcase and take only one piece of luggage per person (you can also carry a small travel bag for reading matter on the plane, then use it later as a beach bag). If you can carry your own bag, you are your own person and not dependent on expensive porters and bellboys and taxis. Having a light bag (or at least one of those wheeled luggage carriers) is practically essential, since it is sometimes difficult to locate porters at the airports, and in small hotels you are usually expected to carry your own luggage. If you happen to arrive at a new place without hotel reservations, being able to manage your own luggage will enable you to look around instead of grabbing anything that gives you a chance to put your bags down. Therefore get yourself the lightest suitcase you can buy (the cloth ones are good, roomy bets), and leave at least one-third of the space for bringing back the things you'll buy in Hawaii. Do buy all your luggage before you go; it will be more expensive in Hawaii.

Most important, don't burden yourself with several large bags. By what we dub the Hammel-Levey Amendment to Parkinson's Law, the contents of a suitcase have a way of expanding to fit the space available.

CONTENTS: What will you need to take with you? Easy does it. It's much simpler to pack for Hawaii than it is for Europe or almost anyplace else. You need only spring or summer clothes and then of the simplest kind. There are no extreme variations in temperature between day and night, so you don't need the usual all-purpose travel coat or overcoat you'd take to Europe or Mexico—unless you're coming from the eastern United States and plan to spend a few days in San Francisco on the way back; then you'll have good use for it. A light raincoat is helpful, and so is a folding umbrella—and let's hope you won't need them! Women will find a stole or shawl useful at night. The only heavy garment that you will require is a warm sweater or hooded parka for exploring the volcano regions on the islands of Hawaii and Maui. Good canvas or other heavy-soled hiking shoes and socks are a must for hiking or for trekking over recent lava flows on Hawaii.

For Men

We're not going to give specifics on what to take, since you know what you like. We will tell you, however, that island dress is extremely casual, and many of our readers say they've never worn a suit in the islands! Some of the fancier places do require a jacket for dinner, however. It's easier to travel with drip-dry shirts and underclothing, but not necessary since the islands are dotted with quick-service launderettes (many apartment-hotels have their own), so you can have a stack of clothes washed and ready to wear in a few hours. Plan on buying a colorful aloha shirt when you're in Hawaii (it's worn outside the trousers and cut a little fuller than the usual sports shirt). You can use it back home for beach or country wear. And do we need to tell you that the "Hawaiian look" is now funky, fun fashion?

For Women

Before you begin to pack your bag, you'll want to know a little bit about what women wear in Hawaii. Allow us to introduce you to the muumuu, the most comfortable garment known to woman. Try one and see. They're loose enough to provide their own inner air conditioning, require a minimum of underwear underneath (the girdle industry must be nonexistent in Hawaii), and look pretty enough to flatter almost everybody—especially large women, who look positively graceful in them. (You'll see more than a few of these hefty Polynesian ladies, by the way, a carry-over from the days when the alii, the nobility, cultivated fat as a royal status symbol.)

The thing we love most about Hawaiian fashion is that many women wear muumuus or other long dresses outdoors, especially at night. Even though many island women are now extremely fashion conscious and favor the same kind of spring-summer fashions that might be seen in New York or Paris or San Francisco, the muumuu is still going strong: it seems Hawaii discovered the maxi back in the days of the missionaries. You'll see full-flowing muumuus (the colorful Hawaiian version of the Mother Hubbards the missionaries forced on the natives); long, slim adaptations of classic Chinese tunics; or, prettiest of all, holomuus, long muumuus, slightly fitted at the waist. (The holoku—a fitted muumuu with a train—is worn mostly on formal occasions.) We strongly urge you to buy a long dress while you're in the islands. You can use it later for an at-home gown, and you'll have a great time walking through the streets with it swishing gracefully at your ankles. Be sure that the muumuu at least touches the instep if you want to look like a kamaaina. And unless you already own a couple of shifts, it's not a bad idea to wait until you get to Hawaii to pick up a few of the local equivalents: the short muumuu, or island-style sundress. The selection is tremendous (see Chapter V), and the prices are at all levels. Of course, many women visitors live in pants and shorts in Hawaii, and there's no reason why you shouldn't. It's just that muumuus are so much more a part of the island scene.

So pack your bathing suits (or get a bikini in Hawaii), your favorite casual clothes, a sturdy pair of sandals (maybe some hiking boots if you're going to go out on the trails), a lightweight woolen sweater, stole, or throw to wear in the evenings, a warm jacket if you're going up into the mountains. Leave your stockings at home; only businesswomen seem to wear them. You'll live in sandals or Japanese zoris, or go barefoot the way many islanders do, especially indoors. (Island kids, by the way, wear shoes as little as possible, usually not even to school, with resulting household crises when they need to find their shoes to go to a movie or restaurant.) The idea, in summer, is to fortify yourself against the heat by wearing open shoes and sleeveless dresses. Leave all your city cottons and little dark dresses at home. In the winter months, when Hawaiian weather can be spring-like, pants and tops, are practically a uniform. And T-shirts are worn everywhere, year 'round. Wash-and-dry clothes are helpful but not crucial since the launderettes are so handy. As for jewelry, the only kind most people wear is island craft, shell or coral necklaces and the like, which can be picked up in any gift shop. The most beautiful jewelry of island women is the natural kind: blossoms in the hair, flower leis around the neck.

A final word on Hawaiian clothing: We don't want to give you the impression that island women never get dressed up. They do, especially for fancy social events. In downtown Honolulu, businesswomen wear more conservative summer clothing, and many men wear regular business suits with tuck-in shirts. But that's for work—not fun.

SUNDRIES: It's not necessary to bring a travel iron from home: most hotels have boards and irons for guests. Get plastic bottles for your liquid toilet articles; they won't break and they take up less space. Seal perfume bottles with wax for plane flights. Get little packets of cold-water soap and scatter them in odd corners of your suitcase. The plastic clotheslines, complete with miniature clothespins and soap, sold in most department stores, are very, very handy. Those inflatable or plastic hangers are good to have too, since you can't always count on finding wooden hangers on which to drip-dry your clothes in an inexpensive hotel. Disposable wash-up tissues are nice to carry with you, particularly on long plane or auto trips.

HOW TO PACK: Everyone's got his or her own theory on this, but ours is simply to put all the heavy things on the bottom—shoes, books, bulky objects—and lay everything else neatly on top. Then, roll underwear, socks, soft articles into the corners and empty spots (inside shoes, for instance). We think it also helps to have plastic bags for organizing underwear, handkerchiefs, sundries. You'll need one large one at any rate for carrying damp bathing suits. Folding tissue into your garments does help avoid wrinkles. And here's a new tip we just learned on how to pack a wide-brimmed sunhat. Place the hat upside down in the bag, then fill the crown with soft items, and tuck other soft items under the brim. This way you avoid either having to wear the hat on the plane trip home or possibly ruining it by folding it (we've ruined quite a few in our time).

SAFETY FIRST: Let's hope your suitcase won't get stolen, lost, or misdirected on the airlines to Australia. But it doesn't hurt to take a few sensible precautions, especially if you're flying in a huge group where bags often get shipped to the wrong hotels and you may have to go without them for several hours. Always tag your bags, inside and out, with your name and home address. Inside each bag, put a note that gives your address in Hawaii; if your bag should arrive at somebody else's hotel, it can easily be sent to yours. Carry with you your valuables, medicines, prescriptions, cameras, and so on—anything that you can't easily replace if your bag is among the missing.

READERS' TRAVEL SUGGESTIONS: "First-time visitors to Oahu (and even those who have been there before but are somewhat vague on their geography) will find a little folder titled 'Map of Waikiki—Hotels and Points of Interest,' available free at any HVB office, invaluable as they attempt to sort out the vast wealth of free tourist literature they encounter on street corners and in hotel lobbies. Major and minor hotels are indexed both alphabetically and by map reference number. All streets, no matter how short, are shown and clearly labeled; and the longer ones have street number indicators to help you locate the exact block where a nonhotel attraction (such as a restaurant) is located" (Leilani Moyers, Patterson, N.Y.).

"I visited Hawaii several years ago, and this year I decided to brighten up the winter by subscribing to the Honolulu Sunday newspaper. Perhaps other readers would enjoy this paper, either to help plan a trip or to read during a cold winter. You can get all the information about subscribing by mail to the *Sunday Star-Bulletin and Advertiser* by writing to Hawaii Newspaper Agency, Circulation Dept., P.O. Box 3350, Honolulu, HI 96801. Last year, the cost was $10.50 for a four-week period" (John Meyer, Sterling, Ill.). [*Authors' Note:* This rate is for ship mail, which takes three weeks; the airmail rate is $19.75.] . . . "A word of caution: Although we were very careful about leaving anything valuable in our car, we had no choice on one occasion, and someone broke into the trunk of the car and took two canvas bags containing all of our newly purchased snorkeling equipment, plus beach and swimwear. The policeman said the trunk can be opened with a screwdriver without damaging the lock. This theft occurred one block from the Pioneer Inn in Lahaina while we were on a sunset dinner sail" (H. Emil Johnson, Darien, Conn.).

"We made the mistake of going to Oahu in late June. Unless you like zillions of teen-agers, don't travel to Hawaii then. It seemed that every high school graduation class in California, bar none, was there. They took over everything. The only escape was the Hale Koa, the military hotel" (Don and Nancy Gossard, Bellevue, Wash.). . . . "It is amazing how finely the Hawaiians have honed their ability to handle great mobs of tourists so that you seldom feel taken advantage of or intruded upon. A great deal of this is probably due to the pride people take in doing their work and in their state, from the lowest paid waitress to the captain of the DC-10 that takes you there. We are sure that Hawaii has its grim sides, since no place is paradise, but with a little common sense the visitor can enjoy the islands to a greater degree than most other places" (Robert and Jean Carroll, Helena, Mont.).

"We brought two round plastic containers from home to fill with ice to put in our insulated lunchbag to help keep our lunches cold. We didn't have to purchase straw mats for the beach as a lot of people did, as I had packed a large sheet for our 'beach blanket.'

Certainly, a lot easier to pack for our trip home. A folding suitcase we had packed came in handy for all the souvenirs we had bought. Our most indispensable item turned out to be a ten-foot length of rope. Since most of our previous traveling has been camping, it just seemed like a natural thing to pack. It was used to secure the trunk of a small car when all the luggage wouldn't fit, to hang wet bathing suits outside, and last, to tie a suitcase when the lock broke" (Beverly Russo, N. Massapequa, N.Y.).

"T-shirts are very much a part of the island scene, worn by every age, it appears. I think it would be more interesting if people wore a T-shirt with the name of their hometown, or area, on it, instead of the local Hawaiian ones; that way tourists could say 'Hi' to anyone wearing a name from their own hometown and probably end up enjoying a great chat. We did see the odd person wearing a 'hometown' T-shirt, and noticed the way passersby obviously read it" (Joy E. Deeks, Victoria, B.C., Canada).

"A terrific packing idea is an inflatable raft. It takes up no room in the suitcase, but can be used to lie on the sand and float in the water" (Mr. and Mrs. R. Bivona, Massapequa, N.Y.). . . . "For an inexpensive souvenir to take back home, just bring a cassette radio recorder and some blank tapes; you can record Hawaiian music from the local radio stations" (Roz and Jim Morino, Colma, Calif.).

"In three weeks in the islands I broke my watchband, my sunglasses' earpiece, my tote pocketbook strap, and my camera carrying-case strap. Therefore, my suggestion is to purchase carrying cases with secure handles, preferably straps that continue all around the bag, including the bottom. This is important for any type of vinyl or plastic bag that will be used for carrying more than a hanky . . . I carried my film (40 rolls) in filmshield bags, which are lead-lined. They can be found in camera stores. Because I made several inter-island flights and went through numerous X-ray machines, the film was protected from the rays. They try to insist it won't damage the film, but professional photographers recommend using the bags because of the cumulative effect of the rays. Where possible I had them hand-examine the film carriers. Some places I was required to remove them from my baggage for examination because the lead lining made them show up as a black, unidentifiable blob on the machine" (Jane Kenney, Kingston, N.H.).

"It's nice to go to the airport early and ask for seating arrangements, as the first row of seats behind first class has more leg room, is less noisy, and has less vibration from the engines. We left three transistor radios at home, but wanted one so badly that we bought one in Honolulu. We recommend one for the packing list" (Mr. and Mrs. Rodney Phillips, Seattle, Wash.). [Authors' Note: More and more letters arrive every year agreeing about transistor radios. Many hotels include neither radio nor television, and the cost of renting a radio is about $3.50 a week. As for going to the airport early to get good seats, it's usually not necessary: try asking your travel agent to reserve seats for you or do so yourself by phoning the airlines a few days before your flight. Unless you've done so, three or four of you traveling together during a busy season may have to be split up, or you may not get to sit in the cabin (smoking or nonsmoking, movie or not) that you prefer.] . . . "I would like to suggest to your readers that they either bring with them or buy as soon as they get to the islands a can of good insect repellent. We were at Waimea Falls Park in June (which wasn't really all that great) and even though we never saw any, we were eaten up by insects. Our tram guide had sprayed himself and at the time I couldn't imagine why, until later when we started itching and scratching. This also happened to us on Kauai when we took the evening Wailua River Cruise to the Fern Grotto. At least that time we saw them flying around" (Muriel P. Maloney, Huntington Beach, Calif.).

"My husband and I agree that a tape recorder is a must for trips. We taped the songs and commentary at the Fern Grotto cruise on Kauai and plan to use the tapes as part of a background to our slides. We also taped our impressions of each day's events before we went to bed. It's so much easier and quicker than keeping a diary, and a great deal of fun to replay" (Joann Leonard, Los Angeles, Calif.). . . . "I suggest taking a featherweight hooded nylon waterproof shell jacket. We were the only ones who could really enjoy the sights around the top of the volcano craters on the Big Island and Maui. Because of the wind, most sleeveless-dressed ladies were miserable." (Mrs. Richard K. West, Glenview, Ill.). . . . "Let me thank the reader who suggested taking a featherweight, hooded nylon waterproof shell jacket—that saved my day many, many times. It was for those sudden showers that it was invaluable during our trip. I had made a special shopping trip before I left home to buy the jacket and found it much better to carry and use than a plastic raincoat; it folds into such a neat package that I could tuck it into my purse. Another helpful item we took with us was a pair of binoculars, and we were the envy of lots of fellow travelers viewing the Waimea Canyon on Kauai, Haleakala on Maui, and the volcanic action on Hawaii—it was very active at that time. They have telescopes at some of the places, but the lines are long! Binoculars need not be expensive or heavy to carry; there are many compact glasses available" (Mrs. Lee Morgan, Vacaville, Calif.).

"In the ten days we were in the islands, my husband didn't have to wear a suit once. Visitors might be safe to bring one, but one is more than enough" (Terry and Lou Cicalese, South Ozone Park, N.Y.). . . . "One item that made our trip particularly enjoyable was a plaid insulated bag. It easily fit into my suitcase on the way over. We thoroughly enjoyed shopping for foods in Hawaii. The produce department was great fun. Each day we packed a lunch, which stayed fresh in our insulated container until we found a delightful place to stop for lunch. This bag saved us considerable time and money. We used it to transport leftover foods when we island hopped. And on the way home we stuffed it with souvenirs" (Marylin C. Haley, Watertown, Mass.).

And now, after a budget flight, we land in the islands. It's time to tour Hawaii on $50 a day.

Chapter II

HONOLULU: ORIENTATION AND HOTELS

1. Hotels in Waikiki
2. Hotels in Downtown Honolulu
3. Hotels in Windward Oahu

AS YOU'VE ALREADY LEARNED, most planes and ships going to the Hawaiian Islands land first on the island of Oahu and deposit you in or near the capital city of Honolulu. For those of us on a budget, that's a marvelously appropriate choice, because Oahu happens to be the cheapest of all the Hawaiian islands—and one of the most fascinating to boot.

THE ISLAND ITSELF: Oahu means "the gathering place" in Hawaiian, and no other name could be so apt. Although it's merely the third largest of the islands in size (40 miles long, 26 miles wide), it boasts the most people (over half a million, and more arriving all the time), the most skyscrapers, the most construction, the most schools, hospitals, radio and television stations—and the most tourists. Honolulu, the capital city, is the center of island life, the metropolis of which youngsters from the other islands dream, a tremendous military stronghold (approximately one-quarter of the island is owned by the military, and defense is a major industry), a bustling boom town, and a cosmopolitan center plunked down in the middle of the Pacific Ocean.

Just about ten minutes away from downtown Honolulu is **Waikiki Beach,** a favorite resort of Hawaiian royalty long before the word "tourist" was invented. For the visitor, this is an ideal situation; it's as if Mexico City were just ten minutes away from Acapulco, Paris a short bus ride from the Riviera. You can, with such geography, have the best of both worlds—as much beach or city, laziness or excitement, as you choose.

The island is dominated by two mountain ranges: the Waianae, along the west coast, and the Koolaus, which form the spectacular backdrop to the city of Honolulu. On the other side of the Koolaus is **Windward Oahu,** which is what islanders are referring to when they talk of going to the country. Commuters tunnel through the mountains to pretty little suburbs that are developing here as the population booms. For the visitor, it's the closest thing you'll see—if you don't get to the neighbor islands—of rural Hawaii: tiny plantation villages, miles of red earth planted with pineapple and sugarcane, a breathtaking succession of emerald beaches, and gorgeous trails for riding and hiking. But we'll get to that later. First, let's get you settled in Waikiki, which in all likelihood will be your center of operations in Honolulu.

ARRIVAL: Honolulu International Airport is about five miles out of town. Although it's easy enough to hop right on the no. 8 Hickam-Waikiki bus that goes from the terminal to the beach area (fare: 60¢), there is one major problem: the bus has no special section for luggage, and even one large bag is no longer allowed on it. So unless you're traveling extremely light, or picking up a car at the airport, your best bet is to take the Greyline Airporter bus which leaves from the lower level of the airport, $5 one way. Regular taxi fare into town runs around $15. Getting back to the airport is also easy: Airport Motor Coach (tel. 926-4747) and Waikiki Express (tel. 942-2177) will pick you up at your hotel about two hours before plane time and deliver you to the airport for a charge of $5.

If you're planning to rent a car, the rates are usually cheaper at places in town than at the airport. Better yet, make your arrangements in advance at one of the less expensive car agencies in town (see Chapter IV).

GETTING YOUR DIRECTIONAL SIGNALS: In order to get your bearings, you should know that no one ever refers to directions in the old-fashioned north-south, east-west way out here. Since the islands sit in a kind of slanted direction on the map, those terms just wouldn't make much sense.

This is how it's done in Hawaii. Everything toward the sea is **makai** (mah-kye); everything toward the mountains is **mauka** (mow-kah). The other directions are **Diamond Head** (roughly eastward) and **Ewa** (roughly westward), named after two of the major landmarks of the city. Once you move out beyond Diamond Head, roughly eastward directions are referred to as **Koko Head** (Aina Haina is Koko Head of Kalani Valley, for example). Once you learn how to use these simple terms, you'll be well on the way to becoming a kamaaina yourself.

HOTELS: Now, with the preliminaries done, we arrive at the initial, all-important, make-or-break project of your Hawaiian vacation—finding a good but inexpensive hotel. As we've discussed in our introduction, inflation is rampant in Hawaii—as it is everywhere else. Many of the cozy little guesthouses that used to enable budget tourists to live comfortably on peanuts just a few years ago have been torn down as part of the masterplan for upgrading Waikiki. In their places, new, more expensive structures have been built. (Some of the remaining guest houses are in such a state of neglect that we won't bother mentioning them here.) However—and this is good news—because of the tremendous number of accommodations in Waikiki, it is still possible to find plenty of good rooms for a very few dollars.

For the purpose of a $50-a-day budget, we will presume that you are part of a traveling twosome, and that between the two of you, you have a total of $100 to spend on a room and meals. If you want to stay on the low side of this budget, check out our selections under "Bargain Beauties." This section covers rooms that average between $25 and $40 a night for two. If you can afford to spend more, then consider the listings under "The Good Buys." These rooms begin at $40 and go to $50 and up. Whatever is left over from the money you spend on your room can go for food. Of course, if there are more than two of you travel-

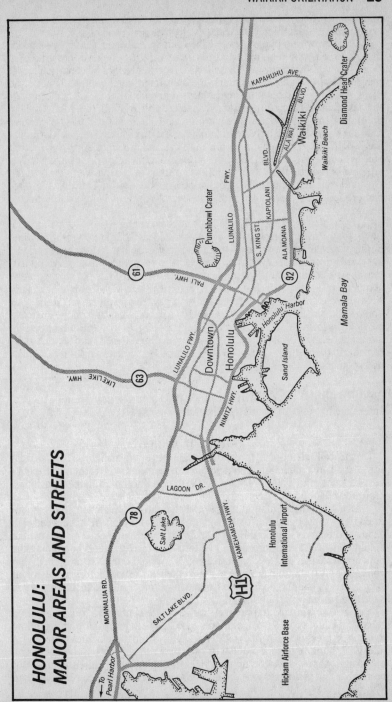

HONOLULU:
MAJOR AREAS AND STREETS

ing in a party, or if you are staying in Honolulu for more than a week or two, you can realize considerable savings on these figures.

Whichever your budget, you will be living sensibly and pleasantly—and far more inexpensively than most tourists, who are led to believe that a hotel in Waikiki under $100 a day just doesn't exist. It certainly does exist, particularly at that Hawaiian wonder of wonders: the apartment-hotel with kitchenette. So many tourists—especially family groups—are enamored of kitchenette units that accommodations of this sort have sprung up all over Waikiki. Many of them are individually owned condominium units. Almost always, they're cheaper than the rooms in the large seaside hotels; they have excellent locations near the beach and mountains; they are fully available to transients; they permit you to reduce expenses by cooking at least one meal in (dishes and utensils are always provided); and most important, they offer what we regard as the most relaxing and enjoyable type of accommodation in Hawaii. We offer names, addresses, and descriptions of several dozen of these establishments below.

If you plan to arrive in Hawaii during the summer season—June through Labor Day—advance reservations are a good idea. They are essential anytime during the peak winter season—roughly from December 20 to April 15. (During the Christmas holiday season, people have been known to reserve up to a year in advance at some of the more desirable places.) While not so imperative at other times of the year, reservations remain the best way of obtaining exactly what you want at the price you can afford to pay. But if you haven't done your homework, all is not lost. Thumb through the pages ahead and phone the likely possibilities from the airport. Or park your traveling companion and suitcases at a seaside bench in Waikiki (get off the bus at Kuhio Beach) and set out to do some serious scouting. That way you won't collapse with exhaustion at the first hotel you find.

A WORD ABOUT CAMPING: For details on camping permits, renting trailers, and where to camp on Oahu, see Chapters IV and VIII.

1. Hotels in Waikiki

Practically all tourists stay in Waikiki, mecca of the malihinis. This is a relatively small area of Honolulu, but within it are concentrated most of the town's best beaches, and therefore most of the hotels and entertainment facilities. Downtown Honolulu is only a short bus ride away.

As a point of orientation, remember that most of the fancy hotels are located right on the beach and on Kalakaua Avenue, the main drag; between Kalakaua and the Ala Wai Boulevard (which marks most of the makai and mauka boundaries of Waikiki) are dozens of tree-lined pretty streets containing the bulk of the smaller and less expensive hotels. Waikiki itself is small enough that you can easily walk from any one of these hotels to the beach; they are also near each other, so you should have no trouble in getting from one to another if you have to do some hotel hunting.

A further word about prices: As we've pointed out above, prices are often cheaper if you stay for a week or more. Also, they can go up or down according to business pressures, so prices may vary slightly from these figures, gathered in mid-1987, but give or take a dollar or two, they will be your best hotel buys on the island. Almost all hotels up their rates during the busy winter months. But remember that in slow seasons you may be able to get rooms at lower prices than the going rates; you can do especially well on weekly rentals. The hotel may eliminate maid service (which is costly), but you may be able to get a very decent apartment for a low price. Please note that we are not responsible for changes in prices: we simply quote the figures hotel owners give us. Also, please do not expect special rates at hotels unless we specifically indicate that the owners are willing to give them to our readers. In addition, and unless otherwise stated by us, all rooms listed below have private bath.

Since most tourists spend far less than a month in Waikiki, we have not covered the apartment buildings that take only monthly or seasonal rentals; if you do plan to stay for at least a month, it may be worth your while to investigate them too. And, of course, many of the apartment-hotels listed here will accept guests for several months or more.

HOTEL TAX: We're sorry to have to break it to you. Hawaii's hotel room tax is now a hefty 9%.

THE BARGAIN BEAUTIES: Although the price range in this category is modest—averaging from $25 to $45 for a double room—the variety of accommodations is surprisingly wide. They range from simple motel-like apartment buildings to graceful small hotels featuring pools, lovely tropical grounds, air conditioning, private phones, and resort-living comfort. We've divided these hotels, and the ones in "The Good Buys" section to follow, into three general areas: **Diamond Head Waikiki,** that part of town closest to Kuhio Beach and Kapiolani Park; **Central Waikiki,** the area centering, roughly, around the International Market Place; and **Ewa Waikiki,** the section near the Hilton Hawaiian Village Hotel and Reef Hotel and the closest area to downtown Honolulu. Two additional subdivisions of the last will be called **Near the Ala Wai** and **Near Ala Moana.** Remember that all these areas are within a few blocks' walking or a short bus distance of each other and all are comparable in terms of comfort and convenience. And they're all near the beach.

Diamond Head Waikiki

We'll begin with an old standby in this part of town, the **Royal Grove Hotel,** 151 Uluniu Ave., Honolulu, HI 96815 (tel. 923-7691), one of the prettiest of Waikiki's small hotels. The six-story pink concrete building is about three minutes away from Kuhio Beach, but if you're really lazy you can dunk in the tiny pool right on the grounds. All told, the Royal Grove has about 85 rooms and a widely varying price range: you can get a room (single or double) starting at $28, a room with kitchenette starting at $34.50, a kitchenette unit with private lanai at $38 to $42—all air-conditioned. One-bedroom apartments average $38 to $75, and it's $10 for an extra person in the room. The accommodations become fancier as prices go up, but all are nicely furnished and comfortable, have tub-shower facilities, and the kitchens are all electric. Subject to availability, you get a day's charge off the weekly rate if you stay for two consecutive weeks in spring or fall. Round-the-clock desk service, twice-weekly or weekly maid service, a health-food shop/restaurant, and a good pizza parlor with outdoor tables are other pluses. Winter sees Canadian and midwestern families here for long stays. Over the years, readers continue to write to comment on the friendliness of the owners, the Fong family, who frequently have potluck dinners and parties so that everyone can get acquainted. Lots of aloha for little price at this one.

The Fongs also rent a number of units at the lovely **Pacific Monarch Hotel**

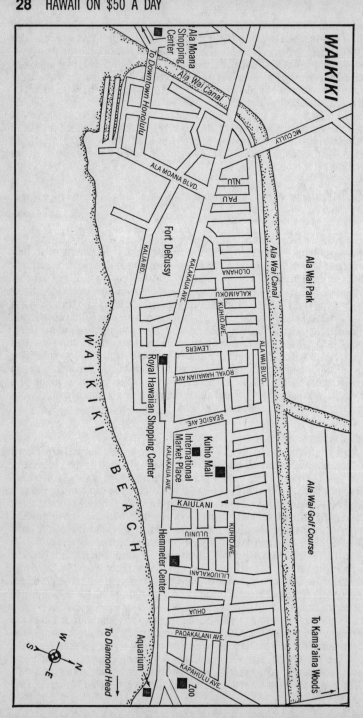

and **Condominium,** just across the street, at higher prices. Inquire about these when you make your reservations.

The **Waikiki Lei,** at 241 Kaiulani Ave., Honolulu, HI 96815 (tel. 923-6656; if no answer, 734-8588), a longtime favorite with our hard-core budget-minded readers, is a pink four-story building with outside staircase (no elevator). All is clean and comfortable, and each of the 19 studio units is furnished with twin beds, a complete, well-equipped kitchen with full refrigerator, and shower-tub combination in the bathroom. TV and air conditioning are optional. The furniture is of a dark, wood-like Formica, offset by bedspreads and curtains in white and bone; the floor is vinyl tile. Best of all, the prices are still very good. The studios usually rent for $28 double, $25 single. (If you stay for less than two weeks, the rates may be a little higher.) An extra person is charged $3. For economy-minded singles, there are just four rooms at $20 with hotplate and refrigerator. (Monthly rates are available, from $450 up.) Other pluses: adequate space for parking (not easy to come by in Waikiki) and coin-operated washer-dryer facilities at hand. There's no maid service (some guests hire one by the hour). You're just half a block from the International Market Place, Hemmeter Center, and the lovely Ala Wai Canal. Also available are six condominium units —studios, and one- and two-bedrooms—with kitchen, air conditioning, TV, view, elevator, telephone, pool, and parking. They sleep two to four persons and rent from $36 per day up, no maid service. Owner Mrs. Vivian Young likes quiet, mature guests, and when she has a congenial group she often plans an outdoor party, especially to celebrate the Chinese New Year. Reserve a few weeks in advance.

The **Continental Surf,** 2426 Kuhio Ave., Honolulu, HI 96815 (tel. 922-2755), is an attractive high-rise with a big, airy lobby and comfortable rooms. The rooms all have color TV, telephone, and individually controlled air conditioning, but no lanai. The decor is tasteful Polynesian, using earthy browns and golds. Prices are reasonable: rooms without kitchenette are priced from $36 to $41, single and double, during the off-season, April 16 to December 20. The rest of the year, add $6. Should you want a room with a nicely equipped kitchen, expect to pay $46 single or double. One-bedroom suites with kitchenette go for $64 to $76 for up to four people during the low season. An extra person is charged $7, but children under 12 may stay free with their parents. The Continental Surf has no pool, restaurant, or recreational facilities; guests use all the facilities of its sister hotel, the Miramar, which is just 1½ blocks away. For reservations, call toll free 800/227-4320 from mainland United States, or 800/663-9671 from Canada.

Amy Lau, the owner of **Edmunds Hotel Apartments,** 2411 Ala Wai Blvd., Honolulu, HI 96815 (tel. 923-8381), has been making newcomers to Hawaii feel at home for well over 20 years now. Amy's establishment is very modest, a small guesthouse with long lanais curving around the building and fronting each of the small, very well-worn, but still okay studio rooms. Best news of all, these rent daily for just $22 single, $24 double, and $4 for each additional person. All rooms have twin beds, good mattresses, private bath, small kitchenette, plus toaster, ironing board, and television set—good value for this price category. There are several more rooms on a nearby street. The hotel faces the cool and breezy Ala Wai Canal and provides a lovely vista, especially at night, of Manoa Valley and the mountains, which goes far in making up for the fact that you do hear automobiles buzzing by. Acceptable for undemanding types.

Tucked away behind the posh Hyatt Regency Hotel, and just a short block from Kuhio Beach is a little gem of a new hotel called **Waikiki Hana,** 2424 Koa Ave., Honolulu, HI 96815 (tel. 926-8841). Actually, the building is not new, but a new management has come in and totally renovated and refurbished an older hotel, creating a sparkling, wicker-chaired lobby and 64 modern rooms that are just as attractive, each entered from the outside. They are furnished smartly in light woods with rose walls, blue quilted bedspreads, color TV, phones, and air conditioning. Refrigerators may be rented for $3 a day; only the top-of-the-line rooms have a kitchenette, which consists of a combination sink, refrigerator, and electric hotplate. Considering that this is a full-service hotel with an excellent location, rates are good: from April 1 to December 19, $41 for a standard double, $44 for a superior, $47.50 for a deluxe, and $52 for a superior deluxe (with kitchenette). In winter, rates are only $6 more per night, still making this one of the better values on the beach. For reservations, write Hawaiian Pacific Resorts, 1150 S. King St., Honolulu, HI 96814, or phone toll free 800/367-5004.

Some of the most reasonable prices in this close to the beach area are offered by the modest little **Waikiki Prince Hotel,** 2431 Prince Edward St., Honolulu, HI 96815 (tel. 922-1544). James Patey, the personable manager, took over this older, six-story, 30-unit hotel, about 3 years ago, and he has been working steadily to improve it: furnishings are acceptable, there is air conditioning and color cable TV in all the rooms, there are new drapes, bedspreads, pots and pans in those 20 rooms that have kitchenettes. The location, however, needs no improvement: it's right behind the Hyatt Regency Hotel, just two short blocks from Kuhio Beach. Many students stay here when school is out. There are no phones, but a buzzer system gets you your messages; rooms are cleaned once a week. Bedding is double or twin; there's a laundry on the premises. Rates, which include the 9% hotel tax, are as follows: from November 28 to December 19, a small studio with no cooking goes for $26; a small studio with cooking, $29; a larger studio with cooking, $33. From December 20 to April 5, those rates are $32, $35, and $38. And from April 6 to November 27, they are $26, $29, and $33, with the seventh day free.

Another budget hotel that's keeping the line on prices is the **Hale Waikiki,** 2410 Koa Ave., Honolulu, HI 96815 (tel. 923-9012), one of those older establishments you'd never confuse with the Hilton, but acceptable in its own right. For $35 daily ($25 daily on a weekly basis), expect small and medium rooms without cross ventilation or views. However, clean tile floors, clean curtains, and clean spreads are a good bet. There is color TV, private bathroom with shower, two beds, a closet and minimal furniture, and cooking facilities. A sidewalk gate leads into a garden that runs along the length of the building, with hanging plants adorning all three balconies. And it's not far from the beach.

There are youth hostels in Honolulu. There's been one in graceful Manoa Valley, near the campus of the University of Hawaii, for 18 years, and there's a smaller one, **Hale Aloha,** which is just the ticket for beach buffs, since it's two short blocks from Waikiki Beach at 2417 Prince Edward St., Honolulu, HI 96815 (tel. 946-0591). The Waikiki hostel is for AYH or IYHF members only (you can become a member by paying a $20 fee), and offers dormitory accommodations at $9 a night for 9 women and 13 men. Two common rooms provide kitchens, TV, and the relaxed comraderie for which youth hostels are famous. Dorms are closed and locked from 11 a.m. to 5 p.m. daily in accordance with the hostel tradition of promoting the outdoor life. Couples might consider renting one of the four studios here at $20 per night, which feature private bath and shower, mini-refrigerators, private entrance, and 24-hour access to the rooms; some have TV. Jack Butrymowicz, Hale Aloha's houseparent, is a veritable font of information on low-cost vacationing and travel. Stays are limited to 3 days; parking is $3 a day on a space available basis.

The **Honolulu International Youth Hostel** in Manoa Valley is the major facility, with 18 beds for women and 20 beds for men. Rates are $7 per night for members, $9 for non-members. Common rooms, a kitchen, ping-pong table, games and a patio under the stars create a relaxed mood here, and again, houseparents Thelma and Susan Akau are helpful sources of information. Facilities are locked between 9 a.m. and 4:30 p.m. daily.

Note: hostels are for "the young at heart, regardless of age," although students—Australian, European, Canadian, Japanese, as well as American—do predominate.

Reservations for both hostels must be made by writing or phoning the Manoa Valley establishment: Honolulu International Youth Hostel, 2323A Sea View Ave., Honolulu, HI 96822 (tel. 946-0591).

Up near the Honolulu Zoo, the **Waikiki Pearl Hotel,** 2555 Cartwright St., Honolulu, HI 96815 (tel. 922-1677) is a fine choice for us budgeteers. This is a modern, eight-story building with some 85 units, not large as hotels go. But standing at the desk in the spacious lobby, with large clocks telling you the time in Hawaii, London, Tokyo, and New York, it's easy to feel you are in a major hotel. Hotel rooms are available at $35, studio rooms with kitchen facilities at $50. Each room has a telephone, color TV, air conditioning, and a tub-shower combo. Most rooms have queen-size double beds, but some with twins are also available. Nicely-furnished one-bedroom apartments are available at $70, penthouse apartments at $80 (the latter for up to four people with no extra perperson charge). In all the other rooms, an extra person is charged $8. This is a fairly new building, so expect modern, clean facilities. There is guest parking, but no swimming pool and no dining facilities. But with the ocean and restaurants two short blocks away, this is no problem.

Central Waikiki

Choicely located a block from the beach and a block from the main drag in Waikiki, the **Coral Seas Hotel,** 250 Lewers St., Honolulu, HI 96815 (tel. 923-3881), is one of the inexpensive hotels in the empire of Outrigger Hotels Hawaii. The rooms and lobby were recently renovated, and now the spacious rooms boast brown carpets, beige wallpaper, green bedspreads with an orange bird-of-paradise blossom print: all have private lanais and air conditioning to keep things cool. Small kitchenettes (with rather minimal cooking equipment) are available upon request. Doubles or singles without kitchenettes are priced at $24 to $40. Doubles or singles with kitchenettes are $35 to $50. Additional person: $15. And there are some larger rooms starting around $40 that can comfortably accommodate four, a real family find. Prices are subject to change. The beach is just down the street, and right in the hotel is a branch of Perry Boys' Smorgy, which offers such good bargains that you may never bother cooking in your room at all.

An important thing to remember about the Coral Seas: If there are no rooms available here, the management may be able to place you in any of several hundred equivalent rooms a few blocks away, all part of the Outrigger chain. For reservations, call toll free 800/367-5170 in continental U.S. and Alaska; in Canada, 800/826-6786.

Another of those ubiquitous Outrigger outposts, the **Waikiki Surf,** 2200 Kuhio Ave., Honolulu, HI 96815 (tel. 923-7671), is well set up for comfortable living. The rooms are spacious, with compact kitchenettes if you ask for them, usually studio beds, air conditioning, and a long narrow lanai that is shared with the next room. Accommodations vary with the price, but all are comfortable. Depending on the season, rooms without kitchenette range from $30 to $45; rooms with kitchenette are $40 to $55. An extra person is charged $15. Two-room family apartments are $55 to $65 for up to four people. The comfortable chairs in the lobby afford a view of passersby on the sidewalk. The bustle of Kalakaua is just one long block away; the Pacific, two. The **Waikiki Surf East and Waikiki Surf West** are part of the same complex, all located close to each other and the beach. They have kitchenettes and slightly lower rates. A nice plus: Waikiki Surf guests are welcome to use the oceanfront beach and pool of the Outrigger Waikiki Hotel, run by the same management. For toll-free reservations, phone 800/367-5170 in continental U.S. and Alaska, 800/826-6786 in Canada. Prices subject to change.

The **Edgewater,** at 2168 Kalia Rd., Honolulu, HI 96815, corner of Lewers (tel. 923-3111), has long enjoyed one of the best locations in Waikiki. Halfway between the ocean and Kalakaua Avenue, the hotel is a two-minute walk to either the peace of sun and surf or the bustle of restaurants, shops, and nighteries. It's a big hotel, with a fairly big swing in prices. Rooms without kitchenettes go from $35 to $50, single or double, depending upon space and view. Kitchenettes range from $55 to $60, single or double, and family suites cost $85. An additional person is charged $15. Rates subject to change. Rooms were recently renovated and are pleasantly furnished; the bathrooms have stall showers but no tubs. Your lanai will be furnished, but nothing will separate you from your neighbor's porch. This is a homey place, with lots of space to stroll around the building, plenty of lobby area and public rooms. The Trattoria Restaurant, right on the grounds, is a Waikiki favorite for northern Italian food. The Edgewater is another of those Outrigger Hotels Hawaii, which means that, for toll-free reservations in continental U.S. and Alaska, you phone 800/367-5170; in Canada, 800/826-6786.

The **Kuhio Banyan,** 2310 Kuhio Ave., Honolulu, HI 96815 (tel. 923-5887) is one of a disappearing breed—a small, low-rise modern hotel in the heart of Waikiki. It's just across from the International Marketplace, two blocks from the beach, and even closer to several theatres. Although Kuhio Avenue is a bit noisy, the hotel itself is set back behind a brick court, and air conditioning permits you to keep the heavy plate glass windows shut. The rate for standard studios is $39 for one or two persons from April 20 through December 14, $49 the rest of the year. A third person is $8 per day, but there is no charge for children under 12.

Every studio has been recently renovated and at this writing a lobby renovation was underway. There are three stories of rooms, all with exterior entrances from rear walkways, by contrast quite secluded and quiet compared to busy Kuhio Street. A two-burner range, refrigerator, and utensils comprise the kitchenette. The bathroom is spacious with a large vanity, and contains a closet and stall shower. Rooms have twin beds, flower print spreads, and a russet rug. Yes, there's color TV, telephone, and maid service. The hotel is part of the Hawaiian Islands Resorts chain, so you can reserve via a toll-free number: 800/367-7402.

Ewa Waikiki

Families are made especially welcome—but then so is everybody else—at the cozy **Malihini Hotel,** at 217 Saratoga Rd., Honolulu, HI 96815 (tel. 923-9644). Situated in an ideal location, across the street from the right-of-way to the beach, the Malihini is a small, older hotel, a homey place with a brick courtyard with barbecue facilities where guests gather to eat and talk. The rooms in the older building, once a private home, are super-plain and the furnishings are well worn, but everything is clean. During the long off-season—from April to December 15—studios are $22 to $24, single or double. The lanai rooms in the newer building are very well maintained and go for $28 to $34, single or double; one-bedroom apartments are $38 to $44 for four to five people. During high season, rates go up a few dollars. There is no air conditioning, but fans keep things cool. Weekly rentals are available, and families are always given the best rates possible. Owner Richard C. Sutton, a cordial host who likes to make everyone feel at home, advises reservations 60 days in advance.

The management of the **Reef Lanais,** 225 Saratoga Rd., Honolulu, HI 96815, is the same as that of the Coral Seas and Waikiki Surf hotels, which we've told you about in the section on "Central Waikiki." The Reef Lanais and the Coral Seas have the same telephone number: 923-3881. Rates are the same for both singles and doubles: $30 to $45 for rooms without kitchenettes, $45 to $60 for rooms with kitchenettes. Add $15 for an additional person. There are also a few suites with kitchenettes for four persons at $70 to $75. Rates subject to change. The beach is a hop-skip-and-a-jump away, since there is a public right-of-way to the beach just across Kalia Road. There is no pool on the premises, but the Reef Lanais' guests may use the one at Waikiki Village, right around the corner on Lewers Street. The hotel is 100% air-conditioned, and although it lacks some of the frills of its sister hotels, it is an excellent value for the price. And the presence of the ever-popular Buzz's Steakhouse on the premises is another plus. For toll-free reservations, call 800/367-5170 in continental U.S. and Alaska; in Canada, 800/826-6786.

One of our favorite streets in Honolulu is Beachwalk, a tiny street running from Kalakaua smack into the ocean and relatively—for Waikiki—quiet. Here you'll find the **Niihau Apartment Hotel,** 247 Beachwalk, Honolulu, HI 96815 (tel. 922-1607), a relaxing place in which to kick off your sandals. The 11-story, 21-unit hotel consists of only one- and two-bedroom apartments, small but cozy, all with air conditioning, cable TV, private telephone, and lanai. The decor is pleasant enough, varying in each apartment: bathrooms (showers only, no tubs) are prettily wallpapered; the modern kitchens are large and very well equipped. And although the rooms are small, the fact that each apartment has several rooms provides a sense of privacy. Prices are good: one-bedroom apartments for a party of two are $35; two-bedroom apartments for up to four are $49. An additional person is $10 a day; parking next door runs $3.50 a day. Manager Hyacinth Hesson (everybody calls her "Hy") runs this place with a firm hand, aims to keep it quiet, and turns away noisy guests. Bravo! Advance reservations advised.

Over the years, we've had very positive input from readers on the **Ilima Hotel,** 445 Nohonani St., Honolulu, HI 96815 (tel. 923-1877). And no wonder—this place is eminently comfortable, it offers many facilities and services, and it maintains a reasonable rate schedule. A walk of less than ten minutes will take you to the beach. You can really kick off your shoes and feel at home here; floors are carpeted, and the studios include one or two double beds, a fully equipped kitchen, color TV, radio, full tub and shower, plenty of storage space, and a private lanai. There's a swimming pool at ground level, two sundecks on the tenth floor, as well as an exercise room, sauna, and Jacuzzi. Generosities not usually found in most hotels include free parking and free local phone calls! If you stick to one of the standard studio units, fourth floor and under, you can get by with $37 single, $42 double, from April 15 to December 15. Views and prices increase as you go up to the moderate rooms on the 5th floor ($42 and $48), the superior ones on the 6th through 9th floors ($46 and $54), and the deluxe ones on the 10th through 16th floors ($54 and $60). Small bedroom apartments for three run from $62 to $84; large bedroom apartments for four are $72 to $90; two-bedroom suites for up to four are $84 to $102. In winter, add $8 to all rates;

a crib or rollaway is $6 extra; a third person is $12. For reservations, call toll free 800/421-0767; in Canada, 800/663-1118.

Near the Ala Wai

A small luxury hotel at budget prices is the **Waikiki Holiday,** 450 Lewers St., Honolulu, HI 96815 (tel. 923-0245), where your willingness to walk about ten minutes to the beach will save you a nice few dollars. This is at the Ala Wai Canal end of Lewers, so don't expect an ocean view, but there is plenty of mountain view—and lots of view inside, where the handsome decor and appointments are the work of Tom Hirai, a top Honolulu designer. All rooms are air-conditioned and have private lanais. There's a perfectly beautiful free-form pool and a tempting Indian restaurant, Shalimar. Now about those attractive rates: singles or doubles without kitchens are $27 to $41; with kitchens, $31 to $63; an additional person is charged $6. One-bedroom suites go from $50 to $78.

Some of the lowest rates in Waikiki are being offered at the **Ala Wai Terrace Hotel,** at 1547 Ala Wai Blvd., Honolulu, HI 96815 (tel. 949-7384), at the very beginning of the boulevard, not far from Ala Moana. This 40-year-old apartment building, now under the aegis of Outrigger Hotels Hawaii, was recently converted into a hotel, and while there's nothing at all fancy about it (don't expect tourist amenities like a pool or restaurant), it does offer clean and comfortable units—with kitchen facilities, air conditioning, and all the necessities—at very decent rates. There are two buildings, the 15-story Tower Building (which has TV in its units), and the low-rise, walk-up Garden Building. Studios in either building are quite small and furnished with a convertible sofa; they rent for $25 daily, $140 weekly, for one or two people. One-bedroom units in the Garden Building are $30 daily, $170 weekly. One-bedroom units in the Tower Building go up in price as they go up in height, from $32 to $45 daily and from $189 to $280 weekly. Monthly rates are available in all categories, and the price stays the same year-round. Rates subject to change. For reservations, phone the central office for Outrigger Hotels Hawaii, at toll free 800/367-5170 on the mainland and in Alaska, 800/826-6786 in Canada.

Jocko O'Nan Realty, P.O. Box 8891, Honolulu, HI 96815 (tel. 943-1776 or 926-4893), formerly known as Apartments Waikiki, is a central source for a variety of condominium apartments. Rather than tell you about all the buildings in which they have listings, we've chosen three that best suit the budget traveler: **Fairway Villa,** 2345 Ala Wai Blvd.; **Island Colony Hotel,** 445 Seaside Ave.; and **2211 Ala Wai,** whose name and address are one and the same. All three are $35 a day in low season, from May 1 to November 30, on both a daily and weekly rate (2211 Ala Wai falls into that category only on those rooms without a lanai; its weekly price is an even lower $30 a day). Amenities differ in all three. Fairway Villa, which requires a minimum stay of one week, offers studios with private lanais and color TV, laundry facilities, swimming pool, sauna, and free parking. Island Colony studios have private lanai and color TV, plus swimming pool and sauna. 2211 Ala Wai offers one-bedroom apartments for up to four people, which have color TV and, on the premises, swimming pool, sauna, shuffleboard, barbecue grills, mini gym, laundry facilities, free parking, and even a Japanese furo bath. Write or phone well in advance for reservations.

Just Beyond Waikiki

Our last recommendation in this category is technically just over the Waikiki border, but not far enough out to be inconvenient. The **Central Branch YMCA,** 401 Atkinson Dr., Honolulu, HI 96814 (tel. 941-3344), is a five-minute bus ride from Waikiki on the no. 8 or Ala Moana bus to Ala Moana and Atkinson Drive. It's a beautiful place, with an outdoor swimming pool and lovely grounds. The newly-painted rooms are small but adequate—"Y-style." Singles with community bathroom and showers are $16.50 daily; with bathroom and shower, $19.50 daily. Add $10 a day for a rollaway bed and you have a double. The Y has a reasonably-priced coffee shop and no end of recreational activities. The single male tourist could hardly do better than stop here. No reservations are accepted.

THE GOOD BUYS: Prices in this category range, roughly, from $45 to $55 and up for a double. Again, savings can be realized by those staying for more than a week and by groups of more than two people traveling together.

Diamond Head Waikiki

A big, bright, modern hotel, the **Aloha Surf,** 444 Kanekapolei St., Honolulu, HI 96815 (tel. 923-0222), is a 15-story, 204-room building offering cheery accommodations in a variety of sizes and shapes. Best suited for our budget are the standard rooms, which go for $48, single or double. They are sunlit, brightly decorated, and air-conditioned. Located higher up, with better views and private lanais, are the moderate rooms, at $52. If you want a kitchenette, you'll have to pay $62. Each additional person in a room is charged $10. There's a nice pool, good service, and a restaurant serving lunch and dinner, and the beach is just a few blocks away. The toll-free reservations number is 800/423-4514.

Readers of past editions of this book who remember the Kuhiolani Hotel will be surprised—very pleasantly—to discover its metamorphosis into **Kaulana Kai,** 2425 Kuhio Ave., Honolulu, HI 96815 (tel. 922-1978). Located in a great spot three minutes away from Kuhio Beach, the tall, modern pyramid-like building designed by Scandinavian architect Jo Paul Rongstad has been renovated inside and out. A strong blue-and-white color scheme predominates, starting in the tasteful lobby, working its way up through elevator and hallways, and into the attractive rooms (58 are available for tourists in the 100-room, partly condominium hotel). These are not large, but they are attractive, done primarily in white, with a white table, white dresser-desk, a white spread with red and blue accents, tasteful prints on the wall. Each room is fully carpeted, with twin beds, small lanai, and a tidy two-burner kitchenette, with refrigerator underneath the range. Studio rooms start at $55, one-bedroom suites (two beds in one room, a double in the other, plus a kitchen) are $78 for up to four people. Manager Alice Bascom and her staff provide courteous and friendly service. Parking is available at $2.50 per day. Attractive and pleasant, this is a bright new find. We heartily concur with the Canadian travel agent who recently described the Kaulana Kai as "one of the best little buys in Waikiki." For toll-free reservations, phone 800/367-5666 from the U.S. mainland.

You can't beat the location of the **Waikiki Surfside Hotel,** right across the street from the ocean at 2452 Kalakaua Ave., Honolulu, HI 96815 (tel. 923-0266). Often a hotel's name belies its location, but this one really is surfside, and its location and front room views are its best features. This older hotel had seen much wear and tear, but a new management has taken over and renovated all the rooms. All of the 80 units are air conditioned and have TVs. Standard rooms go from $39 to $49; moderates, from $45 to $55; superiors from $50 to $60; and $10 for an additional person. For reservations, write Aston Hotels & Resorts, 2255 Kuhio Ave., Honolulu, HI 96815, or phone toll free 800/367-5124 in continental U.S., 800/423-8733, ext. 250 in Canada.

Very welcome in this area is the **Quality Inn,** 175 Paoakalani Ave., Honolulu, HI 96815 (two blocks from Kalakaua, one block from Kapahulu, near Kapiolani Park; tel. 922-3861). It's cheerful, sparkling, and radiates aloha, which you'll notice the minute you approach it. It's smart looking, with a waterfall at the entrance, a golden lobby, and friendly people behind the desk. Prices are lowest in the Diamond Head Tower: $48 single, $51 double, with $12 for each additional person. There are no kitchenettes, but you'll still enjoy your lanai and the view. In the Pali Tower, all rooms have partial kitchenettes; here the rates go up to $57 single, $60 double in low season, $62 and $65 in high season. The air-conditioned rooms are standard size, equipped with call-out phones, dressing areas, and stall showers large enough and deep enough for a bath too. There are two small pools on the third floor. Call toll free, for reservations: 800/367-2317. Rates subject to change.

The **Waikiki Grand**, at 134 Kapahulu, Honolulu, HI 96815 (tel. 923-1511), is one of the most popular places in town for the flocks of Japanese tourists who've discovered Hawaii, and for us that's an extra inducement to stay at this attractive hotel. You can get all the comforts of this hotel at its standard low season (April 15 to December 14) rate of $45, single or twin. At this price you'll get a room with a view of the center of Waikiki and the mountains in the distance; you'll have to go a few dollars more ($50, single or twin) for a breathtaking view of Diamond Head in the other direction. Studio rooms with kitchenettes are $55, single or twin. An additional person is $7; add $5 in high season. Super views or not, the rooms are pleasant if small (very little closet space), feature tub-showers, direct-dial telephones, and air conditioning. There's a pleasant swimming pool in a secluded court, a Japanese restaurant is on the premises, Kapiolani Park and its activities are across the street, and good old Kuhio Beach is just around the bend.

The **Monte Vista**, c/o Lani Properties, Suite C203, 50 So. Beretania St., Honolulu, HI 96813 (tel. 521-0081) is a new, expensively-built, 25-story condominium at 320 Liliuokalani St., corner Ala Wai Blvd. Sometimes a condo hotel starts out as a hotel and begins to sell off units. Other times, as in this case, it starts out as a condominium and owners begin to rent their units. Here, there is no likeness at all to a hotel: no desk, no switchboard, no hotel amenities—just apartments. There is an on-site manager, but he is busy with condominium duties. Thus, you make arrangements with Anita Ho of Lanai Properties, listed above. This place is a good buy for us during the off-season, from April 15 to November 1, when the peak-season rates of $65 to $90 drop to a manageable $45. Furnishings and equipment vary from apartment to apartment, but all are of good quality. There is excellent security, and panoramic views to boot. You may want to cook in here as the nearest restaurant is about three blocks away—which is also about the distance to the beach.

You'll find the **Park Shore Hotel**, 110 Kapahulu St., Honolulu, HI 96815 (tel. 923-0411), a large, cheery place up near Kuhio Beach, Kapiolani Park, and all the goings-on at this end of Waikiki. The Park Shore does have stunning views of the beach and Diamond Head, but these are reserved for the more expensive, spacious rooms. These run from $65 to $110. Best we stick with those rooms without a view, facing the Holiday Inn; they go for $65, single or double. Add $5 during the winter season. It's $10 for an additional person. Tub-shower combos, air conditioning, color TV, and radios are added attractions, while the bright blue-and-green interior creates a cheery ambience. For reservations, phone toll free 808/367-2377.

The **Honolulu Prince**, 415 Nahua St., Honolulu, HI 96815 (tel. 922-1616), is one of Waikiki's older apartment hotels that has seen many years of comfortable, casual living. At the time of our last visit there was talk of a sale to new owners and a major upgrading; that will, of course, mean higher prices, but until that happens, this hotel offers some very neat values. Our favorite units here are the spacious one-bedroom apartments with full kitchens and separate bedrooms, nicely furnished and laid out. These rent for $65 for up to four people. The studio/kitchenettes, furnished with two twin beds and a queen-size sofa bed, are also good buys at $45. And even the studio without a kitchenette is okay, reasonably priced at $35. If there are up to six of you, you can all be accommodated in the two-bedroom kitchen apartments, with two double beds and a sofabed, and plenty of room to putter around in, for $75. Most units have lanais; all have television and telephone, and are air-conditioned. Maid service is provided every other day. No pool, no frills, but a good value, while it lasts.

The towering **Royal Kuhio** condominium building, 2240 Kuhio Ave., Honolulu, HI 96815 (tel. 923-3250), is one of the growing number of such places that has a great number of apartments in the "hotel pool"—which means they are available to visitors for short- or long-term stays. These apartments are quite attractive, nicely decorated, with a bedroom with twin beds that can be closed off from the sitting room or opened to make one big area. The sitting room has sofa beds, and rollaways are available for extra people. The kitchens are all-electric (with dishwashers), the closet space is ample, and every apartment has its own color TV and lanai. A pool and sundeck area, billiard room, Ping-Pong, a shuffleboard court, and a huge laundry room and recreation area all make for easy living—not to mention the location close to the beach. There is weekly maid service. During the long summer season—April 16 through December 14—two people can get a one-bedroom apartment for $49, a mountain-view apartment for $56; rates go up to $72 for a deluxe ocean view. During the winter season, the rate range is $66 to $105. Reservations: Paradise Management Corp., Suite C-207, 50 S. Beretania St., Honolulu, HI 96813. The toll-free number is 800/367-5205.

Central Waikiki

A place that has just about everything going for it is the **Marine Surf,** 364 Seaside Ave., Honolulu, HI 96815 (tel. 923-0277). Located about a block and a half away from the beach, the Marine Surf is a 23-story condominium hotel featuring smartly decorated studio apartments, each of which boasts two extra-length double beds, lots of drawer space, color TV, air conditioning, phone, dressing room, and bath with both tub and shower. Best of all, each studio has a full electric kitchen, just in case you're not prepared to spend the rarified prices at Matteo's Italian Restaurant, one of the finest in town, right on the lobby floor. Rooms, which have been completely renovated; are serviced daily, and a personal safe is available in every unit. Those too lazy to walk to the beach can swim and sun at the lovely pool on the fourth floor. Now for the rates: during the long spring-summer-fall season (from April 8 through December 20), standard rooms are $46, superior are $53, and deluxe are $59, single or double. A one-bedroom penthouse suite is $85. During the winter, rates are $58, $65, $71, and $100. There's no room for a rollaway bed for a third person, but cribs are available at $8. A rate increase is expected. On-site parking is $2 per day. For toll-free reservations, call 800/367-5176; in Canada, 800/663-1118.

Outrigger Hotels Hawaii has a number of establishments in central Waikiki, and of these, one of the most suitable for the budget-minded is the **Outrigger Surf,** 2280 Kuhio Ave., Honolulu, HI 96815, on the corner of Nohonani Street (tel. 922-5777), a short walk from the beach. We like it because it has the greatest number of standard units, all apartments with kitchen facilities, and very good prices: $45 to $65 single or double (from December 19 through March 31, add $10). There are also suites with kitchenettes that can sleep up to four persons at $70 and $80; additional persons are charged $15 each.

Outrigger Surf is a tall, modern building, with 16 floors of comfortable studios, each with a lanai, TV, carpeting, air conditioning, beds in studio arrangement providing a living-room look. There's a stall shower in the bathroom, his-and-hers closets for storage, a two-burner range and basecabinet type of refrigerator for light cooking. The lobby is small but comfortable, and green Astroturf surrounds the lobby-level pool. For toll-free reservations, phone 800/367-5170 in continental U.S. and Alaska, 800/826-6786 in Canada.

Another member of the Outrigger chain that keeps the budget tourist well in mind is the **Waikiki Tower Hotel,** 200 Lewers St., Honolulu, HI 96815 (tel. 922-6424), whose standard rooms are only $45 a day from April 1 through December 18, $55 the rest of the year. Since it's right across Kalia Road from the beachfront Reef Hotel, you can't beat the location. Access to restaurants is just as easy as to the beach: there's the Waikiki Broiler downstairs, Denny's across Lewers Street. The lobby is open to the breezes, blue carpeted, and chock full of convenience desks and shops. The standard rate applies to the lower floors, so don't expect a great view; but they are identical to the higher-up and higher-priced "moderates" ($50 regular, $60 peak season). A large double bed, studio couch, a two-chair lanai, breakfast table, blue carpets, large shoji door closet, color TV, smoke detector, and private in-room safe are just some of the amenities. The two bed lamps have hollow glass bases filled with sea shells—a nice touch. The bathroom is equipped with a stall shower. For toll free reservations, phone 800/367-5170 in continental U.S. and Alaska, 800/826-6786 in Canada.

The **Waikiki Village Hotel,** 240 Lewers St., Honolulu, HI 96815 (tel. 923-3881), is the first hotel we've ever seen with a swimming pool in the center of the lobby! The lobby is a quadrangle built around the pool and there's no ceiling in the center, so you can swim and sunbathe while checking out the new arrivals. The hotel is decorated from lobby to rooms in a bright blending of contemporary and Polynesian styles. Each of the 439 units has air conditioning and a television set; most have lanais. Rooms are all the same, although those on the lower floors are cheaper; the prices, bottom to top, are $50 to $75, single or twin. Kitchenette units—standard, moderate, and deluxe—go for $55 to $75. Family suites are $65 to $130 for up to four persons. These have half-size refrigerators and hotplates. Additional person: $15. The Village boasts its own restaurant, cocktail lounge, and several attractive shops—and a superb location right in the middle of everything and close to the beach. For reservations from the U.S. mainland, phone toll free 800/367-5170. Rates subject to change.

The **Outrigger Malia Hotel,** 2211 Kuhio Ave., Honolulu, HI 96815 (tel. 923-7621), is a bright and beautiful place. The rooms in the Malia wing, the taller of the hotel's two sections, contain two double beds with Polynesian print bedspreads in soft, muted colors and russet wall-to-wall carpeting. All rooms in the hotel have color TV, telephone, and lanai, both tub and shower in the bathroom, as well as small refrigerator, and ironing board. Handicapped people will be glad to know that there are 16 rooms in this wing especially designed for them, with wider doorways, grab bars in the bathrooms, and twin-size rather than double beds for greater wheelchair mobility. Rooms in the Malia wing rent for $45 standard, $55 moderate, and $65 deluxe. Add $10 between December 19 and March 31. Differences in rate depend on the floor; and an extra person in the room pays $10.

Then there's the Luana wing, with its junior suites. These contain a sitting room with two couches and a bedroom with two beds. The lanais in the suites are much larger than those in the bedrooms in the Malia wing. Junior suites, which can accommodate four guests comfortably, go for $65 to $75 ($10 more in winter). An extra person pays $10. Pluses for guests at both wings include a Jacuzzi whirlpool, a rooftop tennis court, and the excellent Wailana Coffeeshop, open 24 hours a day (see Chapter III). And, of course, the beach is just three blocks away. For reservations, call toll free 800/367-5170 in continental U.S. and Alaska, 800/826-6786 in Canada.

You get a really large room at the **Coral Reef,** a modern high-rise hotel at 2299 Kuhio Ave., Honolulu, HI 96815 (tel. 922-1262), directly behind the International Market Place and a short walk from Waikiki Beach. The 243-room hotel boasts every facility—swimming pool, garage, restaurants, shops—and nicely furnished, air-conditioned rooms that have either one or two double beds (or a double and a single), private lanais, and cable color TV. Prices run from $45 for doubles all the way up to $95 for one-bedroom suites on the higher floors. A third person in the room is charged $10; during the winter season, from December 20 to April 1, add $20 per category. Rates subject to change. Cooking facilities are available on request in any category for a $5 daily fee. For reservations, write Aston Hotels & Resorts, 2255 Kuhio Ave., Honolulu, HI 96815, or phone toll free 800/367-5124 in continental U.S., 800/423-8733, ext. 250 in Canada.

Ewa Waikiki

Maile Court, 2058 Kuhio Ave., Honolulu, HI 96815 (tel. 947-2828), is a welcome addition to the Waikiki scene; it's well priced, designed for the easy life, and located at the "Gateway to Waikiki," across the road from the well-known Nick's Fishmarket Restaurant—which means it's within easy walking distance of the beach and all the attractions of Kalakaua Avenue. There's a very pleasant feeling here, evident as soon as you walk into the open-air lobby, so pretty with its statuary, fish pond, maroon-and-beige rugs, and dusty-rose and rattan sofas. With over 500 rooms, this 43-story Colony Resorts condominium resort has a variety of accommodations to offer: 322 hotel rooms, 90 studios, and 88 one-bedroom suites. Rooms are of modest size, but most have views (some, from the higher floors, are spectacular), all have attractive furnishings, flower prints on the walls, cable color TV, and individually controlled air conditioning. There are clocks, radios, tub-showers, phones, but no lanais. Even the hotel rooms boast small refrigerators; studios and suites add a two-burner electric range for light cooking. Prices are $55 to $75 for hotel rooms, $60 to $80 for studios, $95 to $135 for one-bedroom suites (perfect for two couples or a family, with two bedrooms, two bathrooms, and two refrigerators). Children under 12 stay free if they use existing beds; rollaways and cribs are charged at $8 each. There's lots to keep you busy in-house: a pool and a huge, hot Jacuzzi on the large, carpeted sundeck. For reservations at Maile Court, phone toll free 800/367-6046. Inquire about condo-car packages.

Many of the guests at **Hale Pua Nui,** 228 Beach Walk, Honolulu, HI 96815 (tel. 923-9693), are returnees, coming back year after year to this lovely little complex of some 22 large studio apartments run by genial Patrick Glaviano, who can be counted upon to keep his guests smiling. The location is tops—just a half block to the beach at the Reef Hotel, and just around the bend from Fort DeRussy, where the swimming is excellent. The studio apartments are of good size, with either twin, double, or king-sized beds, depending on availability. They are nicely furnished with artistic touches, have cross-ventilation and acoustic walls and ceilings, are thoroughly equipped (even to ironing boards), and have complete kitchens. There's a courtesy phone in the office. The tariff, including all sales and room taxes, is $55.85 for one or two persons, $64.42 for three or four: weekly rates are $367.92 and $413.91. Rates are even less for senior citizens: $41.61 single or double from March 15 through May 31, $44.91 from June 1 through October 14, $41.61 from October 15 through December 14, and $49.28 from December 15 through March 14. Parking is not available here.

A favorite oldtimer in Hawaii, the **Hawaiiana Hotel,** 260 Beachwalk, Honolulu, HI 96815 (tel. 923-3811), just keeps getting more and more mellow year after year. One of the few low-rise garden hotels left in Waikiki, the Hawaiiana is wonderfully located just half a block from good swimming in front of the Reef Hotel and Fort DeRussy. Ninety-five rooms are situated around a gorgeous tropical garden and two swimming pools in the two- and three-story buildings, so you can just step out of your door for a swim in the pool or a complimentary breakfast of juice and coffee out on the patio. Comfortable chairs at poolside are occupied most of the day by guests too content to go out and do much else. Rooms are simply furnished and not fancy, but all have color TV, electronic safe, electric kitchen, excellent beds, air conditioning, phone; most have a lanai. During the summer (April 20 to December 17), rates are $50 to $65 single, $53 to $67 double, extra person $8, for studios with kitchens; one-bedroom suites are $89 with kitchens for up to four guests. During the winter, rates are about $3 to $5 higher. Several package deals offer good value; inquire of the management. Rates are subject to change. The real charm here is in the grounds, and especially in the all-Hawaiian staff, who treat each guest with true aloha, and dispense such welcome extras as pineapple upon arrival, flower leis on departure, free newspapers in the morning or afternoon, Hawaiian shows twice a week, free use of washing and drying machines, free parking at the rear of the hotel on Saratoga Road. A real taste of oldtime Hawaii. For reservations, phone toll free 800/367-5122; from Canada, call collect 808/922-8188.

Those of you who remember the old Kalia Inn will be surprised to find that it's now the **Royal Islander,** 2164 Kalia Rd., Honolulu, HI 96815 (tel. 922-1961). The lobby, small and open to the street, is much as it used to be, but all of the 101 units have been done over and are quite pretty, not large, but nicely decorated with tapa-print spreads and shell lamps, with Hawaiian-type pictures on the walls. Each room has a private lanai, air conditioning, color TV, and a modern bathroom with shower. Studio rooms go for $35 to $60, single or double. Families will do well in the one-bedroom apartments and suites, which range from $75 to $85 for up to four people; add $10 for an extra person. The Royal Islander has a super location, right near the Halekulani and Reef hotels, across the road from a very good beach. There's a McDonald's right in the hotel. And the hotel offers a variety of activities—morning runs in Waikiki, golf and scuba packages—and provides transportation for a number of sightseeing adventures. For reservations, phone toll free 800/367-5170, Central Reservations, Outrigger Hotels, Hawaii.

The modest-looking **Kai Aloha Hotel,** at 235 Saratoga Rd., Honolulu, HI 96815 (tel. 923-6723), is the kind of place whose faithful fans return year after year. They prefer the homeyness of this simple little hotel, the friendliness of the management, and the feeling of intimacy rare at the more impersonal concrete high-rise hotels. The location, very close to the beach and shopping area, is convenient, and the lush tropical plantings add an island flavor. Every unit has either a modern kitchen or kitchenette; apartments have full-size refrigerators, and the studios, half-size ones. All units have a garbage disposal, toaster, and ironing board. There are coin-operated laundry facilities available on the premises. Every unit has air conditioning, although on our last visit the trade winds alone made the rooms delightfully cool on a very hot day. Lanai studios, all with their own little porches, are $41 to $47 double; the one-bedroom apartments are

$52 to $55 double. The latter can comfortably accommodate families of four or five, with twin beds in the living room as well as living-room furniture. There is a charge of $10 for each additional person, and children are welcome. Rates are subject to change.

Although it looks better from the outside than it does inside, **Ambassador Hotel of Waikiki,** 2040 Kuhio Ave., Honolulu, HI 96815 (tel. 941-7777), is still good value for the money. All of the rooms in this high-rise building are approached from outside walkways, and the studios from the second through seventh floors boast private lanais, contemporary furniture, air conditioning, and deep *furo*-type shower-tubs. You can relax at the big pool and sundeck on the second floor, eat at the Café Ambassador, and you're close to all the attractions of Waikiki. Rates for studio rooms range from $42 to $46 single, $46 to $50 double, and there are also deluxe one-bedroom suites, with full electric kitchens, from $80 to $100. Studios with kitchens on request.

The **Waikiki Gateway Hotel,** at 2070 Kalakaua Ave., Honolulu, HI 96815 (tel. 955-3741), manages to stay within our budget for most of the year—from April 15 to December 20. The theme throughout is the Hawaii of bygone days, before the arrival of the missionaries. A well-known island artist is responsible for the murals that decorate the lobby and all of the rooms. Studio rooms are priced from $39 to $49 double, and each has a private lanai, TV set, luxurious bath with both tub and shower, and air conditioning. Deluxe rooms run $59 to $69. During the winter months, it's $8 to $9 more per category. An additional person is charged $10. Rates subject to change. Rooms have refrigerators and hotplates. The beach is less than a ten-minute walk, but if you'd rather swim at home, try the beautiful pool backed by a volcanic rock wall and a spacious sundeck. Adjacent to the pool area is a room with laundry facilities. Toll-free reservations: Aston 800/367-5124 in continental U.S., 800/423-8733, ext. 250 in Canada.

The nice thing about Best Western's **Waikiki Plaza Hotel,** 2045 Kalakaua Ave., Honolulu, HI 96815 (tel. 955-6363) is that it has all the comforts and conveniences of a full-service hotel, but its prices are more in line with those of less imposing establishments. The large 11-story stucco building is located right at the beginning of Waikiki, boasts 250 attractively refurbished rooms, several restaurants and a cocktail lounge, a swimming pool, activities desk, and convenience shops. There's a bellman's desk on the entrance driveway to help with baggage right from your car or taxi door. And parking is free in the underground garage. Views from the rooms are "iffy," as this is a built-up area, but one consolation is the triangular mini-park across Kalakaua where Kuhio Avenue begins. Rooms are nicely decorated, with a walk-in closet, sliding glass doors to the lanai, colorful Hawaiian print spreads color-coordinated in blue or mauve with carpets and draperies. Beds are either two queens or one king-sized; an in-room safe is provided; there's color TV and table and chairs for snacking or card-playing; and a refrigerator can be rented for $2.60 a day. Standard rooms rent for $50 single, $54 double all year; superiors go up to $58 and $62, deluxe to $74 and $78; an extra person is charged $12; no charge for cribs or a child under 12 with existing bedding; $10 for a rollaway bed.

You can also save money by eating right at the hotel, especially early. Baron's Place offers a half-pound prime rib for $6.99 and an all-you-can-eat-spaghetti meal for $4.99 between 5 and 5:30 p.m. (the price goes up just $1 later). Breakfast is served on the mezzanine, open to the breezes, from 6:30 to 11:30 a.m., and it's also reasonable—a platter with egg, two sausages and two pancakes is $1.99. For reservations from continental U.S., phone toll free 800/367-8047, ext. 101; from Canada, 800/423-8733, ext. 101.

Near the Ala Wai

The **Hawaiian Monarch**, 444 Niu Rd., Honolulu, HI 96815 (tel. 949-3911), is one of the newer entries into the Honolulu hotel scene. The skyscraper is situated very close to the Ala Wai Canal and halfway between the Ala Moana Shopping Center and the beaches of Waikiki. It's a well-run first-class hotel, with a mixed international clientele, complete with all the amenities of tourist life: a huge sundeck and regular pool, plenty of shops in the arcade, and the cozy Piko Bar in the main lobby, where there are free pupus during the Happy Hour, plus Hawaiian-style entertainment every night. A free shuttle bus runs on a frequent schedule to shepherd guests to Ala Moana Shopping Center and the heart of Waikiki. Parking is available at a nominal fee.

The Hawaiian Monarch is part hotel, part condo, and the hotel rooms, which occupy the 7th to 24th floors, all have individually controlled air conditioning, color TV, telephone, tub/shower combinations. They are small and pleasantly furnished, of no particular charm, but comfortable enough. The nicest views are those overlooking the Ala Wai Canal. Superior rooms are $43 to $49, deluxe rooms are $49 to $69, and suites go from $89 to $109. A third person in the room is charged $8; children under 12 stay free with their parents. For reservations, call Aston toll free 800/367-5124 in continental U.S., 800/423-8733, ext. 250 in Canada.

Near Ala Moana

Just across the big road from the Hilton Hawaiian Village and a five-minute walk from Fort DeRussy Beach is the attractive **Inn on the Park,** 1920 Ala Moana Blvd., Honolulu, HI 96815 (tel. 923-4511). This is a 230-unit, all-condominium hotel, with smallish but very pretty rooms attractively decorated with floral spreads, nice prints on the wall, and white furniture. Very helpful for those wishing to eat breakfast in and fix a light lunch are the refrigerator under the sink, toaster, and electric coffeepot in each room. (For more serious cooking, you'd have to get one of the deluxe units with kitchenette.) This place would be most suitable for twosomes; families might find it a bit tight. The lobby is wood-paneled, with Oriental rugs and candelabra-style chandeliers. There's a nice pool and sunning area on the fifth floor next to the Inn Beer Garden, another bar on the second floor, and an Italian restaurant on the ground floor. The Pantry Store provides groceries and sundries.

Accommodations here are in three classes: standard (mountain view), superior (ocean view), and deluxe (ocean view with kitchenette). Standard rooms do not have lanais and run $38 single or double. Superior rooms with lanais are priced at $44 single or double. Deluxe units with kitchenette are $54 single or double. All rooms have color TV with 11 channels of programming. For toll-free reservations, phone 800/367-2373.

Friends of ours who love to shop, come every year from Hong Kong and stay at the **Pacific Grand Hotel,** 747 Amana St., Honolulu, HI 96814 (tel. 955-1531). No wonder shoppers love it: it's not only a couple of blocks from the Ala Moana Shopping Center, it's also convenient to a large record/tape store, a smaller shopping mall, and excellent restaurants. Pacific Grand is a large condominium apartment complex, with about 50 hotel units. Since they are all individually owned, decor is different in each studio, but you can be sure each one has two double beds, a telephone, color TV, and a fully equipped kitchenette. There are laundry facilities on every floor, a swimming pool on the third floor, in-house parking. Prices are good: studios go from $40 to $55, depending only on the floor and the view; otherwise, they are all similar. For reservations, write Hawaiiana Resorts, 1100 Ward Ave., Suite 1100, Honolulu, HI 96814 or phone toll free, 800/367-7040.

A new skyscraper in this area, the **Outrigger Hobron,** 343 Hobron Lane, Honolulu, HI 96815, at Discovery Bay (tel. 942-7777), has 600 attractive accommodations to its credit. The 44-story condominium hotel is very popular with tour groups. There are 310 hotel rooms, 140 studios, and 150 deluxe studios. Most of these rooms look similar, the major difference being in height. All rooms have attractive blond wood furniture (desk, vanity, chair), multicolored drapes and bedspreads, air conditioning, and TV; they are small but well appointed, and many offer very good views of ocean, city, mountains, and the nearby Ala Wai Yacht Harbor. Most rooms have twin beds; only four on each floor have queen-size beds, which must be requested in advance. There are also differences in housekeeping facilities: the hotel rooms, which rent for $40 moderate, $45 deluxe, have refrigerators only; the studios, which go for $50 moderate, $55 deluxe, and have mini-kitchenettes. All rates are $20 more from December 19 to the end of March. Rates subject to change. There's a nice pool on the mezzanine level, a sundeck plus Jacuzzi and sauna on the fifth floor. Parking is available to hotel guests at $4 a day. All the excitement of the Ilikai and Hilton Hawaiian Village complexes is about five minutes away. For toll-free reservations, phone 800/367-5170 in continental U.S. and Alaska, 800/826-6786 in Canada.

The **Waikiki Marina,** 1956 Ala Moana Blvd., Honolulu, HI 96815 (tel. 955-0714), is a handsome hotel, just a few steps away from the Hilton Hawaiian Village and Rainbow Bazaar Complex, boasting a large swimming pool and sundeck, plus central air conditioning, and cable color TV. The most inexpensive accommodations here are the standard hotel rooms, which go for $42, single or double, from April 15 to December 16, and $48 the rest of the year. If you want to cook in, however, it's worthwhile to go a little higher and pay $47 moderate, $51 deluxe ($56 and $64 in winter), plus a $5 increment, to get a kitchenette studio. The studios are adequate in size, with sliding glass doors opening onto a lanai. Inside is a kitchenette with base refrigerator and two-burner range, a tub-shower combination, television, and phone. Standard suites are $68, deluxe suites with mountain view are $73 and deluxe suites with ocean view are $78 ($72, $78, and $84 in winter). Rates subject to change. An extra person is $10. For toll-free reservations, phone 800/367-6070.

Another good choice in this neighborhood, the **Hawaii Dynasty Hotel,** 1830 Ala Moana Blvd., Honolulu, HI 96815 (tel. 955-1111), is a high-rise hotel with an inn atmosphere. The accent is on comfort, with medium-size rooms and oversize beds. Twin beds are as big as most doubles, and the doubles are enormous. Rooms are tastefully furnished, with combination tub-showers in the bathroom, TV, and individual air-conditioning units. There are no cooking facilities. A laundry room is available. The pool on the second floor is one of the largest in Waikiki. Now for the prices: doubles at $40 standard, $43 deluxe, $48 superior-deluxe, plus a high-season surcharge of $10 from December 21 through March 31. An additional person is $12. For reservations, call toll free 800/421-6662 outside of California, 800/352-6686 in California.

A Reminder: Unless you want to spend most of your time in this area around the big Ilikai and Hilton Hawaiian Village complex of hotels, stores, restaurants, and beaches, you'd better have a car or be prepared to take the bus; it's a healthy ten-minute walk to either the center of Waikiki or the Ala Moana Shopping Center and Ala Moana Beach Park.

To compensate for not being right where the action is, the **Pagoda Hotel,** 1525 Rycroft St., Honolulu, HI 96814 (tel. 941-6611), keeps a free bus shuttling back and forth between the hotel and the Pacific Beach Hotel in Waikiki. But you won't be isolated here: not only are you near the shopping center, but right on the grounds is one of Honolulu's most spectacular restaurants, the Pagoda, with its colorful displays of flashing carp. Most important, though, is what you'll get for your $50 single or double: a studio room nicely set up for housekeeping, with a full-size refrigerator, four-burner range, and all the necessary equipment. Additional persons are charged $10. You can pay more to go higher up in the building ($4), but don't expect spectacular views here, as you're about a third of a mile from the water (in view over the Ala Moana Shopping Center). One-bedroom apartments go for $60; two-bedroom units for $78. The rooms are air-conditioned, and a swimming pool is here for the dunking. Color TV in all rooms. For toll-free reservations, phone 800/367-6060.

2. Hotels in Downtown Honolulu

Tourists who prefer to stay in downtown Honolulu (an easy bus ride from Waikiki) rather than in the beach area will have somewhat tougher sledding; there are so few hotels outside Waikiki that most tourists never hear about them at all. They are primarily occupied by businesspeople. But there are a few in our budget category, and because this area is ideal for serious sightseeing, you may want to consider them.

There are only 41 units in the **Nakamura Hotel**, 1140 S. King St., Honolulu, HI 96814, just off Piikoi Street (tel. 537-1951), but you may be lucky enough to find a room on the spur of the moment since it's off the tourist mainstream. We say lucky because rates are only $24 single, $28 double, $30 twin, in this clean and quite comfortably appointed building; and because each and every room has wall-to-wall carpeting, large, tile bathroom with a tub-shower combo, good drawer and closet space, even a telephone. We prefer the rooms facing the mountains; even though they do not have air conditioning, they do have those refreshing trade winds. In the air-conditioned rooms, the machine also has to drown out the traffic on King Street (so keep those jalousied windows closed). All these rooms are too small for a third person, but there are a few larger rooms in which a third person is permitted for an additional $4. Mrs. Winifred Hakoda, the personable desk clerk and day manager, advises that no later arrivals (after 10 p.m. on weekdays, after 9 p.m. on Sundays and holidays) are accepted.

Also pleasant is the tastefully modern and newly refurbished **Town Inn**, 250 N. Beretania St., Honolulu, HI 96817 (tel. 536-2377), a Japanese establishment where you'll mingle, so the management promises, "with important personages and travelers of every race." All this cosmopolitanism costs $26 to $41, single or double. Don't expect to sleep on the floor Japanese style: the bedrooms are as Western as the air conditioning. There's a Japanese restaurant, Miyajime, on the premises.

For men, the **Nuuanu YMCA** is a good downtown bet at 1441 Pali Hwy., Honolulu, HI 96813, near South Vineyard Boulevard (tel. 536-3556). It is a modern, $1.3-million facility with 70 dormitory rooms; singles go for $17 a day. Weekly rates are available, and advance reservations are accepted. There's a cafeteria here, and excellent athletic facilities are made available to residents.

For women tourists who'd like to stay at a Y, Honolulu has a terrific answer: the **Fernhurst YWCA**, an attractive tropical residence at 1566 Wilder Ave., Honolulu, HI 96822, about halfway between downtown Honolulu and Waikiki (tel. 941-2231). Women can stay overnight, or for up to one year, as the residence accepts both short- and long-term visitors, many of the latter from countries around the world. So staying here is a good way to get to know people from many countries and backgrounds. The accommodations are double rooms, nicely furnished and decorated, each joined to another room by a common bath. At times single rooms are available. For a double occupancy, each person pays $14 a night with YWCA membership ($18 without), and that includes two meals a day—surely one of the best buys in town! The room-and-board charge for a single room is $20 a night with membership, $25 without. Linens may be rented for a nominal fee if you do not wish to provide your own. Pluses include a swimming pool, garden, laundry room, and a lounge area. Also available for use: typewriters, piano, TV, sewing machine. Advance reservations are accepted with a one-night deposit. Fernhurst recommends that you write first and inquire about future accommodations.

3. Hotels in Windward Oahu

Windward Oahu, as you'll recall from the introduction to this chapter, is the area on the other side of the mighty Koolau mountain range, which serves as a backdrop to Honolulu. The scenery is comparable to what you'll find on the neighbor islands. This is "the country," where many local people spend their vacations, but it's far off the usual tourist track. Although this is a good jumping-off spot from which to visit many of the attractions of the windward side, it's essentially a place where you sit on the gorgeous beach surrounded by sea, sky, and fragrant blossoms and do absolutely nothing at all.

If you're not going to the neighbor islands and you find Waikiki too much hustle and bustle, **Pat's at Punaluu,** 53-567 Kamehameha Hwy., Hauula, HI 96717 (tel. 293-8111), might be just the antidote to civilization you're looking for. Pat's enjoys an enviable setting: the 140-room, nine-story condominium apartment building, directly overlooks a reef-protected beach and lagoon, ideal for swimming and snorkeling. There's a seaside restaurant right on the premises (sandwich lunches every day, a $15 brunch on Sunday), plus a big freshwater pool, gym, sauna (imagine jumping from the sauna right into the ocean!), and other recreational facilities for the comfort of its long-term residents. But about 30 of the apartments are available for short stays; they all have lanais (some rather large) overlooking the ocean, are comfortable (each has been individually decorated by its owners), and decently priced. All studios and apartments can comfortably accommodate up to four people. The smallest unit—called the Lodge ($50 a day)—is definitely not small; it has 622 square feet, and is so arranged that the living area is entirely separate from the sleeping alcove. The Deluxe Lodge ($54) adds another 100 or so square feet of space and boasts wrap-around lanais with ocean and mountain views. The one-bedroom apartments ($58 to $62) are even more spacious. Rates go down several dollars a day if you stay more than one day; monthly rates are also available. Except for the Lodge units, which have limited cooking facilities, all units have full kitchens, complete with dishwashers, washer-dryer combinations, and garbage disposal units. For reservations, and to inquire about apartment/car-rental deals, write to the manager, Jack Chafee, at Pat's at Punaluu, P.O. Box 359, Hauula, HI 96717 or phone 293-8111 or 293-9322.

Located right next door to the Polynesian Cultural Center, the **Laniloa Lodge Hotel,** 55-109 Laniloa St. in Laie, HI 96762 (tel. 293-9282), is a modern, motel-like building offering lots of comfort and a good location not far from many of the attractions of the North Shore. Right at home is a sandy ocean beach and pool; a short drive away is all the swimming, surfing, windsurfing, diving, horseback riding, championship golfing, and the like available in the Sunset Beach and Haleiwa area. Waimea Bay offers some of the world's best swimming (in summer) and best surfing (in winter); Waimea Falls Park is delightful, and Haleiwa has many shops and restaurants and an artsy-craftsy atmosphere. Rooms at Laniloa Lodge overlook the pool and courtyard, have private lanais, color cable TV, and air conditioning; the Lodge is within walking distance of the Brigham Young University Hawaii Campus and the Mormon Temple. Rates, subject to change, are $45 single, $50 double, $55 triple, $61 quad. Family rates are $50, with a maximum of 5 to a room; children must be under 18. Room-car packages, weekly, monthly, and temple patron rates are available upon request.

SOME FINAL WORDS ON LODGINGS: If you'd like to exchange your own home or apartment for a place to stay in Honolulu, it can probably be arranged. Get in touch with the **Vacation Exchange Club,** 12006 111th Ave., Unit 12, Youngstown, AZ 85363 (tel. 602/972-2186), a worldwide home-swapping group. You can be listed in their directory for $24.70 (or receive their directory without being listed for $16) a year and find out what's available in Hawaii (a recent listing, for example, offered a three-bedroom, two-bath house, along with two cars and two bikes, in the posh Kahala region, for a three-month exchange), as well as many other places in the world. Rentals are also available. Vacation Exchange Club provides information only (it is not a travel agency); the actual arrangements are all up to you.

Another organization that provides a similar service is **Interservice/ Intervac,** P.O. Box 387, Glen Echo, MD 20812 (tel. 301/229-7567). Membership fee to be listed in one of their directories, which offers 5,000 home listings, is $29; subscription to the publication only is $23.

The **Shower Tree** at Honolulu International Airport is something every traveler should know about—just in case. In case your plane departure is delayed, or you have to wait several hours to make a connecting flight, or you arrive late at night and there's no inter-island plane service until the next morning, or you simply need a place to be if you've checked out of your hotel early and have a late-night flight. That's where the Shower Tree comes in. This clean and pleasant facility offers showers and eight beds where you can catch a nap for an hour or two or more. The cost for a shower, including soap, towels, shampoo, deodorant, shaving equipment, and hairdryer is $7.50; resting facilities cost $3 an hour, $18 for any eight-hour period, which includes a shower. "Travelers travel under stress," says owner Mona Dunn. "When they walk in this door, the stress ends." Each guest receives personal attention and a real feeling of aloha. There's a perpetual coffee pot brewing, plus a kitchen where flowers or medication can be refrigerated. The Shower Tree is open 24 hours a day. Reservations are advised for sleeping space, as they are usually booked after 10 p.m. So popular has the Shower Tree become, that we may soon see versions of it in other airports in the country. The Shower Tree is tucked away behind the ticket counter for Continental Airlines, on the second level of the main terminal (tel. 836-3044). A refreshing idea.

Bed and Breakfast

The bed-and-breakfast concept is gaining in popularity all over the United States, and Hawaii is no exception. Evelyn Warner and Al Davis started **Island Bed & Breakfast Hawaii** a few years ago, "not as a big business operation, but as a low-key, intimate way for people to visit Hawaii." They offer accommodations in private homes and apartments on all the islands, for rates ranging from upwards of $20 single, upwards of $27 double, including continental breakfast. If you think you'd like to live in a private home in the islands, this might be for you. Write for a free brochure to Bed & Breakfast Hawaii, P.O. Box 449, Kapaa, HI 96746 (tel. 822-7771). Members pay a $10 membership fee, plus $2.40 postage, and then receive a directory of homes and apartments that can be rented.

Doris Epp, the lady who runs **Pacific-Hawaii Bed & Breakfast,** lives in Kailua, that lovely suburb 20 minutes from Waikiki, and most of her Oahu rentals are in that area. It's one of our favorites, too, since both Kailua and Lanikai beaches are superb—and it's also one of the new meccas for windsurfers. Mrs. Epp also has a few listings on Maui, the Big Island, and Kauai. Rates begin at

$25 a day for a room for two with bed and bath, and go up to complete homes or estates that can accommodate up to 16 guests at $275 a day. She requests a fee of $2 for her directory and mailing costs, plus 50% of the cost of the stay for confirmation, promising a partial refund if the room does not meet your expectations and you do not take occupancy because of a serious emergency; she's serious when she says "satisfaction guaranteed." Write to her at Pacific-Hawaii Bed & Breakfast, 19 Kai Nani Place, Kailua, HI 96734.

Discount Discoveries

Club Costa is a new organization that aims to get for its members similar discounts to those that airlines, hotels, car-rental companies, etc., offer to airline employees. The four major islands of Hawaii are their largest areas of operation. On the island of Oahu, they represent approximately two dozen properties (many mentioned in this book), and offer discounts ranging from 10% and 15% to as high as 40% and 50% off regular rates. A yearly family membership is $69 ($20 more overseas to cover the cost of airmailing their publication, *Club Costa* magazine). It might well be worth your time and money to sign up with them. For information, write Club Costa, 9200 Ward Pkwy, Suite 535, Kansas City, MO 64114, or phone 816/361-8404.

READERS' HOTEL SELECTIONS: "I would like to strongly recommend the **Pacific Monarch Hotel** where we have vacationed for the past five years in a row and have booked again for two months in the next season. It is at 142 Uluniu Avenue, Honolulu, HI 96815 (tel. 923-6292). It is ideally located one block from the beach and King's Village and close to many fine restaurants. The Silver family—father Dave, son Dale, mother BJ and Gina—are fine hosts and the whole family is there for the Friday evening cocktail parties to make the guests feel welcome and get acquainted. The skytop pool, Jacuzzi, and sauna with new weatherproofed picnic activity area add to the many pleasures available. Lanais are equipped with table and chairs so that you can have a relaxing meal while watching the beautiful views (many of them oceanfront) and the sunset. Rooms have kitchenettes and include a welcome kit of coffee, tea, etc. Rates are structured by season. The studios with kitchenettes and walkout lanais begin at $62 double. One-bedroom apartments with full kitchens and large lanais begin at $84 for up to three people. There are special weekly rates, and maid service is included. . . . **Hale Koa** at Fort DeRussy is still a marvelous place for active and retired military. In addition to lodgings, they have excellent meals and discount on entertainment. And their Sunday brunch is the best ever, surpassing that at many of the elegant hotels" (Dr. John Lopresti, Jr., Bricktown, N.J.).

"Might I suggest to your readers that they visit Hawaii as I did. I spent six weeks in Honolulu as a student at the **University of Hawaii** at Manoa. The cost of dorm room and board was very economical. Many tours, at special prices, were provided through the university. Our summer student identity cards even got us 'kamaaina' rates at various clubs and attractions. We were often roomed with local students and were thus able to share our different cultures. This is not just meant for single students; there were some dorm facilities for couples. The course selection is wide, ranging from golf and tennis to more academic studies. By the end of six weeks, I was referring to the dorm as 'home' (Susan McEwin, Stratford, Ontario, Canada). . . . "There was a big robbery in our hotel, which occurred only because people on the 12th floor kept their lanai doors open, thinking no one could get in. The robber crawled from the stairway, went from one lanai to another, entering and stealing from purses. Please keep your doors locked at night! We were lucky, as ours was locked" (Dorothy and Mike Capellani, Chicago, Ill.).

"This year was our fourth trip to Hawaii; we decided to go on June 17 and later wished that we had not. No one had told us that Honolulu, along with Miami, is not *the* place to go when school is out. We and our daughter stayed at a Waikiki hotel that is usually very nice. This time it was loaded with high school students who took over the pool day and night and the beaches. They partied and ran from room to room until 3:30 or 4 a.m., jumped up and down in the elevator until it broke down twice. People then had to use the stairs which were littered with broken beer and whisky bottles" (Mrs. Fred J. Criss, Portland, Ore.). . . . "We stayed at the **Hawaiiana Hotel** in Waikiki and loved it. The warmth and friendliness of a small hotel definitely has it over the impersonal atmosphere of a high-rise. When we checked out, however, I foolishly left behind a gold necklace on the shelf of the room safe. Two days later, when I realized what I had done, I called the hotel. The desk clerk said he would check. A day later I called again, and he told me he had found it and would mail it to me. I can't tell you how much his honesty impressed me! It would have been so easy to tell me it wasn't there and keep it. I would never have known. My only complaint about this terrific hotel is the noise from the street. Please advise readers to request a room in the middle of the complex, as it stretches between two busy streets" (Frances S. Kielt, West Hartford, Conn.).

"I selected the **Niihau Apartment Hotel** near Fort DeRussy beach and couldn't have been more pleased! We were there during the season and paid $49 a night for our two-bedroom apartment. We had a nice living/dining area and well-equipped kitchen. The apartment was air-conditioned, and supplied mats for the beach and a cooler for picnics. There were even an iron and an ironing board. Morning noise due to construction in the neighborhood seemed to be a temporary problem. The apartment itself was clean and bug-free. We were able to rent a parking space in the garage for $3.12 a night. It was wonderful to know we wouldn't have to hassle about parking—a problem we had on our first visit" (Barbara Hacht, Decatur, Ill.). . . . "The **Royal Grove** was everything you said it was, and more. . . . There is no question where we would stay if ever again we would be in Waikiki. Why, the bus stop is less than 50 yards from the front door!" (Charles B. Ash, Prescott, Ariz.). . . . "People in Hawaii were absolutely incredible. We stayed at the **Edgewater**—it was everything you said it was. I would never dream of staying anywhere else" (Diane Presser, Marietta, Ga.).

"Please warn people against free offers by employees of **time-sharing companies.** Tourists are assaulted with offers all over Waikiki. They promise you free transportation and free breakfast, which turns out to be coffee, orange juice, and doughnuts. What they don't tell you is that transportation is one-way. We were subjected to high-pressure sales tactics. Three different men with three different approaches worked on us in turn. The 90-minute presentation turned out to be three hours, and then we were informed that we had to find our own transportation back to our hotel at the other end of Waikiki. I strongly feel that if people want to take advantage of the free offers, fine. But they should be prepared for some wicked sales pressure" (Pat Barnes, no address given). . . . "We were very quick to discover the variety and intensity of competition among time-share promoters in Waikiki to enlist visitors to attend 'no obligation' sales presentations. We were very cautious and avoided all the associated discounted tours, sunset sails, etc., until we succumbed to what appeared to be a very generous discount on a compact convertible rental and a 'promised' soft-sell pitch. The next morning we spent 2½ hours subjected to a steadily intensified hard-sell of a condominium time-share on Waikiki. The salespeople tried every approach thinkable to convince us of the affordability of the time-share and the variety of ways we could pay for it. We are both very experienced and skilled at resisting a hard-sell, but this eyeball-to-eyeball team concept tried our intelligence and ingenuity. Only accidentally did we happen upon what we believe to be a foolproof response to such pressure. We ascertained from the sales staff that by Hawaiian state law the time-share property can only be offered for sale within the state of Hawaii. The parties also have five days within which to finalize or negate the contract. So these companies are pressured into completing the sales quickly, at the presentation if possible. We asked them for a property report to take with us (which they repeatedly refused to provide) and told them our attorney back home would have to examine a property statement and all other details of the proposal. This quickly ended the pitch as there were no copies of the property report available and our attorney's involvement would put the sale out of the legal time frame as well as out of the state. If we had known this at the beginning of the presentation, we would have had another morning of our vacation to enjoy in addition to our discounted car rental" (Philip and Vicki Hodgen, Milwaukee, Ore.). [*Authors' Note:* Our own personal reaction to the time-sharing peddlers: Avoid them unless you're seriously interested in buying, or unless you have unlimited time and very strong sales resistance. Otherwise, vacation time is too precious to waste on this sort of hustle.]

"We spent five weeks in Oahu, having previously arranged to exchange homes with a couple who lived in a delightful home in Manoa Valley. Surprisingly, many island people do like to have excursions to the mainland, and home exchange is an ideal way of providing the basis for a really inexpensive vacation. A government employees' bulletin circulates in

Honolulu and elsewhere, and at the University of Hawaii; this provides a good place to advertise" (David Brokensha, Santa Barbara, Calif.). . . . "Some hotels will give a 25% to 50% discount off their published room rates for military personnel and their families. We stayed at three- and four-star hotels at half the normal room rate. I believe that many of your readers are in the U.S. military and would be happy to know about this benefit!" (Joe and Robin Gruender, Wright-Patterson AFB, Ohio).

Chapter III

HONOLULU: RESTAURANTS AND NIGHTLIFE

1. Restaurants in Waikiki
2. Restaurants Around Town (Outside Waikiki)
3. And Elsewhere on the Island
4. The Night Scene

CAN THE AVERAGE TOURIST still find romance, happiness, and a good inexpensive meal in Hawaii? Well, we won't make any rash promises on the first two counts (that's up to you), but on the third we can be quite positive: despite inflation everywhere, Honolulu's restaurants still do very well for the tourist. Although the price for dinner at one of the really elegant restaurants can easily zoom into the stratosphere, most of the good restaurants are in the middle range, which means soup to nuts averaging $12 to $16. And there are also quite a few—praise be—where a good dinner can average under $12. That's where we come in. Even if you wish to spend as little as $20 to $25 a day on food, you should have no trouble figuring about $12 to $14 for dinner, $5 to $6 for lunch, and $3 to $4 for breakfast. To keep on a really tight budget, plan to eat breakfast and at least one meal a day at home; that's when your kitchenette apartment more than pays for itself. Remember that lunch is always cheaper than dinner—often for much the same meal.

THE FOOD ITSELF: The food of Hawaii, like its people, reflects a wide cultural diversity—a lot of American, quite a bit of Japanese, a little less of Chinese, a smattering of Hawaiian, Korean, Filipino, and you-name-it thrown in for good measure. You quickly get used to the ubiquitous sign "Japanese Delicatessen" and to the fact that saimin (a Japanese-type noodle soup with a seaweed base) is just as popular as a hamburger and is often served at the same counter. You soon learn that the exotic-sounding mahimahi is Hawaiian for dolphin, a bland and pleasant-tasting fish—not to be confused with the intelligent mammal of the same name, the porpoise. You'll be introduced to poi, the staff of life of the early Hawaiians, at your very first luau, and you may develop a liking for this purple-gray goo that's one of the most nutritious foods known to man, so high in vitamin B and calcium that it's fed to babies and invalids. Just ignore the old joke that it tastes like library paste; the Hawaiians, and quite a few malihinis, think it's delicious.

Hawaii's fruits are among the islands' special glories. Pineapple, while not exactly invented here, might just as well have been. It's well priced in the markets, served everywhere, and as good as you'd imagine. Pineapple juice is kind of a national drink, something like tea for the English. If you hit the mango season in July, when the local trees are bursting with this succulent fruit, you're in for a great treat. Guavas, coconuts, papayas (one of the most common breakfast foods) are all superb, as are guava juice and passionfruit juice, which you'll often see listed under its Hawaiian name, lilikoi (lilikoi sherbet is wonderful). Macadamia-nut pancakes, as well as coconut ice cream and syrup, are special treats that taste better in Hawaii than anywhere else in the world. We should warn you coffee addicts right here and now—the kind of coffee you'll get everywhere is Kona coffee, grown on the Big Island of Hawaii, and it's so good that you may find yourself drinking innumerable cups a day.

Don't miss the chance to try Hawaii's game fish, caught fresh in local waters, and served up in fish houses under "Catch of the Day." If you're lucky, the catch that day will be ahi (a kind of tuna and a personal favorite), or aki (another tuna), marlin, ulua, opakapaka, rock cod, or a special island delicacy called ono. That word has, in fact, slipped into local parlance as meaning "delicious" —or even "great"—as in "ono ono." At this writing, "Catch of the Day" was selling for about $14 to $16 in most restaurants; save this for a "big splurge" meal.

As for the preparation of these foods, you may not find haute cuisine, but you will find good eating. It is no hardship at all to eat in the budget establishments. Standards of sanitation are very high, and you need have no worries that your food will be anything less than clean, tasty, nourishing, and more often than you'd expect, surprisingly delicious.

1. Restaurants in Waikiki

The most exotic, and the most numerous, budget restaurants are located outside Waikiki. But that doesn't mean you can't have a very good time eating in the beachside area. We'll tell you first about our particular favorites, some three dozen places we call the "fun" restaurants; then move on to the "old reliables," where you can always have a good and inexpensive meal with a minimum of fuss and bother. We've also thrown in a few big splurges—for those moments when you don't mind going slightly beyond your food budget.

THE "FUN" RESTAURANTS: We'll begin with **Perry's Smorgy Restaurants,** which have been offering hearty, American-style buffet meals for as many years as we can remember. They're perhaps the only place in town to offer buffets three times a day. The food is generally very good, there's no limit to how much of it you can eat, and at prices like $6.95 for dinner, $4.95 for lunch, and $3.95 for breakfast (prices subject to change), how can anyone go wrong! Choose any of three Perry's (or try them all); one at the Waikiki Outrigger Hotel, with gorgeous oceanside views and tables for watching the world go by; another at the Coral Seas Hotel at 250 Lewers St.; and the newest location, in a lush, garden setting (the site of the old Banyan Gardens Restaurant) at 2380 Kuhio Ave. At all three, the help-yourself buffet is the same. The table is stacked with about 30 different selections: many fruit and vegetable salads; gelatin combinations; hot vegetables; rice or potatoes; homemade corn muffins and dinner rolls; and lots of hot entrees including southern fried chicken, mahimahi, and Italian spaghetti. Dinner adds a hand-carved round of beef au jus and golden fried shrimp. Fresh island pineapple and local Kona coffee are served at each meal. Breakfast features french toast, blueberry and banana muffins, hotcakes, smoked ham and sausages, and more. You can have as many refills as you like, but no take-home packages, please. Breakfast is served from 7 to 10:30 a.m., lunch from 11 a.m. to 2:30 p.m., dinner from 5 to 9 p.m.

If you can bring yourself to walk past the huge stuffed moose head with a lei around its neck—the first thing you see when you walk in—you'll love **Moose McGillicuddy's Pub-Café,** 310 Lewers St. (tel. 923-0571). It's big and airy—in fact, it's open to the street, with lots of plants and shiny ceramic tile floor. This place is very popular among the local folks, since portions are large and prices very reasonable. Their Early Bird Breakfast Special, served from 6:30 to 9:30 a.m. is one of the best buys in town: two eggs, bacon, toast or rice or potatoes with a fruit garnish, orange juice, all for $1.99. Lunch and dinner menus are the same, and feature "hot'n'juicy" pizzas ($5.25 to $7.50 for small sizes), gourmet hamburgers (most at $4.75 to $5.40), hearty three-egg omelets served with fries, rice, or country potatoes, Texas toast ($4.95), hot soups, sandwiches, and salads. We specially like their pupus: nachos, deep-fried zucchini in beer batter, fried potato skins with beef, chicken or bacon, fish 'n' chips, yummy hot Texas chile ($3.50 to $5.95). Along with your meal you can have some far-out exotic drinks, including terrific margaritas and daiquiris at $4. A rock 'n' roll band plays nightly for dancing in the upstairs pub. McGillicuddy's is a lively spot, the crowd is congenial, and the menu descriptions an entertainment in themselves: look up, for example, the description of "Euell Gibbons' Memorial Omelette." A half-price Happy Hour is on from 4 to 8 p.m. There's another Moose at 1035 University Ave. (tel. 944-5525). That's where the UH kids hang out, and it's lots of fun. Both Mooses are very noisy. There's a third one in Lahaina, Maui, and it's noisy, too. Open every day, from 6 a.m. to 2 a.m.

The budget crowd is kept well in mind at the **Waikiki Broiler,** in the Waikiki Tower Hotel, 200 Lewers St. (tel. 922-6424), a cozy nautical place lit by ship's lanterns and candles, with old seafaring prints and paintings on the wood-paneled walls. The dining room overlooks the pool area of the Edgewater Hotel; in fact, two of the tables are practically in the pool! The Broiler offers low-priced dinner entrees like fish and chips, beef Stroganoff, teriyaki chicken breasts, and mahimahi, from $6.95 to $8.95—in addition to such higher-priced offerings as crab legs, scallops, and roast beef, the specialty of the house. At lunch, there are special sandwiches served with soup or salad (around $5), burgers, and a chef's special salad. Breakfast is served all the way from 6 a.m. to 2 p.m.; waffles or buttermilk pancakes with syrup are a good bet at $1.95.

And there's a long daytime Happy Hour too, from 6 a.m. to 8 p.m., when exotic drinks are sold for the price of standards. Plus entertainment in the evening.

The **Hau Tree Lanai** of the New Otani Kaimana Beach Hotel, 2863 Kalakaua Ave. (opposite Kapiolani Park; tel. 923-1555), is one of those sparkling, over-the-water spots where the atmosphere and food contend for honors. It's so nice to dine here under the hau tree, watching the waves wash up to the shore, in the very setting that Robert Louis Stevenson once favored. Since dinner here is fairly expensive (except for the $10 soup and salad bar), you might want to come by for lunch, when you can have imaginative salads (like papaya and tarragon chicken or crabmeat stuffed in artichoke) from $5 to $8.50, sandwiches (mahi burger, open-faced shrimp and cucumber) from $5.50 to $10.50, and some "fitness selections" (steamed fresh vegetables, Hawaiian chicken curry), from $6 to

$7. Lunch is served from 11:30 a.m. to 1:45 p.m. For a picturesque beachside breakfast, enjoy the view along with your oatmeal, poi pancakes and Kauai sausages, or Belgian waffles. It's served from 7 to 11 a.m.

Another good move is to visit **Scoop Du Jour** at Sans Souci Beach at the same hotel, an ice cream parlor with a history. Late in 1985, a famous hamburger stand on the beach was declared in violation of the building laws and had to be dismantled. Hundreds of beachgoers signed a petition to save it, but to no avail. In its place rose Scoop Du Jour, where you can get very good saimin, jumbo hot dogs, meat sandwiches on onion roll or whole wheat packed with alfalfa sprouts and lettuce, and submarines, from $1.05 to $3.70. Sorry, no hamburgers—the grill would be a building violation—but ice cream sundaes are triple scoop with more chocolate syrup than you probably ever had. Hours vary, but are roughly from 9 a.m. to 5 p.m.

If you're staying in the Diamond Head end of Waikiki, you may want to experience **Marie's,** a popular-priced continental restaurant tucked away on the sixth floor of the Waikiki Sunset, 229 Paoakalani Ave., near Kuhio (tel. 924-2044). If any restaurant has the right to use the word "homemade," this one does, as it is not much bigger than a large home dining room. How Marie is able to turn out a wide variety of continental dishes in the small kitchen is a miracle in itself. Mirrors occupy one wall. Two huge open fans—we'd guess from Thailand —decorate the opposite wall, with about ten tables in between. Dinner entrees come with soup or salad for $9.95 to $12.95, and include chicken scaloppine, linguine with clam sauce, lasagne, stuffed pork chop, and others. Desserts like English trifle and chocolate mousse are so mouth-watering you'll overlook the $3.95 tariff. Marie serves dinner from 6 to 9:30 p.m. daily, and breakfast from 6:30 to 10:30 a.m. Even at breakfast Marie supplies that special touch—our bran muffin was served with butter, jam, and an orchid.

Just because you're saving money, it doesn't mean that you can't dine in style. If, for example, you'd like to have breakfast at one of the most glamorous tropical settings in town, at coffeehouse prices, simply take yourself over to the **Tahitian Lanai Restaurant** of the Waikikian Hotel, 1811 Ala Moana Blvd. (next to the Ilikai Hotel; tel. 946-6541). Seat yourself at an umbrellaed table overlooking the pool, the tropical lagoon, and the Waikiki surf out beyond (or in the atmospheric lanai dining room), and prepare yourself to feast both eyes and palate. Palm trees ring the pool, waitresses are clad in Polynesian costumes, and jungle-like island decor is everywhere. While you're soaking it all up, you can order, as we did, coconut waffles or fresh banana griddle cakes for $3.25, two eggs for $2, and Hawaiian banana muffins for $1.50—recommended! If you're a little hungrier, you could have, perhaps, "Half a Benedict"—eggs Benedict served with hash browns, banana muffins, or a scrumptious popover, $4.75 (a "Whole Benedict" is $6.50). Coffee is robust, and served continuously. Come as early as 7 a.m.; they stop serving breakfast by 11 a.m.

Buffets are very popular in Honolulu, and the **Peacock Room** of the Queen Kapiolani Hotel, at 150 Kapahulu Ave. (tel. 922-1941), is a great place to eat your fill, and then some. Buffets are served at lunch, dinner, and breakfast. You can have a Hawaiian Luau luncheon buffet for $7.25 any day except Thursday and Sunday, featuring all the traditional luau ingredients, along with entertainment by Auntie Leimomi and "whoever stops by"; on Thursday it's a Japanese buffet at $8.95. Or, come by for dinner. The Japanese buffet is served on Wednesday, Thursday, and Friday evening at $13.95; on Tuesday it's another Hawaiian buffet; and on Saturday, Sunday, and Monday, the feature is prime ribs plus two other entrees and an international salad bar, at $12.95. There's live entertainment at all dinner buffets; service is from 5:30 to 9 p.m. Lunch is from

11 a.m. to 2 p.m. And for those of you who can't wait to start buffeting, the breakfast spread is on from 6:30 to 10 a.m. weekdays, to 9:30 a.m. Sundays, at $6.75. Good value for the money here.

You can also have a buffet meal four nights a week at **The Summery,** that strikingly handsome and inviting coffee shop of the Hawaiian Regent Hotel, 2552 Kalakaua Ave. (tel. 922-6611). Dinner buffets are served from 5:30 to 10 p.m.: on Wednesday, it's an Italian buffet for $11.95; Thursday, island buffet, $11.95; Friday, Saturday, and Sunday, prime rib buffet, $13.95. Breakfast buffets are available, too, from 6 to 11 a.m., at $7.95. You may also order from the regular menu here all day and evening, and it includes burgers (from $5.50), hot entrees such as spaghetti bolognese ($6.25) and fried chicken ($7.95), and lovely salads like the pineapple boat ($6.25) and the crab and shrimp salad ($7.95). Seating is indoors and out, under the trees.

Buffet lovers staying at the other end of Waikiki can take their hearty appetites to the **Rainbow Lanai** at the Hilton Hawaiian Village, 2005 Kalia Rd. (tel. 949-4231), once a cafeteria but now a full service restaurant with beautiful views of the beach and sea. Touted as "Hawaiian Fair," the buffet includes Hawaiian chicken, Tahitian curried vegetables, a salad bar of "fresh Hawaiian produce," desserts, and Kona coffee. Price is $12.75 adults, $6.95 children. On Sunday it's a buffet brunch at $15, senior citizens $10. The buffet dinner is served from 5 to 9:30 p.m. The lunchtime menu features sandwiches and salads at medium-to-high prices. Open daily.

One of the most atmospheric "coffee houses" in town is **Pier Seven** at the Ilikai Hotel, 1777 Ala Moana Blvd. (tel. 949-3811), where all of the booths and tables have a view of the ocean and of the passersby on the boardwalk. A window booth gives you the added advantage of a bank of tropical greenery and the marina beyond. There, an early dinner provides a front row seat for the sunset and the Ilikai's nightly torch-lighting ceremony. Most of the prices are a bit over our budget, but we spotted some dinnertime bargains, like the hearty soup and salad bar at just $5.50. Among the low-priced entrees are fettuccine and a steamed vegetable platter at $7.50; fried chicken is about $1 more. Sandwiches and burgers are well worth the $5.75 to $6.50 tab as they are robust and served with all the trimmings. And we'll vouch for the clam chowder, among the richest New England-style chowders we've tasted. Pier Seven is open every day from 6 a.m. to 1 a.m. A stylish spot.

It's not hard to figure out why the **Shore Bird Beach Broiler,** beachfront at the Reef Hotel, 2169 Kalia Rd. (tel. 922-2887), quickly became one of the most popular restaurants in Waikiki. First of all, you can't beat the location: the large, attractively decorated open dining room is right on Waikiki Beach. Second, the food is good; and third, the price is right: that's because you're the chef, broiling your own portion of teriyaki chicken or ribs, seafood or filet mignon kebab, New York steak, ground or top sirloin. Prices run from $5.95 (for mahimahi) to $11.95 (for steak, N.Y. cut). While the fire is doing its work, you can have a few drinks, then fill up on salad bar, chili, plain and fried rice. Coffee, tea, or iced tea are included with the meal; dessert (including their own cheesecake made fresh every day) is extra. Perfect for sunset drinks and dinner. Early Bird specials from 5 to 6:30 p.m. The broiler is hot from 5 to 10 p.m.; from 10 p.m. on the heat is provided by nonstop video, and music and dancing continue until about 2 a.m.

Walk from the Reef's beach to its pool and you'll find more bargain dining; that's at the **Aloha Restaurant** (tel. 923-3111). If you like crabs' legs, you've come to the right place, since they feature an all-you-can-eat crabs' legs dinner, with soup or salad, rice or french fries, and a vegetable, for $11.95. There are also daily specials of two meals for $10.95, which could be barbecued ribs, chicken, or a combination thereof. These are served with soup or salad, fries, and a vegetable. And cheapest of all, a spaghetti dinner special, all you can eat, for $4.99. We've had several letters praising the food and service here. The Aloha Restaurant is open every day from 6 a.m. to 11 p.m. Breakfast is on until 11 a.m., lunch from 11 a.m. to 4 p.m., dinner from 4 to 9:30 p.m. From 9:30 p.m. to midnight, it's back to the lunch menu, which is lighter. Drinks are available from the large and comfy Captain's Aloha Bar.

Everyone likes **Caffè Guccinni,** also in the 2139 Kuhio Ave. cluster (tel. 922-5287), both for the Italian meals and the delectable desserts. This is a modest place, with a counter inside, tables outside, and the menu posted beside the counter. Dinner specials, which average about $7.25, include various pasta dishes on the regular menu (we're partial to the manicotti stuffed with five kinds of cheese), and two or three daily specials, like veal, calamari, quiche, and Italian sausage. Lunch (served Monday to Saturday) is very reasonable: salads, sandwiches, pastas, from $2.95 to $4.25. There's a full liquor and wine bar. Happily, both meals feature those wonderful desserts that made Caffè Guccinni famous. We're always hard put to decide between the merits of a heavenly crème brûlée or chocolate torte, a Sicilian cannoli, or a light and lemony cheesecake. The best solution is to bring a group of friends and share. Desserts are $2 to $2.50. (If you've eaten elsewhere, come here just for dessert.) Along with your feast, have some of the best espresso and cappuccino in the islands, or an ice cream "shake with a shot." Everything is homemade in owner Jocelyn Battista's own kitchen. Open from 11:30 a.m. to 11:30 p.m. Monday to Saturday, from 4 to 11:30 p.m. Sunday.

Here you are in the tropics, but you love the dessert, too. What to do? Ride that lonesome trail to **Peppers Waikiki Grill and Bar,** 150 Kaiulani Ave. (tel. 926-4374), a hybrid of the islands and the southwest, sprouting both cacti and palm trees, and serving some of the best Tex-Mex food in town. It's a casual, sophisticated spot, dominated by a lively bar (watch out for those frosty margaritas!) and yet, with its well-spaced booths and tables, conducive to good conversation. The secret ingredients here are the wood-fired smoke oven that gives a true barbecue taste to the chicken and ribs, and the mesquite grill that turns out super burgers and steaks. Mexican dishes—tacos, fajitas, burritos, and the like —run from $6.95 to $7.95; smoke-oven baby back ribs begin at $7.75; and there are excellent salads like the Cobb salad and the chicken taco salad, from $5.75 to $6.75. Nachos, sandwiches, quesadillas, yummy potato skins, and the like offer inexpensive and tempting possibilities for grazing. For dessert, try hula pie, a specialty of Hawaii, or fried ice cream, a specialty of Mexico (no, it's really not fried, but in such a *simpático* spot, it's hard to quibble). Peppers, in the very heart of Waikiki, serves the same menu from 11:30 a.m. to 2 a.m. every day of the week.

"Waikiki's only San Francisco–style seafood house" is what they call **Blue Water Seafood** at 2350 Kuhio Ave. (tel. 926-2191), a big, busy place decorated with a nautical flair—captain's chairs and lots of brass. Most complete dinners are priced from $7.95 to $13.95 (lobsters higher), and include rice, french fries, sliced tomatoes, and freshly baked bread. Watch for their Early Bird specials, which feature several entrees from $5.95 to $7.25, served with clam chowder and a dinner salad. Entrees of note are fresh fish caught daily, top sirloin steak, scallops, mahimahi, teriyaki chicken, and steak and seafood combinations. Blue Water is also open for breakfast and lunch, serving meals from 7 a.m. to 10 p.m. daily. From 10 p.m. to 4 a.m., it turns into a night spot. And for those who still have the hungries, seafood appetizers are ready and waiting at its fishmarket until 3 a.m.

Ed Greene's Jameson's restaurants pop up in the most interesting places: there's Jameson's Harbor Grille, an ever-popular restaurant and pub in the downtown area: Jameson's by the Sea, a romantic spot for sunset watching on the edge of Haleiwa town, on the North Shore; and now the original and most popular of them all, **Jameson's-on-Seaside Irish Coffee House,** right back where it belongs, after an absence of several years, at 342 Seaside Ave. (tel. 922-3396). Call Jameson's a wee bit of the old country transplanted to Honolulu. There's always a lively crowd at the bar, and the atmosphere is informal and inviting. Jameson's specializes in super-fresh fish and seafood from Hawaiian waters, but does not ignore such Irish standbys as corned beef and cabbage or Mulligan stew, nor island favorites like sesame chicken or shrimp curry with mango chutney. Most dinner entrees run from $6.95 to $11.95, but Jameson's ever-popular burger, served open-face and topped with grated cheddar and fresh mushrooms, plus Irish fried potatoes on the side, is only $5.95. And the huge chef's salad (a combination of Danish ham, chicken, and Swiss cheese, tossed with fresh greens, and topped with grated cheddar) is another super-filler at $6.95. Start your meal with clam chowder (Boston style, of course); end with homemade chiffon pie, or—what could be better—Irish coffee, made with Jameson's Irish whisky and a tall layer of whipped cream. Local people like Jameson's as much as the tourists do, and make it a popular after-theater, movie, or symphony hangout; not many nice places like this serve so late.

Jameson's on Seaside serves lunch (hot and cold sandwiches, salads, chowder, dessert) Monday through Friday from 11:30 a.m. to 5 p.m.; dinner, nightly, from 5 to 10 p.m.; and a late-night supper from 10 p.m. to 1 a.m.

Tony Roma's—A Place for Ribs is getting to be as popular in Honolulu as it is on the mainland, with three restaurants to choose from. One is at the gateway to Waikiki at 1972 Kalakaua Ave. (tel. 942-2121); another is at 4230 Waialae Ave., across from Kahala Mall; and still a third is in Westridge Center, convenient for visitors to Pearl Harbor. The restaurants are big and comfortable, decorated in western style, with lots of wood and leather, walls of brick, shuttered windows, oil paintings on the wall. The staff is energetic and friendly. The menu (which is also your placemat) carries a disclaimer: "Not responsible for meat ordered well done"! All entrees are served with rice, baked potato, or french fries and coleslaw. The house specialty, of course, is ribs: at dinner, a generous serving of St. Louis–style ribs is $10.45; barbecued baby back ribs, $10.95 (lunch orders are a few dollars less). Barbecued chicken is a bargain at $6.45, and so is filet mignon on a skewer at $7.75. Don't miss the famous onion rings at $2.15 for half-a-loaf. Daily specials are $6.95 at dinner, $4.95 at lunch. There's a special keiki menu for kids under 12, and a night-owl menu served from 10 p.m., featuring such goodies as onion rings, fried cheese, potato skins, and steak sandwiches, in addition to ribs. Cheesecake or muddpie, the only desserts, go well with espresso or cappuccino, or French, Irish, or Mexican coffee.

In addition to all this, Tony Roma's features many of Hawaii's premier entertainers—with no cover charge. It also has frequent holiday specials, including popular Thanksgiving dinners with turkey and rib and a not-to-be-missed Waikiki New Year's Eve party. It's open 365 days and nights a year, from 11 a.m. on. Not-so-incidental intelligence: to have those ribs and onion rings delivered wiki-wiki to your hotel or condo, call 947-RIBS in Waikiki, 737-RIBS in Kahala.

Orchids, in the Halekulani Hotel, 2199 Kalia Rd. (tel. 923-2311), is the kind of place you always dreamed of finding in Hawaii, located oceanside at this exquisite hotel. It's a veritable greenhouse, filled with orchids and many other tropical plants and trees. And while dinner here is high for our budget (prix-fixe, complete dinner $28 and up, à la carte entrees from $15.50 to $26.50), lunch is a delightful possibility. There's an enchanting platter of tasty finger sandwiches— ham, roast turkey, tomato, avocado, and cheddar and Swiss cheeses—as well as the Oriental omelet, stuffed with peapods, water chestnuts, bean sprouts, shrimp, and mushrooms. There is a menu section of meals for the diet-conscious (and who isn't?): cold poached salmon in dilled cucumber sauce (about 230 calories), flank steak teriyaki style (220), and breast of chicken Italian style (330) are just a few selections. A menu item called "A Very Fast Lunch" consists of soup of the day, finger sandwiches, and beverage; but who would want to rush through a meal in this lovely setting? Selections are priced from $7 to about $16; luncheon is served Monday through Saturday from 11:30 a.m. to 2:30 p.m., dinner from 5:30 to 10 p.m. There are both brunch and dinner buffets on Sunday, and breakfast daily from 7 to 10:30 a.m.

El Crab Catcher, at 1765 Ala Moana Blvd. (tel. 955-4911), in the Ilikai Hotel area; is decorated in cool green and white—the green is supplied by the abundant green plants. Colorful saltwater fish swim in a big tank that divides the dining room and the oyster and wine bar. The oyster bar is open from 11:30 a.m. until midnight during the week; on weekends, it opens at 4 p.m. Pupus and light meals are featured in this section, so you won't break the budget by eating here. The house specialty is crab-stuffed mushrooms, topped with melted Jack cheese, $5.95. Oysters and clams on the half shell are presented in various ways, from $5.95 to $9.95. The crab custard quiche is heaven; the Crab Catcher sandwich—snowcrab, sprouts, cheese, and tomato baked on cheese bread—is equally delightful ($6.95 and $7.95). In the main dining room, the Light Suppers section of the menu offers crab Louie salad, the above-mentioned crab custard quiche in a larger version, seafood crêpes, and yakitori, $9.95 and $10.95. With dinner entrees, El Crab Catcher serves a salad or soup, vegetable, and a basket of breads. Higher-priced entrees begin at $15.95, and include fresh local fish of the day, and a variety of steaks. El Crab Catcher serves dinner from 5:30 to 10:30 p.m. Monday through Thursday, until 11 on weekends. Open daily.

For a well-priced Japanese meal in Waikiki, try **Odoriko** in King's Village, 2400 Koa Ave. (tel. 923-7368). A big hit with visitors and locals alike is their seafood buffet, usually priced at $13.95 on weekdays, $14.95 on weekends, which offers unlimited servings of crab legs, oysters, clams, shrimp tempura, sashimi, sukiyaki, sushi, as well as roast beef, ham, barbecued ribs, and the like. For those who are counting their yen, they offer satisfying specials from about $7.95 such as: grilled chicken on skewers, broiled salmon with butter, soup, salad, rice, pickled vegetables, and tea. Portions were dainty, but everything was delicious. We had a choice of guava sherbet or vanilla ice cream for dessert.

Odoriko, which has a sister restaurant at the Ilikai Hotel, is a good place to try a meal at the sushi bar, or have some of the robata-yaki appetizers, broiled baby cuttlefish, broiled dried mushrooms, broiled butterfish, and the like, for about $3.50 each. Waitresses wear Japanese costumes and service is cordial. Maiko is open daily from 6 a.m. until 10 p.m.

Most of Honolulu's more authentic Chinese restaurants are outside Waiki-ki, so you'll be as pleased as we were to discover **Five Spice,** 432 Ena Rd. (tel. 955-8706), near the Hilton Hawaiian Village and Eaton Square. Five Spice is a modest restaurant, small but very clean, with no emphasis on decor: all the attention is given to preparing and serving superb dishes from the northern provinces of China, especially Szechuan and Peking, with a few specialties from Canton as well. Let Mrs. Flora Chang, the gracious owner, help you decide what to order: a party of six of us (four of them local Chinese) were delighted with her suggestions. Especially memorable were the tangy fishcake soup (hot-and-sour soup is also very good); Chinaman's Hat, a dish of mixed vegetables, topped with an omelet, and stuffed in pancakes, moo-shu style; shrimp with green vegetables; smoked tea duck; crispy Chinese bread; and Monk's Food, an unusually tasty vegetarian dish (vegetarians have at least 16 choices here). Entrees are very reasonable, most from $4.95 to $7.50, and a satisfying dinner special, which includes soup, entree, rice, stir-fried vegetables, and hot tea, is only $8.95. No liquor is served, so BYOB. Five Spice is open every day, from 11 a.m. to 10:30 p.m.; call for take-out.

A touch of Thai has come to Waikiki. One flight up at 407 Seaside Avenue is the **Siam Inn** (tel. 926-8802), a pretty little place in which to make, or renew, acquaintance with the subtle (and not-so-subtle) spiceries of Thai cuisine. Dine inside in a setting of white walls covered with colorful murals of Thai scenery, crisp green tablecloths, and tile floors; or outside on a little balcony under potted trees. When last we lunched there, the daily specials, $5.95, were Bangkok chicken, served with rice and the chef's special soup, and the chicken masaman curry—slices of tender chicken on a bed of avocado, peanuts, and coconut milk, served with curried rice and cucumber sauce (mild or hot). Other luncheon possibilities are also very reasonable (there are 12 dishes under $6), and include a variety of noodle dishes featuring chicken, beef, pork, or shrimp. Your waiter will ask if you wish your meal mild, hot, or very hot (advice to newcomers to Thai cooking: mild is the safest). Dinner prices are also reasonable, with all the chicken, beef, pork, and shrimp dishes at $7.95, fish specialties at $11.95, and vegetable dishes from $5.25 to $5.95.

Siam Inn opens at 11 a.m. Monday through Saturday and at 5 p.m. on Sunday; dinner is served until 10:30 nightly.

The Godmother, at 339 Saratoga Road (tel. 922-6960), is a bit of Old World Italy in an indoor-out-door lanai setting; its logo is a shapely signora in black tights, a Mafia-style jacket, and slouch hat, carrying a violin case. Dinners are a good buy since they are served with salad or soup and homemade bread and there are many on the low side of the menu, like veal or chicken piccata, with rice or pasta, $12.95. Pasta specialties include lasagne, ravioli, and spaghetti dishes, priced from $6.95 to $7.95, and an especially flavorful spinach fettuccine al Cestare: noodles sautéed in garlic butter, with hot sausage, onions, mushrooms, and fresh tomatoes, "an offer you can't refuse."

The Godmother opens for Happy Hour and late lunch at 2 p.m.; it serves dinner from 6 to 11 p.m. and closes at 2 a.m. daily; piano bar and entertainment from 7:30 p.m. to 1:30 a.m. Wednesday to Sunday.

There's a cute little corner of Mexico at the corner of Kalakaua and Saratoga, and **Popo's Mexican Restaurant,** 2112 Kalakaua (tel. 923-7355), is the name. Popo's has both decor (white walls, tile floors, stucco, serapes, native pottery) and food that is *muy auténtico,* and the prices are right. Come at lunch and you can have dishes like a good and snappy chile relleno for $5.75, or machaca—shredded beef sautéed with bell peppers, tomatoes, eggs, and onions—for $5.95. Combination plates are $6.95 to $9.25, and regular entrees of enchiladas, burritos, etc., are $4.50 to $6.50. Here's your chance to try some new specialties of the native-born Mexican chef: perhaps flautas (deep-fried corn tortillas stuffed with shredded beef and topped with cheeses, guacamole, and sour cream); or chalupa (a boat-shaped flour tortilla filled with picadillo-seasoned beef, cheeses, tomatoes, and guacamole). There's usually a special, like the tasty chicken poblano at $8.95. Dessert? *¿Cómo no?* Guava sherbet with coconut and honey is great, and, of course, there are margaritas, sangría, and Mexican beer at the ready. A *simpático* choice.

So popular has the original Popo's become that two new branches of the same family have opened up, both in Waikiki and both offering good food and good bargains. **Popo's Cantina Mexican Food,** at the corner of Ala Moana Boulevard and Ena Road (tel. 955-3326), usually has a fresh catch of the day, served with rice, beans, and tossed salad, at both lunch and dinner for $7. **Popo's Mar-**

garita Cantina at the International Market Place (tel. 923-8373) is a relaxed spot for sipping margaritas, of course, and for enjoying such inexpensive luncheon and dinner specials as tacos, beans, and rice for just $4.25 at lunch, $6.25 at dinner.

A Chaucerian dining spot in Honolulu? Of course! You'll think you're in Olde England (well, almost) when you step into **Top's Canterbury Coffee Shop & Tavern** at 1910 Ala Moana Blvd. (tel. 941-5277), what with its flowered tapestry chairs, lots of wood, and waitresses in period costumes and mob caps. But the modern menu and 24-hour service make this one briskly up-to-date. Lunch and dinner specials are well priced, and both food and service get good marks. You might have grilled liver for $5.95, grilled mahimahi, or chicken in a basket with french fries, corn bread, and butter, for $6.25 or under; shrimp and vegetable tempura for $8.25. Soup or salad, french fries or rice, vegetable, roll, and butter come with each entree. For dessert, try the tasty cheese or carrot cakes. The menu is extensive, ranging from very good burgers to deli sandwiches to international specialties like nachos and lasagne. Strawberry daiquiris are a specialty. Breakfast is ready all day; we like the silver-dollar-size pancakes at $2.50.

A *Honolulu Advertiser* columnist once named **Emilio's Pizza** as "the best new pizza place in Honolulu." Well, we knew it all along. Emilio's isn't new anymore, but it's still as cozy as ever, with interesting framed pictures and glass shelving lending a homey atmosphere to its quarters at 1423 Kalakaua, near the corner of King Street (tel. 946-4972). This is pizza with a professional touch—deep-dish Sicilian style. They make their own tasty dough fresh every day, and their own sausages and sauces. They also make several specialty dishes like fettuccine Alfredo with artichoke hearts, spaghetti carbonara, meat and vegetarian calzone, spaghetti with white clam sauce, and lasagne ($4.50 to $8), as well as hearty sandwiches, soups, salads, garlic bread. But about those pizzas. . . .

There is a choice of 14 fresh toppings, which are piled abundantly on deep-dish crusts, making a ten-inch pie a filling meal for two to three people. Prices run from about $6.85 for the ten-inch cheese pies with one topping, up to $17.25 for the mind-blowing combo with six toppings. Emilio's is open from 12 noon to 11 p.m. Monday through Thursday, to midnight on Friday and Saturday, from 5 to 10 p.m. on Sunday. And, yes, they will deliver to most hotels and condos in Waikiki.

Pasta and salad are the big light-food crazes these days, and the place to get both, quite reasonably, in Honolulu is at the **Noodle Shop** in the Waikiki Sand Villa Hotel, 2375 Ala Wai Blvd. at Kanekapolei, behind King's Village (tel. 922-4744). With black booths, a bar, soft lighting, big wood-and-rope chandeliers, the atmosphere could be called intimate cocktail lounge. You can try a variety of noodle dishes and help yourself to the all-you-can-eat salad bar, for $4.95 and up. Non-noodlers can fill up with dishes like chicken and fries, beef Stroganoff, filet of mahimahi, plus other entrees, most in the $6.30 to $17.95 range. The Noodle Shop is open daily from 7 to 10:30 a.m. for breakfast and from 5 to 8 p.m. for dinner. (No lunch is served.) There's entertainment nightly, plus a Happy Hour every day from 3:30 to 6 p.m.

At the International Market Place and Kuhio Mall

Few tourists who set foot in Waikiki leave without at least one visit to the International Market Place in the heart of the beach area at 2330 Kalakaua Ave., where throngs of merchants offer everything from grass skirts to wooden idols. Immediately adjoining it, and fronting on Kuhio Avenue, is Kuhio Mall, another lively bazaar. Between the two of them, they offer a number of places sensible enough for our budget. Our old favorite, **Colonial Court,** once a complete cafeteria, now serves only snacks cafeteria style, but it does have a pizza station, an ice cream counter, and a bakery. For a complete meal, and especially if you've brought the kids along with you, you'll have more fun in the Market Place at **Farrell's Ice Cream Parlour Restaurant,** a kicky Gay '90s affair that dispenses—in addition to the huge sundaes, sodas, and staggering banana splits —fresh-ground and handmade burgers ($3.95 to $4.50), hot grilled sandwiches, pizza, jumbo franks, and dinner entrees—filet of fish, chicken strips, hamburger steaks—served with tossed green salad and toasted French bread, at $5.50. Farrell's desserts are a meal in themselves—hot fudge sundaes, mocha nut parfaits, and fudge mint marvel suggest the possibilities. The place is open from 11 a.m. to 11 p.m. on weekdays, until midnight Friday and Saturday. There are other Farrell's elsewhere on Oahu. Good, sensibly priced family fare.

Just below Farrell's is a bit of mittel-Europe in Waikiki. That's the **Hofbräu,** a German biergarten-deli, where the guests sing along and drink along as the Hofbräu Band nightly belts forth polkas, waltzes, and the like. While you're humming along, you can dine (lunch or dinner) on inexpensive plates like bratwurst, knockwurst, and Polish kielbasa for around $4.95, or smoked pork loin for $5.95. Sandwiches, served on country rye, with kosher pickle, include pastrami, ham and cheese, and assorted German sausages, around $4.

For an Oriental meal at the Market Place, try **Yami's Bar-B-Q,** a counter restaurant where you can have barbecue plates from $3.95 to $4.95, plus Korean exotica like hot kuk soo and bi bim bab (noodles in hot soup and rice with vegetables and beef) for low prices.

The culinary adventurers among you will want to experience something different indeed: the **Mongolian Bar-B-Que** at Kuhio Mall. Seems that a very special dish in the northern part of China is strips of beef, barbecued with vegetables and spices, and this is one of the few restaurants we know of in Honolulu that serves it. You select your own meats, sauces, vegetables, and spices and pass them on to the chefs, who then cook them in an open fire pit. The full Bar-B-Que is $9.95, with seconds free ("quick" meals—the chefs make the selection —and "mini" meals are $4.45 and $3.45). Also available: sandwiches on homemade sesame buns, lunch plates, soups, salad, beers, wines, and cocktails. Truth to tell, we find the Bar-B-Que a mite strange tasting, but many local people have become addicted to it. It's one of those things you have to experience for yourself to judge. There's another Mongolian Bar-B-Que in the Cultural Plaza downtown. Open daily from 11 a.m. to 10 p.m.

We can never resist the luscious aromas wafting from the **Hung Yun Chinese Kitchen** at no. 110 in Kuhio Mall, entrance on Kuhio Avenue. It's just a little service-counter place with a few tables, but it's the least expensive place we know to sample a variety of Chinese dishes at penny-pinching prices. Each entree is 99¢ per portion, and they have curry chicken, chicken with black mushrooms, beef broccoli, sweet-and-sour pork, peppersteak, egg foo yung, and spicy Szechuan eggplant. Open every day during mall shopping hours.

Keep in mind that Kuhio Mall also has several good fast-food outlets, among them **Pizza Hut** and **Taco Hut.**

At the Waikiki Shopping Plaza

Time was when budget dining at the Waikiki Shopping Plaza, at 2250 Kalakaua (corner of Seaside), was limited to the basement snack shops (see "Old Reliables," ahead), while its upper floors harbored some of the more glamorous and expensive international restaurants in town. But then the **Marco Polo Eating and Drinking Establishment** took over one of these attractive enclaves and all that changed. Not only does Marco Polo offer steak and seafood at reasonable prices, but it will also reserve good seats for you at the entertaining free show, "Hawaii Calls," which is presented at the Plaza every evening. Make your reservation for 5:15 p.m. to see the 6:30 p.m. show or at 6:15 p.m. for the 8 p.m. show. Entrees—which include soup or salad, pilaf rice or potato, and homemade bread and butter, run from $7.95 to $9.95, and include teriyaki chicken or steak, barbecued spareribs Chinese style, sautéed mahimahi, and London broil. There's usually a steak and shrimp special at $8.95; a lobster, steak, and shrimp combo for $15.95; plus a few pasta dishes from $5.95 to $7.95. Marco Polo also offers a daily luncheon special under $6, like beef curry, mahimahi sandwiches, or omelets. With its intimate, multilevel setting, lively bar, and Happy Hour prices from 11 a.m. to closing—it's hard to beat this one. Open for lunch Monday to Friday from 11 a.m. to 2 p.m., for dinner every day from 5 to 10 p.m.

For a touch of opulence at the Waikiki Shopping Plaza, try **Lau Yee Chai** (tel. 923-1112), the famed Waikiki Cantonese restaurant, whose magnificent furnishings, irreplaceable today, come from the original Waikiki Lau Yee Chai, which opened in 1929. The main dining room, big enough to hold 600 people, is decorated with gleaming lacquered furniture, rich woodcarvings, a huge brass gong that would put the J. Arthur Rank one to shame, and real gold in the exquisite wall panels. The golden calligraphy characters spell out poetry in the Cantonese dialect. Considering the splendor befitting an Oriental emperor, the prices are surprisingly democratic, and the food is very good. Most à la carte entrees run between $5.50 and $7.50, and in this price range you could have mushroom chicken, lemon chicken, scallops with vegetables, almond chicken or duck, stuffed duck, beef chow mein, and shrimp with vegetables. Should you favor shark-fin soup (a rarified taste), it's $4.95.

For the Steak Set

When the whole family wants to eat steak and you don't want to break the budget, there's a terrific answer: find the nearest **Sizzler Steak, Seafood, Salad.** Luckily, there are seven of them in the Hawaiian Islands, including one right in Waikiki, at the corner of Kalakaua and Ala Moana. The big round building has comfy booths and tables, plants, and a pleasant atmosphere, and it's open 24 hours a day. The Jamboree Breakfast, served from midnight until 11 a.m., offers eggs, bacon, and all the hotcakes you can eat for $2.99. For lunch and dinner, Sizzler serves steaks that are a good size and good quality, amazing values for the money, considering the cost of meat at the supermarket: an order of sirloin is $6.89; New York–cut steak, $8.29. Along with your steak comes tangy, cheesey Sizzler toast, plus a choice of baked potato, french fries, or rice. All Sizzlers now have salad bars, soup, and serve beer and wine. There's also seafood, including steak and shrimp at $9.99. Salad, desserts, and coffee and iced tea are extra, but refills on the beverages are free. There are more Sizzlers elsewhere on Oahu and a very pretty one at Koko Marina, overlooking the waterskiing area.

The Exotic East

A longtime favorite for the cooking of the exotic East—of India and Pakistan—is the small and intimate **Shalimar Restaurant,** in the Waikiki Holiday Hotel, 450 Lewers St. (tel. 923-2693), a lovely spot with a gracious, subdued atmosphere, Oriental carpets on the wall, and at least one or two of the Karim brothers—who have owned and managed restaurants in Lahore, New York, and Chicago—on hand to explain the subtleties of Pakistani-Indian cooking to you. We followed Tariq Karim's suggestions at a recent meal and chose the Khansameki Sifarish, a seven-course dinner consisting of mulligatawny soup, tandoori chicken, shish kebab, cubed lamb curry, vegetable curry, and rice pilaf, at $12.50; as well as a tasty Shakahari Thal vegetarian platter which included homemade yogurt with spicy potatoes, samosa vegetable patties, creamed spinach with potatoes, vegetable curry, and much more, at $11.95. (More inexpensive dishes run $7.50 to $8.95.) Flavors were subtle, the food gently and exquisitely spiced. With it we had a big order of naan—unleavened bread baked in a clay oven—as delicious a bread as can be found anywhere; we could have happily made a meal on that alone. Well-priced wines are available by the bottle or carafe. If you have room for it, the pasha coffee—a combination of liqueurs, coffee, and whipped cream, looking like a pasha with a turban—is fine for leisurely, after-dinner dawdling. Dinner only, served from 6 to 10 p.m., seven days, and reservations are essential, as this small place is constantly growing in popularity.

At the Royal Hawaiian Center

If we had to take all our meals in Honolulu under one roof, we'd pick the roof of the Royal Hawaiian Center, right in the middle of Waikiki at 2233 Kalakaua. There, on the third floor are The Great Wok of China, Las Margaritas, and the Bavarian Beer Garden. Cafe Copenhagen is on the second, and downstairs, on the ground level, is still another winner, It's Greek to Me.

Wok cooking is becoming almost as popular in the United States as it is in China. To see a master perform the art at your own table, take your chopsticks to **The Great Wok of China** (tel. 922-5373), a spacious and handsomely decorated room. The kitchen is largely Cantonese but various dishes also represent Mandarin and Szechuan cuisines. You'll be seated at tables for eight, with two woks in the center; you place your order for, perhaps, the Celestial Celebration Chicken at $8.85, the Shanghai Vegetarian (vegetables and tofu) at $8, or whatever the Wokmaster's Special is for that night, at $7.85. While the chef is busy in the kitchen with his cleaver cutting up the ingredients for your main dish, you'll be served, first, a delicious bowl of hot-and-sour soup, followed by a Chinese chicken salad—tiny shreds of chicken with lettuce and a sesame-based dressing —very tasty. Then the chef goes to work at the wok, tossing up a succulent (and happily, smokeless) meal. Of course, there's a pot of tea, and fortune cookies for dessert. Dinner is served daily from 5:30 to 10 p.m. At lunch, daily from 11 a.m. to 2 p.m., you can sample some Imperial Salads, like the Kwongung Tofu Salad (with shrimp, vegetables, and egg), the Hanchow Salad (cold meats and vegetables), and the Four Winds Salad (chicken, sprouts, mushrooms), all between $3.75 and $4.25. Sunday brunch, 11 a.m. to 2 p.m., is $11. The 4 to 6 p.m. Happy Hour features low prices and free egg rolls. Cooking classes are often held here on Friday afternoons.

Mexican restaurants are no longer a novelty in Honolulu, but any restaurant as beautiful and tasteful as **Las Margaritas** (tel. 923-2906) certainly is. Stepping into **Las Margaritas** is like entering another realm, one of mirrored ceilings, thick carptes, canopies over round tables, subtle Aztec designs on the walls. The room is done in the colors of sand and is cool and restful. You can be sure the food is very good and authentic. The family in charge, Oscar and Gloria Amezcua, come from a long line of Mexican restaurateurs—and it was Gloria's father, Danny Herrera, in fact, who invented the "Margarita" in 1942 for a young starlet named Margaret King (facts you never knew department). Margaritas, of course, are a specialty here—come by for Fiesta Hour between 2 to 4 p.m. and you can have a giant one (a full quart) for $3.75—but also special are dishes like the fajitas, enchiladas verdes, pollo al carbon, burritos mariachi, and a variety of combination plates, all from $7.25 to $9.95. Only a few beef and seafood dishes go higher. All entrees come with a choice of soup or salad, plus spicy seasoned rice, frijolitos, and tortillas. Cantina La Gloria serves up a neat menu of snacks—potato skins, deep fried cheese, chicken wings, nachos—most of which are available as appetizers for dinner. A strolling mariachi band serenades you at night. A good place to relax with friends.

Las Margaritas is open weekdays from 11 a.m. to 10 p.m., weekends from 5 p.m.; the cantina stays open until 2 a.m.

Did you know that lots of Danes visit Honolulu? They regularly sign the guest book at **Cafe Copenhagen,** on the second floor of the Center, right next door to Copenhagen Cones (tel. 923-7227). But you needn't be Danish to enjoy this one. A Danish family—Paul Krogh, the former Danish consul; his wife, Inger; their daughter, Marianne, and son-in-law, Gilbert—have created a neat little Danish cafe right here in Honolulu, complete with pictures of the King and Queen of Denmark on the walls, an antique armoire, and Danish posters. A self-service counter dishes up such goodies as frikadeller (Danish meatballs) at $4.95; open-faced sandwiches like the Little Mermaid Shrimp Salad at $3.95; half-sandwiches of turkey or ham, pastrami or tuna on freshly baked European breads (cracked wheat, country French, light rye). A combination consisting of a half-sandwich and homemade soup (split pea and ham, vegetables and beef, etc.) makes for a neat light meal at $2.95. Even if you're not ready for a meal, be sure to stop off for a snack; you'd have to go to Denmark to get a Danish pastry (totally unlike anything that goes by that name in the states) as good as Inger's home-baked one, a flaky wonder made with butter and marzipan. Along with that, have a cup of freshly brewed Lion chocolate-macadamia coffee and know the meaning of contentment. The coffee is also available to take home by the bag.

Cafe Copenhagen is open every day from 8 a.m. to 10 p.m. The same people also have a kiosk called "Hello, Doggy" on the ground floor, where they serve hot dogs with roasted onions from Denmark, sauce rémoulade, and cucumber salad, at $1.95, $2.35, and $2.75.

If you'd like some hearty German fare, then go to the top of the Center and visit the big new **Bavarian Beer Garden** (tel. 922-6535). Here you can dine on a good selection of wursts and weiners and the like, modestly priced, from $2.35 to $8.95, listen to accordian music from 5 to 7 p.m., and even get up and do a waltz or a polka or two once the five-piece Bavarian band starts oom-pah-pahing around 8 p.m. There's no cover, but a $5 minimum after 8. Open every day from 5 p.m. to 1 a.m.

Come down to earth now, to the ground floor and Building A, where **It's Greek to Me** (tel. 922-2733) provides the answer to a lot of dining needs. You can stop here anytime and get a quick sandwich at the counter, or sit down at one of the comfortable tables indoors or in the garden and enjoy a delicious meal. We have so many favorite lunch foods here—for example, the tasty gyro sandwich at $3.95, the falafel plate at $5.95, the light and flaky spinach pie at $3.25—that it's hard to choose. On our last visit, we went with a refreshing tabouleh salad at $3.95, and a wonderfully tasty chicken souvlaki sandwich at $4.50—that's a skewer of charbroiled marinated chicken breast, onions, and pepper rolled in warm pita bread and topped with tomatoes and lettuce—ummm! We like taramasalata (a fish roe spread) for an appetizer, an honest-to-

Zeus baklava for dessert. At dinner, salads and sandwiches are a bit higher and entrees run $8.95 to $14.95. Daily specials include fresh fish and lamb souvlaki. One of our readers, L. Faulstich of Dallas, Texas, writes to recommend the great apple and cherry pastries, made fresh on the premises every day; now, with Häagen-Dazs ice cream, they're better than ever. For liquid refreshment: a greatly expanded wine and beer selection, plus espresso and cappuccino, in addition to the usual. Open daily.

At Discovery Bay

Discovery Bay, a two-level shopping area topped by a huge condominium, at 1778 Ala Moana Blvd., opposite the Ilikai Hotel, boasts three excellent restaurants. **Cafe 33** (tel. 955-0775) is the newest, French all the way (despite its Japanese-style plastic replicas of dishes in a showcase up front), with red-and-white tablecloths sparking the rather muted decor. Come for lunch or come for dinner; the menu is largely the same, except for some pricey dinner specials (like crevette aux champignons, king prawns with mushrooms in a cream sauce, at $17.95) prepared at table. You might start your meal with an excellent coquilles St-Jacques ($5.90) or the soup de jour ($3), and have an entree like chicken breast with liver mousse, at $8.95. Pêche flambé is a delightful, if splurgy, dessert at $5.95. Ex-Bagwell's manager George Dubuisson is your host. Lunch is served Monday through Saturday from 11:30 a.m. to 2 p.m., dinner seven days from 6 to 10 p.m.

Renown Milano in the same building (tel. 947-1933) is more within our reach. Lunches start at $4.95, dinner at $6.95. For that price you can have a heart-shaped pizza spiked with ham, pepperoni, and green peppers. There are 15 pasta dishes priced at $6.95 to $9.75 ($2 less at lunch), and these include very good lasagne or cannelloni. This is a long, sedate room with brown and yellow striped chairs. Art on the walls, plants in abundance, and piped-in music make you feel you are in a more expensive restaurant. Renown Milano serves lunch from 11:30 a.m. to 2:30 p.m., dinner from 5:30 to 10 p.m., daily.

Our favorite restaurant here is **Bon Appetite,** (tel. 942-3837), master chef Guy Banal's contribution to the cause of haute cuisine. Dinner here can be a rather expensive if you order off the à la carte menu, so save yourself some francs by having their complete gourmet dinner: four courses for $22.50, $18.95 if you eliminate course one or two. The menu changes daily, but the day we were there, course one was duck and morels mushroom soup with vegetable; course two was Maui tomatoes with shrimp salad and avocado dressing. Course three was a choice of sirloin of beef or broiled island fish with lobster champagne sauce. And course four, your choice from the incredibly good dessert menu. You dine at windows overlooking Ala Moana Blvd. on royal red chairs. There is an excellent wine list, and a popular wine and appetizer bar as well, the biggest in town. Bon Appetit serves dinner only from 5:30 until 10 p.m. Closed Sunday.

And if it all sounds too high for your budget, Discovery Bay also has a McDonald's!

More Fun Choices

Fans of Ward Centre's **Compadres Mexican Bar and Grill** (and there are many—the restaurant has been voted "Best Mexican Restaurant" in Hawaii by the *Honolulu* Magazine Poll) can enjoy the same great food and atmosphere at a sister restaurant in the Outrigger Prince Kuhio Hotel, 2500 Kuhio Ave. (tel. 924-4007). See our report under "At Ward Centre," below.

The cheerful little **Harbor Pub and Pizzeria,** just below the Chart House at

1765 Ala Moana Blvd. (tel. 941-0985), is usually filled with a "fun" crowd in the evening. It's a favorite watering hole for people employed at nearby hotels and offices. The fare is not terribly varied here, but what there is is just fine. All sandwiches—roast beef, breast of turkey, submarine, and tuna melt—are under $5. The specialty is pizza: plain cheese pies are $5.50 small, and the Harbor combo, with everything, is $8.25 small. This is the sort of place where everyone talks with everyone else and the atmosphere is friendly and fun. Hours are 11 a.m. to 1:30 a.m. daily.

THE OLD RELIABLES: Now we come to the standbys, the places you can always count on for fast service, and good, basic food. And if there's anything more basic than a McDonald's hamburger, we've got to find it. There are three **McDonald's** in Waikiki, one at 2204 Kalakaua Ave. and two in the Royal Hawaiian Shopping Center at 2233 Kalakaua. All are attractively decorated (outdoor tables at the first are great for people-watching), and staffed with employees who can give sightseeing advice as well as dish out the Big Macs. A collection of primitive Hawaiian art is featured at the shopping center. Breakfast, served from 6 to 10 a.m. (Egg McMuffin and Sausage McMuffin served until 11 a.m.), features inexpensive scrambled eggs, sausages, muffins, and hash browns. For the rest of the day, it's Big Macs at $1.45, Filet-O-Fish sandwiches at $1.05, plus other sandwiches, desserts, and drinks. A special blessing is the fact that these places close late (midnight on weekdays, 1 a.m. on weekends), so that the grownups can have a snack while junior and company are fast asleep.

Woolworth's, in the Bank of Hawaii Building on Kalakaua (tel. 923-1713), is another family-type spot that can be relied on for decent and inexpensive food. The atmosphere is pleasant and the prices are right: every day there's a $3.15 luncheon special like pineapple chicken, and regular luncheon entrees run $3.30 to $4.95. Franks with french fries and coleslaw are $3.30; other sandwiches are $4.95 tops; a seafood salad bowl costs $4.95. Prices are also low at night—a turkey dinner is $4.10. Japanese and Chinese dishes are also served, and you can have southern fried chicken to go. Note, too, Woolworth's Oriental Snack Bar in the back of the store, where you can sample all kinds of strange goodies. We'll give you more details in our section on Japanese restaurants, ahead. You'll find a larger, equally bustling and cheerful Woolworth's restaurant at Ala Moana Center.

Princess Bernice Pauahi Bishop (the very lady after whom the Bishop Museum was named) is also honored in the **Princess Coffee Shop Restaurant,** on the ground floor of the Royal Hawaiian Center, 2233 Kalakaua Ave. She and her husband once made their home on this location, near the enormous banyan tree in front of the Royal Hawaiian Hotel. The restaurant is tastefully decorated in Hawaiian monarchy decor, with prints and portraits on the walls; the food is nicely presented American fare with island accents, at very reasonable prices. Dinner specials like stuffed peppers or roast chicken or beef sukiyaki run from $6 to $8, and are served with a choice of soup or salad, vegetables, potato or rice, hot roll, and butter. Always available are offerings from the "Fry Kettle" —fish and chips, deep-sea scallops, seafood platter, from $4.95 to $7.25—as well as grilled items like beef liver and onions, and Hawaiian chopped steak. Specials like corned beef and cabbage with mustard sauce or shoyu chicken, from $4 to $5.75, will make for a filling lunch. Doors open at 7 a.m. for breakfast, close at midnight, seven days a week. Their outdoor Garden Bar is a relaxing spot for a drink. It's open from 11 a.m. to 11 p.m., with music every evening.

Denny's, in the Imperial Hawaii Hotel at 205 Lewers St. (tel. 923-8188), is a good-size coffeeshop-style operation that's always open. There are comfortable booths, silent ceiling fans, and abundant greenery. And the glass façade affords a panoramic view of the passing parade. Lunch or dinner entrees are priced the same all day. Such entrees as chicken fried steak or fried chicken, broiled rainbow trout, meat loaf, New York steak, or steak and shrimp range from $4.15 to $8.69, and are accompanied by vegetables and potato, roll and butter. Our breakfast favorite here is the french toast with strawberries ($3.05), but eggs Benedict is another winner. Other Denny's can be found in the Miramar Hawaii Hotel on Kuhio Avenue, at 1909 Ala Wai Blvd., and on the mezzanine level of 2586 Kalakaua.

There are two **Jolly Rogers** in Waikiki: the newer one is in the Outrigger East, at the corner of Kuhio and Kaiulani; the original has been holding forth at 2244 Kalakaua Ave. for just about as long as anyone can remember. The new place has green carpets and a cheery atmosphere; there's a cocktail lounge too, where a trio entertains nightly. The other place gives you a choice of sidewalk tables right out on the busy avenue or, more peacefully, tables inside under umbrellas; there's also the **Crow's Nest** above the restaurant with nightly entertainment and a Happy Hour every day from 4 to 8 p.m., when maitais are priced at $1.59. Both restaurants offer a casual ambience and American coffeehouse-style food, quite tasty, at good prices. Complete dinners—served with soup or salad, potatoes or rice, and dinner roll—include such entrees as chicken polynesian or baby beef liver with onions or bacon, and most are under $8.50. There are daily specials like roast beef or steak and shrimp. Burgers, salads, and sandwiches are also available. Breakfast is a special treat, since that's when you can get the "Mac-Waple." Reader Teresa Tydings of Olympia, Washington, wrote us about this one: "It consists of a waffle covered in sliced, spiced hot apples topped with macadamia nuts. Positively sinful." The doors are open from 6:30 a.m. until 12 midnight, cocktail lounge till 2 a.m.

Located just across Kalakaua from the International Market Place, **The Rigger,** in the Outrigger Hotel, 2335 Kalakaua Ave. (tel. 922-5544), is one of those places you can always depend on for a reasonably priced meal in attractive, comfortable surroundings. Hamburgers are a specialty here, and they're good. The surf burger is $3.55; the fancier variations—mushroom burgers, teriyaki burgers, avocado burgers, and the like—slightly higher. Dinner is an excellent buy. Entrees like paniolo steak, teriyaki chicken breasts, fried shrimp platter, and beef liver and onions, run from $6.45 to $8.45, and are accompanied by soup or salad, a choice of rice or potato, and a dinner roll. Light lunches are served with a green salad, roll and starch, and include choices like mahimahi, pollo con salsa, and teriyaki steak, from $4.45 to $5.95. The doors stay open from 6 a.m. to 1 a.m. every day.

While shopping at the **Waikiki Shopping Plaza,** 2250 Kalakaua, corner of Seaside, can be expensive, and most of its upper-level restaurants are pricey, its below-street level is a veritable bonanza for the budget-conscious diner who wants something a little bit different. Start in the Japanese sector at **Ramen** for freshly made Japanese noodles. You can have them seated at the open tables or at the Japanese counter flanked by Japanese lanterns. Prices start at $3.75 for shoyu rahmen and go to $5 for gyoza—Japanese noodles Chinese style—and to $5 for shrimp tempura; a combination plate is $5.75. You'll see Japanese visitors enjoying rahmen at all hours of the day; in fact, this is one of the few Plaza spots that opens early, at 10 a.m. There are no tables at the next Japanese fast-food outlet, **Okazu-Ya Bento** ("Bento" means take-out). Here, they custom-design your take-out lunch or dinner, filling the large plate with Japanese favorites at tiny prices: yaki soba, meatballs, chicken cutlet, cone sushi, from 40¢ to $1.85. All items are in view in a glass showcase, Japanese style, so you can just point, or take their combination plate for $3.75. To round off this Japanese trio, there's

Plaza Sushi, a tidy little restaurant that serves a mostly all-Japanese crowd, offers various sushis from $3.90 to $7.50.

Want more variety? You can have a deli lunch at **Plaza Deli,** perhaps a baked ham or roast beef sandwich at $3.95. Salad bar is $3.75, daily soup and sandwich specials are $3.15. **Plaza Burger** is versatile: it serves a quarter-pounder for $1.44, plus a taco dinner at $3.75, and a fried chicken dinner at $4.85. The **Chinese Kitchen** has lots of goodies, like lemon chicken, sweet-and-sour fish, and roast duck, from $2.95 to $4.95. **Plaza Pizza** is one of the welcome few places around town where you can get pizza by the slice, $1.30, plus daily specials; and of course there has to be a **Plaza Ice Cream,** with soda chairs and tables, offering cooling cones, sodas, and sundaes.

Your best all-around choice here is the huge **Plaza Coffee Shop,** where changing lunch specials go from $4.25 to $5.25 and include the likes of boneless barbecued chicken, corned beef and cabbage, and sautéed red snapper. Similar specials are $5 to $8 at dinner.

At last count, there were something like 16 **Jack in the Box** restaurants in Honolulu. We were especially happy to find one right in the midst of the beach area, at 2424 Kalakaua Ave. (tel. 923-4487), across the road from the banyan tree at Kuhio Beach. This is a bright, cheery spot with blue and beige tiled floor, blue leather booths, and an open feeling. They have everything from croissant breakfasts to dinners-in-the-box, pizza pockets, good salads (seafood, pasta, taco), and, of course, those good "jumbo jacks" at $2.09. Good for a quick bite any time of day.

An always dependable establishment at the oceanfront in the Reef Towers Hotel is the **Islander,** at 247 Lewers St. (tel. 923-3233), famous for its fresh baked orange bread, served hot with dinner or as french toast or dessert. Copper trim and copper fixtures against a cocoa color scheme accent this impeccably clean and attractive place, open most of the day (6 a.m. to midnight). Breakfast is served all day; $2.95 buys a waker-upper of egg, two slices of bacon, and toast with jelly. Lunch and dinner menus and prices are largely the same. At dinner, along with your entree—perhaps teriyaki steak, mahimahi, or roast pork, at prices ranging from $5.85 to $7.45—you get homemade soup or salad, potatoes or rice, plus hot orange bread. Don't miss one of their great desserts, and if you order pie, ask them to heat it up for you.

For an authentic Japanese meal at a very low price, **Ezogiku,** 2038 Kuhio Ave. (tel. 941-1646), fills the bill. It's a tiny, lunch-counter-type place, with perhaps ten seats surrounding the cooking area and a limited number of menu items. The "menu" is posted over the counter. One of our readers, Lester S. Hyman of Washington, D.C., recommends this as a great place for kids; they not only love watching the chefs do their antics in front of a roaring stove, but they can also skim the colorful Japanese magazines and comic books stacked beneath the counter. And the food is amazing considering the prices. Noodles, or ramen, is the specialty here; miso, butter, or shoyu ramen, which also contains bean sprouts, vegetables, and meat, is $3.75 for a big bowl. There's a curry rice plate at $4 and a fried noodle plate at $3.75. Lunch and dinner prices are the same. A find!

Prices are about 50¢ higher at four other Waikiki Ezogiku locations: at 2310 Kuhio Ave. (Waikiki Marketplace); 2420 Koa Ave. (behind the Hyatt Regency Hotel); 2546 Lemon Rd. (behind the Hawaiian Regent Hotel); and 2141 Kalakaua Ave., at Beachwalk.

Unless somebody told you, you wouldn't think the **Wailana Coffee House** was a budget place, because it looks so imposing and expensive, located as it is in the exclusive Wailana Condominiums at 1860 Ala Moana Blvd. (corner John

Ena Road), opposite the Hilton Hawaiian Village dome. But go! It's never closed, and the prices will surprise you. The nicest thing about the Wailana is that lunches and dinners are the same price—the tab does not go up after 5 p.m. as it does in so many other places. So any time of the day you can have the soup and sandwich lunch for $3.75, or the delicious "broasted" chicken, juicy and tender, served with a generous helping of french fries, coleslaw or salad, roll, and honey, for $4.95. Other good buys are the old-fashioned beef stew at $5.50, the beef liver with fried onions or bacon at $5.75, the top sirloin at $9.50. All of these entrees are served with a choice of soup, salad, or fruit cup; and you get plenty of potatoes, hot rolls, and butter, as well as salad bar between 11 a.m. and 10:30 p.m. Prices subject to change here.

The attractive **Wailana Malia Coffee Shop** in the Outrigger Malia Hotel at 2211 Kuhio Ave. (tel. 922-4769) is owned by the same firm as the Wailana Coffee House on Ala Moana, and it too is open 24 hours a day. The food, again, is delicious and inexpensive. We like the breakfasts here a lot, especially the Irish breakfast: grapefruit juice, a three-egg omelet stuffed with corned beef hash and topped with cheddar cheese, grilled fresh pineapple spears, hash-brown potatoes, toast and jelly, and coffee, at $5.75, guaranteed to put you on top of the morning. Lunches and dinners, served all day, include baby beef liver, knockwurst and cabbage, oyster-sauce beef with onions, and the like—all served with soup, salad, or fruit cocktail, french fries, baked potato, or rice, hot vegetables, and rolls and butter, for only $5.50. Broiler favorites begin at $6.50 for hamburger steak and go up to $7.75 for teriyaki steak and $9.75 for top sirloin. There's a salad bar at lunch and dinner. Cakes and pies are good here, and best of all is the cheesecake with strawberries. Another Wailana winner for Waikiki.

It's rare in Honolulu to find a restaurant where you can get pizza by the slice (as well as by the pie), so we were happy to discover **Slices**, at 870 Kapahulu Ave. (tel. 735-6441), on the Diamond Head border of Waikiki, near the Honolulu Zoo. A mere 89¢ will buy you a very good-size slice of cheese-and-tomato pan pizza. You can pile on as many extras as you like—homemade Italian sausage or anchovies or whatever—for 30¢ each. Sub sandwiches are also a treat, especially the steak sub at $2.80. Beer and wine are available. You step up to the shiny-clean counter to order and pay for your food, then take it with you to sit at one of the little tables outside. Slices has won "The Greatest Pizza in Honolulu" contest for two years in a row. Open Monday to Saturday from 10 a.m. to 2 a.m., on Sunday to 10 p.m. They make deliveries to Waikiki and surrounding areas.

There's a sidewalk pizza-calzone parlor with seats at umbrellaed tables a block from Kuhio Beach, at 151 Uluniu St., at the side of the **Royal Grove Hotel** (tel. 922-1622). Carlton Fong, one of the owners of the hotel, has been having great fun creating pizzas that he swears are just as good as those in New York—and they really are. The pizzas are thick crusted, and can be had by the pie ($3 for an eight-incher) or by the slice ($1.25), either plain or with a variety of toppings; the veggie pie, with mushrooms, olives, bell peppers, zucchini, tomatoes, and green onions, is a special treat at $5, small. And if you've never tried calzone—a pizza dough filled with ricotta, mozzarella, sauce, and seasonings—here's your chance; they are $3.25 each, and the Mexican calzone, with beans, olives, onions, tomatoes, and ground beef, is a winner at $5.50. Spaghetti and other daily pasta specials are $3 to $4. Ask about their hot garlic bread and hot cinnamon bread, baked right on the premises. Open daily from 11 a.m. to midnight. Happily, they will deliver in Waikiki, between 5 and 10 p.m.

If you're nuts about macadamia nuts—as well as cookies, chocolates, shakes, sundaes, ice creams and other fattening temptations—stop in for a sweet snack at **The MacNuttery,** an attractive shop and sidewalk café at 2098 Kalakaua Ave., not far from Fort DeRussy (tel. 942-7798). In addition to the above-mentioned goodies, they also serve a nice chef's salad, turkey or ham sandwiches, and a hot-dog platter, all from $3.50 to $4.29, and all with macadamia nut bread. Eat in the shop or at ice-cream chairs and tables right out on busy Kalakaua.

RESTAURANTS THAT NEVER CLOSE: If you get the "hungries" after a late movie or show—or even at 3 a.m.—there's no need to despair in Honolulu, for this is definitely not a town that shuts down tight at 9 in the evening. You could take yourself to **Top's Beachwalk Coffee Shop,** at 298 Beach Walk (tel. 923-2302), a nifty coffeehouse with a touch of Tiffany decor, breakfasts served around the clock, and lots of daily specials: many breakfast specials are under $3; complete dinners begin at $4.95. The pastry shop with fresh baked goods is also open 24 hours a day. You might have seafood dishes like mahimahi and deep-fried shrimp or a big Hawaiian pineapple fruit boat for $4.50, or a tasty light-eater meal from $4.95—plus burgers and sandwiches, of course. Lunch is served in a unique pub, open from 11 a.m. to closing; and there's a daily Happy Hour from 11 a.m. to closing too.

And remember, as mentioned above, these other Waikiki 24-hour favorites: **Top's Canterbury Coffee House & Tavern, Sizzler Steak Seafood Salad, Denny's, Wailana Coffee House,** and **Wailana Malia Coffee Shop.**

2. Restaurants Around Town (Outside Waikiki)

Once you leave the Waikiki area, your choice of restaurants—in all categories—becomes much greater. The following are all within easy driving or bus distance of Waikiki, and they're listed according to the type of food they serve and/or the geographical area in which they're located.

AMERICAN RESTAURANTS: These aren't necessarily your basic steak-and-baked-potato/hamburger-and-fries/fried-chicken-and-mashed-potatoes places. Not in Honolulu U.S.A., where teriyaki beef is as American as apple pie. So many ethnic specialties have come into the local repertoire that Japanese, Chinese, and Polynesian dishes (among others) are listed right along with—yes, steak, hamburger, and fried chicken. In a few pages we'll concentrate on the "foreign" restaurants—those that specialize solely in ethnic food. Right now, it's a little bit of everything.

From Waikiki to Downtown Honolulu

In this area, which stretches from the ewa end of Waikiki to downtown Honolulu (Kapiolani Boulevard is the main thoroughfare), we'll begin with the charming **Victoria Station,** 1599 Kapiolani Blvd. (tel. 955-1107), where you'll dine surrounded by mementos of the English railroad era—antique boxcars out in the front and on the side, red and gold railway signs all over. "Inflation-fighting" lunches feature cheeseburgers at $4.25 and teriyaki chicken at $4.95, quiche and soup at $4.95. Soup-and-salad luncheons are $5.95. At dinner, you can eat light entrees—London broil, jumbo fried shrimp, chicken stir fry, and the like—from $7 to $10, or go the complete dinner route from $11 to $18. Salad bar is included with many entrees. A nonsmoking section is available.

We always wonder why Honolulu's tourists haven't yet caught up with **King's Bakery and Coffee Shop,** 1936 S. King St. near McCully (tel. 941-5211), which has been a popular local rendezvous for years. Even though it's open 24 hours a day, seven days a week, it's always jammed and you sometimes have to wait a few minutes for a seat at the counter, tables, or booths—that's how well liked it is. Certainly it's not because of the decor, which is perfectly plain with plastic-topped tables. It is because of the good service, the good food, and the fact that breakfast, lunch, and dinner menus are the same and are served around the clock. This means you can always count on a plate of hot, lusty beef stew, Hawaiian chopped steak, crispy fried chicken, sautéed mahimahi, or breaded veal cutlet, from $3.75 to $5.30. Daily specials at $4.95 to $5.10 include pot roast pork, short ribs, and mushroom chicken, served with a tossed green salad, vegetable, rice or potatoes, butter, and roll. We mention the roll last because this is also a bakery, and a good one. People come from miles around to shop for King's bread and rolls and their delicious pies and cakes. After you've had your fruit pie, or cream cheese pie, you may be tempted to join the crowd at the bakery counter and take some home with you—and don't forget the very special sweet bread, $1.70 per loaf. (Try it for french toast!) Send some home to your friends—King's has them already packaged—and they'll bless you forever.

You can also get the standard sandwiches here at low prices, plus soups, salads, and soda-fountain concoctions. King's also has two other locations, at the Kaimuki Shopping Center, 3221 Waialae Ave., and at Eaton Square, on Hobron Lane.

The **Pagoda Floating Restaurant,** 1525 Rycroft St. (tel. 941-6611), is one of those rare places where the scenery alone is worth the price of admission. The glass-enclosed Koi Room on the first floor, which specializes in seafood, and the more elegant La Salle (see, ahead, under French/Japanese Restaurants) look out over a lotus-blossom pond stocked with almost 3,000 brilliantly colored Japanese carp. Walkways lead out to individual pagodas seemingly afloat in the pond. Although the pagodas are reserved for groups of eight or more, the view from the main dining rooms is quite beautiful. At dinner, entrees go from $12.95 to $18.95. The house specialty, mahimahi Blue Hawaiian, is $14.50. Lunch is always a buffet, priced at $8.95, and served daily, from 11 a.m. to 2 p.m.; dinner is from 5 to 10 p.m. Try to plan your visit to catch the grand show at carp-feeding time—8 a.m., noon, or 6 p.m. Bring the kids and the cameras.

In the Ala Moana Area

A popular spot for calorie counters (and who isn't, these days?) is the **Guiltless Gourmet,** located a block from Ala Moana Center at 1489 Kapiolani Blvd. (tel. 955-6144). This place has become so popular that they've added a large new dining room and expanded their menu to include breakfast. Everything is made with "no added fats or oils, no added raw or refined sugars, no added starches or preservatives, and no guilt." And calorie counts are listed for every dish. In addition to the yummy desserts made with "Skinny Delite" (their frozen ice milk), they feature appetizers and snacks like cheese nachos and ratatouille; Latin favorites like chicken enchiladas and tasty tostadas; international fare on the order of vegetarian Stroganof, zucchini lasagne, chicken parmesan, and vegetarian "chicken curry." (Obviously, a good place for vegetarians to hang out.) Soup and salad meals; chicken, ribs, and seafood dishes; sandwiches and Stuffed Skinny Spuds, baked potatoes filled with such stuffings as veggie chili, nacho cheese sauce, veggie curry, at $3.29, are also winners. Most dishes are $4 to $5. Sandwiches are served on the house's own "Guiltless Bread," which runs about half the calories of regular bread. You can have non-alcoholic beer or wine to go with your "lite" meal. Now, about those desserts. Skinny Delite is available in dozens of flavors, like English Toffee, Swiss Chocolat,

Tootsie Roll, various fruit flavors, and many more. It tastes divine and it's only 20 calories per ounce! The Hot Fudge Cake (200 calories) is very popular; it's a chocolate brownie served with a scoop of ice milk and topped with hot-fudge sauce, $2.59. Our favorite is apples à la mode—steaming hot apples topped with Skinny Delite, 130 calories for $1.89. Skinny Delite also comes in cups, cones, and take-out containers. Guiltless Gourmet is open until 9 p.m. daily.

The **Original Pancake House,** at 1221 Kapiolani Blvd. (tel. 533-3005), is a pleasant place to have breakfast or lunch on your way to or from the Ala Moana Center. We especially like to sit out in the pretty little garden, where one is sure to be visited by English sparrows, doves, Brazilian cardinals, and mynahs, all looking for a handout. Pancakes and crêpes include cottage cheese pancakes (one of our favorites!), at $4.10; cherry crêpes, made with liqueur, at $6.25; blueberry pancakes, at $3.70; and the house special, apple pancakes (allow 30 minutes), at $6.75. Among the many omelets, all served with three buttermilk pancakes, our favorite is the potato—made with green onions and bacon bits and served with a flavorful sour cream sauce, $4.70. Beef Stroganoff crêpes and crêpes Palestine (filled with sour cream and Triple Sec) are unusual and special; they're priced at $4.30. There are also hot sandwiches such as teriyaki, steak, and french dip in the $4.30 to $4.70 range, and daily specials like mahimahi, chicken-fried steak, spaghetti, and beef stew, priced from $4.50 to $7.95. The restaurant is open from 6 a.m. until 2 p.m. every day.

There is another Original Pancake House in the Waikiki Marina Hotel, 1956 Ala Moana Blvd., across from Fort DeRussy (tel. 947-8848), open 6 a.m. until 9 p.m., Sunday until 2 p.m. Their dinner specials might include lemon chicken and mahimahi, from $4.50 to $7.95.

One of our favorite places to pick up wonderful, portable food for a picnic or the beach—or just to take back to our hotel—is **Chicken Alice's,** at 1470 Kapiolani Blvd. (tel. 946-6117). The stellar attraction here is Alice Gahinhin's flavorful fried chicken. It's ever-so-delicately spiced and definitely habit-forming. And you can't beat the price—$4.25 for a small box containing 10 pieces; $6 for the large box, 18 to 20 pieces; $20 for some 60 pieces (in case you're throwing a party or have a very large family to feed). Chicken pieces are also available: a breast is $1.27, thigh or drumstick, 99¢. We also like the combination Korean plate: kal-bi (tender barbecued ribs), chicken, rice, and kim chee, for $4.75. The plate lunches here are king-size, to say the least. Chicken Alice's is open from 9:30 a.m. to 9:30 p.m. Monday through Saturday, to 7:30 p.m. Sunday.

A real haven for the hungry and high-price weary, **Hana,** 636 Sheridan St. (tel. 537-1523), is worth the five-minute walk from the Sears end of the Ala Moana Shopping Center (it's one block mauka of Kapiolani Boulevard). It wouldn't do Hana justice to call it just a delicatessen—it's a combination deli, cafeteria, restaurant (although tiny, with fewer than a dozen tables), and a picnic kickoff spot. The main reason for coming here is their broasted chicken: nibble on a wing (75¢) or a breast ($1.29), or order either the regular chicken box (two pieces, french fries or rice, salad) for $2.59, the queen-size with three pieces at $3.12, or the king-size with four pieces for $4.49. You're ready for your picnic. There's another Hana at Pearlridge Center.

Although J.C. Penney's, the huge department store at Ala Moana Center, is right up-to-date with its fashions, the prices they charge at **Penney's Restaurant,** on the third floor, went out of style years ago—which makes it a great place for us. Every year we get letters from readers telling us about the good, inexpensive meals they've enjoyed here. It is a good deal, for breakfast, lunch, or dinner. At lunch, for example, hot plates are mostly under $4.75; we like their teriyaki plate at $4.35. A roast beef sandwich is $3.50. At 4 p.m. some dinner items are added to the menu, like grilled beef liver or choice sirloin steak. Entrees, from $5.50 to $7.50, are served with potatoes, vegetable, dessert, and beverage. Try to avoid the peak lunch hour unless you don't mind queuing up for a few minutes' wait. Open from 8 a.m. to 8 p.m. on weekdays, on Saturday from 8 a.m. to 5 p.m., and on Sunday from 8:30 a.m. to 4 p.m. Early arrivals must use the special third-floor entrance.

The kamaainas are mad about **Zippy's,** and it's no wonder. The food is plentiful and the prices are as reasonable as you'll find anywhere in Hawaii. There are 17 Zippy's restaurants on Oahu, (they're all listed in the phone book), including one convenient for us at Ala Moana Center. Two of their most popular specialties are chili and fried chicken. In fact, many local clubs and children's athletic teams sell tickets for the chili to raise funds, and they sell like . . . Zippy's chili! A big bucket of this taste treat (seven servings) is $6.50. Fried chicken is $10.15 for a 12-piece bucket. And everyone loves Zippy's plate lunches: big platters of beef or pork teriyaki, breaded beef cutlet, fried chicken, spaghetti with meat sauce, hamburger steak, or mahimahi, including rice or fries, are priced from $3.45 to $4.45. There's good news for the diet-conscious, too: Zippy's huge salads—we especially like the taco and chef's salads—are all $4 and under. Zippy's are self-service restaurants where you place your order at one window, pay, and collect it in very short order at the next window. A few of them have table-service dining rooms as well, and several have a Napoleon's Bakery (their local TV commercials feature a somewhat addled emperor who is never sure whether it is he or the pastries that the announcer asserts are "flaky"). Waiting to fatten you up are luscious haupia and dobash cakes; wonderful doughnuts, danish, and cupcakes; freshly baked Portuguese sweet bread, French, and raisin breads; and great pies, from apple to macadamia cream. And all the Zippy's eateries are open 24 hours a day.

Note: For a rundown of other restaurants at the Ala Moana Shopping Center, see Chapter V.

If you're shopping at Ala Moana Center and want to escape the "madding throng," note that the adjacent Ala Moana Hotel has several restaurants, including the charming and reasonable **Tsukasa** (tel. 955-4811). It's open for breakfast, lunch, and dinner, but don't expect scrambled eggs or Danish for breakfast: the Japanese eat rice, miso soup, fish and raw egg for the morning meal. At dinner you can have a combination dish of sashimi for $8.95. Soba and udon noodles are fillers at $4.75 to $6.50, tempura style. Other tempura style dishes include shrimp at $6.75, vegetables at $5.50, combination at $6.50. Prices are lower at lunch, but the selection is more limited. Service at Tsukasa is with the traditional Japanese graciousness; the surroundings are 20th-century Tokyo. The location is on the street level of the lobby. Breakfast time is 6 to 10 a.m., lunch 11:30 a.m. to 2:30 p.m., dinner 6 to 11 p.m.

Close to Town

For years the Flamingo restaurants have been offering terrific quality for the money. There are two such restaurants close to town: the **Café Flamingo,** at 574 Ala Moana (tel. 538-6927), and the **Flamingo Kapiolani,** 871 Kapiolani Blvd. (tel. 538-6931). We have a slight preference for the latter if only because it's nearer Waikiki; both are attractive and specialize in good service and delicious food. There are something like 22 main dishes on the menu priced from $5.25 to $8.95. And here's what a typical dinner for that price would be like. It starts with soup or fresh mixed fruit cup (we tried both: the soup was a very satisfactory chicken mulligatawny; the fruit cup was out of the ordinary since it was made with fresh papaya); an entree of deep fried butterfish with lemon butter sauce; spinach, rice, and salad on the side; delicious banana pie or chocolate pudding for dessert; and coffee or tea, or fruit punch to drink. If you choose spaghetti with meat sauce for a main course, the price of the entire meal is only $5.25. The quality of the food and the variety of choices are remarkable for the prices. At lunch prices go down about 50¢. Note to late eaters: You can get dinner at the Café Flamingo until 1 a.m. weekdays, until 2 a.m. on Friday and Saturday; the Flamingo Kapiolani serves dinner until 8:45 p.m., cocktails until closing. The Café Flamingo opens at 6 a.m. for breakfast, the Flamingo Kapiolani at 6:30 a.m. weekdays and 7 a.m. on Sunday.

The same top-notch management also runs the **Flamingo Chuck Wagon,** at 1015 Kapiolani, where lunch starts at $4.25 and at dinnertime you can eat as much prime rib or fried chicken as you like, served chuckwagon style, for under $10. In the central business district downtown, the **Flamingo Coffee Shop,** and **Arthur's Restaurant,** at 173 Merchant St., are big local favorites. Luncheon in the coffeeshop starts at around $3.95, and at Arthur's at $5.95 (for sandwiches).

News dominates the conversation at **Columbia Inn,** 645 Kapiolani Blvd. (tel. 531-3747), a favorite hangout for the staffs of Honolulu's two daily newspapers just a few doors away. The news about food is also good at this large, wood-paneled spot with its leather booths. At lunch you can choose from 28 complete lunches between $5.20 and $8.75, and that includes boiled brisket of corned beef and cabbage, clams in the shell cooked in garlic butter, pepper steak with rice pilaf, all accompanied by fish chowder or fruit salad, dessert, and beverage. Order à la carte and the range is $3.95 to $7.50. At dinner there are some two dozen choices for $10 and under, beginning at $5.95 for a complete meal. Columbia Inn is open 24 hours a day seven days a week—except during the wee hours of Monday morning—but full meals are served only from 11 a.m. to 4 p.m. (lunch) and 4 to 10 p.m. (dinner).

George's Inn, 1360 S. King St. (tel. 949-7222), has offered value and quality for as long as we can remember. The cozy restaurant is lit by hanging Japanese lanterns and furnished with shiny booths upholstered in black. Friendly waitresses wear bright happi coats over long pants; Oriental scenics and plants decorate the dining room. The menu features complete meals served with soup, salad, or fruit cup, mashed potatoes or rice, vegetables, and bread. No need to spend very much here; you can do very nicely with breaded mahimahi, hamburger steak teriyaki, filet of sole, or liver and onions for just $5.25; seafood platter is $6.75. À la carte choices include breaded shrimps, oysters, or scallops at $5.25. Sandwiches and burgers too. George's is open from 7 a.m. to 9 p.m. every day except Sunday and holidays.

Not too long ago, *Aloha* magazine had an islandwide search for the best hamburger on Oahu. The winning burger was the one offered by the **Bakery Kapiolani Coffee Shop,** 1221 S. King St. (tel. 523-1291), and it only costs $1.15—$1.35 with cheese! The hamburger and cheeseburger deluxe are $1.60 and $1.80 respectively. Also available in this basic coffeeshop with lunch counter, booths, and bakery in the middle, are the likes of teriburgers, chili dogs, saimin, and coconut pies; and what must be the world's last surviving 40¢ hot dog. All sandwiches are served on home-baked buns or bread. Open 5:30 a.m. to midnight daily.

When a restaurant has been going strong for over 30 years, you know it must be doing something right. Such a place is the **Wisteria,** 1206 S. King St. (tel. 531-5276), very popular with the local crowd (at a recent lunch we and one other couple were the only tourists present). Save for a few murals with wisteria branches, there is very little decoration. The atmosphere is pleasantly businesslike, the service swift and professional, and the deep leather booths comfortable. The menu leans to the Japanese side, but there are also quite a few American-style specialties. If you're in the mood for Japanese food, you can choose from various sushi dishes at $5.10 to $6.30, or select from a wide range of donburi, tempura, and sukiyaki specials (sukiyaki dinners of chicken, beef, or pork) are $5.80 to $9. Treading on more familiar ground, you might order such American-style dishes as roast chicken, baked meatloaf, or seafood creole, from $4.95 to $6.95 at lunch. The house special is an excellent sizzling rib steak: $9.35. Our Japanese meal (we chose the daily specials of tempura soba and chicken araimo) included eggdrop soup garnished with scallions in dainty black bowls, pickled vegetables, rice, and a pot of tea. Two of us had more than enough to eat for $10.65. The Wisteria is open daily from 6 a.m. until 10:30 p.m., on Friday and Saturday until 11 p.m. The cocktail lounge is open from 11 a.m. to 1 a.m.

Everything about **TGIFriday's,** at 960 Ward Ave., corner of King (tel. 523-5841), is delightfully different—from the *big* menu with some 160 items to the art nouveau leaded-glass hanging lamps and lovely antique furniture and accessories. It's obvious that no expense was spared in making this a delightful place to dine or have a drink. Friday's is insanely popular, and since reservations are not accepted, it's first-come, first-served.

The food, too, is far from run-of-the-mill. It was here that we first discovered potato-skin plates, a TGIF specialty. The skins are baked, then fried to a delightful crispness. You can order them plain or with sour cream and chives for dipping ($3.35), or "loaded," that is, slathered with a quarter pound of cheese and crumbled bacon, plus the sour cream dip ($5.65). Or try a potato-skin dinner, with chicken and asparagus and cheese, at $6.75. Another tasty treat is chicken nachos (like the Mexican original but substituting chicken for refried beans), $5.75. The quiches, priced from $5.50 to $5.95, are exceptional. Even the salads are something out of the ordinary—how about an avocado-crab salad in a flour tortilla, for $8.40? Seafood selections include fried clams in a basket with wedge fries at $7.25, and fried shrimp at $11.50. Omelets can be custom designed, and there are tacos and burgers of all descriptions, and sandwiches on the order of chicken, french dip, or steak, priced from $4.95 and up. We like their steak on a stick too: three skewers of beef marinated in teriyaki sauce and served with fries and a big onion ring, $7.95. TGIFriday's is open every day from 11:30 a.m. until 2 a.m. Weekends opening time is 9 a.m. We love it.

Hawaiian Bagel—how's that for a marriage of concepts? This wholesale-retail delicatessen with a few tables for those who can't make it out the door is at 753 B Halekauwila St. (tel. 523-8638), in a new contemporary-style building located in the rundown but picturesque Kakaako section of Honolulu. The sights and scents are surpassed only by the tastes. Needless to say, proprietor Stephen Gelson is not a full-blooded Hawaiian. Nor are the bagels, blueberry muffins, and homemade rye bread. But the little restaurant and takeout bakery deli is a hit with the local folk. And our readers love it, too. We quote from a letter from Samuel Meerkreebs of Washington, D.C.: "We were met with such gracious, kosher, aloha spirit that we had to write you on behalf of Hawaiian Bagel. We were not informed that it closed at 3 p.m. on Saturday. When we arrived around 3:30, the door was locked and things were all put away. Mr. Gelson finally opened the door and explained they were closed. I mentioned that we had come from the Hyatt, had called earlier, and added, 'My wife will kill me after bringing her all the way out here!' Steve left and brought back a 'care package' containing bagels, blueberry muffins, and cream cheese, and refused any money. His actions were different from the crass, commercial demeanor we had encountered around the island. A hearty mahalo for having the Hawaiian Bagel in your book; it was a pleasure to run into a 'mensch' along our holiday path."

They carry ten varieties of bagels, including onion, sesame seed, and poppy seed, priced at 30¢ and 32¢ each. The sandwiches are typical deli variety: roast beef, lox or whitefish and cream cheese, corned beef, liverwurst, turkey, pastrami, and the like, from $2 to $3. In true deli tradition, they even serve celery tonic. You may want to take home a fragrant, round loaf of fresh-from-the-oven rye bread. Hawaiian Bagel is open weekdays from 6:30 a.m. to 5:30 p.m., until 3 p.m. on Saturday. There is parking on the premises.

Auntie Pasto's, 1099 S. Beretania St., corner of Pensacola (tel. 523-8855), resembles a little trattoria in Florence or Rome, with its brick interior, cafe curtains, and checkered cloths. The food here is marvelous, and at lunchtime the place attracts a lively crowd, many of whom work at the shops and medical clinics in the neighborhood. Special lunches, $4.50 to $5.50, include frittata (an open-faced omelet), a mortadella scramble, pan-fried sausage and vegetables, and a club sandwich served with pasta salad. Also very popular are Auntie's big sandwiches (meatball, salami, subs), $3.95 to $5.75, and her super pastas, especially those with clams and spinach, from $3.95 to $6.50. At dinnertime, pastas are priced a little higher, and there are also some flavorful specialties like stuffed calamari, poached salmon, veal parmigiana, and osso buco, all from $6.95 to $7.95. Auntie does business Monday through Friday from 11 a.m. until 10:30 p.m.; Saturday, Sunday, and holidays, 4 p.m. until 10:30 p.m.

At Fisherman's Wharf

For a nautical meal in a nautical atmosphere, **Fisherman's Wharf,** 1009 Ala Moana (tel. 538-3808), is a Honolulu tradition. If you're counting pennies, though, it's best to go at lunch, since the menu on the whole is too expensive for our budget. At lunch, however, you can get dishes like fish 'n' fries or fried Pacific oysters for $5.25, and sandwiches from $3.75; a chowder and mahimahi sandwich lunch is $6.25; Fisherman's Wharf soup—a thick, delicious brew—is $3.25 a bowl. This place fully deserves its popularity; there are huge picture windows for viewing the sampan fleet outside, and the waitresses wear intriguing uniforms that look like French sailor suits. Happy Hour in the Snug Harbor Inn is from 4 to 6 p.m. daily, when pupus are served along with beer and bar drinks.

Want some local color in your vacation life? You can join the fishermen and other local types who frequent the **Kewalo Ship's Galley Restaurant** at 1125 Ala Moana Blvd. at Kewalo Basin (tel. 521-6608). It's been here for at least 25 years, first under the name of Sampan Inn, then Seaside Inn. Owner Zenen Ozoa made news recently when he agreed to pay the State of Hawaii $150,000 over the next five years to keep operating the restaurant. He promises he won't raise his prices very much, although he does have plans for reconstructing the place and adding a seating area outdoors near the waterfront. At this writing, it looks like a very worn 1950s diner, complete with juke box, and with 1950's prices to match: a one-pound lobster, served with french fries or rice, salad, soup, and coffee, was all of $12; a one-pound sirloin steak dinner was $6, mahimahi and pork chops, $4 each. Doors open at 5 a.m. to accommodate the fishermen and stay open until about 2 a.m., when popular entertainers or who-knows-who are likely to drop by.

At Ward Warehouse

Just opposite Kewalo Basin is the delightful **Ward Warehouse** shopping complex, and there are several charming restaurants here that match the appeal of the shops. The **Chowder House,** for one, is a bright, bustling, and inexpensive seafood house, where you can watch the boats of Fisherman's Wharf through the glass wall behind the bar and have a light seafood dinner for as little as $5.95.

We recently lunched on a good-size fresh salad, two slices of French bread, and filet of red snapper with french fries for that price. Most of the other seafood dinners are $6.10 to $9.85 (prices stay the same in the evening; there's only one menu). Fish sandwiches, also served with fries, go from $3.90 for mahimahi to $4.65 for bay shrimp; there are salads, seafood, cocktails, fish fries, and three kinds of chowder, all reasonably priced. Open from 11 a.m. to 10 p.m., to 11 p.m. weekends.

Upstairs at Ward Warehouse, the same management operates the much fancier **Orson's Restaurant,** a spacious dining room with a peaked roof, bamboo and a delightfully open and breezy feeling. Although there are a number of seafood specialties in the higher-price ranges, there's plenty to choose from under $10: filet of mahimahi, sautéed calamari, filet of red snapper meunière, for example, as well as several pasta dishes and a good variety of fish and seafood sandwiches, from $5.25 to $8.75. Orson's is open from 11 a.m. to 9:30 p.m. weekdays, to 10:30 p.m. weekends.

If you like spaghetti and you like low prices, then you're going to love the **Old Spaghetti Factory** at Ward Warehouse (tel. 531-1513), which has to be the most stunning budget restaurant in town. It's worth a visit just to see the setting, which might be described as "fabulous Victorian," the rooms brimming with authentic European antiques and Oriental rugs, ornamental lampshades, overstuffed chairs, many mirrors, and huge chandeliers. You may dine in an authentic trolley car or, more likely, at large, comfortable tables on colorful plush velvet seats, some with backs made from giant headboards. So popular is this place that you can always anticipate a wait for lunch and dinner, even though the main dining rooms seat 350 and the bar upstairs about 125! The menu is modest, concentrating mostly on spaghetti, and the food is not as dazzling as the surroundings; but you will eat heartily and well for very little. Complete dinners, from about $3.75 to $6.75, include a good green salad with choice of dressing, sourdough bread with marvelous garlic butter (a whole loaf is brought to your table with a knife, and there are seconds), beverage, and spumoni ice cream in addition to the main dish. It's fun to have either the Pot Pourri, a sample of the four most popular sauces, or the Manager's Favorite, which serves up two different sauces. Our favorite sauces are the clam and the browned butter with mizithra (a Greek cheese). Lunch runs from about $2.85 to $5.25, has smaller protions, and does not include beverage and dessert. Beer, wine, and cocktails are available. Note the hours: lunch from 11:30 a.m. to 2 p.m. Monday through Saturday; dinner from 5 to 10 p.m. Monday through Thursday, till 11 p.m. on Friday and Saturday, from 4 to 10 p.m. on Sunday.

For a quick bite at Ward Warehouse, try the **Food Express.** Central outdoor seating serves a number of fast-food stands offering saimin, Mexican food (**Taco Delta** has the usual array of enchiladas and tortillas), burgers, hot dogs, and sausages. Our favorite here is the **Juice Shop,** where you get freshly squeezed, delicious, and healthful juices, smoothies, and slushes, as well as a variety of gourmet sandwiches, from $1.99, and delicious, freshly-made salads. Two winners: the Boston clam chowder at $1.95 and the strawberry smoothie at $2.75.

Dynasty II, an elegant Chinese restaurant at Ward Warehouse, offers a popular weekday lunch buffet from 11 a.m. to 2 p.m. You can eat all you want, and the price is only $6.95. For a splurge, you might want to come back here for dinner. Appetizers like stuffed crab claw at $4.25 and entrees like the Peking Duck at $28 (the whole bird), deep-fried crispy chicken at $5.50, and the seafood combination plate at $12.75 have earned for this restaurant *Travel Holiday Magazine*'s 1986 recommendation as "one of the outstanding restaurants of the world." Even before you dine, you will be impressed by the impeccably coutured maître d', the Oriental carpets, and the distinctive serving ware. Dinner is served 5:30 to 10:30 p.m. every day.

At Ward Centre

The elegant Ward Centre shopping/dining complex at 1200 Ala Moana Blvd. and Auahi Street, a block from Ward Warehouse, boasts a number of first-rate restaurants. We could spend weeks eating here and not needing to go anywhere else. A few of our favorites:

The quality of the food and the charm of the surroundings make **Crêpe Fever** (tel. 521-9023) on the street level, inside the Le Pavillon shopping area, quite special. Red tile floors, oak tables, pastel pennants overhead, plus tables in the pretty garden outdoors, set a sparkling background for a menu that is not limited to just crêpes. It has a lot to offer vegetarians, sophisticated "grazers," and those who just want to eat delicious, healthy food at very reasonable prices. Our favorite lunch here used to be the homemade soup served in a bowl of scooped-out cracked wheat bread; with salad, it's a satisfying lunch for $3.95. But now that owner Sandee Garcia has come up with her new Grains & Green Express Bar, it's a tossup. Here you build your own vegetarian meal from a selection of complimentary protein combinations that changes everyday; grains, legumes, greens, beans, and seeds are provided in a variety of ways that might have a Mexican or Italian or Indian accent. Have a medium-size bowl at $3.50 or a huge bowlful for $4.80. Begin with a cup of that wonderful homemade soup and you've got a super meal. Now for those crêpes: they're filled with the likes of chicken and ham, tuna salad melt, and lemon spinach (with cream cheese), and so are croissants, and either can be had with soup or salad or both for an under-$5 meal. Desserts are yummy too: cheese blintzes topped with sour cream, fresh strawberries and cream and bananas and cream crêpes, $3.95 and $4.25. Since Crêpe Fever serves the same menu continuously, Monday to Saturday from 8 a.m. to 9 p.m., Sunday to 4 p.m., you can have breakfast anytime: three-egg omelets, waffles, and (especially good) their french toast: thick slices of Hawaiian sweet bread, garnished with bananas, $3.75.

Right next to Crêpe Fever, the same management has opened **Mocha Java,** an espresso fountain bar with a variety of hot and iced gourmet coffees, plus real milk shakes, and unbelievable flambé sundaes. Take anything from here as a dessert for your Crêpe Fever meal: perhaps a simple but satisfying choice like espress over a scoop of vanilla ice cream at $1.85. Crêpe Fever was expecting to get a liquor license at the time of this writing: meanwhile, wine and beer plus Irish coffee were available. This one is open Monday to Saturday from 8 a.m. to 10 p.m., weekends until 11 p.m.

The most picturesque restaurant here must surely be **Keo's at Ward Centre** (tel. 533-0533), the latest creation of Thai restaurateur Keo Sananikone. Keo runs four restaurants in town (see ahead, under Thai Restaurants, for a description of the cuisine), and this one is exquisite, with lovely plantings, flowers, a fountain splashing into a languid pool, pink tablecloths, black bentwood chairs, seating indoors and out—just beautiful! Enjoy the European-Asian café ambience at either lunch or dinner for reasonable prices: most entrees run between $6.95 and $8.95. While you're here, you can pick up a copy of *Keo's Thai Cuisine,* so you can try your hand at creating these delicate wonders back home. Open Monday to Saturday from 11 a.m. to 10:30 p.m., from 5 p.m. on Sunday.

There comes a time when the wandering traveler, far from home, suddenly develops an irrepressible longing for, say, a corned beef on rye, a bowl of matzoh-ball soup, or a big plate of brisket of beef. Happily, a remedy is at hand right here in Honolulu: **Big Ed's Deli** (tel. 536-4591), which packs in the crowds at its counter and large table section at Ward Centre. Big Ed serves up all kinds of delicatessen delights, super sandwiches, salads, deli platters, and hot meals. You can start your meal with a wonderful borscht ($1.75 for a large bowl) or a chicken matzoh-ball soup for $2.25. House specialties are the brisket of beef dinner with potatoes and vegetables at $7.65 and chicken in the pot with matzoh balls and noodles, $6.95. Or have a sandwich: corned beef, pastrami, liverwurst, beef tongue, and roast beef are priced from $4.25 to $5.35. Salad and delicatessen platters—our favorite is smoked salmon with Maui onions—range in price from $4.75 to $10.95. Beer, wine, and cocktails are available, and the atmosphere is cheerful and hearty. Open from 7 a.m. to 10 p.m. Sunday to Thursday, to 11 p.m. Friday and Saturday.

Monterey Bay Canners (tel. 536-6197) offers a tremendous variety of seafood specialties, many of which we've not seen elsewhere. It's a big, bustling, nautical-type place; you'll want to linger over dinner here. If you're lucky enough to get a table by the window, you can overlook Kewalo Basin, where the commercial fishing charters are berthed. Lunch fits better than dinner into our budget, since you could order a delicious seafood tostada (a tortilla stuffed with seafood, cheddar, avocado, etc.) for $6.95, a big bowl of bouillabaisse for $9.45, or Pacific red snapper for $5.45. But dinner too has a number of entrees on the low side of the menu, like ono at $12.25, or mahimahi at $10.95. And at both lunch or dinner you can order catch of the day—which might be opakapaka, ono-wahoo, ahi, or ulua—priced according to availability (several of the local radio stations carry MBC's "Fresh Catch" report several times a day). Drinks are quite special here: when was the last time you had a watermelon daiquiri! Sunday brunch, 10 a.m. to 3 p.m., is the time for seafood crêpes, with any number of other delightful brunch specialties, priced around $6.95.

Monterey Bay Canners serves lunch from 11 a.m. to 4 p.m., dinner from 4 to 11 p.m. Sunday through Thursday, until midnight on Friday and Saturday; cocktails available from 11 a.m. to 2 a.m. all week. There are sister restaurants at 2335 Kalakaua Ave. and at Pearlridge Center.

Fans of the **Yum Yum Tree,** that delightful pie shop and restaurant at Kahala Mall (see below), are thrilled to have another branch at Ward Centre. That makes it all the easier to stop in whenever the urge—for, say, macadamia nut or lemon crunch or English toffee pie—becomes overwhelming to take home a whole pie, or just have a delicious slice here. The menu is the same as at Kahala, and the setting is charming, both inside and out, with the feeling of a big country house with a large porch, shady and cool, thanks to the big blue umbrellas. This Yum Yum Tree serves breakfast food from 7 to noon and again from 11 p.m. to closing, lunch also from 7 a.m. to 5 p.m., dinner from 5 p.m. to 1 a.m. (until 3 a.m. on weekends), and cocktails from 11 a.m. to 2 a.m.

Long a dazzler here at Ward Centre is **Ryan's Parkplace** (tel. 523-9132), a big, rambling, stunner of a room with highly polished wood floors, gleaming brass, lazily revolving ceiling fans, windows all around, myriad lush plants, and a shiny kitchen open to view. What impresses most is the pride the attractive staff takes in this knockout place, as well they should. Ryan's is seriously committed to "foods for all moods"—and that means quality in everything from gourmet dishes to simple fare, from recipes that are low in sodium, fat, and cholesterol to sinfully rich creations for sybarites. "Unstructured dining" is the operative term here: the menu reads "We do not want you to spend or consume more than you wish." So whether you're in the mood for a light snack or fancy dinner, you can get exactly what you want here. And that includes meat, chicken, and fish broiled with native Hawaiian kiawe charcoal from Niihau (superior to mesquite), fish fresh from Hawaiian, mainland, and Alaskan waters, pasta made fresh daily, and desserts that range from low-cal Tofutti and fresh-fruit gelato to chocolate truffle pie. Check the list of daily specials, and tell your server of any special dietary needs; he'll be happy to oblige as much as possible. Prices, considering the high quality here, are quite reasonable. Consider, for example, stir-fried chicken, Mediterranean chicken salad, a sensational lasagne —all between $6.95 and $8.50. We're partial to the Three-Salad Sampler, which includes Mediterranean chicken salad, Ryan's pea salad (fresh peas and bacon in a heavenly herb dressing), and the pasta salad with pesto, quite a meal at $7.50. We've also enjoyed a lovely chilled lemon-cucumber soup (there's a different chilled soup every day), a hearty French onion soup, and a tasty-kiaew-broiled Cajun chicken, $9.50. Like everything else at Ryan's, the bar list is generous: a good selection of California wines is available by the bottle, or by the glass from the unique Cruvinete wine machine, which guarantees freshness. There are also temperature-controlled beer selections and a moderately priced bar list. Ryan's serves lunch from 11 a.m. to 5 p.m. except on Sunday, and dinner from 5 to 11 p.m.; the bar is open until 1:30 a.m. Reservations are accepted. Try not to miss this one.

Another star at Ward Centre is **Andrew's** (tel. 523-8677), perfect when you're ready for a slight splurge. This is gourmet Italian and although the prices are not low, they are not as high as the excellence might warrant. Muted rose and browns from floor to ceiling produce a sedate effect, reinforced by the upholstered banquettes with dropped lamps, fabric-covered walls, and flowers on the tables. Lunch is à la carte, with your choice of a dozen pastas that range in price from the house cannelloni, filled with veal and spinach, at $7.75, to linguine filled with lobster, scallops, calamari, and shrimps, at $12.75. There are choices galore of fish and fowl in the same price range; beef and veal run a little higher. Daily specials, like Italian sausage with green pepper, run about $7.75.

Considering that complete dinner meals include antipasto, mixed green salad, minestrone, ice cream or Italian ice plus beverage along with your entree, the price range of $13.75 for eggplant parmigiana to $20.95 for the broiled filet with jumbo shrimps scampi is not exorbitant. We chose à la carte at a recent dinner and found the cannelloni di mare (stuffed with seafood) at $12.50 a tasty and filling meal. Half-a-dozen other pasta choices go for around $8, and there are a few seafood and chicken dishes at about $10. Drinks are moderately priced. And skilled service contributes to a memorable experience.

Andrew's serves lunch Monday to Saturday from 11 a.m. to 5 p.m. On Sunday, a regular lunch is served from 10 a.m. to 5 p.m., and there's a special brunch until 3 p.m. Dinner starts at 5 p.m. nightly, and is served until 10 p.m. Sunday to Tuesday, until 11 p.m. Wednesday to Saturday.

Mexico is represented at Ward Centre by **Compadres** (tel. 523-1307), which gets a resounding *ole!* from us. We're not at all surprised that it was voted "Best Mexican Restaurant" in Hawaii by the *Honolulu* magazine poll, for two years in a row. It's a big, very attractive place with comfortable rattan basket chairs and soft lights, and a young and energetic staff to serve you. The food is *muy bueno,* and the prices won't damage your budget. The same menu and prices are in effect all day long. The sandwiches, like the chicken and avocado at $5.95, are all served with thick-cut deep-fried potatoes and Mexican salad, but you'll probably want to sample such Mexican specialties as the various platillos, which include refried beans, Mexican rice, and salad; they run from $4.95 to $8.95, for enchiladas rancheros. Arroz con pollo at $9.75 and chicken mole at $8.95 are both good, and everybody loves the house specialty of fajitas—grilled, marinated meat or chicken, sliced thin and stuffed into warm tortillas with a great salsa, $8.95 and $9.95. Baby back ribs (a half order for $7.50) and chicken deliciously marinated in white wine ($9.75) are other favorites. As for the desserts, we can't resist the apple chimichanga—brandied apples in a flour tortilla, deep-fried and topped with vanilla ice cream or cheese, at $2.75. Compadres opens for breakfast at 7 a.m., offering a wide assortment of omelets, plus chili relleños, "Huevos Dos Ricardos," and much more. The complete menu is served from 11 a.m. until midnight daily.

Note: There's a sister Compadres right in Waikiki, in the Outrigger Prince Kuhio Hotel, 2500 Kuhio Ave. (tel. 924-4007), which serves the same menu beginning at 4 p.m. every day. More about its incredibly popular Corona Cantina under our nightlife section, ahead.

Ward Centre has some eat-and-run spots that are not the usual fast food "joints." Take **Chez Sushi,** for example, which calls itself a Japanese bistro—a delicate balance of Japanese cuisine and French flair. You can sidle off the red brick walkway of the Centre's Colonnade onto the red and gold chairs of a sushi bar when you can order rice balls and rolls filled with red snapper, yellow tail, or 10 other choices, including abalone, from $2.25 to $4, with half and double orders available. Should you have time for a sitdown meal, walk around the bar and there's a formal dining room with only a few tables but a complete menu. A la carte dishes run from tofu at $2.50 to sashimi (raw fish) at $10.75. Complete dinners include soup, rice, pickles, and Japanese tea, with entrees that range from chicken katsu (breaded chicken cutlet) at $8.75 to sashimi at $11.50. Their specialty is Daymio, a choice of items all simmered together in broth: you select scallops, crab, shrimp, fish, chicken, and vegetables, at $12.50. For dessert, why not green tea ice cream? Chez Sushi is open for lunch from noon to 3 p.m., dinners 5 to 10 p.m.

Downtown Honolulu

A good place to eat in the downtown area is in the YWCA Building, 1040 Richards St. long home to M's Garden Buffet, a bargain standby with Honolulu business people. M's is gone now, but in its place is **Simply Delicious** (tel. 521-8760), and the lovely large room with beamed ceilings is still a cool place to go when the sun has gotten to you. Outside there are tables under pretty awnings. A sit-down lunch is served between 11 a.m. to 2:30 p.m. There's a soup-and-salad buffet at $4.50 and hamburgers at $3.95. Breakfast, 6:30 to 10:30 a.m., features a daily special omelet at $4.75. When you finish, stroll around the Y a bit; we especially like the scene at the pool, with parents earnestly watching their serious-faced youngsters learning to swim.

You'll have to look sharp to spot **Harold's Restaurant,** behind the Bank of Hawaii in the King Center, 1451 S. King St. (tel. 946-0295), but it will be worth the effort. This cozy place, with its curtain pattern on the walls and blue carpeting, serves good food at reasonable prices at all three meals. There are always luncheon specials priced around $4.95, like braised turkey wings or teriyaki chicken cutlet. The price includes fruit cup or soup, salad with choice of dressing, roll and butter, and rice, potatoes, or steak fries. Standard lunch-menu items range from spaghetti with meat sauce to roast turkey at $5.25 to the seafood platter at $6.95. Come dinnertime, many of the same dishes are served and the prices rise only about 30¢. Shrimp tempura is $6.95. Portions are generous and the menu is varied. You get a feeling of "home-cooked." And breakfast is good too, with eggs and omelets at $3 to $4.50. Harold himself will probably seat you or greet you at the cash register on the way out. Booths add privacy, and the bar is separate. There is plenty of parking in the bank parking lot. Harold's is open daily from 6:30 a.m. to 10 p.m.

Jake's Downtown Restaurant, at 1126 Bishop St. (tel. 524-4616), is a tremendous favorite with people who work downtown. Don't let the lunchtime line scare you away; the turnover is quick and the wait is never long. Jake's is a most attractive place of the brick-wall, stained-glass, cozy-booth, wood-paneled variety; the food is excellent and the service quick and courteous. Although the usual breakfast and lunch items are here in abundance, the stars are the wonderful pancakes, waffles, crêpes, and blintzes: buttermilk pancakes, blueberry or strawberry crêpes, macadamia-nut pancakes, blintzes with fruit compote and sour cream, and strawberry and blueberry waffles, served with hot fruit compote and sour cream, and dusted with powdered sugar, are special favorites, from $2.50 to $4.50. Plenty of omelets too, and eggs Benedict served with home fries, at $5.50. There's homemade seafood chowder every day, as well as a variety of meat sandwiches, most under $6. Save some room for either the carrot cake or the cheesecake, plain or with fruit compote: heavenly! Jake's is open from 6 a.m. to 3 p.m. Monday through Friday, and 7 a.m. to 2 p.m. on Saturday and Sunday. No dinner is served.

It's tiny. You might call it a "hole in the wall." But it's a giant pleaser for downtown weekday lunches. The **Red & White Café** is located on the walk behind Bishop Square at Tamarind Park (tel. 531-0744). When you enter, you stop immediately at the hot plate counter. There your order is filled in a jiffy and you're a half step from the cashier who packs it for comfortable picnic dining on nearby outdoor tables or on the stone sitting walls in the park. But here's the best news: delectable dishes such as artichoke pasta salad, brown rice and vegetables, chicken with mushrooms, Thai chicken curry, linguine with clams, and vegetable lasagne are priced from only $3.50 to $3.75. A different specialty is featured each day, like Italian sausage fettuccine on Monday, chicken enchiladas on Tuesday, spaghetti with meatballs on Wednesday. Hot soup—the corn chowder was chock full of kernels—is $1.25. This is a health-minded place. Everything is prepared fresh daily; the rolls are whole grain, and no MSG is used. They open at 6:30 a.m. for continental breakfast and close at 4 p.m. Closed Saturdays and Sundays.

There's more to eat than just croissants at the **Croissanterie,** at 222 Merchant St. (tel. 533-3443), a charming, airy place with abundant potted palms and whirring ceiling fans. Sure, there are 36 different kinds of croissants served here, priced from 95¢ to $3.95, and including such innovations as the Gobbler's Enchantment (turkey and cream cheese) and our favorite, fresh strawberries and cream cheese topped with brown sugar; but they also have very good sandwiches, laden with sprouts and served on nine-grain bread, as well as deli sandwiches with potato salad or coleslaw, from $2.50 to $4.50, and good salads and quiches too. An especially good buy is the Croissanterie Deluxe, served among the luncheon specials, from 11 a.m. to 2 p.m.; it's stuffed with ham and cheese or turkey and cheese or roast beef and broccoli, two kinds of sauces, and includes a tossed salad, all for $3.75. As if this weren't enough, there are espresso, cappuccino, café mocha, and other assorted coffees. Croissanterie is open from 6 a.m. to 8 p.m. weekdays, to 4 p.m. on Saturday. Closed Sunday.

For a quick, inexpensive, and very good lunch while shopping or sightseeing downtown, pop in at the tiny **House of Soup** at 1148 Bishop St. (tel. 531-8660). You can tell it's good because of its popularity with the office workers and shop workers. A big bowl of Portuguese bean soup is $4.50; pigs' feet or oxtail soup is $5, won ton $3.50, and saimin $3. And generous plate lunches are just $3.25, burgers from $1.50. Open from 6 a.m. to 2:45 p.m. Monday through Friday only.

If you're sightseeing by car and want a clean, reasonable, fast-service restaurant where the food is above "fast service" average, try **Kenny's Coffee**

House, a local favorite at the Kam Shopping Center. Likewise Highway and North School Street in Kahili (tel. 841-3733). How Kenny's manages to keep the prices so low is hard to figure out. Standard broiler items like steaks, chops, and chicken run from only $5.95 to $6.75, and most are accompanied by fruit cocktail, soup or salad, and roll and butter. Two daily specials at around $4.75 are noteworthy: the oxtail soup served with rice is a meal in itself, and the teriyaki butterfish melts in your mouth. The menu is the same all day, from 6 a.m. to 11 p.m., until 1 a.m. on Friday, Saturday, and Sunday. There's a dinner special each night, ranging from Swiss steak to seafood platter, roast pork, and roast beef—all from $5.95. Kenny's is a bright, cheery place with high ceilings and floor-to-ceiling windows. The bright-green booths and yellow-and-orange color scheme reinforce the cheery mood. You'll be well fed and well pleased here.

If you prefer a picnic, try Kenny's take-out deli next door, where meat and chicken picnic trays are just $3.75, and the chicken isn't fried, but broasted. Tasty.

In the University Area

Now that the cafeteria at the impressive East-West Center has closed, the best place to eat at the university is the **Student Activities Center,** close to University Avenue in the middle campus. Its huge upstairs cafeteria serves weekday breakfast and lunch from 7 a.m. to 2 p.m. Depending on the day, you may get lemon chicken, mahimahi, veal cutlets, or barbecued ribs, from $1.50 to $3.50. A variety of salads and desserts are available too, and more of the latter can be purchased at the Bake Shop (open until 1 p.m.) and the Ice Cream Shop (open until 4 p.m.). The lower level of the campus center features "local" foods such as loco moco, Bentos, chili rice, and plate lunches at the Snack Bar for $1 to $2.50 (open 9:30 a.m. to 3 p.m.).

If you want to party with the students, **Manoa Garden,** in Hemenway Hall, is open from 10:30 a.m. to 9 p.m. weekdays and from 8:30 a.m. to 3:30 p.m. on Saturday. It features deli sandwiches to order and salad by the ounce. You can get a cold pitcher of beer here, and Thursday and Friday feature live outdoor entertainment. You can sit indoors or, if the sun is shining in Manoa Valley, try the lanai and throw some crumbs to the Brazilian cardinals, sparrows, and doves.

Bagpipes sounded, the Union Jack waved, and British accents were rampant when **Cockney Fish & Chips** opened at 1010 University Ave., corner of King Street (tel. 949-8533). Today local people and tourists are making it one of their favorite fast-food spots. The fish comes in three varieties: New Zealand red cod, Alaska cod, and prawns; three pieces of fish with chips and coleslaw cost $3.75, $4.60, or $6.95 depending on which you choose. The luscious lumps of fish are delectable. Owner Barbara Cheney has been working on bringing Britain's favorite fast food to the islands since 1980. She offers dinner specials every night to introduce new varieties of fish, plus other traditional favorites like steak and kidney meat pies at $2.50, and bangers ("British sausages") with chips, $2.60. Her clam chowder (95¢) is delicious, and so is the seafood mornay, a creation of prawns, shrimp, and fresh fish with cream sauce and cheese served in a pastry shell. It's $5.80 and includes chips. Desserts are fun too: fruits dipped in batter with sugar and deep-fried. The restaurant has several booths, a stand-up counter, and a free parking lot shared by other stores in the small Varsity Center. It's open daily from 11 a.m. to 11 p.m.

Another popular destination in the same Varsity Center is **Bubbies,** 1010 University Ave. (tel. 949-8984), a favorite after-theater spot. Keith Robbins, who hails from the East Coast and named the shop after his grandmother, serves wonderful homemade ice cream and desserts—in addition to delectable ice cream ($1.25 the dip), you can have cheesecake or apple pie or chocolate-chip or macadamia-nut cookies along with your coffee. Curtains at the window, fans overhead, plants, an old-fashioned pendulum time clock, and a photograph of "Bubbie" complete the scene. Open from noon to midnight, until 1 a.m. Friday and Saturday.

Manhattan–style delicatessens may be catching on in Hawaii. **Bernard's of New York** is certainly getting kudos. Located at 2633 S. King St. (tel. 946-7477) in University Square where there is plenty of parking (Diamond Head makai corner of University Ave. and King St.), Bernard's is kosher style from chicken soup to apple strudel. New Yorker's will get homesick just reading the menu: half boiled chicken with matzo balls and carrots, stuffed cabbage rolls with potato pancakes and salad, two kosher beef knockwursts with baked beans and salad are all $6.95, as is gefilte fish with borscht and matzo. You might want to start your meal with a bowl of "homemade" chicken soup or cold schav or borscht with sour cream. Then perhaps on to a deli sandwich of corned beef or chopped liver, hot pastrami or kosher salami, from $3.50 to $3.95. Any side dishes you're fancying, like potato latkes, potato knishes, stuffed derma? They're all available. So are blueberry or cheese blintzes with sour cream, $3.95, and delicious apple noodle pudding, $2.25.

Bernard's is a full-service restaurant with spanking white table tops, cane chairs, and checkerboard floors. It's open 11 a.m. to 9 p.m. Monday through Friday, 9 a.m. to 9 p.m. Saturday. Closed Sunday.

The Buzz's restaurants have been popular with residents and visitors alike for as long as we can remember. Our favorite of these handsome places is **Buzz's Original Steak House,** just off University Avenue at 2535 Coyne St. (tel. 944-9781). The decor is art nouveau, with wood paneling, stained glass, and wonderful '30s light fixtures. Steak and seafood are the mainstays of Buzz's bill of fare, so prices run a bit above our budget, but they also have one of the best salad bars in town, at just $5.95. A perennial dieter friend of ours swears by it. This is one place where we wouldn't want to pass up the pupus: sautéed mushrooms, artichoke surprise, escargots ($2.75 to $5.50). A good dinner choice is the kal-bi platter (marinated beef ribs, Korean style), at $9.65. Other specialties on the low side of the menu include Buzz's beef kebabs at $8.95 and top sirloin (six ounces) at $8.95. All entrees come with bread, veggies, and that salad bar. And don't miss Buzz's incredible ice-cream pies, at $2.50 a serving. Buzz's in the university area is open Sunday to Thursday from 5 to 10 p.m., on Friday and Saturday to 10:30 p.m.

The longtime mecca for pizza lovers in this area is **Mama Mia,** at 1015 University Ave. in Puck's Alley (tel. 947-5233), and real "New York pizza" it is too, since the owner is a transplanted New Yorker. There's a pie for every taste (even a vegetarian pizza with whole-wheat crust—$8.76); terrific spaghetti and lasagne dinners for under $7; some really lusty and crusty hero sandwiches; plus soda, beer, and wine. The place stays open until 1 a.m., so it's fun to come here —and sit at the sidewalk café if you like—after the evening's entertainment. Occasionally there's entertainment here too—perhaps a grownup puppet show, or just music.

One of our favorite places for submarine sandwiches in these parts is **Mr. Sub,** 2600 S. King St. in Puck's Alley, a clean and cheery spot that is very, very popular. (At a recent chic Honolulu cocktail party, the pupus turned out to be six-foot-long Mr. Subs!) All the subs are good, but our favorite is the No. 4 supersub—prosciutto, pressed ham, salami, cappicola, and cheese, covered (as are all the subs here) with lettuce, tomatoes, onions, and dressing, $2.25 for a half, $4.50 for a whole. The place closes at 10 p.m. The people here really work hard at maintaining quality, quantity, low prices, and super-fast service!

At Kahala Mall

A big favorite in the lovely Kahala residential area is the **Yum Yum Tree Restaurant and Pie Shop** (tel. 737-7938) in Kahala Mall. This is such a pretty place, with seating both on the lanai and in the wood-and-stone inside room. Service is fast and friendly, and the food is good: we like the grilled tuna, tomato, and cheese sandwich on sourdough bread at $4.45; the salads; and the main dishes—mahimahi, sirloin, country fried chicken, and the like, served with soup or good salad (choice of dressing), fries or baked potato, roll, and butter—all $8.95 at dinner, closer to $6 at lunch. Best of all are the yummy pies for dessert, baked in their own kitchens; the pie display at center stage makes it difficult to resist taking a whole one back to your hotel. It's rumored that folks who stay at the posh Kahala Hilton Hotel a few blocks away like to come here now and then for a quick and inexpensive change of pace.

It's open for all three meals, starting at 7:30 a.m. with breakfast, until 11 p.m. daily. There's a newer Yum Yum Tree at Ward Centre (see above).

For a little bit of mittel-Europa in Kahala Mall, stop in at the **Pâtisserie** (tel. 735-4402), a bakery that also serves sandwiches and pastries at its sparkling counter and several little booths. Sandwiches, served on their home-baked breads (we like the country Swiss), with sprouts or lettuce, run to the likes of Black Forest ham, head cheese, roast beef, bratwurst, and pastrami; prices go from $2.95 to $3.95. And there's hot German potato salad, quiche Lorraine, and carrot salad too. If you don't want anything quite so heavy, Black Forest cake, dobosh, and freshly baked pies should be just right. Open weekdays from 7 a.m. to 9 p.m., until 7 p.m. on Saturday and Sunday. Check their shops too, at the Edgewater and Outrigger West Hotels in Waikiki.

THE NATURAL LIFE: Healthy fast foods is an idea whose time has come, and it's come in great style to Honolulu. **Healthy's Natural Fast Foods,** at 2525 S. King St. (tel. 955-2479), is the brainchild of Kathy Hoshijo, a Hawaiian woman who owns Down to Earth Health Foods, right next door, and has a syndicated television cooking show. This is a pretty, inviting place with cool tile floors, ceiling fans, and tons of healthy (naturally!) green plants. You order at a service counter, then take your food to a table either on the street floor or in the dining gallery a few steps up, lined with attractive artworks (all of which are for sale). We're very partial to their wonderful veggie pizza pie: cheese, tomato, onions, and peppers on a whole-wheat crust, $2.25 for a big square. Also good is the Texas chili, which is made with beans, soy protein, and onions in a savory tomato sauce; an eight-ounce size, with cheese, is $2.10. Burgers here are not made with beef: they are created of nuts and veggies, tofu, or tempeh; can be topped with melted cheese; and are surprisingly tasty, at $3.25. Tofutti, you might guess, is the favorite dessert here. A local friend of ours swears that all she asks of life is a big slab of Healthy's veggie pizza and one of their root beer floats; it's made with Tofutti and Rooty Rush, a natural root beer. Sounds good to us! Healthy's is open every day from 6 a.m. until midnight.

Wherever you see the name **"Vim and Vigor Foods,"** you can be sure you're getting very fresh, tasty natural food. There are two Vim and Vigors in town. Their take-out and drink counter at Ala Moana Center keeps huge lunch crowds happy with luscious sandwiches like avocado, tuna, or egg combinations on whole-grain breads with sprouts, from $2.95 to $3.50. Plenty of honey ice creams, fruit smoothies, and the like too. The Vim and Vigor at Kahala Mall has a small salad-sandwich bar in back of the health-food store that dishes out big portions of very tasty food, plus lots of home-baked cookies and pies. Don't miss their wonderful breads up at the front counter, especially the whole-wheat cinnamon-raisin bread.

What a treat to find a handy health-food store, restaurant, and juice bar right in the heart of the busy Waikiki scene. **Ruffage Natural Foods** is there at 2443 Kuhio Ave. in the Royal Grove Hotel (tel. 922-2042), just a block from the beach. It specializes in organic foods and those that are as free as possible of processing, all modestly priced: freshly squeezed juices; good fruit and vegetable salads; lunch and dinner dishes on the order of vegetarian curry or vegeburritos ($2.65 to $3.95); sandwiches like zucchini cheese or tofu tuna ($2.95 to $3.75); yummy shakes and smoothies. The atmosphere is health-food counter, but the food is fresh and good; take it out and go to the beach, or dine there at one of the several open-to-the-street tables. While you're there, pick up a few organically grown papayas to take back to your hotel with you for breakfast. Ruffage is open daily from 8 a.m. to 9 p.m.

To experience a vegetarian meal in a serene setting, visit the **Syda Meditation Ashram Hawaii** at 1929 Makiki St. (tel. 942-8887), high in the hills in the Makiki section of town. Here, followers of Swami Muktananda and his successor, Gurumayi, lead the Yogic life, but you need not be a devotee to have a meal here, take part in their programs, or even stay a few days (those who are willing to share in the activities of the ashram can get dormitory-style accommodations plus meals for about $20 per night). As for the meals, dinner features a different ethnic vegetarian entree each night, usually Indian, Chinese, or Italian, and costs $4; lunch is a soup-and-salad meal for $3.50. Meals are served promptly at noon and at 6:25 p.m. Reservations should be made 24 hours in advance. You pick up your food in the kitchen and eat outside on the dining lanai, surrounded by the sounds of birds and the rustling of trees. Ah, so peaceful. When you call, inquire about their Sunday morning and Monday through Saturday evening programs.

DINING FOR A GOOD CAUSE: Now here's your chance to have two good meals for two good causes in two picturesque settings. The atmosphere in both is decidedly tea-roomy, but men *are* allowed. The first of these, lunch only, is the **Garden Café,** at the Honolulu Academy of Arts, 900 S. Beretania, where the dining lanai is under the trees just outside one of the world's great art collections. The waitresses, the cashier, even the cooks are all volunteers, and all profits from your meal go to further the work of the academy. Lunch is served from Tuesday through Friday at either an 11:30 a.m. or 1 p.m. sitting, and every day there is a different soup, salad, and sandwich. Almost everything has a gourmet touch: the soups include chicken curry and crème mongole; you might get green-bean and bacon salad (delicious), or green salad with sliced fresh mushrooms; as for sandwiches, it's turkey, ham, and roast beef. Lunch is $4.75; beverages are 75¢; wine and beer are available. The desserts, $1.50 extra, include ice cream with homemade chocolate sauce, brownies, or special dessert bars. Only one menu is served each day. Lunch reservations are recommended: call 531-8865.

Since there is usually a film or lecture at the academy at 7:30 Thursday nights, the volunteers also serve a Thursday supper at $6.50 (tax included) for a light meal of international cuisine. Wine and dessert are extra. Reservations are required. *Note:* The Garden Café is open from a week after Labor Day through the Friday before Memorial Day; closed Christmas and Thanksgiving.

Lunch at the **Waioli Tea Room,** 3016 Oahu Ave. in Manoa Valley, has been a Honolulu tradition since 1922. The food is good and well priced, and the surrounding grounds are beautiful enough to justify the 15-minute trip on The Bus no. 5 from Ala Moana Shopping Center; and all profits benefit Salvation Army programs. A bountiful salad bar featuring island treats ($5.95) and a special entree ($5 to $7) are offered daily, as well as a selection of hot and cold sandwiches and a "chickenut" salad made from a special recipe with a secret ingredient. Old time favorites include Waioli fried chicken and coconut mahi. Waioli's famous coconut cream pie or macadamia-nut cream pie is a must for dessert. Lunch is on from 11 a.m. to 2 p.m. Tuesday through Sunday; on Sunday, it's a brunch buffet for $9.50. Reservations are advised for Friday and Sunday; phone 988-2131. Do walk around the grounds, visit the gift shops, and view the Memorial Grass House of Robert Louis Stevenson, the chapel, and the stained-glass windows; this is some of the lushest, most exotic scenery in all Honolulu.

KIDDIE TREATS: So you're traveling with the kids? By all means, take any youngsters up to age 12 or so to **Showbiz Pizza Place** (tel. 373-2151), at the Aina Haina Shopping Center out on Kalanianaole Highway, not far from the Kahala Mall. There's a big stage at the front of the dining room, and every so often the curtains part to reveal very cleverly designed, life-size mechanical animal musicians and singers, such as Beach Bear, Mitzi Mouse, and Fatz the Gorilla. These ingenious creations appear most lifelike, and they "sing" and "play" instruments. There are also people in animal costumes who circulate in the dining room and visit with young diners. As if that weren't enough, there are myriad video games. This is a most popular place for local kids to celebrate birthdays. And the food isn't half bad. The pizzas—Super Combo (cheese, sausage, beef, pepperoni, etc.), Aloha Delight (cheese, ham, pineapple, toasted almonds), Vegetarian Favorite, and Taco Pizza sell for $8.75 small, $12.10 medium, and $15.45 large. There's a salad bar with a good variety of fixings, $3.49 for all you can eat. You can even buy the kids a Showbiz Pizza T-shirt. Showbiz Pizza Place is open every day except Christmas.

SPLURGES: Call **Hackfeld's,** on the ground level of Liberty House at Ala Moana Center (tel. 945-5243), an elegant bistro; the food has a French–continental accent, and the artful presentations make dishes as pleasing to the eye as they are to the palate. Prices are most reasonable at lunch, when entrees run from $6.25 to $8.95, and include dishes like coquille of scallops and escargots, Thai curry, and New England crab cakes, all served with a choice of soup of the day or salad. The dinner menu, with entrees priced from $8.95 to $13.50 is also intriguing. Try escargots maison or fettuccine Alfredo among the appetizers, the wonderful Burnt Crème (or any of the French pastries and tortes) for dessert. In between are dishes such as fresh catch of the day, teriyaki steak, sirloin peppersteak, and veal classic, all served up with soup of the day or salad, plus garlic pasta, fresh mashed potatoes, potato pancakes, or steamed rice.

Hackfeld's serves lunch from 11 a.m. to 2:30 p.m. Monday through Saturday; dinner, Monday through Friday only, from 5 to 9 p.m. Closed Sunday.

A dinner-only spot that combines a fine meal with an educational experience is the **Pottery Steak and Seafood Restaurant,** in the Waialae-Kahala area, at 3574 Waialae Ave. (tel. 735-5594). Not only is your meal served in unusual pottery—eating and drinking vessels fired in kilns right on the premises—but you can see the potters in action up front. And when you've finished your meal, you can buy the dishes and take them home! As you might expect, this attractive restaurant is decorated throughout with clay vessels that re-create some of the history and romance of early world pottery. And the food is excellent. If you want to stay on the low side of the menu, have the Potter's Delight, ground New York sirloin, at $8.50. Like all the other entrees, it comes with a choice of soup or salad, rice or a baked potato with a variety of garnishes, vegetables, and loaves of garlic bread that continue to toast in their hot ceramic loaf-shape containers. Or splurge and order fresh fish of the day (quoted daily) or a variety of steaks from $10.75 up to $23 (for steak and lobster). We can recommend the Cornish game hen at $13.75, moist and tender and fired in its own clay vessel— you get to keep the pot. For dessert, go all out with the special potter's coffee, laced with rum, topped with whipped cream and served in a handsome mug. The Pottery is open from 5:30 to 10 p.m. daily, and reservations are advisable.

The dining critic of the *Honolulu Star-Bulletin* has called **Alfred's European Restaurant** "one of the top five restaurants in the city." We couldn't agree more. A visit to chef/owner Alfred Vollenweider's gracious dining room on the third floor of Century Center, 1750 Kalakaua Ave., corner of Kapiolani (tel. 955-5353), is like visiting a fine restaurant on the continent where every detail is handled perfectly, from the china on the table to the attentive service by the waiters to the superb French-continental cuisine. Everything is prepared fresh, using only the best market ingredients. And nothing comes out of the kitchen until Alfred—who spends part of each evening walking around the restaurant in his tall chef's hat, checking on everything—makes sure that it is perfect. While a meal here is not inexpensive, neither is it overpriced by today's standards, and it offers top value for the dollar. Dinner starts with four or five salad-relish dishes prepared according to the season, plus a basket of European-style breads. Soup de jour follows that, and then it's your choice of such dishes as a flavorful wienerschnitzel, coquilles St-Jacques au beurre blanc, Long Island duckling, tournedos de boeuf, live Maine lobster, or fresh fish taken from local waters and sautéed or steamed or poached in a light champagne sauce. Prices range from about $16 to $22 for the complete meal. Desserts are extra but more than worth the price, especially for creations like the soufflé glacé Grand Marnier, or the unforgettable strawberries Romanoff, fresh strawberries marinated in liqueur and topped with Häagen-Däzs ice cream, served in a tall champagne glass. Wines are decently priced, as Alfred shops around for the best values and passes the savings on to his customers. Irish, Swiss, and other specialty coffees, English and herbal teas, plus brandies and cordials top off the meal. Lunch is also pleasant and well priced, from about $7 to $12 for egg dishes, salads, fresh fish, sandwiches, plus a daily chef's special that includes soup or salad, for $8.75.

Alfred's is open every day but Sunday, serving lunch Monday to Friday from 11 a.m. to 2 p.m., and dinner Tuesday to Saturday from 6 to 10 p.m. Reservations are advised. Valet parking is available.

Soft Spanish background music, abundant flourishing plants displayed against ornate trellises, candlelight, elegant table settings, and colorful paintings combine to create an enchanting atmosphere at **Casa Madrid** in Eaton Square, 444 Hobron Lane (tel. 955-3333). Despite its name, Casa Madrid is not strictly a Spanish restaurant: Italian and Portuguese influences are equally as strong here. At lunch, for example, you might have cold gazpacho or hot straciatella for your soup course, or a main dish of gnocchi or fettuccine Alfredo (pastas are in the $6 price range). But the house specialty, paella valenciana, is, of course, one of the great classics of the Spanish kitchen: it's a treat, and only $8 at lunchtime (at night, it is reserved for a minimum of two persons, at $16 each for a Light Eater portion, $19 for a regular serving). All entrees come with Spanish potatoes and fresh vegetables; many are available in Light Eater portions. Especially popular are the supremo de pollo a la flamenco (stuffed boneless breast of chicken), cordero asadera (rack of lamb), and filetes de Ternera (broiled, sliced beef tenderloin). Dinner entrees are in the $12.50 to $18.50 price range. Luncheon is served Monday through Friday from 11 a.m. to 2:30 p.m., dinner nightly from 5:30 to 11 p.m.

HAWAIIAN RESTAURANTS: You'll probably have your first experience with Hawaiian food at a luau, and then you'll find the same dishes appearing again and again in Hawaiian restaurants and on the "plate lunch" menus of other restaurants all over town. We'll first tell you about the major Hawaiian food specialties, then give you some tips on a "poor man's luau," and finally show you where to find the budget-priced Hawaiian restaurants.

The Food and How to Eat It

You're already on speaking terms with poi. The other basic dishes are kalua pig (pig steamed in an underground oven, or imu), laulau (ti leaves stuffed with pork, salt fish, bananas, sweet potatoes, and taro shoots, and steamed), chicken luau (chicken cooked with coconut milk and taro or spinach leaves), sweet potatoes, pipikaula (jerked beef), and lomi-lomi salmon. The last is a triumph of linguistics over gastronomy: lomi-lomi means massage, and this is salmon "massaged" with tomatoes and chopped onions, then marinated. Haupia (coconut pudding) and a piece of coconut cake are the usual desserts, along with fresh pineapple.

Food is served on paper plates and the proper way to eat is with your fingers; plastic spoons are provided for the timid. The correct way to eat poi, by the way, is to dip one or two fingers in it (in the old days you could actually order "one-" or "two-finger" poi), scoop it up quickly, and attack. But nobody expects that of a malihini.

Poor Man's Luau

Luaus are fun affairs—everyone comes dressed in aloha shirts and muumuus, a great ceremony is made of putting the pig in the imu (camera buffs have been known to go wild with joy at this part), there's lively Polynesian entertainment, and of course there's the equally delightful food. But most of the commercial luaus cost from $30 to $35, enough to destroy a minimum budget for a week.

Here's our answer to the high cost of luaus: check the local tourist papers for news of the frequently held church luaus. There's a neat irony about all this: the early missionaries forbade the Hawaiian songs and dances, and now, just a century later, the churches raise money by presenting them. At any rate, it's the local equivalent of a cake fair or card party; the price is usually about $12 for adults, $6 for children; and the food and entertainment is as good—or better—than at many a commercial shindig. Visitors are warmly welcomed.

Budget Restaurant Recommendations

Close to Waikiki, a very popular place to find ono Hawaiian food is **Ono Hawaiian Foods,** at 726 Kapahulu Ave. (tel. 737-2275). It's a little place, with about ten tables, its walls covered with photos of popular local entertainers who are patrons. Try the kalua pig at $4.11, or the laulau plate at $4.32, or just go mad and have the combination kalua pig *and* laulau at $5.25. These and other plates come with pipikaula (Hawaiian beef jerky), lomi-lomi salmon, poi or rice, and haupia. The atmosphere here is very friendly; the place may be short on size, but it's definitely long on aloha. Open Monday through Saturday from 10:30 a.m. to 7:30 p.m.

Another spot close to Waikiki for good Hawaiian food is **Aloha Poi Bowl** at 2671 S. King St. in University Square (tel. 944-0788). There are only six booths and a few big white plastic-topped tables in a plain, store-like room, but the food is the star. In addition to those luau staples like laulua, lomi salmon, kalua pork, tripe or beef stew, and chicken long rice, which run from $1.80 to $2.80, there's always a daily special; the day we were there it was fried akule fish at $4. Combination orders run $3.50 to $4.50. Be sure to top off your meal with that coconut dessert called haupia, 60¢. Open daily, 10:30 a.m. to 9 p.m., Sunday, 3:30 to 9 p.m.

People's Café, 1310 Pali Hwy. (tel. 536-5789), is another favorite place for authentic, inexpensive Hawaiian food; the local office workers come here when they have a hangover and want some of that nice, soothing-to-the-tummy poi. Poi plate lunches go for about $6.50 to $7.50, and always include kalua pig and laulau. The prices are the same at lunch and dinner. A good place to remember for take-out orders; there's a $3 Bento box. Open every day, from 10 a.m. to 7:30 p.m., Sunday from noon.

JAPANESE RESTAURANTS: Japanese cuisine has so permeated the islands that you'll find Japanese dishes—beef hekka, shrimp tempura, saimin—on menus everywhere. Hekka is a kind of poor man's sukiyaki (a beef and vegetable stew) and tempura means anything deep-fried in batter. Saimin (known in Japan as *rahmen),* the seaweed-chicken-noodle soup that we mentioned earlier, is just the thing for the starvation budget; a large bowl, which will cost about $3, will do for a whole meal, and you can get it almost anywhere. You can even make it at home: instant saimin, direct from Japan, is sold in the food departments of most Japanese stores, like Shirokaya at Ala Moana. Sooner or later you'll be introduced to sushi or sashimi, probably served among the pupus (hors d'oeuvres) at a bar, and you'll think it's delicious unless somebody spoils the fun first and tells you it's raw fish. Forget your prejudices and enjoy it. Sushi bars are great favorites, and can be found in many Japanese restaurants.

A good place for your first experience with Japanese food—and for one of the best bargain lunches in Honolulu—is the **Oriental Snack Bar** at Woolworth's on Kalakaua Avenue in Waikiki or at Ala Moana. Both are big hits with office workers and shoppers, and both offer you a chance to sample authentic Japanese dishes for just pennies. The prices vary minutely at the two; an order of beef hekka or butterfish runs $1.35, and a bowl of saimin is $1.80 to $3.25. The Kalakau Avenue store has a Sushi Bar and Bento (take-out) lunches. We slightly favor the Ala Moana Woolworth's since, after filling up your paper plate, you can go out and sit in the pretty mall watching Hawaiians mill about you as you nibble. Incidentally, two "cone sushis" (cold, marinated rice cakes) tucked in your bag make a tasty lunch-on-the-run.

When you dine in a regular Japanese restaurant, all you order is your main course; it will come served on a tray with several small dishes like pickled vegetables, soup, rice, and tea. Nobody will think you're a square if you ask for a fork, but why not live dangerously? You'll get the hang of chopsticks, more or less, by the end of your first Japanese meal.

Many of Hawaii's Japanese restaurants are pretty expensive affairs, complete with kimono-clad waitresses and lavish settings. We have a couple of favorites, however, where you can dine quite reasonably at lunch and pay an average of $10 to $12 for complete dinners.

First, we've always liked **Suehiro,** at 1914 King St. (tel. 949-4584). Try to get one of their ozashiki or tatami rooms, where you sit on the floor and dine at a low lacquered table (you take off your shoes before you enter, of course); the setting will immediately put you in a tranquil mood, ready for a different kind of experience. You usually need a party of eight and a reservation for these rooms, but if a room happens to be open you may double up with other waiting guests. On one visit we teamed up with a big, charming family of Japanese-Americans, and had dinner at $12.95 per person that included a tasty miso soup (a clear broth made with soybean paste), namasu (pickled cucumber), lobster salad, sashimi, shrimp tempura, fried lobster, and beef sukiyaki. All of this was served with several side vegetables, sauces, rice, dessert, and plenty of tea. It was a colorful and memorable experience. At the regular restaurant tables, you may order a similar dinner special for $25 for two people, and there are several "combination dinners" at $16.95 per person, again with all the extras. At lunchtime, the combination plates are an especially good buy: shrimp tempura and broiled fish or barbecued chicken at $4.50, both served with tossed green salad, soup, and rice. *Note:* You can also get a tasty Japanese box lunch here, for picnics and trips.

Kabuki Restaurant Kapiolani, 600 Kapiolani Blvd. (tel. 545-5995), is a very pretty restaurant—light-wood paneling, lots of mirrors, white stoneware dishes with blue flowers, an attractive little sushi bar—that offers a chance to sample many Japanese foods at reasonable prices. Yakiniku dinners, with a choice of beef, chicken, boneless kal-bi, tenderloin, or beef tongue, served with fresh vegetables, range from $12.50 to $13.50; a tasty teishoku dinner with a main course of fried scallops, plus sashimi, tempura, vegetables, soup, rice, and tea, is $7.75. And combination teishoku dinners—with main courses of beef, tonkatsu, fried scallops, etc., accompanied by rice, soup, pickled vegetables, and tea—are the best buys of all, just $8 to $8.75. For lunch, the combination teishoku meal is only $5.50. And they have enjoyable breakfasts as well, everything from corned beef hash to miso soup and Kabuki fried rice. Breakfast is served from 6 to 10 a.m., lunch from 11 a.m. to 2 p.m., dinner from 4 to 9 p.m. Sunday to Thursday, until midnight on Friday and Saturday.

Although one of our longtime favorites, the quaint little Japanese fish house called Horitsuji's Aala Diner in the Little Japan area of town has closed, the tradition of terrific food continues at the new **Horitsuji's,** in much larger and fancier downtown quarters on the second floor of Kukui Plaza, 50 S. Beretania St. (tel. 531-3277). There's comfortable seating in booths and tables, and traditional Japanese decor sets the scene. Don't worry about breaking your budget: most dishes are in the $5.45 to $7.95 range, and that includes all the side dishes. We finally decided on ahi teriyaki with tempura (melt-in-the-mouth tender), at $6.75; an entire steamed mullet at $5.50, with a piquant, delicate flavor in a spicy sauce; and chicken teriyaki, the best we've tasted in the islands, accompanied by shrimp, meat, and vegetable tempura, at $6.45. Our dinner started with a tasty fish soup, followed by a pickled salad, and yet another pickled salad. Our steaming pot of green tea was brewed with brown rice, which made it hearty and satisfying. Service was fast and efficient, but not rushed. And the total bill for a superb meal for three was under $18! Horitsuji's is open from 11 a.m. to 2 p.m. and from 5 to 9 p.m. Monday to Saturday. Closed Sunday.

A favorite with the local people, **Kamigata,** in the Manoa Marketplace, 2756 Woodlawn Dr. (tel. 988-2107), is a very attractive spot, all reds and golds and low lights. Come at lunch and try one of their three combination specials: each starts with shrimp tempura. Add shoyu chicken and the price is $4.25; with beef teriyaki, it's $4.35; and with broiled butterfish, $4.50. These are served with rice, tsukemono, and soup. Other complete lunches run up to $7. At dinnertime, you can have sushi plates, from $7.25 to $9.25, yakiniku dinner for $9.50 (for a minimum of two people), a king crabs' legs dinner for $12, New York steak for $9.75. If there are at least four of you, call ahead to reserve one of Kamigata's lovely tatami rooms: here you can have their festive Bun Raku or

Kabuki dinners ($11.75 and $12.75), in addition to the choices mentioned above. Kamigata is open for lunch from 11 a.m. to 2 p.m. Monday through Saturday, and dinner is served nightly from 5:30 to 9 p.m. (to 9:30 p.m. on Friday and Saturday).

For Japanese food with a local flavor, there's **Irifune** at 563 Kapahulu (tel. 737-1141). Although short on decor, it's long on good food, large portions, and low prices, which are the same at lunch and dinner. It's only $4.95 for a meal consisting of miso soup; pickled vegetables; three skewers of barbecued chicken and veggies; a salad of lettuce, tomatoes, and chopped cabbage with a delicious house dressing; rice, and green tea. Chicken udon with noodles and mushrooms is $3.50. Specialties are the breaded fried tofu and shrimp tempura. Unlike most Japanese restaurants, Irifune does serve dessert, and a delicious one at that: sliced mango crêpes with ice cream, large enough to satisfy the sweet tooth of two or more diners at $2.50.

Those who are really into sushi—and there are many these days—know that a meal of these exotic raw fish delicacies can really add up. **Kats Sushi,** 715 S. King St. (tel. 526-1265), has you fanatics well in mind, and offers an incredible all-you-can eat sushi dinner for just $14.95! This tidy little Japanese place seats about 25 people and has a simple decor—but it's the sushi you'll be noticing. Dinner is served from 5 to 11 p.m. Monday to Saturday. On the regular lunch menu, weekdays from 11 a.m. to 2 p.m., there's sushi à la carte from 30¢ to $6.50, donburis from $2.85 to $3.50, soba noodle dishes from $2 to $4, and Bentos at $3.

On the way to Sea Life Park (Bus no. 57) or Hanauma Bay, you may want to stop at the Aina Haina Shopping Center on Kalanianaole Hwy., the home of **Otomi** (tel. 377-5700). From exterior to interior, from the classic decor to the exotic taste sensations, you'll think you're in Kyoto, not Honolulu. Hanging Japanese lanterns, framed rice paper collages, other folk art touches, and waitresses in colorful happi coats add to the illusion. We often see Japanese visitors dining here at the polished wood tables. Check the plastic replicas of dishes in the showcase before you enter—just like on the Ginza in Tokyo. Lunch dishes range from $3.25 for zaru soba, a Japanese noodle, to $7.95 for tempura sashimi, with dishes like pork tofu and beef sukiyaki in between. Dinner features a number of entrees like fried chicken, butterfish, miso or seafood platter, from $6.95 to $9.75; more exotic dishes like shabu shabu for two go up to $19.75. You may want to take out a Bento lunch of shrimp and seven other items, $3.75, and continue on your outing.

Otomi is open daily from 11 a.m. to 2 p.m. for lunch, from 5 to 10 p.m. for dinner, and in between times, the cocktail bar and sushi bar are open. There's plenty of free parking.

A JAPANESE/FRENCH RESTAURANT: In the Pagoda Gardens, famous for their multi-colored Japanese carp, and above the Pagoda Floating Restaurant which it encircles, is a new gourmet restaurant that makes a commendable effort for excellence without extravagance. **La Salle,** 1525 Rycroft St. (tel. 947-7373), is a circular room, done in shades of pale rose and mauve that enhance the feeling of opulence, as does the huge chandelier that dominates the decor. Take your choice here of Japanese or French food, at either lunch or dinner; lunch is about half the price, and the more rigid dinner dress requirements (no shorts or zoris) are not enforced at lunch.

Japanese entrees are a good buy at lunch: pork cutlet, chicken tofu, shrimp tempura, and teppanyaki chicken, among others, are priced from $6.50 to $10.95, and served with miso soup, rice, and Japanese salads. French entrees are in the same price bracket and include a delicate poulet farce mousseline (boneless breast of chicken stuffed with shrimp and poached in wine sauce), quiche, and crab Louis. These are served with soup or salad. Luncheon sandwiches include stuffed croissants, French dip, and crab Monte Cristo, $5.95 to $7.50. At dinner, prices go from $15.95 to $19 (for lobster), and the entrees are more gourmet, like New York steak and shrimp Milanaise, parmesan-accented shrimp in a garlic-butter-caper sauce. Lunch is from 11 a.m. to 2 p.m., dinner from 5 to 10 p.m., every day.

CHINESE RESTAURANTS: Cities with large Chinese populations always have enough inexpensive restaurants to keep you going for some time, and Honolulu is no exception. It's especially good for us budgeteers, since many of the restaurants are quite lavish and yet offer a number of surprisingly reasonable dishes. The problem here is choosing from an embarrassment of gourmet riches: local friends each swear that their favorite is "the best." Remember that since most of Hawaii's Chinese came from the southern districts, most restaurants feature Cantonese dishes; but happily, the more subtle Mandarin cooking of the northern provinces and the fiery Szechuan cooking that's so popular on the mainland have found their way to several of our budget choices.

One of the most popular Chinese restaurants in town is **Yong Sing,** 1055 Alakea St. (tel. 531-1366). It's a huge place occupying all of a recently renovated downtown building, and the vast dining room is nicely, if not elaborately, decorated in red and gold. There's a huge menu from which to choose, and the selections run the gamut from a $3.75 luncheon plate—pork chop suey, fried shrimp, sweet-and-sour spare ribs, pot roast pork, crisp wonton, and fried rice—to a $130 nine-course dinner to feed a party of ten. In between, there are loads of well-priced goodies. The last time we were here we had a succulent almond duck ($4.75) and chicken with oyster sauce, the house specialty ($4.50). An excellent $17 dinner for two people includes egg flower soup, almond chicken, sweet-and-sour pork, beef broccoli, and fried rice. For something unusual, ask the waiter for a dim sum lunch. This consists of many different varieties of Chinese dumplings: either steamed, baked, or fried, some filled with sweetmeats and served as main dishes; others, dainty pastries for dessert. Five or six of these and plenty of the free-flowing tea—and you've had a lovely, inexpensive treat. But be sure to get there between the hours of 11 a.m. and 2 p.m. for the dumplings; otherwise: so sorry, all sold out today. Yong Sing also has cocktails at reasonable prices, take-out orders anytime, and plenty of parking available. It's open from 7:30 a.m. until 9 p.m. seven days a week.

Shoppers at Ward Warehouse have only to cross the road in the rear of the complex, and there's **The Chinese Chuckwagon** at 1020 Awahi St. (tel. 537-5208). Every night this new restaurant offers a nine-course buffet meal for just $9.95 adults, $5.95 children. The menu changes every week, but there are always at least ten hot dishes: such as roast duck, sweet-and-sour fish, clams with ginger and garlic sauce, barbecued spareribs, beef Szechuan, stuffed tofu, and chicken with vegetables. Soup, hot tea, and an almond float dessert are also included. The buffet is on from 5:30 to 8 p.m. daily; other dishes are served from 6:30 a.m. to 5 p.m., and most cost only $1.10 to $1.25. This is a very plain place that looks like a luncheonette, but it has comfortable booths, and a few tables outside.

The **Golden Inn,** 1272 S. King St., between downtown Honolulu and the university area (tel. 523-6988), used to be relatively unknown to the haoles. Not that it was waiting to be "discovered": the Chinese population came in droves for some of the best Chinese food anywhere. Now that the word's out, people are flocking here from everywhere. The restaurant is elegant inside and out, adorned with Chinese art and plaques on the outside, with elaborate woodcarvings within. The food is equally elegant: if you're a seafood lover, don't miss the fried shrimp at $5.25, or the lobster at $13.50. The chef also does magical things with specialties like Peking duck and shark-fin soup, as well as the more common Cantonese fare. Prices are reasonable, and most dishes—like the chicken and duck entrees at $4.25 to $4.50, and the pork and beef dishes at $3.25 to $5—are big enough to serve three. And there are noodle dishes galore in the $3.50 range. The Golden Inn is open every day from 11 a.m. to 8:30 p.m., and the same menu holds all day long.

There are precious few North Chinese restaurants in the islands, so praise be for **King Tsin**, 1110 McCully St. (tel. 946-3273), an attractive, pleasantly decorated place popular with both visitors and local folk. The food is reasonably priced, subtly flavored, and most fun to eat with a group, as we did the last time we were there. A Chinese friend had ordered for us over the phone, and our soup and appetizer were whisked to our table moments after we arrived. Our party of four began with pot stickers, small dumplings stuffed with pork, two orders at $3.25 each, and two orders of sizzling rice soup at $3.25 per order. For our main courses, we had mu shu pork, $5.50; dry-fried beef—superhot—at $5.75; King Tsin chicken, $5.75, a delicate combination of tender white meat of chicken and pea pods; braised bean curds, $4.95; and sweet-and-sour fish, an entire rock cod, complete with tail and head, smothered in sauce, around $12, depending on size. We all ate until we couldn't manage another bite—and still had a huge doggie bag to take home. Lunch prices are about 10% cheaper than dinner. With the exception of the aforementioned beef—about which the menu warns you—the food here is not overly spicy, as it can be at other northern Chinese restaurants. Open daily for lunch from 11 a.m. to 2 p.m. and dinner from 5 to 9:30 p.m.

Vegetarians who love Chinese food swear by the **Yen King Restaurant** in the Kahala Mall Shopping Center, near the Kahala Hilton Hotel (tel. 732-5505) —there are at least 30 meatless dishes on the menu! So do lots of other folks who've discovered this attractive restaurant that specializes in the cuisines of Peking and Szechuan. There's a lot to choose from here (most dishes run $3.95 to $7.50), but two dishes that we never miss are their famous Singing Rice Soup (it "sings" when the crispy rice is added to the hot broth), and Chinaman's Hat, which consists of very light "pancakes" that you stuff and wrap at the table with a luscious filling of pork and vegetables. From then on, choose what you like: crackling chicken, lemon beef, sautéed clams—they're all good. So are the new Peking-style dumplings and noodles among the appetizers. As for those vegetarian dishes, we found the lo hon chai vegetable dish delectable. Desserts at Chinese restaurants are usually unimaginative, but not here. If they're not too busy, they might make you their fried apple with honey: flaming apple cubes covered with a honey-maple syrup sauce are dipped into ice water right at your table. The result? A treat you won't forget. Everything on the regular menu is available for take-out, and take-outs during the dinner hours (5 to 9:30 p.m.) are only charged lunchtime (11 a.m. to 2:30 p.m.) prices. Yen King has full bar service, and is open seven days a week.

Fortune Gate Seafood Restaurant, 100 N. Beretania St. (tel. 538-7081), is a popular new addition to the restaurants in the downtown Cultural Plaza. Although the decor and length of the menu are lavish, prices are very much down to earth, and whether you're alone or in a large party, you can feast on a variety of dishes for very little money. Although there's a little bit of everything here, from vegetarian dishes to fowl, beef, and pork, the emphasis is on seafood: at least 15 shrimp dishes, eight squid offerings, eight variations of crab, 14 kinds of shellfish, four lobster preparations, and half-a-dozen fresh fish dishes. (Most of these are alive and swimming in the tank in the rear of the restaurant.) Prices range from about $3.95 to $7.95, higher for crab and lobster. If there are at least four of you, try the seafood gourmet dinner at $8.95 per person. It starts with either bird's-nest soup or crispy wonton, and includes entrees like steamed fish, sea bass with vegetables, clam with black-bean sauce, and deep-fried oyster. A nice choice, with many happy Chinese families bubbling about. Fortune Gate is open every day from 8 a.m. to 9 p.m. From 8 a.m. to 3 p.m., a variety of Hong Kong–style dim sum is served.

Seafood is also the specialty of the house at **Won Kee,** another very popular spot in the Cultural Plaza (tel. 524-6877). The dining room is pleasant enough, decorated in cool greens with scenics on the wall that depict birds; the carpeting is thick and plushy, and wind chimes tinkle faintly. But the star attraction here is the food. The menu abounds with such fish and seafood delicacies as sautéed Dungeness crab with ginger and garlic sauce, $13.50; steamed island prawns with long rice, $10.95; and a 1¼-pound Maine lobster, Won Kee style. Delicious! Steamed island fish is highly recommended; at various times they have kumu, golden perch, sea bass, opakapaka, and other varieties, priced according to the current market value. On the low side of the menu ($7.50 to $8.50), you can feast on deep-fried crispy oysters, sweet-and-sour crispy fish filet, or seafood casserole. And if you'd rather not have fish or seafood, you'll be happy with dishes like sliced beef with seasonal vegetables, sweet-and-sour pork, golden crispy chicken. Won Kee serves lunch from 11:30 a.m. to 2:30 p.m. and dinner from 5 to 10 p.m. every day. *Note:* There's another Won Kee at 444 Kanekapolei in Waikiki (tel. 926-7606).

Also in the Cultural Plaza on the block bounded by Beretania, Maunakea, Kukui, and River Streets, is the downtown branch of the **Mongolian Bar-B-Que Restaurant** we told you about at Kuhio Mall (see above). This is a very tidy, neat little place; lunch is served from 11 a.m. to 2 p.m. Monday to Friday; dinner from 5 to 9:30 p.m. daily.

Rating high with the local Chinese community is **Maple Garden,** at 909 Isenberg St. (tel. 941-6641), a small, most attractive dining room with Chinese decorations on the walls, wood paneling, and soft lights. The Szechuan dishes are so tasty and authentic that a doctor friend of ours from Taiwan says that he takes all of his visiting friends and relatives there. Mr. Robert Hsu, the owner, is constantly adding new delights to the menu. The house specialty is Szechuan smoky duck, crispy on the outside and tender on the inside, served with steamed buns—you tuck the meat into the buns. A very generous order (you'll probably need a doggie bag) is $6.50. If you really like the super-hot Szechuan-style cooking, you'll love the eggplant with hot garlic sauce or the pork with hot garlic sauce, $5.25 and $9.75; they're real eye-openers. (The eggplant recipe has received an award from the *Los Angeles Times.*) There are more than 75 entrees on the menu priced at $6.50 or less, including hard-to-find singing rice—actually it's more of a whistle—served either with pork and vegetables or with shrimp, $5.95 in either case. Lunch is from 11 a.m. to 2 p.m. Monday through Saturday; dinner from 5:30 to 10 p.m., seven days. There's ample parking space; and you can phone for easy bus or auto directions from Waikiki.

Just about ten minutes away from Waikiki, in the area of McCully and King Streets, is the ever-popular **New Golden Duck,** 930 McCully St. (tel. 947-9755). It's a tremendous dining room furnished with red leather booths and chairs, extremely popular with local Chinese families for big parties and receptions. Almost everything on the large and varied menu is under $7, with most items about $2.75 to $4.50. Some of our favorites include lemon chicken and shoyu chicken, shrimp with broccoli, beef with sweet-and-sour cabbage, shrimp vegetable noodle, and oyster roll. The portions are so generous and the food so good that you'll want to visit this one again and again. New Golden Duck opens at

10:30 a.m. daily and closes at 1:30 a.m. on Friday and Saturday, at 12:30 a.m. the rest of the week. From Waikiki, take the no. 2 bus to Kalakaua and King, transfer to a no. 1 bus going Diamond Head on King Street (or walk) four blocks to McCully Street.

One of the most popular Chinese restaurants in Honolulu since 1963, and still going strong, is **Hee Hing**, at 449 Kapahulu Ave. (tel. 734-8474), not far from Waikiki in a Diamond Head direction, near the Honolulu zoo. There's a good reason for this popularity: it's a handsome, spacious restaurant, with good-luck murals, paintings, and collages adorning the walls, plates brilliantly bordered with Chinese "Walls of Troy"—and a superb Cantonese cuisine, worthy of the finest traditions of Chinese cooking. And the prices for these delicious, authentic Chinese treats are always reasonable. The menu is voluminous, so take a little time to study it, or ask the waiter for advice. Don't miss trying the dim sum here; they serve over 75 Hong Kong–style dim sum every day. The house specialty, exclusive to Hee Hing, is drunken prawns—live prawns, marinated in white wine, cooked tableside, priced seasonally. There's a vast variety of other live seafood dishes, too, as well as fresh fish prepared in a choice of five different styles. Or, you might decide to feast on one of the sizzling specialties—like sizzling chicken with black-bean sauce, sizzling tenderloin of beef, sizzling pork chops with onions—from $6.25 to $7.95. Earthen-pot casserole dishes, $5.95 to $9.95, are a whole other way to go. Then there are taro nest specialties, the usual chicken, pork, duck, and beef dishes, at least 16 vegetarian offerings, and a vast array of "soup-style" noodle dishes, rice soups, and more. Everything we've tried here has been excellent. For dessert, forgo the fortune cookies in favor of a seasonal fruit pudding or fried apple fritters. A great find.

When local Chinese families want to celebrate a special occasion, they gather up at least ten friends, call **The Chinese Menu** a few days in advance, and gather for a banquet of crispy, crackling Peking duck. But even if there are just a few of you, a visit to this highly praised restaurant at 2600 S. King St., in Puck's Alley (tel. 946-1633), is well worth your while. It's a big, attractive, local place, full of scurrying waiters and people chomping down the delectable dishes that owners David and Georgiana Li and their staff produce. Everything is reasonably priced: four of us ate dinner here recently, from soup to dessert, for just over $20. Wonton soup, at $3.50, enough for all of us, was outstanding; main dishes like lemon chicken at $4.50, fresh scallops sautéed with a choice of vegetables and green onions at $5.95, and sweet-and-sour pork at $3.95 were all delicately prepared. Fresh seafood, like Hawaiian prawns at $9.50, and king clams at $7.95, are house specialties. We finished our meal with cooling almond floats, turned our teapot top upside down to signify that we wanted more tea, and left feeling happy and contented. Lunch is also a good bet, with most dishes running around $2.95 to $4.50. A lunch plate is $3.50; a dinner plate, $4.25. Bar service is available. The Chinese Menu is open for lunch from 11 a.m. to 2 p.m.; for dinner, from 5 to 9 p.m., seven days.

A PHILIPPINE RESTAURANT: At last there is a restaurant offering Philippine cuisine that we can recommend enthusiastically. At 750 Palani Ave., Plaza Manila, in Kapahulu (tel. 734-0400), **1521** (named for the year in which the Philippines were discovered by Magellan) is a handsomely appointed place. The walls are "papered" with woven straw fans, the tablecloths are lavishly embroidered cotton, and a beautiful mural depicts Magellan's galleon *Victoria*. The attractive staff members are very proud of their heritage and their restaurant. As the menu states, the food here is "just like the Filipino people, partly Malaysian, Spanish, Chinese, Japanese, European, American. It is, at the same time, very Filipino." We suggest that you start your meal with soup, so you can sample such delicacies as the tinolang manok (a ginger-flavored chicken soup) or the pancit molo (a stuffed noodle soup with chicken, pork, and shrimp). Salads are equally interesting: the Mindanao salad consists of cucumber slices dressed with a coconut-cream vinaigrette and tossed with fried fish flakes; char-broiled eggplant with onions and tomatoes and a coco-ginger dressing comprise the Bicolono salad. Entrees are accompanied by vegetables and a choice of either garlic fried rice or steamed rice. There are all kinds of authentic selections to choose from: we like the chicken and pork adobo, flavored with garlic and pepper; the bistek Tagalog, grilled filets of beef in a soy-lemon sauce topped with butterfried onions; and especially the prawns in coco—giant prawns sautéed in coconut cream, braced with chili peppers and garlic. These are priced from $4.50 to $8.50. House specialties include roast duckling with mango sauce, paella, and solomillo Manileño (beef tenderloin with an oyster, cream, and brandy sauce), and priced from $9 to $19. Desserts are unusual and luscious: we find it hard to choose between Manila Holiday (mango crêpes stewed in liqueur with chantilly cream and chocolate sauce), $4.50, and cassava Bibingka (a pudding of cassava baked with a topping of sweetened coco cream), $2.50.

The 1521 is located in a cluster of handsome buildings modeled after those on the famous Parker Ranch on the Big Island; they were built several years ago by Richard Smart, the owner of Parker Ranch. The little complex, which also houses a boutique offering Philippine-made handcrafts and native souvenirs, is known as Plaza Manila. At 1521 lunch is served from 11:30 a.m. to 2 p.m. and dinner from 5:30 to 10:30 p.m. every day except Monday; reservations are advised. For a grand splurge at $30, catch their "Philippine Fiesta," presented every Tuesday and Saturday at 6 p.m.; it's a cultural extravaganza, plus a buffet featuring the mouth-watering lechon (roast suckling pig).

AN INDIAN RESTAURANT: The **India House,** at 2632 S. King St., near Puck's Alley (tel. 955-7552), is owned by Ram Arora, formerly the specialty chef at the elegant (and super-expensive) Third Floor Restaurant at the Hawaiian Regent Hotel. His own place, besides being very much more within our reach, is attractive, cool, and relaxing. Brass lamps and lush plants abound in the small dining room that accommodates perhaps a dozen tables. A sari-clad hostess will greet you, make you welcome, and assist you in ordering. At dinner, you'll do well with boti kebab, fish tikka, or tandoori chicken, priced at $9.75 and $10.75, and served with pullao (rice pilaf) and wonderful naan bread, all from the tandoor— that's a clay oven which imparts a delicious flavor to the food baked within. Combination dinners run $9.95 to $14.95. There are plentiful à la carte choices —curries, keema, chicken, shrimp, lamb, or vegetarian dishes, from $4.95 to $5.95. A particularly good dessert choice is the gulab jaman, a "dairy delicacy served in rosewater syrup." We'd call this one a thoroughly delightful dining experience. India House is open for dinner every day from 5 to 9:30 p.m. and for lunch Monday to Friday from 11 a.m. to 2 p.m.

THAI: Every now and then one discovers a place where the food is exotic and delicious, the staff cordial and attentive, the atmosphere warm and cozy, and the prices painless. Such a find is the **Mekong Restaurant,** a charming bit of Thailand at 1295 S. Beretania St. between Keeaumoku and Piikoi (tel. 521-2025 or 523-0014), where a meal is a cultural experience. The small dining room sparkles with white linen tablecloths and blue linen napkins, posters on the wall, and a pretty latticed ceiling. An upstairs room is usually open. The voluminous menu will explain the basics of Thai cooking to you, but you'll do just as well to tell your waiter what you like and follow his suggestions. Thai cooking is a cross between East Indian and Chinese, and while it can be highly spicy, almost every dish can be ordered either mild, medium, or hot. Our waiter explained to us that the hottest—and most popular—dishes are Thai green curry (beef, pork, or chicken sautéed in green chili and curry in fresh coconut milk), $5.50; and Evil Jungle Prince (beef, pork, or chicken sautéed with hot spices with either hot or sweet basil leaves), $5.25. We chose, however, a number of mild dishes which were exquisitely spiced: not-to-be-missed spring rolls (you "sandwich" them at table in fresh lettuce and mint, top with a flavorful carrot-based sauce, and sprinkle with ground peanuts—incredible!), $4.95; a memorable chicken ginger soup in a fresh coconut-milk base, $5.50; a dish of thin, crisp noodles with tiny bits of chicken, $3.75; water chestnut fried rice, $4.95; and the special of the day, king crab sautéed with green onions, eggs, and bean sauce, $8.25. Bring your own bottle if you want wine. Dessert was another unforgettable treat: tapioca pudding unlike any you've ever tasted, in a warm coconut milk; and half-ripe Thai apple-bananas, again cooked in coconut milk. Thai teas are just a little bit different, brewed with vanilla beans and served with condensed milk to make them quite sweet. Eating at Mekong is such a delight that you might be tempted to end your culinary wanderings right here. Open for lunch from 11 a.m. to 2 p.m. Monday to Friday, and for dinner from 5:30 to 9 p.m. every day.

So successful has the Mekong Restaurant been, that owner Keo Sananikone has gone ahead and opened two more temples of Thai cuisine nearby: **Mekong II** at 1726 S. King St. (tel. 941-6184), which does serve beer and wine, and the grandest of them all, **Keo's Thai Cuisine,** at 625 Kapahulu (tel. 737-8240 or 737-9250). So spectacular, in fact, is the latter, that if you're going to have only one Thai meal, we suggest you pay a little more for the same items this one time, and eat here, imbibing the beauty along with the luscious food. Keo has created what might be called a garden-jungle atmosphere: tiny lights strung into the plants, umbrellas over some of the tables, ceiling fans overhead, straw chairs with blue cushions, statues, carvings, portraits on the wall, orchids everywhere —it's a stunner. Dinner only is served here, daily from 5:30 to 11 p.m. Reservations recommended.

The newest outpost of the Keo empire is **Keo's at Ward Centre,** which we've told you about, above. Prices are the same as at Keo's Thai Cuisine, and the setting is similarly beautiful. The advantage for us is that this one is in a more convenient location, and it does serve lunch. Reservations: 533-0533.

Just a block mountainside from the Ala Moana Shopping Center is another Thai winner, **Siam Orchid,** 638B Keeaumoku St. (tel. 955-6161). The setting is charming: fans, Thai posters on the wall, rattan chairs, pink clothes under glass, orchids on the tables, banquette seating. The menu is thoroughly authentic, reflecting the different styles of the various regions of the country. And prices are modest, at both lunch and dinner. What to choose? There's a huge array of dishes, some hotter than others (ask your waiter), but you can't go wrong with appetizers like stuffed chicken wings or squid salad (most run $4.95 to $5.95). Or, begin your meal with a white tofu or fresh cabbage clear soup ($4.95 to $7.95 for soups), and choose from such entrees as fresh chili chicken, beef on a sizzling platter, pork with ginger curry sauce, or Thai garlic shrimp. Most entrees run from $5.25 to $6.95, with the seafood dishes a few dollars higher. As in most Thai restaurants, there's a healthy list of specialties for vegetarians. Lunch is always a good buy, with half-a-dozen noodle specials around $5.

Siam Orchid is open every day, serving lunch from 11 a.m. to 2 p.m., dinner from 5:30 to 9:30 p.m.

Not only is **Bangkok Garden** at 802 Kapahulu Ave. (tel. 734-3887) within walking distance of hotels in the central and Diamond Head areas of Waikiki, it will also deliver to your hotel! This is a plain, attractive dining room with Thai buffalo-hide shadow puppets under the glass table tops, an extensive menu, and very reasonable prices. The reasonable prices become even more reasonable at lunch time, when $5.95 dishes like Mee Krob—shrimp and bean sprouts on a bed of crisp noodles mixed in a tamarind sauce—are priced at only $3, and are served with rice. Before your main course at either lunch or dinner you may want to try some of the delectable appetizers like shrimp fritters or deep-fried bean curd (most are $3.95) or perhaps start with a hearty soup like the seaweed soup we had, with sliced chicken and scallions in a clear, aromatic broth, from $2.50 to $2.95, small. A new taste experience is a Thai "yum"—this is a finger food delicacy served on a lettuce bed. Steak, shrimp, squid, or ground pork is grilled and marinated in a spicy lime mixture, quite tasty, from $5.95 to $7.95. Then you can choose your way through a menu of 14 seafood dishes; 16 chicken, beef, or pork choices; five vegetarian dishes, and several unique desserts. House specialties include honey duck and scallop curry, and range from $5.95 to $8.95. Be careful of the spices; you can order either mild, medium, or wow!

Bangkok Garden serves lunch weekdays from 11 a.m. to 2 p.m., dinner every day from 5 to 11 p.m.

KOREAN RESTAURANTS: So few cities in the world give you a chance to sample good Korean cuisine that you shouldn't pass up the opportunity in Honolulu. Koreans make up a relatively small part of the islands' population, but their culinary tradition has left its mark, especially in the ubiquitous kim chee—pickled cabbage seasoned with red-hot peppers. You'll find it in grocery stores, on menus everywhere in Honolulu, and even at the beach stands along Waikiki where they serve kim chee dogs. But the cuisine has much more to offer: barbecued meat dishes, hearty noodle soups, tasty meat dumplings, fish filets sautéed in spicy sauces, and daintily shredded vegetables are some of the other standbys. A few, but by no means all, of the dishes are served with fiery hot sauces; if you're not accustomed to that sort of thing, check with the waitress before you order.

Honolulu has only a handful of Korean restaurants, and the oldest and best of these, the **House of Park,** at 2671D S. King St. in Moiliili, on the way to the university (tel. 949-2679), is the kind of family-style place that gives you a real experience in nontourist dining. Small and tidy with white walls and flower arrangements—an attempt at decoration—it caters to local Korean and other Oriental families (lots of cute keikis spill about), and a smattering of university students. There are a few booths and tables up front (at one, a man may be rolling dumplings for the soup), from which you can see the big open kitchen in the back. We love the combination of mon doo and kuk soo—hot noodle soup with Korean dumplings stuffed with beef, pork, and vegetables. The waitress once explained to us that this is "New Year's Soup, but so popular we make it every day." The house specialty is kal-bi, barbecued short ribs, and it's excellent. Most dishes run $3 to $5. The plate lunch—barbecued meat, na mul (Korean-style vegetables and fish fried in an egg batter), and rice is a buy at $3.80. Kim chee and hot sauce come with all orders. While you're here, try the famed Korean ginseng tea. The restaurant closes each night at 8 p.m. and all day Sunday. While you're in Moiliili, by the way, note that there are a number of similarly small, family-style Oriental restaurants, with low prices and, we suspect, good food.

Ted's Drive-Inn, 2820 S. King St. (tel. 946-0364), is a small Korean lunch-counter operation that features, in their words, "Seoul food." Although the spelling differs here and there, the dishes are quite similar to those at the House of Park. You could have bul gogi (barbecued beef) at $2.75, kal-bi (barbecued meat) at $4.50, and Kal-bi with mon doo (dumplings) at $4. Non-Korean offerings include beef curry plates and a teri-beef burger. A recent *Honolulu Advertiser* survey rated Ted's as serving "among the top 10 best plate lunches in Honolulu."

Small, sparkly clean, and friendly pretty much sums up **O-Bok** in Manoa Marketplace, 2851 East Manoa Rd. (tel. 988-7702), a little Korean place that serves wonderful food at very moderate prices. All entrees here are served with na mul (vegetables), kim chee (best described as a fiery cole slaw), and rice. The most popular Korean specialty in Hawaii seems to be kal-bi, tender barbecued short ribs. They are particularly good here, and priced at $5.99. Other very good dishes, priced from $3.85 to $5.20, are the barbecued chicken, the fish or meat jun (breaded with an egg batter), and the bi bim bap (mixed vegetables, beef, and fried egg on rice). Very tasty too are the mon doo (a kind of Korean wonton); try them in soup or fried, as a side dish. To explore several of these taste sensations, order one of the mixed plates: the special plate at $4.35 includes kal-bi, barbecued chicken, mon doo, tae-ku (dried codfish), and na mul. The lunch plate (which you may also order at dinnertime), consists of barbecued beef, chicken, na mul, kim chee, and rice. Westerners tend to think of Korean food as being extremely spicy; in reality, it is only the kim chee that makes your eyes water. Open every day, except Monday, from 11 a.m. to 8 p.m.

ITALIAN: **Castagnola's Italian Restaurants,** at Manoa Marketplace (tel. 988-2969), reminds us of the little trattorias one sees everywhere in Rome and Florence—even though you more likely than not will be served by a friendly Oriental or Polynesian waiter. Decor is fresh and simple, the food terrific, and the prices reasonable. Complete meals, offered all day, can be ordered in a regular portion or for the light eater; this means that rigatoni ricotta, linguine marinara or with white clam sauce, and eggplant parmigiana are all $8.90 regular, $6.30 for the light eater. Similarly, veal—be it scaloppine, alla marsala, milanese, piccata, or parmigiana—is either $13.90 or $9.80. Castagnola's homemade bread and tossed salad are served with all of these. There are lots of luncheon specials under $5, and an individual pizza is just $2.40. Castagnola's is one of the few places in Honolulu where you can find cannoli, those flavorful ricotta-filled pastries. Try this, or chocolate gelato, spumoni, or zabaglione for dessert. Castagnola's is open Monday from 11 a.m. to 3 p.m., Tuesday through Saturday from 11:30 a.m. until 10 p.m. Closed Sunday.

Che Pasta, at 3571 Waialae Ave. (tel. 735-1777), is a charming Italian restaurant in the Kaimuki neighborhood: we found the food to be quite special and the service impeccable. The dining room is elegantly furnished, yet the ambience of the place is warm and friendly. Dinner can be quite reasonable here if you stick with the pastas, like the delicious saffron cannelloni ($11) or the linguine al pesto ($8). We sometimes come here and make a whole meal on the $5.50 antipasto. A flavorful house specialty is the cacciatore espresso, breast of chicken with tomato, mushroom, olives, onions, and garlic, $11.75. The lunch menu features a variety of salads, notably spinach and goat cheese, pasta salad, and Che Pasta's lovely antipasto, all priced between $4.50 and $6.25. Sandwiches too, plus some delicious pasta entrees like the fettuccine Alfredo, $7.95. It's a great temptation to overdo on their wonderful fresh Italian bread (a new supply is whisked to your table as soon as your basket is empty), but be strong and save room for the gelato and sorbet, or the chocolate Grand Marnier cake. A *bellisimo* treat. Lunch is served from 11:30 a.m. until 2 p.m. weekdays only; dinner hours are 5:30 to 10 p.m. every day.

Note: If you're in downtown Honolulu, you can enjoy similar cuisine at slightly lower prices at **Che Pasta, A Bar & Grill,** at 1001 Bishop St., at Bishop

Square. The same philosophy and practice prevail here: "A fresh approach to Italian cuisine, using only the finest and freshest ingredients available."

FROM RUSSIA WITH LOVE: A Russian snackbar in downtown Honolulu is a cultural anachronism, but we don't mind a bit. **Rada's Piroshki,** 1144-1146 Fort Street Mall, specializes in the piroshki—a delicate, flaky bun stuffed with beef, cheese, cabbage, mushrooms, whatever combination suits your fancy. Whenever we're downtown, we simply can't resist the chicken, mushrooms, and cheese piroshki, but the other combinations are also delicious. Along with a drink, one big piroshki, $1.30, makes a satisfying meal. The chicken soup is also marvelous, and the Russian fried squid, $1 a bag, are . . . uh, different. Rada's is a family operation, and the people in charge make you feel welcome. But alas, they close at 6:30 p.m. every day, and are open only from 1:30 to 3:30 p.m. Sunday. Warning: Piroshkis may be habit-forming.

VIETNAMESE: Vietnamese food is rare in Honolulu, with just a few restaurants offering this subtle cuisine, which combines a number of Asian and sometimes European influences. Local friends swear by Mark Fu, well known for his catering work and as chef of **Hale Vietnam,** 1140 12th Ave. in Kaimuki (tel. 735-7581). Chef Fu specializes in the cuisine of the Mekong Delta region, and serves it in a casual setting of Oriental art and tropical plants. Lunches run from $2.50 to $3.75 and include an appetizer of Imperial Rolls, crisp South East Asian delights wrapped in rice paper and filled with seafood, pork, and fresh herbs. You may choose to have them unfried and they're just as good that way. The prices also include a hearty Vietnamese beef noodle soup. Prices for the same items are a little higher at dinner. If there are two or three of you, try the "hot pot" which will serve all of you for $18.95; it consists of pork, chicken, fish, shrimp, crab meat, mushrooms, and vegetables all cooked together. Beef or a spiced chicken dish are grilled at your table. Plan on spending between $8 and $10 for dinner, including entree and beverage. Be sure to try the Chao Tom, shrimp on sugar cane, for an exotic taste. Unless you're an old hand at Asian food, ask that your dishes be done "mild" or "medium."

Chef Fu closes Hale Vietnam on Wednesday, but it's open every other day from 10 a.m. to 10 p.m., with prices remaining the same all day. Plenty of municipal parking is handy.

3. And Elsewhere on the Island

RESTAURANTS IN KAILUA: One of Honolulu's very finest restaurants is just a short drive across the Pali in pretty little Kailua town. It is **L'Auberge Swiss,** at 117 Hekili St. (tel. 263-4663). The owner, who is also the chef, is Alfred Mueller, formerly head chef for Hilton Hotels Hawaii. Only dinner is served at this charming place, Tuesday through Sunday from 6 to 10 p.m. The dining room very much resembles the little country inns one sees in Switzerland, Mueller's boyhood home. The food is superb and the service friendly; the dining room is presided over by Mrs. Mueller, who was born and raised in Hawaii. It's difficult to choose what to start with: there's country pâté, bay shrimp cocktail with avocado, oysters Rockefeller, escargots bourguignon—and the French onion soup gratinée, which is sheer poetry! L'Auberge's specialties—none of which go above $15—are all magnificent: take your choice of the likes of chicken piccato albergo (boneless breast of chicken on pasta); weinerschnitzel; émincé de veau zurichois (tender pieces of veal in a rich cream sauce with mushrooms and rösti potatoes); or scallops and shrimp sautéed in a delicate sauce, served with pasta. And then there's that great Swiss favorite, cheese fondue, with dinner salad, for at least two lucky people. Light Swiss dinners, such as bratwurst on toast with ham and melted Swiss, and the fresh pasta of the day, are all about $6. Fondue is $8. Reservations are a must; kamaiinas comes from all corners of the island to dine here.

Family restaurants often have that special warmth and conviviality that other restaurants find hard to match, and that's part of the success story behind **Florence's,** 20 Kainehe St. (tel. 261-1987), in Kailua. Florence—Mrs. Gerardo Jovinelli—is an Italian-American woman who learned all of mama's recipes and has translated them into a superlative cuisine that's been keeping the local people coming for the past 30 years. We promise you won't forget Florence's giardiniera, a mouthwatering combination of lasagne, eggplant, ravioli, spaghetti, and beef ragoût that's served with minestrone and side dishes: $6.75 at lunch, $10.75 at dinner. Every night, there's a $10.50 Bohemian dinner that consists of minestrone soup or tossed green salad, vegetables or spaghetti, French bread, beverage, and an entree of the day, which could be anything from scampi veneziana to veal scaloppine to lobster Marseille! Desserts are special too; try the lemon cheesecake at $1.50. Lunch features lots of salad 'n' sandwich meals (meatball sandwich, $2.85; crabburger on toasted bun, $3.75), but do try the Italian dishes; they're too good to miss. The place is uncrowded and unpressured, far from the milling tourist scene. From downtown, take the Pali Highway, which becomes Kailua Road, and watch for the intersection of Kailua with Kanehoe; Kainehe is the first street on the left before entering Kailua.

Cinnamon's, at 315 Uluniu St. (tel. 261-8724), is named in honor of a bear in a charming French children's story that was owner Bonnie Nam's favorite when she was a little girl. A big, plush replica of Cinnamon, sporting a crisp white baker's cap decorated with a red heart, waits to greet you just inside the front door. The restaurant is on the ground floor of an attractive neighborhood shopping plaza. It's so popular that on weekends they have to put extra tables out on the mall to accommodate everyone. The restaurant itself is small and cozy: four of the tables are under a pretty white gazebo. And the tab will be very reasonable. For lunch, we like the chicken cashew salad, $4.95, and the grilled cheese deluxe sandwich, with Monterey Jack, American, and Swiss cheeses, $2.95. Country quiches with salad, the garden vegetable platter, and burgers are all very popular, too. At dinnertime, pick one of the house specials and you'll have a complete meal from $7.95 to $10.95, with such entrees as chicken fantasy, with broccoli hollandaise; kebabs of lamb, chicken, beef, pork, or fish; and broiled top sirloin. These are accompanied by soup or salad; rice, fries, or baked beans; vegetables; and hot dinner rolls. On the à la carte dinner menu, the fiesta taco grande salad and the chef's super salad (described as "a salad bar brought to your table") are fun, as are the roast pork with apple dressing, fried chicken with country gravy and vegetables, seafood crêpes florentine, seafood platter, and fresh fish, all $6.50 to $11.75. Doors open at 7 a.m. for breakfast (freshly baked cinnamon rolls, coffee cake, croissants, muffins, corn bread, and pancakes) and do not close until 9 p.m. every day.

The **Plush Pippin,** at 108 Hekili St. in Kailua (tel. 261-7552), is a sparkly little tea room–type place where the house specialty is pies: sour cream lemon (or, for that matter, sour cream blueberry, apple, cherry, and pineapple), cream cheese, apricot, peanut butter, German chocolate, and many more. While you're picking one up to take back to your hotel (they're about $5), have lunch or dinner, very reasonably priced. The Pippin's all-day menu offers sandwiches, burgers, and quiches, from about $2.80 to $4.35. Dinners, ready from 5 p.m., are served with a choice of soup or salad and bread; you may choose from roast beef, boneless chicken breasts, mahimahi, or ham steak in a price range of $6.25 to $7.95. For dessert? Pie, of course, what else? The Plush Pippin opens every day at 7 a.m. for breakfast (served until 11 a.m. weekdays and 11:30 a.m. weekends, it features Belgian waffles, hotcakes, blueberry cornbread, and much more), and closes at 11 p.m. Monday through Thursday, at midnight on Friday and Saturday, and at 10 p.m. on Sunday.

Coffee fanatics have their own hangout in Kailua, a place called **Kailua and Cream,** in the same building as Plush Pippin, 108 Hekili St. (tel. 262-9729). Sit down at one of the widely scattered tables—there's a feeling of living-room privacy here—and choose from among 20 to 30 types of coffee, a large selection of teas (herbal and regular), and a variety of pastries including a super banana cake: fresh, moist, and deliciously iced. Owner Ken takes pride in serving you coffee or tea just the way you like it, and prices are modest: 80¢ for the daily specials, espresso for 95¢.

When we first saw Doug & Don's, we exclaimed, "Gee, a deli!" That turned out to be its name. **Gee . . . A Deli!** is at 418-F Kuulei Rd., Kailua (tel. 261-4412), directly behind McDonald's. You'll know this is a New York–style deli right away: sandwiches are automatically served on rye and are inches thick. There are all the usuals, including a very good beef tongue at $5.25, plus a dozen or more clubs and combos, bagels with cream and lox, too. Although this is an extremely popular place, service is fast and efficient. And there are two or three large tables, so you don't have to eat in the car. Hours are 10 a.m. to 6 p.m. Monday to Saturday, 11 a.m. to 5 p.m. Sunday.

There's another interesting place to eat in Kailua, should you happen to be out this way. That's the cafeteria of the **Castle Medical Center,** 640 Ulukahiki St., over the Pali at Waimanalo Junction. The hospital is run by Seventh Day Adventists, and everything served is vegetarian, delicious, and at old-fashioned prices. All the hot entrees—like meatless Oriental stew and herb loaf—are 85¢ to $1; a salad-and-sandwich bar is available at 15¢ an ounce, so you can easily put together a very reasonable meal. Take the elevator or stairs down one flight as you enter the hospital and you'll see the cafeteria. It faces a rear garden and a beautiful view of the Pali. Meals are served to the public Monday through Friday from 11 a.m. to 1:30 p.m. and from 4:30 to 6 p.m. À la carte breakfast—pancakes, eggs, fresh fruits, and beverage, at $3—is served between 6:30 and 9:30 a.m.

AROUND THE ISLAND: The very cheapest way to eat on your round-the-island journeys is to bring your own picnic lunch, but there are also a few restaurants that make fine budget-wise refueling stops. The several shopping malls in Kaneohe offer a bonanza of inexpensive eateries. At the new enclosed Windward Mall, for example, the standout restaurant is **Marie Callender's** (tel. 235-6655), a charming, airy spot, where $7.50 brings you a terrific pot pie lunch. It's served in a ceramic casserole, has an all-vegetable crust, and is a meal in itself. Quiches, salads, and desserts are all fantastic here. At the same mall, be sure to try **Cinnabon** for a singular experience. Customers start lining up before opening time (10 a.m.) to buy these incredible cinnamon rolls, each measuring about 5 inches in diameter and about 3 inches high, topped with a mound of whipped cream. You can watch the team of bakers turn them out. People have been known to make a meal out of them—although not exactly a balanced one. They're $1.35 each. Pizza fans have **Harpo's,** and brag of their fresh veggies on hand-rolled dough, and sausages, by a local maker. Two slices of their deep-dish–style pizzas will set you back $4.90 for pepperoni, $4.30 for special vegetables. If you've been to Ala Moana Center, you know that **Patti's Chinese**

Kitchen is great. Now there's a Patti's here, too, and it's inexpensive and filling. Plenty of tables at the mall, plus lots of other fast-food outlets.

For a meal in a splendid setting, turn mauka just past Kaneohe and proceed about a mile toward the mountains and **Haiku Gardens,** an oldtime kamaaina favorite surrounded by two acres of gorgeous gardens and grounds that you may want to tour (see details in Chapter VIII). Lunch is a very pleasant and not expensive affair; you can have an open-face sandwich of barbecued teriyaki, hot beef, or mahimahi, served with coleslaw, coffee, or tea for $4.25 to $5.25. At $8.25 for adults, $5.95 for children, you get a serve-yourself Haiku buffet special —all you can eat of four hot entrees, salad, fruit, vegetable, dessert, and beverage. Dinner entrees run about $9.50 to $15.50.

Farther along, you'll find Swanzy Beach, a scenic picnic spot. If you haven't packed your own, stop in at **Kaaawa Country Kitchen,** across the street. It has some outdoor tables, plus lots of take-out items, like plate lunches of teriyaki beef or fried chicken, $3.50 to $3.95. Tacos too, and hot apple pie. It's next to the Kaaawa Post Office.

The **Texas Paniolo Café,** 53-146 Kamehameha Hwy., in Punaluu (tel. 237-8521), is our favorite fun stop on this route, even though we still can't quite bring ourselves to try the specialty of the house—rattlesnake chili! The place has a rustic, western appearance inside and out; it's a wooden frame building with a front porch and the interior walls resemble adobe. Country-western wails from the jukebox during the day; at night, there's live entertainment. You'll just love the stuffed rattlesnake on the walls! And if you're braver than we are, you can also have that rattlesnake chili at $7.25, whose menu notation states "in season (?) when available." If the rattlers are not available, however, there is plenty of other very tasty Tex-Mex food. Among the appetizers, we vote for the chili con queso—a crock of melted cheese, tomatoes, and green chilies with tostitos for dipping, $4.95. A half-pound bowl of beef chili with rice or beans and crackers is $4.95; a chiliburger or jalapeño burger with cheese is $5.95. Dessert offerings include such Texas treats as pecan pie. Open every day except Sunday from 11 a.m. to 11 p.m.

Where can you get the best sandwich on the North Shore, maybe in all of Oahu? We'd cast our vote for **Kua 'Aina** (tel. 637-6067), a sparkling sandwichery across the street from the courthouse in Haleiwa. It's tiny, neat as a pin, with wooden tables, framed pictures of local scenes, a few tables on the porch. And the atmosphere is casual, with people coming in off the beach. We haven't stopped raving yet about the sandwiches we had on our last visit: mahimahi with melted cheese, Ortego pepper, lettuce, and tomato at $4.25, tuna and avocado ("the tastiest combo in the Pacific") at $3.40, and a great baconburger at $3.85. Sandwiches are hearty enough to be a whole meal, and are served on either a Kaiser roll, honey wheat-berry bread, or earth rye. Kua 'Aina is open daily from 11 a.m. to 9 p.m.

Haleiwa is, in fact, an ideal place to break for lunch, for this little town is surfers' headquarters, and when they come off those mighty waves, surfers have to eat. You can join them at several spots, in addition to Kua 'Aina, mentioned above. In the Haleiwa Shopping Plaza you can get tasty Mexican dishes at **Rosie's Cantina** (tel. 637-3538), an attractive, high-tech looking spot, where à la carte dishes run about $1.75 to $4.95. Rosie's serves all three meals, features delicious tortas (hamburger or chicken with fries or beans on thick bread with hollowed-out insides), and offers tacos for an astonishingly low 79¢, beer for 89¢, and margaritas for 99¢ when Taco Tuesday—that's every Tuesday between 4 and 6 p.m.—rolls around. On the other side of the shopping plaza, there's **Kiawe Q and Deli** (tel. 637-3502), a pleasant-looking spot with comfortable chairs, natural woods, plants, and Hawaiian music. If you like kiawe wood-smoked meats, you'll love their barbecued ribs, chicken, hot sandwiches, and burgers, modestly priced from $1.95 to $5.95. They also have smoked locally caught fish, homemade desserts, and freshly ground Hawaiian–roast coffee. Take-out available.

You can have a cozy lunch in an elegant setting at **Steamer's Restaurant & Bar** (tel. 637-5071), in the Haleiwa Shopping Plaza on Kam Hwy. It's a big, low-lit, wood-paneled place, with shiny brass accents and an enjoyable outdoor dining area. And the food lives up to the decor. Lunch offers a hearty seafood omelet at $6.45; it, and other omelets, from $5.25, are served with rice or fries and blueberry or French crumb muffins. A good variety of hot sandwiches—opakapaka, teriyaki, french dip, Reuben, and good old hamburgers—are priced from $4.50 to $6.50. All the hot sandwiches are accompanied by salad and rice pilaf or fries, so they make quite a satisfactory meal. One of our favorite dishes here, the Steamer's Delight Platter, is a tasty assortment of tempura vegetables: onion rings, zucchini, artichoke hearts, and mushrooms deep-fried in batter, $8.25. Dinner here is a splurge; mahimahi is low on the menu at $9.75, petite top sirloin steak is $10.25, steak and seafood crêpes are $15.95, and other steak and seafood combos go up to $21. All entrees are accompanied by seafood chowder or house salad, Steamer's bread, rice pilaf, and fresh steamed vegetables. Save room for the special cheesecake or carrot cake. Steamer's is open from 11:30 a.m. to 11:30 p.m. (food service until 10 p.m.), seven days. The bar is busy until 2 a.m.

Another wonderfully picturesque spot for lunch or dinner is **Jameson's by the Sea,** on the outskirts of Haleiwa at 62-450 Kam Hwy. (tel. 637-4336). Take in the harbor, the sunset, and great food and drink; it has a seafood menu similar to that of Jameson's on Merchant in downtown Honolulu, and to Jameson's-on-Seaside, described in our section on Waikiki Restaurants (see above). Even if you're eating elsewhere, you might want to stop here just for a nip of their famous Irish coffee—made with Jamesons' Whisky, of course.

To give yourself a very special treat at the end of your around-the-island journey, stop in for dinner at **Kemoo Farm,** 1718 Wilikina Dr. (tel. 621-8481), overlooking Lake Wilson in Wahiawa, holding forth in these parts for 70 years and still going strong. And no wonder: this is a place where the spirit of Old Hawaii still lingers, with excellent food and drink, gracious service by caring waitresses, a gentle mood. The price of your entree includes a complete dinner, and that means a delicious homemade soup (the seafood chowder we sampled recently was thick with potatoes and chunks of shrimp, crab, and mahimahi), tossed green salad, fresh vegetable, and fresh baked bread. You might order fresh Idaho rainbow trout, boneless Polynesian duck with wild rice stuffing, or mahimahi, all on the low side of the menu at $8 to $10.50. Nice little extras on the regular meals include a loaf of hot bread on its own serving board that arrives as soon as you sit down (and keeps being replaced), and crispy wontons. Add another $1.25 to the price of your meal and have Kemoo's pine-mint tea; they make it right here by marinating the pineapple in a simple syrup with fresh mint—quite wonderful.

If you happen to be in town on a Wednesday or Sunday, we have a suggestion to make: drive up to Wahiawa just for lunch at Kemoo Farm (it should take about an hour from Waikiki via the H-2 Freeway). It will be well worth your time, for that's when "Hawaii's Greatest Voice," Charles K.L. Davis, presides over a lunchtime show that is truly a Hawaiian classic. Davis, whose operatic career has taken him to the great stages of the world, hosts the show, and before introducing other talented island entertainers—these might include such luminaries as Emma Veary or Moe Keale—he spends about an hour doing his own satirical, sometimes slightly naughty, numbers. The kamaaina crowd, dressed up in aloha finery, loves it when he sings lyrics like "Ooga, ooga, mushka—it means I love you in the Yukon" for the Eskimos in the audience; or, for the realtors in the crowd, "I'll make some jack on that little grass shack in Kealekekua, Hawaii." The show lasts for about two hours (be there by 11:30 a.m. or 12 noon and make reservations), and includes a delicious "Plantation Buffet"—for all of $10. Surely one of the great entertainment values anywhere, plus a chance to be part of nontourist, kamaiiana Hawaii.

Other days, lunchtime offers some unusual salads (like Japanese somen), in addition to regular entrees and sandwiches, from about $4.95 to $7.50. And Sunday brunch is special, with many eggs Benedict and Florentine dishes, and an unusual filet of trout and eggs. Kemoo Farms serves lunch from 11 a.m. to 2 p.m. Sunday through Friday, and dinner from 5 to 8:30 p.m. every day of the week.

A WORD ABOUT SHAVE ICE: A unique treat that's loved by just about everyone in the islands is a phenomenon called shave ice. Not "shaved" ice—shave ice. When it's pointed out to them, mainland visitors often sneer. "Oh, we have that at home—we call them snow cones" (or ices, or slushes). It isn't any of those things, it's just wonderful Hawaiian shave ice. Half the fun of having it is watching the ice being shaved. You can have a "plain" shave ice—that's just the incredibly fine ice particles bathed in syrup—and there are all kinds of syrups. Strawberry is the most popular, but there's also vanilla, guava, lemon, cherry, orange, root beer, coconut, and combinations of the above, known as "rainbow." Or you can have ice cream on the bottom, or azuki beans (a sweet Japanese bean used in desserts); or throw caution to the winds and have ice cream *and* beans on the bottom). Shave ice is served in a cone-shaped paper cup, with both a straw and a spoon.

Shave ice places abound, but after years of diligent sampling and research, we offer our two favorites: **Matsumoto's Grocery** at 66-087 Kam Hwy. in Haleiwa, across from the intersection of Emerson Street, is a family operation and on weekends the lines can be long, because the local people drive out from all over the island; it's a pleasant wait, everyone is friendly. **Malia's** lunch wagon parks across from Sandy Beach at the intersection of Kalanianaole Highway and the Kalama Valley road every day except Wednesday and Thursday. The effervescent Malia has created a new shave ice called "The Snowy Delight." Prices at both places vary slightly, from about 60¢ for a small plain shave ice to $1 for the large size with ice cream and beans. There's usually a 5¢ extra charge if you want rainbow—that's three or more flavors in a fetching striped motif.

Caution: Shave ice is definitely habit-forming.

4. The Night Scene

Contrary to what you'd expect, the night scene in Honolulu is not all hula girls in grass skirts and sentimental songs on the ukulele. Sure, there are palm trees and schmaltz aplenty, but there are also ultrasophisticated jazz groups, authentic Polynesian music and dances, songsters, psychics, comedians, discos, sing-alongs at the piano, and no dearth of gorgeous seaside gardens where you could easily while away a few years. We'll tell you about the free shows first, then take you on a tour of the "in" bars and cocktail lounges, and on to a rundown of what we consider the most exciting entertainment in town.

But you really don't need any planned entertainment to enjoy Waikiki at night. There's a great show going on wherever you look: you can observe the people, browse in the shops, or stand in front of the clubs and dig the sound, free of charge, at the International Market Place. Or watch the newcomers parade up and down Kalakaua Avenue, survey the scene at the big hotels, or take our favorite walk, the "scrounger's stroll."

THE SCROUNGER'S STROLL: Here's how you do it: at the Diamond Head end of the Surfrider Hotel, there's a paved path leading to the ocean. Follow it along the back of the Surfrider Hotel and onto the beach in back of the Moana next door; here you can gaze at the floodlit shore and listen to the music drifting from the Moana's romantic Banyan Court, just behind you. You can even have a nighttime swim if you want to; no one will stop you (all the beaches are public property up to the high-water mark), or just meander barefoot along the sands ewa until you come to the beach of the Royal Hawaiian Hotel. If you've timed your scrounger's stroll correctly, you'll arrive in time to watch from afar the show at the Royal's fancy Monarch Room; it's not exactly a ringside table, but it's fun.

Wander down the beach to the Outrigger Hotel, where the very popular **Chuck Machado Luau** takes place Tuesday, Friday, and Sunday at 6 p.m. There'll be lots of people watching the show from the sand. Emcee Doug Mossman usually acknowledges the scroungers; he calls them the "graduating class." Join the fun and see the $19.50 entertainment gratis.

A free beach show gets rolling every Sunday at 8 p.m. on the beach in front of the **Reef Hotel.** A crowd of young people comes to watch the professional beach boys (you'll see them on the beach during the day) sing, play the uke, and try to impress the girls. Girls who have taken hula lessons get up and perform too, and there's often a noisy community sing. It's all done by amateurs, but it's friendly fun—and always packed. The show may be canceled in poor weather; you may want to check with the hotel.

BARFLY'S TOUR: If you'd like to watch the sunset in luxury, arrive early (about 6 p.m.) at the cocktail lounge of **Reef's Aloha Bar** for a front-row seat. The most intriguing bar at the Reef? **That's Harry's Underwater Bar,** reached via the basement and located right under the swimming pool. You can watch the swimmers above while you drink up.

Head Mauka on Kalakaua Avenue to the smart-looking Princess Kaiulani Hotel for a pleasant drink poolside at the **Kahili Bar.** Cross the street (Koa Avenue) to King's Village for a drink at an English pub, the **Rose and Crown.** Brews from the mother country, of course, plus an assortment of beers and cocktails, sing-along piano, darts, ladies' night on Tuesday, tequila night on Thursday, and tropical drink specials on Aloha Sunday. Plus all-day Happy Hours. The **Lobby Bar** of the Hawaiian Regent Hotel is pleasant, and so is **The Library,** a contemporary wine bar and lounge overlooking the beach, where it's fun to meet people and discuss wines or relax over a drink. And there's a snug feeling about the **Sandwich Island Pub** at the Holiday Inn, an intimate room for drinks, pupus, and good music on the jukebox.

In the mood for a Mexican party? The **Corona Cantina** at Compadres Waikiki, in the Outrigger Prince Kuhio Hotel, has become one of the most madly popular bars in town. Try their "Back Bar Margaritas" (made with Grand Marnier) or, if you dare, their "Headrest Margaritas," where the bartender pours all the ingredients right into your mouth, and the first one is on Compadres!

A big favorite with the Honolulu theater crowd is **South Seas Village** at 2112 Kalakaua Ave.; they come to hear John Saclausa at the piano bar, every evening except Sunday from 9 p.m. until closing. John plays, people get up and sing, and everybody has a good time. Wine coolers are $2.25.

Viewpoints

Waikiki is full of gorgeous rooms with a view, but for the most sensational of all, take the glass elevator (on the outside of the hotel; it's eerily exciting going up) to **Annabelle's** at the top of the Ilikai. This 30-story-high, glass-walled aerie is to Honolulu what the Top of the Mark is to San Francisco: the place to see the million lights of the metropolis dazzlingly spread out before you. Before 9 p.m., standard drinks are $2; after 9 p.m. they're $4. Dancing starts at 5 p.m. with Big Band sounds and favorite oldies; from 9 p.m. until closing at 4 a.m., the sound is disco. Alas, there's a $4 cover. But even if you're not a drinker or a dancer, don't miss the ride up in the glass elevator, from which the view is also spectacular, and at least peek at the room. (Incidental note for parents looking for ways to amuse their kiddies: They love a ride in the glass elevator.) More about discos ahead.

Another thrilling view is to be had from **Windows of Hawaii Revolving Restaurant** atop the Ala Moana Office Building, a merry-go-round for sybarites. Twenty-three stories up, and affording an almost identical view to that of Annabelle's, the room slowly revolves, affording spectacular views of mountain, sea, and city. Cocktails are served all day. New Englad–style cuising is featured.

At the center of Waikiki is another glamorous revolving restaurant, the **Top of Waikiki,** in the Waikiki Business Plaza Building at 2270 Kalakaua Ave. The top tier of this gigantic wedding-cake of a restaurant is the cocktail lounge, very glamorous by candlelight and starlight. Views of all of Waikiki are yours for the price of a drink: beer from $2.75, exotics from $4.50.

At the Sea

For one of the most majestic views in town, try the glorious **Hanohano Room** of the Sheraton-Waikiki; the panorama stretches all the way from Diamond Head to Pearl Harbor. Drinks are pricey: beers will cost you $2.75, imported beers are $4.05, and mai tais cost $5.95. There's entertainment and dancing nightly, from 9:30 on. No cover, no minimum.

If ever you've dreamed of picture-perfect Hawaii, treat yourself to sunset cocktails at **The House Without a Key,** the oceanside lounge at the recently rebuilt Halekulani Hotel. Here, under a century-old kiawe tree, you can watch the waves splash up on the breakfront, the sun sink into the ocean, and hear the music of a top island group, Sonny Kamahele and the Islanders (Sunday, Monday, Tuesday, Thursday, 5 to 9 p.m.) and the Jerry Byrd Trio (Wednesday, Friday, Saturday, 5:30 to 9 p.m.). Kanoe Miller, a former Miss Hawaii, does some beautiful dancing. Draft beers at $2.50, exotic drinks higher. A sunset cocktail pupu menu is served from 5 to 8:30 p.m. daily. Don't miss this one.

The Moana, one of the classic oceanfront hotels in Waikiki, is another neat place for a drink near the water's edge. Its **Beach Bar** offers mixed drinks from $3.75, beer from $2.50.

At some of the Waikiki hotels, the cocktail gardens overlook the lagoon—and one of our favorites is the **Tahitian Lanai** in the Waikikian Hotel (a superb example of modern Polynesian architecture; as you walk through to the garden, note the hotel's cave-like lobby with the roof of an ancient spirit house). Beer is $2 and up; gin and tonic, $2 and up (about a quarter more when music begins at 8:30).

Another romantic spot we favor greatly is the **Hala Terrace** of the Kahala

Hilton, a short drive from Waikiki. You can sip your drinks on the beachside patio and watch the surf roll in. At 9:30 p.m. a cover descends for the Danny Kaleikini dinner show, about which more later.

Pupus and Happy Hours

Now we come to the more practical side of pub-crawling: how to drink at half the price and get enough free food for almost a meal at the same time. The trick here is to hit the bars during their Happy Hours (usually from 4 to 6 p.m. but sometimes greatly extended), when they serve free pupus or lower their prices, or both. Note that these hours and prices are apt to change often, but these places always offer a good deal of one sort or another.

There's a generously long Happy Hour (11 a.m. to 8 p.m.) at the **Crow's Nest,** located above the Jolly Roger at 2244 Kalakaua Ave. Several readers have written to praise this place for being "the friendliest and cheapest bar in Waiki-ki." Mai tais are just $1.50. No cover, no minimum, entertainment nightly from 8 p.m., and plenty of free peanuts, whose shells cover the floor . . . **Rose and Crown,** that jolly old English pub at King's Village, offers mai tais at $2.50, beer and standards from $1.25, at its 11 a.m. to 7 p.m. Happy Hour . . . From 6 to 9 p.m., the **Waikiki Broiler** in the Waikiki Tower Hotel, 200 Lewers, brings out the mai tais and chi chis at standard drink prices. There's entertainment after-noons and evenings . . . Nothing skimpy about the Happy Hour at **Monterey Bay Canners Lounge** in the Outrigger Hotel. It runs from 7 a.m. to 7 p.m., and during all that time, mai tais are $1, daiquiris $1.50. As if that weren't enough, there's a double Happy Hour between 4 and 7 p.m., when all well drinks are $1.95. Oysters and clams on the half-shell are 75¢ each. And—you won't be-lieve this—there's still a third Happy Hour, from 10:30 p.m. to closing. That's when well drinks are $1.25, Irish coffee and chi chis are just $1.50 . . . Ever-popular mai tais are just $1.25 during the long (6 a.m. to 6 p.m.) Happy Hour at the **Rigger** in the Outrigger Hotel, and from 6 to 10 a.m. Bloody Marys are 95¢. There's a big-screen TV for sports events, entertainment nightly beginning at 9 p.m. with no cover charge, and popcorn served free all day . . . There's anoth-er very long Happy Hour in the **Plaza Lounge,** downstairs at the Waikiki Shop-ping Plaza, from 11 a.m. to 11 p.m. Standard drinks are around $1.10.

Marco Polo, on the fourth floor of the Waikiki Shopping Plaza, has one of the longest Happy Hours around—from 11 a.m. to closing. Different drinks are featured each day at low prices . . . It's half-price for all draft beer and liquors (except for ice cream drinks) during the 4 to 8 p.m. Happy Hour at **Moose Mc-Gillicuddy's Pub-Café** . . . The **Aloha Restaurant and Bar** at the Reef Hotel of-fers all drinks for $1.50 to $2.50 during its 11 a.m. to 6 p.m. Happy Hour. Over at **Las Margaritas,** that lovely Mexican restaurant at the Royal Hawaiian Shop-ping Center, it's called Fiesta Hour, from 4 to 7 p.m. And fiesta you will if you consume one of their giant—one-quart—margaritas for $3.75; $2.75 is the price for the usual kind. Nifty pupus are available at Cantina La Gloria . . . During the 4 to 6 p.m. Happy Hour at the **Great Wok of China** at the Royal Hawaiian Shopping Center, standard drinks are $1.10; mai tais, $1.35; hot pupus are free on Friday . . . One of the most *simpático* Happy Hours in town takes place be-tween 4 to 7 p.m. daily at **Compadres Waikiki,** when margaritas are $1.50 the glass, $7.50 the pitcher . . . It's $1.50 for beer and standard drinks from 4 to 8 p.m. Happy Hour at the **Surfboard Bar** of the Waikiki Beachcomber Hotel.

THE DISCO SCENE: The disco scene is bigger, better, and noisier than ever in Honolulu. A recent look around revealed something like a dozen clubs packing them in, and more on the way. Besides offering plenty of exercise, the local discos are mostly inexpensive; usually they have a modest cover charge or none at all, and just a few insist on a two-drink minimum and/or a fee. Live bands usually alternate with disco, and the action gets under way between 9 and 10 p.m. in most clubs and only ends when everyone drops from exhaustion—anywhere between 2 and 4 a.m. Here's a rundown on the action, as of this writing.

One of the most popular disco spots and perhaps the biggest singles scene in town, is **The Point After** at the Hawaiian Regent Hotel, (tel. 922-6611), with European decor, twin dance floors, and hi-tech video dancing that features popular rock tunes as well as "oldies but goodies." A $3 cover charge . . . **Zone Seven** calls itself an "ultrasonic discotheque." Designed by a top Japanese disco impresario, it's an audio-visual experience new to the islands. Entertainment starts at 6 p.m., dancing begins at 9:30, and continues on and on. There's a $3 cover on Friday and Saturday. It's at 1910 Ala Moana Blvd. (tel. 941-5277) . . . A joint cover charge of $3 will gain you access to two of the town's newest, most progressive disco clubs. **Masquerade,** at the corner of Kalakaua and McCully (tel. 949-6337), boasts "the heaviest sound system in Hawaii," **Phaze,** at the corner of the Ala Wai Blvd. and McCully (tel. 941-8383), "Alternative-European"–style music . . . The staff of colorfully costumed characters at **Bobby McGee's Conglomeration** in the Colony East Hotel (tel. 922-1282), really attracts the guests. It's a lively spot also known for good food. There's a live DJ, a great sound system, and dancing until 2 a.m. . . . **Spats,** in the Hyatt Regency Hotel, is a handsome and immensely popular room, where you're likely to run into (or bump into) a big crowd on weekends.

There's a fancy feeling and dress code to match at **Rumours,** at the Ala Moana Hotel (tel. 955-4811), which features disco, musical videos, a light show complete with smoke, and a London DJ as backup. There's a game room, too, for the backgammon crowd. Disco is on from 9 p.m. to 3 a.m. weekdays, to 4 a.m. weekends; and they also offer ballroom dancing from 5 to 9 p.m. Sunday and Wednesday. During the Friday 5 to 9 p.m. Happy Hour, they play music from the late '60s and early '70s, which they call "The Big Chill" (no dress code during this time).

Then there's the **Shore Bird Bar** of the Reef Hotel (tel. 922-2887), which provides live entertainment from 4 to 8 p.m. and dancing to nonstop videos from 8 p.m. to 2 a.m. The Shore Bird is great for a broil-your-own meal and sunset right over the beach.

JUST DANCING: Remember the Big Band days of the '30s and '40s, when people actually did the fox trot, the tango, and the waltz? Well, they still do, thanks to the Royal Hawaiian Hotel Monarch Room's Monday afternoon Tea Dances. From 5:30 to 8 p.m., Del Courtney and the Royal Hawaiian Hotel Orchestra provide the sounds. You don't even need to order a drink; tea and coffee, as well as harder stuff, are available. Cover charge is $4 (tel. 923-7311).

ACCENT ON ENTERTAINMENT: Let us be perfectly honest. To see the top nightclub shows in Hawaii, you're going to have to break your budget—and then some. When a big name is entertaining, the local clubs usually impose a cover charge of a few dollars, plus a minimum of two drinks, which can swiftly add up to more than you'd think. On top of that many of them prefer to accommodate their dinner guests only—and dinner at these places is usually in the $25 to $40 and up bracket. However, for those times when you're willing to go all out, here's the information on the top names and places. Check the local tourist papers when you're in town for exact details; a top star might just happen to be on the mainland when you're in the islands, but somebody new and unknown might be making a smashing debut. Prices quoted here are subject to change.

We'd give up almost anything to catch a show by **The Brothers Cazimero,** featured entertainers at the Monarch Room of the Royal Hawaiian Hotel. They are beloved champions of authentic Hawaiian music and dance, and their songs, and the dances of their company, featuring the incredible Leina'ala, are truly from the heart of Hawaii. No need to spend $34 for the dinner show unless you want to, when the cocktail show is only $18.50. It's presented Tuesday through Saturday at 9 p.m. and again on Friday and Saturday at 11 p.m. Local people say this late show is the best one of all, a time when Robert and Roland "let their hair down" for a mostly local crowd. If The Brothers aren't in town, don't fret: the Monarch Room will have another top artist, perhaps songstress Emma Veary. Reservations: 923-7311.

Note: If you're in town on May 1, which is "Lei Day" in Hawaii, you'll get a chance to see The Brothers Cazimero for even less—$12.50—when they entertain in a giant outdoor production at the Waikiki Shell.

Don Ho, who is probably Hawaii's best known entertainer, seems to be permanently ensconced at the Hilton Hawaiian Village Dome Showroom. Don heads up an exciting Polynesian extravaganza, for which you'll have to pay $39 for adults, $25.50 for children, if you want dinner. It's still expensive—but more sensible—to come for the Friday or Sunday 10:30 p.m. cocktail show, which will set you back only $20 for adults, $15.75 for children, and includes a tropical drink, tips, and taxes. Reservations: 947-2607.

Again, try the cocktail show—it's yours for the price of two drinks plus an $8 cover—rather than spending $52 for the dinner show to see **Danny Kaleikini** at the Hala Terrace of the Kahala Hilton Hotel. Seating is at 8:45 p.m. nightly except Sunday. Danny is undoubtedly one of the islands' top entertainers, a brilliant musician who dances, sings, plays a variety of instruments (including the nose flute), and watches over a talented company of Hawaiian entertainers. The show is deliberately low-key and in excellent taste. Reservations: 734-2211.

Al Harrington, the "South Pacific Man," can always be counted on for an excellent show; he's an island favorite. You can catch him at the Polynesian Palace of the Reef Towers at $23 for adults, $15 for children at the cocktail shows, Sunday through Friday at 5:45 and 8:45 p.m. Should you want to dine, there's a sit-down dinner at 5 p.m., and a hot entree buffet at 8:30 p.m., each at $37 for adults, $20 for kids under 12. Reservations: 923-9861.

The show put on by the seven talented entertainers who call themselves the **Society of Seven** is just a little bit different: it's a history of popular music, from the 1950s up to today. Music, imitations, comedy routines, skits, are all a delight; this show is a perennial favorite. It's held at the Outrigger Waikiki Main Showroom at 8:30 and 10:30 p.m. nightly except Sunday (on Wednesdays, 8:30 p.m. show only). Dinner will cost you $33.50 for adults, $25 for those under 12. Or, come for the cocktail show, which, at $18 for adults, $11.50 for children, includes tax, tip, and either two standard drinks or a cocktail. Students 13 to 20 years old may attend the cocktail show for $13.50. Reservations: 922-6408 or 923-0711.

There are several good Polynesian shows on the beach, but one of the most consistently well received is the **Moana Hotel Polynesian Revue,** which takes place out under the stars in the hotel's Banyan Court. Although the tab is $38.50 for grownups, $25 for kids (free under age 4), the value is excellent: an hour-and-a-half-long authentic Polynesian show, an excellent prime rib buffet, and one drink. Buffet seating is at 5:15 and 7:45 p.m. Or have just cocktails and see the show at $19.50 for adults, $13.50 for children. Reservations: 923-9826.

It will cost you $17 to see another long-running Polynesian spectacular: that's **Kalo's South Seas Revue** at the Hawaiian Hut of the Ala Moana Hotel. This price entitles you to watch the show and have one drink: if you want to feast on a lavish prime-rib buffet beforehand, the cost is $29.50. Reservations: 941-5205.

Although a lot of his material is local, **Frank De Lima,** who plays at the Noodle Shop, seems to be adored by both islanders and tourists alike. Frank is a musical comedian rather than a standup comic, and he uses the guys in his back-up group (who are also very funny) in his zany song parodies and skits. Frank is not smutty, just crazy, so you can feel perfectly comfortable bringing older children. His show is on Wednesday through Sunday at 9:30 p.m., with sometimes an 11 p.m. show, depending on the crowd. There is a two-drink minimum (beer and wine at $2.75, mixed drinks for $3), plus a $4 cover.

Praise be for small favors. There still are places that levy no cover or minimum charges where you can watch the show for the price of a few drinks. One of our favorites among these is the **Blue Dolphin Room,** a cozy place with a turn-of-the-century atmosphere, poolside at the Outrigger Hotel. Sometimes you can catch standing, old-style Hawaiian entertainment here. During the show, from 10 p.m. to midnight, beer is $2, mixed drinks from $2.50; exotics are $4. All meals are served here, indoors and outdoors, right beside the sands of Waikiki beach.

Again, you need only pay the price of the drinks when you go to hear **Herb Ohta,** who sometimes plays at the Colony Lounge of the Hyatt Regency Hotel. And go you should—Herb is a true virtuoso, and his touch is uncanny.

Traditional Bavarian biergartens in Waikiki? Of course! Waikiki now has two of them. Newest is the **Bavarian Beer Garden** on the top floor of the Royal Hawaiian Shopping Center, with Waikiki's biggest dance floor. Hubert Haneman and his five-piece band play polkas, waltzes, and the like from 5 p.m. to 1 a.m. every day, and there's inexpensive German food. No cover, but a $5 minimum after 8 p.m. Long on the Waikiki scene is the **Hofbräu** in the International Market Place. Between the omm-pah-pah band's sets, the waitresses, in authentic costumes, dance polkas with the customers. Food and drinks are inexpensive, and there is no cover or minimum.

Michael W. Perry and Larry Price, Honolulu's top-rated morning-drive radio personalities, do their radio show live every Saturday from the **Hanohano Room** of the Sheraton Waikiki Hotel, beginning at 8 a.m. They have lots of guest stars and give away prizes. Breakfast features eggs Benedict or blueberry pancakes, and the tab is $10.95 per person. Reservations (tel. 922-4422) are a must.

READERS' RESTAURANT AND NIGHTLIFE SELECTIONS: "One of our favorite Friday afternoon pastimes is to sip cocktails at **Harry's Bar,** by the atrium fountain of the Hyatt Regency Waikiki, while watching Auntie Malia Solomon's 'Pau Hana' show, complete with hula dancers and the mellow singing voice of Joe Ah Quinn. 'Pau Hana'—literally, work's finished—is the local equivalent of T.G.I.F. and the show starts at 5 p.m. There is no cover or minimum" (Leilani Moyers, Patterson, N.Y.). [*Authors' Note:* Check local papers when you arrive to see if this show is on when you're there.] . . . "I went back several times to the **Perry's Smorgy** at 2380 Kuhio Ave. for the breakfast buffet. What a feast for $3.95! Breakfast included fresh papaya and pineapple, grapefruit, bananas, stewed prunes, applesauce, bananas rolled in coconut, sausage, eggs, bacon, french toast, pancakes. A very mild ham was being sliced off the bone right in front of you. There was fresh Kona coffee, urns filled with orange juice and pineapple juice, three kinds of sodas, and three kinds of donuts. And the tropical decor was beautiful. The Perry's dinner I had at the Outrigger Waikiki, overlooking the sunset, was also great. . . . If you're driving out to Kailua, have a meal at **Someplace Else,** 33 Aulike St. (tel. 273-8833). They have reasonable pastas, chicken, and broiler items, a few Mexican dishes. And the decor is so pretty, with lots of greenery, and a few tables outside under the umbrellas" (Marietta Chicorel, New York, N.Y.).

"One of the few high quality fast-food eateries in Waikiki is the **Jack-in-the-Box** restaurant next door to the Waikiki Grand Hotel on Kapahulu. Here the customer can have his choice of window booth dining with views of the Honolulu Zoo across the street, sitting at one of the tables in back facing a pool and courtyard, or simply ordering 'to go.' This establishment is efficiently co-managed by a former Chicago insurance agent with personality plus who, with his staff, knocks himself out to provide swift service and food satisfaction to all. Highly recommended, among the many fine budget offerings which include hamburgers, chicken, steak sandwiches, and shrimp, are the various Breakfast Crescents stuffed with combinations of bacon, eggs, ham, and cheeses, all under $2. Another standout is the very tasty Pizza Pocket, a substantial mixture of pizza meats, veggies, and Spanish olives wrapped in thick pita for only $1.99. This spot deserves recognition!" (Connie Tonken, Hartford, Conn.).

"The **Hau Tree Gang,** a group of locals and seniors, meets from 1 to 4 p.m. on weekdays, under the Hau tree in front of the Reef Hotel, on the beach, and they put on an interesting musical show. . . . **Kapahulu Chop Suey,** on Kapahulu, is a popular 'local' place with good, inexpensive Chinese food. . . . **Fog Cutters** in Makaha is a good, reasonable place for lunch when you're up on the Leeward Coast, but steer clear of fancy drinks like mai tais, as they are $4.25" (Dorothy Astman, Levittown, N.Y.). . . . "The **Pizza Parlor** in the Rainbow Bazaar of the Hilton Hawaiian Village served a delicious cheeseburger with the works for $3. A side of coleslaw, which was shared since the portion was so large, was 75¢. Delicious" (Alice Christaldi, Lindenwold, N.J.). . . . "**Kamaina Suite** at the Willows, 901 Hausten St., tel. 946-4804, was superb. It charges a fixed price for each person, and wine and drinks are extra. The price is something like $42. With tax and tip, it's virtually impossible to get out for under $100—but it's worth it. In fact, this restaurant may well be worth the trip to Hawaii, all by itself. We will definitely return to Oahu if only to experience Kamaina Suite again" (Barbara Bazemore and Dave Butenhof, Hudson, N.M.). . . . "As vegetarians, we especially like the Chinese restaurant, **Five Spices,** which had a lot for us to choose from; especially good was the dynamite eggplant in Szechuan hot sauce. . . . We also recommend **Galaxy Juiceworks** in Haleiwa, which serves first-rate fruit smoothies for $2 to $2.50, and vegetarian specials like veggie tamales" (Will Ernst, Federal City, Wash.). [*Authors' Note:* See review of Five Spices in text.]

"Eating in Hawaii can be lots of fun, whether at the local restaurants or in your condo. One could have a gourmet/gourmand tour of the Pacific Rim in Hawaii alone. If you're trying sushi (which is not raw fish; raw fish is sashimi), watch out for that little pile of green stuff. That's not a decoration: that's *real* horseradish. Danger, beware, mix it with a little soy sauce before tasting. That pink leafy stuff on the plate, sometimes arranged in the form of a rose, is pickled ginger, and is refreshing between different types of food" (Roz and Jim Morino, Colma, Calif.).

"We recently visited Waimea Falls and found ourselves past lunchtime and hungry. A lengthy search for a decent place to eat produced only a couple of 'greasy spoons' and two places we walked out on (a rarity for us) when we saw the ridiculous prices on their menus. Then we found a gem—**Rosie's Cantina** in the Haleiwa Shopping Center, right at the highway. The mental image created by the name was quickly dispelled when we went inside and found a light, airy, spotlessly clean café with attractive decor. The menu was surprisingly varied and prices were modest. Best of all, the food was absolutely top-notch" (Walter and Pat Rector, Penn Valley, Calif.).

"The **Super Chef** is a new restaurant at 2424 Koa Ave., right behind the Hyatt Regency Hotel and next to King's Village (tel. 926-7199). The owner is Robert Chou, who also owns the Won Kee Restaurants in the Aloha Surf Hotel and downtown Honolulu. At the time of our visit, Super Chef was running two-for-one dinners. We had a choice of rack of lamb or Châteaubriand at $15.95 for two. They also had a lobster and filet mignon dinner for only $9.95, with complimentary hors d'oeuvres. This place has a nice atmosphere. From many of its tables, you can watch the chef working at the grill. . . . The **Beachcomber Hotel** at 2300 Kalakaua Ave., serves a very nice prime-rib buffet for only $8.95 before 6 p.m., in an attractive new dining room. Italian chicken, mahimahi, and salad bar are also included. . . . **Lam's** Chinese restaurant on Kapaulu Ave., across from the zoo, served the best shrimp chow mein I've ever eaten, for only $5.75, and there were plenty of luscious shrimp. . . . The Crazy Austrian Band at the **Hofbräu** in the International Market Place provides two hours of wild entertainment and dance music while you enjoy the very good German food. We like the smoked pork chops with sauerkraut and potatoes for $6.95. . . . Not only does the **Pizza Hut** on Kuhio Avenue, next to Kuhio Mall, serve good pizza, but it has a delicious spaghetti and meat sauce platter with hot garlic bread for only $2.95 at lunch and dinner" (Dr. John Lopresti, Jr., Bricktown, N.J.).

"We stayed at the **Turtle Bay Hilton** which is a wonderful hotel. For lunch one day we had their buffet at $8.50. The selections were varied and delicious, and especially nice was their scrumptious dessert bar with out-of-this world cakes and tarts. . . . We also stopped at a little restaurant called **D'Amicos** in Sunset Beach. The facade was not very impressive, but the pizza was very good and they make the most delicious homemade ice cream cookie sandwiches. It's worth a stop for this special treat" (Eloise Weissbach, Hauppauge, N.Y.). . . . "For **coupons** and **bargains** intended for Honolulu residents—not us tourists —pick up the *Sunday Star Bulletin and Advertiser.* You will find coupons that do not appear in the throwaways at the corner of every Waikiki street. . . . Singles may feel alone on a sunset sail, but not on the **Leahi Catamaran Sunset Mai Tai Sail.** The green-sailed catamaran is docked at the Sheraton Waikiki Hotel, and leaves at 5 p.m. every day for a 1½-hour sail. Drink as many mai tais as you want. I stopped counting after *ten.* There's live music on board, a hostess, and the captain even had pupus the night I sailed. The price: around $18. During the day, there are one-hour sails, without drinks, for $9. . . . For a late-night date with an ocean view, try the lounge on the upper lobby of the **Outrigger.** Sit at a table for two on the lanai, overlooking the beach, and order a $10 drink for two, served with two very long straws. It will make you feel warm, tingly, and tipsy" (Robert Pray, Los Angeles, Calif.).

"Even though we stayed at the Hilton, we kept our food budget under $10 a day with no problem, eating very well indeed. To do this, you have to buy groceries for breakfast, and sometimes a light lunch, in your room. Our groceries averaged $10 a person per week. We are not big eaters in the morning, so we just bought muffins, sweet rolls, cereal, fruit, milk and orange juice. From home we brought coffee, packets of sugar, paper bowls and plates, and plastic utensils. **The Pâtisserie,** in the Edgewater Hotel on Beach Walk, sells muffins, rolls, and bread at half price when they are one day old. These keep very well for three or four days. Also, **King's Bakery** on Hobron Lane has excellent bran muffins and delicious Hawaiian sweet bread that keep very well for days" (Karen and Joan Polsen, Halifax, Nova Scotia, Canada).

"One of the highlights of our stay was the **Windjammer Cruise.** It consists of a 2½-hour sail, from 5:15 to 7:45 p.m., aboard the *Rella Mae,* Hawaii's largest sailing vessel. The price of $39 per person includes transportation from major Waikiki hotels to the *Rella Mae* and back, open bar, a delicious, seated dinner, terrific revue dinner show, and dancing to an exciting live band. We were amazed at how well organized the whole operation was and how gracious, helpful, and cheerful all the crew were. It was a real fun trip from beginning to end. We highly recommend the Windjammer Cruises, 2222 Kalakaua Ave., Suite 600, Honolulu, HI 96815 (tel. 521-0036 or toll free 800/367-5000)" (Mr. and Mrs. Norm Johnson, Ontario, Calif.). [*Authors' Note:* Windjammer Cruises also offers a moonlight cruise from 8:30 to 11 nightly that can be bought as a dinner-and-cocktail sail or a cocktail sail only. Tickets are $39 per person for dinner and cocktails, or $25 for cocktails only. Prices do not include tax.] . . . "Be careful with **outdoor buffets** in the hot weather. They seem to be worth the money in terms of quality, but we got food poisoning at one of the 'better hotel' buffets" (Pat Connor, Arlington, Mass.). . . . **"New Tokyo Restaurant** on Beach Walk near Kalakaua Ave. serves authentic, really good Japanese dishes at moderate price. On a typical hot day, try cold buckwheat noodles with tempura, called 'tenzaru' ($5.95); it is so refreshing. They also serve sushi, cutlet, teriyaki, etc. Above all, the service is very good, and the waitresses are very helpful and friendly" (M. Komoto, San Francisco, Calif.).

"Waioli Tea Room was exactly as mentioned—delightful—and one of the fun things to do is to watch the almost constant weddings going on in the little chapel. Apparently, package tours are sold in Japan, including a traditional church wedding, music, pictures, videotaping the ceremony, honeymoon, etc. The only people present at the ceremony we observed were the minister, his wife, and the photographer. However, the bride and groom were in traditional formal attire and we found ourselves wanting to wave as they were leaving the chapel. We saved **The Willows,** 901 Hausten St., for our last night in the islands and what a perfect choice. It was expensive—$50 with wine, tax, tip, etc., but worth every cent of it. The atmosphere outside is incredible; the three-piece ensemble playing 'Hawaii City Lights' reduced me to tears. The food was superior, as was the service; all in all, a must" (Sheila Pritchett, Villanova, Pa.). . . . [*Authors' Note:* The Willows is one of the islands' most gracious "Old Hawaii" restaurants, situated on a beautiful pond amid the garden surroundings. Try it for a big-splurge meal; at dinner, most à la carte entrees are in the $15 to $20 range; a complete dinner is around $30. Call 946-4808 for reservations.]

"For great decor with your meals, try the Chinese and Japanese restaurants in Waikiki; they are all authentic. We were warned against going into the Chinatown area at night because of the thefts. Please inform your readers that it is not a safe place after dark" (Barbara Smith, Winnipeg, Manitoba, Canada). . . . "For breakfast, you cannot do better than **Wendy's Old-Fashioned Hamburgers,** a chain with half-a-dozen restaurants listed in the Oahu telephone directory. The place where I ate is at 2310 Kuhio Ave. All their food is good, but the French toast was a particular treat, with a generous portion of butter or syrup and a second helping for the asking" (T.S. Holman, Clifton, N.J.) . . . "The **Reef Broiler,** the **Pagoda Restaurant, Victoria Station,** and **Chuck's** all have marvelous salad bars—all you can eat in a beautiful atmosphere. **Victoria Station I** and **Sizzler Steak, Seafood, Salad** have no smoking—a real blessing not to have someone blowing smoke in your face" (Mr. and Mrs. Michael F. Henely, Honolulu, Hi.).

"Our hint: We took from home silverware, paring knife, can opener, two-cup coffee pot, and the makings for morning coffee. Every one of our hotel rooms had a small refrigerator. We bought orange juice, papaya, danish, whatever, and had breakfast on our lanai each morning before leaving. Many days we stopped in the grocery store and got sandwich fixings, canned iced tea, and fruit, and had a picnic on the beach. We not only saved money, but time as well. Many days we saw the tourists lined up at the coffeeshops trying to have breakfast before catching a tour bus" (Mary Lou and Davie Bregitzer, Cleveland, Ohio). . . . "When you cannot get a hotel with a kitchenette, take along the following equipment, which will fit right in with your clothes in the suitcase: a four-cup percolator or hotpot; an eight-inch electric frying pan; one pancake turner; one sharp paring knife; plastic or stainless-steel cutlery; coffee mugs; a plastic pot scraper; paper plates; two or more plastic margarine dishes to use for soup, cereal, salad, or dessert dishes; salt and pepper shakers. With these utensils I cooked up some really adequate meals. The little frypan holds four eggs at a time, and if you cut bacon strips in two, you can fry up a good panful. Two small steaks can be cooked, and then add and cook some frozen vegetables in a bit of water, and you have a meal in a dish. The little hotpot is for beverages as well as instant soup or porridge. One night I cooked an exotic creamed shrimp and hot rice dish by buying frozen 'boil in a bag' food. The extra plastic trays used for the meat become service trays, etc. It is a challenge to cook up imaginative meals and it can be done!" (Mrs. Margaret Springett, Moose Jaw, Saskatchewan, Canada). . . . "If you're going to be doing some cooking, save your pill bottles, remove the prescription labels, and fill them with all the spices you will need (salt, garlic salt, pepper, etc.), and label the containers. These take very little room and won't break" (Mrs. I. Hodgeman, Bloomington, Minn.).

"We went to see **'This is Polynesia'** at the Polynesian Cultural Center, and as far as I am concerned, it was the best thing I saw in Hawaii. The sound effects and scenery were fantastic, as were all the dancers. My children loved the fire dancers the best, especially when they sat on the fire mats in their grass skirts! The show is worth every penny you spend on it" (Ruth E. Dishnow, Wasila, Alaska). . . . "I recommend **Eggs 'n' Things,** which is in the heart of town. They have a special $1.49 breakfast, which is delicious. They are open from 5 to 9 a.m. and 1 to 2 p.m., and are friendly, polite, and busy" (Ricky A. Blum, Los Angeles, Calif.). [*Authors' Note:* Eggs 'n' Things is at 436 Ena Rd., and an old favorite. Each year we get more letters of praise for it!] . . . "For readers who may be staying in or near the downtown area, here are some suggestions. **McDonald's** serves Portuguese sausage with rice and eggs for breakfast at the Fort Street Mall branch, as well as the usual choices. You can walk across the street to **Woolworth's** and get baked goods or a wide variety of prepared ethnic foods. Try the bread pudding at Woolworth's if they have it that day. Sit on the bench on the mall and watch the little birds circle you, watching for food" (Mark Terry, Alameda, Calif.).

"Here are some ideas that have worked beautifully on our Hawaii trips and have saved us well over $100 on breakfasts alone. (1) Buy one of those small Styrofoam beer coolers, put in a few cubes of ice, and you have a refrigerator you can use in your room, or take with you on day trips, to keep your milk, butter, sandwich meat, etc., fresh and sweet. It can be easily carried from one island to another too. (2) On King Street in Honolulu, **King's Bakery** makes a Hawaiian sweet bread that has the unique quality of not drying out even after being cut. The taste is delicious, something like a sweet roll, and it will keep fresh in your room for days. (3) In the islands, orange juice comes in a quart glass 'milk' bottle. Fill this almost full of cold water, put in a few spoonfuls of instant coffee, insert one of those pigtail immersion heaters (made for heating liquid in a cup and available in most variety stores), using a clothes pin to stop it from going too far down, plug in, and voilà!—a quart of excellent coffee in about five minutes" (Sheldon Myers, Berkeley, Calif.).

Chapter IV

TRANSPORTATION WITHIN HONOLULU

From Buses to Cars to Rickshaws

IN THE CHAPTERS immediately following we'll discuss the sightseeing and activities of Honolulu and its suburbs. In this chapter, we deal with the cheapest ways to get to those activities and see those sights.

So many people think it's difficult to get around the islands that they succumb in advance to those package deals that wrap up your whole vacation in advance: transportation, hotels, sightseeing from the limousine window, all for one flat—and unnecessarily high—fee. And even if they've already discovered the do-it-yourself trick of staying at budget hotels and eating at low-cost restaurants, panic strikes when it comes to sightseeing—and how else to "do" Honolulu unless someone takes you by the hand on a guided tour?

Tours are okay, of course, pleasant and useful if you have only a day or two and want to pack in as many sights as you can. And you may want to take one (or else rent a car) when you circle the island of Oahu (see "Guided Tours," below). But for sightseeing in Honolulu, at your own pace, there's a method that's much cheaper, and much more fun—

THE BUSES: We refer, of course, to the MTL buses (known as TheBUS) owned by the City and County of Honolulu and operated under contract by the private firm of MTL, Inc. MTL has routes all over the island, which gives you a chance to mingle with the island's nontourist population. (You'll really feel like a kamaaina when someone asks you how to get to a certain place!) The friendliness of the Hawaiian drivers too will be quite an experience, especially if you come from an overcrowded city on the mainland where every passenger is a potential enemy. In a bus dispute some years ago, the drivers figured out a novel way to show their dissatisfaction with the company: they just refused to collect fares from the passengers!

But don't count on that. You'll pay 60¢ for a ride on TheBUS. Exact change in coins is required. Children pay 25¢. Free transfers, which can extend your ride considerably in one direction, must be requested when you board and pay your fare.

Bus schedules are not, unfortunately, available on the buses themselves, but if you have any questions about how to get where, simply call TheBUS information number at 531-1611. A free brochure, "Hawaii Visitors Guide to The-BUS," is very helpful. Keep in mind that the buses you will take from Waikiki to Ala Moana Shopping Center or to downtown Honolulu must be boarded on Kuhio Avenue; buses on Kalakaua go only in a Diamond Head direction.

Note: Senior citizens (65 or over) may ride free on the buses at all times. Appropriate proof of age (driver's license, or birth certificate, or passport, or baptismal certificate with seal), is required, and processing of passes takes three to four weeks. Apply at the MTL office, 725 Kapiolani Blvd.

If you're staying in Honolulu and doing extensive bus riding for any length of time, it may pay for you to buy a monthly pass. They cost $15 for adults, $7.50 for youths up to high school age (generally considered 19 or younger). Bus passes are available from the 20th of the month preceding the month in which they are valid to the 19th of the month in which they are valid. They are available at TheBUSPass Office at 725 Kapiolani, at the Manoa Campus Center of the University of Hawaii, at Foodland and Emjay Supermarkets, Satellite City Halls, and at Pioneer Savings Bank. All purchases must be made in cash: checks or credit cards are not accepted. Fares are subject to change.

RENTING A CAR: This alternative to the buses is more expensive, of course, but it's awfully nice to have a car at your disposal. And you can save money on meals by driving to inexpensive restaurants or drive-ins outside the tourist area. If you do decide on one, you'll have your choice of just about any type of vehicle, foreign or domestic, from the numerous U-Drive agencies in town. The most inexpensive cars are Gala Jeeps and foreign compacts like the Datsun, both with manual shifts; if you want an automatic shift, you'll have to pay about $2 to $3 more. Prices are also higher for standard-size cars. And rates are always higher—as much as $5 or $10—in the busy winter season than in summer. As for the car-rental agencies themselves, they are very much in competition for your business, and since rates are constantly changing and new attractive deals are offered all the time, a little comparison shopping at the time of your arrival will pay big dividends. We'll give you the names of the top budget companies and their rates as of this writing, and we'll pass on the warning they gave to us: "Rates are subject to change at any time without notice." Most of the companies offer flat rates with unlimited free mileage.

All-Island Rentals

If you're going to visit several of the major islands, the easiest way to rent your cars is to make one telephone call to a company that provides service on all of them. Give **Alamo Rent-A-Car** a call and find out if they're offering one of their "Sun Sale" specials if you're traveling in the winter. They often offer a good deal on an economy two-door Chevy Chevette; last year it was $21.99 per day, $79.99 per week. Regular rates are about $27.99 per day, $97.99 per week for an air-conditioned, automatic, economy car, all with unlimited free mileage. Alamo is in Honolulu, Waikiki, Maui, Hilo, Kona, and Lihue (cars at airport terminals in neighbor islands, courtesy bus in Honolulu). Call Alamo toll-free at 800/327-9633, 24 hours a day. If you're already in town, local phone numbers are 924-4444 in Waikiki (142 Uluniu Ave.), and 833-4585 at the airport (3055 Nimitz Highway). Certain restrictions apply, including age and credit card requirements. Rates do not include gas, tax, or a nominal under-25 surcharge.

With a fleet of over 7,000 cars, **Budget Rent-A-Car** the well-known mainland and international car-rental agency, offers a vehicle for every taste and pocketbook. Compact, sedan, Jeep, Mercedes, Lincoln Town Car, you name it. Since rates fluctuate so much, Budget does not care to quote them, but you can be sure that they are always competitive. Free coupon books chockfull of free admission to Hawaii's major visitor attractions, free meals, and free gifts are given to all renters. There are offices at 2379 Kuhio Ave. in Waikiki, plus many Waikiki branches (tel. 922-3600). There are locations at Honolulu and neighbor island airports, and also on Maui, Kauai, Molokai, and the Big Island at a number of places. For reservations, call toll free 800/527-0700, or write Budget Rent-A-Car of Hawaii, Central Reservations, P.O. Box 15188, Honolulu, HI 96830-0188.

Friendly service and good deals are available at **Tropical Rent-A-Car Systems,** 550 Paiea St. (tel. 836-1041). They offer flat rates only (no mileage charges), compacts for as low as $22.95 a day, $139 per week; air-conditioned cars for $23 a day, $149 a week. They also have station wagons. Tropical has offices on all the neighbor islands, and rents to drivers 25 to 70 only, and not to campers. Tropical has two offices in Waikiki (call 949-2002) and a toll-free reservation number: 800/367-5140. Tropical can pick you up at all the airports; call them on the courtesy phones when you arrive in the baggage claim area. Rates are subject to change.

A variety of good deals are available from **Traveler's Rent-A-Car** of Hawaii, which is one of the fastest growing car rental companies in the state. It services all major islands and offers their standard transmission cars—Toyota, Datsun, Chevrolet, and Ford—for as little as $12.95 a day, $95 weekly; these cars with automatic transmission are as little as $14.95 a day, $109 weekly. Written reservations should be sent to their Central Reservations Office at 2880 Ualena St., Honolulu, HI 96819 (tel. 833-3355). They do not have airport space at Honolulu International Airport (they do at all other airports), but they'll pick you up when you arrive and take you to their offices two blocks away.

Dollar Rent-A-Car of Hawaii is another enterprising outfit. They have numerous locations on the five major islands (including 12 in Honolulu alone, five in Maui), and offer flat rates. For their compact cars with standard transmission, it's $24.95 daily, $149.95 weekly; compact deluxe automatics go for $25.95 daily, $154.95 weekly. They will rent to drivers over age 21 who have a major credit card. The local reservations number is 926-4200. For toll-free reservations, phone 800/367-7006.

National Car Rental of Hawaii, 3001 Nimitz Hwy. (tel. 834-7156), has convenient locations at the airports on Oahu, Hawaii, Kauai, and Maui, and offers competitive unlimited-mileage rates for all types of cars, including station wagons, convertibles, sports cars, and vans. The toll-free number is 800/CAR-RENT.

Thrifty Rent-A-Car has locations on Oahu, Maui, and Kauai (but not on Hawaii). They have direct-line courtesy phones at all baggage-claim areas. Usually, standard compacts rent for $21.99 daily, $109 weekly. New models, no mileage charge. Call 833-0046 in Honolulu for reservations, or write to them at 3039 Ualena St., Honolulu, HI 96819.

United Car Rental, 234 Beach Walk (tel. 922-4605), rents cars on three major islands (it is right at the airports at Maui, Kauai, and Kona) and offers attractive rates on its fleet of late-model cars, from compacts to Cadillacs, vans, and Jeeps. Compact standards are $18.95 daily (sometimes they will go lower), $113.70 weekly; automatic compacts are $21.95 daily, $131.70 weekly.

Avis Rent-A-Car, Honolulu International Airport (tel. 834-5564), serves all five major islands, and offers a special for seven days of driving an automatic Chevy, Chevette, or similar car on a combination of two or more islands—about $198 a week. *Note:* Avis will rent to 18-year-olds who have a major credit card. For toll-free reservations, phone 800/331-1212.

Hertz Rent-A-Car, 233 Keawe St., Room 625 (tel. 523-5181), features an

All-Island touring rate that covers seven days or more on any combination of the four major islands. Days do not have to be consecutive and there is no mileage charge. The seven-day rate starts at $140 for a stick-shift car, or $25.99 for one day. Daily rates offer free unlimited mileage. For toll-free reservations and information, call 800/654-8200; in Honolulu, 836-2511. Hertz has offices at airports and hotels on all the major islands.

Honolulu and Maui Only

V.I.P. Car Rentals, 2025 Kalakaua Ave., Honolulu, HI 96815 (tel. 946-1671), has been offering consistently low rates for a number of years; we've had good readers' feedback on them. A standard compact rents for $14.95 daily, $98 weekly; an automatic compact is $16.95 a day, $110 weekly. Minimum age is 21.

Honolulu Only

If you don't mind not driving the newest models, you'll be able to save a few dollars at **Maxi Experienced Cars,** 413 Seaside Ave., Honolulu, HI 96815 (tel. 923-7381). Their fleet has had a bit of experience—cars are a few years old —but they rent them for just $12.77 a day, and most of these are automatics. Maxi will also rent to 18-year-olds, who usually must pay $18 to $22 (no credit card needed).

There's a local franchise of the nationwide **Ugly Duckling Rent-A-Car** company in town, at 1152 Waimanu St., Honolulu, HI 96814 (tel. 538-3825), and it's offering some terrific deals in well-cared-for, used cars. If you choose from their "Fleet C," you can get a standard economic Chevrolet Sprint for $9.95 per day, $62.95 per week; an economy, automatic, air-conditioned Dodge Colt for $12.95 per day, $81.60 per week; a compact, automatic, air-conditioned Chevrolet Spectrum for $15.95 per day, $100.50 per week, etc., up into higher-priced models. "Fleet B" starts at $16.95 per day; "Fleet A" at $22.95 per day for similar cars, newer models. Ugly Duckling rents to drivers at least 21 years old. For toll-free reservations, phone 800/843-3825.

General Notes

Remember that automatic-shift cars always cost more than the standards and that there's a state tax of 4% added to all charges. Check, too, whether your rental charges include insurance and if so how much. Insurance should include public liability, property damage, fire, theft, and collision (usually $100 deductible, although many companies have much higher deductibles). If you carry insurance on your car at home, you might want to use your own insurance coverage for the rented car; this is sensible if your policy provides higher limits and if your company can furnish fast claim service in the islands. Using your own insurance can save you as much as $5 to $10 per day on rental charges. It would be a good idea to obtain the name of your company's local claim representative in Hawaii before you come; also, bring your policy or identification card if you plan to do this.

You can arrange to have the car delivered to your hotel and picked up when you're finished with it. Usually, though, most people pick up and return their cars at the airport. A further tip: Since cars may not get regular servicing during the busy season, it would be a good idea to give yours a test run of a few hundred yards before the agency representative leaves you. They've been known to have quirks.

Also, it's a good idea to jot down the mileage on your car before you start out with it and just before you return it to the rental agency. This is a useful check on mileage charges.

And a final, important, word of warning. Don't be misled by those companies that offer cars for "$1 a day." Add to that mileage charges, plus a *50-mile daily minimum,* plus the cost of gas and insurance, and you're paying as much, probably more, than you would at the other agencies.

Advice for Younger Drivers

In the course of the years this book has been published, we have occasionally received letters from young readers who have had trouble renting cars in the islands. We have checked into the situation, and have come up with the following findings. Hawaii state law prohibits anyone under 18 from driving with an out-of-state license (even though islanders can get licenses at 15!). As far as we know, there are only two agencies willing to rent to those 18 to 20: **Hertz** and **Maxi Experienced Cars,** both mentioned above. Maxi's regular rates are $12.77 a day; 18-year-olds do not need a credit card, but they will have to pay $18 to $22. At Hertz, a major credit card is necessary, and there is usually a daily charge for overall collision insurance. The same conditions apply to those under 25. There may be special stipulations for 21- to 24-year-olds. When you reach 25, of course, you can just sign the papers anywhere and drive away.

RENTING CAMPERS AND TRAILERS: If you're used to camping out on your vacation, you can do it in Hawaii as well. It's a good way to save money on both car rentals and hotel rooms, not to mention the pleasure of cooking your own meals just a stone's throw from the beach, and getting to know the local people in a way that few other tourists do. The camping areas on Hawaii's beaches and mountains are truly lovely, and immensely popular. All of the campers come fully equipped with good beds, pillows, blankets, pots and pans, stove, refrigerator or icebox; more deluxe models come with toilets and showers. You provide the gas. The best budget choice here would be **Beach Boy Campers** (Beach Boy Mobile Holidays), which serves only Oahu. They have five mini-motorhomes, all with shower-toilet, refrigerator, and furnishings, from $50 to $70 per day. They service their clients seven days a week except on Christmas, New Year's Day, and Thanksgiving. The price includes linens, dishes, and cookware. Collision insurance is $250 deductible.

The other major camping outfit is **Travel/Camp,** P.O. Box 11, Hilo, HI 96720 (tel. in Hilo: 935-7406). The oldest camper company in the business but serving only the Big Island, Travel/Camp rents only motor homes, from economy class to deluxe. They are fully furnished and contain propane stoves, ovens, refrigerators, johns, hot-water showers, etc. Excellent U-Drive camper-oriented maps and complete itineraries are provided. Prices go from $47 to $94 per day (plus mileage), $68 to $115 per day (with 100 free miles), $335 to $576 a week, with 500 free miles, for up to five sleepers, depending on the size of the vehicle. The rental center is at 1266 Kamehameha Ave. in Hilo.

Note: See Readers' Suggestions in Chapter X for more details.

WAIKIKI TROLLEY: It's cheaper than your own car, more expensive than The-Bus. But the new Waikiki Trolley service presents an entertaining alternative means for getting around the busiest tourist areas. **E Noa Tours** runs two quaint-looking motorized trolleys that recall the spirit of turn-of-the-century Honolulu. From 8:45 a.m. to 11:45 p.m., they ply the route between Diamond Head Waikiki and the Ala Moana Shopping Center, making 29 scheduled stops en route, the driver all the while pointing out places of interest and presenting a painless lesson in Hawaiian history. If you buy a $5 all-day pass, you can hop on and off as much as you like. One-way fare is $2; children 11 and under, $1. Phone 941-6608 for routes and schedules.

BIKING AROUND: Honolulu, like big cities everywhere, has become very cycle conscious. Bicycles used to be available for rental at a number of locations, but lately most of the hotels and rental agencies (like Hertz) have stopped renting them because of the high equipment mortality rate. "We kept finding them in the ocean," said one supplier. But we did find *one* place where they can still be rented: **Aloha Funway Rentals**, at 1982 Kalakaua Ave. (tel. 942-9696), offers them from $10 to $15 per 24-hour day; they also have tandems, Mopeds, and motorcycles, as well as snorkel equipment and boogie boards.

SKATING AROUND: Roller skating is no longer a big fad here, but should you get the urge, you can rent a pair from the above-mentioned **Aloha Funway Rentals** for moderate fees—$5 for 24 hours.

RICKSHAWS: Here's a novel—if not exactly inexpensive—way to get around Waikiki! Two pedicab companies—**Felicity and Paradise**—have a number of them traveling on Kuhio and Kalakaua Avenues and connecting streets, between the Hawaiian Village Hotel and the Colony Surf Hotel (which covers a good part of the main part of Waikiki). Each pedicab driver is an independent contractor and may charge passengers as he pleases. The ones we talked with asked $10 for 15 minutes, but they love to haggle and, if business is slow (as it often is due to the large proliferation of pedicabs), you can ride for much less. Just be sure that you and the driver agree on price and distance before you hop in. The young people who sit on the bicycle seats and pedal you around, incidentally, all appear to be in excellent physical condition, tanned and handsome—making rickshaw drivers, unlike their counterparts in the Orient, altogether Hawaiian.

TAXIS: Good news! It's now very easy to get a cab in Waikiki. Simply step out into any major thoroughfare, lift your hand to signal, and within five minutes, you'll undoubtedly be on your way. Although they are not cheap (the first flip of the meter is usually $1.40), taxis are useful for emergencies and for short trips, and could be practical if a few of you are traveling together. If you want to call a cab in advance, your hotel desk can usually get one for you, or you can call any of the numerous companies listed in the telephone book.
    Here are the telephone numbers of a few taxi companies:
    Charley's Taxi—531-1333
    Aloha State Cab—847-3566
    Sida of Hawaii—836-0011

GUIDED TOURS: If you're traveling alone, you'll have to invest about $25 (maybe more) for a guided tour around the island of Oahu. But if there are at least two of you, renting a car slices the per-person expense considerably. Even more cheaply, you can travel almost all the way around the island of Oahu for a mere $1.20 in bus fare (details in Chapter VII). And economics aside, we believe there is no travel thrill like that of a do-it-yourself exploration of a new part of the world, where you make your own discoveries at your own pace, free to follow the intriguing bypaths that don't always appear on a planned itinerary. Best of all, you can throw your lunch and bathing suit in the back seat for a picnic or swim whenever you feel like it.

ADVICE FOR DRIVERS: A few words about driving in Honolulu. First of all, there's a remarkable extension of the aloha spirit to pedestrians, who are often considered fair game elsewhere in the world. The custom dates back to an old law from the days of the Hawaiian monarchy when the pedestrian had the right to lie down in the street. We doubt if you'll see anyone doing that, but traffic does stop for pedestrians crossing the street, provided they stick to the lights and the painted crosswalks at intersections and, of necessity, even if they don't. However, progress is catching up with the islands, and as it does, traffic—and manners—can get almost as bad as in the big mainland cities. But not quite—at least not yet.

Many of the major thoroughfares of Honolulu are now one-way streets, which helps the flow of traffic, but often makes it seem that you are driving miles out of your way to reach a specific destination; downtown Honolulu is an especially confusing place to drive in. You may want to keep in mind that in this area Beretania Street is ewa, King Street is Diamond Head, Pensacola traffic now heads makai (to the sea), and Piikoi cars go in a mauka (to the mountains) direction. In Waikiki, Kalakaua traffic is Diamond Head most of the way, with a short stretch downtown running in both directions; Kuhio Avenue and the Ala Wai Boulevard are ewa for most of their lengths.

Those painted white arrows on the various lanes are not to be ignored. They indicate in what directions you are permitted to drive from each lane: right only, left only, left and straight ahead, or right and straight ahead. It's legal to make right turns when the light is red at most intersections—but not all, so read the signs first. And if you come across a sign reading "We appreciate your kokua," it's not an invitation to pay a toll. Kokua means cooperation in Hawaiian.

Parking for the night can be a problem in the Waikiki area, where you may find yourself driving around and around the block. *Tip:* Ala Wai Boulevard, along the canal, is less crowded than other main thoroughfares (but cars must be off one side of the street by 6 a.m.). In the downtown area, there are both municipal and private parking lots. Street meters charge only one cent per minute; in some busy locations the meters allow no more than 12 to 24 minutes. Read each meter carefully.

Mainland driving licenses may be used until expiration date. After that you'll need a Hawaiian license, obtainable from the Department of Motor Vehicles for $8.50, for those 15 and older.

READERS' TRANSPORTATION TIPS: "If a person is going to visit some of the attractions and/or plans to eat even one meal at other than the Jack-in-the-Box, and intends to rent a car for a drive to points around the island, rent the car before seeing the attractions. The freebies and discounts that come with many of the car rentals add up to some real savings. In other words, don't do something like taking a dinner cruise on a catamaran at full price and then learn you could have gone for free or at a substantial savings with a coupon that comes with a car rental" (The Ed Glassner Family, Kent, Ohio). . . . "Several of those places that advertise 'used cars' to rent for $7 to $9 a day are using false advertising— telling us that they don't have any of those types of cars in now and that they expect one in three weeks or so—a come-on!" (Paula Fisk, Greenwood, Ind.). . . . "If you're renting from an agency that gives out free coupons, note that you can only use your coupons while you are renting the car. You must show your car keys and/or your contract when you try to use a coupon. I don't really know if the free coupons are worth it. It might be cheaper to rent from an agency without coupons" (Carl and Debbie Adams, St. Louis, Mo.). . . . "I rented cars on all the islands except Lanai, and found parking at hotels and motels was quite limited in some cases. Fortunately, I always managed to get a spot. It would be wise to check that a hotel has parking available if you plan to rent a car. Also, be aware that some of the hotels, particularly in Honolulu, charge for parking" (Jane Kenney, Kingston, N.H.). . . . "If you're parking your car in Waikiki, try Fort DeRussy's huge parking lot (it's free) or the side streets near Kapiolani Park" (Jack Nakamoto, Ottawa, Ontario, Canada).

"When you arrive at the airports in Hawaii and have already reserved a car, don't call the car agency trying to speed things along before you've retrieved your luggage. They ask if you've gotten your bags yet. If you haven't, they'll tell you to get them and them call back. Only then will they send their airport pickup bus to get you" (Norman Saulnier, S. Ashburnham, Mass.).

"Suggestions to drivers: You can be tagged for even one or two miles over the speed limit. Watch parking directions carefully. We parked in a driveway, in the evening, that had a closed fence around a vacant lot and obviously wasn't being used for anything that year—and received a ticket. Also, watch the meters: around Fisherman's Wharf, for example, they *do not* stop at 6 p.m." (Sheila Pritchett, Villanova, Pa.).

"The average tourist who rents a car should be aware of the deductible requirements of most rental agencies, as well as of coverages and limitations of their own auto insurance policies. Ordinarily, the standard personal auto policy (most states) has an exclusion whereby coverage for a rented auto that is assumed by the individual under a form of contractual liability is limited to $1,000, yet most rental agencies have a $3,000 deductible for physical damage to the rented car. The renter is liable for damage to the car, whether or not at fault in the loss of the car. I am referring only to the collision coverage to the auto. There are other provisions to cover or waive coverage for medical coverage or bodily injury. Every traveler should take the precaution of checking this point with his insurance agent or company. To 'buy back' the deductible at this time is about $7.95 per day just for the collision. This increases considerably the cost of rental. The rental companies want to sell the 'buy backs' as it is a good deal for them. Incidentally, responsibility for coverages mentioned above are further complicated in a state such as Hawaii that has no-fault laws that put the damage back on the individual driver" (Joe D. Kinnard, Greer, S.C.).

"Please remind people to lock rental cars even if leaving them just to take a picture. We met several people who stopped just to see a particularly scenic view and came back in less than five minutes to find coolers, cameras, whatever, gone" (Sandy Abramovich, Thomaston, Conn.). . . . "It was interesting to take **TheBUS** to the New Windward Mall in Kaneohe (take no. 56 'Kailua—Kaneohe' or no. 52 'Kaneohe—Kailua'). The mall has a Liberty House (with lunch specials), Penney's, Sears, etc., and is enclosed. The bus route over the Pali and Kaneohe Bay on no. 56 is scenic" (Marge O'Harra, Portland, Ore.). . . . "We found TheBUS quite difficult in Honolulu—usually crowded, slow, and uncomfortable, as well as hard to determine schedules. However, the Guide from a local paper helped" (Melvin H. Boyce, Corte Madera, Calif.). . . . "You are absolutely right about TheBUS. We could have gotten along without a car for a few more days by using TheBUS. It's easy to catch onto the routes as plenty of free information is available, and for price, TheBUS has to be one of the last bargains left on earth" (Robert and Jean Carroll, Helena, Mont.).

SHOPPING IN HONOLULU

1. Shops in Waikiki
2. Ala Moana Center
3. Around Town

MUUMUUS AND MACADAMIA NUTS, koa woods and calabashes, tapas and tiki figures—these suggest the exotic items for which you'll shop in the islands. Although Hawaii is not one of the great bargain shopping areas of the world (no free-port prices or favorable money exchange for dollar-bearing Americans), it still offers a fascinating assortment of things Polynesian, Oriental, and American for the inveterate browser and souvenir hunter. We'll skip the expensive items—jewelry, objets d'art, Oriental brocades and silk, elegant resort wear—and stick to the good buys for the shopper who wants quality and low prices—which is where you, the $50-a-day'er, come in. Lately, a number of new shopping complexes, some of them geared to the affluent Japanese tourists, have opened in Honolulu and elsewhere on Oahu; we'll cover them here and tell you about shopping in the neighbor islands when we get to them.

1. Shops in Waikiki

Much of your island shopping can be done right in Waikiki: along Kalakaua Avenue and in the hotel gift shops, and at the International Market Place, King's Village, Royal Hawaiian Shopping Center, the Atrium Shops at Hemmeter Center, the Waikiki Shopping Plaza, and the Rainbow Bazaar. First we'll cover Waikiki in general, listing our recommendations by type of merchandise. Then we'll head for the special shopping areas and see what's up.

HAWAIIAN WEAR: Begin on Kalakaua Avenue if you're looking for island muumuus, holomuus, aloha shirts, and such, which we've suggested you plan to buy here, in our earlier section on packing. Almost every shop carries these items, but be sure to take a look at the reliable Waikiki branches of Honolulu's major department stores—**Liberty House**, and **McInerny's**—where there are extremely attractive selections of clothing for men and women, and children too. There's nothing provincial about Liberty House, by the way; it has everything from swimsuits for baby at $6 up to designer sportswear separates at $300 and more. There are so many stores, on Kalakaua and in the hotels and shopping centers, that you could spend days and days just going from one to another. A store we like very much is **Casa-D' Bella II** at 2352 Kalakaua. They carry some stylish designs from New York and California as well as local resort wear. And they have a very nice collection of fashion shell jewelry, too. The manufacturers of Hawaiian clothing we like best include **Malihini of Hawaii, Bete, Sun Babies, Princess Kaiulani, Tori Richards, Cooke Street** (better men's apparel), **Hilda,** and **Malama;** you'll find these brands all over town. Note too that most of the specialty shops will make up muumuus for mother, aloha shirts for dad, and junior versions of both for the kiddies in matching fabrics, and will also make clothes to your special size. (We should tell you that locals consider this very "touristy.") Many will make bikinis to order, or at least allow you to match the top of one to the bottom of another. Made-to-measure work usually takes just a day or two and in most cases costs no more than ready-made garments.

Prices for Hawaiian clothes are pretty standard everywhere: better muumuus average $30 to $50 short, $70 and way up long. To realize substantial savings on aloha wear, your best bets are four places we'll tell you about outside of Waikiki, ahead: Hilo Hattie's Fashion Center, Island Muumuu Works, Especially for You, and Muumuu Factory.

SOUVENIRS AND SMALL PRESENTS: Scads of Honolulu tourists swear by the low prices at the **ABC Discount Stores.** There are two dozen ABC stores in Honolulu, in all the tourist areas. You can usually expect to save 20% to 25% here on small items, sometimes more. Hawaiian perfumes and macadamia nuts are always a bargain at ABC stores. Most are open seven days a week, from 7:30 a.m. to midnight. Most ABCs also have drugs, cosmetics, grocery sections, gift packages ready for mailing, deli, fresh produce, and liquor, and usually the lowest prices anywhere on Hawaiian scenic postcards.

A number of other stores cut the regular prices on standard items—perfumes, cosmetics, souvenirs—and you'll find quite a few of these shops on Kalakaua in the area just Diamond Head of Uluniu Avenue, up toward the Queen Kapiolani Hotel. You can also count on good buys at **Holiday Mart,** which you'll read about ahead. **Woolworth's,** in the Bank of Hawaii Building on Kalakaua, now charges more for some standard souvenir items than ABC and some of the other shops, but their discount on jade, coral, opal, and 14-karat gold items is good. (It's nice to know that they'll mail your gifts and souvenirs home for you.) **Long's Drugstore** in Ala Moana is another excellent source for small items; their values are consistently tops.

What to buy? Hawaiian perfumes make delightful small presents. Royal Hawaiian and Liana are the leading brand names for island fragrances—pikake, ginger, orchid, plumeria—all of them sweetly floral and worlds away from the sophistication of Paris. Gift packages complete with artificial orchids begin around $3. Royal Hawaiian's higher priced perfumes have a real orchid right in the bottle.

Another idea for an authentic Hawaiian present—perhaps for yourself—is a bottle of kukui-nut oil. This is a new item for us and we've seen no claims for it being anything other than a skin emollient, but we tried it on a recent trip and found it makes the skin look wonderful! It's not available in too many places, but look for it at the Hawaiian Country Store at the Royal Hawaiian Shopping Center, or the Aloha Health Food Store at Ward Warehouse, or at any of the Vim and Vigor health food stores. Cost is about $6.50.

For Hawaiian jewelry that's both unusual and inexpensive, take a look at Pele's Tears and olivine, two stones found in fresh lava. Pele's Tears are drops of natural silica in dark-brownish to black shades; they make interesting earrings, which can be found for about $4 and up. (They are reputed to be good luck stones that keep a traveler safe.) Olivine has a lovely green cast and is sometimes called green diamond. Earrings run from about $5, and the stones are also used to decorate compacts and cigarette lighters.

An unusual fashion in island jewelry is real flowers dipped in gold; prices start about $15 for orchid pins. We've also seen plumeria preserved in plastic so realistically that it looks natural, about $6.

Black coral, mined in the waters off Maui, is handsome in small tree shapes (about $12), and in numerous other pins and pendants. An exquisite pink coral called angelskin has also been found off Maui waters. Blue coral is the "look" with jeans and casual tops. You'll see all of these, in abundance, at jewelry stores all over the islands.

You can buy Hawaiian delicacies—such exotic tastes as guava jelly, coconut syrup, passionfruit ambrosia—at almost any grocery store, but should you want to send a package home, the best and most reasonably priced places are **Long's Drugs, ABC Discount,** and the **Waikiki A-1 Superette.** Prices for gift packages average $10 or $15.

There are shell stores in every beach city in the world, but to see shells treated as objects of art is something else again, and that's where **Shellworld Hawaii,** 2381 Kalakaua (near the Surfrider-Moana Hotel), comes into its own. Some of the shells are rare, some are simply naturally beautiful, many are mounted for sculptural display, and all come from Pacific waters—the Philippines, Japan, Australia, the Hawaiian Islands. Most shells are not inexpensive, but you could surface with a cowry shell for $1.35. Be sure to see their stunning shell-framed wall mirrors. Shells for serving salads and sauces are from $2.95 up. There are more Shellworld shops at the Royal Hawaiian Shopping Center and the Kahala Hilton Hotel.

INTERNATIONAL MARKET PLACE: The oldest and most colorful shopping area in Waikiki, this place is still fun, despite the fact that there are now so many booths and so many tourists that it sometimes reminds us of rush hour in the New York subway. And prices are apt to be a mite higher on the same items than they are in the department stores or Ala Moana Center. Still, with its enormous range of Hawaiian and Polynesian specialties—lauhala hats, shell and ivory earrings, woven placemats, tiki figures, woodcarvings, scrimshaw pendants, resort wear for the whole family, as well as other items ranging from T-shirts to Oriental rugs—there's nothing quite like it anywhere else. Informal, semi-open shops set around a giant banyan tree and interspersed among tropical plantings stay open until 11 at night, giving you plenty of time for al fresco browsing. Directly behind it, with an entrance on Kuhio Avenue, is Kuhio Mall with more of the same. A very entertaining scene, especially in the cool of evening.

You should be aware of two things when you shop at the International Market Place. One, comparison-shopping pays off; one booth might be selling T-shirts for $12, another one around the corner for $8 or $9. And lately we've noticed a bit of bargaining going on—it doesn't always work, but it could be worth a try.

There are two items in particular you might want to look for at the Market Place. One is polished kukui nuts, which resemble large black jewels, and sell for about $3. They usually come with their own black chain and make a handsome pendant. For around $25 to $35 you can treat yourself to a kukui nut lei (the same kind the male nightclub entertainers wear), a true island treasure. (*Note:* there are many cheaper kukui nut leis available, but they are likely to be made in the Phillipines, or plastic.) The other is tapa, an unusual fabric made from the bark of a tree and stenciled in handsome patterns; it was the original clothing of the primitive Polynesians. It can be worked into handsome tablecloths or draperies, but in quantity it's expensive. You might, however, pick up a two-foot square, back it with wood when you get home, and have an unusual wall hanging for just a few dollars. You can usually find tapa—as well as many other Polynesian crafts—at Kalo's Polynesian Handicrafts. Baskets, hula skirts, and wood carvings are other specialties here.

Shops come and go at the Market Place with great rapidity, so our best advice is simply to roam where fancy leads you. But do stop in at **Diamond and Ivory;** you can't miss it—you'll hear its windchimes tinkling in the wind. Wonderful windchimes go for all prices here, beginning with ones of ceramic pineapples at $8, of dolphins at $10, small ones start at $3. . . . **Diamond Palace** has everything from Playboy Bunny watches on up, including 14-karat gold Hawaiian charms from $10. They also offer a 40% discount on 14-karat gold chains. . . . **Harriet's Custom Made and Ready to Wear** has good selections of resort wear, and custom service if you desire. . . . We liked the dolls from Thailand, the lamps, windchimes, and jewelry at **Capricorn.** . . . At **Tongan Tapu Woodcrafts** you can watch Tongan carvers work magic on a piece of wood. They'll even carve to your request. Plaques, snakes, carved figures, and small, inexpensive tikis are part of their stunning display of craftsmanship. Our favorite was the "Tiki of Peace."

At the rear of the Market Place, up one flight of stairs, you get a chance to pose for a picture standing on a surfboard, with a simulated 14-foot Banzai Pipeline tube wave cresting behind you. Your photo will be made up into postcards (three for $6.95, six for $10.95) and will be ready to send home to gasping, admiring friends in just two hours.

AT KUHIO MALL: Kuhio Mall is directly behind International Market Place and very much like it. The most exciting store here, for our money, is **Swimsuit Warehouse,** which offers stupendous savings in name-brand swimsuits. At our last visit, they were offering every swimsuit for $18.95, two for $35. This is a wholesale operation, and the prices are about half of what you'd pay elsewhere. There are suits for serious swimmers, suits for everybody else, in every style from bikini to skirt, high and low cuts, with special sections for larger women. Junior sizes run 5 to 13, missy sizes 8 to 22. No decor to speak of, just racks of great suits! *Note:* There's a second Swimsuit Warehouse at 870 Kapahulu. (Another wholesale swimsuit operation is **Swim City USA** which also offers low prices and has two locations in Waikiki: at the Reef Hotel, 2169 Kalia Rd. and the Outrigger Waikiki Hotel, 2335 Kalakaua. Their warehouse/showroom is behind Ala Moana Center at 1540 Makaloa, Room # 206).

ROYAL HAWAIIAN SHOPPING CENTER: Across Kalakaua from the International Market Place is Waikiki's newest shopping center, and in many respects its most exciting and sophisticated. "An oasis of green in Waikiki" is what the builders promised when ground was broken a few years ago, and despite the outcry against the lavish use of concrete, it's pretty much what they've delivered. Occupying three city blocks along Kalakaua Avenue between the Outrigger Hotel and Lewers Street, this stunning 6½-acre, 120-store complex is indeed graced with flowers and trees, ferns and shrubbery, and hundreds of trailing vines and Hawaiian plants. A high level of taste is evident in the shops, restaurants, and huge variety of entertainments, enough to keep the visitor happy and busy for a long time. The ground floor is usually awash with "sidewalk sales" and some pretty good ones at that, but don't stop here: the more interesting merchandise is on the upper levels.

Number one on anybody's list here has to be the **China Friendship Store,** occupying much of the second and third floors of Building C. With its unique collection of affordable gifts and apparel from the People's Republic of China, this could well be the biggest Friendship Store anywhere ("Friendship Store" is the name the Chinese give to tourist stores selling arts-and-crafts merchandise). There are over 21,000 different items here, ranging in size from jewelry to furniture, in price from a few dollars up to the thousands: carvings, clothing, carpets, lacquerware, hand-embroidered linens, pure silk fabrics, bamboo, Peking glass, hand-turned vases, just to name a few. Even if you're just looking, thanks, be sure to drop by: frequent lectures (we wandered into one on acupuncture), arts-and-crafts demonstrations, even a visit by a giant panda can be entertaining. Some changes may be in the offing here soon.

Chinese goods, sold on a much smaller scale, but all of excellent taste and at very fair prices, can be found in **China Marketplace** in Building C and **Peking Marketplace** in Building A. At China Marketplace, note the hand-painted goose eggs and Ping-Pong balls, $1.45 each; the whimsical animals—turkeys, owls—fashioned of split bamboo, from $2.95; and the cut wheat-stalk pictures at $1.95. Stop in to pick up a paper fan perhaps, only 49¢ at Peking Marketplace. Arts and crafts of Thailand can be found at **Pacific Marketplace.**

Andrade's, long known for fine clothes for both men and women, has its largest store here on the second floor. Stop in to browse through its Princess Street boutiques and keep an eye open for bargains—we recently saw some large canvas shopping bags with the Andrade logo for only $3.50. Then stop for some refreshments—perhaps a pastry and a 25¢ cup of Kona coffee—at the Sweet Shoppe. Adjoining is the Bargain Attic, which discounts items from the Friendship Store.

Ready to treat yourself to something special? Stop in and visit Marlo Shima who runs **Boutique Marlo** on the second floor, Building A. Marlo designs and sews exquisite women's clothing of silk, cotton, and other natural fabrics, and although dresses go for about $60 to $120, you can find many modestly priced scarves, necklaces, fabric bags, and the like, with the same high standards of workmanship and beauty.

Be sure to visit the **Little Hawaiian Craft Shop** on the third floor, where a fantastic assortment of unusual finished jewelry sits alongside buckets and barrels of raw materials, the same kinds that were used by the ancient Hawaiians. This is a workshop for craftspeople using natural island materials in both traditional and contemporary styles. Replicas of museum pieces sit among $4.50 hand-carved tikis and buckets of 50¢ shells. They have some wonderful hard-to-find sandalwood necklaces—fragrant, lovely, and well priced, from about $18. Almost everything here is handmade in Hawaii. Great ideas for presents include tapa tote bags from $16, kukui nut rings at $4.50 (many kukui rings, pendants, and necklaces), Hawaiian exotic wood key chains at $3.50 each. They also have a small booth on the main floor, where they sell that very popular 14-karat-gold Hawaiian heirloom jewelry, engraved with your own name. The goldsmith promises a completed product in 24 to 48 hours.

Adjoining the Little Hawaiian Craft Shop and under the same management is the **Hawaiian Wood Shed,** an outstanding wood gallery that shows local woodworkers of the calibre of Pai Pai, known for his woodcarved replicas of Hawaiian and Pacific images, along with stone replicas by Salote. Only island woods—among them koa, mango, Norfolk pine, milo, macadamia, ohio lehus, and keawe—are used. Prices range from $3.50 to $3,000.

On the other side of the Little Hawaiian Craft Shop is the museum-style **Pacific Island Artifacts** with both traditional and contemporary handcrafts from islands of the Pacific—Fiji, New Guinea, Tonga, the Solomons, Micronesia, Polynesia, Melanesia—with an ever-changing kaleidoscope of spirit figures, tapas, weavings, war clubs, drums, masks, spears. The owners make frequent trips to these areas to find these treasures. Well worth a look.

If you know any lefties or are one yourself, don't miss **Lefties, Etc. . . .** (third floor, Building A). Owners Mary Murphy and Maria Zimmer have put together an engaging and unique shop, the only one of its kind in Hawaii. Here corkscrews and can openers move counter clockwise (so do clocks), and notebooks, rulers, scissors, and such all cater to the left-handed. We love the sayings on T-shirts and greeting cards, especially the one that reads: "If the right side of the brain controls the left side of the body, then only left-handed people are in their right mind."

Although Oriental storekeepers sell it in Honolulu, the ginseng available at **Ginseng King** is grown in Wisconsin. Stop in at their store, learn about the therapeutic effects of the centuries-old root, and perhaps buy a few tea bags (35¢ each), or a large bunch of the root itself ($25) to be used in making ginseng chicken soup.

If you've bought too much on your shopping rounds and are wondering how to get it all home, visit **GBC** on the second floor. They'll do professional packing, wrapping, and shipping, or sell you the materials—corrugated boxes, mailing tubes, sealing tapes, etc.—that you need to do it yourself. United Parcel Service is available here, and there's a U.S. Post Office just next door.

A popular stop on the first floor is the **Hawaii Country Store,** a busy, modern rendition of the old general store. It's a good place to pick up fresh fruit, cards, macadamia nuts, monkeypod carvings, and the like. We doubt if you could get a cup of espresso or cappuccino in a real country store, so its tiny café is most welcome, as is the snackbar, which dishes out sandwiches for about $1.30 to $1.95 and plate lunches around $3. This may be just the time to experience a real Hawaiian shave ice. The snack counter is open daily from 7 a.m. (8 a.m. on Sunday) until 8:30 p.m.

Where else can you eat here? We've already told you about some of our favorite sit-down restaurants in Chapter III (**Great Wok of China, Las Margaritas,** and **It's Greek to Me**). For a drink outdoors under the umbrellas, it's the **Princess Coffee Shop;** for a look at a private collection of Hawaiian art, it's **McDonald's,** on the second level. For a traditional Japanese meal (complete to the plastic replicas of the food in the window), it's **Daruma;** for Danish open-faced sandwiches, *frikadeller,* and the best Danish pastry this side of Copenhagen, it's **Café Copenhagen. Chubby's Barbeque** on the first floor is a busy, inexpensive, self-serve spot for charbroiled burgers and a variety of plate lunches. The **Coffee Connection** at McInenery's has marvelous exotic coffees and teas, plus bakery desserts on the order of baked cream cheese, strawberry shortcake, and Mocha cake with macadamia nuts, from $1.50 to $2. And don't forget another favorite, **Copenhagen Cones,** with ice cream stuffed into waffle-like cones baked in an old-fashioned oven brought all the way from Scandinavia to Honolulu.

Before you leave the center, try to make time to see the absorbing film about the voyage of the *Hokule'a,* a 60-foot, double-hulled canoe that sailed from Hawaii to Tahiti and back in 1976, using only the navigational techniques of the original settlers. The 23-minute film, produced by the Polynesian Voyaging Society, is shown continuously between 9 a.m. and 5 p.m., Monday through Saturday, on the third level, Building A. Admission is free.

Plenty of free entertainment, arts and crafts exhibitions, hula lessons, and the like take place at the center on a continual basis; check the local papers for a schedule. Should you need information on where to find any of the shops or restaurants, or where to locate particular items, you can talk to a computer—or a real person on the computer screen—at the first-floor **information booth.**

AN ORIENTAL EXCURSION—RAINBOW BAZAAR: Can't make it to Hong Kong or Tokyo for a shopping spree this year? Honolulu has a substitute of sorts: the Rainbow Bazaar at the Hilton Hawaiian Village Hotel. Authenticity has been stressed in the creation of this unique shopping complex, both in products and atmosphere; you enter through a Chinese moon gate, are serenaded by Japanese music in the background, and can shop for an intriguing selection of gifts from Japan, China (both the mainland and Taiwan), Korea, and the South Pacific. While some of the objets d'art, jewels, and brocades can get quite costly here, there are also loads of small things you can pick up, and it's certainly well worth your while to come and browse. You can have an inexpensive lunch or dinner at **Hatsuhana** or **J's Pancake House** while you're here. Have a look, too, at the grounds of the Hilton Hawaiian Village Hotel, which we always consider an entertainment in itself.

It's nice to wander where fancy leads you here, but let us tell you about a few of our personal favorites. **House of Jade** has beautiful baubles at fantastic prices, as well as pretty trivia like ivory rings from $3 to $6 and pearl earrings at $15. . . . Jewelry lovers should also look in at **The Coral Grotto, Golden Boutique, Jewels of the World,** and **Maxim Jewelry.** . . . True to its name, **Topazerie** has lots of topazes, but also many other things. We saw great necklaces in amethyst, jade, onyx, coral, pearls, and lapis. . . . **Nautilus of the Pacific** is the place for all manner of shells and items crafted from shells; we spotted sea urchins at $10.95 each. . . . **Exotic Fair** is known for footwear; if you need an extra pair of shoes for touring the islands, have a look here. Sandals for $15 come in all colors. Or, pick up a pair of Magna sandals that give your feet a massage as you stroll, also $15. . . . Have a look at the Oriental accessories and handbags at **Pagoda Shop.** . . . **Royal Creations** features quilts as well as attractive women's wear. . . . **Far East Antiquities** has a wide range of treasures, from folding fans and brass abacuses for under $1 to Mandarin necklaces from 18th-century Tibet, in silver, coral, jade, and turquoise, $200. . . . **T's Galore** has a shirt that reads, "Hawaii, It's the Only Place." We agree. . . . We saw beautiful woodcarvings—bowls, figurines, wood roses—at **House of Kea.** . . . Trusty branches here, too, of Honolulu's better known stores like **Alfred Shaheen** and **Liberty House.**

KING'S VILLAGE: It's supposed to look like a 19th-century European town, with its cobblestone streets and old-fashioned architecture, but King's Village is very much a part of modern Honolulu. Behind the gates at the corner of Koa and Kaiulani Avenues (across the street from the Hyatt Regency Waikiki, at Hemmeter Center) is a cozy bazaar that contains a variety of shops, several restaurants, and an open market—all done up in a style that recalls the 19th-century monarchy period of Hawaiian history, when royal palaces were built in Honolulu, and Hawaiian kings and queens journeyed to London to be presented at the court of Queen Victoria.

The shops, however, are not so much European as the typical Honolulu-international mix, with lots of Oriental and Polynesian crafts, plus plenty of Hawaiian resort wear and souvenirs. All are small and in good taste; King's Village is a commercial venture, certainly, but there's no commercial ugliness about it. We think you'll enjoy browsing here.

As at Rainbow Bazaar, prices go from just a little to quite a lot. Despite its name, **Harriet's Custom Made and Ready to Wear** is not expensive; prices for ready-to-wear begin at $18.95 for short muumuus, $13 for men's shirts. For custom work, prices go from about $35 to $65, depending on fabric, size, and style. Your garment will usually be ready in a day or two. (We've had excellent comments from readers over the years on the quality and care of their workmanship.) . . . We love the Japanese garments at **Kitamura's.** Buy your favorite samurai back home a samurai T-shirt for $14 or a handkerchief for $4.75, ogle the magnificent wedding kimonos from $200. . . . You may want to get yourself a simulated "diamond" ring in a 14-karat-gold setting, from $125 at **Brilliant Creations.** Their motto is: "Counterfeit Jewels—that won't tell unless you do." . . . You can take home a wooden tiki for all of $7, courtesy of **Hime,** an intriguing woodcarving shop, which also has a milo woodcarving of Madame Pele for $2,700. . . . The **Royal Peddler** can always be depended upon for quality brass gifts with a nautical theme. . . . **Cal-Oahu Fabrics** features vibrant prints with which to make your own aloha clothing, plus patterns. The fabric is hung in the shape of a dress and matched with appropriate necklaces. Two panels, enough for a dress or a skirt, begin at $34.50. . . . There's a large branch of the ever-popular **Crazy Shirt** here: we love the outrigger canoe/paddling-cat design.

Defense d'Afficher has three stores in Paris and three in Honolulu, one of them right here. Designs and prints are striking; check out their wildlife T-shirts at $28. *Formidable!* . . . Kids will love the dollhouse miniatures at **My Favorite Things,** the Mickey Mouse clothing and toys at **Gift Doll.** . . . If you have to buy a present for a "golfer who has everything," the people at **Jobi's** can help you out: they have Hawaiian golf shoes—thongs with cleats. . . . You can find some disinctive women's clothing at **Annie's Fashion.** We like their all-cotton dresses. . . . Beautiful haku leis (head leis) made of silk and dried flowers can be found at **High Ling Flowers** for $25. Put them on a straw hat for a smashing effect. You can also have your picture put on a plate here for $8.

Unless you've wisely chosen to visit King's Village early in the morning or after the sun goes down—it tends to get very hot in midday—you may want to sit around the fountain up top and cool off for a bit under the canopy. You can also cool off very nicely and have a pleasant lunch or meal at **Waikiki Light House,** decorated in old-world fashion within. Displayed outside in a revolving case are luscious pastries, like macadamia-nut cheese cake, ambrosia cream pie, Black Forest cake. Inside, to go with them, are coffee, espresso, and cappuccino, plus a menu that runs from omelets to burgers to local-style lunch and dinner plates, most in the $5 to $6 range. Everything served any time of day, from 7:30 a.m. to 11 p.m. **Country Cupboard** has subs, Texas chili, nachos, and lemonade at low prices. And it's always good fun to stop by for a drink or a meal (steak-and-mushroom pie, quiche Lorraine, a variety of salads, and hearty sandwiches, in the $4.50 to $6.50 range) at a new-old English pub, **The Rose and Crown.** There's a long Happy Hour here, from 11:30 a.m. to 7 p.m.

There's more to do at King's Village than shop and eat. There are the King's Village Honor Guards to watch, so wax-like that they should be at Madame Tussaud's. The changing of the guard ceremony takes place every night at 6:15. There are often free shows; watch the papers for specific times.

THE ATRIUM SHOPS AT HEMMETER CENTER: Towering 44 stories above Kalakaua Avenue between Kaiulani and Uluniu Avenues, the multimillion-dollar Hemmeter Center, topped by the very posh and expensive Hyatt Regency Hotel, houses a beautiful and elegant shopping complex. You may do more sightseeing than actual shopping here, but see it you must. The shops surround the central courtyard in three tiers; a spectacular waterfall splashes from the third tier into a crystal pool in the courtyard below. The center part of the courtyard is open at the top, a massive metal sculpture hovers above, and beyond that is the sky. Striking metal sculptures inhabit the pool too. At night the courtyard is lit by massive polished brass lampposts. Combined with the brick-red ceramic tile floor, it all creates an effect that is at once modern Hawaii and Hawaiian monarchy, each style complementing the other superbly. Sweeping staircases lead to the two upper tiers of shops, as do unobtrusive escalators.

As for the shops, they are a quality collection, and many—like **Gucci** and **Bugatti**—are in line with the pricey atmosphere of this place. But there are several others for the budget-wise: **Watumull's** offers family-priced clothing, as do **Leilani, K. & K. International,** and **Hawaii Fashions.** . . . The **Royal Peddler** is known for gifts in depth, including handsome chess sets and nautical curios. . . . **Cotton Cargo** has some neat togs for women. . . . **Happy Fashions** has a selection of clothes and accessories for children and teenagers, as well as adult resort wear. Have a look at their selection of carry-on bags for the plane; we bought one here last time for all of $12, and it worked perfectly. . . . Jewelry and gifts are moderately priced at **Treasures World.** . . . **Tarbo** is stocked with stylish jewelry, some of it using native materials. . . . Dresses and caftans in vibrant Tahitian prints can be found at **Tahiti Arts.** Prices begin about $55 for dresses. . . . **Cal-Oahu** is a worthwhile source for really good shoes, plus lightweight luggage, hats, and bags. . . . Mickey Mouse shirts and paraphernalia can be found at **Yokahama Okadaya.** . . . There's a trusty branch of **Liberty House** here. . . . Pick your favorite gems: there are plenty of sources to choose from. The **Coral Grotto, House of Opal, House of Jade,** and the **Pearl Factory** are all here. . . . There's lots of fancy footwork to be seen at **Islander Thongs.** . . . Ogle the handsome sculpture at **Bennett Sculpture,** the works of international and Hawaiian artists at **Images International.**

A variety of free events take place here every afternoon. Monday, Tuesday, Thursday, and Saturday, it's songs and guitar music from 4 to 6 p.m.; a fashion show Wednesday at 4 p.m.; and the delightful Aloha "Pau Hana" show Friday at 5 p.m., when locals and visitors alike celebrate the end of the work week with dance, song, and story. The Atrium Shops are open daily, from 9 a.m. to 11 p.m.

WAIKIKI SHOPPING PLAZA: The first impression one gets on seeing the enclosed Waikiki Shopping Plaza, 2250 Kalakaua Ave., corner of Seaside, is that it more properly belongs in New York or San Francisco or some sophisticated European city. Shops like Roberta di Camerino, Courrèges, Bally of Switzerland, Ferragamo, and many versions of the ubiquitous Paris shops have little to do with the islands. But as you ascend the escalators to the four shopping floors, it gets better and more versatile, with more of an island flavor. The traffic-stopper here is the five-story fountain by island designer Bruce Hopper, a wondrous, half-million-dollar creation with lights that change colors, and fascinating Plexiglass spheres and bubbles that make the waters dance. There's a different point of interest at each level, creating new surprises as you ride the escalators.

As you walk in, you can check out those pricey boutiques in the **Yokahama Okadaya** store, and then turn to the serious business of buying all kinds of souvenirs, food, aloha wear, and more at the enormous **Hawaii Discount Mart.** Intriguing holographic pendants run around $20. . . . Check the racks at **Villa Roma,** a high-fashion shop for women (they often run clearances on sports items for women), and also ogle the pretties at their other shop, **Chocolates for Breakfast,** with delectable designer women's clothing. . . . **Maleka's Attic** has charming women's clothing too, with a lot of crochet work. . . . You can pick up some cute Japanese novelties for children at **Okadaya,** which has a lot of trendy Mickey Mouse items. . . . Art lovers will enjoy the **South Shore Gallery,** an artist-cooperative gallery which maintains high standards of taste. . . . **Ali Baba** is a wholesale outfit that imports and exports leather accessories. Among the huge display of merchandise, we saw well-made eelskin wallets for $22.50 and bags for around $60. Eelskin, in case you hadn't noticed, is extremely popular in Hawaii, and "wholesale outlets" abound. This is one of the better sources. . . . **Ocean Sports & Wear** has good bargains: factory-direct purchases, special buys, and closeouts. . . . Stock up on some reading matter at **Waldenbooks,** which has a very large selection.

While most of the shops at the Waikiki Shopping Plaza are not budget-oriented, the basement restaurants certainly are, with a bevy of fast-food counters offering varied ethnic foods. **Marco Polo,** on the fourth floor, also has great prices (see Chapter III's restaurants). On the third floor, a pleasant **Coffee Bar** sells Kona coffee by the pound, as well as sandwiches, espresso, and cappuccino. And in the fourth-floor showroom, nightly at 6 and 7:15 p.m., there's a hula show, **Waikiki Calls.** You and your cameras are welcome, free.

MILITARIA UNLIMITED: Once part of the Fort DeRussy Museum, **The Military Shop of Hawaii,** 1921 Kalakaua Ave., may well be the largest store of its kind in the country. Soldiers, military patches from all the services, military models, camouflage clothing, and accessories are all for sale. And there's a large selection of military books as well. For those interested in such things, a fascinating spot. Open every day of the year except Christmas.

BEATING THE HIGH PRICE OF POI—FOOD SHOPPING: If you're going to do any cooking in your kitchenette apartment, you're also going to be shocked when you do your first shopping for groceries. Food costs in Honolulu are substantially higher than in big cities on the mainland (almost one-third more, in some cases), and if you pick up your groceries in the hotel shops, sometimes much more than that. (We were stunned recently to have to pay almost $1 more on a quart of grapefruit juice in a hotel shop than it cost in a nearby supermarket.) The hotel shops are a convenience, and we're glad to have them, but if you're going to do any serious shopping, you're far better off to take your U-Drive and head for the supermarkets. The big Honolulu chains are **Star, Times, Safeway,** and **Foodland** (and **Emjay's,** a subsidiary of Foodland.) There are several of each of these, with addresses in the phonebook. **Gem** on Ward Avenue, and **Holiday Mart,** 801 Kaheka St. (two blocks mauka of the Ala Moana Shopping Center), also offer low prices. In Waikiki, the best food prices (albeit on limited selections) are at the **ABC Discount Stores.**

Natural foods are generally not inexpensive, so we were delighted to find "healthy food at prices that don't make you sick" at **Down to Earth Natural Foods,** 2525 S. King St. (tel. 947-7678), near University Avenue. A recent poll taken by *Honolulu* magazine rated this friendly place as the best overall natural-food store in Honolulu. As big as a supermarket, Down to Earth has dozens of bins of grains and beans, a large refrigerator case of organically grown fruits and vegetables, and a Natural Medicine Center that features, among other items, Chinese herbs, including ginseng and "dragon eggs." All products, including vitamin and mineral supplements, are totally vegetarian. Open from 7:30 a.m. to midnight Monday to Saturday, until 9 p.m. on Sunday. Also on the premises is a terrific natural fast-food restaurant called **Healthy's** (see Chapter III on restaurants), which serves from 6:30 a.m. until midnight seven days a week.

Just down the block, at 2357 S. Beretania St., is **Kokua Co-op Natural Foods and Grocery,** a membership co-op where, in addition to natural foods, you can find items like Hawaiian Reef Fish T-shirts. They have fresh sandwiches, cold drinks, and a wide variety of snack items like bagels with cream cheese, cookies, and cheese wrapped in individual portions. Nonmembers pay 10% above shelf prices. Open daily.

Terrific baked goods—freshly baked whole-grain breads (oatmeal, raisin, cinnamon, sprouted wheat), pies, and cakes—are the main reason for tracking down one of the popular **Vim and Vigor** stores: you can find them at Ala Moana Center, Kahala Mall, Pearlridge Shopping Center, and elsewhere in Oahu. They also have good prices on an extensive selection of dried fruits, nut butters, fresh produce, and many other natural and organic items. Their snackbars are great too.

If you'd like to shop for produce, fish, and meat with the local people, be sure to visit the **Ala Moana Farmer's Market** (a block in from the Ala Moana–Ward intersection at Auahi Street), where the atmosphere is pungent and the prices low. It's a great place to get acquainted with local Hawaiian foods and taste sensations. The long, low building is lined with a number of stalls, some with ready-to-eat items. Here you can sample poi, raw fish, and other delicacies such as ogo, palu, and tako. In case you're not feeling all that adventurous, you can settle for a 12-ounce can of New Zealand corned beef or imu kalua pig, both cooked and ready for your own private luau. At **Haili's Hawaiian Foods,** in business since 1867, we saw one-day and two-day poi and even sour poi, all quite difficult to find.

Get yourself downtown to **King's Bakery** at 1936 S. King St. (tel. 941-5211), which makes an incredibly delicious sweet bread that they will package and airmail to the folks back home. A charge of $10.50 covers the shipping box, two loaves, and postage. You can sometimes find these breads sold at the airport, just before you reach the gate to board your plane.

Need cookies for dessert or a nibble? Wally Amos, better-known as Famous Amos, is a local celebrity who is active in many charities. His name is found on his delicious chocolate chip cookies, all made with fresh ingredients and pecans or macadamia nuts. There are two **Famous Amos** shops in Waikiki, at 2301 and 2330 Kalakaua Ave., plus a new shop in the Windward Mall in Kaneohe, and others scattered around the island. Prices are 70¢ a piece, or from $5.25 to $6.25 the pound.

SHOPPING FOR SURFERS: If you're really serious about surfing, or learning to surf, let us point you in the direction of **Local Motion** at 1714 Kapiolani Blvd., near the Ala Moana Shopping Center (tel. 944-8585). Any surfer will tell you that in order to learn to surf safely and joyously you need good instruction and a well-constructed board. Many of those for rent at beach stands are outdated. Hence the need for a source like Local Motion. You can rent a board for $15 for the first day and $10 for every day thereafter. By the week, it's $50. And they also sell snappy sports and leisure clothes. Local Motion is also at the Windward Mall in Kaneohe and at Kuapa Kai in Hawaii Kai.

2. Ala Moana Center

Honolulu's fabulous modern shopping center (one of the largest open-air malls in the world), just across the Ala Moana Beach from Waikiki, is an example of island architecture at its best. Landscaped with trees, flowers, fountains, and a meandering stream down its Central Mall, which is graced with large works of sculpture, Ala Moana Center is always packed with enough island families to make it worth seeing for that reason alone. But the stores are, of course, the main attraction—more than 150 of them, an international bazaar full of intriguing wares. We'll mention just a few, but shopping buffs will come back here many, many times. (From Waikiki, take the no. 8 bus; it runs on Kuhio Avenue every ten minutes.) The center is only ten minutes away.

One of Hawaii's biggest department stores, **Sears Roebuck,** is here, with the usual mainland amenities and the unusual Hawaiian specialties—like orchid plants (Sears will ship to the mainland and guarantees live delivery), and a tremendous selection of muumuus and island clothing at very reasonable prices.

J.C. Penney is known for fashion and for excellent value in all departments, as is **Watumull's.** The flagship store of **Liberty House** is here, and most striking it is, its eaves decorated with Hawaiian tapas.

We always enjoy browsing around the large Japanese department store, **Shirokiya,** which has everything from state-of-the-art stereo to kids' T-shirts that glow in the dark, for $8. It has superb and often elegant wares: fashion that ranges from designer to traditional, housewares, china, audio and video innovations, furniture, fine arts, and a gourmet food department, a great place to try sushi and other Japanese delicacies. It also has, uncharacteristically, a European-style bakery called **St. Germaine,** where you might get a passion fruit or strawberry mousse for around $1. *Fashion note:* Shirokiya stores also carry socks, with a separate space for the big toe, to wear with zoris.

There are also dozens of small shops in the center, reflecting just about every interest and taste. **Summer's Place** is a lovely gift shop full of precious stuff, notably scrimshaw, dollhouse miniatures, windchimes, and unusual greeting cards. They have another shop at Pearlridge Center. . . . **Paniolo Trading** has clothes and accessories for the equestrian (paniolo means "cowboy" in Hawaiian). . . . **Laura Ashley** of London, Paris, and New York, is here in Hawaii, too, with a shop full of distinctive prints that translate into utterly feminine clothes and charming fabrics and accessories for the home. . . . And **Benetton** brings the Italian sense of style here in vibrantly colored sportswear. **Banana Republic** is a must if you're going on safari, going on a trip, or just want to look stylish. These are not bargain stores, but everything is of great quality for the price.

Quality is also the word at **Villa Roma,** the fashion boutique always first with the newest—be it the classic, contemporary, or nostalgic look, local crafts, what-have-you. The Japanese high-fashion designers are all the rage here at the moment. . . . **Chocolates for Breakfast** has the sort of elegant clothing for women that never goes out of fashion. . . . **Prides of New Zealand** seems a bit incongruous in hot Hawaii, selling woolen sweaters, sheepskin rugs, and sheepskin car seats, but the people here swear that sheepskin is cool. . . . Stop in at **Musashiya** for wonderful patterns and fabrics, or pick up a surfboard at lively **Hawaiian Island Sports.** . . . You'll find a great selection of hand-carved pipes at **Tobaccos of Hawaii.** . . . **Tahiti Imports** takes Tahitian prints of their own design and makes them into muumuus (short muumuus average $46.95; long ones, around $70.95), aloha shirts, bikinis, and pareaus. They also sell their exquisite hand-printed fabrics by the yard.

The Sharper Image, the catalog store to end all catalog stores, is a fabulous playground for adults, so even if you have to push along the aisles with the crowds, don't miss it. Come in and try their exercise bikes, the self-massage table or massage chair (soothing after a hard day's shopping), and scads of other curiosities.

We picked up several gifts on our last trip from **The Compleat Kitchen and More.** A company called "What a Melon" creates charming designs of Hawaiian flowers and fruits with a motto reading "Grown in Hawaii," and puts them on potholders ($3.75), aprons ($13), towels, tote bags, and more. . . . There's always a sale of some sort going on at **Island Shells.** We spotted lapis necklaces from $22.95. And their shell flower arrangements are very beautiful. . . . It's fun to go fly a kite in Honolulu, and the place to get your equipment is at **High Performance Kites,** right near the Centerstage. Many of their kites come from one of our favorite places on Molokai, the Big Wind Kite Factory. . . . Also near the Centerstage, and in a sense the "heart" of the shopping center is the **Honolulu Book Store,** with superb selections in every category, especially Hawaiiana, and newspapers that may—or may not—make you nostalgic for home, like the *Los Angeles Times,* the *San Francisco Chronicle,* the *New York Times,* and the *Wall Street Journal.*

Feet getting to you? The **Slipper Shop** is a good place to replace whatever wornout sandals you're trudging around in. They claim to have the widest selection of casual footwear in the state, with over 400 styles of made-in-Hawaii shoes, including hard-to-find golf slippers with cleats, for $19. . . . Check out the **Pocketbook Man** for a wide selection of quality bags and luggage. . . . **Chantelle's of Hawaii** boasts unusual jewelry, like stunning mastodon ivory pendants, inlaid with precious gems.

Need some decorating ideas? Striking posters, many with an Oriental motif, begin around $30 at the **Art Board.** . . . **Peach Blossom** is as graceful as its name, with superb handmade Oriental crafts. Their hand-painted wooden ducks start at low prices. . . . **Iida's** is crammed with colorful Japanese giftware. . . . For clothing, **Carol & Mary** is tops on our personal list, with sophisticated styles that looks at home in Honolulu—or anywhere on the mainland. Hard-to-find junior lines are available here, and they have some really gorgeous full-tilt tutu (granny) muus in distinctive fabrics. New here is a Calvin Klein boutique. As you might imagine, it's not inexpensive. . . . **Fumi's** is another show-stopper for women's clothes, with a line that might be described as demure but come-hither. . . . Best known for conservative men's and boy's wear, beautifully made and well priced, **Reyn's** also features good-looking women's clothes as well. Many shops on Oahu, Maui, and Kauai. . . . **Irene's Hawaiian Gifts** features unusual carvings from native woods and collectors' items, like Hawaiian dolls, made locally and sold at good prices. . . . Candles in the shape of Hawaiian tikis and pineapples make novel presents. You'll find them at the **Hale Kukui Makai Candle Shop.** . . . Check in at the big **Vim and Vigor Health Food Store** for excellent selections of honey, nut butters, whole grains, organic foods, superb home-baked goods that should not be missed, and other healthies. . . . Stop in, too, at the **Crackseed Center,** if you want to know what island youngsters clamor for (crackseeds, originally a Chinese confection, are a cross between seeds and candies, very sticky, very tasty).

Chocaholics will find the temptations at Ala Moana hard to resist. If you're trying to break the habit, pretend you don't know that there's usually a woman working in the window at **La Maison de Chocolate,** hand-dipping plump, luscious, fresh strawberries into chocolate, and that you can buy one, sold by weight, for about $1. And forget we ever told you about **Mrs. Field's Chocolate Chippery,** which turns out warm and moist cookies studded with chips, sold individually, or by the pound at around $5.25.

One of the most intriguing stores at Ala Moana is the **Foodland Supermarket.** It's like an international food fair, reflecting the cultures that make up Hawaii—and the rest of the world. You walk along seemingly endless aisles of exotic foods: fresh-frozen coconut milk, packages of weird-looking Japanese dried fish, health foods, tortillas, English biscuits, French cheese, you name it—if it's edible, this place has got it. The salad bar includes kim chee, lomi lomi salmon, and fresh poi, so create your own lunch. You can, in addition, pick up some okolehao, Hawaii's potent ti-root drink, in the large liquor department. If life has become boring in that little kitchenette of yours, don't miss a visit here. There's also an inexpensive souvenir section.

For more bargains in souvenirs and small items at Ala Moana, it's trusty old **ABC Discount Stores, Long's,** and **Woolworth's.**

The best bargains at Ala Moana are available when the stores take to the sidewalks—the ground-floor level that is—displaying racks and racks of clothing for very low prices.

Remember the center, too, for free entertainment during local holidays and at special ethnic celebrations; you may catch a Japanese or Philippine dance group, a Hawaiian show, or some of the island's top nightclub entertainers. For years now, the **Young People's Hula Show,** presented every Sunday at 9:30 a.m. on the Centerstage, has been a Honolulu institution. Don't miss it. A more-or-less continuous program of local events and entertainment takes place on the Centerstage.

RESTAURANTS AT ALA MOANA: Ala Moana Center has always been one of the best locales in town for inexpensive dining. Now, with the advent of the 850-seat, glass-enclosed dining court called Makai Market, on the makai (sea) side of the Center, the possibilities for entertaining eating are better than ever. We'll begin at the Market, then move on to some other Center choices.

At Makai Market

Makai Market is served by a score of self-service specialty kitchens. Name your desire—Hawaiian, Italian, New York deli, seafood, Japanese, Chinese, health food—the food is here and you can put together a meal for around $3 to $4 at lunch, $5 to $6 at dinner. You serve yourself, then take your food to the pretty tables under the bright buntings overhead. You can start with a drink from the center bar with its "Let's Make A Daiquiri" neon sign; daiquiris, pīna coladas, and other favorites are about $3 to $4, and there are smoothies and non-alcoholic cocktails as well.

Take a look around and see what you might like. **Thirst Aid Station** has "Remedies and Prescriptions" that include shakes, smoothies, yogurt, and soup, 50¢ to $2. . . . **Poi Bowl** features local favorites like tripe stew, $2.95, up to a luau special for $4.50. . . . At **Sharro Pizza,** folks line up for baked calzone at $2.89. . . . We counted 10 noodle varieties from $2.95 to $4.50 at Tsuruya Noodle Shop. . . . **Yummy Korean Barbecue** offers plate lunch dinners from $3.95 to $4.50. . . . **Panda Express** is a Chinese cafeteria with such choices as spicy chicken with peanuts, hot Szechuan shredded pork, and vegetable chop suey. Two items are $2.95; three, $3.75; and four, $4.45.

Healthy's offers a cholesterol-free pizza at $1.25 a slice, and others with choices of five toppings up to $2.25 a slice, plus a selection of salads, chile, and potato dishes, $2.25 to $3.25. . . . Then comes **The Kitchen Garden** with croissant sandwiches from $3.50 to $3.95, salads from $2.95 to $4.25, and baked potatoes, plain and fancy. . . . **Plush Pippin,** an outpost of the full-service restaurant upstairs (see below) offers quiche at $2.25 a slice, soups at $1.35 a cup and $1.95 a bowl, and pies galore that you can sample at $1.95 the slice, or $5.50 the works. . . . **Orson's Chowderette** is an outpost of the popular Orson's in Ward Warehouse. Finger foods like fish nuggets and clam strips are $2.10; chowders—New England, Manhattan, or seafood—$1.90; salads like shrimp and crab, $3.95 to $4.95; and burgers of mahimahi, shrimp, or oysters, $2.25 to $2.65.

Interspersed among these but not yet open at the time of this writing were **La Rôtisserie, Shop DC, Smoked Salmon Etc., Joni's, Patti's Chinese Kitchen** (they may close their other Ala Moana restaurant only 1,000 feet away when they open here), **Little Sicily Pizza,** and **Lyn's Delicatessen,** formerly in this spot. Lyn's has long been one of the best kosher-style delis in town, known for thick corned beef and pastrami sandwiches, lox and bagels, fragrant and garlicky hot dogs, plus plate lunches, and very special buys on steak dinners.

As for **Patti's,** it's been a byword among locals and visitors alike for many, many years. Plate lunches with rice or noodles and a choice of any two items are $2.65; it's $3.30 for three items, $3.90 for four. These might include Peking-style roast duck, beef with broccoli, shrimp roll, lshoyu chicken, sweet-and-sour fish, crispy almond duck, ad delicious infinitum. Considering that these dishes are not cooked to order, they are still tasty and are certainly a lusty bargain meal.

At the time of this writing, Makai Market was open weekdays from 9:30 a.m. to 9 p.m., to 5:30 p.m. on Saturday, and from 10 a.m. to 5 p.m. Sunday. However, business has been so good that the owners have been talking about opening from 7 a.m. to midnight. Makai Market occupies a half acre of space and employs over 500 people—who obviously don't starve.

Ala Moana Restaurants Outside Makai Market

Should you feel the need for something a little more in the peace-and-quiet department, where you might sit down with friends in comfortable booths and enjoy a reasonably priced meal, try **Plush Pippin** (tel. 955-2633), a bright new restaurant, very popular with locals as is its original restaurant in Kailua (see Chapter III, Honolulu: Restaurants). Pink and green tones, whirling fans overhead, plants, a sunny, relaxed atmosphere are the big pluses. And the food is good: you could have a hot entree like quiche or pot pie or half a Cornish game hen, served with soup or dinner salad, from $4.75 to $6.25. There are good burgers from $2.95 to $3.75, a tasty vegetarian sandwich of guacamole and veggies at $3.50, and an all-you-can eat salad bar for $5.25. For dessert, it's either old-fashioned fruit pie, the house specialty, or an ice cream treat from a branch of Bubbie's, right in the restaurant (the original is a big favorite in the University area, see Chapter III). Breakfast is served from 7 a.m. to 11 a.m., until 11:30 on weekends, so it might be a nice idea to come here for banana pancakes before or after the young people's hula show on Sunday. Plush Pippin is open every day from 7 a.m. to 10 p.m.

Another sit-down spot with a pleasant atmosphere—a gazebo and colorful murals on the wall—is **Bella Italia** (tel. 955-7891), on the lower oceanside level of Ala Moana. It caters to local families (kids get free reusable bibs) and serves up well-prepared, tasty Italian dishes. Complete lunches start at $3.95, full-course dinners begin at $4.50. Antipasto plus veal and seafood specialties are popular at dinner, and for lunch, it's pizza, pasta, and subs. If you come by for breakfast, try their Belgian waffles.

If you want a wonderful cup of coffee, a flaky butter croissant, or some light food served in a cheery bistro setting, *allez vite à* **Michel's Baguette** (tel. 946-9233), on the mauka side of Ala Moana's street level. This Gallic addition to Ala Moana is very popular, and the prices are *bon marché:* omelets with two fillings, $2.75; salade maison, $3.60: soup du jour, $1.65, just to give you an idea. Half-a-dozen specialties include a Basque rib meal with beverage, for $5.25, and quiche with salad for $3.45. Service is cafeteria style, and you sit at spanking white tables and chairs. Check their sidewalk bakery department and take home some of the French breads, rolls, croissants *par excellence,* and baguettes, for breakfast munching at your hotel. Better yet, come back here; they serve a continental breakfast, from 7 a.m. Monday to Saturday, from 8 a.m. Sunday.

For an all-American meal, there's **Peppermill** (tel. 946-4044), a few doors away. Again, it's cafeteria style with pleasant seating: tables are wood, chairs reed, tiled floors beige. Lamps add a colonial touch. Thick liverwurst and onion sandwiches, $3.60, and roast beef, $3.95, are very popular. Homemade soup and salad are served with a freshly baked half-loaf of bread at $3.55. A half avocado filled with chicken mango or shrimp is $4.80. Hot specials like beef and mushroom in Burgundy sauce, chicken with vegetables, and prime rib, are in the $4 to $5 bracket. We found the portions liberal and a cut above standard fast food.

There must be plenty of natural-food enthusiasts in Honolulu; they mob the wonderful take-out counter at **Vim and Vigor** every lunchtime. Not only are there "unreal" vegetarian sandwiches like tofu burger, Vigor burger, wham salad (like ham), and tuno salad (like tuna), all bulging with sprouts, shaved carrots, and sunflower seeds, and only costing $1.95 to $3.50, but there are now "real" sandwiches, still health-oriented, like bull burger, which has less than 2% fat, and bacon and pastrami sandwiches with no nitrates ($2.50 to $3.50). There are "real" plate lunches, pizzas with many toppings ("real" or "unreal"), delicious salads, and tasty "dip wiches" of babaganush, guacamole, or hummus, served with pita and bran crackers ($2.50). Yogurt-dophilus and tofu-dophilus desserts are low in fat. Try one of their cooling smoothies, or fruit drinks made to order from fresh island fruits, in the middle of a hot Honolulu afternoon. Too bad there's no seating area, but there are benches outside. If you like unusual breads, take home a loaf of whole-wheat sweet bread, sprouted wheat, or carrot-onion!

There's a fresh, natural feeling about **The Haven,** a charmingly decorated spot (tile floors, murals on the wall, banners hanging from the ceiling); you can sit down at tables to enjoy your meal. Sandwiches and salads are featured here, and they are imaginative and delicious: you could have a Pacific Catch (albacore tuna salad, Monterey Jack cheese, and avocado), or a Mauna Kea (cucumber in dill sauce with three cheeses) among the sandwiches, which run from $2.95 to $5.25, and can be served on nine-grain bread, a French baguette, or sourdough. Salads, $4.50 to $5.25, include a tasty Greek salad called Athena's and The Waterfront, an avocado stuffed with shrimp salad. Thick, homemade soups, quiche platters, and stuffed baked potatoes are also featured. We never miss having the banana nut bread (80¢) here. End your meal with hot, spiced apple cider, herb teas, fresh juices, or a 50¢-cup of Kona coffee with as many free refills as you like. Come early and enjoy some good breakfasts here too.

There's another branch of The Haven at 841 Bishop St., in the Davies Pacific Center, in downtown Honolulu.

On that same rear level, you can join local Japanese families having dinner, from 4 to 9 p.m., at **Wong's Okazu-ya.** That's when they prepare such Japanese specialties as shoyu butter fish with tofu and vegetables, sukiyaki, and combination tempura plates, from about $4.25 to $7. Meals include soup, tsukemono, rice, and tea. The rest of the day, from 8 a.m. to 4 p.m., they'll fix you up with a hearty bowl of wonton min, saimin, or special rahmen for $3 to $3.75. In addition, you can choose your own plate lunch from their delicatessen, which has over 55 items, including sushi, chow mein, fried rice, and teriyaki. The average plate lunch costs $3 to $4.

Bad news for dieters! **Lappert's Aloha Ice Cream,** the rage of Kauai, is now in Honolulu, with flavors like Grand Marnier, brownie fudge, blueberry cheesecake, or pink bubblegum! Scrumptious! Singles are $1.44.

VITAL STATISTICS: Most Ala Moana Center establishments stay open seven days a week, opening at 9:30 a.m. Monday through Saturday, at 10 a.m. on Sunday. They close at 9 p.m. Monday through Friday, at 5:30 p.m. on Saturday, and at 5 p.m. on Sunday. From Kalakaua Avenue in Waikiki, you can take the no. 8 bus and you'll be at Ala Moana in about ten minutes. Parking areas are numerous—and they even have coconut palms coming through the concrete!

3. Around Town

WARD WAREHOUSE: One of the most eye-catching of Honolulu's shopping centers is Ward Warehouse, located on Ward Avenue between Auahi Street and Ala Moana, across from Fisherman's Wharf. More than 75 shops and restaurants occupy the handsome two-story structures fashioned out of great rough-hewn planks, and there seems to be a higher-than-usual level of taste and selectivity here. Many are decorator shops of interest primarily to residents, but there is an equal number to delight the visitor.

Right up at the top of the list is Agnes Chin's **Future Heirloom Collectibles,** a gallery/shop that concentrates on superb arts and crafts collected from all over Asia. The price range is vast here, so while you might spend $500 to $600 for an authentic museum piece from Thailand or $1,000 for an elaborately carved screen from China, you can also garner such treasures as a hand-painted porcelain bud vase from Thailand at $4, a $40 woodcarving from Borneo, or a one-of-a-kind precious stone from $30. There is a small, very well-selected collection of ethnic clothing, like the magnificent Ikat Samurai coats for $200 that we saw on our last visit. And Chinese "Little Freedom" dolls, complete with I.D.s, China's answer to the Cabbage Patch dolls, are $35. Be sure to note the exquisite hand-carved and meticulously hand-painted wooden ducks made by a master from Hong Kong, very reasonably priced at $55 each. . . . Another dazzling showplace for handcrafts is the **Artist's Guild,** a gallery and outlet for many local craftpersons: you'll see beautiful ceramics, leaded glass, fine furniture made of local hardwoods, flower pillows, jewelry, modern and traditional metal sculpture, soft sculpture, and finely detailed leather goods. Have a look at the Gyotaku—fish rubbings by island artist Michael Hemperly. These are prints of local schools of fish done in iridescent colors, according to the ancient Japanese technique. From $40, framed—not bad for a fine home decoration. Note the Old Hawaiian prints (from $12), and lovely notepapers, too. . . . You'll find art posters from Hawaii—and just about everywhere else—at the **Art Board,** which shows Luigi Fumigalli, among other popular local artists. Note their collection of original photographs, and enchanting mugs by Laurel Burch, well-priced at $9.25. . . . Fine art posters, art reproductions, and original prints may also be found at **Frame Shack.** Nicely matted small prints begin at $7.50. . . . If you're in town for a while and want to learn the fine art of making artificial flowers, stop in at **The Extra Dimension,** which sells beautiful flowers and gift items and represents the Miyuki Art Flower Studio of Hawaii. All the flowers are made of different fabrics and are quite handsome.

Those weary of seeing the same clothing in every store should stop in to see **Kinnari,** where Yupin, a lissome Thai lady, designs creative dresses, skirts, and blouses; a touch of appliqué floral design, patchwork, or hand-embroidery sets each apart from the others. Considering the quality and the fact that minor alterations are included in the price of the garment, the price for long dresses—$80 and up—is competitive. There are dresses for children too, from sizes 1 up to 9 or 10. . . . **Birkenstock Footprints** is the place to buy those ugly-looking, marvelous-feeling naturally contoured Birkenstock sandals that give you a "barefoot on the beach" sensation even on hard surfaces. They're for men, women, and kids of all ages, and the average price is about $55 for adults, $45 for children.

With your feet all nice and comfy, you're ready to continue your explorations of Ward Warehouse. You may want to pick up some Christmas ornaments from **Kris Kringle's Den,** some fine music boxes at **Erida's,** or lovely Japanese clothing and prints at **Manyo Gallery.** Check out the furoshiki blouses at Manyo; they are made of rayon fabric with interesting prints, used to wrap gifts in Japan. The pieces are sewn together here, and make an unusual blouse, $29. The same shop also has fabrics by the yard, plus magnificent Japanese wedding kimonos that cost from $200 to $300. . . . The **Executive Chef** is for the compulsive cook: we saw wine glasses, cookie molds, French copperware, and other kitchen joys, at good prices. One of their most popular items is a foil cutter for wine bottles, $5.50. A great T-shirt reads: "Life is too short to drink bad wine."

Conscientious Honolulu mommies shop **Child's Play** for creative play and learning materials, educational toys, and books. An excellent selection. . . . They collect dollhouse miniatures in the gigantic dollhouse that is **My Favorite Things**. . . . And moms-in-waiting, or those who've already delivered, find **In Bloom** just what they've been looking for: attractive maternity and baby clothes under one roof.

Pause 'n' Paw has the veritable something for everyone, from stuffed animals and pop-art home decor to nautical knickknacks. Note their excellent collection of island jewelry, including hologram necklaces at $22. . . . **J. W. Dohrman's** is known for exquisite china and the best in European, Oriental, and American art. But there are many small gift items here, like sachets, potpourri, and graceful pillboxes made of crushed marble, $11. . . . You can get gorgeous fans among the Chinese arts and crafts at **Chien Ho Gallery,** the traditional pottery of Okinawa at **Arts of Okinawa.**

End your excursion, perhaps, at the **Coffee Works,** a charming shop that purveys all manner of imported coffees, teas, and chocolates, as well as some very attractive vessels from which to sip them. Coffee makers too. Happiness is a slice of carrot cake and a cup of café Vienna, served from their coffee bar. Adjoining is a new café whose specialties are roast beef, Black Forest ham, and smoked turkey sandwiches, served with lettuce, tomato, bell peppers, provolone, pickle and dressings, quite a mouthful for $3.95.

We've told you about the **Chowder House** for a quick seafood meal, the **Old Spaghetti Factory** for pasta in a fabulous setting, and **Dynasty II** for a Chinese buffet lunch, **Inakaya** is a lovely double-decker Japanese restaurant with a rustic air about it and cobbled floors, very attractive. **Start Anderson's Cattle Company** is locally famous for their $10 prime ribs and chicken dinners, served in an upbeat setting with a great view of Kewalo Boat Basin. For light snacks, choose among the fast-food stands (seating in a central courtyard) at the **Food Express** (everything from burgers to saimin to health-food salads), or visit **Yami Yogurt, Harpo's** for pizza, and **Dave's Ice Cream** (with 40 flavors, including passion fruit, guava, and pineapple sherbet) for calories. There are outside tables on the lower level. While you're snacking, you can watch lunchtime entertainment, Monday and Friday at the amphitheater stage, Wednesday at Food Express.

Ward Warehouse shopping hours are 10 a.m. to 9 p.m. Monday through Friday, until 5 p.m. on Saturday, and from 11 a.m. to 4 p.m. on Sunday. Restaurants stay open until late in the evening. From Waikiki, take any bus no. 8 (except those marked "Waikiki Beach and Hotels") mountain side of Kalakaua, Kuhio Avenue, or Kalia Road. It's about a 15-minute ride from Waikiki.

WARD CENTRE: Down the road a block at 1200 Ala Moana Blvd., Ward Centre is a worthy follow-up to Ward Warehouse, another sophisticated collection of boutiques and restaurants, all with a high level of charm and taste. The emphasis is on small, very expensive boutiques, so we usually find ourselves coming here to eat at some of our favorite restaurants—**Compadres, Crêpe Fever, Macha Java, Keo's at Ward Centre, Andrew's, Monterey Bay Canners, Ryan's Parkplace,** and **Big Ed's Deli** (see Chapter III on Honolulu: Restaurants) and doing a lot of just looking, thanks, at the pricey shops. But it is fun to explore boutiques like **Peony Arts,** with fragrances, potpourris, and other accessories for bed, bath, and table. We especially like the hand-embroidered linens from Portugal and the People's Republic of China. Treat yourself, at least, to a handkerchief, from $2.50 to $9, depending on the workmanship, or pick up some bit of fragrance, like English soap leaves, $1.50 each. The wonderful scents permeate the air. . . . Have a look at the award-winning jewelry designs by Harry Haimoff, at **Haimoff & Haimoff.** You could pick up a gold Hawaiian pineapple charm with a diamond chip for as little as $65. . . . **Allison's Wonderland** is a very special store with a wide variety of classic toys, great dolls, wonderful stuffed animals—even a life-size Shetland pony, for the kiddy who has everything. From the good selection of children's books you might pick up "Legends of Hawaii as told by Lani Goose," a tape and coloring book at $4.95. And there are cute stamp pads at $5.95.

Of course, you'll want to stop by **Mary Catherine's** for "an extraordinary bakery experience"; this European-style bakery uses only fresh and natural ingredients, avoids additives and imitation flavors, and produces divine breads (brioches, baguettes, challah, a very popular French sourdough, multigrain), as well as even more divine cakes and pastries on the order of chocolate mousse cake or "snowberry"—whole raspberries folded into imported white chocolate cream. If you just can't wait to sample the goodies, repair to the tables a few steps up, in the rear. . . . While your taste buds are thus activated, saunter over to **R. Field Wine Co.** at the opposite end of Ward Centre: in addition to fine wines, it stocks the likes of dried morels imported from France, smoked butterfish, Beluga caviar, and spiced and pickled asparagus. The last time we were there they were selling chocolate covered potato chips—"weird but good."

Have a look at the fine-arts collection at **Images International,** which shows some of Hawaii's top local artists. They also have Oriental prints, which begin around $40. . . . Check out the latest books at **Upstart Crow & Co.,** sample the divine champagne truffles created by **Neufchâtel Chocolates at Chantilly, Ltd.,** which also has a great card collection. . . . You can pick up attractive women's shoes, handbags, and sportswear at **The Shop** for **Pappagallo,** and spend big bucks for those little polo player emblems at **Polo/Ralph Lauren.**

Ready for a bit of a splurge? Have lunch or especially dinner at **Il Fresco;** it's one of the best northern Italian–Cajun style restaurants anywhere, and their goat-cheese specialties are extraordinary.

To reach Ward Centre, again take bus no. 8 from Waikiki, a 15-minute ride.

DESIGNER DISCOUNTS: Just opposite Ward Centre, at 1112 Auahi St., is a shop known to few tourists; but **The Ultimate You** (tel. 523-3888), which might be called the "Bergdorf Goodman of the consignment shops," is a very well known, indeed, to Hawaii's most fashion conscious women. This is where they come for new and next-to-new high fashion at surprisingly low prices. Owner Kelsey Sears has contacts with socialites and celebrities in the islands, in California, and in Europe; when they get slightly bored with their designer duds after a wearing or two (or when they've compulsively bought five-of-a-kind sweaters and never worn them), they send them to Sears; who resells them for anywhere from 50% to 90% off retail price. She insists that everything be in "pristine condition." Half of the store consists of brand new merchandise which is also heavily discounted, much of it from European designers. Obviously, the stock here changes daily, so you never can tell what you will find, but it's worth a look-see. Some examples: A $3,000 Gucci alligator handbag sold for $495; a $600 Yves St. Laurent skirt for $90; brand new, $150 Hermes scarves for $29; and $300 garments worn once or twice for $80 or $90. A $100 dress could go for as little as $49, a $75 silk blouse for as little as $25. "Every day mini-miracles happen here," Sears says.

Since the shop deals with the island's best-known celebrities, we asked the inevitable question. No, there has been no sign of Imelda Marcos's shoes.

The Ultimate You is open from 11 a.m. to 6 p.m., Monday through Saturday.

DOWNTOWN HONOLULU: Downtown is where the local people do most of their shopping, and we'll let you in on a kamaaina secret known to very few tourists. Head for 1 N. King St., where **Liberty House's Penthouse** is located. Discounted merchandise from all the Liberty House stores around town is brought here, and the initial reduction is a whopping 50%. On top of that, the price is automatically dropped 25% every 14 days. Most of the items consist of women's and children's clothing and women's designer shoes, but occasionally you'll see men's aloha shirts and other men's wear, as well. On a recent shopping foray we found $40 handbags at $20, $35 dresses at $18, and $30 aloha shirts at $15. Enough said? This is one of those places where on some days you'll find nothing suitable, on other days you'll strike it rich!

The rest of Liberty House and the other Fort Street stores have merchandise similar to what you find in their Waikiki and Ala Moana branches, but perhaps a shade more citified, since they cater mostly to a local trade. It's fun to come here during the lunch hour, when island people are shopping, eating lunch on the many stone benches and seats that dot this fountained area, and watching their kids play in the sand. Traffic is closed off, creating one long window-shopping promenade. If you're hungry, stop off at any of the restaurants or fast-food stands mentioned in Chapter III (**Rada's Piroshki** is at 1144-1146 Fort Street Mall).

If garment factories appeal to you, there's one you can be taken to, free and with extras thrown in. The **Hilo Hattie Fashion Center,** at 700 Nimitz Hwy., offers something like 40,000 Hawaiian fashions to browse through, all for sale at factory prices, plus free refreshments, free alterations, a lei greeting, and even a free bus trip to its doors. (They'll also take you to the Dole Pineapple Cannery.) Phone 537-2926 or check the tourist papers to find out where you can pick up the Fashion Center Fun Bus, or simply take bus no. 8 marked "Airport" from Waikiki or Ala Moana.

Anyone who likes stuffed bears will be delighted with **A Bear in Mind,** 1171 St. King St. at the corner of Piikoi. Owners Al and Amy stock hundreds of collectible bears, from Steiff all the way down to little travel bears you can carry in your pocket, as well as anything you can think of in bear-related items, such as stationery, erasers, pencils, T-shirts, rubber stamps, or notepads. Open weekdays from 10 a.m. to 5:30 p.m., Saturday only until 3:30 p.m.

THE CHINATOWN LEI SELLERS: When local people need to buy leis, they usually head for Chinatown—and so should you. Although leis are sold all over town, especially at the airport and on the ocean side of Kalakaua Avenue, the best prices and finest quality can usually be found among the Chinatown lei sellers. There are several stores on Maunakea Street; three of our favorites are **Cindy's Lei Shoppe** at no. 1034, **Violet's** at 1165 Maunakea, and **Jenny's Lei Stand** at no. 1036. **Lita's Leis** is around the corner at 59 N. Beretania St. Local friends advise that Lita sells beautiful hako-head leis that dry splendidly and can be worn for a long time. Cindy's carries the largest selection of flower leis in the state, and all four make up orchid, plumeria, double carnation, and other leis, at prices ranging from $2 to $8 and up, depending on the season and the availability of flowers. Should you want to send leis to your friends back home—a lovely but no longer inexpensive gift—the price, by Express Mail, will be about $25. We also like the flowers—and the low prices—at **Chiyo's,** located inside and at the front of the Thrifty Drugstore at 3610 Waialae Ave. in the Waialae-Kahala area. You can shop by phone (tel. 734-6337 or 737-5055), and be assured that your order will be well and speedily taken care of. They'll bill you later.

If you'll see your friends within a day or two of your arrival, it's cheaper to carry flowers with you. Better still, give your friends the flower leis your Hawaiian friends will doubtless drape around your neck as they bid you aloha—if you can bear to part with them.

Buyers beware: The most expensive times to buy leis are May Day, the graduation season (end of May), and New Year's; that's when $2.50 vanda leis can suddenly become $12!

MORE CHINATOWN SHOPPING: Some of the old buildings in Chinatown have been refurbished in the last few years. Now you'll find, in a five-block area, a couple of new luncheon spots, and five or six art galleries. Have a look at the **Pollitt Galleries,** 139 Nuuanu Ave., which, in addition to some interesting art that includes painting in all media, shows glass ceramics, Hawaiian sculptures in fiber and clay at $48, and handmade papers items by local artists, from $75 up. They also carry Austrian and Italian cotton knits from $125 and up, one-of-a-kind pieces of jewelry by local craftspersons, batik silk scarves for around $30, and unique batik ensembles, by Asiann, who lives and works in Hawaii.

The gallery is run by June Pollitt, a dynamic lady who was born in Capetown, grew up in New York, and has been a resident of the islands for many years. Hours are 10 a.m. to 4 p.m. weekdays, Saturday to 1 p.m., closed Sunday.

FOR RENT: If you need to rent something while you're in Honolulu—maybe a TV set or a radio, a stroller, even wheelchairs or crutches, we have a terrific place to recommend: **Dyan's Rental.** Their rates are low, they deliver to your hotel cheerfully and promptly, and they're very nice to do business with. Just call them at 531-5207 and a delivery boy will emerge from their huge downtown warehouse with exactly what you need.

BARGAIN HUNTERS' HEAVENS: A mecca for penny-pinchers, **Holiday Mart** is in a residential neighborhood at 801 Kaheka St. (two blocks mauka of the Ala Moana Shopping Center). It's a huge discount store, jammed with local people busy buying everything from groceries to books to toys to toasters, all at fat discounts. Buys are especially good in Hawaiin wear for men, women, and keikis. We also spotted a swim board for which we had paid $6.95 at a gift shop on Kauai for $3.99 here; a boogie board on sale for $40 here, regularly $55 (and $59 in other stores); macadamia nuts at $2.79 for a five-ounce tin; kukui-nut leis for $4.49; and Hawaiian records for $6.99—all very good prices indeed. Holiday Mart is now owned by the Daiei Corporation, and is better than ever.

Those who sew should note the selection of Polynesian fabrics from about $4.49 a yard. And while you're here, stock up on groceries and booze—the prices are excellent, much better than in the smaller stores at the beach. If it's time for lunch, you can join the crowd at the outside Chinese cafeteria deli, which has a good take-out department, as well as some 20 items on the steam table. Holiday Mart is open every day, from 8 a.m. to midnight, until 10 p.m. on Sunday.

Visit the factory store of **Blair's,** at 404-A Ward Ave., for good buys in seconds of their fine monkeypod, koa, and other woodcarvings, known for many years for excellent quality. Some of these factory store items may have small flaws, but they can be repaired, and the savings are huge. (Many of our readers have been happy with their purchases here.)

WHOLESALE HEIRLOOM JEWELRY: Greg Reeser is an extremely talented young man who wholesales Hawaiian Heirloom Jewelry to the public. His company, **Precious Metals Hawaii,** 1600 Kapiolani Blvd., Suite 1616 (tel. 955-6657), is not only the largest manufacturer of such jewelry in the state, but also aims to have the best prices as well: these begin at $36 for a solid gold bracelet enameled with either your name in Hawaiian or with initials. When the last Hawaiian queen, Liliuokalani attended Queen Victoria's jubilee, she was given a gift of a bracelet that inspired this style of jewelry, so popular in Hawaii today. When a return gift was brought to the current Queen of England, Greg Reeser was chosen as its designer. In addition to bracelets, he created special rings, pendants, rope chains, and earrings. Hours are Monday through Friday from 9 a.m. to 5 p.m., Saturday to 4 p.m.

MUUMUU MADNESS: Saving money on muumuus is great fun: Why pay $70 or $80 or more for a muumuu in a department store or fancy resort shop when you can pay about half if you know where to look? In addition to **Hilo Hattie** (see above), we have some special bargain favorites. **Island Muumuu Works,** 660 Ala Moana, sells Hilda of Hawaii muumuus at just one price: $37.50. They also have pretty head or hat leis made of silk flowers and leaves, which go for about $24. Open Monday through Saturday from 9 a.m. to 5 or 6 p.m. There's a second store at Maui Mall in Kahului, Maui.

Especially for You has eight locations in Honolulu: the closest ones are downtown at 1133 Fort Street Mall, in the heart of the business district, and at the Kahala Mall; see ahead. All of the very pretty muumuus here are made by Jacqueline of Hawaii; short muumuus begin at $25.95, long ones at $29.95. When sale time comes, the prices go down even lower, to $19.50. Open Monday through Saturday from 9 a.m. to 5 p.m.

Attractive muumuus by Naili'i Fashions, which sell for $60 to $80 in the regular stores, go for $35 at the **Muumuu Factory** at 818 Keeaumoku St. During their very frequent sales—which seem to last for weeks—prices are even less: all long muumuus are $25; all shorties, $19. This is a good-size shop with wall-to-wall muumuus, and while the number of styles is limited, each style comes in a variety of fabrics in all sizes, so you're very likely to find the dress you want in the fabric you like best.

RESORT WEAR: Stunning savings—as much as 40% to 70% off regular retail prices—make the 20-minute-or-so drive out to **Malia: The Factory Outlet** at 2200 Dillingham Blvd. eminently worthwhile. But don't expect to see muumuus and aloha shirts here: Malia does strictly contemporary resort fashion—jackets, big shirts, cotton sweaters, skirts, dresses. On a recent visit we walked away with a beautiful $64 silk sweater for $15 (they were selling at two for $25). The selection changes constantly, but typical examples would include $76 dresses for $56, $28 shorts for $15, $35 T-shirts for just $10. Great fun, good buys. Open Monday to Saturday from 9 a.m. to 5:30 p.m., Sunday from 11 a.m. to 4 p.m.

AT THE ZOO: Honolulu Zoo has a gift shop called the **Zootique,** filled with toys, books, kites, apparel, jewelry, and novelties with bird and animal themes. Our special favorites are the T-shirts made especially for the zoo with sayings like "Lion on the Grass at Honolulu Zoo" or "See You Later, Alligator," with appropriate line drawings underneath. Perhaps you'll walk away with some pop-up books, a stuffed animal or two, and some souvenirs sporting the zoo's logo. The Zootique is open from 8:30 a.m. to 4 p.m. every day (except Christmas and New Year's), and all proceeds go to the Honolulu Zoo Hui, a nonprofit organization of friends of the zoo who raise funds for zoo improvements and educational programs.

KAHALA MALL: Still haven't had enough of shopping malls? Hop into your U-Drive, go up Kapahulu to Lunalillo Freeway East, exit at Waialae, and you'll find yourself at Kahala Mall, part of the big Waialae Kahala Shopping Complex that the local folks love. Kahala Mall is an enclosed shopping center, with a main lobby like that of a hotel—carpeted and decorated with a beautiful fountain and plantings. Stretching out in various directions from the lobby are a bevy of interesting stores. The big chains like **Liberty House, McInerny, Carol & Mary, Andrade, Long's Drugs, Waldenbooks,** and **Woolworth's** are represented, of course, and so are smaller boutiques like **Benetton** with its marvelous Italian knit sweaters; **Pappagallo** with stunning shoes and chic women's wear, and **Plush,** which stocks smart styles for that previously forgotten woman, the one who wears sizes 14 and up . . . **Cotton Cargo** bursts at the seams with lovely, pricey clothes—mostly from Mexico and India. . . . Both custom-made and ready-to-wear couture clothing, plus accessories and jewelry, draw the cognoscenti to **Fabrications.** . . . Unhappy with the high price of most muumuus? Try **Especially for You,** which has beautiful ones, and all at about half the going rate. They have seven other shops around town (see above). . . . The **Curious Porpoise** is chock full of tasteful and unusual gifts. . . . We like the selection of beautiful stationery, cards, desk accessories, bookmarks, and calendars at **San Francisco Paper World.** . . . **Jennie's Garden** has a good selection of leis, cut flowers, arrangements, and quality houseplants. . . . The size range goes up to 14 at **Familiar,** which has darling clothes for children. . . . A full line of silk-screened and iron-on decal shirts are a specialty at **India Imports International.**

Worth a special trip is **Following Sea,** a shop-gallery that represents the work of some 350 professional craft artists from 40 states, and sponsors outstanding monthly exhibitions. Everything is unique, and the inventory changes constantly. Prices range from a little to a lot, but there is a fine selection of ceramics, woodwork, and jewelry in the $15 to $20 range. Their most popular items are hand-blown oil lamps, from $38. On a recent visit we saw koa, a native Hawaiian hardwood, beautifully crafted into notebook covers, chimes, jewel chests, and unique boxes from $25 to $300; plus exquisite leaded-glass boxes each with a beautiful seashell set into the top, from $53 to $75. Following Sea is working with local crafts people to develop new and unique items. Save this place for gifts for some special person—or for yourself.

After you've explored the mall, go outside and see the other stores in the shopping complex; **Vim and Vigor,** for example, has one of the best assortments of natural-food items in the city. Top off your shopping excursion with a snack or a meal at the **Yum-Yum Tree,** a restaurant enormously popular with the neighborhood people for its well-priced food, deft service, and friendly atmosphere. Be sure to try a slice of their incredibly good pies—strawberry cheese and English toffee are among the choices; you'll want to take a whole pie home with you. Or enjoy a delicious northern Chinese meal at **Yen King,** one of the best such restaurants in these parts. There's also a Chinese cafeteria and, for Mexican food, **Chi Chi's.**

KILOHANA SQUARE: A far cry from the sleek modernity of Kahala Mall, **Kilohana Square** looks as if it comes right out of Hawaii's past. Drive up Kapahulu Avenue from Waikiki to the 1000 block (one block makai of the H-1 Freeway), and you'll come to a cluster of buildings surrounding a square and a parking lot.

The atmosphere is more European flea market than shopping center, and indeed Kilohana Square seems more devoted to arts and crafts than to ordinary commerce.

You'll have fun browsing through the antique shops, galleries, craft stores, and boutiques, whose wares spill out into the street. Most of the items at **Something Special!** are just that: bamboo chopsticks with burnt-in designs ($1.40 for a bundle of ten); colorful tableware from China and Japan (from 50¢ to $10.50); hand-screened T-shirts of favorite local foodstuffs ($7.50 for children, $10.50 to $22 for adults), sushi refrigerator magnets, and their charming ceramic manapua (Chinese dumpling) paperweight, packed in a Chinese restaurant take-out container, are just a few of the selected items from at least ten different countries.

Needlepoint, Etc., could get you interested in the art if you're not already addicted. They have hundreds of beautiful needlepoint kits and canvases, with both Hawaiian and Oriental themes. . . . **The Trunk** specializes in muumuus and casual wear for queen-size ladies—size 16 and up. It's one of the few stores in Hawaii that does so. And they also have a full line of swimwear and lingerie for "big, beautiful women." . . . Lovers of rare and out-of-print books will have fun browsing through **Pacific Book House.**

AT MANOA MARKETPLACE: One of the most charming shops in Honolulu has to be **Distractions,** in this neighborhood shopping center at 2752 Woodlawn. Dr. Teddy bears are a big item here (we're partial to the pastel rainbow-striped ones with blank faces), as are teddy bear T-shirts, posters, and stationery. There's a varied collection of unusual greeting cards and gift wraps, as well as beautifully designed writing paper and all sorts of bright desk accessories, including hand-painted wooden letters and ornaments to glue onto plaques for signs. Prices are modest. We never seem to be able to leave here without getting something new and different.

If you love to browse among books for children, be sure to visit the charming **Story Hour.** And if you and some little ones can make it on a Saturday morning, from 11 to 11:30 a.m., you're likely to hear local or visiting authors reading from their own books. You'll enjoy chatting with proprietor Terri, a former teacher, who chooses books from pre-school up through young adult. You'll also find cassettes, posters, and stuffed animals that go with a number of books. The shop is open from 10 a.m. to 5 p.m. Monday to Friday, on Saturday to 4 p.m. (Phone 988-7795 for driving directions.)

NEAR THE BISHOP MUSEUM: Nake'u Awai, at 1613 Houghtailing St., is a bit out of the way—unless you combine it with a visit to the Bishop Museum—but it is worth a trip if you like the unusual in fabrics and design. Joel Nake'u Awai is a young Hawaiian designer whose beautiful silk-screened fabrics are a blend of the traditional and the contemporary in Hawaiian art. After he designs and executes the textiles, he has them whipped up into long skirts, shirts, muumuus, bags, and sun dresses. While not cheap, the prices are certainly competitive with those of the better department stores and specialty shops; and the designs are exclusive. We also saw some very good-looking T-shirts with Hawaiian designs for $12 and up, and an interesting array of locally crafted items—lauhala fans, floppy-brimmed hats, gift cards, woven bags, and books of Hawaii—for $4.16 and up. Inquire about his fashion shows. If you can catch one of them you're in for a treat. They're as imaginative as the clothes and include appearances by guest luminaries. The shop is open only until 3:30 p.m. weekdays, until 2 p.m. on Saturday; closed Sunday.

PEARLRIDGE SHOPPING CENTER: Out in Aiea, about a half-hour drive from Waikiki, is Pearlridge Shopping Center, a multimillion-dollar complex that tops even Ala Moana in size and is a big favorite with the local people. Its design is unique. The two, huge, air-conditioned malls at Pearlridge are built on opposite sides of an 11-acre watercress farm. Shoppers travel between the two malls in Hawaii's only monorail train, "The Pali Momi Express." From your perch in the Hawaiian-looking, orange and yellow monorail, you enjoy a panoramic view of Pearl Harbor along the way.

As at most of the shopping centers catering to the local trade, familiar names like Liberty House, Sears, J.C. Penney, and Long's Drugs dominate the scene. Daiei, Tokyo's largest retailer which once had a huge department store here is gone now (replaced by 12 Consolidated Chain theaters) but **Shirokiya** shows the Japanese influence, with many captivating art objects from the Orient. And for those who must have the very latest in far-out fashions, Pearlridge is an embarrassment of riches. **Contemporary Casuals, Casual Corner, Brooks, San Francisco Rag Shop, Town & Country, Wildflowers, Pepperkorn, The Body Shop, American Denim Company, Ethel's, Jeans West, Runway 7,** and **Foxmoor Casuals** all stock the foxiest of threads. **Princess Lea** offers muumuus beginning at $19.99, and they're quite attractive.

The kids will love **Playwell,** jammed with just about every imaginable kind of toy. The $750,000 **Fernandez Fun Factory,** in the Pearlridge Makai (toward the sea) Mall, must be one of the world's fanciest "penny arcades." It features the newest, most elaborate electronic games. This is the main one; there are four branches around the island.

Hungry? Pearlridge "brings the world to you" with **Chuck's Steak House; Monterey Bay Canners; Anna Miller's** coffeeshop, with a fancier restaurant, the **Round House,** downstairs; two Chinese restaurants, **Hong Kong Garden** and **Shanghai Restaurant.** A new food court includes that popular island favorite, **Patti's Kitchen,** plus **Pizza Hut, Capuchino's Italian Restaurant,** and **Denny's,** a family-style dining spot. More were being built at the time of this writing. With a dozen or more fast-food emporiums here, there's truly something for every taste. *Note:* **Hong Kong Garden, Anna Miller's,** the **Round House,** and **Baskin-Robbins** are in a section removed from Phases I and II; they are "behind" Phase I, all the way down on Kam Highway.

Official store hours at Pearlridge are from 10 a.m. to 9 p.m. weekdays, 10 a.m. to 5 p.m. on Saturday, and 11 a.m. to 4 p.m. on Sunday. You can easily squeeze your visit to Pearlridge into your trip to Pearl Harbor or to Makaha. If you're driving to Pearl Harbor on Kam Hwy., you see it on your right just after you reach Pearl Harbor's entrance to the *Arizona* Memorial. If you're driving out the H-1 Freeway, take the Aiea exit. When driving out the Lunalilo Freeway from downtown, you'll see Pearlridge on the freeway directory signs. By bus, take the no. 20 from Waikiki to Pearlridge.

READERS' SHOPPING SUGGESTIONS: "Because Honolulu was our first stop, we were reluctant to shop there, afraid we would see something we liked better later on. This was a mistake. Honolulu was definitely cheaper on most souvenir items. My daughter found lovely shell bracelets for her friends in the posh Royal Hawaiian Shopping Center for 50¢. The same bracelets were $1.50 in Maui. The same was true for other items of jewelry and T-shirts. Also, most vendors in the International Market Place rapidly came down from their original prices when we hesitated. Bargaining seemed to be an acceptable way to do business" (Frances S. Kielt, West Hartford, Conn.). . . . "Warn your readers about the way they can get taken by some of the saleswomen in the gift shops. They would quote a price on an unmarked item, then up the price at the sale. We thought we all heard wrong until we compared stories in the car!" (Clareana Berched, Medford, Mass.). . . . "Tell people to buy the straw beach mats for 89¢ or 99¢ at the drug stores. I've seen them sold for $3 at the beach" (Karen J. Sinnreich, New Brunswick, N.J.). . . . "The Mission Houses Museum Shop in Honolulu had a wonderful selection of interesting items, all reasonably priced. I was able to buy most of my gifts in that one place. In contrast, I found gift items at the Polynesian Cultural Center to be overpriced" (Nancy E. Sephton, Berkeley, Calif.).

"**Records Hawaii** at 404 Piikoi St. and **Tower Records** at 611 Keeaumoku St., both near Ala Moana Center, have good selections of Hawaiian music and they often have sales. You can buy an album at $6.99 on sale, while other stores charge $7.99 or $8.99. Especially at Records Hawaii, they are very friendly and helpful; one time, they played quite a few LPs for me to choose from. If you like mellow music, try the following albums: *This is Our Island Home* by the Beamer Brothers; *Island in Your Eyes* by the Brothers Cazimero; *Best of Country Comforts* by Country Comforts, and *Like a Seabird in the Wind* by Olomana" (M. Komoto, San Francisco, Calif.). . . . "For a sampling of different Japanese treats, visit **Shirokiya Department Store** in Ala Moana Shopping Center. Half of the second floor is devoted to Japanese food, and what they sell is available to sample in the containers with toothpicks and napkins. They sometimes have a buffet where you can try hot items quite inexpensively. The foods are quite exotic, so I would recommend it for the adventuresome. . . . Aloha shirts are 'in' now on the mainland, so for the benefit of readers who want a good selection, here's what I found. I shopped for hours in Waikiki and came up with little I liked. The stores I visited all seemed to have limited selections. But guess which store had the best selection I saw on the island? **Sears** at Ala Moana Center! They had some of the finest makers and the shirts were attractively displayed. I brought eight home for Christmas gifts" (Eric Schuman, Topeka, Kans.).

"Jewelry and leather goods can be bought wholesale, for about one-third or one-half of what they cost at other shops at **Ali Baba**, which has two locations: at the Waikiki Shopping Plaza, 2250 Kalakaua, and at the Waikiki Business Plaza, 2270 Kalakaua. The only problem is, it's not Hawaiian. It's jewelry from India, but it's lovely" (Rue Drew, New York, N.Y.). . . . "For a bargain on popular T-shirts or sweatshirts, try **Crazy Shirts Factory Outlet** at 1095 Dillingham Blvd., in Kokea Center. Discontinued models, overruns, or slightly flawed men's, women's, and children's sizes. Selection would vary. 'Open daily, 9 a.m. to 6 p.m.' (Marge O'Harra, Portland, Ore.). . . . "**The University of Hawaii Bookstore** is a delightful place to shop for take-home goodies: they have a wide variety of sweatshirts, jackets, caps, track bags, etc., all with the U.H. logo, plus lots of stationery, cards, etc." (Brenda English, Fox Creek, Alberta, Canada). . . . "Buy postcards at **ABC** stores for the best buy. We were able to purchase ten for 90¢. Don't forget to bring 14-cent stamps from home, as you lose money on those small stamp machines. . . . We found the best buy for cans of macadamia nuts to be at **Hilo Hattie's**. . . . Instead of buying the pearls at the stands for $5 each, look for the oysters in a can, at three for $5 at some places. These pearls are very nice, and the equivalent of what you can get at the International Market Place. . . . T-shirts of fair quality were on sale at **ABC** stores for $1.98 each—what a bargain!" (Ricky A. Blum, Los Angeles, Calif.).

"After taking the free bus tour to Hilo Hattie's Fashion Center at 440 Kuwili St., we noticed the **Salvation Army store.** We asked if they minded if we walked over there after visiting their factory, and they said, 'Of course not, just come back anytime for the free bus trip back to Waikiki.' I found three muumuus and three Hawaiian skirts for $20. Wow —what a good deal, and fun to boot!" (Mark and Kay Irwin, Phoenix, Ariz.). . . . "If you can cook, see if you can find uncooked macadamia nuts and roast them yourself: 12 ounces cost me $4, considerably cheaper than 5 ounces for $2 in a can. They are unsalted, and will keep in a refrigerator or freezer. Occasionally there are sales on macadamia nuts at the **Macadamia Nut Factory** stores on Kalakaua that even beat the prices at Long's Drug Store and other comparable places. I purchased six five-ounce cans of whole nuts for $10.95" (Barbara Karchin, Naperville, Ill.). . . . "We found the shopping centers to be well planned, very modern, and quite expensive. We discovered that the **Swap Meet** at Aloha Stadium was a bargain-hunter's paradise. So very many new items, never before used, with prices sometimes at only one-fifth the cost of what the downtown shopping centers were asking. It was open each Saturday and Sunday from 7 a.m. to 3 p.m." (Jerald R. Borgie, San Diego, Calif.). . . . "We received many, many bargains at the **Aloha Stadium Swap Meet:** for example, Hanes T-shirts going in Waikiki for $8 and up, three shirts for $10; hanging shell mobiles for as little as $3, baseball hats for $2, and many other souvenir items we found throughout the island at much higher prices. The Swap Meet is easily reached from Waikiki by taking TheBUS and transferring at the Ala Moana Shopping Center and straight to Aloha Stadium. Entrance fee is 25¢" (Phyllis M. DiChiara, Yonkers, N.Y.). [*Authors' Note:* Another popular flea market called **Kam Swap Meet** is held on Wednesday, Saturday, and Sunday, across from the Pearlridge Shopping Center at Kam Twin Drive-In Theaters. Admission to drivers is 35¢. At any swap meet, you can get great bargains, but remember—you can also get taken! We've compared prices on the same item, and found as much as a $6 difference, below or above the regular retail price. Careful shopping is in order.]

"There is a U.S. Post Office in the **Royal Hawaiian Shopping Center,** also an ABC store. We found it convenient to purchase a six-can box of macadamia nuts in packages all ready for mailing, then go right up to the post office. Mail service to the mainland is very good, and we didn't have to carry the packages home and mail them later" (Pearl B. Weber, Brick Township, N.J.). . . . "The **Bishop Museum** is always a 'must' on our list, but I want especially to recommend the museum bookstore and gift shop. It really is the only place to buy good books on Hawaii, beyond the picture books that have nice color pictures and price tags and little else, which one finds everywhere. Two special purchases: *A Hawaiian Reader,* edited by A. Grove Day and Carl Stroven. This little paperback gem is a collection of short chapters by 30 different authors, including Mark Twain and Robert Louis Stevenson, organized chronologically and 'providing an informal history of Hawaii' in a most enjoyable way. It features diaries and firsthand accounts in particular ($3.95). Also special is a little pamphlet entitled *Current Facts and Figures About Hawaiians* by George S. Kanahele. This is a little book of statistics that was a real mind- and eye-opener for us. The information is a bit depressing, but explains a lot of what the observant tourist must notice about daily life in the islands. The chapters are: population, land, health, education, crime, business and employment, income, welfare, voter registration, and Hawaiian agencies" (John and Anne Duffield, Costa Mesa, Calif.). [*Authors' Note: A Hawaiian Reader* has long been one of our favorites (see the Introduction). We have also found an excellent selection of books on Hawaii at the **Honolulu Book Store** at Ala Moana Center.]

"I recently began a series of allergy shots and, to continue their effectiveness, decided to take my serum along. My physician suggested contacting one of the Kaiser hospitals. I did so and had my weekly shots in the outpatient section each week. It was low cost and very accommodating to me" (Mary M. McAndrew, Farmington, Minn.). . . . "A tip for those who intend to take pineapples home: Many places take orders for pineapples to be delivered to the airport or shipped home—often for as much as $5 each. We waited until we were ready to depart, then picked up three in a handy carrying case at a good price at the **Aero Shop** in the Honolulu airport" (Jeffrey S. Campbell, Colorado Springs, Colo.). [*Authors' Note:* Aero's pineapple stands are located by the baggage check-in counters of the major airlines. They sell pineapples in 3-packs, 6-packs, and 12-packs, and the latter two can be checked with your baggage.] . . . "Visit the swap meets on weekends at drive-ins around the island. You can find monkeypod bowls, etc., for much less than at 'tourist traps' and also soak up the local feeling. Check the classified section for swap announcements" (Mrs. Christine Newman, Kaneohe, Hi.).

"If you are buying liquor, note that it is cheaper at the **ABC stores** than at liquor or wine stores. For example, Tia Maria was more than $1 cheaper at ABC, and prices were also lower on certain wines" (Karen and Joan Polsen, Halifax, Nova Scotia, Canada). . . . "We found an absolute treasure on Kuhio Avenue near Kuhiolani called the **Food Pantry.** Prices there were the cheapest we found anywhere for food and drinks (hard and soft!), sometimes nearly a dollar cheaper than at the ABCs. They have a rather small selection of souvenir and gift items, but these too are cheaper than elsewhere" (Michael C. Healy, Victoria, Australia). . . . "If you are visiting someone in the U.S. Navy, you can shop at the **Exchange** on Oahu if you bring your returning plane tickets with you (this proves that you're not a resident). The prices in the Exchange are reasonable, and the quality of the merchandise is higher than in many 'tourist' stores" (Debbie Tait, Burlington, Mass.).

"The seven **Goodwill** stores on Oahu are great places to find good, 'gently used' muumuus from such stores as Liberty House, McInerny, Watumull, etc. They have a large selection, all dry-cleaned, for $7.95, sometimes less on sale. . . . I stopped in a **Salvation Army** store one day, and enjoyed it so much I went back. It was very clean and neat, and they had a big selection of muumuus, priced from $1.55 and up, about $10 for lovely Oriental brocades! I bought many, some just for the materials, others to wear. One day, I got five long muumuus! They also have bathing suits for 89¢ and up, and monkeypod from 49¢. [*Authors' Note:* There are seven Salvation Army stores on the island.] . . . "I also liked the Thrift Shop at the **University of Hawaii** for books, Hawaiian clothes, jewelry, household items. It was open only Tuesday, Wednesday, and Thursday, so check before going (also closed during the month of August). The thrift shop at **Central Union Church** on Beretania, near Kalakaua, is one of the best. It's large, bright, clean, and well stocked with nice items at reasonable prices. . . . I found a new thrift shop, the **Laniolu Good Samaritan Thrift Shop,** 333 Lewers St., open Monday, Wednesday, and Friday 9 a.m. to noon. It is in the Lutheran Senior Retirement Center, and profits go to the Center" (Mrs. Joseph Astman, Levittown, N.Y.).

"My husband and I both wear large sizes, and we have never enjoyed shopping any-where as much as we did in Honolulu. We could walk into almost any store and find racks of attractive things to fit us" (Mrs. Norman Cohen, Swampscott, Mass.). . . . "We pur-chased a lovely ukulele from **Kamaka Hawaii, Inc.,** 550 South St., where factory seconds are priced $95 and up. [*Authors' Note:* Visitors are welcome to visit their small factory, where they hire predominately handicapped workers and train them as craftspeople.] . . . Shopping at the Japanese department store at Ala Moana Center is a must if you are a short person—my wife found racks and racks of size 5 dresses; the average Japanese being short, it follows. However, when shopping, we had to watch ourselves when it came to style. Many things that were conservative there are considered wild by mainland stan-dards" (William D. Devlin, San Francisco, Calif.). . . . "There is so much to photograph that one can easily run out of film. In spite of our good stock of film, we had to buy more. We strongly recommend **Long's Drugstore** in the Ala Moana Center, where we found the best bargains in town. Long's price on both the film and the processing was lower com-pared to others, resulting in a net saving of $1.25 per film. Slide films were also cheaper than elsewhere. An excellent place for this kind of shopping" (B. K. Mehra, Mississauga, Ontario, Canada) . . . "The view of Pearl Harbor from the monorail at Pearlridge is great. My two-year-old nephew really loves it. He thinks 'Pearlridge' and 'monorail' are synonyms" (Florence Klemm, Colorado Springs, Colo.). . . . "We found the shops and the people at **Ward Warehouse** gave the most unusual selections and friendliest service of anywhere we've traveled" (Mrs. Eric Jones, St-Eustache, Québec, Canada).

Chapter VI

HONOLULU ON THE HOUSE

1. Something for Everybody
2. Ethnic Hawaii

THE FANTASTIC BARGAIN of Honolulu is the enormous amount of entertainment and activities—free or at low prices—that are available to the visitor. Few communities in the world share their activities so wholeheartedly with the newcomer.

Part of the reason for this, of course, stems from Hawaii's real need to attract tourists—for tourism is one of the islands' largest industries. But commercial motivations aside, there's enough genuine aloha to go a long way—and to give you so much to do that it becomes hard to decide what to sample and what to pass up!

There are three vital areas where the action takes place; they surround each other like concentric circles.

First, there's Waikiki, the heart of the tourist scene. Some people never leave it and feel they've had a marvelous vacation. Just beyond that is the big, exciting world of Honolulu, one of the great cities (the 12th largest in the United States, in fact). And beyond that, Windward Oahu and the joys of country life and rural beauty. We think you ought to try some of the doings in all three areas —as much as you have taste and inclination for.

The activities described below will give you the broad, overall picture. For up-to-the-minute, day-by-day news of what's going on, consult the *Waikiki Beach Press, Guide to Oahu, This Week on Oahu,* or *Key,* free papers given away in most hotel lobbies, on Kalakaua Avenue, and elsewhere. (These papers also carry many bargain discount coupons, which could add up to considerable savings on shopping, restaurants, car rentals, and the like. Be sure to check them out.) The "Aloha" section of the *Sunday Star Bulletin & Advertiser* provides a rundown of events for the coming week. *Oahu Drive Guide,* available at the offices of the U-Drive companies, has plenty of information, plus excellent driving maps. Finally, you can pay a visit to the Information Office of the **Hawaii Visitors Bureau,** on the eighth floor of 2270 Kalakaua Ave. (tel. 923-1811); they also have a booth at the Royal Hawaiian Shopping Center. Innumerable brochures highlight current activities.

1. Something for Everybody

ON THE BEACH: The best place, of course, to get your basic training for a Hawaiian vacation is on **Waikiki Beach,** that fabled stretch of sand that curves from the Ala Wai Canal to the shadow of Diamond Head. Stretched out among other bodies in various states of pose and repose, you can calmly watch the frantic traffic out in the breakers where the surfboard and outrigger-canoe crowds are busy trying to run each other down. The blue Pacific, the coconut palms, the trade winds—everything around you induces a lotus-land lethargy that has caused more than one vacationer to tear up his return ticket home ($50-a-day'ers, naturally, should cash theirs in). The best part about all this is that it's absolutely free; there's no need to stay at any of the lush seaside caravansaries to use the beach. All of the beach area is public property, up to the high-water mark, even though some of the big hotels do rope off special areas for their guests. Swim in front of the hotels if you like, but you'll have just as much fun at **Fort DeRussy Beach,** near the Ewa end of the beach (a good bet for families, but you can't buy anything at the snackbar unless you have a military card), and at **Kuhio Beach Park,** one of the best natural beaches in Waikiki and headquarters for the surfing and bikini crowd. The beach has been considerably widened, and now its' better than ever. However, we should warn you that there is at least one 22-foot-deep hole in the midst of otherwise knee-high (for an adult) water, and there is no way such anomalies in the ocean floor can be corrected—fill them in one day and they'll be back the next. Parents of small children and non-swimmers should exercise caution here. In fact, Ralph Goto, director of water safety for the City and County of Honolulu, suggests that visitors always check with the lifeguard on duty at a beach before swimming.

Kuhio Beach begins Diamond Head of the Surfrider Hotel, at Uluniu Avenue. Incidentally, it is named for Prince Jonah Kuhio, who once lived on the site. He was the last titular prince of Hawaii, a hereditary high chief and for ten consecutive terms the territory's delegate in Congress. We like the name the Hawaiians gave him: Ke Alii Makaainana—the People's Prince.

If you'd like to learn to surf, try the concessions at Kuhio Beach, or in front of the Sheraton Waikiki, Moana, or Hawaiian Village Hotels, or inquire at the Recreation Desk of any large hotel. A beach boy will teach you (and one or two others) for just about whatever the traffic will bear ($10 an hour is a usual fee). You've got to be a strong swimmer. According to the experts, you'll need three months to become a real surfer, but if you're reasonably well coordinated, you should be able to learn enough to have some fun in a day or two. If you're not, don't torture yourself. Take a ride in an outrigger canoe instead. With six or seven others in the canoe, you paddle out to deep water, wait for a good wave, and then, just as the surfer does, ride its crest back to shore. It's a thrilling experience, slightly strenuous, but with little possibility of broken bones.

Looking for a beach far from the maddening crowd (well, as far as you can get)? Take the bus going Diamond Head on Kalakaua Avenue (on the Makai side) to **Queen's Surf,** just across from Kapiolani Park, a lovely beach area frequented mostly by island families (and, at the Diamond Head end, mostly by the island's gay population). There's a snackbar here, plus locker rooms, showers, and picnic tables. Another good family beach, practically surfless, is the one at **Ala Moana Park.** And if you drive out to the marina behind the Hotel Ilikai, all the way to the left, you'll find a delightful beach between the Hilton Hawaiian Village and the marina. It's kind of an "in" spot for kamaainas, but tourists don't seem to know about it. There's also plenty of space for free parking here (a rarity in Waikiki).

Want to see how the other half lives? Here's a chance to get a ride to one of Hawaii's most elegant resort hotels—the **Kahala Hilton**—and to spend as much time as you want at Waialae Beach Park next door—at minimal expense. A shuttle bus drives back and forth between the hotel and the Ala Moana Hotel every hour on the half-hour from 8:30 a.m. to 10:30 p.m. (with the exception of Sunday, when the last shuttle is at 8:30 p.m.). The charge is $4 each way, and en route to the Kahala, the shuttle stops in front of the Surfrider Hotel in Waikiki. It then takes you along a lush tropical route spilling over with trees and flowers, past millionaires' villas (Clare Boothe Luce had her residence here), to the Kahala Hilton Hotel in the residential section of Kahala. The hotel's architects and decorators have done a masterful job of translating the old Hawaiian motifs in a contemporary setting; the splendid round rugs in the lobby are an example. You can stroll around the lovely grounds and watch the mini porpoise show in the lagoon near the swimming pool. Feeding times are at 11 a.m., and 2 and 4 p.m. daily. If you get hungry, there's the **Hala Terrace** surfside for food and drink, and the new and lovely **Plumeria Café,** a courtyard café, for sandwiches, ice cream, snacks, and full meals. After you've explored the grounds, you're off for a swim at **Waialae** (a bit rocky, however), reached by walking in an Ewa direction from the Kahala sands. Buses will take you back to Waikiki from the Kahala every hour. If you're driving, parking charges are modest.

SNORKELING: Once you start traveling around the island, there are literally dozens of beaches, one more beautiful than the next. One of the nearest of these beaches, and an ideal one for snorkeling, is **Hanauma Bay** (you can rent snorkeling equipment at many places in Waikiki, and other snorkelers are always willing to help beginners). And you don't need your own car to get to Hanauma Bay, or to Sandy and Makapuu Beaches, which are big favorites with the surfing set. Simply board the **Beach Bus.** It runs every day during June, July, and August, the rest of the year on weekends and holidays, departing from Monsarrat Avenue near the Kapiolani Park bandstand. Departures: 9:20 and 10:20 a.m., and every hour on the hour from 11 a.m. to 4 p.m. You can also take the no. 57 bus, "Hawaii Kai–Lunalilo Home Road" and walk up to the bay. (For more details on Hanauma Bay, see Chapter VIII, "Around Oahu," and the Readers' Suggestions, ahead.)

Note: Serious snorkelers who will be touring the neighbor islands may wish to write for a copy of "Dive and Snorkel Guide," published by Destination Hawaii, a nonprofit association. Over 40 locations, about 10 on each island, are mapped and described. Send $3 (includes postage and handling) to Destination Hawaii, P.O. Box 90295, Honolulu, HI 96815.

HIKING, TENNIS, AND OTHER SPORTS: If you'd like to discover what those mountains are actually like across the Ala Wai, the **Hawaiian Trail and Mountain Club,** will take you on a hike along one of the numerous beautiful trails around Honolulu, where you'll feel far removed from both city and beach. You pack your own lunch and drinking water on these hikes, which usually start from the Iolani Palace grounds at either 8 a.m. or 1 p.m. The fee is minimal, usually about $1 to cover the cost of the drive to the hiking site. For information on hiking schedules for Oahu and all islands, send a legal-size stamped, self-addressed envelope plus $1 to P.O. Box 2238, Honolulu, HI 96804. You can join a group of hikers on most Sundays. Also check the local papers. . . . Many people choose to go hiking on their own (see the Readers' Activities Suggestions, ahead, for some comments), but before you do so, check with the outdoor recreation section of the State Department of Land and Natural Resources (tel. 548-7455). They have a list of 13 hiking trails that are considered dangerous because of a recent history of holdups of tourists. There are many illegal growers of marijuana in the wilderness areas, and encounters with them are not advisable.

Tennis in Honolulu? Certainly. It's free at 26 public courts. Pick up the brochure called "Golf and Tennis in Hawaii" at the Hawaii Visitors Bureau for complete listings. The **Ilikai Hotel** has a lot of tennis action: six specially surfaced courts, one court lit for night play until 10 p.m., ball machines, a full-time tennis pro, private lessons, daily clinics. The pro shop rents racquets and does overnight stringing. They'll even help you find suitable partners (tel. 949-3811). . . . If you've got wheels, you can take your racquets out to the **Pacific Islands Club** in Hawaii Kai, about a 20-minute drive from Waikiki. This is a private tennis and swim center, open to visitors from 9 a.m. to 5 p.m. weekdays. Two people can rent a court for $20 per hour, four people for $30. Phone 385-3300 for information. They're at 6800 Hawaii Kai Drive. . . . There are 14 public golf courses on Oahu, most with surprisingly low greens fees. The nearest one to Waikiki is the 18-hole **Ala Wai Golf Course** at 404 Kapahulu Ave. Reservations are taken by phone (tel. 296-4653) one week in advance starting at 6:30 a.m. All reservations are usually given out by 7 a.m. Huge lines of local people start to form before dawn to take advantage of any cancellations. Ala Wai is reputedly the busiest golf course in the world, with over 500 persons playing daily. Visitor rates are $8 weekdays, $12 weekends. Cart rental is $10.40; club rental, $6. With a car, you can drive to Hawaii Kai and the **Hawaii Kai Golf Course,** 8902 Kalanianaole Hwy., in about 20 minutes. It has an 18-hole par-3 course, an 18-hole championship course, and a driving range. Rates for the par-3 are $9 weekdays, $10 weekends; for the championship, $30 weekdays, $35 weekends. There's a restaurant on the premises. Phone 395-2385 for information and reservations. If you're planning a drive out to the North Shore, you can take advantage of the little-known (to visitors) **Kahuku Municipal Golf Course,** which has the benefit of an ocean view and very low greens fees. The 2,725-yard course is usually not crowded, except occasionally on weekends. On weekdays, rates are $2 for 9 holes, $2 more for the second nine holes ($4 total). On weekends, it's $3 and $6. Note that there is neither pro shop nor restaurant here. Tee times are required only on weekend mornings. For information, phone 291-5842. For a listing of golf courses elsewhere on Oahu, see again, "Golf and Tennis in Hawaii," available from the HVB. . . . **Kapiolani Park** is certainly one of the world's most active recreational areas. It has archery and golf driving ranges, fields for soccer, rugby, and softball, courts for tennis, and volleyball, a jogger's circuit training course, and lots more. For details, call the Department of Parks and Recreation headquarters at 523-4631 (they can also give you information on swimming lessons). . . . Oahu also has loads of facilities for riding, waterskiing, skindiving, plain and fancy fishing, even birdwatching. (Look for listings of Audubon Society programs in the daily papers.) The Hawaii Visitors Bureau can direct you to the right places. . . . You can even go glider riding, out at Dillingham Airfield on the north shore, using the facilities of the **Honolulu Soaring Club.** You can get instruction in doing it yourself or go for a joy ride on a sailplane ($45 for two passengers, $32 for one). Look ma, no engines! Phone Bill at 677-3404 for information. No reservations are required, and things glide along here seven days a week, 10 a.m. to 5:30 p.m. Bring your camera.

We realize that you probably didn't come to Hawaii to go **ice skating,** but if that's your pleasure, Honolulu has a beautiful rink: the Ice Palace Chalet. Located in the new Stadium Mall, across from Aloha Stadium and Castle Park, this place has really caught on with the local folk. Admission is $5 for adults, $4.50 for students, and $3.75 for children 11 and under; the admission price includes rental of skates. The rink is open daily; phone 487-9921 for public skating hours. Don't fret if you forgot to pack warm hats, mittens, and gloves; there's a little shop here that will sell them to you.

FITNESS, HAWAIIAN STYLE: There's no need to let up on your fitness program just because you're on vacation. There are several free or low-cost exercise classes, and undoubtedly it's more pleasant to do your workout in the great out-of-doors. There's always a good crowd at the entrance to the Honolulu Zoo weekday mornings at 8:30 a.m., on Saturday at 9 a.m., getting in shape with **Ursula Hare.** You're welcome to join them. Ursula is a colorful lady, her classes are sponsored by People for Pets, and it's all free. . . . There is also a free exercise class every day except Sunday from 9 to 10:30 a.m., at the beach at **Fort DeRussy.** . . . Jogging is big in Honolulu, as just about everywhere else. You can join those getting in shape for the Honolulu Marathon (it's held the first or second weekend in December) at a free **Marathon Clinic,** every Sunday at 7:30 a.m. at the bandstand in Kapiolani Park. . . . **Janis McDonald,** a local fitness expert and TV personality conducts her classes in Low Impact Aerobics at the Waikiki Shell—Monday, Wednesday, and Friday at 7 a.m.; Tuesday, Thursday, and Saturday at 8 a.m. A single visit is $8 (tel. 948-3408). . . . And **World Gym,** 1701 Ala Wai Blvd. (tel. 942-8171), stays open 24 hours a day to accommodate those who want to work out with weights, Universal Pulleys, and Nautilus equipment.

After all this exertion, you may be in need of a massage. The **Honolulu School of Massage** at 1750 Kalakakaua Ave., Suite 401, is a reputable, state-licensed organization that offers low-cost massages by its apprentice massage therapists. Cost is $12 for a half-hour, $20 for an hour. And, oh yes, massage helps relieve jet lag, too. Phone 942-8552 for an appointment.

SPECTATOR SPORTS—THE SURFING SCENE: Some visitors to Hawaii find that watching others exert themselves is the most fun of all—and this usually means gazing at the surfers on Waikiki Beach. It's an incredible and never-ending show, especially enjoyable if you've brought your binoculars. If you'd like a closer view, try to catch one of the surfing movies that are shown frequently in the summer at places like the **Waikiki Shell** and **McKinley Auditorium.** They're instructive and thrilling—and much more dramatic than watching the scene from afar at the beach.

Surfing, by the way, was the favorite sport of Hawaiian royalty and originally had religious connotations; in the early part of this century, Jack London, among others, helped revive the sport, and today it's an absolute passion with every able-bodied islander, far surpassing the interest of the mainlander in, say, baseball or skiing. Of course, many mainlanders move to Hawaii for the lure of the surf. (A T-shirt we saw on our last trip proclaimed, "Work is for those who can't surf".) Radio weather reports always include a report on the latest surfing conditions. A special phone (tel. 836-1952) also gives the latest reports. And the proudest possession of any island teenager is, naturally, his or her surfboard.

From time to time, special surfing clinics free to the public are held at Kapiolani Beach Park. Subjects include body-surfing, canoeing, skindiving, and the like. For information, phone 523-4361.

Other island spectator sports that you might like: football, baseball, and soccer at the **Aloha Stadium** in Halawa (tel. 487-3877); auto racing Friday and Saturday nights at **Hawaii Raceway Park** at Ewa Beach (tel. 682-4494). World-class polo is played each Sunday during polo season (early March through July) at the **Hawaii Polo Club** at the Mokuleia Polo Grounds in Mokuleia, one of the three polo fields in the world located on a beach. The game is at 2 p.m., but the gates open at 11 a.m. for some pretty fancy tailgate picnics. Admission is $5; children under 12 get in free. Last year, the British, French, Australian, Argentinian, Chilean, and San Franciscan teams were invited to play with the local club. For information, phone 637-7795 or 533-2890.

Basketball, karate, wrestling, boxing, Japanese sumo wrestling, and such are held at the **Neal S. Blaisdell Center Arena.**

THE HULA AND OTHER ETHNIC DANCES: Just as you expected, everyone
in Hawaii does the hula except the lame (being old or blind is no hindrance). Island youngsters learn the hula just as mainland children take ballet or tap lessons. Social directors and hotel instructors patiently instruct the malihinis, and wherever you look there's a hula show underway. All this is fun and some of it is good dancing, but much of it is a bastardization of a noble and beautiful dance, Hawaii's most unique contribution to the arts.

The original hula dances were sacred, performed in honor of the goddess Laka (who supposedly entertained her sister, the volcano goddess Pele, with the first hula). Laka's devotees lived under a strict system of kapus (taboos), studying the hulas as well as the chants and meles, by which the myths of the race were transmitted from one generation to another. In the whaling days, some of the hulas became a bawdy entertainment for the sailors, and the good missionary fathers, who would have found dancing sinful on any account, naturally forbade it. But the hula managed to survive. Today the styles of hula range from the most serious to the most comic—the so-called hapa-haole hulas.

Happily, there's been a great revival of interest in serious hula lately, and if you're lucky you may get to see outstanding dancing at some of the better nightclub shows (the Brothers Cazimero at the Monarch Room of the Royal Hawaiian Hotel, for one) or at concert presentations. True devotees of hula should visit the islands during the month of April. That's when the **Merrie Monarch Festival** is held in Hilo, on the Big Island of Hawaii, a week-long virtual Olympics of hula, with dancers from all the various hula halaus (schools) of the islands competing in both ancient and modern hulas. You probably won't be able to get tickets to the events themselves (they are usually sold out by the preceding Christmas), but they are fully covered on television, and are a true joy to watch. On a recent trip, we sat enthralled for nights in a row viewing the competition and the judging—as did just about everyone else on the islands.

One of the most delightful hula shows, in our opinion, is the **Young People's Hula Show,** presented every Sunday morning at 9:30 on the Centerstage at the Ala Moana Shopping Center. The children, all students of Ka'ipolani Butterworth, ranging in age from about three to the teens, are talented nonprofessionals bursting with charm and aloha. It's all free and more enjoyable than many an expensive nightclub show. (Their new video, "Hawaii's Children in Dance," could be a memorable gift.)

Look for notices in the papers of concerts presented by **Dances We Dance,** an educational and performing organization which sponsors both ethnic and modern dance concerts throughout the state. On our last trip we were lucky enough to catch a concert by The Ladies of Na Pualei O Likolehua, as part of a special season of Hawaiian dance. Performances are usually held in state-of-the-art Mamiya Theatre at St. Louis Center for the Arts, on the St. Louis–Chaminade campus, 3140 Waialea Ave. To see a noncommercial dance presentation by a respected hula halau like this one is a very special experience.

You'll note, by the way, that hula dancers—who can just as well be men as women—tell the story with their hands while their feet keep up a steady rhythmic pattern. They often use instruments to help them: the smooth stones or pebbles that they click together, that sound like castanets, are known as ili ili. The seed-filled gourd that sounds like a South American maraca is known as the uli uli. The hollow gourds are called ipus. Pui li, splintered bamboo sticks, produce a rattling sound, and kalaau are hard wooden sticks struck together to make a noise like that of a xylophone.

According to the experts, probably the best ethnic dancing in the islands is that done by the dance group at the **Polynesian Cultural Center,** which we'll tell you about in Chapter VIII. They often do free mini-shows at the Royal Hawaiian Shopping Center. Watch for outstanding programs of Japanese and other Asian dances at the University of Hawaii.

DO-IT-YOURSELF DANCING: You too can do the hula! Hula-dancing lessons are given everywhere—at the Ys, at the university, and at any number of private dance studios. The **Department of Parks and Recreation** (tel. 955-1551) offers hula classes (as well as other classes pertaining to Hawaiiana) for a nominal fee. Free classes are sometimes given at hotels and shopping centers, but since the times of these lessons change with the seasons, it's best to consult the local tourist papers. Lessons are usually given on Wednesday and Friday at 10:30 a.m. at the Royal Hawaiian Shopping Center.

For square-dancers, there's something going on almost every night of the week. The locations change frequently, so the best thing to do is to call the Hawaii Visitors Bureau (tel. 923-1811). The **Square Wheelers** is an excellent group that welcomes visitors at Ikapiolani Bandstand, Mondays from 8 to 10 p.m. (tel 941-1607).

MUSIC: Classical music lovers have no cause for complaint in Honolulu. Western concert artists of the stature of Andrés Segovia and Emanuel Ax stop here en route to the Orient or on round-the-world tours; Japanese soloists and orchestras pay frequent visits. You might catch opera companies and the like from China. You can enjoy subscription concerts by the **Honolulu Symphony,** which performs under the baton of its music director, Donald Johanos, and famous guest conductors. Soloists include internationally acclaimed virtuosos, and programs include choral works and appearances by the San Francisco Ballet. Pops concerts and the Starlight Festival in the Waikiki Shell are among the most widely attended symphony events, as are the annual presentations of *Nutcracker* and *Messiah.* Associate conductor Henry Miyamura conducts the very popular Youth Concerts, Youth Opera, and the annual Keikis' (Children's) Concert at the Waikiki Shell where guest stars have included Big Bird.

Try to attend a performance of the **Hawaii Opera Theater,** which holds a yearly Opera Festival in February and March, featuring world-renowned opera stars and lavish sets. And the islands' most gifted young musicians play with the **Hawaii Youth Symphony,** which performs during the year.

Chamber music in a scenic setting is offered by the **Hawaii Chamber Orchestra.** Its ten-concert winter-spring "Soundscapes-by-the-Sea programs are held every other Friday night from January through May at Calvary-by-the-Sea Lutheran Church in Aina Haina. The concerts begin at 8 p.m., and the audience is encouraged to come early and enjoy a sunset picnic dinner on the lawn and beach areas overlooking the ocean. Free coffee, punch, and wine are served before and after the concert and during the intermission as well, when concertgoers can mingle and chat with the musicians. Single tickets are available at the door for $7. Check the papers for details or phone 734-0397.

During the summer months, from late June through late August, the **Hawaii Chamber Jazz Players,** under the direction of the Hawaii Chamber Orchestra's music director Herb Ward, offer Jazzscapes-by-the-Sea on Friday nights. September and October finds the Hawaii Chamber Orchestra at Dillingham Hall on the Punahou School campus presenting a season of opera.

THEATER: Hawaiian theater, long of the tired-businessman, light-entertainment school, is getting more mature and more varied all the time. Very popular here is the **Honolulu Community Theater,** an able group that presents a year-round program of current Broadway shows, revivals, and musicals old and new. Performances are held in the Ruger Theater on the slopes of Diamond Head. Tickets range from $6 to $12. For information, call 734-0274.

Now in its 16th season, the **Hawaii Performing Arts Company (HPAC)** provides an intimate setting for a broad spectrum of theatrical offerings. Their 150-seat Manoa Valley Theater at 2833 E. Manoa Rd. brings the lights up 42 weeks of the year on a variety of productions ranging from the Bard to Broadway, from classics to musical comedy. Tickets are priced at $11 and $12. Call 988-6131 for dates and availability of seats.

Hawaii's newest professional theater company, **The Aguilar Organization,** stages musicals plus dance and concert programs. Tommy Aguilar is a Broadway musical comedy performer who was featured in "A Chorus Line" both on Broadway and tour. Each production features at least one star turn. Performances are held Wednesday through Sunday nights with a Saturday matinee, at the beautiful Richard T. Mamiya Theatre (named for Hawaii's foremost open-heart surgeon) on the St. Louis–Chaminade campus, 3140 Waialae Ave. All seats for all performances are $12.50. Reservations: phone 735-4896 and 735-4897.

Up at the **John F. Kennedy Theater,** the University of Hawaii's outstanding Department of Drama and Theater presents the great classics of the Orient and the West—Shakespeare, kabuki, and modern plays, as well as ballet and modern dance. Besides the eight or so major productions staged each year, they present at least six shows produced by Kumu Kahua, a theater group that performs plays written by Hawaiian residents. For information on tickets and productions, call 948-7655.

Should you find yourself on the windward side of the island, you might stop in to see an offering by the **Windward Theater Guild,** a good local company. Performances are held in the Kailua Elementary School auditorium; tickets are $6 for adults, $5 for all others; and you call 261-4885 for information and reservations. Also outside of Honolulu, Broadway theatrical productions and name entertainment shows, some of them free, are presented at **Schofield Barracks** and **Fort Shafter.** Call 655-9081 or 438-2831 for information and reservations.

HUNA PHILOSOPHY:
The old Hawaiians were very practical psychologists, and some of their ancient Huna practices are gaining the attention of psychologists and educators today. If you'd like to learn some of the secrets of that ancient wisdom, updated for today's world, try to catch one of the free evening lectures on Ho'oponopono (the art of problem-solving and stress reduction), given by Morrnah Simeona and her staff at **The Foundation of I,** 1649 Kalakaua Ave. A native Hawaiian, Morrnah is renowned throughout the islands as Kahuna Lapa'au, a healer, herbalist, and authority on the Hawaiian teachings; she has recently been named a "Living Treasure of Hawaii." Among her colleagues is a clinical psychologist, Stanley Hew Len, Ph.D. We attended one of these free lectures and a Ho'oponopono workshop (for which there is a fee) on a recent trip and found it fascinating. For information, phone 955-1236.

CHANOYU: THE JAPANESE TEA CEREMONY:
As refreshing as a quick trip to Japan, the twice-weekly demonstrations of the Japanese tea ceremony held at 245 Saratoga Rd. (near Fort DeRussy), offer a fascinating look at the ancient "Way of Tea." Sponsored by the **Urasenke Foundation of Hawaii,** a nonprofit group whose goal is "to find friendship in a bowl of tea," the demonstrations are held every Wednesday and Friday (excluding holidays) from 10 a.m. to noon:

donations are welcomed. Seated in a formal Japanese tatami room in a garden setting, guests are introduced to the proper customs for the preparation and partaking of tea, and are served a sweet and powdered green tea from exquisite "tea bowls." You may ask questions and take pictures if you wish. A must for lovers of Orientalia.

Monthly Tea Gatherings are also held. For information, phone 923-3059.

THE STUDENT LIFE: Here's a tip that can save you literally scads of dollars. The **University of Hawaii at Manoa** sponsors a number of low-cost activities for the benefit of its students. But nonstudents may join in the fun and savings simply by paying an activity fee that covers a six-week summer session. Inquire at Campus Center, Room 212, on the Manoa Campus of the University of Hawaii.

FREE SHOWS: There are quite a few of these, and most of them are worth your time. The best known, the **Kodak Hula Show,** takes place next to the Waikiki Shell in Kapiolani Park. Even without benefit of a light meter, you should enjoy this big free show of authentic music and dance by talented performers. Naturally, it's nirvana for photographers. There is special seating for the handicapped. Show times: Tuesday through Friday at 10 a.m. Get there early for a good seat, because even with new bleachers that seat 4,000 people, it's always crowded. . . . **Waikiki Calls,** a 45-minute production using live dancers and a computerized audio-visual program, is presented every night at the Waikiki Shopping Plaza. Show times are 6:30 and 8 p.m.; if you have dinner at one of the Plaza restaurants, like Marco Polo, they will arrange for reserved seating. . . . Everybody loves the **Young People's Hula Show** at the Ala Moana Shopping Center (details above). And from mid-June through August, free Hawaiian entertainment is also scheduled at 2 p.m. on Tuesday and Thursday at Ala Moana. . . . Check the papers for dates of free entertainment at Pearlridge Shopping Center. . . . Kuhio Mall presents a free **Royal Aloha Extravaganza** every night at 8. . . . Don't miss the free show at the beach in front of the **Reef Hotel** every Sunday, from 8 to 9:30 or 10 p.m. Lots of bright amateurs get into the act. . . . Free concerts and cultural shows are given in the Great Hall of the **Hyatt Regency Waikiki,** often at noon or 5 p.m., but since the schedule varies greatly, you should check with the Hyatt Hostess Desk (tel. 922-9292) for exact times. . . . Hawaiian music and dance performances are presented at the **Atherton Halau** of the Bishop Museum, Monday through Saturday and the first Sunday of every month at 1 p.m.

Free concerts are generally held Sunday afternoons at 1 at the **Kapiolani Park Bandstand.** Entertainment includes Polynesian revues, ukulele clubs, visiting mainland troupes, jazz and rock musicians, and usually the famed Royal Hawaiian Band. Call 926-4030 for more information. . . . You can nearly always be sure to catch the Royal Hawaiian Band at its Friday noontime concerts at the **Iolani Palace bandstand.** These lunchtime concerts are very popular with the local people who work nearby; bring a lunch and have a listen. . . . On Wednesday evenings during June, July, and August you can see "The Wildest Show in Town" at the **Honolulu Zoo.** The zoo stays open until 7:30 p.m., and there's a show at 6 p.m. on the stage in the main courtyard. Most families bring a picnic supper to eat during the show. We've seen the Honolulu City Ballet, a troupe of Scottish bagpipers (many of them Japanese and Hawaiian!) in full regalia, the Honolulu Boys' Choir, puppet shows, kabuki theater, and a New Orleans jazz group. . . . The Waikiki-Kapahulu branch of the **Hawaii State Library** system, 400 Kapahulu, offers varied programs for adults and weekly story hours for 4- and 5-year-olds. It's also pleasant to just sit and read in the bougainvillea-shaded lanai at this library in a coconut grove at the foot of Diamond Head. The building itself is an architectural gem, built of sandstone, wood, and glass, with koa furniture. Visitors are also welcome to borrow books, free of charge. . . . There's free entertainment galore at the **Royal Hawaiian Shopping Center:** check the local papers for the schedule.

THE ART SCENE: A lot of good artists are coming out of Hawaii—young people with a mixture of backgrounds whose work shows multiple influences. Perhaps because of the natural beauty that surrounds them, their paintings tend to be more representational here than in other art centers, but ways of seeing are as modern as they are in Paris or New York. Not a few have married Oriental atmosphere with Western techniques, another example of the fortuitous cross-fertilization that goes on in every area of Hawaiian life.

Right in Waikiki are three places which features the work of top island talent. There's the distinguished **Royal Gallery** in the Royal Hawaiian Hotel and the newer **Island Gallery,** at the Halekulani Hotel, where we noted stunning collages, oils, and mixed media painting by Gloria Foss, among other noted local artists. And we've always been impressed by the works of local artists in many media that we've seen at the **South Shore Gallery,** an artists' cooperative at the Waikiki Shopping Plaza.

Downtown, the impressive **Contemporary Arts Center,** on the first floor of the News Building at 605 Kapiolani Blvd., (tel. 525-8047) is a showcase for leading island artists and specializes in individual exhibitions. By the time you read this, the Center should have completed its renovation of the 1920s Spaulding Estate at 2411 Makiki Heights, which will provide eight additional galleries on three-and-a-half acres of landscaped gardens. . . . For the past 15 years, **Territorial Savings and Loan Association** has been presenting exhibitions by Hawaii's artists as a public service (no commission is taken) at its Downtown Office Gallery, Ground Floor, Financial Plaza of the Pacific, corner of Bishop and Merchant Sts. Exhibits are open Monday through Thursday from 8 a.m. to 3:30 p.m., and Friday to 6 p.m., every month except December (tel. 523-0211). . . . The **AMFAC Plaza Exhibition Room** at AMFAC Center, Fort Street Mall and Queen Street, has interesting group exhibitions of contemporary paintings, crafts, sculpture, and photography, as well as cultural and historical presentations. Exhibits are scheduled the first part of every month, 8:30 a.m. to 5 p.m. weekdays, Saturday to 4 p.m. (tel. 523-1440).

The largest concentration of galleries featuring local artists can be found in—of all places—**Chinatown.** Old buildings have been refurbished, a small artistic colony has moved in. You can see the works of Pegge Hopper at her own gallery at 1160 A. Nuuanu Ave., those of pen-and-ink artist Ramsay at 1128 Smith St. and also at 119 Merchant St. Pollitt's Gallery shows crafts, clothing, and the work of local artists; it's at 1139 Nuuanu Ave.

Hale Naua III, founded by sculptor and artist Rocky Jensen, is composed of native Hawaiian craftspeople and artists, who draw on the inspiration of ancient Hawaiian legends, history, and chants. Jensen is the first native Hawaiian ever to have a show on the mainland. For information on their work, exhibits, or to visit their workshop, phone 487-6969. . . . John Young, one of the islands' most outstanding artists, displays his own paintings and prints, along with a superb collection of primitive art, at the **John Young Studio,** Poka Place (tel. 732-2496). . . . On Saturday and Sunday, local artists exhibit and sell their work on the zoo fence near Kapiolani Park—sort of a twice-a-week Greenwich Village Art Show. . . . At **Hawaii Koko Marina Artists Gallery** you can meet the local artists and watch them work (open every day). . . . When you travel to the North Shore, stop in to see works by local artists and craftsmen at the **Fettig Art Gallery,** 66-051 Kam Hwy., in Haleiwa (tel. 637-4933).

Art is, in fact, everywhere in Honolulu; the builders of large public facilities are becoming more and more art-conscious and you will find monumental pieces of sculpture, some outstanding, such as a Henry Moore in Tamarind Park at Bishop and King St. downtown, some less distinguished, in such places as the Ala Moana Shopping Center, Hemmeter Center, Royal Hawaiian Center, the Waikiki Shopping Plaza, the University of Hawaii, the State Capitol Building, and at Sea Life Park in Windward Oahu. The fountain sculptures at Ala Moana are particularly worth a look.

To see some excellent works by Hawaii's talented craftspeople (and perhaps to pick up some distinctive small presents), pop into some of our favorite places. **Following Sea,** at the Kahala Mall Shopping Center, 4211 Waialae Ave. (tel. 734-4425), is a visual experience. It represents the works of many American craftspeople in ceramics, glass, jewelry, fiber, woodwork, and one piece is more glorious than the next. Many island artists are represented. . . . A high level of taste and artistry is evident in all the works chosen for **Rare Discovery,** a contemporary gallery/shop at Ward Warehouse. . . . Similar high quality is found at another longtime favorite, **Artist's Guild** at Ward Warehouse. . . . A wide range of handcrafts is shown at **Bazaar** at the Waikiki Shopping Plaza, all of it in excellent taste.

Keep an eye out for these artists: Randy Hokushin in pottery; Bumpei Akaji in welded sculpture; Jewel Lafferty and Jeanne Robertson in watercolors; Louis Pohl in mixed media; Shirley Hasenwager and Dodie Warren in prints and drawings; Hiroshi Tagami and David Lee in oils; Connie Hennings-Chilton for Polynesian portraits. This is but a partial list of the talented island artists whose works are increasingly being recognized outside the islands. Incidentally, Hawaiian art is considered a good investment and is being scooped up by mainland people.

Crafts Fairs and Craftspeople

Hopefully, you'll be in town for one of the several arts-and-crafts fairs that happen in Honolulu at odd times throughout the year. The Mission Houses Museum hosts two of them, one on Kamehameha Day (June 11) and one around Thanksgiving. There are two big, beautiful fairs at Thomas Square Park, one right before Christmas, the other before Easter. Several two-day fairs are held at Ala Moana Park, and there is usually a fair in July, at Kapiolani Park. On the North Shore, there are two two-day fairs each year—one in late June or early July and one in November—at Waimea Falls Park. (You needn't pay the park admission fee to go to the fair.) All of these are held on weekends. Some talented artists and craftspeople to watch for are the following: *(note:* telephone numbers are given when craftspeople have indicated they will show their work in their own studios to seriously interested people.) Barbara Engles for jewelry; Erica Karawina for stained glass (you'll find a stunning example in the Contemporary Arts Center); Edward Brownlees for bronze sculpture (examples at the Hyatt Regency Hotel and the Federal Building, downtown); Bonnie Lum for Hawaiian floral pillows and hoop stitchery (tel. 623-0574); Hoaliku Drake for authentic Hawaiian quilts, feather leis, koa woodcarvings, lauhala woven items (tel. 668-1800). For bags with Hawaiian themes, there's Wailani Originals (tel. 261-8756). Marvelous seascapes are a unique art form created by Alan and Viki Lai-Hipp (tel. 839-5959). For gold-on-wood Hawaiian jewelry—bracelets, earrings, pendants, and rings—phone Dolly Bosque on Maui (tel. 878-6529). If you're out Kaneohe way on the Windward side, and want to visit a gallery of exquisite pottery, phone Sandy and Alex Anderson at 247-1582 for directions. Their work is housed in a glorious tropical setting.

The Art Establishment

Hawaii, of course, has her art establishment, names that are known in art circles everywhere. Perhaps the greatest of these is the muralist Jean Charlot, who, along with Orozco, Siqueiros, and Rivera, brought the art of the mural to revolutionary heights in Mexico in the '20s and '30s. An islander by choice since 1949, Charlot has contributed much to Hawaii's art world. Other prominent figures include painters/muralists Herbert Kawainui Kane and Juliette May Fraser; painters such as Pegge Hopper (who does incredible Polynesian portraits), Guy Buffet (a Frenchman who paints the Hawaiian scene with remarkable élan), Reuben Tam, Peter Haywood, Ben Norris, Tadashi Sato, Kenneth Bushnell, Edward Stasack (also known for sculpture), the late Harry Baldwin, and Isami Doi; and the brilliant young ceramist Shugen Inoye, a Buddhist priest who died at the age of 29. John Kelly, who died some years ago in his 80s, was Hawaii's master printmaker; his colored etchings of the Polynesians are considered the best of their kind ever done. They are widely reproduced and frequent exhibitions are held.

A great lady of the arts in Hawaii was Madge Tennent, who came to Hawaii at the turn of the century via South Africa and Paris and broke away from the academy and its conventions to record on canvas her massive portraits of the Hawaiian people. You can visit her gallery, the **Tennent Art Foundation,** at 203 Prospect St., from 10 a.m. to noon Tuesday through Saturday, 2 to 4 p.m. on Sunday, or by special appointment: call Elaine Tennent at 531-1987. Closed Monday.

Don't leave Hawaii without a visit to the **Honolulu Academy of Arts,** 900 S. Beretania St., where you'll see the work of island artists and much more as well. The academy is one of the most beautiful art museums in the world; it offers a look at the best of both Eastern and Western art. The physical plant is ideal for viewing art, divided as it is into a series of small galleries that open into tranquil courtyards; the Chinese garden, in particular, is exquisite. There's a superb collection of Asian art—a magnificent sculpture of Kwan Yin, the Chinese goddess of mercy, Chinese scrolls and carvings, Korean ceramics, Japanese screens—as well as a good representation of Western masters, including works of Picasso, Braque, Monet, and Van Gogh. Note also the Kress Collection of Italian Renaissance painting. Stop in the bookshop for prints and other distinctive gift items and have a lovely lunch in the Garden Café (seatings at 11:30 a.m. and 1 p.m., September through May, reservations suggested). The museum is open Tuesday to Saturday from 10 a.m. to 4:30 p.m., on Sunday from 1 to 5 p.m. Supper is served in the Garden Café on Thursday evening at 6:30, about $7, beverage and dessert extra. Reservations required (tel. 531-8865).

Admission to the academy is free. Locked lockers are provided, free of charge, for visitors' parcels. The academy is about a 15-minute ride from Waikiki on the no. 2 bus. Closed Monday.

MISCELLANEOUS ACTIVITIES: The **Honolulu Senior Citizens Club** welcomes newcomers to its social and recreational activities every Wednesday from 9 a.m. to 2 p.m. at the Ala Wai Clubhouse. There's bridge, canasta, and checkers. Membership is only $5 a year, and it's certainly worth that to go on some of the club's regular outings—sightseeing tours, picnics, etc. These usually start from the Ala Wai Clubhouse (on the other side of the Ala Wai Canal) on Wednesday mornings, under the auspices of the city Recreation Department. For more information on other activities for senior citizens, contact the **Hawaii State Senior Center** (tel. 847-1322). . . . Visitors are welcome at the **Siddha Meditation Ashram Hawaii,** 1925 Makiki St., where followers of the late Swami

Muktananada and his successor, Gurumayi, follow a Yogic way of life. Programs, lasting an hour-and-a-half, are usually held Monday through Saturday evenings at 7:30 p.m., and an introductory program is given on Sunday morning. The ashram is up in the hills, in a beautiful residential area of Honolulu. Visitors may also have a vegetarian meal at lunch or dinner. For information, phone 847-1322 or 942-8887. There's a group for just about every interest in Honolulu, from barbershop quartet singers to coin collectors, and they all extend their aloha to the visitor. Check the papers for news of their meetings. Bridge buffs will find duplicate bridge games at local hotels practically every night of the week. Meetings of mainland fraternal organizations take place constantly.

SERVICES FOR THE HANDICAPPED: Handicapped people are made very welcome in Hawaii: there are more than 2,000 ramped curbs on Oahu alone, hotels provide special facilities, and tour companies provide many services. Helpful brochures are available for each island. For details, send a legal-size, self-addressed, stamped envelope for each brochure desired (Oahu, Maui, Kauai, Big Island of Hawaii). Each brochure lists accessibility features of Hawaii's major hotels, shopping malls, beach parks, and sightseeing and visitor attractions. Write to **Commission on the Handicapped,** Old Federal Building, 335 Merchant St., Room 353, Honolulu, HI 96813 (tel. 548-7606). **Handi-Cabs,** a private company (P.O. Box 22428, Honolulu, HI 96813; tel. 524-3866), and **Handi-Van,** a city service (1585 Kapiolani Blvd., Suite 1554, Honolulu, HI 96814; tel. 955-1717), provide special transportation facilities. Handi-Cabs also provides sightseeing tours.

MEDICAL SERVICES: We hope it won't happen, but should you need medical assistance while you're in Honolulu, you have several possibilities. Should you need a house call—or hotel call—contact **Doctors on Call (DOC).** They're on duty every day, 24 hours a day, and a phone call to 926-4777 will bring them to your hotel room promptly; the charge is $64. Of course, in a medical emergency you can always call 911 and get an ambulance, or go to the Emergency Department of the Queen's Medical Center, 1301 Punchbowl St. (tel. 547-4311). If you have medical questions but you're not sure you need a doctor, you can call **Ask-A-Nurse,** a 24-hour health care information and physician referral service sponsored by Queen's and Castle Medical Centers. Dial 533-NURS for assistance.

FREE AND LOW-COST CLASSES: If you'd like to learn to make feather or flower leis, do Hawaiian quilting or lau hala (fiber) plaiting, attend one of the demonstrations of traditional Hawaiian folk crafts, held Monday through Saturday, from 9 a.m. to 3 p.m. at the **Atherton Halau of the Bishop Museum.** Cost is $5 plus materials. We have enthusiastic reports on these delightful classes each year. For information, phone 847-3511. . . . The **Hawaiian Electric Company** has occasional free cooking demonstrations in the evening featuring the foods of one of the major ethnic groups in Hawaii each time. Call 548-3511 for further information. . . . Free classes in hula, fresh-flower lei making, and Hawaiian ti-leaf hula-skirt making, as well as displays of the art of Hawaiian quiltmaking, are featured in the Great Hall of the **Hyatt Regency Waikiki** at various times. Specific information is available by calling 922-9292. . . . You can learn how to slice a pineapple, make a flower lei, weave a coconut frond, and lots more, in the huge array of classes presented at the **Royal Hawaiian Shopping Center.** Consult the local papers for schedules. . . . Honolulu's **Department of Parks and Recreation** has an extensive recreation program for adults, teenagers, and children. Visitors are welcome to participate in classes (of up to ten sessions) in such subjects as quilting, Hawaiian, ukulele, and hula. Events are announced in the local papers. If you're staying in town for a month or two, you may want to sign up for one of the short-term, low-cost, noncredit classes at the **University of Hawaii at Manoa,** (see "Tour 3" section, below). On the agenda one summer: Kundalini yoga, batik, folk guitar, occult numerology, belly dancing—and then some!

FREE AND LOW-COST TOURS: Roasters roast, grinders grind, and packages get packed at a free, fascinating tour held at the factory headquarters of **Lion Coffee,** 831 Queen St. Lion is fast gaining a reputation as Hawaii's premier gourmet coffee (we agree). You'll learn all about the Arabica beans from which Lion coffee is made (they have half the caffeine and almost double the natural sugar of other beans) and watch millions of them being noisily roasted in their state-of-the-art roaster. After the tour, you're invited to sample any of the four different coffees brewed that day (we are personally insane about their chocolate macadamia-nut coffee, and it comes in decaf, too). Of course you're going to want to take some of this coffee home, and you can buy it right here, with a savings for quantity purchases. They make great gifts and it's easy to bring home the beans: just take the box to the plane and ship it through as baggage. Tours are held every weekday at 10:30 a.m. To get to Lion Coffee, take the #6 Pauoa bus from Ala Moana Center. For driving directions or information, phone 521-3479. . . . Free refreshments and more than 40,000 fashions to select from at factory prices are available at **Hilo Hattie Fashion Center,** 700 Nimitz. Call them at 537-2926 and they'll tell you where their free bus will pick you up in Waikiki. . . . It's always Christmas at the **Emgee Corporation,** 3210 Koapaka St., in the airport industrial area. You're welcome to take a free tour of the factory and see artists handcrafting unique and whimsical wooden Christmas ornaments from over 400 original designs. Then you can browse in their Christmas Shop. A catalog is available. Call 836-0988 for details. . . . If you'd like to see how Hawaiian gift items—toys, hula skirts, jewelry, Hawaiian dolls, and kitchen accessories, etc.—are made, you can take a free tour of **Lanakila Crafts** at 1809 Bachelot St. Lanakila is a private, nonprofit organization that provides vocational training and employment for many handicapped adults. Their products are sold in the finest gift stores. Gift shop hours are 8 a.m. to 3:30 p.m. weekdays. Closed on holidays. Call 531-0555 for information on the tours, which are held on Tuesday and Thursday at 1 p.m. . . . Don't forget the **Dole Cannery** tour, which we describe in full in Chapter VII. Admission is $2.

HAWAIIAN WEDDINGS: What could be nicer than getting married in Hawaii? You can get married and honeymoon in the same place, and the cost need not be exorbitant. The idea has become so appealing that thousands of visitors are now seeking out Hawaiian weddings in offbeat settings—perhaps on the beach, on top of a mountain, aboard a catamaran, in a lighthouse—even in a church. For help in planning a Hawaiian wedding, you can contact several private services, suggested by the Hawaii Visitors Bureau. **Damien Waring Photography** arranges weddings in a tropical garden on the grounds of their Honolulu oceanside estate: 5253 Kalanianaole Hwy., Honolulu, HI 96821 (tel. 373-2141). . . . **Aloha Wedding Planners** takes care of every detail, from the minister to the photographs: P.O. Box 90865, Honolulu, HI 96835 (tel. 734-8169). . . . **SOL-Hawaii** offers weddings in the great outdoors: P.O. Box 8494, Honolulu, HI 96815 (tel. 923-7066); and so do a couple of ministers named **Edwards** who specialize in "strange settings" (tel. 395-9631). . . . **Waimea Falls Park** is a popular North Shore wedding setting, with a botanical garden, nature trails, and waterfalls: Tinker Bloomfield, Waimea Falls Park, 59-864 Kamehameha Hwy., Haleiwa 96712 (tel. 638-8511).

Planning to marry in Maui? **A Hawaiian Wedding Experience** specializes in West Maui weddings, although it services other islands as well: P.O. Box 11093, Lahaina, Maui, HI 96761 (tel. toll free 800/367-8047). . . . Nothing could compete with a sunset wedding at the lush **Kona Village Resort** on the Big Island of Hawaii: P.O. Box 1299, Kaupulehua-Kona, HI 96745 (tel. toll free 800/367-5290). . . . On Kauai, **Coco Palms Resort** has been a favorite wedding and honeymoon spot for years, with its private wedding chapel nestled amidst a lush, 45-acre coconut grove. They'll do everything from selecting the minister, music, and flowers, to providing a Hawaiian conch-shell blower and setting up a helicopter "shower" of island blossoms: P.O. Box 631, Lihue, Kauai, HI 96766 (tel. toll free 800/42-MARRY).

2. Ethnic Hawaii

Now we come to perhaps the most colorful aspect of the Hawaiian scene—the life of its various cultural groups. For us, this is what most makes Hawaii a marvelous place to visit. All the ethnic festivals and celebrations are exciting; just take in whatever is going on when you're there. Some people even plan their trips to the islands around the festival calendar; we wouldn't go that far, but we would advise you never to miss a festival that's going on when you're there—it might be the best part of your trip.

THE FESTIVAL CALENDAR: Now we'll turn to the ethnic events, plus other events of interest, that take place only on certain dates. We've set them forth in roughly chronological order.

New Year's Eve. Celebrations are much like those on the mainland, except that the firecrackers are noisier (Oriental style), costume balls are held at the leading hotels, and purification ceremonies are performed at Buddhist temples, to which visitors are welcome. January 1st is open house among island Japanese families.

Narcissus Festival. For three weeks before and five days after the Chinese New Year (which usually falls in the first week of February), the community blows its collective top in a running series of lantern parades, fashion and flower shows, banquets, house-and-garden tours, the crowning of the Narcissus Queen, and dancing in the streets.

Cherry Blossom Festival. A Japanese cultural and trade show, this is held in February or March, complete with a queen, pageant, and a coronation ball, plus demonstrations of tea ceremonies, flower arranging, and more.

Japanese Girls' Day. Japanese girls are presented with dolls on the first March 3rd after their birth and every March 3rd thereafter. In accordance with this delightful custom, public displays of dolls—usually costumed in the dress of a royal court—can be found in windows of the big Japanese department stores.

Prince Kuhio Day, March 26. Hawaii's beloved "people's prince" and first delegate to Congress is honored with impressive ceremonies first at Iolani Palace and later at his tomb at the Royal Mausoleum. At Kuhio Beach in Waikiki, the site of his home, a memorial tablet is decorated with leis. Hawaiian societies hold special programs and events.

Merrie Monarch Festival, April. This all-island competition between Hawaii's best hula halaus (schools) is held yearly on the Big Island of Hawaii, is sold out months in advance, and is enthusiastically watched on TV by just about every man, woman, and child in the state of Hawaii. Wonderful!

Lei Day. On May 1, everybody wears a lei, and there are contests for the most beautiful leis (judging at Kapiolani Park) and a wonderful Lei Day concert at the Waikiki Shell by the Cazimero Brothers in the evening. Tickets are about

$8 for general admission. Come early, bring a picnic supper and a blanket, and join Hawaii's people for a joyous event.

Japanese Boys' Day. You needn't be Japanese to have your family fly a brightly colored paper-and-fabric carp in your honor. Many island families have taken up the custom; watch for the flying fish each year on May 5.

Kamehameha Day, June 11. This is a state holiday (many offices will be closed) and one of the biggest celebrations of them all; there are parades and festivities all over the islands.

Japan Festival in Hawaii, June 13 to 15. One of the newer annual events in Honolulu, it includes a Bon Dance Festival (see below), a Tabishibai of the samurai period, a Japanese folk dance show, and, of course, a parade.

Bon Odori Festival, late July. One of the most colorful events in the islands, these traditional dances are done to welcome the arrival of departed souls in Paradise. The dances are usually sponsored by Japanese temples whose members practice their steps for months. Watch the local papers for dates.

Aloha Week. Mid-September to mid-October. Take the celebrations of all the ethnic groups, roll them into one, and you'll get some idea of Aloha Week—or Aloha Weeks, as they should more properly be called, since this is a moveable festival, taking place on different islands in a more-or-less progressive order. The Oriental, Polynesian, and Western groups all get together for this hoolaulea (gathering for a celebration), each vying to demonstrate the warmth and beauty of the wonderful Hawaiian aloha. The eight-day-long spree features music and dance events, demonstrations of ancient arts and crafts, a beautiful orchid show, water sports, an enormous flower parade, pageants, the crowning of both a king and a queen, and even a Molokai-to-Oahu Canoe Race (terminating at the Hilton Hawaiian Village Beach). This is a great time to come to the islands. Check with the Hawaii Visitors Bureau for the exact dates of Aloha Week celebrations; as stated, they vary from island to island.

Bodhi Day. On the nearest Sunday to December 7, the enlightenment of Buddha is commemorated with religious observances in the Buddhist temples and with Japanese dance programs and ceremonies elsewhere.

Princess Bernice Pauahi Bishop's Birthday. Hawaiian societies and schools state a moving expression of remembrance for the beloved princess at the Royal Mausoleum on December 19.

Christmas. What could be nicer than a Polynesian Christmas? There aren't any chimneys, so Santa might arrive in an outrigger canoe or on a surfboard. He might—it's not as bad as it sounds—be wearing a hula skirt. Carols are sung to ukulele accompaniment. If you happen to be in Lahaina during the Christmas season, you'll see two imaginative coral Christmas trees. Elsewhere, Christmas lights are hung on everything from evergreens to bamboo. There are special programs for the children at the Honolulu Academy of Arts. The stores are jammed, just as they are on the mainland, but surprisingly, a view of the bustling crowds (thronging the mall at Ala Moana Center, for example) is one of the prettiest of holiday pictures. The Christmas greeting: "Mele Kalikimaka!"

READERS' ACTIVITIES SUGGESTIONS: "The **Adventure V Pearl Harbor Cruise,** with daily departures from Kewalo Basin at 9:15 a.m. and 1:15 p.m., is a fine recreational and historical value at $8.50. We go aboard every visit just for the sheer pleasure of an almost-three-hour scenic cruise featuring the Honolulu waterfront, the Koolaus, and the Waianaes. The Pearl Harbor portion of the trip is, of course, fully narrated, and the script is as accurate as it is engrossing—you can take that from someone who saw the show with the 'original cast' on December 7, 1941. There is a snack bar on board, and reasonably priced souvenir booklets and slides are available for purchase. A nice new touch noted on this year's visit is the 50¢ mini-leis you can buy (if you've forgotten to bring your own) to cast into the water next to the *Arizona* Memorial as a tribute to our 1,102 sailors entombed there. For reservations, call 923-2061" (Leilani Moyers, Patterson, N.Y.). . . . "A fish auction is held every Monday through Saturday at 6 a.m. at **United Fishing Agency,** 117 Auhi St. We went about 7 a.m. and saw fish we didn't know existed, such as a 114-pound moon fish. This auction was far bigger than others we've seen and the people were more than happy to answer our questions. . . . Rent an underwater camera for $10 to $12, including a 24-exposure roll of film, from almost any scuba or snorkel shop, and you will get more comments on these pictures than on any others of your trip" (Kenneth Kendall, Omaha, Nebr.).

"Tourists who are needlework enthusiasts should know that they can learn Hawaiian quilting at the **Bishop Museum** on Monday and Friday from 9 a.m. to 3 p.m. Lei making and other crafts are featured other days. For $5, you receive personal instruction for the entire day! Kits containing everything you need to complete a quilted pillow are $25, and a book authored by teacher Kepola Kakalia is available for $8 (they take personal checks). The class is held in the Atherton Halau building on the museum grounds. The ambience is strictly 'hang loose,' with sides of the building open to the sunny breezes and the museum's two short musical presentations taking place at 10 a.m. and 2 p.m. on the stage in the same room. You can come and go if you wish to see the museum exhibits or the planetarium show. The day I was there happened to be the teacher's 70th birthday: in honor of the occasion, she was wearing several fresh-flower leis and also did a hula dance as part of the 10 a.m. musical presentation. At noon an array of Oriental foods ranging from lobster to who-knows-what was brought on and the 15-or-so quilters enjoyed a delicious birthday lunch! On the days she is not teaching at Bishop, 'Aunt Debbie' Kakalia demonstrates quilting at a shopping center" (Janet Bryan, Stockbridge, Ga.). [*Authors' Note:* Evening classes are also held in many crafts. For information, call 847-1443.]

"On Sunday we went to the worship service sponsored by **Waikiki Beach Chaplaincy** on the shore outside the Hilton Hawaiian Village hotel. It ran from about 10:30 a.m. to noon and included a good deal of music and a sermon. People were there in every form of dress and undress imaginable—perhaps 300 to 400 persons. The services have been conducted there 15 years. We decided that it was one of the best services we had ever attended. Certainly God could be worshipped in this way in this beautiful place, and it was fitting to pause and thank Him for His gifts to us, including the particular one of being in Hawaii. The preacher, in his early 30s, told us afterward that he was not a Southern Baptist, but for all the world he sounded like one!" (Jim Cox, Middletown, Ky.). . . . "For a truly unique, beautiful experience—during the summer months a **Hawaiian Catholic Mass** is held on the beach at Fort DeRussy every Saturday night. All the participants are dressed in Hawaiian costumes. All the hymns and some of the prayers are said in Hawaiian. There is even dancing during some of the hymns! Picture taking is encouraged. As you'll be sitting on the sand, bring along a mat" (Marian Ruggiero, Brooklyn, N.Y.).

"For those who wish to try the **snorkeling at Hanauma Bay,** we recommend the 'Early Bird' trip which leaves at 7 a.m. When we arrived, the beach was relatively quiet, but by the time we were ready to leave, it was practically standing room only" (Judy and Geoff Horner, Abbotsford, British Columbia, Canada). . . . "It is our opinion that Hanauma Bay is not really a place to stop for a swim, but a wonderful place to snorkel *or* see fish without snorkeling gear. No one was swimming: mobs of people were sunning themselves, snorkeling, or just standing in the water feeding the fish that are all around. To get the most enjoyment from the place, the reader should know ahead of time to bring food—particularly frozen peas—to feed the fish. We wish we had" (Marjorie Diamond, Tiburon, Calif.). . . . "As a first-time visitor to Hawaii, I truly enjoyed the **snorkeling** at Hanauma Bay. A bit of advice for anyone who is considering bringing food for those beautiful fish. First, an investment in some Ziploc bags. They keep the food, especially bread, from getting soggy and falling apart. The best food that I have found is frozen peas" (Lynn Dalton, Stony Point, N.Y.). . . . "Our son had a lot of fun swimming at Hanauma Bay in the clear water. A professional scuba-diver told him to feed cheese to the tropical fish and it worked great, better than bread. The cheese that comes in a tube and squeezes out is the best" (Ingo Platzer, Omaha, Nebr.).

"For the second time we were privileged to view the annual **orchid show** at Neal Blaisdell Center around the middle of October, and we highly recommend it for those with an interest in flowers. Cacti and anthuriums are also on display and have been judged. The picturetaking opportunities are endless, and chatting with growers and other visitors was an extra for us. Attending right after lunch, midweek, was less crowded than at other times. . . . We always check the Honolulu paper immediately after arrival to find out what is on display at the Academy of Art. We were able to view an antique Portuguese quilt show this year; last time, it was Japanese screens. The permanent collection is always good to see, and the building itself is charming. And it's a quick trip by bus from Waikiki" (Elizabeth Greer, El Cerrito, Calif.). . . . "We were handed a flyer on Kalakaua Avenue for a moonlight cruise on the *MV Adventure* for the half-price of $18. We went and had a marvelous time. We think it is one of the best bargains in Honolulu because, for that price, we had live entertainment, dinner, and drinks! Hawaii still has its charm" (Mrs. Marilyn Wade, Bainbridge Island, Wash.).

"Persons wishing to take noncredit courses should inquire at the **University of Hawaii at Manoa,** College of Continuing Education, 2530 Dole St., Box N, Honolulu, HI 96822, for course information, schedules, and fees. They will mail a copy of their brochure about a month before the classes are scheduled—timing basically follows the quarter system. One would not have to be in Honolulu for a long stay to take advantage of some of these courses; some are one-day seminars" (Dian Presmanes, Atlanta, Ga.). . . . "We each bought an inflatable raft for $3.99, and loved going way out where the waves were breaking: It took practically no room to bring the rafts home. We felt sorry for the people who bought beachmats; many had to hand-carry them on the plane because they were too wide to fit into suitcases" (Carl and Debbie Adams, St. Louis, Mo.). . . . "Do not carry extra money to the beach—leave your wallet with a friend, or put your money and keys in a **waterproof wallet** that you can wear swimming. Thieves seem to love Waikiki Beach" (Nancy Grant, South Easton, Mass.). . . . "Please advise your readers against **cashing travelers checks** in banks. There is a minimum fee of $2 for this service. If the check is cashed in a store, restaurant, or hotel, no fee is charged" (Marian Ruggiero, Brooklyn, N.Y.).

"For the more active visitor interested in hiking, phone or write the **Hawaii Geographic Society,** P.O. Box 1698, Honolulu, HI 96806 (tel. 538-3952), for maps and advice on hiking or camping on Oahu or other islands" (Jim Drouin, Edmonton, Alberta, Canada). . . . "The climb to the top of the stairway at the **Omega Coast Guard Station** is a must for those who enjoy hiking. From the top of the stairway, on a clear day, the islands of Molokai, Lanai, and Maui, and Mauna Kea on the Big Island, are visible, plus an excellent view of Pearl Harbor and the leeward coast of Oahu. The Omega Station is located at the mauka end of Haiku Road in Kaneohe. Phone Chief Warrant Officer Brian Whitaker at 235-4981 for permission to climb the stairway" (Martin Schmidt, Minden, Nebr.).

"For those planning to be in Honolulu for Christmas, we would recommend attending **Christmas Eve services** at historic **Kawaiahao Church** in downtown Honolulu. The beautiful Christmas music is sung in both Hawaiian and English, giving the visitor a chance to sing along, and feel the island blend of cultures" (Mrs. John O'Harra, Portland, Ore.). . . . "My husband played **raquetball** for free almost every day at the court at the Diamond Head end of Fort DeRussy Park—Wilt Chamberlain beat him, though" (Diana Lofstron, Prince George, B.C., Canada). . . . "We enjoyed being in Waikiki for May 1st, **Lei Day.** There were lei-making exhibits all over and a contest at the park, where we saw the very impressive coronation ceremony of the Lei Day Queen and also a large craft show with many beautiful things, some very reasonable" (Kay Loesch, Cordova, Alaska).

"We learned the hard way that tourists are open season at **Wiamanola Beach Park.** The park is absolutely gorgeous and we love to swim there because the waves are big enough to have fun on, but not too big for our youngsters. Last summer we swam there almost every day during our vacation, but this summer was different. While changing in the dressing room, my husband was jumped by three young Hawaiians who were after his wallet. He was able to fend them off with his fists and a lot of hollering, and saved us from what would have been a terrible fate. Our travelers checks and credit cards were in his shorts' pocket. We reported it to the police, but without a good description, nothing could be done. We told other people about this incident, and they all confirmed that Wiamanola is not a good place for tourists to go swimming. I would advise anyone not to go into a dressing room there without someone else they know" (Ruth E. Dishnow, Wasila, Alaska). . . . "Sharks are occasionally seen offshore, sometimes only 100 yards off the beach, but newspaper reports indicate that only five persons have been killed by sharks in Hawaiian waters in the past 85 years. Drowning is fairly common, though. It seemed that at least five were drowned every week or so. Visitors should be impressed with the extreme hazards of swimming in the surf in winter and even in just sitting on rocks where the occasional extra-large wave can sweep you off" (Jack and Ruth Phillips, Summerland, B.C., Canada).

"The beach at **Kailua** is great for children. There are good waves without dangerous undertow. . . . **Ala Moana Beach Park** is much more desirable for children than Waikiki. The water is shallow and there are no rocks or coral" (Kim Andrews, Lincoln, Nebr.). . . . "I would like to suggest that your Protestant readers attend **Waikiki Baptist Church,** 424 Kuamoo St. They have a special Sunday School class for 'first-timers,' in which the history and culture of Hawaii are explained. We both found it the most interesting part of our trip" (Morgan and Kay Tallman, Westland, Mich.). . . . "Please check local papers the day you arrive. We did not do so and missed a beach fair on the one afternoon that we did not have rain when we were in Honolulu" (John Ruble, Hillsboro, Ohio). . . . "I would like to suggest that Hawaiian malihinis turn on their AM radios to 1420, **KCCN,** the only radio station playing strictly Hawaiian music. This immediately sets them in the mood for the Hawaiian experience" (Diane Miyazaki, Wahiawa, Hi.).

"The **Hyatt Regency Waikiki** continues to provide great free entertainment. Check the tourist papers. On New Year's Eve in their Great Hall we danced to big-band entertainment with hundreds of balloons sailing down at midnight, vendors with Maui potato chips, pretzels, and other inexpensive treats—a very pleasant evening. Speaking of New Year's Eve, Waikiki was much quieter, with new fireworks regulations and great supervision by HPD. . . . The best fun is still free, wading in the warm surf at midnight in December while friends at home are shoveling snow" (Mrs. John O'Harra, Portland, Ore.).

"Those interested in other murals of Jean Charlot should stop off at the **Leeward Community College** exit and look at the mural painted in the lobby of the theater there. I think it's one of his best so far. You can see the fresco from the upper-level glass doors. . . . Check with the **State Department of Land and Natural Resources** for hiking maps, or check with the **Sierra Club** for information on local trails. To me, you haven't seen Hawaii until you have hiked up the mountains, eaten the wild fruits, and seen the magnificent tropical plants along the way. There is hardly any mountain trail where you will not find guava when it is in season. . . . The **State Foundation on Culture and Arts** can give you a schedule of what's happening culturally for the month. Some things are free" (Shirley Gerum, Haleiwa, Hi.). . . . "The **Prince of Peace Church** is an interesting attraction on Waikiki Beach; it's on the 12th—top—floor of 33 Lewers, and is referred to as 'the church with a view from the pew' and that is certainly true" (Jerald R. Borgie, San Diego, Calif.).

"I have a suggestion for vacationers who would like to make a very reasonable trip. My mother took two very interesting but not difficult courses at the **University of Hawaii,** one on the geography of Hawaii, the other on the botany of Hawaii. Both courses enhanced our trip very much. My mother is a teacher, and with these credits she moved up one notch in her income bracket—about $1,000! Also, for the time she was in school (about two months), the trip was deductible from her taxes!" (Bonny Warner, Mt. Baldy, Calif.). . . . "In winter and spring, watch for the fairs and carnivals held at local schools such as **Punahou, McKinley High, Iolani,** or the **University of Hawaii.** They have lots of local color, good ethnic foods (great Portuguese malasadas), interesting white elephant and antique booths, carnival midway areas, etc. They are usually free and are fun to attend. There are sometimes local fundraising events at the **Blaisdell Center** or on the large stage at **Kapiolani Park,** at which the name Hawaiian entertainers, like Don Ho or Danny Kaleikini, appear, and these events cost little—much cheaper than going to see the same performers at a nightclub. We saw an excellent show with some of the best island talent and Don Ho as emcee at the park, in a benefit for Life of the Land, the local ecology group" (Mrs. Joseph G. Astman, Levittown, N.Y.).

"You can visit the **Kahala Hilton Hotel** by city bus. Take the no. 1 bus on South King Street, transfer on the corner of Waialae and Koko Head, and take the no. 14 bus to the corner of Pueo Street and Kahala Avenue. From here, turn left and walk a few blocks to the hotel. If you pack a lunch, there is a nice spot to eat before going home—the Waialae Beach Park—and the view of Koko Head is absolutely gorgeous. It's really a paradise on that part of the island" (Sharon Perna, Honolulu, Hi.). . . . "I found the **Hawaii Trail and Mountain Club's Sunday walks** one of the most enjoyable parts of my vacation, introducing me to wild country that I should certainly not have seen on my own. An easy walk within Honolulu may be worth a mention. By getting prior permission from the National Guard in Diamond Head (open 8 a.m. to 4 p.m. Monday to Friday), we walked to the top of Diamond Head Crater, an easy 35-minute walk, although the last part involves a steep iron ladder, and needs a flashlight. Worth doing for fantastic views and orientation" (David Brokensha, Santa Barbara, Calif.).

"**Fort DeRussy Beach** is extra nice because of the grass and trees and benches. True, it is primarily for the armed forces, but just walk up the beach and you can stay there all day. We watch the papers closely and always attend native celebrations and gatherings; sometimes news of one is passed on to us by a native. Enjoy them as an honored guest; you will be richly rewarded" (Mrs. S. R. Kranek, Brocksville, Ohio).

SIGHTSEEING IN HONOLULU

NOW WE COME to the serious center of any trip to a new place—seeing the basic sights. If you want to know what makes the 50th state tick, you must explore the city of Honolulu. And if you really want to experience the sights and sounds and feel of a city, the best way to do it is to get out and walk. Happily, it's also the cheapest way and the most fun.

Commercial tours are expensive and can only skim the highlights. We think the city merits more attention. The local buses of the MTL, a good pair of walking shoes, and the instructions that follow will get you to all the major places. And more important, you can go at your own pace, devoting the most time to what most interests you—and you alone.

These itineraries have been set up as basic touchstones for seeing Honolulu. Improvise at your pleasure. Take two days to do a one-day trip and spend the other half of each day at the beach, if that's what suits you. We've set forth eight different tours of Honolulu and vicinity, only one of which (the trip to Pearl Harbor) will involve more than $1.20 in transportation costs. In following our directions, please remember once again that makai means to the sea, mauka is to the mountains. Diamond Head is in the direction of Diamond Head crater, and Ewa is away from Diamond Head.

If you have any questions about what bus goes where, phone MTL at 531-1611 for information. You may phone anytime between 5:30 a.m. and 10 p.m.—and the people here are really knowledgeable and friendly. If you're at Ala Moana Center, you can use the no-cost direct telephones to MTL, which are located at the bus stops on the north and south sides of the Center. You should also note that traffic on Kalakaua Avenue, Waikiki's main thoroughfare, goes Diamond Head most of the way. Except for a short stretch between the end of Kuhio and the Ala Wai Bridge, buses running from Waikiki downtown should be boarded on Kuhio Avenue. Remember that bus fare is 60¢ (exact change in coins required), and that senior citizens can use the buses free at all times by showing a bus pass. (However, it takes four weeks to get a pass, making it meaningless for most tourists. Information: 531-7066.) Oh yes, they call it **TheBUS.**

Tour 1. Downtown Honolulu

Plan to spend at least a full day on this trip, which covers the major sights of the city: the Honolulu Academy of Arts, the Mission Houses, Kawaiahao Church, Civic Center including the State Capitol, Aloha Tower, the *Falls of Clyde,* the financial and shopping districts, Chinatown, and the downtown Japanese neighborhood. It's a long trip, but once you've done it, you'll have seen the heart of Honolulu. If you prefer, break the trip up into a two- or even three-day jaunt.

THE ACADEMY OF ARTS: Your first destination is the Honolulu Academy of Arts, which you reach by taking the no. 2 bus in Waikiki right to the academy at the corner of Ward and Beretania (that's how the early Hawaiians pronounced Britain), and you'll spot the low, pretty building of the academy. Magnificent art treasures await within. (See "The Art Scene," Chapter VI, for details.) Open Tuesday through Saturday from 10 a.m. to 4 p.m., and Sunday from 2 to 5 p.m. Closed Monday and major holidays. Admission is free.

NEAL S. BLAISDELL CENTER: Now retrace your steps back across Thomas Square to King Street; coming into view is the dazzling Neal S. Blaisdell Center ("NBC" to the locals), a giant $1.25-million complex with an arena, a concert theater, and a convention hall. There are no official tours of the building, but apply at the administration office if you are seriously interested in seeing it; they will have someone show you around. Don't forget to ask for a schedule of coming events while you're there; some big names in the entertainment world may be appearing. The Arena, which can seat up to 8,800, has seen such recent stars as Lionel Richie and Whitney Houston. Home court of the University of Hawaii Rainbows, the center is the scene of many sporting events, from boxing and wrestling through gymnastics, tennis, and basketball. Family entertainments include the Ice Capades and the circus. The Concert Theater, home of the Honolulu Symphony, hosts ballet, opera, modern dance, national touring theater shows, and many other specials: noted pianist John Browning was presented here recently. The Exhibition Hall has numerous displays and trade exhibits presenting many items unique to the islands. Since this is Hawaii, all is landscaped in a tropical setting with lovely gardens and a lagoon, a perfect natural backdrop to this modern-day marvel.

Note to Parents: Kids will enjoy feeding the tame ducks and geese that live in the ponds on the grounds. They are lovingly cared for by the staff of the City Auditoriums, but are always happy for a handout! You often see local keikis and their moms feeding them loaves of day-old bread.

THE MISSION HOUSES: Now we go back to the Hawaii of old. Cross Ward Avenue on the Ewa side of the center, then turn left on King Street and walk Ewa three short blocks to King and Kawaiahao Streets. There you will come across the Mission Houses Museum, three 19th-century buildings that will give you a tremendous insight into the lives of the missionaries in Hawaii—and the unlikely intermingling of New England and Polynesia. One of the houses, the

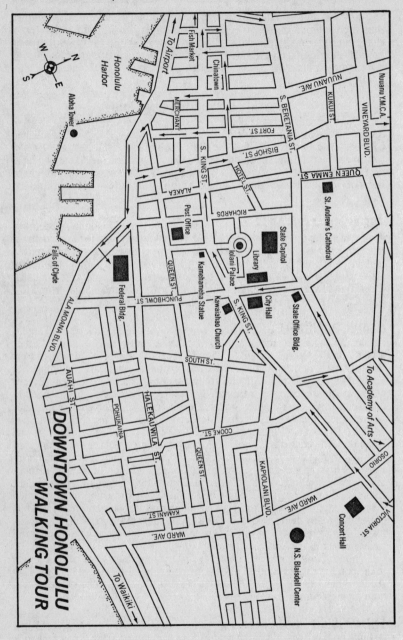

DOWNTOWN HONOLULU WALKING TOUR

home of missionary families, was built of ready-cut lumber that was shipped around Cape Horn from New England; a second, made of coral, houses a replica of the first printing press in the islands, which produced a Hawaiian spelling book in 1822; the third, also of coral, was the warehouse and home of the mission's first business agent.

A huge renovation and restoration project has been completed here and the museum is more attractive than ever. Restored to the period 1821–1860, the Frame House includes furnished parlors, bedrooms, kitchens, and cellar, a collection of original missionary furniture and other personal artifacts, documenting the lives of the families who lived and worked here. This house makes possible the study of a lifestyle and set of cultural values that had a profound influence on Hawaii's history. A new gallery in the 1831 Chamberlain House holds changing exhibits.

If possible, plan your visit for a Saturday. That's when history goes live at the museum as costumed players portray the missionaries in a program entitled, "A Social Gathering at the Binghams." (Admission fee is the same as during the week.)

The Mission Houses are open daily, 9 a.m. to 4 p.m. Admission, which includes a 45-minute guided tour, is $3.50 for adults, $1 for children 16 and under, free for children under 6. Be sure to pick up a copy of the Mission Houses' 75¢ booklet guiding you through "Historic Downtown Honolulu"; it's very helpful. Also note that a guided walking tour of that area leaves the Mission Houses Museum every weekday morning at 9:30. The fee, including museum admission, is $7, $2 for children 6 through 16. Reservations are advised (tel. 531-0481). If you happen to be in town in June for the Kamehameha Day celebration, don't miss the Fancy Fair on the grounds; about 50 booths are set up to sell local handcrafts, plus refreshing things to eat and drink.

KAWAIAHAO CHURCH: Outside the Mission Houses Museum, turn left and cross Kawaiahao Street to Kawaiahao Church. Inside, the tall, feathered kahilis signify at once that this is royal ground. You're standing in the Westminster Abbey of Hawaii, the scene of pomp and ceremony, coronations, and celebrations since its dedication in 1841. On March 12, 1959, the day Hawaii achieved statehood, the old coral church was filled with ecstatic islanders ringing its bell noisily and giving thanks for the fulfillment of a dream long denied. The next day, the Rev. Abraham Akaka linked the spirit of aloha with the spirit of Christianity in a sermon that has since become a classic in the writings of Hawaii. Note the vestibule memorial plaques to Hawaiian royalty and to the Rev. Hiram Bingham, the missionary who designed the church. Note, too, the outstanding collection of portraits of the Hawaiian alii by artist Patric. If you have time, come back on a Sunday morning at 10:30 when you'll hear a Hawaiian-English service and some beautiful Hawaiian singing. You can visit the church from 9 a.m. to 3 p.m. weekdays, on Saturday from 9 a.m. to noon. Group tours can be taken during the week by appointment.

Behind the church, and seven to eight years older than it, is an adobe schoolhouse, one of the oldest school buildings in the state.

CIVIC CENTER AND IOLANI PALACE: On the sidewalk outside the church, walk across King Street to the neo-Spanish City Hall, or **Honolulu Hale.** Just Diamond Head of Honolulu Hale are two very attractive New England–style red-brick buildings with white trim. These house such city and country departments as Municipal Reference and Records. Continuing in a Diamond Head direction, on the expanse of rolling lawn between these buildings and the towering gray stone monolith beyond, you'll see a highly controversial piece of art acquired by the city and county at a cost of $120,000. Created by famed Japanese-Hungarian sculptor Isamu Noguchi, this sculpture is entitled **"Sky Gate."** It consists of four pieces of what is apparently a gigantic stove pipe, painted flat black and welded together. Three of the pieces are supporting "legs" for the fourth—forming a sort of eccentric quadrangle—which rests atop them. One is meant to stand on the concrete walk beneath the quadrangle and look at the sky through it. This acquisition created a veritable storm of controversy and was the subject of thousands of letters to the editors of Honolulu's two daily newspapers. You'll either love it or hate it!

The aforementioned gray stone monolith is the **Honolulu Municipal Building,** 650 S. King St., which houses the Departments of Transportation, Buildings, and Public Works, and much more. Like *Sky Gate,* this building was greeted with something less than unmitigated joy by Honolulu's citizenry, many of whom feel that its architecture is out of keeping with the rest of the Civic Center, which consists of low-rise structures. When you stand in front of the Municipal Building by the flagpoles, the very attractive gray building with the terracotta roof that you see is the **Hawaii Newspaper Agency,** which houses the two daily newspapers. Many consider it one of the loveliest monarchy-style buildings in the city. Walk through the Municipal Building and out the other side, cross the little park area, and on the other side of Beretania Street you'll see the **Board of Water Supply,** a lovely pale-green building with a beautiful lawn and fountain.

Now retrace your steps in an Ewa direction, this time along Beretania Street; the beautiful new building you see across from the rear of Honolulu Hale is **Kalanimoku** (Ship of Heaven), a state office building. It houses the state Departments of Land and Natural Resources, Fish and Game, and Forestry, among others. The building has a cool, wonderfully open design, and at night, softly colored lights filter through the cut-out designs at its top. It is gorgeously landscaped with plantings of natal plum, giant zinnias, lau'e fern, various species of palms, and bright Shasta daisies.

The Punchbowl side of Kalanimoku is directly across from the **State Capital.** It's time to take a look now at this magnificent structure, completed in 1969 at the cost of $25 million. The open-air roof sweeps skyward like the peak of a volcano, reflecting pools signify an ocean environment, and Hawaiian materials and motifs have been used tastefully throughout. If the state Senate and House of Representatives are in session, you're invited to come in and see politics in action in the 50th state. You are also invited to visit, browse, and "experience" the offices of Hawaii's governor and lieutenant-governor during regular working hours (8 a.m. to 4:30 p.m., Monday through Friday); Hawaii is one of the few states that allows the public to visit its Executive Office without an appointment or on official business. Be sure, at least, that you see the building; it is a glorious architectural achievement. Note, too, Marisol's controversial statue of Father Damien, and other works of art in front of the building, facing Beretania Street. Just outside the makai side of the building are two relatively new works: a replica of the Liberty Bell and a statue of Hawaii's last reigning monarch, Queen Liliuokalani.

After viewing the State Capitol, go back the same way you came in. Walk makai and you are at the central building of the **Hawaii State Library.** It's a Greco-Roman edifice with a delightful open-air garden court. Visit the Edna Allyn Children's Room to see Hawaiian legend murals by Juliette May Fraser, and take in the other paintings hung throughout the library; those by Madge Tennent are of particular interest. Library hours may differ with the season but are usually from 9 a.m. to 8 p.m. on Tuesday and Thursday, until 5 p.m. every other day, but closed on Sunday. Don't forget to ask about free programs at the

State Library and other public libraries on Oahu. They include films, puppet shows, story hours, music recitals, and ethnic programs.

Directly across King Street is the **State Judiciary Building,** and right outside it is the famous statue of **King Kamehameha,** dressed in a royal feathered cape and a helmet that looks curiously Grecian. A symbol of Hawaii (you'll see it in countless pictures and on postcards), this larger-than-life statue of the unifier of the islands is not a great work of art, but it's appropriately heroic. On Kamehameha Day, June 11, the local citizenry decks the statue with huge leis.

Just Ewa of the library you'll see a streamlined building, the **Archives of Hawaii.** Inside are invaluable documents, journals, photographs, and other records, the largest collection of Hawaiian in existence. Visiting hours are Monday through Friday from 8 a.m. to 4:30 p.m.

The Archives are on the grounds of **Iolani Palace,** which is Diamond Head of the building, at King and Richards Streets. Take a good look at the only royal palace on American soil. Until 1969 the State Capitol, it was built during the glittering golden era of Hawaii by King Kalakaua and his queen, Kapiolani. But it housed its royal tenants for only 11 years, from 1882 until the monarchy was overthrown in 1893 by a group of haoles linked to American sugar interests. Kalakaua's successor, his sister, Queen Liliuokalani, spent nine months in the royal bedroom under house arrest after the abortive coup to restore the monarchy. (She is known for her song of farewell, "Aloha Oe.")

Now, after nine years of work and for a total cost of $7 million (the original palace came in for $343,595 in 1882), a massive restoration has been completed by the Friends of Iolani Palace and the Hawaiian flag flies over it once again. Some of the furnishings are still being restored, but several rooms are ready for the public, and the American-Florentine building is eminently worth seeing. Tours are conducted by extremely knowledgeable docents who will fill you in on plenty of Hawaiian history as they show you the throne room with the king's tabu stick (made of a 17-foot narwahl tusk and topped by a gold sphere, it was endowed with mana or spiritual power); the King's quarters, with his books, dressing table, and card table; the entry hall with its portraits of the alii of old Hawaii; and the dining room with its royal portraits of European monarchs. While it becomes difficult to imagine the daily life of a royal household in such quiet, almost ghost-like surroundings, the splendid woods and carvings, the gleaming bannisters and shining mirrors, the remarkable plaster reliefs on the ceilings, have a hauntingly beautiful effect.

The Friends of Iolani Palace conduct 45-minute tours every 15 minutes up until 2:15 p.m. Wednesday through Saturday. Reservations are requested, and tickets not claimed 15 minutes before the start of a tour will be sold to anyone who happens to be waiting for a cancellation. The charge is $4 for adults and $1 for children ages 5 to 12 (children under 5 not admitted). You'll have to don enormous khaki "airplane slippers" over your shoes to protect the delicate wooden floors. We thought the tour overlong, but worthwhile nonetheless. Call 523-0141 for reservations.

Look Ewa across King Street and you'll see a beautiful pink Spanish-style building with palm tree sentinels; it houses the U.S. Post Office and other federal agencies. Where else but Hawaii could a post office look positively scenic?

Ready for lunch? Check our "Downtown Honolulu" suggestions in Chapter III for some good restaurants.

HAWAII'S WALL STREET: The downtown shopping area is next on your tour. Walk back to King Street and turn right for a three-block walk to the **Fort Street Mall,** a lively shopping thoroughfare lined with fast-food stands and throngs of local people. You'll find Liberty House here, one of Hawaii's leading department stores, as well as a big, fascinating Woolworth's where you can buy grass skirts to send home to your niece—cheap. If you walk four blocks makai on Fort Street you'll come to the **Aloha Tower** at Pier 9 on the waterfront. The tower, open 8 a.m. to 9 p.m. daily, provides a good cool view of the harbor and city in all directions and is a fine spot for nighttime photography of harbor lights and the downtown area. At the Aloha Maritime Center here, you can see the **Maritime Museum,** the *Hokule'a* (that's the Hawaiian double-hulled canoe, which is a replica of the one in which the first Hawaiians are believed to have sailed from the Society Islands) when she is in port, and the *Falls of Clyde,* a 19th-century sailing vessel, all for $3. The Center is open daily from 9:30 a.m. to 4 p.m.

Walk across Ala Moana Boulevard to see the newest (June 1977) buildings of the State Civic Center Mall. These are the $37-million **Prince Jonah Kuhio Kalanianaole Federal Building** and **U.S. Courthouse,** two unusual low-lying structures with terraced roofs in the style of Nebuchadnezzar's Hanging Gardens of Babylon. (They are situated on the ocean side of the Civic Center; the State Capitol is on the mountain side, and Iolani Palace is in the middle.) Two outdoor sculptures here have also caused quite a stir, mostly of the favorable variety. In the courtyard, George Rickey, known for his kinetic and moving sculptures, has fashioned the 31-foot-tall **"Two Open Angles Eccentric,"** and that's just what they are—two huge stainless-steel open and transparent frames that slice through the air but never collide as they frame buildings and sky. In the plaza is Peter Voulkos's 25-foot-long and 6-foot-tall bronze called **"Barking Sands,"** composed of serpentine and geometric forms. Be your own art critic and give your verdict. Some lovely fiberworks by Ruthadell Anderson and Sharyn Amii Mills can be seen in the lobby and on the fourth floor of the courthouse.

Two blocks mauka of the Federal Building is Merchant Street—the Wall Street of Hawaii—where the "Big Five," the great financial powers of the islands, have their offices (money and the sea are always closely linked in seaport cities around the world). You'll see the handsome offices of Castle and Cooke, Ltd., Davies Pacific Center, Dillingham Transportation, Amfac Center (at Merchant and Bishop), and the almost-Oriental decor of the Alexander and Baldwin, Ltd., building. (The Ltd. appearing after all these names is a remnant of the days when British influence was strong in the islands; so is the Union Jack, which coexists with the American Stars and Stripes in the Hawaiian flag.)

Now, retrace your steps and walk mauka on Bishop Street four blocks to Hotel Street; turn left here and walk Ewa five short blocks to Maunakea Street. On the Ewa corner you'll see the pagoda-like headquarters of Wo Fat, and you'll know you're in Chinatown.

THE ORIENTAL NEIGHBORHOODS: Now we leave money, power, and the affairs of state for a look at Oriental Hawaii. **Chinatown** begins at Maunakea Street (walk left), with its jumble of shops laden with crafts, herbs, and Chinese groceries. There are several Chinese acupuncturists and Hong Kong herb doctors here (the local people swear by them) should you feel the need. It's fun to poke around on your own, but if you want something organized, two tours are available. If you're free on a Tuesday morning, make arrangements for the **Chinese Chamber of Commerce tour,** whose leader is the well-known local TV and film celebrity, Yankee Chang. The four-hour tour includes visits to shops and two temples. The price is $3 (optional lunch, $4). The tour leaves at 9:30 a.m. from Chinese Chamber of Commerce headquarters at 42 N. King St. (tel. 533-3181 or 533-6967). The **Hawaii Heritage Center,** at 1024 Nuuanu Ave., has a tour on Wednesday and Friday (except holidays), from 9:30 a.m. to 12:30 p.m. Cost is $4 per person. For information and reservations, phone 521-2749. If you're on your own and it's time for lunch, join the local folks at any of the plain little restaurants in the neighborhood, or at **Wo Fat,** where a window table will give you a good view of the goings-on below.

The **Chinese Cultural Plaza** itself—which occupies the block bounded by Beretania, Maunakea, Kukui, and River Streets—somehow never really took off as a major cultural-shopping area, and often seems half-deserted. This is not one of our favorite shopping centers, since many of the goods seem to be overpriced. We do, however, like **Hakubundo,** a Japanese "book shop" that sells many things besides books, like Japanese art supplies, ricepaper, martial art supplies, etc.; **Dragon Gate Bookstore,** with dragon puppets, books, and calendars (in Chinese, of course); and **Excellent Gems** and **Bin Ching,** both of which do jewelry repairing and carry pearls and jades. There are several enjoyable restaurants here that we've told you about in Chapter II: **Fortune Gate,** the **Mongolian Bar-B-Que,** and **Won Kee.** In their midst is a Japanese restaurant, **Hisumi.** You might stop in at the **Exhibit Hall** to see the current show.

As you wander through Chinatown's little streets, you'll notice that a renaissance of culture has taken place here. Old buildings have been refurbished and many artists have opened galleries. The renowned pen-and-ink artist Ramsay has two galleries in the neighborhood, one at 119 Merchant St. and another at 1128 Smith St. Pegge Hopper, whose works are seen all over the island, is shown in the Pegge Hopper Gallery at 1160 A. Nuuanu Ave. Pollitt's Gallery, a unique combination of a boutique featuring hand-made styles and a gallery showing the work of local artists, is at 1139 Nuuanu Ave. Most of these galleries are open weekdays from 10 a.m. to 4 p.m., until 1 p.m. Saturday, and closed Sunday.

On to Japan. Walk three blocks mauka from King Street until you come to Beretania Street. Turn left and walk Ewa a block or two to the Nuuanu Stream, where the ambience is slightly Southeast Asian. Across the street on Beretania, half a block Ewa, is the modern Town Inn facing Aala Park. Much of the old Japanese neighborhood—scrubby little saimin stands and pool halls, fish and grocery stores under quaint Oriental roofs—has been torn down to make way for new construction. Here's where you'll find the **Kukui Market Place,** with its distinctive blue roof and a pretty courtyard to rest in.

Keep going now, for the best is yet to come. A few blocks mauka on River Street, on the other side of Vineyard Boulevard, is a green-roofed Taoist temple. Slip off your shoes and walk inside for a face-to-face contact with Eastern religion. Joss sticks and incense burn at the altar, food offerings calm the ancestral spirits, and the U.S.A. seems far, far away. This is the **Kwan Yin Temple.** (There's another statue of Kwan Yin—far more splendid, we think—in the Honolulu Academy of Art.)

Tour 2. Punchbowl, Lower Tantalus, and Nuuanu

Here's a compact tour that's typical of the variegated texture of Hawaii: a U.S. military cemetery, a summer home for Hawaiian royalty, some beautiful residential districts, the resting place of the Hawaiian nobility, two Buddhist temples, and one of the most exciting botanical gardens in the world.

To take this half-day ramble, start with a no. 2 bus on Kuhio Avenue heading for town (request a transfer). Get off at Alapai Street and walk a quarter of a block left, where you can pick up the no. 15 bus ("Pacific Heights"). This leaves every hour on the half hour, so time your trip carefully. Get off at Puowaina Drive and walk for ten minutes to your first destination, the **National Memorial Cemetery of the Pacific** in Punchbowl Crater. Buried inside the crater of an extinct volcano (which had, with prophetic irony, been named the Hill of Sacrifice by the ancient Hawaiians) are some 26,000 American servicemen who perished in the Pacific during World War II, the Korean War, and the Vietnam conflict. Also listed here are the names of all Pacific war service people who have been recorded as missing or lost or buried at sea. (Visiting next of kin of any service person reported as missing during World War II, Korea, and Vietnam are urged to visit the Administration Office for information regarding grave locations.)

Parents from all over the mainland and from the islands come to Punchbowl on pilgrimages. The endless rows of gravestones of young men form a sobering sight, an awesome monument to the futility of war. When you've had enough, walk for another ten minutes to the lookout at the crater's rim for a sweeping panorama of Honolulu just below. Punchbowl is open to the public every day from 8 a.m. to 5:30 p.m. September 30 to March 1, until 6:30 p.m. the rest of the year.

Walking back to the bus stop, get another no. 15 bus and continue on it for a grand ride through the residential district of Pacific Heights. At the end of the line, another breathtaking view of the city and the Pacific awaits. When you pay for the return trip, get a transfer and leave the bus at Pauoa Road, along which you walk right two blocks to Nuuanu Avenue and bus no. 4R ("Nuuanu–Dowsett"). This bus will take you through damp, lush **Nuuanu Valley,** glorious in scenery and island history (here Kamehameha won the battle that gave him control of Oahu). Unfortunately, there's no bus to the Nuuanu Pali with its magnificent view of Windward Oahu.

The first stop on this leg of the trip is the white frame mansion on the left side, the **Queen Emma Summer Palace.** Emma and her consort, King Kamehameha IV, called this Victorian country retreat of theirs Hanaiakamalama, and it is faithfully maintained as a museum by the Daughters of Hawaii. Hawaiiana mingles comfortably with the 19th-century European furnishings of which Hawaiian royalty was so fond. Stop in at the gift shop for Hawaiian books, notepapers, postcards, and other tasteful items. The museum is open daily from 9 a.m. to 4 p.m. Admission is $4, $1 for ages 12 to 18, 50¢ for under-12s; there are conducted tours through the rooms for all visitors.

Ride on the same bus farther down Nuuanu Avenue, past the brightly colored Chinese Consulate to the **Royal Mausoleum,** on the right. Here's where the last of the Hawaiian alii, the Kamehameha and Kalakaua dynasties, and others of royal blood are buried. You can browse around from 8 a.m. to 4:30 p.m. weekdays. Closed weekends and most holidays except for Kuhio Day (March 26) and Kamehameha Day (June 11).

Resuming your makai trip on the no. 4 bus, ride down to the **Soto Mission of Hawaii,** a Buddhist temple of the Zen sect, at 1708 Nuuanu Ave., between School and Kuakini Streets; just look for its severe central tower and eight smaller octagonal ones (these represent Buddha's Path of Life). The interior is as ornate and Japanese as the exterior is austere, somewhat Indian. Walk in and have a look. They'll be happy to answer any questions. Free. Call 537-9409.

Leaving the temple, walk mauka to Kuakini Street, then turn right one block to Pali Highway, and right again for half a block to the **Honpa Hongwanji Mission Temple** on Pali Highway; this is the cathedral of the Jodo Shin Buddhist sect in Hawaii.

Now retrace your steps to Nuuanu Avenue and walk makai two blocks to Vineyard Boulevard. Turn right and you'll find the entrance to **Foster Botanic Garden** about one block away at 180 N. Vineyard Blvd. This is a marvelously cool oasis on a hot day and one of the most impressive botanical collections to be found anywhere. There are 15 acres of rare trees, flowers, plants, and unusual species of vegetation, many of them brought from the Orient. Orchids bloom throughout the year. Here you can measure the minuteness of man against a tree 20 times taller than you are, and ogle such rare specimens as the cannonball tree, the bombax, and the sunshine tree. On the grounds is a C-shaped granite monument, presented in 1960 to Honolulu by its sister city of Hiroshima, from which most of the first Japanese immigrants came to work the island plantations. A free, self-guided tour brochure is available at the reception office. There are also three free guided tours: a Hawaiian tour on Monday, and a general tour on Tuesday and Wednesday. All tours begin at 1:30 p.m., and reservations are necessary (tel. 531-1939). Foster Garden is open daily, 9 a.m. to 4 p.m. Admission is $1 for adults.

For the return, walk back to Nuuanu Avenue below School Street, board the no. 4 bus to Hotel and Bethel Streets, where you will transfer to a no. 2 bus back to Waikiki.

Tour 3. The University of Hawaii at Manoa, East-West Center, and Manoa Valley

Here's your chance to see what all those bikini-clad coeds are doing when they're not on the beach at Waikiki. Just as they do, take the Route 4 bus that runs from the corner of Kapahulu and Kalakaua right to the university campus. From here you can meander around the beautiful grounds of the university, one of the most relaxed institutions of higher learning we've seen anywhere. Nobody thinks it's unusual for that fellow in the library poring over the card catalog to be barefoot, so why should you?

Although many of Hawaii's socially conscious families still send their children off to mainland colleges (in the old days it was the Punahou–Yale route), the island's own university is the goal of thousands of other youngsters. Established in 1907 as a small agricultural and mechanical arts college, the university has grown into an important center for the study of tropical agriculture, marine biology, geophysics, astronomy, linguistics, and other fields. Its student body of more than 21,000 reflects the multiracial composition of the population of Hawaii. In addition, students come from all 50 states (about 2,000 per year) and more than 60 foreign countries (some 1,200 each year).

The **East-West Center,** a separate institution at the Manoa campus, is particularly worth your attention. A meeting place of Oriental and Occidental cultures, it brings students, professionals, and research scholars here from Asia, the Pacific islands, and the mainland United States in an exciting exchange of ideas. All students have been given awards that send them first to the University of Hawaii and later out on field work—in the mainland United States for the Easterners, in Asia or the Pacific for the Americans. Later, most of the Asians will go back home to teach or work in government posts, and most of the Americans too will go to live and work in Asia.

Walk over to see the starkly simple East-West Center buildings, a masterful architectural blending of Eastern and Western styles. Free tours leave Monday through Thursday at 1:30 p.m. from **Thomas Jefferson Hall,** but it's easy enough to walk around yourself. The lounge area of Jefferson must certainly be one of the most interesting student centers in the world. Where else might you pick up copies of *Thailand Illustrated,* the *Wall Street Journal,* and *Social Casework,* all from one rack? Asian and other art exhibitions are frequently held in the lounge art gallery.

Walk now to the rear of Jefferson for a peaceful moment at the lyrical Japanese garden, with its waterfalls, stone ornaments, lanterns, and flashing carp. And be sure to see the **John Fitzgerald Kennedy Theater,** one of the best equipped in the world for staging both Western and Oriental dramas. It's the official home of the university's drama department, and a technological center that draws theater people from both sides of the Pacific to study, teach, and produce plays. Naturally, this is a great boon for the Honolulu theater-going community; a typical season might include productions of a Japanese Kabuki classic, Shakespeare, and a contemporary Broadway comedy. An authentic Beijing opera was recently staged here—in English.

You'll want to tour the rest of the University of Hawaii campus too. Stop in at the University Relations office in Hawaii Hall, Room 2, to get maps and directions for a self-guided tour. You'll find plenty to see, especially if you're interested in art—the university definitely is: there are two art galleries, and frescoes, sculptures, and works in other media are seen everywhere, from the **Campus Center** to the systems administration center, **Bachman Hall.** Begin on the first floor of that building with Jean Charlot's impressive two-story fresco depicting old and new Hawaii. At **Bilger Hall** are four more murals of old Hawaii, done by leading artists: Juliette May Fraser, Richard Lucier, David Asherman, Sueko Kimura. Artist Murray Turnbull is represented by a stained-glass window in **Keller Hall** and in a series of murals in the **Music Building.** A ceramic work graces one entrance to the Campus Center.

Students of modern architecture will want to see the **Biomedical Sciences Buildings,** designed by Edward Durell Stone.

Nature-lovers can have a treat here too, trying to identify the 560 or so varieties of tropical plants and trees that bloom all over campus. If you need help, check the **University Relations Office** at Hawaii Hall for a map showing names and locations. We'll give you a start: the tree on the side of Hawaii Hall, which looks as if it has large sausages dangling from it, is a native of West Africa, where the oddly shaped fruits are used externally for medical purposes. Here, however, they're just decorative.

Take a gander at the bulletin board in the Campus Center, the student union. You may pick up a tip on a surfboard, a plane ticket to Los Angeles, or someone with a room to share. Need a haircut? The barbershop at **Hemenway Hall** has women barbers; haircuts for both men and women are always a good buy.

Want to take a summer course? The university enrolls over 17,000 summer students in some 500 courses. Get into Hawaii's social and cultural mix with, perhaps, some Asian Studies courses in history, languages, literature, etc. For a physical view of the islands, try Botany 105 (ethnobotany), Geography 368 (geography of the islands), or Oceanography 201. For a catalog and details, write in advance to the Summer Session Office, 101 Krauss Hall, 2500 Dole St., Honolulu, HI 96822.

The university's noncredit summer courses are also intriguing. How about sailing, stained-glass craft, Ikebana (Japanese flower arranging), hula, ESP, and self-hypnosis—for starters?

Lush **Manoa Valley,** in which the university is located, is one of the most beautiful residential areas in Honolulu and well worth an exploratory trip. You can see its flowering streets and graceful old homes from a no. 12 bus, which you board on University Avenue, back where you entered the campus. The ride up East Manoa Road to Woodlawn will take you past an interesting Chinese cemetery (marked with a big Chinese gate) at the intersection of Akaka Place, where there are often food offerings on the graves.

Taking the same bus back (on the opposite side of the road) toward the university, get off at the intersection of Manoa Road and Oahu Avenue. If you walk a little way to the right on Oahu Avenue, you'll discover the cozy **Waioli Tea Room,** a pleasant restaurant in a gorgeous tropical garden. The Little Chapel on the grounds was designed for the children of Waioli, and it's rumored that Robert Louis Stevenson courted the muse in the little grass shack now rebuilt as the Robert Louis Stevenson Memorial Grass House. You can stop here for lunch, 11 a.m. to 2 p.m. Tuesday to Sunday (tel. 988-2131). All proceeds go to the Salvation Army.

The shuttle bus will take you right back to Waikiki.

Tour 4. Bishop Museum and the Dole Cannery

Today's trip takes you to one of the Pacific's most important museums and then on to observe one of Hawaii's major industries in action. It takes half a day.

To reach your first destination, the **Bishop Museum** at 1525 Bernice St., board the no. 2 "School–Middle Street" bus and ride it all the way past the center of town to School and Kapalama Streets, where you get off and walk one block makai on Kapalama, then turn right on Bernice Street. The museum complex entrance is at midblock. Inside its stone walls (which look more like those of a fortress than a museum) is housed a world center for the study of the Pacific—its peoples, culture, history, artifacts. Most fascinating for visitors is the Hawaiian Hall, where special exhibits illustrate particular aspects of early Hawaiian culture. Note the collection of priceless feather cloaks; one uses half a million feathers from the rare mamo bird (each bird produced only a few feathers, so the kings built up feather treasuries—which were among the prime spoils of war). Other exhibits re-create the way of life of the Hawaiians, showing the outrigger canoes, a model heiau, weapons, wooden calabashes; trace the history of the Hawaiian monarchy; explore the marine and plant life of the Pacific. All this, plus the fascinating exhibits of primitive art, make for a rewarding visit, worth as much time as you can give it. You can have an inexpensive snack at the Museum Lanai Restaurant. Stop in too at Shop Pacifica for Hawaiian gifts, a cut above the usual: good books on Hawaiiana such as *Hawaiian and Polynesian Miracle Health Secrets,* children's games, a collection of Hawaiian ethnic dolls, and reproductions of Polynesian artifacts and ancient jewelry. The museum is open from 9 a.m. to 5 p.m. Monday through Saturday and the first Sunday of each month; closed Christmas Day. Admission is $4.75, $2.50 for those 6 to 17 years old, and includes a show at the adjacent Atherton Halau and entrance to Kilolani Planetarium. For information, call 847-3511 or 847-1443.

Note: If you're interested in studying **Hawaiian crafts,** you've come to the right place. Lei Making is one class you can count on. At this writing, it is held on Tuesday, 9 a.m. to 3 p.m., and costs $5, plus $3 to $5 for the flowers. Another class is Hula-Implement Making, Wednesday 9 a.m. to 3 p.m., $5; still another is Quilt Making, Friday, same time and cost. Classes are held in the Atherton Halau, (phone for schedules) also the site of special events which are usually held on weekends.

Sharing the museum grounds is **Kilolani Planetarium** a great spot for anyone interested in space exploration and astronomy. The planetarium has the only observatory in the islands available to the public; it is open after the fascinating evening sky shows on Friday and Saturday at 8 p.m. Shows are also held weekdays at 11 a.m. and 3:15 p.m. Admission is $2 for adults, $1 for youths 6 through 17. Children under 6 are admitted free (with paying adults) on Saturday and Sunday.

After leaving the Bishop Museum grounds, you can face the modern industrial world again at the **Dole Pineapple Cannery.** To get there from the museum, board the no. 2 bus at School and Kalihi Streets, disembark at Hotel and River Streets, and transfer to the no. 8 bus on the opposite side of the street (make sure it reads "Airport–Hickam"). If you come direct from Waikiki, take the no. 10 "Airport–Hickam" bus on Kuhio direct to the cannery. The walk-through tour of the cannery, for which there is a charge of $2, is given only on the days the cannery is in operation; always call in advance to make sure that tours will be given that day (tel. 536-3411). Anytime of the year, however, you can see a free film tour of the canning process. And you can be taken directly to the cannery—as well as to Hilo Hattie's Fashion Center two blocks away—by free bus from major Waikiki hotels. For bus schedules, see the local tourist papers or phone 537-2926.

Now, about that walk-through tour held during the canning season. The 45-minute tour, led by personable guides through the world's largest fruit cannery, is a fascinating one; the sheer size and efficiency of the operation is most impressive. You'll see thousands and thousands of pineapples bobbing along on huge conveyor belts, looking oddly like lambs for the slaughter. There's an amazing machine (the Ginaca) that can peel and core 100 pineapples in 60 seconds! And there are rows of workers checking and sorting the fruit before it goes into the cans; during the height of the summer harvest season, when the cannery operates at peak capacity, many of these workers will be high school and college students earning next year's tuition. Before the tour, you're free to imbibe as much pineapple juice as you like and you get a delicious fresh slice during the tour. That silly-looking pineapple on top of the building, by the way, is not filled with pineapple juice; it's the water tower. There is a charge of $2 for the tour, 50¢ for children under 17.

To return to Waikiki, take the no. 8 bus outside the cannery on Iwilei Road in the opposite direction.

Tour 5. Pearl Harbor

Anyone who remembers—or has heard about—December 7, 1941, should not leave the Hawaiian Islands without seeing Pearl Harbor. The cheapest way to get there is by TheBUS; bus no. 20 goes right from Waikiki to Pearl City. From Ala Moana Center, you can take no. 50, 51, or 52. The trip should take about an hour. Ask the driver to let you off at the **U.S.S. Arizona Memorial.** You can also take private bus services direct to the *Arizona* Memorial via the *Arizona* Memorial Shuttle Bus, $4 round trip (tel. 926-4747).

The new $4.2-million Visitor Center, administered by the National Park Service, provides an ideal starting point for your trip to the U.S.S. *Arizona* Memorial. Its museum relates the early history of the war at sea and life in wartime Hawaii. Step up to the Information Desk, where you will be given a tour number, and find out approximately when your shuttle boat will leave. Because the crowds can be enormous—up to 5,000 on very heavy days—you may have to wait for two hours or more, unless you arrive before 9:30 a.m., when the wait should be a bit less, although it may still be more than an hour. While you're waiting, you can study a detailed mural of the *Arizona* or check out the books and souvenirs in the bookshop. When your number is called, you enter the theater to see a 20-minute film, and then are ferried on a navy boat to the U.S.S. *Arizona* Memorial. Tours operate daily from 8 a.m. to 3 p.m. and are free.

Dedicated in 1962, the memorial is a covered white concrete bridge rising starkly above the hull of the battleship *Arizona*, victim of a direct hit on the day that bombs fell on Hawaii, and the tomb of over 1,000 American servicemen (some 2,403 in all were killed that day). The outlines of the ship shimmer just below the water, and, as if warning that the story is not yet finished, oil slicks still rise from the rusting hulk. Like Punchbowl Cemetery, it is an eloquent witness to the fury and folly of war. A big experience.

Note: If the weather is stormy, call the *Arizona* Memorial at 422-0561 to find out if the boats will be operating. Children under 45 inches in height are not permitted on the shuttle boats, but they are permitted at the Visitor Center and in the theatre; those 6 to 10 must be accompanied by an adult; bathing suits and bare feet are taboo.

If you have time, you can take a short walk from the *Arizona* Memorial to visit **Bowfin Park,** where the U.S.S. *Bowfin,* a World War II submarine launched one year after the attack on Pearl Harbor, is moored. Admission of $3 for adults, $1 for children 6 to 12, includes a self-guided tour. Open daily, 9:30 a.m. to 4:30 p.m.

Tour 6. Paradise Park

We recommend this place especially to families traveling with children; all of you can have a good time. Public transportation can get you here within 45 minutes (no. 8 bus to Ala Moana, then the no. 5 bus with the sign reading "Paradise Park"), but since there's a free shuttle bus from Waikiki, that's a much better solution. Call 988-2141 or visit their booth at the International Market Place, and they will arrange free transportation for you.

The most exciting focus at Paradise Park is birds—mostly from South America and Africa (Hawaiian birds can be found in the Honolulu Zoo). You'll see rare birds as they are found in their natural habitats, in lush jungle and forest settings of great beauty. As you arrive, you'll descend into a mammoth cage with a circular walkway and all the parrots and macaws come up to you for a handout. Scheduled shows held at the Kamehameha Amphitheater offer birds that play poker, ride bikes across a tightrope, and do other amazingly human things. There is also a trained duck show ("Animal Quackers") on the grounds, and special shows at various times featuring different ethnic entertainment (the parks theme is a multicultural one) and children's entertainment. You can also take the marvelous jungle trails (don't miss the grove of Asian bamboos), see demonstrations of Hawaiian arts and crafts, gawk at and photograph what seem like millions of orchids, trees, flowers, and plants. And you're sure to enjoy the "Dancing Waters" show. Plan on 3½ to 4 hours to enjoy it all.

Henri's Hawaii Restaurant overlooking the grounds is a beauty, and prices are not overly expensive. Or you can fill up on hot dogs, soft drinks, and ice cream at the modestly priced snackbar. Admission to Paradise Park is $7.50 for adults, $6.50 for juniors 13 to 17, and $3.75 for children 4 to 12. It is open daily, except Christmas Day, from 10 a.m. to 5 p.m.

Note: After a three-year interlude, Paradise Park has returned to "show biz" with a Hawaiian revue. At the present writing, the show is part of a five-hour package tour that begins at 2:30 p.m. and encompasses all the attractions of the park, plus an all-you-can eat buffet, ending with the show "Magic in Paradise," presented at 6:15 p.m. Monday through Friday only. The $32 price includes transportation from Waikiki.

Tour 7. Castle Park

This is another trip we recommend particularly to families with children, but we don't see why everybody shouldn't enjoy a visit to Castle Park, the first major theme amusement park—à la Disneyland—to hit the islands. Castle Park is much smaller than Disneyland—just 16 acres—but it packs a lot of fun into that space, with such attractions as a real fairytale castle with drawbridge and moat (inside it's filled, paradoxically, with Space Age electronic and video games); three 18-hole miniature golf courses whose strange and wonderful obstacles include haunted houses and windmills; a batting range with authentic major-league baseball and softball pitching machines; the Grand Prix racing car ride, where you hope not to bump into other drivers, and Bumper Boat Lake, where you do. All in all, plenty to keep everybody in the family occupied for a full day's worth of fun. There's a snackbar on the grounds.

There is no general admission charge to enter Castle Park. Each attraction has its own price, or you can purchase passes for a variety of attractions at discount rates. To reach Castle Park, which is open every day from 10 a.m. on, take the H-1 Freeway and follow the Aloha Stadium signs. It's about an eight-minute drive from downtown Honolulu.

Tour 8. A Waikiki Checklist

We're not going to map out any formal tour of the Waikiki area, since you'll be spending so much of your time here anyway. We'll simply remind you of some of the attractions you can see more or less anytime, before or after a swim at the beach.

The big hotels, of course, are great for strolling in and out of in the evening (see Chapter III). While you're at it, check out the sleek modernity of the **Ilikai,** the tasteful Polynesian architecture of the **Waikikian,** the graceful airs of the **Moana,** the old-world splendor of the **Royal Hawaiian.** The **Hawaiian Regent,** one of the newer hostelries, is done in beautiful taste, with its open-air lobby surrounding a central court aglow with a fountain and two lagoons. Walk up two flights of stairs to the pool and the Ocean Terrace, and you'll be rewarded with one of the most beautiful open daytime views in Waikiki. The hotel seemingly juts out right over the beach (even though it's across the street), and the glorious colors of ocean and sky surround you wherever you look. The famed **Halekulani Hotel,** the last of the low-rise, Hawaiian-style cottage hotels on the beach, has been totally rebuilt. The $100-million project has preserved the main two-story structure as an indoor-outdoor dining area and added five interconnecting high-rise buildings. It's luxury all the way here, in the first world-class hotel to be built in this area in 25 years. The **Hilton Hawaiian Village,** which has just undergone a major, $80-million upscaling, represents Henry J. Kaiser's first contribution to Hawaii (he sold it to Hilton some years back and moved on to even bigger projects). It's a fascinating cornball beach city of its own, with 20 acres of tropical gardens, an artificial lagoon, a vast array of indoor and outdoor bars and restaurants, six pools, a beautiful beachfront, even its own post office. The array of shops here includes the Rainbow Bazaar, which we've detailed in Chapter V. Walk around for a few minutes and you'll view a cross-section of Hawaii's visitors—anybody from a group of Shriners on one side to a gaggle of blushing young Japanese couples on another.

Near the Hilton is the **Fort DeRussy Military Reservation,** a great low-cost recreation area for the military on a prime strip of Waikiki Beach. Fortunately, the beach is now open to the public, and many claim it's the best in Waikiki. You can usually park there too. (The 15-story Hale Koa Hotel here offers attractive, well-priced rooms to active and retired military, dependents, and widows of retired personnel.) You may want to stop in for a quick visit to the **U.S. Army Museum** in Fort DeRussy Park, which contains military memorabilia dating from ancient Hawaiian warfare to the present. It is housed in Battery Randolph, built in 1909 as a key installation in the defense of Honolulu and Pearl Harbor. Exhibits include "Hawaiian Military History," "Coast Artillery Defense," "The Pacific War, Korea, and Vietnam," and "A Hawaiian Gallery of Heroes." On the upper deck, the **Corps of Engineers Pacific Regional Visitors Center** graphically shows how the Corps works with the civilian community in managing water resources in an island environment. The museum is open Tuesday through Sunday from 10 a.m. to 4:30 p.m., admission free (tel. 543-2639).

You will, of course, want to spend a lot of time shopping and browsing at the **International Market Place, King's Village,** and the **Royal Hawaiian Shopping Center** (details in Chapter V). Check the local tourist papers for news of free entertainments and events.

Of course you'll have to see **Hemmeter Center,** a stunning architectural landmark encompassing the super-luxurious Hyatt Regency Waikiki Hotel, plus a shopping center, restaurants, and cocktail lounges. The entire area is dramatically landscaped, with tropical foliage, trees and plantings, huge sculptures, many-storied waterfalls, flowing lagoons, picturesque kiosks, and Polynesian objets d'art. The Hyatt Regency, however, is slightly out of our range: penthouses at $550 per day, other rooms from $95. It's on Kalakaua, between Uluniu and Kaiulani Avenues.

There are more than a few things to see at the Diamond Head end of Waikiki, up near Kapiolani Park. Past Kuhio Beach, at Kapahulu Avenue, the **Honolulu Zoo** looms up on your left (the entrance is at 151 Kapahulu Ave.). It's noted for its collection of native Hawaiian and other tropical birds. You'll see Australia's national bird, the "Laughing Jackass" (more politely referred to as the kookaburra); gorgeously colored flamingos; handsome blue- and purple-crowned pigeons from New Guinea; and various bird-jungle habitats. The kids will get a kick out of the four primate islands surrounded by moats. There's also the usual array of Bengal tigers, Asiatic elephants, a lion, and three adorable Himalayan sun bears. With Diamond Head providing the background, plenty of trees and flowers (including a giant banyan and date palms), white doves, and keikis tumbling about, it's one of the most charming zoos anywhere. At the moment, it's undergoing a multimillion dollar renovation: Phase I, "The African Savannah," is now underway. The zoo is open every day (except Christmas and New Year's Days) from 8:30 a.m. to 4 p.m. During June, July, and August, the zoo stays open until 7:30 on Wednesday evenings, with free entertainment starting at 6 p.m. at the stage under the earpod tree, just behind the flamingos. Take a picnic supper and join the fun. Local artists hang their work on the fence outside on Saturday, Sunday, and Wednesday. Be sure to stop in at Zootique, the charming gift shop (described in Chapter V). Admission to the zoo is $1 for adults, free for children 12 and below.

From here on, Kalakaua Avenue is a regal, although narrow, tree-lined drive. And a little farther on, where Kalakaua meets Monsarrat Avenue, **Kapiolani Park** begins (those are the Koolau Mountains in the background). The 220 acres of the park have facilities for just about everything, from soccer to rugby to picnicking; also archery, a golf driving range, and tennis. The Royal Hawaiian Band plays frequently in the bandstand, and major musical events take place in the Waikiki Shell. For a particularly beautiful view, note Diamond Head framed in the cascading waters of the splendid Louise C. Dillingham Fountain.

Bordering the ocean on the right is a stretch of wide, palm-dotted grass lawn with a fringe of sand to let you know you're still at the beach. Swimming here is excellent, since the surf is quite mild; it's a big favorite with island families. **Kapiolani Beach Park,** with locker room, rest rooms, picnic tables, and snackbar, is just ahead.

The **Waikiki Aquarium** is also up here, just past the beach, and it's a lot of fun. Here's your chance to see, among other creatures of the deep like giant clams and sharks, the lauwiliwilinukunukuoioi; if you can't pronounce it, just ask for the long-nosed butterfly fish. The museum features an exhibit entitled "Hawaiians and the Sea," focusing on the early Hawaiians' love of and dependence on the sea. The aquarium is open daily from 9 a.m. to 5 p.m. Admission is free for children under 16, but donations of $2 from adults are invited—to help them feed the fish. Stop in to see their attractive giftshop called Natural Selection. Everything in it, from T-shirts with fish designs, books, posters, cards, linen, and home accessories relates to the ocean and its life-forms. They have a good selection of children's toys and books, too.

Now it's time to rest your feet—and see something new—by hopping aboard a no. 14 bus going Diamond Head on Kalakaua Avenue. The bus will take you through the lovely **Waialae-Kahala** area and **Kaimuki** suburbs, and up the mountain to **Maunalani Heights.** From there, you can look straight down into **Diamond Head Crater.** Koko Head on the left, Waikiki slightly to your right. For your return trip, change to a no. 2 bus, and you'll be back in Waikiki. Or if you prefer, stay on the no. 14 and ride up to **St. Louis Heights** for a magnificent panorama of Honolulu. A forest of beautiful Norfolk pines with picnic tables and a splendid view of Manoa Valley awaits you here at the **Waahila Ridge State Recreation Area.**

Note: If you're making this little trip on wheels, you can actually drive right inside Diamond Head Crater—the only drive-in crater on Oahu, except for Punchbowl. Here's how you do it. Follow Kalakaua until it circles left, just past the Colony Surf Hotel; then make your first right to Diamond Head Road. Come up Diamond Head Road, past the lighthouse on the right. Take your first left before the triangular park; you are now entering the Fort Ruger area. Watch for the Diamond Head Crater sign on the left and follow the road to the left. Go through the tunnel, and you're in Diamond Head State Monument. Hiking trails go up to the rim of the crater. The area looks quite undramatic, but where else, but in Hawaii, can you drive into a volcano!

WAIKIKI TROLLEY: For a more organized look at Waikiki, it's lots of fun to ride the new Waikiki Trolley. Recalling Honolulu's turn-of-the-century streetcars, these jaunty red motorized trolleys with an old-fashioned look (etched glass windows, polished brass rails, handcarved oak interiors), traverse the route from Waikiki to Ward Warehouse, Fishermen's Wharf and the Ala Moana Shopping Center, while an entertaining driver/tour guide points out interesting spots and historical sites. Since there are 29 scheduled stops, you can use it almost as a Waikiki taxi, jumping on and off as much as you like for the cost of a $5 all-day pass. One way fare is $2; children 11 and under, $1. Trolleys operate every 45 minutes from 8:45 a.m. to 11:45 p.m.; the complete trip takes 90 minutes. For schedules, phone E Noa Tours, one of our favorite tour companies, at 941-6608.

TOURS FOR THE HANDICAPPED: Handi-cabs of the Pacific offers special tours for handicapped passengers, in specially equipped vans that can handle six wheelchairs. Typical city tours cost $23 per person. For information, phone 524-3866.

READERS' SIGHTSEEING SUGGESTIONS: "I would like to put in a good word for **E Noa Tours** (tel. 941-6608). We had a delightful city tour in a van with two other families for $14 each, $11 for children. We had a charming and helpful guide who gave us loads of tips for a great stay in Hawaii" (Ken and Dorothy Gimblin, Sacramento, Calif.). [*Authors' Note:* We get many letters each year praising E Noa and their warm hospitality that makes each passenger feel like a personal guest.] . . . "Perhaps you could suggest that people lock their cars, especially when stopping at scenic spots. This was the first thing my family in Hawaii warned us about, as there has been a lot of trouble with tourists' cars being robbed while they viewed the sights. One time when we were at the Blow Hole, we heard a police officer stop a couple and ask the woman if she had left her purse in the open car. When she said 'yes,' he politely but firmly told her to go back to get it, and lock the car. He also said, 'You people are careless, then you come to us and expect us to do something about it when your things are stolen'" (Mrs. Joseph Astman, Levittown, N.Y.). . . . "Please advise all visitors to do their sightseeing on their own. Bus sightseeing trips consisted of a few ten-minute stops at scenic points and too many long stops at tourist traps, always trying to sell something. Also, they *all* seem to arrive at a point at the same time, dumping hundreds of tourists together trying to see the same sight in the same ten-minute time limit, and generally raising havoc" (John C. Schmid, Line Lexington, Pa.).

"For those who *like* walking we would recommend the three-hour **walking tour of**

Historic Old Honolulu, which includes the State Capitol Building, a worthwhile visit in itself. Here we were warmly welcomed by a receptionist who gave us a couple of very interesting and beautifully printed pamphlets on the capitol buildings, with terrific color pictures, including aerial shots of the grounds and Iolani Palace, and packed with facts on Hawaiian history, geography, culture. A really nice souvenir!" (Lloyd and Shirley Kilby, Hope, B.C., Canada). . . . "Just past Paradise Park on Manoa Road, the road ends. We parked and took a delightful 45-minute hike through the lush ferns and plants to a beautiful waterfall. This trail is mostly known only to locals and is well worthwhile" (Richard Marks, Lodi, Calif.).

"Unless someone is an avid, strong hiker, I suggest passing up the trail to Manoa Falls. The trail will take half an hour to an hour going up, and is filled with rocks and roots and slippery spots. It is a difficult trail with many opportunities to twist an ankle or fall and break something. If you get hurt on that trail, who is going to carry you out? You can see plenty of Hawaiian jungle, cultivated and uncultivated, just by visiting the nearby **Lyon Arboretum,** which is free. And the trails are much better" (Mark Terry, Alameda, Calif.).

Chapter VIII

AROUND OAHU

1. The Seaside Drive
2. The Pali and Makiki Heights
3. Tips for Tourists

YOU HAVEN'T REALLY SEEN HAWAII until you've left the urban sprawl of Waikiki and Honolulu and traveled to the other side of the mountains for a look at Windward Oahu. And what a look that is! There are jagged cliffs and coral beaches; Stone Age ruins and tropical suburbs; a vast military concentration; backwoods country towns sleeping in the sun; endless stretches of breadfruit, banana, papaya, hibiscus, lauhala, coconut palms—the glorious vegetation of the tropics so ubiquitous as to be completely taken for granted. And best of all, some of the most intriguing sightseeing attractions in the 50th state are here: Sea Life Park, the Byodo-In Temple, and the Polynesian Cultural Center.

Not one advertising billboard defaces the landscape; they're kapu in Hawaii. The only signs you will see are those of the Hawaii Visitors Bureau's red-and-yellow warrior pointing to the places of interest. There are dozens of spots for beachcombing and picnicking, so pack your bathing suit and lunch. If you get an early start, you can certainly make this trip in one day, but there's so much to see that two would be much more comfortable. We'll provide a basic itinerary, around which you can plan your time.

TRANSPORTATION: You can see a good part of the island by sticking to public transportation. The Wahiawa–Kaneohe bus no. 52, which leaves Ala Moana Center every 15 minutes from 6:15 a.m. to 10:15 p.m. daily, will enable you to see many island points of interest: the big surf at Haleiwa, Sunset Beach and the North Shore, the Polynesian Cultural Center, to name some. (The cost will be at least $1.20, with no transfers; you'll have to pay 60¢ every time you reboard the bus.) Many of our readers make this trip and praise it highly. But since it is a commuter service, not a sightseeing bus, and would take you many, many hours, we personally believe it's not the best way to go. We therefore recommend that you part ways with the public transportation system and rent a car. If you're traveling alone or don't want to drive, you can, of course, take any of the standard around-the-island sightseeing tours. (We've had excellent reports, over the years, on those offered by **E Noa Tours**—tel. 941-6608; for a report, see the Readers' Suggestions at the end of this chapter.) A new and highly recommended tour company is **Na'Ike,** which promises "a real Hawaiian experience"; they'll adopt you for a day for a family outing, visiting attractions off the beaten path along the windward side and the north shore. Lunch is prepared by a former chef to two Hawaiian governors. En route, you're entertained by Hawaiian singers and dancers. Full-day tours cost $45 for adults, $41 for children under 12 (tel. 621-2655). For two or more, of course, it's far cheaper to rent a car for the day (total costs should come to about $30), and the really akamai way to do it is to find three or four other people and split the expenses down to practically nothing. But the main thing is to make the trip, whatever way you decide. You might even consider hitching; since the bus strike a few years back, it has not been against the law to hitch, and many people do. *If you're driving, remember to lock your car doors and take your valuables with you when you get out to look at the sights.*

A NOTE ON OUR MAPS: The maps in this book are for the purpose of general orientation. When doing any extensive driving, we suggest you follow a more detailed road map. We have personally found the maps in *Drive Guide to Oahu,* free from any car-rental company, to be excellent.

ON YOUR WAY OUT OF TOWN: You start at Waikiki, driving Diamond Head on Kalakaua Avenue past Kapiolani Park; this will lead you into Diamond Head Road, which runs into Kahala Avenue past the sumptuous residential area of Black Point (Doris Duke's seaside mansion is nearby). Sculptor Kate Kelly's monument to Amelia Earhart is just past the Diamond Head Lighthouse. At the end of Kahala Avenue, where it hits the Waialae Golf Course, turn left on Kealaolu Avenue; follow this road to Kalanianaale Highway (Rte. 72); the entrance will be on the right. Before you turn, you come to **Waialae Beach Park,** with modern facilities, covered pavilions, and wide, wide beaches, right next door to the prestigious Waialae Country Club. The swimming here, however, is not too good, since there are many rocks in the water. Next door is the splendid Kahala Hilton Hotel; you might want to have a look at the lovely grounds.

Just before you reach Koko Head, you'll pass the entrance to Henry Kaiser's once-controversial **Hawaii Kai**—a 6,000-acre, $350-million housing development that's a small city in itself. You can drive in for your own tour of inspection. (A resident advises us that there is a beautiful view at the top of the hill past the Hawaii Kai Golf Course overlooking the ocean and the south end of Windward Oahu.) While you're in this area, you may want to stop in at **Waterfront Village,** a charming small shopping complex perched right out on the waters of Koko Marina, and tied in by walks and a shared parking lot with the much larger Hawaii Kai shopping center.

Koko Head and **Koko Crater,** now coming into view ahead, are reminders that Oahu, like all the Hawaiian islands, is a volcanic mountain spewed out of the Pacific. During Oahu's last eruption (volcanologists say it happened at least 10,000 years ago), these craters and the one that houses *Hanauma Bay* were born. One side of Koko Head has been washed away into the sea and the result is an idyllic beach, one of the most popular in the islands. Since the placid turquoise waters cover a cove in the purple coral reef, it is a perfect place for beginning and advanced snorkelers. (Rent snorkels in Waikiki or bring your own; none is available here.) Hanauma Bay is now a marine reserve, and so gentle have the fish become that parrot fish, bird wrasses, and others will eat bread from a swimmer's hand. There are dressing facilities, and camping, barbecue, and picnic areas. Although the beach is a very long walk from the parking area, the driver can drive all the way down to the beach, discharge his passengers, and then drive up to park. Or all of you can take a train from the parking lot to the beach for a small fee. *Be sure to lock your car and remove any valuables!* Needless to say, the islanders love this place, and the only problem is that you've almost always got to share it with quite a lot of them. (Before you begin this stretch, see "The Pali and Makiki Heights" below.)

1. The Seaside Drive

For the next few miles, you'll be driving along one of the most impressive stretches of rocky coastline in the islands. The black lava cliffs hurtle down to the sea to meet a surging purple Pacific, all set against a brilliant blue-green background of sky, trees, and flowers. Park the car at any of the designated areas, or at the popular **Blow Hole,** where the water geysers up through an underwater vent. (The areas before the Blow Hole are just as pretty, much less crowded.) With the wind in your hair and the surf crashing below, you'll feel light years away from the trivialities of civilization. Just beyond the Blow Hole is **Sandy Beach** (where you might stop off for one of those shave ices we described in Chapter III at **Malia's Lunch Wagon,** parked across from the beach at the intersection of Kalanianaole Hwy. and the Kalama Valley road). Beyond that is **Makapuu,** where people are actually surfing on those horrendous waves. These two beaches are strictly for the experts; beginners had better watch from the sand. More important, this is the site of a big island sightseeing attraction—

SEA LIFE PARK: There's plenty of entertainment here for the whole family. First, there's a show in the Ocean Science Theater, a live training session in which porpoises and penguins show off their agility and brains. Shows alternate with those in the Whaler's Cove, in which a replica of a whaling ship, two whales, and several species of porpoise, together with a beautiful Polynesian girl, re-create Hawaii's early whaling history in a narrated pageant. At the 300,000-gallon Hawaiian Reef Tank exhibit, you may descend three fathoms below the surface for a skindiver's-eye view of a typical offshore coral reef, full of brilliantly colored marine creatures, some 2,000 of them. Dangerous black-tipped sharks are just inches away—on the other side of the glass. An exciting new exhibit called "Rocky Shores" re-creates the surf-swept intertidal zone of Hawaii's shoreline. A 20-foot tower will have the capacity to drop 600 gallons of water into the exhibit every 45 seconds. A sea lion feeding pool has become a popular attraction: you may feed the splashy animals fish and try your luck at coaxing them to do a trick or two.

In addition, you'll want to check out the mini-lectures at the Bird Sanctuary, which shows species of marine birds seldom seen by the public (the red-footed booby, masked booby, and albatross, among others); and visit the Turtle Lagoon and the Pacific Whaling Museum, which houses the largest collection of whaling artifacts—scrimshaw, harpoon, rope work—in the Pacific.

Stop in at the Sea Chest gift shop with its collection of distinctive artifacts. Note the rubbings of ancient Hawaiian petroglyphs, original marine paintings, stunning stained-glass fish, and a fine selection of marine books for children and adults.

Admission to Sea Life Park is $8.25 for adults, $6.50 for juniors 7 to 12, and $2.75 for children 4 to 6; free for children under 4. (Prices are subject to change.) The park is open daily from 9:30 a.m. to 5 p.m. The last series of shows starts at 3:15 p.m. Inquire about special behind-the-scenes tours. Call the park at 259-7933 or the Waikiki office at 923-1531 for information. Note that several tour companies run excursion trips to Sea Life Park several times a day, with Waikiki hotel pickups. MTL buses also make hourly runs to the park. You can call MTL at 531-1611.

A SIDE TRIP TO KAILUA: It's possible now to make a little side trip to Kailua,

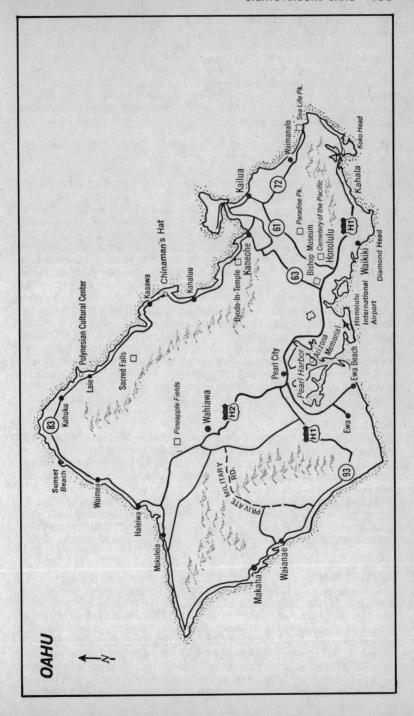

OAHU

←N

one of Honolulu's most pleasant suburbs, by staying on Hwy. 72 until it intersects with Hwy. 61, then turning right on 61 until you reach Kailua, a few miles down the road. The reason for this trip is the beach: **Kailua Beach Park,** and especially **Lanikai,** are absolutely beautiful, with gentle waves, white sand, and much smaller crowds than you see at Waikiki Beach. We always feel this is what Waikiki must have been like in the old, pre-tourist days. There are several attractive restaurants in Kailua, too, like Florence's and Cinnamon's, which we've told you about in Chapter III. (Alternatively, plan a visit to Kailua for another morning or afternoon's excursion.)

ON TO HEEIA: Retrace your way back to Hwy. 72 now, and continue north. Off Rabbit Island, the water turns turquoise. The inland view along this coast is also spectacular, thanks to the towering **Koolau Mountains;** their corrugated slopes (an example of the forces of erosion at work on volcanoes) are a neat balance to the restless sea on your right.

Just past Sea Life Park, you'll find **Waimanalo Beach Park,** which many island families consider the best beach on Oahu: pleasant surf, grassy knolls, picnic tables, the works. You may want to come back here for a long stay. For now, drive on for a few more miles and you'll come upon what was long considered one of Oahu's most magnificent beaches by the few people lucky enough to enjoy it—the military. This is **Bellows Beach Park,** nestled against the mountains, a 46-acre strip of fine sand, lively but not dangerous surf, and wooded picnic groves of palm and pine. After long years, Bellows has been opened to the public, but on weekends only, from Friday noon to midnight Sunday; and on federal and state holidays. There are public bathhouses. (It's a favorite spot for tent and trailer camping; permits from the Recreation Department, City and County of Honolulu.) Bellows is a perfect place for a picnic lunch (bring your own, as there's nothing to buy), or a swim, the only danger (aside from occasional Portuguese man-of-wars) being that you may be tempted to spend the whole day and forget about your exploring. Keep going, for the best is yet to come.

Haiku Gardens

Your next stop might be a chance to stretch a bit at Haiku Gardens. The main house of this old kamaaina estate is the **Haiku Gardens Restaurant,** where you can stop by for a decently priced luncheon (see Chapter III for details). But you don't need to eat here or pay any other admission to tour the grounds, which are open during daylight hours. A lily pond dominates all, and from it, trails lead off which will take you to, among other things, a lovely grove of golden bamboo from Java, Hawaiian grass huts, a palm grove, a bird sanctuary, fragrant plantings of ginger and anthurium, and exotic fish ponds. To reach the gardens, turn left off the highway at Haiku Road and proceed mauka about a mile.

Byodo-In Temple

For devotees of Orientalia, we know of no more rewarding spot in the islands than the Byodo-In Temple in the Valley of the Temples, which should be your next destination. It's about two miles from Haiku Road, and you can reach it by driving back to Kahekili Hwy. from Haiku Gardens and proceeding north. (If you haven't stopped at Haiku Gardens, continue on Kamehameha Hwy. to Pineapple Hill, proceed to the intersection, then turn left the way you came onto Kahekili Hwy.; you'll come to Valley of the Temples in about half a mile.) Byodo-In is an exact replica of the venerable Byodo-In, reputed to be the most beautiful temple in Kyoto, Japan, constructed at a cost of $2.6 million and dedicated on June 7, 1968, almost 100 years to the day after the first Japanese immigrants arrived in Hawaii. The temple sits in a magnificently landscaped classical Japanese garden fragrant with pine, plum, and bamboo. Inside, you can gaze at the intricately carved screens and panels, and pay obeisance to the magnificent gold carving of Amida, the Buddha of the Western Paradise. Many of the Buddhist faithful in the islands come here, of course, but a visit is every bit as much an aesthetic, as well as spiritual, experience. While you're meditating, turn the kids loose in the gardens, supply them with a package of fish food (thoughtfully sold in a tiny tea-house gift store), and let them feed the flashing carp in the two-acre reflecting lake. The shop also imports religious items and other Japanese gifts from Kyoto. Have a look. Admission is $1.50 for adults, 75¢ for children.

Heeia

For a change of pace now, get back on Hwy. 83 and retrace your way to Heeia, on Kaneohe Bay. This is a good place to stop, stretch your legs, and switch to another mode of transportation. Glass-bottom boats at **Heeia Kea Pier** take you on a narrated excursion at a charge of $7.50 for adults, $3.50 for children under 12. Cruises depart every hour daily. Make advance reservations by calling 239-9955. Also, check to see if the water is clear that day; if not, there's not much point in going out. The **Deli Snack and Gift Shop,** right on the pier, offers local-style plate lunches (around $3), as well as the usual snacks.

THE ROAD TO LAIE: Outside of Heeia, it's one awesome view after another as you weave along the coast, past acres of tropical flowers and trees whose branches frequently arch across the whole width of the road. You can't miss spotting **Pineapple Hut** on the right, which has a good selection of carved wood, shells, macramé planters, and the like, at reasonable prices. As you drive along, keep your eyes peeled for stands selling "Ice Cold Coconuts"; there's usually one out here, another on the road at Waimanalo.

You're now coming to the end of Kaneohe Bay, and the next HVB marker you'll see will point to an island that looks like its name, **Mokoli'i** (little lizard); it's sometimes also called Chinaman's Hat. On the other side of the road, tangled over by weeds, are the ruins of a century-old sugar mill. Cane grown here was once shipped by boat to "distant" Honolulu.

This is the area, by the way, where you're likely to see people out dune-cycling on three- or four-wheeled vehicles, or doing some "land sailing." If you'd like to join them, **Kualoa Ranch** can fix you up with all the necessary equipment at rates of about $15 per hour. Phone first: 237-8202. They are located on Kamehameha Hwy., mauka from Chinaman's Hat.

In a short while you'll come to a rocky cliff that reminded the old Hawaiians of a crouching lion, hence its official name—**Crouching Lion.** The scenic **Crouching Lion Inn** is just in front. This area is fine for a picnic: **Kaaawa Beach Park** has good swimming, and so does **Swanzy Beach Park,** just before Punaluu and fully equipped with the amenities. The next beach, at **Kahana Bay,** is safe for swimming inshore, but there are no dressing facilities and the bottom is muddy.

As you approach Hauula, you'll see the HVB marker pointing to a side road leading to the 87-foot **Sacred Falls.** Even though the trail is lined with impressive trees and flowers, our considered advice is to pass this one up; in order to see the falls and the mountain pool below, you have to hike for about an hour on a rough, rocky path. Over the past few years, there have been a number of drownings and tragic accidents here; locals definitely consider this place bad news. Coming up now, the beach park at Hauula is well equipped with the usual bathing facilities, and the swimming is safe inshore. But keep going; you're about to reach the picturesque village of Laie, one of the high points of your Windward Oahu sojourn.

Laie: Polynesia in Miniature

Laie is Salt Lake City with palm trees. No slouches at missionary work, the Mormons arrived in Hawaii not long after the first Protestants; over 100 years ago they founded a large colony of Hawaiian and Samoan brethren of The Church of Jesus Christ of Latter-Day Saints, whose descendants still live here.

In 1919 the Mormons established a Hawaiian Temple, the first Mormon house of worship outside the mainland; in 1955 the Brigham Young University–Hawaii Campus, a fully accredited liberal arts institution; and in 1963, the **Polynesian Cultural Center,** a loving re-creation of Polynesia in miniature. On beautifully landscaped grounds, seven authentic Polynesian villages—Tahitian, Marquesan, Samoan, Maori, Tongan, Fijian, and of course, Hawaiian—have been built, peopled with islanders who demonstrate the ancient crafts of making tapa (barkcloth), pounding taro roots into poi (a Hawaiian food staple), weaving baskets of lauhala, woodcarving, and the like. All this is part of the church's effort to revitalize the ancient Polynesian cultures by giving them a dramatic showcase and, at the same time, to provide job opportunities for Polynesian young people who need to work their way through school.

A visit here is an absorbing excursion into long-ago, far-away culture. You'll find such curiosities as a splendidly carved Maori war canoe, all 50 feet of it carved from a single log (it took two years to make—in ancient times, it would have taken 20); a native queen's house; Tongan grass huts lined with tapa; and Samoan sleeping quarters for a high chief. Most striking of all, perhaps, is the Maoris' sacred house of learning, with its carved and woven inside panels. The veddy British accent of the Maori guides, dressed in island costumes, may come as a bit of a shock until you remember that they are New Zealanders, Commonwealth subjects. As you make your way around, either on foot or by tram or canoe, you'll find that they and the other guides who explain their traditions with such deep feeling are the most impressive aspects of the Cultural Center.

Various events are scheduled throughout the day, like the "Pageant of the Long Canoes": it takes place in the Hale Aloha amphitheater at 1, 2, 3, and 4 p.m. The stellar entertainment here is a spectacular production of Polynesian dancing and singing called *This Is Polynesia.* It's just a trifle showbiz (colored waters, tricky lighting), but the performers—people brought from Polynesia to man the villages, or students at B.Y.U. Hawaii—are quite good, and some of them, such as the Fijian men in their traditional war dances, do probably the best ethnic dancing in the islands.

To see everything at the Polynesian Cultural Center, including *This is Polynesia,* you will have to purchase the "Voyager Passport" $30 for adults, $15 for juniors (12 to 15), $10 for children 5 to 11 (free under 5), with rates of $35, $18, and $11 June through August. Although the price makes it a splurge for us, considering that it encompasses your daytime activity plus dinner and a show, the value is good. For just about everything except the buffet dinner and show, take the "Explorer Passport" at $20, $10 and $6. *Note:* it is suggested that visitors arrive no later than 2 p.m. to enjoy the full experience. If you're staying for the evening, you may want to plan this as a special excursion, rather than as part of an all-day, around-the-island trip.

Visitors can pick up tickets at the center's ticket office on the ground floor of the Royal Hawaiian Shopping Center, Building C. While you're there, check the schedule; there are often mini-performances on Thursday and Saturday morning, 9:30 to 11:30 a.m. You can also book round-trip motorcoach transportation at about $7 per adult.

The Polynesian Cultural Center is open Monday through Saturday, closed Sunday, Thanksgiving, Christmas, and New Year's Day. For further information, call the box office at 293-3333 or toll free 800/367-7060, or the Waikiki ticket office at 923-1861. If you are driving directly to Laie from Honolulu, take the Pali Hwy. and turn north on Kamehameha Hwy.

While you're here, you'll also want to see the **Hawaiian Temple;** it stands back from the road on high ground, above a pond, an illuminated fountain, and at the head of a long avenue of royal palms. Best approach for a Taj Mahal-like vista is to leave the highway at Halelaa Boulevard. A complimentary Historical Laie Tour is available. You'll tour the Mormon Temple, Brigham Young University Hawaii, and the Laie community on a re-created 1903 Hawaiian streetcar. By the way, not all the students here are Mormons; the school is open to others, provided they take the pledge not to smoke or drink, and "to live good Christian lives."

Laie Beach used to be the scene of the Mormon hukilaus, once considered one of the island's top visitor attractions. The ocean at **Laie-Maloo** is safe for inshore swimming, although the beach is not a public park and has no dressing facilities.

You won't want to leave Laie without a drive out to **Laie Point** (the turn-off is just past the entrance to the Cultural Center), where you get a dramatic view of the rugged coastline. Walk out over the porous lava rock as far as you can safely go for the best view of all. Some old Hawaii hands swear it's the best view in all the islands. Sunset devotees shouldn't miss this one.

THE HALFWAY POINT—KUILIMA, SUNSET BEACH, AND HALEIWA:
Now the road runs inland through sugar country, starting with the village of Kahuku, the halfway point of your trip. (In summer, stop off at one of the roadside stands for the home-grown watermelon—the best on the island.) It reaches the shore again at Kuilima, where you might want to have a look at the sumptuous Turtle Bay Hilton and Country Club (formerly the Hyatt Kuilima Resort), one of the most beautiful in the islands. The scenery is spectacular here, especially the view at the swimming pool, perched atop a cliff overlooking the ocean on two sides as the waves pound in. (If it's time for lunch, you might want to try the 11 a.m. to 2:30 p.m. "mini-deli" buffet for about $7.50 in the scenic Bay View Lounge. There is a charge for parking here, but the fee can be validated at lunch.)

Back to the car again for a drive along **Sunset Beach,** with its huge breakers crashing in at your right. It's safe for summer swimming, but in winter it's a wild, windy stretch, exciting to walk along; better still, you may be lucky enough to see some spectacular surfing here, for this is Oahu's North Shore, currently *the* place for the surfing set. Traffic may be jammed for miles, from here to Haleiwa, if there's an important surfing contest going on. If you're wondering whether you should try it yourself, be advised that the surfing areas range from pretty dangerous, to very dangerous, to one that's called "Banzai Pipeline" (remember the wartime suicide cry of the Japanese?). **Waimea Bay,** just below Sunset, has the distinction of having Hawaii's biggest waves, sometimes crashing in as high as 30 feet. However, in the summer months Waimea Bay is tranquil, the waves are gentle, and swimming here is close to perfection.

While the surfers are tempting fate, you can survey a more primitive form of human sacrifice (and this time we're serious) by turning left on Pupukea Road (it's one of the few paved roads here, and you should note that it's opposite a fire station and next to a market). As soon as the road begins its ascent up the hill, take your first right and continue on up to **Puu O Mahuka Heaiu.** Here, on a bluff overlooking Waimea Bay (another view-collector's spot), are the ruins of a temple where human sacrifice was practiced. When Captain Vancouver put in at Waimea Bay in 1792, three of his men were captured and offered to the blood-thirsty gods. Today all is tranquil here, and the faithful still come, offering bun-dles of ti leaves in homage.

For a refreshing change of pace, head back to nature now at **Waimea Falls Park,** opposite Waimea Bay Beach Park, 1,800 beautiful acres where you'll find an impressive collection of tropical and subtropical plants in the Waimea Arbo-retum, a bird sanctuary for many species including the rare Nene goose and Koloa duck, and hiking trails as well. It's fun to take the minibus up to the beau-tiful 45-foot waterfall (a three-quarter-mile walk), and then walk down; some of the lovely gardens cannot be seen well from the road. Of special interest is the site for ancient Hawaiian games (located near the upper meadow), where tour guides demonstrate and teach such games as Hawaiian checkers and spear throwing. Ancient hula and cliff-diving shows take place several times a day. **Charlie's Country Store,** with books on Hawaiiana, plus jams, jellies, and jew-elry, is fun to browse. There are a number of natural picnic spots in the park; you can get sandwiches, snacks, and hot lunches from the **Country Kitchen** if you haven't brought your own. Guided walking tours go through the gardens and Hawaiian historical sites. The **Proud Peacock Restaurant** (medium to high prices and well recommended) has a soup, salad, and sandwich bar from 11 a.m. to 3 p.m. and dinner nightly. The park is open daily from 10 a.m. to 5:30 p.m. Admission is $7.50 for adults, $5.25 for juniors (7 to 12), $1.75 for children (4 to 6); 3 and under, free. Park phone: 638-8511.

Incidentally, Waimea Falls Park is a very popular location for **weddings.** Contact Tinker Blomfield, Waimea Falls Park, 59-864 Kamehameha Hwy., Ha-leiwa, HI 96712 (tel. 638-8511) for information. Ms. Blomfield advises that cus-tom wedding packages are available, with prices ranging from "$50 to $550 or thereabouts."

Pupukea Beach Park in this area has good swimming and outstanding snor-keling in the summer months. A few miles farther along, at **Haleiwa Beach Park** on Waialua Bay, you'll find the last swimming spot before you strike into the heart of Oahu. It's a fine family-type place—lawns, play areas, pergolas, dress-ing rooms, showers, fishing, camping, and picnicking area.

The Youth Scene at Sunset Beach and Haleiwa

If you're seriously interested in—or part of—the youth culture, you'll be welcome among the inhabitants of Sunset Beach and Haleiwa, an area that at-tracts a number of young people who want to live close to nature. They're not putting on a show for sightseers or tourists, just quietly doing their thing—and an attractive thing it is. Haleiwa is like a very tiny version of Cape Cod's Prov-incetown, with its distinctively artsy atmosphere, small gift shops, and bou-tiques. Hand-painted dresses and original designs, most of them made in the area, are offered by Inga Jausel at **Oogenesis Originals** at 66-249 Kam Hwy. Japanese-inspired designs grace tops, pants ensembles, and simple dresses that can be worn belted or unbelted. Prices are reasonable. Inga's other store, **Rix,** 66-145 Kam Hwy., offers contemporary designs in fashion. . . . **Deeni's Bou-tique** at 66-079 Kam Hwy. in Haleiwa specializes in swimwear, T-shirts, and sportswear. . . . at 66-119 Kam Hwy. is **Iwa Gallery,** which shows the work of North Shore artists, hand-carved candles by owner Scott Bechtol, and, in a little annex around the corner, Tahitian pareaus, hand-dipped and dyed in Tahiti, no two alike; they go for $23.95.

Have a look, too, at the **Fettig Art Gallery,** 66-051 Kam Hwy., an impor-

tant outlet for the local painters and potters. You might come up with a miniature for as little as $5; standard-size works run from $50 to $125. There are also
handcrafted pottery, locally made candles, and sculpture.

Hungry? You've come to the right town. Some of our favorite North Shore
restaurants are here (see Chapter III), like **Kua'Aina** for super sandwiches,
Steamer's for island fish and seafood in a glamorous setting, and **Jameson's-by-
the-Sea** (a sister restaurant to the Jameson's Irish Coffee Houses in Waikiki and
downtown Honolulu), open to beautiful views and breezes as it overlooks Haleiwa Harbor. Wherever you eat, skip dessert and drive over to **Matsumoto's
Grocery** at 66-087 Kam Hwy. in Haleiwa (across from the intersection of Emerson Street) for the ultimate shave ice experience. Local people drive out from all
over the island to queue up here, while no fewer than four girls form an "assembly line" to shave and season the ice. We won't swear that you'll really love
shave ice with ice cream and azuki beans on the bottom ($1), but can you say
you really know Hawaii unless you've tried it? Matsumoto's also sells nifty T-
shirts, caps, and sweatshirts with their logo in pretty colors—great souvenirs.

Since Sunset Beach is a spiritually attuned community, it abounds in centers for yoga, Zen, and other such disciplines; the people at any of the shops can
give you information on any groups that may interest you. This area is a world
apart from the urban crush of Honolulu, the tourist scene at Waikiki, and the rat
race everywhere. Try to schedule your visit in time for the fantastic sunset,
which turns the horizon to a brilliant blazing red.

THE RETURN TRIP: At the intersection of Rte. 82 (Kamehameha Hwy.), turn
left and follow it as it climbs to **Leilehua Plateau.** Here the tall sugarcane gives
way to seemingly endless miles of pineapple—dark-green and golden against
the red earth. It's the largest pineapple area in the world. Just as you're beginning to feel like the Ancient Mariner (you can't pick any), you'll find a pineapple
stand on the left side of the road as you come out of the pineapple area. Buy a
whole "pine" or get a half-dozen delicious spears, fresher than any you've ever
tasted. The custom here is to sprinkle a little unrefined Hawaiian salt on the
pineapple; it helps cut the acidity. Unfortunately, Dole does not conduct tours
through the fields, but many operations are visible from the highway. In case
you're curious, the variety of pineapple grown here is called Sweet Cayenne.

In the midst of these Wahiawa pineapple fields, one mile past the pineapple
hut, is the Del Monte Corporation's **Pineapple Variety Garden,** right at the junction of Hwys. 82 and 809. It's small, but well worth a brief stop to see a huge
variety of species and pineapple plants from all over the world—Asia, Africa,
South America, and various small islands. Just ignore the tremendous spiders
that build their webs among the plants; they're nonaggressive and totally
harmless—to people and/or pineapples.

Next stop is for the history-anthropology buffs: a Stone Age spot where the
royal chieftesses of Hawaii gave birth. Just before **Wahiawa,** watch on the right
for a dirt road leading into a clump of eucalyptus trees in a pineapple field on the
Kaukonahau Gulch—the **Place of the Sacred Birthstone.** The large flat stone
protruding several feet above the ground was a primitive delivery table; legend
had it that a son delivered on this stone would be born with honor.

Now take Hwy. 99 into Wahiawa, a dreary-looking town that serves as a
center for personnel stationed at **Schofield Barracks** (where James Jones met his
muse) and **Wheeler's Field.** It's also a huge pineapple depot. The bright spot
here is **Kemoo Farm,** a restaurant overlooking Lake Wilson that's been a big
favorite with the kamaainas since 1927. Besides the very good food (see a complete review in Chapter III), Kemoo Farm sells some attractive gift items in its
"country store" lobby. Try to catch one of their lunch shows on Wednesday and

Sunday with outstanding island entertainers. In this area you may also want to visit the **Schofield Museum,** with its military and historical documents (weekdays only), and the **Wahiawa Botanical Garden,** at 1396 California Ave. (east of the highway), 1,000 feet high, where you can wander through four lovely acres of rare trees, ferns and shrubs, many orchid plants, and a Hawaiian garden. Don't forget your camera. Admission is free.

You'll pass through more sugar fields as you drive along the now four-lane Kamehameha Hwy. (Hwy. 99) or the new Interstate Highway H-2. From here on, it's fast sailing home. At the intersection with Rte. 90, take that road to the left; it will take you past Pearl Harbor (you might visit the U.S.S. *Arizona* Memorial if you have the time; see Chapter VII for details) and the Honolulu Airport. At Middle Street, turn right onto Rte. 92 (Nimitz Hwy.), which will take you past the harbor; take Ala Moana and Kalakaua into Waikiki.

But before you settle into your hotel, consider the following two other points of interest, which you could take in at the start or at the end of your trip—or save them for another day.

2. The Pali and Makiki Heights

The only major attraction you haven't seen on this trip is the view from the **Nuuanu Pali,** a glorious panorama of Windward Oahu from the top of a jagged cliff. It's a historic spot too, because it was here that Kamehameha the Great vanquished the Oahuans in a fierce battle in 1795. Thousands of the defeated fell to their deaths on the rocks below. (You could start the round-the-island trip via the Pali, but you'd miss the scenery in the Koko Head area, which we find more appealing.) You can see the Pali by turning left off Nimitz Hwy. in downtown Honolulu onto Nuuanu Avenue (or Bishop Street, which runs into Pali Hwy.), which you follow until it hits Pali Hwy., and on to the Pali.

Just before you reach the Pali, however, you might want to stop at one of the island's newer points of interest. If you drive about a mile up the Pali and turn left at Jack Lane, you come upon the beautiful **Tendai Mission of Hawaii** and its enormously impressive 25-foot statue of Senju Kannon, the Thousand-Armed Goddess of Mercy. The Tendai sect of Mahayana Buddhism ended 1,200 years of confining its worship halls to Japan when it opened the Hawaii mission in November 1973. You're welcome to inspect the grounds and building any day during regular activity hours. (There are no specific times of opening or closing.) Occasionally, you'll see local groups using the facilities for flower-arranging, tea ceremonies, and handcraft exhibits.

Another spectacular view that we think you shouldn't miss is the one from **Makiki Heights.** In a way, we like it better than the Pali, since this is a top-of-the-world view, completely unobstructed. Here's how to get there: from Waikiki, take Kalakaua Avenue until it ends at South Beretania Street; go past Makiki to Keeaumoku Street, turn right, go across Hwy. 1 and turn right on Wilder. Go one block, then make a left on Makiki, which runs into Round Top Drive, then Tantalus Drive, and up, up, up. The road, which is excellent all the way, goes through the Round Top Forest Reserve. Stop at **Puu Ualakka State Park** and have a look at the glorious view from Round Top. Back in the car, continue in the same direction you were going; you'll end up just about where you started, having come full circle.

3. Tips for Tourists

SWIMMING: Don't attempt to swim at any beach that is not also a public park; dressing-room facilities will give you a clue. Although dangerous areas are usually posted, the signs may be missing, or you may not see them. The following beaches on this drive are *unsafe* because of undertow or heavy surf: Koko Head Beach, Waimea Beach and Sunset Beach on the North Shore (in winter), and Light House Beach at Makapuu. Never swim where there is a steep beach, a rocky shoreline, or large waves. In case of trouble, call the police at 911 or dial zero.

CAMPING: If you want to join the island families camping on some of the beaches (besides the beauty, a really cheap way to cut overnight costs), obtain a permit from the Department of Parks and Recreation on the first floor of the Honolulu Municipal Building, 650 S. King St. Call 523-4525 for details, plus a list of the parks that have facilities: water, toilets, sometimes sinks and barbecue stoves. Note that all city beach park campgrounds are closed to camping every Wednesday and Thursday. There is no charge for camping permits.

Should you decide to camp in style, you may want to rent a camper (a truck with a little house on top) or a trailer (to which you attach a car). Both campers and trailers come equipped with everything from pots and pans to blankets, have their own toilets, stoves, and running water, and offer a family of four or more a terrific way to save money. For details on where and how to rent, see Chapter IV. See the Readers' Suggestions, ahead, for a warning from a local resident.

READERS' SUGGESTIONS IN WINDWARD OAHU: "Mention should be made about the hazards of camping in certain areas overnight. People come here expecting 'Paradise' and find that violence is the same all over. Many bad incidents have recently occurred to overnight tourist campers in the **Waianae** and **Waimanalo** areas. These two areas have many people of low economic situation who know tourists have money and are easy marks. Local folks don't even camp alone on the beaches in these two areas. A warning should be given" (Alton Rogers, Honolulu, Hi.). *[Authors' Note:* Local friends report the Waianae area is still dangerous for tourists, but that Waimanalo is safe during the daytime.]

"Rather than take one of the big tours, where there are so many people and the whole experience is so impersonal, I strongly recommend that people take the small 8- to 11-person tours. I went with **E Noa Tours** (tel. 941-6608) on an around-the-island tour and it was the best day I spent in Hawaii. Since the cost is $40 including lunch and snorkeling lessons, it's not cheaper than renting a car, but I would not have learned as much as I did about the Hawaiians, their land, culture, and values. Not only that, but when you get on the bus, the driver asks if there are any places in particular you would like to see, so you don't miss a thing. There were eight of us on our tour, and in that full day of traveling I made some beautiful friends. The driver knew so much about everything—there wasn't much he couldn't answer—and he had us constantly rolling with laughter. The tour is complete with snorkeling at Hanauma Bay and a multitude of sights" (Kristin Fry, Calgary, Alberta, Canada).

"Pass up the hike to **Sacred Falls,** Hauula, unless you're a vigorous and determined hiker. Even experienced hikers cannot reach Sacred Falls in an hour's hike. The trail has been neglected and jungle has leaned over the path; one must duck under and climb over trees. The path is indeed rough, rocky, and usually muddy. Plan an hour and a half up, an hour back. . . . At Punaluu there's **Kahana State Park.** An excellent trail starts up the mountain toward the Koolau range. It quickly becomes pitted with mudholes, but is still a good foot trail and gives a good opportunity to see Hawaiian mountain jungle. There are a few papaya and banana plantings, and some oldtime-style Hawaiian dwellings. An hour's hike brings one to a freshwater swimming hole; it is possible to cross a dam here for an extended hike. Allow half an hour to return to Kam Hwy. A permit to hike is required, but may be obtained, free, at Kahana Park Headquarters" (David Moore, Phoenix, Ariz.). . . . "On our first full day in Hawaii, six of our party rented a full-size, air-conditioned Lincoln and used your book as a guide. The highlight of the day was our lunch stop in a little town named **Wahiawa,** and the name of the restaurant was **Kemoo Farm.** It was a great, relaxing spot, overlooking a small lake, with a pineapple field beyond. The food was superb. If you like fresh pineapple, what a spot! Pineapple on the salad bar and large wedges of pineapple in the iced tea. We just had to let you know how much we enjoyed Kemoo Farm" (Richard and Angie Ager, Hyattsville, Md.).

"At **Sunset Beach,** beside the waves, which *did* reach 30 feet, we joined in with beachcombers who were sifting puka shells in the sand. We stayed here for about half an hour sifting the sand through our fingers and found several dozen beautiful shells" (Dave Kaiser, Fort Lauderdale, Fla.). [*Authors' Note:* A word of caution: Shell-hunters should never turn their back to the ocean when the surf is high; more than one person has been swept out to sea by a high wave.]

"Regarding your advice about **Makaha Beach,** some islanders told us not to miss that end of the island, so we decided to make the trip in spite of your advice that the locals might not be friendly to tourists. Here's why I liked Makaha: First, it was the only place where we discovered great tidepools. They were teeming with aquatic life of every possible variety (visit when the tide is out). Second, the snorkeling was wonderful. Be sure to wear sneakers when walking over the tidepools or snorkeling because there are thousands of spiny urchins on the sea floor. And third, the Hawaiians we met on the beach were as friendly as anyone we met in Hawaii. One fine lady even showed us how to find the best shells, and invited us to her home to take boxes of them home with us! I would recommend placing your beach mat and belongings close to where others are; we felt quite safe there. It was also April, so the ocean was quiet" (Eric Schuman, Topeka, Kans.).

"Your readers should know about the park at **Kualoa,** near Chinaman's Hat. It is marked on the makai side of the road just past Kualoa Ranch. The road is pretty poor (purposely so). Take the first turn right after you pass the gates. Soon you will reach one of the most respected places: this is where the Hokule'a was launched, just because of this. Be sure to take a look" (Mrs. Clarence Gaber, Kailua, Hi.). [*Authors' Note:* Swimming is poor here, but it's a beautiful park, a place where island families like to camp.] . . . "Please caution people not to leave any valuables in their car, even if it's locked. There must be many other seasoned travelers accustomed to traveling the continental United States and stopping at overlooks with all their luggage, cameras, etc., in the cars and having no one disturb their property. We started our circle tour and got to the lookout just beyond Hanauma Bay and went over the fence to take pictures. We were gone five minutes at the most. When we returned, the car's lock mechanism had been removed and all camera equipment, tape recorder, binoculars, and purse were gone. At Koko Marina, the police told us there are people who make their living doing this, so they are very quick" (Linda Loreny, Toledo, Ohio).

Chapter IX

THE ABC'S OF HONOLULU

HERE'S A CAPSULE LIST of names and numbers to help you find your way around town. Some is a recap of what you'll find explained in more depth in other chapters, and some of it is new.

AAA HAWAII: The local office of the American Automobile Association is at 590 Queen St. (tel. 528-2600; road service, 537-5544).

AIRPORT: Honolulu International Airport, about five miles from Waikiki, is easily reached by bus no. 8 ("Airport") or bus no. 20 from Waikiki and Ala Moana Center, without luggage. With luggage, try Airport Motor Coach (tel. 926-4747). For visitor information at the airport, call 836-6413.

ANIMAL HOSPITAL: Twenty-four-hour emergency care for pets is provided at **Care Animal Hospital,** 1135 Kapahulu Ave. (tel. 737-7910).

AREA CODE: All telephone numbers in the State of Hawaii have one telephone area code: 808.

BABYSITTERS: Check first at your hotel desk. You can also try **Patch**—People Attentive to Children (tel. 523-6436), and **Aloha Babysitting Service** (tel. 732-2029).

BANKING HOURS: Normal hours are 8:30 a.m. to 3 or 3:30 p.m., until 6 p.m. on Friday.

BUS INFORMATION: Call **MTL,** which operates TheBUS, at 531-1611, or visit their information booth on the street level of Ala Moana Center, open daily from 9 a.m. to 5:30 p.m., to 4:15 p.m. on Sunday.

BUSINESS HOURS: Most office workers in Hawaii are at their desks by 8 a.m., sometimes even earlier, and it's *pau hana* (finish work) at 4 or 5 p.m., the better to get in an afternoon swim or round of golf. Hawaii may be the only place where even executives can be reached by 8:30 a.m.!

CAMPING PERMITS: For information about camping permits for city parks, phone 523-4525; for state parks, phone 548-7455.

CAR RENTALS: Major car-rental companies, which rent automobiles on all four major islands, include **Alamo Rent-A-Car,** 3055 N. Nimitz Hwy. (tel. 833-4585 or 924-4444, or toll free 800/327-9633); **Budget Rent-A-Car,** 2379 Kuhio Ave. (tel. 922-3600, or toll free 800/527-0700); **Tropical Rent-A-Car Systems,** 550 Paiea St. (tel. 836-1041, or toll free 800/367-5140); **Avis Rent-A-Car,** Honolulu International Airport (tel. 834-5836, or toll free 800/831-8000); **Hertz Rent-A-Car,** 233 Keawe St., Room 625 (tel. 836-2511). See Chapter IV for details.

CLIMATE: Among the best in the world. Hawaii's climate is subtropical, which means that temperatures average about 75° Fahrenheit, rarely going more than six or seven degrees above or below that point. In summer months, the temperature is usually in the 80s; winter months, November through March, can bring slightly lower temperatures and occasional rain and storms.

CONSUMER PROTECTION: To reach the Office of Consumer Protection, phone 548-2540.

DENTISTS: **Royal Hawaiian Dental Service,** 1450 Ala Moana Blvd. (in Sears Roebuck at Ala Moana Center) has a dentist on call from 9 a.m. to 9 p.m. Monday through Friday, until 5 p.m. Saturday.

DOCTORS: House calls are available from **DOC** (Doctors on Call), 24 hours a day, seven days a week (tel. 926-4777), charging $64. For health care information and physician referral service, call **Ask-A-Nurse,** a free, 24-hour service of Queen's and Castle Medical Center. Dial 533-NURS for assistance.

DRINKING AGE: Sorry, kids, the legal drinking age in Hawaii is now 21.

DRY CLEANERS: Quick service is available from **Al Phillips the Cleaner** in the Waikiki Market Place, 2310 Kuhio Ave. (tel. 923-1971).

EMERGENCY: Dial 911 for fire, ambulance, or police; if you cannot reach 911, dial 0 and the operator will assist you.

HANDICAPPED SERVICES: Handi-cabs provides private transportation and tours (tel. 524-3866); **Handi-Van** provides public transportation (tel. 955-1717). For free brochures describing accessibility features of Hawaii's major hotels, shopping malls, beach parks, and sightseeing and visitor attractions, on all islands, write to **Commission on the Handicapped,** Old Federal Building, 335 Merchant St., Rm. 353, Honolulu, HI 96813 (tel. 548-7606). Enclose a legal-size, self-addressed, stamped envelope for each brochure desired.

HAWAII VISITORS BUREAU: The **HVB** is located at 2270 Kalakaua Ave., eighth floor (tel. 923-1811). There is also a booth at Ala Moana Center.

HOLIDAYS: Just about all businesses and banks will be closed on the major holidays: Christmas, New Year's, Easter Sunday, Thanksgiving Day. In addition to the legal holidays observed throughout the United States—Memorial Day, July 4th, Labor Day, Columbus Day, Election Day, and Veterans Day—there are specific Hawaiian holidays on which many business establishments close: Prince Kuhio Day (March 26), Kamehameha Day (June 11), and Admission Day (the third Friday in August).

HOSPITAL EMERGENCY ROOM: **Queen's and Castle Medical Center,** 1301 Punchbowl, has 24-hour emergency-room service and offers outstanding trauma care (tel. 547-4311).

LAUNDROMATS: Should your hotel not provide washers and dryers (most do), try **Waikiki Laundromats,** with four central locations. They also provide irons, ironing boards, and hair dryers. Addresses are 2335 Kalakaua Ave., across from the International Market Place; Outrigger West Hotel, 2330 Kuhio Ave.; Outrigger East Hotel, 150 Kaiulani Ave.; and Edgewater Hotel, 2168 Kalia Rd. These are open daily from 7 a.m. to 10 p.m. The location at the Coral Seas Hotel, 250 Lewers St. (tel. 923-2057), is open around the clock.

PHARMACIES: In Waikiki, try the **Outrigger Pharmacy** at the Outrigger Hotel, 2335 Kalakaua Ave. (tel. 923-2529), or the **Kuhio Pharmacy,** Outrigger West Hotel, 2330 Kuhio Ave. (tel. 923-4466); at Ala Moana Shopping Center, **Long's Drug Store,** 1450 Ala Moana (tel. 949-4010). **The Pillbox Pharmacy,** 1133 Eleventh Ave. (tel. 737-1777), is open seven days a week until 11 p.m. and provides 24-hour emergency service (for prescriptions only).

POISON CENTER: 941-4411.

POST OFFICE: The main post office in Honolulu is at 3600 Aolele St. (tel. 423-3930), open 8 a.m. to 4:30 p.m. Monday to Friday, until noon on Saturday. In Waikiki it's at 330 Saratoga Rd., next to Fort DeRussy (tel. 941-1062).

PUBLIC PHONES: Cost of a local call is 25¢ from any one part of an island to another. Inter-island calls are billed as long distance.

SHOPPING MALLS: Most shopping malls are open Monday to Friday from 9 or 10 a.m. to 9 p.m., on Saturday until 5 p.m., and for a shorter period on Sunday, usually until 4 p.m. Individual establishments at these malls will vary their hours, some closing earlier than others.

SUNDRIES: ABC Discount Stores offer a little bit of everything one might need under one roof, from suntan lotion to sandwiches, from groceries to gifts, from postcards to photo processing and film, and much more, all at bargain prices. There are at least two dozen ABCs in town, and most of them are open from 7:30 a.m. to midnight. Walk a block or two from where you are and you'll find one. The **7-11 Food Stores** now have 34 shops on Oahu; two convenient locations are at 1901 Kalakaua Ave. and 707 Kapahulu Ave. They carry everything from grocery and toiletry items to pantyhose, hot food, soft drinks, etc. Open 24 hours.

SURF REPORT: 836-1952.

TIME ZONES: From the East Coast of the United States to Hawaii, one crosses five time zones. That means that when it's noon Hawaiian Standard Time, it's 5 p.m. Eastern Standard Time, 4 p.m. Central, 3 p.m. Mountain, and 2 p.m. Pacific. Hawaii does not convert to Daylight Saving Time as the rest of the nation does, so from May through October, noon in Hawaii would mean 6 p.m. Eastern, 5 p.m. Central, 4 p.m. Mountain, and 3 p.m. Pacific Time.

VISITOR INFORMATION: Hawaii Visitors Bureau, 2270 Kalakaua Ave., eighth floor (tel. 923-1811); they also have a booth at Ala Moana Center and the Royal Hawaiian Shopping Center.

WEATHER REPORT: In the Honolulu area, call 836-0234; for the rest of Oahu, phone 836-0121; for the Hawaiian waters, dial 836-3921.

Chapter X

TO THE NEIGHBOR ISLANDS

Polynesia with Plumbing

TOO MANY TOURISTS start and end their island holidays in Honolulu —and think they've seen Hawaii. Yes—and no. They've seen the one major city and the major resort area, but far more awaits: a Hawaii at once more gentle and more savage, where the old gods still have powers. To see the desolate moonscapes of the volcanoes and Hawaiian cowboys riding the range, to see beaches so remote and pristine as to make Waikiki seem like Times Square, and to visit South Seas villages just coming into the modern age, you'll have to venture to the three other important Hawaiian islands: the Garden Island of **Kauai,** the Big Island of **Hawaii,** and the Valley Isle of **Maui.** You may also want to visit **Molokai,** which remains much as it was 50 years ago; it is also the home of Kalaupapa, the settlement for the treatment of Hansen's disease—leprosy. The island of **Lanai** is almost wholly given over to growing pineapples and, as yet, does not have much to interest the average tourist; but there is talk of resort development here, and you may want to splurge on one of the sailing-ship cruises out of Lahaina, Maui, that spend half a day or so there for a figure of about $90. Going to the neighbor islands requires a little effort for the budget traveler, but we strongly urge you to try.

THE MONEY FACTOR: Most people do it the easy way, by simply taking one of the various package tours around the islands. A flat fee, paid in advance, covers your plane fare, hotels, meals, sightseeing. There is, of course, nothing wrong with this method except that it's expensive, even when you go as an economy tourist. We think you can do much better on your own. Besides, on a tour you've got to go where you're taken—in a group—thus missing all the fun of discovering the off-the-beaten-pathways that appeal to *you!*

Another alternative is to "flightsee" the islands from the air, landing briefly for meals and hurried sightseeing, and returning the same night; theoretically, you've "seen" five islands, but that's just a once-over lightly, about as satisfying as those European jaunts that take you to seven countries in six days. And the one day costs about $175 to boot!

The best way to see the neighbor islands is on your own; and doing that will cost you just a little more than you've been spending in Honolulu. You should be able to stay within a reasonable budget here. You can almost always find a good hotel room averaging about $50 (you should, of course, be traveling with a companion); there are plenty of restaurants where you can get $7 to $10 meals; and the supply of kitchenette condo apartments (where you save money by doing your own cooking) is enormous.

A money-saving plan is to check the special car-hotel deals that the major airlines—Aloha, Hawaiian, and Mid-Pacific—often make in conjunction with the leading car-rental companies and some of the island hotel chains. If the airlines are sold out on any of these special programs, try a local travel agency; they'll often be able to help you.

You can also save money on hotels and condos, as we've mentioned in our chapter on Honolulu hotels, by joining **Club Costa.** Dick Bodner, a veteran airline pilot, set up the new enterprise a few years ago, and is able to offer some nice discounts—ranging anywhere from 10% and 15% to as much as 40% and 50%—on excellent properties on the four major islands. Many of their selections are mentioned in these pages. A family membership of $69 a year also commands a 5% discount on airline flights, and a subscription to the club's quarterly publication, *Club Costa* magazine ($20 more overseas). Write Club Costa, 9200 Ward Pkwy., Suite 535, Kansas City, MO 64114; or phone 816/361-8404.

Your major expense on the outer islands will be transportation. Only one city on one island—Hilo, on the island of Hawaii—has anything resembling a public transportation system, and even that is not very extensive. There is also bus service in Lihue, Kauai, and in the Lahaina-Kaanapali and Kihei areas of Maui, but none of the buses run for any great distances. So unless you want to stay put, you have only two choices: taking expensive sightseeing tours or renting your own car. The latter is not cheap either, especially on days when you must pile on a lot of mileage, driving from one end of an island to another. If you're a couple or a family, of course, your car costs per person will be fairly low. In any case, you won't be sorry you made the trip.

WHICH TO CHOOSE: Each of the three major neighbor islands is fascinating and important to visit, and we strongly recommend that you make the circuit tour. (We suggest Molokai as an added attraction, after you've seen the others.) If you decide to go to only one island, read carefully the chapters ahead on the sights of Maui, Hawaii, and Kauai before you make your decision. Each has its special fascinations. **Maui** has become the most popular of the neighbor islands, especially appealing to an affluent condo crowd; it has some of the best golf courses in the state of Hawaii. Its great natural wonder, and its chief claim to fame, is Haleakala, the largest dormant volcano in the world, with a moon-like crater that you can explore on foot or horseback. The popular, picturesque old whaling town of Lahaina, remote and lovely Hana, and a succession of golden beaches are strong lures. The Big Island of **Hawaii** is the most varied, geographically, of the islands, almost like a small continent in miniature. It has few beaches (except in the Kona area), but it has the islands' second-biggest city (Hilo), the volcanic wonderlands of Mauna Kea and Mauna Loa (Volcanoes National Park is a must on any itinerary), and a cattle ranch big enough to belong to Texas. **Kauai,** our personal favorite, is perhaps not as well known as it should be; it is still refreshingly rural, small, beautiful, and easily assimilated. The damage done by Hurricane Iwa in 1982 is largely repaired. Waimea Canyon, a smaller version of the Grand Canyon, is its principal natural attraction. It also has a string of unforgettable beaches (you've seen them as Bali H'ai in the movie version of *South Pacific* and as Matlock Island in the television production of *The Thornbirds*). For advice on itineraries, see suggestions on inter-island travel in Chapter I.

CAMPING ON THE NEIGHBOR ISLANDS: Camping is popular on all the outer islands (as well as on Oahu, of course), and throughout these pages you will find various references to camping. For information on renting a camper (make arrangements in Honolulu or Hilo), see Chapter IV. You can, of course, bring your own equipment (see the Readers' Suggestions ahead for some interesting tips), but note that permits in advance are required. Check with the offices of the Hawaii Visitors Bureau (you can write them in advance; their addresses are given in the Introduction) to find out where to get permits for each island. And note references to various special camping grounds and cabins in the pages ahead. Note too, alas, that camping, especially tent camping, is no longer as safe as it used to be: readers report better luck renting campers.

AND KEEP IN MIND: Driving distances on the neighbor islands can be great, particularly on the Big Island of Hawaii, and you may have a lot of trouble finding gas stations, especially ones open on Sunday: keep the tank full. Be sure to check your U-Drive carefully before going on a long trip, and get a phone number where you can reach the agency at night in case of problems. Remember, too, to ask the agency for some good road maps indicating distances, and don't hesitate to ask questions and directions before you take off.

Also, even though it's easier than it used to be to find inexpensive places to eat as you scoot around the islands because of the rise of fast-food outlets, it can be a long drive between meals. It's always a good idea to throw a few sandwiches and some fruit in your beach bag, along with the suntan lotion and the road maps.

A NOTE ON PACKAGE TOURS: If you do decide on a package deal, remember that there are all kinds, sizes, and shapes. The most expensive ones park you at the luxury hotels and take you sightseeing in private limousines; the cheapest put you up in standard hotels, take you sightseeing in motor coaches, and may not provide meals. If they don't, you have a chance to shop around for inexpensive restaurants, which will charge much less than what the tour companies figure on as the cost of three meals. Do some careful studying and comparing before you sign up for one. Here, to aid in that task, are some of the major travel companies that offer tours to the outer islands:

Island Holidays Tours, 2255 Kuhio Ave., Honolulu, HI 96830-0519 (tel. 945-6000).

Hawaiian Holidays Tours, 2222 Kalakaua Ave., Honolulu, HI 96815 (tel. 926-9200).

Trade Wind Tours of Hawaii, 150 Kauilani Ave. (P.O. Box 2198), Honolulu, HI 96815 (tel. 923-2071).

Akamai Tours, 2270 Kalakaua Ave., Honolulu, HI 96815 (tel. 922-4685).

Pleasant Hawaii Holiday, 270 Lewers St., Honolulu, HI 96815 (tel. 923-7611).

American Express, with offices in all major mainland cities, can also arrange comprehensive inter-island tours for you. And every travel agency in Hawaii will deal, if you wish, with these companies.

READERS' SUGGESTIONS ON SEEING THE NEIGHBOR ISLANDS: "We were one week on each of the islands of Kauai and Maui, and four days on Oahu. We took our tent, air mattresses, and sleeping bags in two duffle bags; the sleeping bags were unnecessary, and next time we will take a washable blanket sewn into a bag, across the bottom and part way up

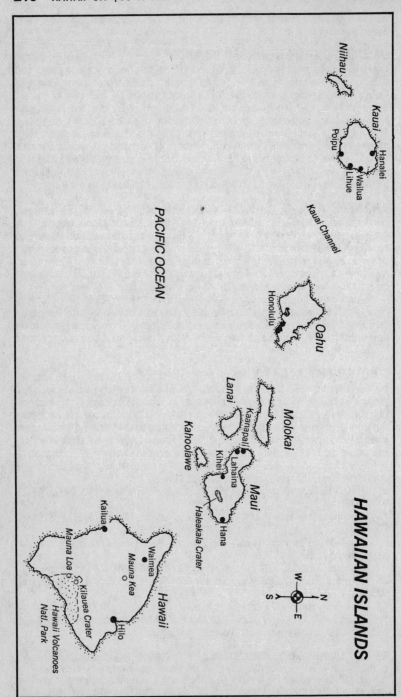

the open side. Our other necessities were carried in two small army knapsacks and my shoulder bag. . . . Since our accommodation costs—camping permits and $10 for a cabin at Hana—totaled less than $25 for the entire time on the islands, we could well afford to rent a car and travel as much as time would permit. So we saw a great deal more of each island than anyone on a tour. . . . **Camping** there is quite a different experience from what we are used to in Canada. On the islands, you have to use a small stove that uses fuel or charcoal, and since the fuel for the little stoves cannot be taken on the plane you have to refuel on each island; the driftwood and coconut husks you can gather are usually too damp to burn. Charcoal takes a long time to be ready. Personally, we were seldom at camp during the day other than for breakfast, so we just tucked any burnable garbage in a bag and picked up any odd sticks we came across in our travels. This was sufficient to boil a couple of cups of water for coffee or a cup of instant soup. Some camps have fireplaces, but if there was no cooking facility, we would just make a ring of three or four beer cans— no lack of them, either!—and put our small cook-whatever-you-are-having-in-the-skillet over the small fire built between the cans; it worked very well. . . . I am 55 years of age and my husband past 60, so we were usually the oldest campers around, and what a fine, respectful, yes, even admiring attitude did we receive from everyone we met. By the time we reached Oahu I was feeling so much a part of the scene that I found myself feeling sorry for those tourists on the buses!" (Mr. and Mrs. C. G. Huffman, Saskatoon, Saskatchewan, Canada). [*Authors' Note:* Bravo!]

"Seeing **Lanai** is like reliving the life of the ancient Hawaiians. Many ancient sites have remained unidentified to protect their preservation. It's best to rent a Jeep—about $60 a day but worth it—because most of the sites are along dirt roads (make reservations a few weeks in advance by phoning 565-6952). After you've seen Shipwreck Beach, the Kahe'a Heiau and Petroglyphs, and the Ho'Okio Battlegrounds (get James A. Bier's map in the bookstores), you're ready for swimming and snorkeling at Manele Bay, which is, in my opinion, the most beautiful beach in Hawaii. You are sure to enjoy Lanai. This is one place that will always keep its Hawaiian charm, as long as modern civilization doesn't overtake it. Even if the things that you see most are pineapples, you'll remember what the Hawaiian spirit is like for the rest of your life" (Liam Kernell, Honolulu, Hi.).

"If you wait until you get to Hawaii to book your trips to the other islands you can take advantage of the overnighter packages available, which include round-trip airfare for two and a room and rental car for two nights, for as little as $155, from **Roberts of Hawaii.** You have to be in the islands to make these reservations" (Kenneth Kendall, Omaha, Nebr.). [*Authors' Note:* There are many deals like this that can only be booked from Hawaii, since the companies are usually forbidden from advertising them outside the islands; they are mainly for kamaainas. It's wise to check these out when you are in the islands.]

Chapter XI

THE ISLAND OF KAUAI

1. Island Hotels
2. Island Restaurants
3. The Night Scene

ABOUT 15 JET MINUTES out of Honolulu and 110 miles to the west, your plane lands you in a tropical Switzerland. This is Kauai, the northernmost and oldest of the major Hawaiian islands, one of the lushest tropical spots on earth.

Kauai (pronounced correctly Kah-*wah*-ee, lazily Kah-*why*) is the oldest Hawaiian island in both geologic and historic time. The fantastic verdure of its cliffs and canyons was formed over millions of years of volcanic growth and collapse, by the endless workings of streams and ocean waves on its bleak cinders and craters (contrast these with the newly formed volcanoes on the island of Hawaii for an idea of the awesome powers of nature). In island lore, Kauai was the original home of Pele, the goddess of fire and volcanoes, before she moved southward. It was also the homeland of a race of pre-Polynesians, whose origins are anybody's guess—including anthropologists'. Some believe they were the survivors of the lost continent of Lemuria. In legend they're called Menehunes, South Sea leprechauns who stood about two feet tall, worked only in darkness, and accomplished formidable engineering feats in the space of a night's work.

The first Polynesian settlers chose Kauai too, landing at the mouth of the Wailua River somewhere between A.D. 500 and 900. They crossed the Pacific in outrigger canoes in a voyage of many months, probably from the Society Islands. Other Polynesians came later, but time stood still on Kauai and the rest of the Hawaiian Islands until 1778, when Captain Cook arrived at Waimea and the modern history of Hawaii began.

So much for history. Geographically, Kauai is a small island, about 32 miles in diameter. Its central mountain receives an average of 500 inches of rainfall a year, making it one of the wettest spots on earth, which accounts for the lushness of the surrounding landscape. You can see all the important things in Kauai in three days—but the longer you stay, the luckier you are.

Although Kauai bore the brunt of Hurricane Iwa in November of 1982, the storm and the damage it wrought are largely only memories now. Kauaians picked up quickly and made their beautiful island more beautiful than ever before.

ARRIVAL: Your plane will land in **Lihue** on an airstrip amid towering sugarcane. From here to Lihue, you'll either have to drive in your own rented car or take a cab.

U-DRIVES: For information on the major budget U-Drive companies—offering excellent flat-rate packages on all the islands—see Chapter IV. If, however, you haven't done so, or prefer a time-plus-mileage deal, simply walk up to any of the car-rental agencies just across the road from the airport. **United Car Rental,** Booth 4, Lihue Airport, offers flat rates on standard-shift compacts of $17.95 to $21.95 a day, $24.95 to $28.95 for automatics. Their phone is 245-8894. **National Car Rentals** (tel. 245-3502) can fix you up with a compact stick-shift car for $28, an automatic with air conditioning for $30.88.

Outside of the airport area, **Rent-A-Wreck of Kauai,** 3156 Hoolako St. (tel. 245-4755) doesn't exactly deal in wrecks; they do rent good used cars at rates starting at $16.95 for a stick-shift automatic. Don't let the name fool you. . . . **Kauai Rent-A-Jeep,** 3137A Kuhio Hwy. (tel. 245-9622) is the only place on Kauai to rent four-wheel drives. Jeeps are $29.95 to $59.95 a day. They also have older used cars (1970 to 1980 models) for $10 to $15 a day. They have an agency in Maui, too. . . . **Westside U-Drive** (tel. 332-8644) offers free delivery and pickup in the Poipu Beach area, as well as good rates; standard compacts at $22.95, automatics at $24.95; with air conditioning, $26.95.

Remember that in busy tourist seasons, prices may go up considerably, and advance reservations are always advisable.

1. Island Hotels

IN LIHUE AND ENVIRONS: The tiny town of Lihue and its immediate surroundings are the most centrally located places to stay in Kauai, since they're the starting point for your eastern and western tours of the island. Lihue is also the county seat and the center of Kauai's government, commerce, and culture. Here are a few acceptable budget accommodations.

The **Ahana Motel-Apartments,** at 3115 Akahi St. (tel. 245-2206), are a longtime favorite with budget travelers to Kauai. Located in the center of town and about a three-minute drive from the Westin Kauai and beautiful swimming at Kalapaki Beach, they offer clean and cozy rooms that are comfortably, if quite modestly, furnished. There's TV in every room, and a picnic and recreation area outdoors in the garden away from the street. The tab is low: singles and doubles, $16; singles and doubles with kitchenette, $22. A one-bedroom apartment is $22. Some of the apartments are connected units and can be used as two-bedroom suites. There's an extra charge of $4 for each additional person. Children are heartily welcomed. Two two-bedroom units, each with two bathrooms, rent for $38 for four, okay for two couples who want to share the cooking. Mr. and Mrs. Ah Sau Ahana's little place is very popular, despite its lack of fanciness, so write well in advance for reservations to P.O. Box 892, Lihue, Kauai, HI 96766. Rates subject to change.

Motel Lani, at Rice Street where it meets Kalena (tel. 245-2965), is a pleasant place patronized by both island people and tourists. The ten small but modern rooms rent for $17 to $20, single or double; $24 to $28 triple. All have a small refrigerator. There's an extra charge of $7 per person for any number over three, with rollaway cots provided. Rates are subject to change without notice. Two nights' deposit required. Janet Naumu suggests that you reserve in advance by writing to P.O. Box 1836, Lihue, Kauai, HI 96766.

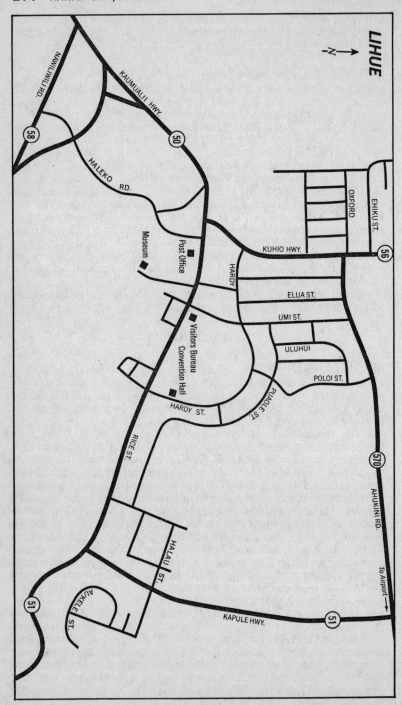

A few blocks away, at 3173 Akahi St., the **Tip Top Motel** (tel. 245-2333) offers 34 rooms at $19 single, $25 double, $29 triple, $33 quad. All rooms are air-conditioned. It's right above the Tip Top Restaurant, Bakery, and Cocktail Lounge, big favorites with the locals. The rooms are pleasant if plain, and the place seems to us more efficient than resorty, but it's comfortable, and the price is right. Prices may rise this year. Reservations: P.O. Box 1231, Lihue, Kauai, HI 96766.

COCONUT PLANTATION: Nine miles out of town, near where the Wailua River meets the ocean, is the site of the Coconut Plantation complex of hotels in Wailua. These are more expensive than the ones in the Lihue area since they are situated directly out on the ocean, but here on the windward side of the island the surf is rougher (and the weather apt to be rainier) than on the leeward side. If you have a car it's no problem, since it's a short drive to the splendid beaches of leeward Poipu. If you don't have a car, however, and want ocean swimming, we recommend choosing a hotel in Poipu (see ahead).

In this area—which has the advantage of beautiful scenery, the Coconut Plantation Market Place, and lots of good restaurants—your best budget choice is the attractive and informal **Kauai Sands Hotel,** part of the hospitable chain of Hukilau Hotels. Both the dining room and bar look right out onto the beach, and there are two swimming pools. The rooms are nicely done in greens and blues borrowed from the ocean hues; they are all carpeted and air-conditioned. Single or double, standard rooms are $46, superiors are $52; deluxe are $55; with kitchenette, $59. The hotel's dining room, Al and Don's, is inexpensive, serving dinner entrees between $4.95 and $8.75, and features "fresh catch of the day" nightly. The cocktail lounge offers good prices during a long 2:30 to 6 p.m. Happy Hour.

Even more bargains await you: Kauai Sands offers a hotel, car, and breakfast package for two that is quite impressive. It includes your hotel room and a Budget car with free mileage. The price of this package for two is $59 standard, $65 superior, $68 deluxe, $72 with kitchenette; and $10 for a third person. For reservations, write to Kauai Sands Hotel, 2222 Kalakaua Ave., #714, Honolulu, HI 96815; or phone, toll free 800/367-7000.

It's not easy to get an apartment at **Mokihana of Kauai,** 796 Kuhio Hwy., in the Coconut Plantation area (tel. 822-3971) in the busy winter months; that's when this handsome condominium complex is usually chock full of owners. But during the summer season, May through September, it's possible to get a rental. The 81-odd studio apartments are nicely furnished with limited kitchen facilities, bath, and/or shower; they're right on the oceanfront and two miles away from a championship golf course. Mokihana also boasts an 18-hole, par-36 putting green, shuffleboard, a large swimming pool, and a barbecue area. And the original Bull Shed Restaurant, a superb steakhouse right on the waterfront, is here. Apartments rent for a low $45 per night, single or double. Readers who've managed to wangle a place here have sent good reports. For information, contact Hawaii Kailani, 119 N. Commercial, Suite 1400, Bellingham, WA 98225 (tel. 206/676-1434).

KAPAA: Farther up Hwy. 56 you'll hit the area of Kapaa, which boasts the cute little **Hotel Coral Reef** (tel. 822-4481), right on the ocean and close to everything. You could even make do without a car here, as within minimal walking distance is a pretty good public swimming beach, a freshwater swimming pool, a tennis court, a library, and a laundromat—and several great little budget restaurants. The hotel has a stretch of white, sandy beach, and there is good swimming and snorkeling in the deep water between the reefs. We hardly recognized the place when we last visited Kauai; the new owners have done wonders with this older hotel. Michael and Linda Warriner proudly showed off their "baby"— completely refurbished inside and out. The buildings have been painted sand color with deep-red trim on the lanais, all of the rooms have fresh paint and pretty new bedspreads. In the newer, oceanfront wing, the rooms have private lanais and refrigerators, and are furnished with double or twin beds. The ground floor rooms have brown terrazo-tile floors; the upper units are carpeted. These rooms are $40 per day, single or double. In the older building are one- and two-bedroom units; these do not have lanais, but they are comfortable; it's $25 nightly for the one-bedroom units, $40 for the larger ones. Children under 12 years old stay free with their parents if they use existing beds; there is a $5 charge for a rollaway bed or crib. For reservations, phone toll free, 800/843-4659, or write to Iron Mike & the Princess, Inc., 1516 Kuhio Hwy., Kapaa, Kauai HI 96746.

One of our favorite places to stay on Kauai is the comfortable and very attractive **Kapaa Sands,** 380 Papaloa Road, Kapaa, Kauai HI 96746 (tel. 822-4901). It's just a few minutes' walk from Coconut Plantation, yet there's a secluded feeling at this friendly hostelry right on the beach. The pretty, two-story green buildings house studios and two-bedroom apartments. All rooms have color TV. Studios, with lanais and separate, fully equipped kitchens, go for $49 garden view, $59 oceanfront. The two-bedroom units are charming duplex apartments (two bedrooms and full bath upstairs, sofa bed and half-bath downstairs), each with two lanais, that go for $69 garden view, $79 oceanfront. Minimum stay is three days in summer, seven days in winter. Incidentally, the gracious and friendly manager, Mrs. Harriet Kaholokula, is the mother of two members of the very popular island cabaret and recording group, Na Kaholokula. Write for reservations to the address above, or phone toll free, 800/222-4901.

For a touch of luxury in Kapaa at a very good price, **Kapaa Shore,** 4-0900 Kuhio Hwy., may be just the ticket. This 81-unit condominium complex is right at the beach, and each and every apartment has a view of ocean, garden, or pool. They are beautifully furnished, many in avocado-and-white decorative schemes, with full electric kitchens, washers and dryers, and patio furniture to make dining on your lanai a treat. To help you prepare your meal, the kitchen is fully equipped, and includes a frost-free refrigerator, automatic dishwasher, and garbage disposal. The one-bedroom apartments can sleep up to four people in two twins or a queen-size bed in the bedroom and a queen-size sofa in the living room. Six people can be cozy in the two-bedroom apartments, which are duplexes with vaulted ceilings; they have a queen-size bed in one of the bedrooms, two twins in the other, and a queen-size sleeper-sofa in the living room. One-bedroom apartments are $75 for garden view, $85 for ocean view; two-bedrooms are $85 and $95. Pluses include the tennis court, 40-foot swimming pool, sunbathing deck, and barbecue area. For information and reservations, you can write Kapaa Shores at 4-0900 Kuhio Hwy., Kapaa, Kauai, HI 96746; or phone toll free 800/367-7040 or 367-7041. The local phone is 822-3055.

NEAR POIPU BEACH: In the other direction from Lihue, 12 miles south, stretches the idyllic Poipu Beach area, dry and sunny, where the surf crashes a Mediterranean blue-green on palm-fringed, white-sand beaches. This area is, of course, more expensive than Lihue, but you are right at the beach, and a glorious one it is—in our opinion, the best on Kauai. An old favorite here is the **Garden Isle Cottages,** a group of private cottages set in Hawaiian flower gardens, offering island ambience and scattered within a two-block area along the Poipu coast. The hospitable owners, Sharon and Robert Flynn, an artist, work hard at preserving the feeling of Old Hawaii in all of their cottages by using batiks, ethnic fabrics and furniture, and Bob's paintings and sculpture. There are no phones or TVs. Hale Melia, across the lane from a small sunning beach and gentle lagoon for floating and snorkeling, has three accommodations: two studios, each with bath and lanai with a partial ocean view; the smaller is $36 and the larger runs $44, double. You'll be in heaven if you can land the apartment below; it has a very large living/dining room with an open-beamed lahala ceiling, kitchen, and bath, surrounding an enclosed tropical garden patio that you will probably never want to leave. It rents for $65 double.

Then there are the Sea Cliff Cottages, whose unique location—perched on a cliff over Koloa Landing, where the Waikomo Stream meets the ocean—gives them an ambience that can only be described as idyllic. They each have not one, but two lanais—a morning lanai for watching the sun come up over the water, an evening lanai for watching it set over the mountains. They are beautifully furnished with a spacious living/dining room, kitchenette, one bedroom, bath, plus washer-dryer, and rent for $80 double. A new deluxe accommodation consists of a one-bedroom apartment with living room, dining room, and kitchen, plus a lanai on the ocean and a patio in a tropical garden, it's $100 double; with two bedrooms and two baths, suitable for up to four persons, it's $130. A studio apartment with lanai on the ocean, toaster, coffeepot and refrigerator, is $60 double.

Hale Waipahu, located on the highest point in Poipu at Poipu Crater, epitomizes luxurious tropical island living with a breathtaking, nonpareil 360-degree view of mountains, ocean, sunrises, and sunsets. Your own private "lap pool" overlooks the Poipu coast. Charming wood shutters, open beamed ceiling, and wicker furniture in the living room, latticed dining room, full kitchen and bath, and one bedroom: it all goes for $100 double per night. An extra bedroom/bath suite is $50 double.

The office of Garden Isle Cottages is located in Robert's gallery at 2666 Puuholo Rd., Koloa, and is open only from 9 a.m. to noon. Good restaurants are nearby, but remember that you'll need a car to get around here. Write to Garden Isle Cottages, RR 1, Box 355, Koloa, Kauai, HI 96756 (tel. 742-6717).

When people are traveling they need a friend. And Den and Dee Wilson, the hospitable owners/managers of the **Prince Kuhio Condominiums,** have such a talent for friendship that staying with them gives one the feeling of coming home. And it's a good place to come home to! The nicely furnished apartments here overlook either Prince Kuhio Park on one side or a lovely pool in a garden setting on the other; there's a beach known for good snorkeling right across the road and there are good swimming beaches nearby (the one we like best is in front of the Hotel Sheraton). The famed Beach House Restaurant is a few steps away. A variety of studios and apartments are offered. Twin-bedded studios are $39 double daily, $234 weekly; regular one-bedroom apartments for four are $46 daily, $276 weekly; and deluxe one-bedroom units for four are $55 daily, $330 weekly. Prices may be slightly higher from December 15 to April 15. All the units are fully equipped for housekeeping with kitchen and comfortable living space; all have private lanai and cable TV. There is no maid service unless requested upon arrival. The central barbecue is a popular spot, and this is the kind of place where it's easy to make friends. Contact Prince Kuhio Rentals, P.O. Box 1060, Koloa, Kauai, HI 96756 (tel. 742-1409).

Just across from Prince Kuhio is another large condominium complex, the 74-unit, 12-year-old **Kuhio Shores.** The big attraction here is its location on the waterfront: one side of the building faces ocean waves, another a more peaceful harbor; every room has a water view. The units have very large living rooms and fully equipped kitchens with dishwashers and garbage disposals, and are very nicely furnished. The one-bedroom units rent for $60 to $75; the two-bedroom/ two-bath apartments run from $90 to $110. There is a four-day minimum stay. For information, write to R & R Realty & Rentals, RR 1, Box 70, Koloa, Kauai, HI 96756; or phone toll free 800/367-8022.

Many people dream of moving to an island, having a lovely home of their own, and renting out a handful of cottages in their garden. Hans and Sylvia Zeevat (he is Dutch, she is Dutch-Indonesian), who came to Hawaii from Holland, have realized that dream on Kauai, and the result is four wonderful, reasonably priced accommodations for those lucky enough to get into the **Koloa Landing Cottages,** 2740 Hoonani Rd. The Zeevats are exceptional hosts (see the Readers' Selections, ahead, for several personal comments), and they delight in treating their guests like family: they ply them with fresh fruit from their own trees, loan them fishing equipment, give them tips on where to snorkel and what to feed the fish. ("This is just a family operation, nothing fancy," says Sylvia.) They have two cottages and two studios: spacious and tastefully decorated (many batiks reflect Sylvia's background), they have open-beamed ceilings, cross-ventilation, well-equipped kitchens (blenders, dishwashers, mixers, etc.), cable TV, and—hard to find in Poipu—telephones with their own private numbers! Guests like to barbecue out in the garden; restaurants and good swimming beaches are all within walking or very short driving distances. Each cottage has two bedrooms (double beds), two baths, and a lovely living room; they rent for $60 for one or two persons, $70 for three or four, $5 each for up to two more people. The studios are $40 for one or two people (one of the studios has no steps, so would be convenient for a handicapped person). A minimum stay of four days is required. Since so many guests book again for the next year when they leave, reserve as far in advance as possible. Write to Dolphin Realty, RR 1, Box 70, 2827 Poipu Rd., Koloa, Kauai, HI 96756, or phone Sylvia Zeevat at 742-1470.

Note: Whether or not you stay at Koloa Landing Cottages, you should know that Sylvia Zeevat has her own custom-sewing business called **Radja** right on the premises and is known for her fine work. She does anything from alterations to upholstery to custom garments. Just bring her some fabric and she will whip up muumuus (from $45), aloha shirts (from $20), kimonos in aloha prints, and lots more. Again, phone her at 742-1470.

If your idea of bliss is a hammock strung between two coconut palms and overlooking the pounding surf, then you might want to get one of the five rooms at **Gloria's Spouting Horn Bed & Breakfast,** 4464 Lawai Beach Rd., Koloa, Kauai, HI 96756 (tel. 742-6995). It's located on an idyllic rocky coastline within sight and sound of the surf and the famed Spouting Horn saltwater geyser, and the hammock is right out there, behind the house. Gloria Merkle's small cottage was being extended at the time of our last visit to make room for more B&B accommodations. The house is charmingly furnished with American oak and English walnut antiques; there's a Baldwin piano, TV, and VCR in the living room; most guest rooms have queen-sized beds, private lanais, and shared bath. All but one have a view of the ocean. Continental breakfast consists of papaya and other fresh, locally grown fruits; croissants or brioches or bagels; coffee, tea, cocoa, or hot cider. Rates vary from high season (December 15 to April 19 and June 15 to Labor Day) to the rest of the year, from about $45 to $70 for the different accommodations. Gloria's daytime office number is 245-8841; in the evening, call 742-6995.

Evie Warner and Al Davis, the very nice people who run the statewide Hawaii Bed & Breakfast Service we've told you about several times in this book, have recently built some very attractive vacation rental units behind their house on their own tropical acre of land, just up the road from Poipu Beach Park, one of the best places to swim in this area. This is **Poipu Plantation,** 1792 Pe'e Rd. (tel. 742-7038 or 822-7771), which consists of nine good-sized units, all of them attractively furnished, done in tropical decor, with ceiling fans, excellent modern kitchens, phones, and TVs. Washers and dryers are outside. Three one-bedroom units on the garden level go for just $50 a night for two, $10 for each additional person. The one-bedrooms with ocean view are $60. There are also several duplexes, luxury accommodations with two bedrooms, two baths, even marble floors in the bathrooms. These rent at $80 for two, $100 for four. There's a gazebo out in the garden, which is quite lovely, with its apple trees, blossoming plumerias, bougainvilleas, and gardenias. Evie and Al are friendly hosts and see to it that everybody is well cared-for. Write to Poipu Plantation at Rt. 1, Box 119, Koloa, Kauai, HI 96756, or phone the above numbers.

The **Poipu Beach Hotel** (tel. 742-1681), blessed with a perfect location right on the beach, has long been one of our favorite places on Kauai. Rates have jumped quite a bit here in the past year, but if you want an on-the-beach resort hotel, this is still a fine choice. Standard rooms are $89, single or double, and since all the rooms in this hotel are exactly the same, the only thing that determines the difference between an $89, $99, or $115 room is its location; at the higher prices you'll be facing the pool or the ocean; at the lower, the mountains. But the rooms are all good, spacious, nicely furnished, with private lanais, a huge dressing area, and best of all, a compact little kitchenette unit that makes fixing breakfast or a quick meal a breeze. The three buildings surround the pool and grassy area, the dining room is right in the middle of it all, and on some nights there's a Polynesian show; sit out on your lanai and you'll hear the whole thing. There are six tennis courts, with a pro shop next door. The management is attentive, service prompt. The neighboring property, Waiohai, has been completely rebuilt and is now an exquisite resort hotel, all of whose guest services you can use, including the Waiohai Physical Fitness Center (gym, Jacuzzi, sauna, massage, etc.). Reservations: Amfac Resorts, P.O. Box 8520, Honolulu, HI 96830, or phone toll free 800/227-4700.

The furnishings in the **Poipu Shores Resort Condominium** are luxury-plus: in fact, the same may be said of the whole complex. Rattan and cane furniture with oceany-colored upholstery in Oriental leaf prints highlight the cool, spacious apartments. Each unit has an all-electric kitchen, a color TV set, and a lanai. The low-rise buildings are surrounded by lush gardens and located in a secluded area right on the ocean. The one-bedroom, 1½-bath apartments are $100 a day, placing them out of our budget range, but savings can be realized in the larger units, if you're bringing the family or are two couples traveling together. The two-bedroom, two-bath apartments are $130 for up to six people; the three-bedroom, two-bath units and the two-bedroom town houses, with 2½ baths, are $150 and $140 respectively, for up to six people. Rates are lower on weekly stays. Summer rates are $20 less. If you truly want to get away from it all, this is the place to do it—in style. For reservations, write Poipu Shores Resort Condominium, RR 1, Box 95, Koloa, Kauai, HI 96756 (tel. 742-6522), or call toll free 800/367-5686.

If you are really into the great outdoors—but not enough to backpack it and sleep under the stars—**Kahili Mountain Park** might be the place for you. Seven miles from Poipu Beach, the park is off Hwy. 50 west, just beyond the 7-mile marker. Mount Kahili rises majestically behind the little cabins and cabinettes nestled near a small swimmable and fishable (bass) lake. The park is owned and operated by the Seventh Day Adventist Church; their school is on the premises. The less expensive of the two types of accommodations, the cabinettes, go for $18.50 double, $4 for an extra person. They are grouped in a circle around the bathroom-and-shower buildings. They each have one room, with a small dining lanai where there's a tiny refrigerator, a two-burner hot plate, and a sink. Cookware is furnished. Cabins, consisting of either one large room or two small ones, have a bathroom with a sink and toilet; the only showers are those near the cabinettes. Cabins have a full-size refrigerator, as well as the two-burner stove and sink. They go for $32 double, $4 for an extra person. All of the accommodations have screened windows with outside canvas awnings that can be pulled up for protection against wind and rain. Linens are furnished. These facilities are very, very plain. There is a laundry room on the premises, as well as basketball and tennis courts. Prepayment in full is required for all reservations, a minimum stay is two days. For reservations, write Kahili Mountain Park, P.O. Box 298, Koloa, Kauai, HI 96756 (tel. 742-9921).

PRINCEVILLE: Think of Princeville, on the north shore of Kauai, and you think of luxury living, of championship golf and tennis amid a green sweep of mountains and valleys. You don't think of budget accommodations here, but we've found some sensible values in two resorts. First is a place called **Sandpiper Village,** a 75-unit condominium complex that features *only* two-bedroom, two-bath apartments, and two-bedroom-plus-loft, 2½-bath apartments at prices of $85 (up to four guests) for the smaller units, $100 (up to six) for the larger. (An extra person is charged $7; kids under 12 free; rollaways and cribs, $7.) Rates are subject to change. And each unit is like a lovely little house, high-ceilinged and fully carpeted, with ceiling fans, handsome dark bamboo furniture, superb decorator's touches wherever you look. Kitchens are of generous size, with dishwashers and washer-dryers. A cable hookup can be rented for the television set. From your windows you can sometimes watch the waterfalls coming down the mountains. The units are set in shaded gardens and clustered around a central area where the whole family can have fun—large swimming pool, sauna, Jacuzzi, recreation building, barbecue pits.

From your apartment here you're a short distance from the Princeville Makai golf course, rated among "America's Top 100," and its six outdoor tennis courts. There are half a dozen enjoyable restaurants right at Princeville. You can drive down to the beach at Hanalei in about five minutes, or get your exercise hiking down to the shore. For reservations (best make them three to six months in advance from December 15 to Easter and June 15 to Labor Day) write Sandpiper Village, Princeville, Hanalei, Kauai, HI 96714; or call toll free 800/367-7040. The local phone is 826-9613.

The Cliffs at Princeville is the largest condo complex in the area (210 units). Set amid graceful lawns and gardens, and perched atop cliffs overlooking the ocean far below, it offers as much of peace and privacy, sports or excitement, as one would wish. On the grounds are four tennis courts, a putting green, a large pool area with Jacuzzi, and a recreation pavilion complete with a huge fireplace, wet-bar, an indoor whirlpool bath and sauna, Ping-Pong, and pool tables. All of the suites are perfect little one-bedroom, two-bath houses, fully carpeted, beautifully and individually furnished in bamboo and oak, with oak doors, completely equipped kitchen, and cable TV. All have been decorated in excellent taste. These suites can be divided to provide the following possible combinations: a hotel room with a garden view (small executive-size refrigerator instead of kitchen) for one or two people at $50; a one-bedroom, two-bath unit with garden view for one to four people at $90 ($10 more for ocean view); and a one-bedroom-with-loft, two-bath unit for one to four people at $130—

garden view, $150—ocean view. Weekly rates are available. Whatever the size of your family or group, the very helpful management will work with you to provide a highly livable and affordable setup.

There are amenities and service aplenty at the Cliffs. These include daily maid service, beach mats and ice chests for taking to the beach or touring, daily morning coffee klatches with slide presentations and afternoon cocktail parties, charcoal barbecues available at the pool area and at the Gazebo. And the Gazebo is something special—a romantic spot overlooking the water, the ideal place to watch the sunset or the crashing surf far below.

Again, the Princeville Makai Golf Course, designed by Robert Trent Jones, is right at hand; the sandy beach at Hanalei is about a five-minute drive; and opportunities for horseback riding, surfing, windsurfing, scuba-diving, and much more are all close by. It's a good choice for Na Pali Coast hikers, as they will store your luggage while you're off hiking the trails.

For reservations, call toll free 800/367-6046, or write to Colony Resorts, 733 Bishop St., Suite 1600, Honolulu, HI 96813.

Would you believe it's possible to rent a bedroom and bath for $49 a day in the Princeville area? It's not advertised, but it can be done by closing off one of the bedrooms in the two-bedroom units at **Pali Ke Kua,** a two-story condominium complex overlooking the ocean from a point high on the cliffs. The one- and two-bedroom apartments are expensively furnished in modern decor, boast full kitchens with washers and dryers. From April 20 to December 14, one-bedroom apartments with mountain or garden view are $75; two-bedroom apartments (for up to four persons) are $105; ocean-view apartments are $90 and $110, ocean front $105 and $120. Rates are $10 more during high season. An extra person is charged $8. For reservations write to Hawaiian Islands Resorts, Inc., P.O. Box 212, Honolulu, HI 96810 (tel. 531-7595 in Honolulu, or toll free 800/367-7042). The Kauai address is Pali Ke Kua, P.O. Box 899, Princeville-Hanalei, HI 96714 (tel. 826-9066).

KOKEE: Forty-five miles away from Lihue, in Kokee State Park (just beyond Waimea Canyon), you'll find **Kokee Lodge,** 3,600 feet up in bracing mountain air. The cabins are owned by the state but operated by a private firm, and the prices are low—a practice we'd like to see imitated all over Hawaii. This is a place only for those who have enough time to really linger in Kauai (on a two- or three-day trip, a stay would be impractical, since the time and cost of driving to the other sights of the island would outweigh the savings here). The cabins vary in size from one large room, which sleeps three, to two-bedroom units that will accommodate seven. Each cabin rents for a flat $25 per night. The cabins are rustic, furnished with refrigerators, stoves, hot showers, basic eating and cooking utensils, blankets, linens, and pillows. You can buy a pile of wood and make a fire in the fireplace when the night air gets nippy in this cooler northern Kauai that seems a world away from beaches and coconut palms.

Daytime activities at Kokee include driving or hiking on gorgeous trails and swimming in hidden freshwater pools. You can also hunt boar and wild goat, fish for trout in the nearby mountain streams, or just laze in the sun. Kokee Lodge Restaurant serves breakfast, lunch, and snacks daily from 8:30 a.m. to 5:30 p.m., dinners from 6 to 9 p.m. The restaurant provides take-out orders and snacks for outdoor picnics, and for those wishing to cook, there's a simple grocery store on the premises. (Bring your own supplies, however, if you're planning on cooking anything fancy.) There's also a cocktail lounge and a gift shop. For reservations: Kokee Lodge, P.O. Box 819, Waimea, Kauai, HI 96796 (tel. 335-6061). Management advises making early reservations, since holiday weekends are very popular here, and so is the trout-fishing season in August and September.

BED-AND-BREAKFAST: For information on bed-and-breakfast lodgings in Kauai, see details at the end of Chapter II, "Honolulu Hotels."

2. Island Restaurants

IN LIHUE AND ENVIRONS: Lihue has some excellent budget restaurants frequented mostly by the local people, and you'll be glad you joined them. One of the best is the **Lihue Barbecue Inn** on Kress Street (tel. 245-2921), where the cuisine is Japanese, American, and Chinese—and very good too. There's a bar and lounge off to one side of the restaurant. You'll know why the Barbecue Inn has been going strong for some 47 years now when you have a look at the prices: a typical dinner menu lists 40 complete dinners—and that includes soup or fruit cup, tossed green salad, vegetable, beverages, and dessert, accompanying such main courses as shrimp tempura, baked mahimahi, broiled teriyaki pork chops, corned beef brisket with cabbage, chow mein chicken with spare ribs—for $7.95 and under! (Complete meals start at just $4.85.) Seven more dinners go up in price to as high as $16.95, for baked lobster tail with steak and fried rice. Fresh fish is served whenever it's available. Complete lunches are even cheaper; we counted 32 of them for $4.25 and under! These often include seafood platter, Chinese chicken salad, mahimahi sandwich, or pastrami on rye. The menu changes daily, but whatever you have here will most likely be good—especially the freshly made pies and the homemade bread. Do try the green tea—the hospitable owner Henry Sasaki let us in on the secret; it's brewed with rice and popcorn! One of the most appealing inexpensive restaurants in Lihue, the Barbecue is patronized by family groups; and over the years we have had consistent letters of praise from our readers about it. It's open from 7:30 a.m. to 1:30 p.m. and 4:30 to 8:30 p.m.; closed Sunday.

Another place that's long been popular with the locals is the **Tip Top Café,** in shiny air-conditioned quarters at 3173 Akahi St., just north of the Lihue Shopping Center. It's a family-style restaurant, the prices are modest, and while the food is not of gourmet quality, it's dependable. Service is apt to be on the slow side. We often have breakfast here (pancakes are served all day, and the macadamia-nut ones, $2.50, are delicious). There's a Chinese plate lunch for $4, and lunch entrees like pork chops for $3.75. Dinner entrees such as teriyaki pork, breaded fish filet, and ground round steaks with eggs average $5.50, and that includes soup, salad or potato salad, rice or potatoes, and coffee. The Chinese combination plate dinner is $5.75. Prices subject to change. This is a good place to remember if you need a box lunch for an all-day excursion; either American- or Oriental-style take-out lunches are available at $3.25. Before you leave, take a look at the omiyage (gift) department. Besides pastries, orchids, and souvenirs, it has some memorable homemade jams; you might want to pick up a bottle of passionfruit, pineapple, or guava-macadamia-nut to take to the folks back home. And the Tip Top Bakery is famous for its macadamia-nut cookies and Portuguese sweet bread, baked fresh daily. The Tip Top stays open from 6:45 a.m. until 8:30 p.m. daily (tel. 245-2343 or 245-2333). There are clean motel units next door (see above).

A favorite with the local folks is **Ho's Garden Restaurant,** at 3016 Umi St., corner of Rice Street (tel. 245-5255). The atmosphere is plain, but it's the food that counts, and fragrant and tasty it is. Most lunch entrees run from $4 to $5;

the day we were there we enjoyed two delicious specials: tempura mahimahi in a black bean sauce, and roast duck with rice and oyster sauce. Dinner entrees such as lemon chicken, almond duck, abalone with black mushrooms, and squid with sour cabbage are mostly $4.50 to $6, and often include specials like crab with black bean sauce and roast duck with hoisin sauce. Vegetarians take note: specialties like tofu tomato flower—golden-brown tofu and tomato sautéed in a scrambled-egg sauce—are quite tasty; most are under $5. Ho's is open weekdays from 10:30 a.m. to 2 p.m. for lunch, from 4:30 to 9 p.m. for dinner; on Saturday, it's 5 to 9:30 p.m. Closed Sunday.

For authentic Hawaiian food—and American and Japanese dishes as well —local people recommend **Dani's,** at 4200 Rice St. (tel. 245-7894), whose menu lists something like two dozen dishes from $4.50 to $7.95, and includes such entrees as roast pork, chicken cutlet, seafood platter, teriyaki chicken, and Hawaiian plates, accompanied by salad or soup, rice, roll with butter, and beverage. Most lunch dishes, served with salad, run between $2.95 and $4.50, for the likes of hamburger steak, pork cutlet, or breaded mahimahi. Hawaiian breakfast and lunch specialties include kalua pig, lomi salmon, and rice for $3.85. Don't be surprised if you're the only tourists here. Dani's serves breakfast and lunch Monday through Saturday from 5 a.m. to 2 p.m.; no dinner; on Sunday it's breakfast only, from 6 to 11 a.m.

Casa Italiana, at 2989 Haleko Rd., across from the Lihue Shopping Center (tel. 245-9564), serves up *delizioso* Italian cuisine in a comfortable setting furnished with outdoor chairs and tables, soft lighting, and lots of wrought iron. It's a dinner-only place, nightly from 5:30 to 10 p.m. You can dine quite reasonably by sticking to one of the pasta dinners, which include a trip to the salad bar and Chef Tony's sublime garlic and pepper breads. Fresh pasta is prepared daily on the premises. Your meal of spaghetti or ravioli, with such accompaniments as red or white clam sauce, Italian or Portuguese sausage, meatballs, olives, or shrimp marinara, will cost from $7.95 to $11.95. Or, go for a variety of chicken or veal specialties, from $14.95 to $16.95. A bowl of spumoni and a bit of cappuccino will top off your meal nicely.

The local people rave about **Kauai Chop Suey** at Harbor Village (tel. 245-8790). Our favorite local couple love this place, and take all their visiting friends to dinner here. Despite its unimaginative name, it serves superior food, all in the Cantonese style. There are about 75 items on the menu, at least 70 of them under $5, so the budgeteer cannot go wrong here. There's something for everyone: roast duck, egg foo yong, squid with vegetables, shrimp with broccoli, lemon chicken, stuffed tofu, sweet pork, or char sui (an island favorite), and much more. And the soups—seaweed, scallop, abalone—are quite special. The place is large and comfortable, decorated in typical Chinese style. Large parties are seated at round tables with revolving centerpieces, similar to our "Lazy Susans," the better to sample all the delicacies. Kauai Chop Suey serves lunch Tuesday to Saturday from 11 a.m. to 1 p.m.; dinner, Tuesday to Sunday from 4:30 to 9 p.m. Closed Monday.

There's a mixed menu and name at **Denmar's Pancakes and Mexican Restaurant,** also at Harbor Village (tel. 245-3917), an attractive place with an open-air feeling. Pancakes are the specialty—delicious concoctions like papaya-nut or banana-macadamia pancakes—but they also have other "things": at lunch and dinner they whip up moderately priced Mexican specialties like quesadillas at $4.75 and the tostada suprema at $6.50. Early Bird specials—prime rib, mahimahi, and pineapple chicken—are $5.95 to $6.95 from 5 to 6:30 p.m.

One of the old-standby restaurants in Lihue is **Club Jetty,** overlooking the Pacific at Nawiliwili Harbor; it's the only restaurant and cabaret in Hawaii partially built on the water. Try to get a window seat here, so you can keep an eye on harbor activity: Coast Guard boats, a freighter swaying gently at anchor, small craft, the luxury liner *Constitution* if it happens to be Thursday. The food here is a combination of American and Chinese, with good values in both. American-style dinners start at $8.95. Chinese entrees are mostly $3.95 to $6.95. Music starts at 10 p.m. Tuesday through Saturday. Club Jetty is at the end of Rte. 51 South (tel. 245-4970). Dinner only, 4:30 to 9:30 p.m. (Happy Hour from 4:30 to 5:30 p.m.); closed Sunday.

The **Eggbert's: Kauai's Family Specialty Restaurant** is a long name for a friendly little restaurant at 4483 Rice St., in the Haleko Shops. It's an attractive place, with wooden partitions, ferns, flowers, and ceiling fans to keep the trade winds moving. The day starts here at 7 a.m. with a variety of terrific omelets from $2.85 to $6.45. Also excellent: Eggbert's Benedict at $5.95 for the vegetarian version, $6.95 with country ham and turkey. Their handmade hollandaise is quite special. All breakfast/brunch items are served until 2 p.m., but lunch dishes are added on at 11 a.m. That's when you can have soups, salads, sandwiches, and burgers, $2.95 to $4.25. A special lunch menu of sandwiches, salads, and soups, plus bar service, continues until dinner, which is served Wednesday through Saturday from 5:30 to 9:30 p.m., featuring fish, chicken, beef, pork, and omelet specialties along with good salads, freshly made soups, and desserts. Complete dinners run from $7.95 to $12.95. Reservations are suggested (tel. 245-6325). Bar prices are very reasonable. Eggbert's is almost always open, and you can always get something tasty and decently priced here.

The tiny **Restaurant Kiibo** at 2991 Umi St. (tel. 245-2650) is a comfortable, nicely furnished place where the food is outstanding. The pretty little sushi bar up front gives way to a small dining room with ten or so tables. Japanese lanterns supply the soft lighting, and examples of Japanese folk art adorn the walls. Two of us had a lovely dinner here for less than $14. Our meals included a flavorful miso soup, rice, tsukemono (pickled salad), and tea. We enjoyed our $7 chicken sukiyaki and $5.50 beef teriyaki to the accompaniment of soft Japanese music in the background. Other good choices include a big plate of shrimp and vegetable tempura at $7, and donburi, a huge bowl of rice topped with sukiyaki or teriyaki or something equally interesting, at $5. A child's dinner is available at $5. Lunch offers similar dishes at slightly lower prices. Chances are good that you'll be the only haoles at the Kiibo; it's a local favorite, off the usual tourist beat. Closed Sunday and holidays.

Kukui Grove

Kauai's multimillion-dollar shopping center, **Kukui Grove,** just outside Lihue on Rte. 50 toward Poipu Beach, has several attractive eating possibilities for us. Our favorite is not a traditional restaurant at all, but a café area in the middle of Rainbow Books called **Rainbow Coffees.** Freshly roasted coffee is sold by the pound and its fragrant aroma makes everything you eat here—at the cozy counter or tables—taste wonderful. There are always coffees of the day, a variety of espressos and cappuccinos, herbal teas, and coffee specialty drinks such as coffee cream soda, coffee grog, café mocha. You can dine lightly here on soups and sandwiches, perhaps vegetable soup and sourdough bread or a croissant sandwich with meat and cheese, all from $3 to $4. Have some of their home-baked cake—it may be our favorite, chocolate raspberry decadence. A lovely place for a sophisticated snack. Rainbow Coffees is open most days from 9:30 a.m. to 5:30 or 6 p.m., to 9 p.m. Friday, Sunday from 10 a.m. to 4 p.m. Call 245-6654 for takeout orders.

Probably the most popular specialty restaurant here is **Rosita's Mexican Restaurant** (tel. 245-8561), in an attractive indoor-outdoor setting: many plants, stained-glass lanterns, ceiling fans, stucco walls, cozy booths. You can dine leisurely here, at lunch and dinner, on Mexican and American favorites and sometimes a combination of both, like the hamburger ortega and hamburger ranchera lunch specials at $5.75. Combination plates run $5.35 to $7.65. Their seafood tostado is good at $6.75, and so is the arroz con pollo at $8.95. Dishes tend to be highly spiced. Don't pass up Rosita's famous margaritas—when was the last time you had a *banana* margarita? Friendly owners Rosita and Rick Shaw keep this lively place open seven days a week, from 11 a.m. to 10 p.m. Where else can you go between 2 and 4:30 p.m.? They present entertainment—Thursday and Friday nights and Happy Hour music—Wednesday, Thursday, and Friday.

The **Kukui Nut Tree Inn** (tel. 245-7005) is a family restaurant, serving all three meals in a summerhouse atmosphere. Latticework arching over the booths and on the ceiling make this nicer than your average coffeeshop. The food is American with island touches, and prices are quite reasonable. The day starts at 7 a.m. (7:30 a.m. on Sunday) with omelets and pancakes, plus local foods like taro cake or an Oriental breakfast—miso soup, tsukemono, grilled mahi, and rice, for $3.75. Lunch features at least 15 entrees under $7—and that includes the likes of the mahi tempura and teri combo, honey-stung fried chicken, grilled beef liver with onions and bacon. Entrees are served with hot vegetables and starch; they are preceded by soup or fruit cocktail, and accompanied by garden greens and rolls with butter. Especially popular are such salads as vegetarian chef, tofu, and Moloaa papaya with turkey salad, all served with unique dressings made locally: papaya seed, passion fruit with herbs, and Maui onion dressing. At dinner, the bill goes up about 70¢, but dessert is included. With prices like these, it's no wonder this place is always crowded. There are also special menus for keikis and kupunas (under 12 or over 65). Drinks are available. The kitchen closes at 8 p.m., except on Friday (9 p.m.) and Sunday (3 p.m.).

If you're in the mood for a quick Japanese lunch, join the locals here at **Joni-Hana,** a neat little red-and-white spot, where you can get sushi to go, sushi Bento (a box lunch of assorted sushi with chicken and steak teriyaki for $3), or hot lunches like beef cutlet or sesame fried chicken wings for $3 for one choice, $3.50 for two. It also has a cute little back room with a mirrored wall where you can sit at chairs and tables. Next door it runs a fast-food place called **Local Grinds.** Hot lunch grinds are $3.25 to $3.75. Hot sandwich grinds are $2.75. And grinds in a bowl, over rice, $1.25.

Brick Oven Pizza, long one of our favorites in Kalaheo (see ahead), has a new and attractive restaurant now here at Kukui Grove. It's a large, comfy place with red-and-white checkered tablecloths, ceiling fans overhead, and a family atmosphere. Hearth-baked pizzas, wholewheat or white, begin at $5.75, and there are hot sandwiches, a salad bar, and wine and beer. For pizza to go: phone 245-1895.

Other snacking possibilities at Kukui Grove include the very attractive **Yogurt Patio** with its blue-tiled floor and white chairs, where you can get stuffed potatoes (bacon and cheese, broccoli and cheese, etc.) from $2.49 to $2.69 as well as frozen yogurt; **Family Kitchen,** which feeds a local crowd with hearty breakfasts, $3.85 plate lunches, sandwiches, burgers, saimin, and sushi, in a pleasant self-serve, sit-down setting; and **Ed & Don's,** known around the islands for good sandwiches and ice creams.

At Kilohana Plantation

One of the nicest restaurants to open in Kauai in many a tropical moon is **Gaylord's,** at Kilohana, the legendary plantation estate of the 1930's that has been lovingly restored and is now open to the public. Gaylord's (tel. 245-9593) is a courtyard restaurant open to a manicured green lawn around which tables are arranged on three sides. The restaurant is done in whites, pinks, and greens, with soft cushioned chairs, white tablecloths, pink napkins, fresh flowers on every table. It would be a delight even if the food were not special—but we can assure you, it is. Dinner at Gaylord's *is* pricey (entrees from $17.95 to $22.95), but at lunchtime you can have a first-class dining experience for a modest tab. We sampled quite a few specialties at a recent lunch and can tell you that the oriental chicken salad (tossed with romaine lettuce, toasted almonds, wonton strips, and topped with an unforgettable dressing) is a winner at $7.95; so is Gaylord's Papaya Runneth Over, island papaya stuffed with delicate baby shrimp salad, and its tangy seafood fettucine. Gaylord's chef does some wonderful treatments of fresh island fish, market-priced daily at about $7.95 to $8.95. And you can't beat the vegetarian selection of the day for freshness, since 80% of the greens are grown right on Kilohana's acres. Duck, pheasant, and venison frequently appear in lunch (and dinner) specials. Entrees are served with a fresh garden vegetable, a choice of soup or salad or steak fries or rice, and fine wines, of course. And don't miss dessert here; Kilohana mud pie, $2.75, is a classic, and chocolate amaretto mousse and cheese with fresh fruit topping also merit serious attention. Lunch is served Monday to Saturday from 11 a.m. to 4 p.m.; Sunday brunch, with a special menu ($6.95 to $12.95), is on from 10 a.m. to 3 p.m. Reservations are usually not needed at lunch, essential at dinner.

If the atmosphere at Gaylord's is decidedly patrician, it's downright downhome at the other restaurant on the Kilohana Plantation estate, this one called **The Carriage House** (tel. 245-9393). Every night, from 5 to 9 p.m., there's an old-fashioned cookout, live music from the 20's, 30's, and 40's and dancing too, in the historic sugarcane plantation camp. The price of the entree—which you first select, then pick up from the grill when your name is called—is quite reasonable, considering that it comes with an unlimited and generous salad bar, oven baked beans, rice, dinner rolls, plus desserts, and beverage. Broiled half chicken is $11.95, pork or beef spare ribs are $13.95, broiled Alaskan salmon is $13.50, boneless rib steak is $14.95, and so on, up to fresh island fish, priced daily. Salad bar alone is $7.95; so is a keiki's menu. There's a full-service bar. Choose this one when you want hearty food and a lively atmosphere; it's not conducive to quiet conversation. Reservations suggested.

Hanamaulu

It's well worth making a short trip from Lihue (about two miles north on Hwy. 56) to dine at the **Hanamaulu Restaurant and Tea House.** It's an attractive place, and the Japanese garden is really something to see, beautifully landscaped with stone pagodas, pebbled paths, and a pond filled with flashing carp. We suggest you call a day in advance and reserve one of the charming ozashiki, or tea-house, rooms; you take off your shoes, sit on the floor at a long, low table, and the shoji screens are opened to face the lighted garden. (You may be able to get one of the rooms without reservations, but it's best to call ahead; tel. 245-2511). The food here is excellent and inexpensive; the Chinese and Japanese plate lunches at about $6.50 are good buys. You'll get soup, fried chicken or shrimp, chop suey, spare ribs, rice, and tea on the Chinese menu; miso soup, pork tofu or teriyaki steak, takuwan, rice, and tea on the Japanese. For dinner, the special plates start at $7, entrees like chicken sukiyaki go for $6, and you can feast on a veritable Oriental banquet for about $13 per person. An excellent sushi bar is an attraction here. Owner Roy Miyake is a cordial host. The restaurant is open from 11 a.m. to 1 p.m. and from 5 to 9 p.m. Closed Monday.

Mile Two, named after the roadside sign in front of it, is a new addition to the Hanamaulu scene. It's a nice, dim, cool place with a big lanai where you may eat if you choose. In addition to a variety of burgers and sandwiches ($4.25 to $6.95), lunch features such entrees as barbecue pork ribs, teri chicken, a deep-fried shrimp platter, and kiawe-broiled New York steak, served with salad or homemade soup, rice or fries, plus vegetables, all for $5.95 to $7.50. You can't go wrong at dinner either, since, on the low side of the menu are such entrees as chicken Budapest, chicken teriyaki, fettuccine florentine, and barbecue ribs at $9.95, served with salad with homemade dressing (blue cheese and buttermilk dill are tasty), homemade soup, rice or other starch, and fresh garlic bread. Prime rib au jus and fresh fish, broiled over kiawe, are good buys at $12.95 and $12.50. And children's meals are available for $5.95. Mile Two serves lunch every day from 11 a.m. to 2 p.m.

RESTAURANTS ON THE EASTERN AND NORTHERN ROUTE: This is the most populous part of the island, with many budget restaurants.

In Wailua and Kapaa

Exquisite is the word for the dining experience at **Restaurant Kintaro,** 4-370 Kuhio Hwy., between Coco Palms and Coconut Plantation (tel. 822-3341), a sparkling bright restaurant, authentically Japanese down to the prettily wrapped chopsticks on the table. The rather bland exterior does not even suggest the harmonious Japanese scene inside: kites and kimonos on the walls, blonde woods, shoji screens, a long sushi bar from which the chefs turn out tender marvels. Have a seat, read the menu, sip a glass of sake or a cocktail while you're reading, and you'll be pleasantly surprised: a complete dinner runs from about $11.50 to $14.75 and includes a variety of delicious small dishes. First you are served chilled buckwheat noodles in a flavorful sauce, presented on a *zora*, a wooden box with bamboo top. Next, also served on traditional wooden platters, arrive miso soup, rice, Japanese pickled vegetables, and your main course—it could be the delicious chicken yakitori (boneless broiled chicken, onion, bell pepper, and teriyaki sauce and salad) or salmon yakitori that we sampled. Or it could be the yosenabe, a Japanese "bouillabaisse" of many kinds of seafood cooked with vegetables and served in a clay pot; a tasty tempura combination; or fresh fish of the day. Kintaro is justifiably proud of its teppan cuisine, including steak, shrimp, lobster, and fresh island fish with scallops, from $15.95 to $23.50. Green-tea ice cream, which we find delicious, is included with the meal; it was even more delicious topped with Suntory Green Melon Liqueur ($2.95)! A pot of green tea accompanies your meal. There are various sushi and sashimi combinations for appetizers or for those who wish to eat at the sushi bar. All in all, an ah-so-harmonious experience. Kintaro serves dinner only, every day from 5:30 to 9:30 p.m.

A favorite of steak and seafood lovers, the **Bull Shed,** 796 Kuhio Hwy., just north of Coconut Plantation, behind the Mokihana of Kauai condos (tel. 822-3791), is a Kauai tradition. The atmosphere is great: a large, airy, wooden frame building overlooking the ocean. If you're watching the budget or your waistline, you can make do with visits to the superb salad bar (salad bar alone is $5.95). Or splurge on some of the specialties; entrees, which run from $12.95 to $17.95, include prime rib, prawns and scallops in a delicate sauce, lobster tail, New Zealand rack of lamb, teriyaki chicken, and more; and all entrees include a trip to that salad bar. Open from 3:30 daily for cocktails; dinner is served every night from 5 to 10 p.m. Reservations advised.

At lunchtime, when the hungry crowds come off the boats from the Fern Grotto, the **Wailua Marina Restaurant** at Wailua Marina (tel. 822-4311) is the kind of place we like to avoid. But at dinnertime, when the mobs have gone, it's an entirely different story. Then, all is peaceful and quiet in the huge dining room with its slanted ceilings, murals, stuffed fish and turtleshells on the wall—and it's then that you can really enjoy the good food and attentive service at prices that are ridiculously low. How they manage to serve almost two-dozen dishes from $5.75 to $9—and that includes boneless chicken stuffed with crab and pork, crispy teriyaki chicken, salmon steak, fried mahimahi, baked stuffed pork chop, and breaded veal cutlet—is a mystery to us, especially since every meal includes delicious hot rolls with butter and a green salad with choice of dressing (the bleu cheese is excellent), plus vegetables and potatoes for that same low price. Our teriyaki chicken was quite good, and the salmon steak, although frozen, was nicely done. Another dozen or so entrees, including seafood specialties like Alaskan snow crab claws and broiled lobster tail, range from $10 to $17.95. Homemade pies costs $1.50. Dinner is served from 5:30 to 9 p.m. daily, lunch from 11 a.m. to 2 p.m., breakfast from 8:30 to 11 a.m. Free transportation from Wailua area hotels in the evenings only. A find.

If you're in the mood for a treat now, stop and have lunch with the rich at the glorious **Coco Palms Hotel**. Lunch is an extravagant buffet with several hot entrees—usually including chicken and roast beef—and many, many choices of vegetables, potatoes, salads, breads, yummy desserts, and fresh fruits, priced at $11. And it's so nice to sit in the lovely open dining room overlooking the palms and the lagoon, where, in the early evening, their famous torch-lighting ceremony is held. Lunch is served from 11:30 a.m. to 2 p.m., salads and sandwiches between 2 and 4:30 p.m. Be sure to walk around the beautiful grounds and browse through their museum and shops.

Just opposite the Lagoon Dining Room is the newer Flame Room at Coco Palms, a dinner-only spot you should definitely plan to come back to. Make your reservations early, in time for the torchlighting ceremony, which is held at dusk, and ask for a seat as close to the lagoon as possible. Silence descends and you're transported back in time to the Hawaii of old as the runner lights torch after torch along the black lagoon; then, the coconut groves alit, the festivities may commence. The festivities here including dining on such entrees as chicken Wailua, beef brochette, steak and chicken combos, Indoneasian steak, prime rib, from $9.75 to $14.95. All entrees include salad bar, fresh sautéed vegetables, and either rice pilaf or cottage fries. You could also have the salad bar alone, a very good one, with freshly baked rolls, for $6.50; and that modest price alone could be your admission to this dramatic spot. Our favorite dessert here is poha berry cheesecake, an island treat. Dinner is served from 6 to 10 p.m. nightly. Reservations: 822-4921.

If you've developed a taste for real Hawaiian food, you can satisfy it in plain surroundings at the **Aloha Diner** in the Waipouli Complex, 4-971 Kuhio Hwy. (tel. 822-3851). Best bets are the lunch specials from $4.75 to $5.75, including kalua pig or laulau, lomi-lomi salmon, rice or poi; and the more elaborate dinner special from $6.75 to $8.75—kalua pig or laulau, lomi-lomi salmon, chicken lau, poi or rice, and haupia (coconut pudding). À la carte entrees, from $3 to $4, include beef stew, squid lau, and other favorites. Several readers have praised this one. Open Monday to Saturday from 11 a.m. to 9 p.m.; closed Sunday.

The little town of Kapaa offers a bonanza of budget restaurants, all on or near the main street, Hwy. 56. A real favorite here is **Kountry Kitchen** (tel. 822-3511), a dressed-up diner with carpets, Tiffany-type lamps, gingham curtains at the windows, and a flavor of olden times. The flavor of the food is pretty good too: you can have complete dinners like fresh local fish, all-vegetable quiche, baked ham, Kountry beef ribs, sesame shrimp, or steak and shrimp, from $6.35 to $8.75, and your entree is accompanied by vegetable soup or salad, vegetables, rice or potatoes, and a loaf of home-baked bread. Beer and wine are available at dinner, which is from 5 to 9:30 p.m. Lunch, served from 11 a.m. to 2:30 p.m., runs to sandwiches, super burgers, and dishes like fried chicken, grilled mahimahi, chef's salad, and roast beef, from about $4.40 to $5.20. Breakfast, from 6 a.m. to 2 p.m., offers crispy hashbrowns, a big favorite with all omelets and egg orders on the complete breakfast. The omelet bar is popular at breakfast, especially the build-your-own combination, since such unusual ingredients (for omelets) as hamburger, tuna, raisins, and kim chee are all ready and waiting. On our last visit we breakfasted on the chef's sour cream omelet—filled with sour cream, chopped bacon, and tomatoes, served with hot corn bread and hash browns, it was a huge filler at $4.65. The coffee was great too.

"Ono" means "delicious" in Hawaiian, and that's what to expect— delicious food for the whole family—at **Ono-Family Restaurant,** 4-1292 Kuhio Hwy. in old Kapaa town (tel. 822-1710). Pewter plates and fancy cookware hang on the wood-paneled walls; ceiling fans create a pleasant breeze: European and Early American antiques and paintings add to the charm of this warm and inviting place. This is a family-owned operation, and it shows in the care and attention that the Geralds and the Smiths lavish on their guests, especially senior citizens and children; many come back year after year because of that warm welcome. Omelets are featured at breakfast, and so are Canterbury eggs (grilled English muffins topped with turkey, ham, veggies, eggs, and cheese), at $4.95, and quite a way to start the day. The lunch menu has "Special Delights" from $3.65 to $5.25 (the $4.25 fish sandwich we dined on recently, with vegetables, cheese, sprouts on grilled Branola bread, was a meal in itself), super burgers from $3.50 to $4.95, and shrimp, fish, burger, and chicken plate lunches from $4.75 to $6.25. Dinner is nicely priced between $8.95 and $11.95 for dishes like teriyaki chicken, southern pork chops, barbecued ribs; all dinners are served with Portuguese bean soup or salad, rice pilaf or french fries; plus fresh sautéed vegetables and flavorful molasses rye bread. Some tasty linguine dishes, fresh fish, and burgers, round out the dinner menu. Desserts can be fun, especially macadamia cream or coconut pie. You can pick up a postcard here with the recipe for their famous Portuguese bean soup. Open Monday to Saturday from 7 a.m. to 9 p.m.

Chic's Café, a block from Pono Kai in the center of Kapaa (tel. 822-9816), has a casual and comfortable atmosphere, and reasonably priced breakfasts, lunches, and dinners: delicious pizzas, foot-long submarine sandwiches at $3, charburgers from $2.30, local-style plate lunches, roast chicken, freshly baked goods—and they'll deliver to your Kapaa-Wailua hotel or condo.

Tropical Taco, a cozy little Mexican cantina in the Kapaa Shopping Center (tel. 822-3622), has some of the best Mexican food and lowest prices in Kauai. Terrific tacos, burritos, nachos, and other Mexican standbys range from $2.75 to $5.95. The café part of the operation is open from 11 a.m. to 9:30 p.m. or later, and the cantina (try the margaritas!) from 11 a.m. to closing.

Local friends who live in Kapaa swear that the sandwiches at **Chico's Subs,** in the same Kapaa Shopping Center, are the ultimate—in freshness, quality, taste. Chico's is especially well known for its beach packs and picnic baskets, so if these are in your plans—or if you're just munching in the car as you drive along—stop in. Regular subs at $5.99 are a foot long and stuffed with goodies. Other sandwiches include Cheese & Chilies (grilled wheat bread filled with

Monterey Jack cheese and green chilies) at $3.25; the enormous half-pounder corned beef and pastrami at $5.90; and the Veggie Delite (Swiss and Provolone cheese with mushrooms, onions, tomato, and lettuce) at $4.10. You can phone your order in advance: 822-3898.

There are a few other places fine for quick sandwiches and snacks. At **Kinipopo Pizza and Subs** (tel. 822-9222), the locals will be sitting out on the porch indulging in the likes of "toadstool pizzas" (from $6.85) and hamburgers at $2.55. The tidy little blue-curtained dining room has hoagies, subs, chicken pieces, meatball sandwiches. . . . And you know you can't go wrong at a **Zippy's** anywhere in Hawaii; the new one at 4-919 Kuhio Hwy. in Waipouli, mountain side of the road, is no exception to the rule. Burgers start at $1.55, taco salad is $4.30, Zippy's special chili with rice (ono!) is $2.20 for a large bowl. A variety of plate lunches, like beef teriyaki, breaded veal cutlet, fried chicken, etc., with rice and salad, go from $3.75 to $5.10. Best of all—Zippy's is always open!

So successful has the new **Sizzler Restaurant** on Hwy. 56, opposite Kinipopo Shopping Village become, that it's now far and away one of the most popular budget restaurants in Kauai, with people traveling all the way from the west side of the island just to eat here. At last count, Sizzler was serving up to 1700 people a day! The reasons for its popularity are evident as soon as you come in: the place is spacious and pretty, done in tones of pink and light green, with comfortable booths and tables, overhanging flower baskets, ceiling fans and skylights, and plenty of tables on the large lanai. Unlike some others in the Sizzler family, this is not a self-service operation. Instead, you place your order at the counter and pay for it as soon as you come in, then you sit back at your table while the waiter brings you your food and serves you coffee. The *pièce de resistance* is the fresh fruit and salad bar, really outstanding, with luscious papayas and avocadoes grown a few trees away, delicious pasta and protein salads, breads, rolls, and sweets. You could easily make a complete meal of this alone: it's $4.49 for all-you-can-eat. An all-you-can-eat soup bar is $3.69, and that is not a bad idea either, since the soup selection includes seafood chowder, chili, french onion, Cajun jumbo, and vegetable beef. However, most people do opt for the meat and fish dishes; their steak, as always, is excellent, and only $6.39. Some other examples are: prime ribs platter, $8.19; steak and hibachi chicken, $7.59; New Zealand white fish, poached in white wine, $5.49. On Sunday, they serve fresh fish of the day, which could be mahi, ono, ulus, ahi, yellow fin tuna, among others—truly an outstanding value at $6.47. Breakfast is another bargain bonanza: $2.99 for eggs benedict, $3.75 for omelets, $1.89 for french toast. And there are great drink specialties, too, like mai tais, margaritas, and piña coladas, from $2.50 to $2.75. With prices like this, cooking at home could become obsolete! Sizzler is open from 6 a.m. to 10 p.m. Sunday to Thursday, until midnight Friday and Saturday. No need to make a reservation: just come, with a big appetite. Perfect for families.

At Coconut Plantation

It's hard to decide what's more fun, shopping or eating at the Coconut Plantation Market Place, but there are temptations aplenty in both areas. There's an international assortment of restaurants and snackbars here, and most are in the budget range. . . . See the people at **Don's Deli & Picnic Basket** if you need a picnic lunch. They'll custom-make it for you, with meats, cheeses, breads, fresh fruits, ice-cold drinks, and give you directions to secluded beaches as well. They also have good sandwiches to eat right there. Sandwiches start at under $3; picnic baskets for two are under $12, and packed in unique, local boxes. . . . Jim Jasper, the very one who owns the more expensive J.J.'s Broiler in Lihue, and J.J.'s Broiler Room in the Market Place, both very popular for steak, fish, and salad bars, also runs a quality low-budget operation at **J.J.'s Dog House.** Ground fresh USDA choice chuck hamburgers start at $2.30, all-beef hot dogs are $1.95, and they cut fresh potatoes for natural french fries. Chili sausage dogs and kraut sausage dogs are $2.60. Wine coolers and ice-cold draft beer are at the ready, and there's a pleasant shaded terrace for eating.

Waldo's Fried Chicken has more than just delicious fried chicken (plates start at $2.25); they make beautiful salads of fresh local fruits and garden vegetable salads with a choice of tuna or crab; and they have a daily plate-lunch special for around $3.98. Also good: their hot chicken hoagie and boneless breast-of-chicken sandwiches. They'll make picnic lunches, too. . . . The **Fish Hut** has tasty goodies galore: fish and chip platters at $2.95 and $3.95; a lunch of grilled cheese or tuna with homemade clam chowder at $3.95; and a pupu platter for $3.95. . . . For tacos and burritos, try the "**Outrageous Burrito**"—from $3.45 at **Ramona's Mexican Foods.** . . . Pizza is available by the slice ($1.50) at **Mineo's Gourmet Pizza,** and so are meatball heros ($3.75) and lasagne ($5.95). . . . Tempting Hawaiian ice creams, fresh fruit smoothies, rainbow shave ice, and macadamia-nut waffles for breakfast are the special treats at **Sugar Mill Snacks.** . . . And you can always count on **Farrell's of Kauai** for a snack or a meal or a super hot-fudge or passion-orange sundae. It's open from 8 a.m. until 10 p.m. every day. . . . **Tradewinds, A South Seas Bar,** has all the atmosphere its name suggests, and is especially relaxing during the 4:30 to 6:30 p.m. Happy Hour.

The **Jolly Roger** restaurant (tel. 822-3451), adjacent to the Coconut Plantation Market Place, is always busy, and with good reason. It's part of a family of restaurants in the islands that offer consistently good food and service. There's everything you ever wanted for breakfast, including the heavenly Mac-Waple, a golden-brown waffle smothered with spicy cinnamon apples and macadamia nuts, about $3.25. There are dozens of lunches under $5; we're partial to their fabulous quiche Lorraine, served with fresh spinach salad and fresh fruits; teriyaki or mahimahi luncheons are also good, both with salad, rice or potato, and bread. And for dinner, choose from the complete meals, such as stuffed chicken breast; mahimahi; a delightful scallop, shrimp, and mahi platter; chicken Polynesia, with a fragrant, sweet-and-sour sauce, accompanied by salad, rice or potato, dinner roll, and fresh fruit; and the pañiolo, a char-broiled sirloin steak smothered with fresh sautéed mushrooms, bell peppers, and onions; all are well under $10. *Now* do you see why it's so popular?

In the lounge, you can catch guitarist Jimmy Limo, who plays anything from rock to contemporary, seven days a week. Jolly Roger is open daily, serving breakfast from 6 a.m. to noon, lunch from 11 a.m. to 3 p.m., dinner from 3 to 10 p.m., cocktails till 2 a.m.

You're in no danger of missing the **Kapaa Fish and Chowder House** on Kuhio Hwy., just past the Market Place (tel. 822-7488). It's the only building in the area—and probably on the island—with a boat on its roof. Yes, there it sits, cargo nets hanging down over the roof's edge; the interior decor is nautical as well. This delightful spot and its sister restaurant, Koloa Fish and Chowder House on the other side of the island, attract a lively and fun-loving crowd every night. Dinners are terrific, there's so much to choose from. There are wonderful chowders, of course, New England or Manhattan clam chowder and Kapaa fish chowder, $2.75 to $3.25 for a pot. Most entrees run from about $9.25 to $13.95, but you can stay with the low side of the menu happily by ordering kiawe broiled chicken at $8.25, Ipswich clams at $8.95, or the luscious Kapaa Fish House Casserole (fresh fish, mushrooms, cheddar), $9.95. Along with your entree, choose fries, pasta, steamed rice, or coleslaw and sourdough bread and butter. Lunch features the same chowders, as well as fish and chips, clams and chips, salads, sandwiches, fish burgers, and more, from about $5 to $8. For dessert at either meal, you can indulge yourself in cheesecake—chocolate espresso, or lilikoi—perhaps topped with raspberry sauce. Sublime! Open from 11:30 a.m. to 3 p.m. for lunch, from 5:30 to 10 p.m. for dinner every day.

As you buzz along Kuhio Hwy. now, going north, you'll soon find yourself in Anahola. Look for the U.S. Post Office on the ocean side of the road, and you'll spot **Duane's Ono Burgers,** a shrine to the humble hamburger for many years. Friends of ours swear by their avocado burgers and their great french fries. Try the fish burger at $3.25; you can get it on grilled bread, with lots of sprouts, tomatoes, and onions. Terrific.

RESTAURANTS ON THE WESTERN AND SOUTHERN ROUTE: You
should have no problem dining on your trip around the southern and western end of the island, for there are several excellent choices. Not all, however, are in the budget category.

Old Koloa Town
If you don't like the way your food is done at the **Koloa Broiler** (tel. 742-9122), on Koloa Road in Old Koloa Town, a few miles from Poipu Beach, you have no one but yourself to blame. This cute little place is one of those broil-it-yourself affairs—and that way, they really manage to keep the prices down. You can choose from top sirloin, marinated beef kebab, mahaimahi, barbecue chicken, beef burger, from $7.95 to $8.95 (fresh fish is sometimes available at market price); and with your entree comes salad bar, baked beans, and rice. Lunch offers the same choices, but the burger is $3.50. The only dessert on the menu is macadamia-nut ice cream, so you may want to skip the dessert on here and walk over to the Koloa Ice House (see below) for mud pie. Koloa Broiler is a lively, fun kind of place, simply decorated (try to get a seat out on the lanai), with a jolly bar, a neat list of exotic drinks, and lots of local people enjoying their meals. You will too. Koloa Broiler is open from 11 a.m. to 10 p.m. every day.

The **Koloa Ice House** (tel. 742-6063), two blocks away from Koloa Broiler and across the street from the U.S. Post Office, is housed in a green wooden historic building and has just a few tables and booths inside, but it's also fun to sit at any of the eight tables in the garden lanai. You can get a good variety of deli and veggie sandwiches here, as well as a mahimahi sandwich, quiches, nachos, bagels and cream cheese, burritos, homemade soup, veggie burgers, and the like (most items run between $4 and $5). On our last visit we tried the mahimahi burger and the tofu veggie burger on an onion roll, each $4.33 and real fillers, stuffed with heaps of lettuce, sprouts, tomatoes, and onions, with a pickle on the side. They're famous for their mud pie—a cookie-crust ice-cream pie at $3.75—and a number of other sweet treats. Everything here is available for take-out.

The **Koloa Fish and Chowder House** (tel. 742-7377) in the same block, has a virtually identical menu to that of its sister restaurant, Kapaa Fish and Chowder House, described above. No, there's no boat on this one, but it is handsomely decorated in nautical fashion with ship's lanterns, captain's tables and chairs, and an antique oak bar. Another highly enjoyable scene. Open from 11:30 a.m. to 2:30 p.m. for lunch, from 5:30 to 10 p.m. for dinner every day.

If you like a deep-dish pizza, you'll be well pleased with the tasty pies at **Fez's Pizza** in Old Koloa Town. Call ahead (tel. 742-9096) and they'll have your choice ready to take out. Or you can eat at the little garden lanai. Medium pizzas are $7 with one topping, $8 with two, $9 with three; you can also have pizza bread (made on a French roll) for $3.90, a delicious meatball, pastrami and cheese, or vegetarian sandwich for $4.50, plus pastas, from $5.50 to $6.25. Choose from 20 varieties of beer, wine, or soda, to go with your meal. The menu is the same at lunch and dinner.

Taquería Norteños, next to the Kukuiula Store in Koloa, is a tiny take-out taco bar that packs a mighty wallop. Owner Ed Sills, former chef at the prestigious Plantation Garden Restaurant, and his wife, Morgan, decided to do their own thing: turn out excellent food, but keep the prices low. When you want some good Mexican munchies for a picnic at the beach or a meal on the run, come and see them. Tacos are $1.35 and $2; burritos, $1.85 to $2.85; tostados, $1.65 to $2.35, chips and salsa, 95¢, nachos, $1.65.

Poipu, Kalaheo, and Hanapepe

Poipu's famed **Beach House Restaurant** was destroyed by Hurricane Iwa in November of 1982, but we're happy to report that a new and beautiful Beach House is firmly established on Sprouting Horn Road (tel. 742-7575), and, if anything, it's even better than before. Nestled right on the sand, it's still an idyllic spot, perhaps the best around for viewing the sunset, the surfers, maybe an occasional whale or two in winter, or just waves crashing on the beach beneath the stars. Decorated in elegant, understated modern lines, adorned with many flowers, the restaurant has more than doubled in size, so now there are 22 of those fabulous window tables. Wherever you sit, though, you'll enjoy gracious service and excellent food. You can splurge or not, here, as your choose. If you order one of the lower-priced entrees, like teriyaki chicken, sirloin kebab, sautéed boneless breast of chicken, or the eight-ounce cut of USDA prime rib, you can dine for under $15, and that price includes fresh green salad; a choice of baked potato, rice, or shoestring fries; and the special Beach House Bread and Butter Crock. The night we were there, it sheltered wonderful homemade macadamia-nut/pumpkin muffins (apple/macadamia-nut muffins are another favorite). If you want to spend a bit more, however, you can have the Beach House's succulent crabs' legs at a "pre-hurricane" price of $19.95, a variety of seafoods that go up to about $24, superbly prepared fresh fish (market price), or steaks that run about $12.50 to $15. The pupus are so good that we recommend you try the Malihini Pupu Platter ($7.50), so two of you can sample sashimi, manapua, deep-fried snorkler sea rolls, and more. Ice-cream desserts are outrageous, especially the Bunga-Bunga Snowball (vanilla ice cream rolled in fresh coconut, topped by strawberries and meringue), or any of the blended ice-cream and liqueur drinks. There's a good list of French and California wines, and several pleasing house wines at $2 the glass. In short, a place to relax, celebrate, throw cares and calories to the winds. The Beach House serves dinner only, from 5:30 to 10 p.m. (bar open from 4:30 p.m.). Reservations are requested to assure the best tables.

Although **Brennecke's Beach Broiler** on the second (and top) floor of the new little building across from Poipu Beach Park (tel. 742-7588) is the new kid on the block, it has quickly become one of the most popular places in the Poipu area. Decorated with window boxes blooming with bright flowers and the names of island fish spelled out in big white letters on the wall above the kitchen, this is a most attractive place—and it attracts a happy, fun crowd every evening. A variety of original tropical drinks with unlikely names (such as Big Nickel Bill, Brown Nipple, Pink Hawaiian) might get the meal off to a good start. The menu, all à la carte, offers plenty of possibilities, so choose anything from a sandwich to a full dinner. Beach burger, teriyaki steak, and french dip au jus sandwiches are ensconced in Sandwich Baskets, along with nachos, $5.75 to

$7.95, and are served with pasta or green pea salad, or chilled gazpacho. On the low side of the menu, chicken (teriyaki or with garlic baste) is $9.95; imported durum wheat pasta, cooked al dente with butter and vegetables in the lightest of cream sauces, is $7.95; the same pasta with fresh clams is $10.25. And fresh fish, kiawe broiled and served with pasta primavera, is $13.95. You can order salad cart, chowder, and garlic bread for an extra price. Several keiki dinners go from $4.25 to $7.25. Brennecke's is open from 1 p.m. until 1 a.m. every day, with full dinners beginning at 5 p.m.

We think you'll agree that **Keoki's Paradise,** at the entrance to the Kiahuna Shopping Village on Poipu Road (tel. 742-7534), is aptly named. Open and airy, it overlooks a gem-like little lagoon dotted with water hyacinths. Soda fountain chairs at the bar, are painted cheerful reds; the bar, with its own roof, looks like a little Polynesian house. The bar and the seafood and taco bar open at 4:30 p.m. and closes at midnight; dinner is served nightly from 5:30 to 10 p.m. All dinners are accompanied by tossed green salad with house dressing, a basket of freshly baked muffins and French rolls, and steamed herb rice. Staying within the lower reaches of the menu, we can recommend the Kushiyaki, a brochette of marinated chunks of chicken breast and sirloin, $9.95; and that island favorite, huli-huli chicken, $7.95. Seafood selections and prime ribs are higher. It's fun to start with the Fisherman's Chowder (ono!) at $1.95, and sample the side dish of Maui onions and mushrooms, $3.50. Come early—between 5:30 and 6:15 p.m.—and you can enjoy some good Sunset Specials at $7.50; entrees like petite New York steak, huli-huli chicken, small sirloin, mahimahi, and ginger chicken brochette are served with salad, rice, and bread. Keoki's Paradise claims that its Hula Pie is "what the sailors swam to shore for." The idyllic setting and the friendly ambience here are sure to make you want to linger . . . and linger. Keoki's Paradise, by the way, is run by the same talented management which runs some terrific restaurants on Maui: Kimo's Leilani's, Kapalua Grill & Bar, and Chico's.

Pizza Bella in the Kiahuna Shopping Village is much more than your average "pizza parlor." It has an attractive layout—black-and-white tile floors, white wicker chairs, greenery, ceiling fans, even a few outside tables. Here you can dine on eight-inch, California-style gourmet pizzas—topped with homemade sauce and four cheeses; or with barbecued chicken, cilantro, and smoked Gouda cheese; or perhaps with a melange of seafood, red onions, pesto, and sundried tomatoes—from $7.95 to $8.50. Less nouvelle tastes might go for the old-fashioned pies, $1.95 a slice, $8 for a medium, twelve-inch pizza. Then you have regular lasagne and veggie lasagne, $5.50 each; pasta marinara with or without meatballs, $3.75 and $5.50; and a variety of hot and cold sandwiches. There's wine, beer, and a nice atmosphere. Since Pizza Bella is open every day, from 11:30 a.m. to 10 p.m., keep it in mind for lunch or a light dinner if you're staying in the neighborhood. They deliver in the Poipu area: tel. 742-9571.

About 40 years ago, Gwen Hamabata's parents and her grandmother started a simple little restaurant in Hanapepe and called it the **Green Garden** (tel. 335-5422). It's doubled and redoubled its size many times over in those years, and today it's one of the most charming local spots around, with the kind of flavor and tradition that can only come from a family business where everybody cares. Gwen and her mother, Sue, are the "working bosses," who make sure that all the guests, whether they be the faithful locals or the scores of visitors (we get letters every year praising this place), enjoy their modestly priced and delicious Oriental, American, and Hawaiian food. (As for the locals, we were told that in the aftermath of Hurrican Iwa in 1982, when much of the island had no electricity, Green Garden, which had its own generator, fed everyone in the neighborhood nonstop—and refused to accept payment!) You'll feel as if you're sitting in the middle of a greenhouse, with orchids on the tables, plants surrounding you everywhere, an entire screened wall facing a garden, bamboo chairs, and white walls. For a real treat, do as the locals do: have a family-style Oriental meal. Just tell them what you like and what you want to spend, and they'll create a meal for you. We did this recently and were treated to an incredible banquet; highlights were the luscious barbecued chicken, shrimp wontons, vegetable-stuffed eggrolls, tempura aki, shrimp omelets, and scallops with noodles. Reserve this meal at least half an hour in advance.

More simply, you can dine on a complete hot lunch for $5.95 and under (beef cutlet, roast beef Korean style, boneless barbecued chicken), or a complete dinner for $5.25 and up, choosing from such entrees as sweet-and-sour spare ribs, breaded filet of mahimahi, or shrimp tempura. Fresh fish goes for $6.85 and up. Broiler specialties are also reasonable, like filet mignon at $10.75 and the East-West Special (char-broiled petite teriyaki steak and shrimp tempura) at $6.95. With your main dish comes soup or fruit cup, a crispy green salad with a good dressing, hot dinner rolls, rice or potatoes, plus tea or coffee. And whatever you do, be sure to save room for Sue's homemade pies, $1.35. We'll vote for the macadamia nut and lilikoi, but then again, the chocolate-cream pie is divine too! Open from 7 a.m. to 2 p.m. and from 5 to 8:30 p.m.

Note: If a tour bus happens to disgorge its hungry passengers here, things can get a bit hectic. Better to come on the late side of the lunch hour, or, even better, at night, when you can enjoy the peace.

Brick Oven Pizza, on the main road in Kalaheo, is a nice cozy little place with red-and-white gingham tablecloths: it stays open until 11 p.m., so you can stop here just about anytime hunger pangs strike as you're driving this road. Pizzas start at $5.75 for a 10-inch plain cheese pie, and go all the way up to $17.95 for a 15-inch pizza-with-almost-everything combo. In addition to pizza, there's a vegetarian sandwich with cheese, mushrooms, olives, squash, etc., for $3.75, and a Hot Super Sandwich with Canadian bacon, salami, and a variety of cheeses and vegetables, for $4.10. A spicy Portuguese smoked sausage sandwich is $4.25. Green salads are available, and so are wine and beer. Open 11 a.m. to 11 p.m., every day except Monday.

In Princeville and Hanalei

Chuck's Steak House (tel. 826-6211) is rightfully one of the most popular places at the Princeville Shopping Center. An attractive porch, plants, ceiling fans, dark walls, secluded booths, paintings, and antiques everywhere set a cozy scene. Lunch is fun here, especially when you have a hearty sandwich like shrimp, crab, bacon, and melted cheese, with fries ($8.25); or a mahimahi sandwich ($4.75); or barbecued beef ribs ($4.75 small, $5.95 large), or one of Chuck's one-third pound burgers, $4.95. There's a salad bar, too, $4.95. Dinner features steaks and prime rib from about $12.50 to $17.95, seafood, and fresh fish specials, from $14.95 to $18.95. All meals include salad bar, hot bread and butter, and steamed rice or pilaf; the salad bar is available on its own for $7.25. For dessert, hesitate not: the mud pie is divine. Chuck's is also known for great tropical drinks and fine wines. Chuck's serves lunch from 11:30 a.m. to 2:30 p.m. weekdays only, dinner every day from 6 to 10 p.m. Cocktails are served on weekdays from 11:30 a.m. to 11:30 p.m., on weekends beginning at 5 p.m.

The best time to come to **The Flats,** a grill and bar at Princeville Shopping Center (tel. 826-7255) is on a Tuesday or Saturday night; that's when they have an all-you-can-eat barbecue-ribs feed for just $11.95. Another good time is Thursday and Sunday night when they present a hula show by a local Hawaiian family—and the waiters dance, too. Stucco walls, tile floors, ceiling fans, and a lively cantina lined with *ojos de dios* on the walls create a south-of-the-border mood, but the menu is only partially Mexican: potato nachos, cheese quesadillas, chimichangas, Mexi-skins (fried potatoes), and the like are available for lunch ($5.95) and as pupus all day. Lunch also offers burgers and a daily special. Dinner features a combination of broiler, seafood, and Cajun dishes, from $10.95 to $16.95—teriyaki chicken, steak and scampi, blackened fish, chicken creole, New Orleans–style shrimp are all served with soups or salad, steamed rice or potatoes, vegetables, and rolls. Lunch is served daily from 11 a.m. to 5 p.m., dinner from 5:30 to 9:30 p.m., and the bar is open a long, long time: from 11 a.m. to 2 a.m. every day.

Natural foods restaurants come and go with some rapidity in Kauai; let's hope the newest one, **The Oasis** (tel. 826-1449), at Princeville Shopping Center, will stay. This is a small place (next to the Bank of Hawaii), very casually put together, with booths and a few wooden tables. Out of a hole-in-the-wall kitchen in back, owner Mikel Jay turns out some very tasty dishes, using only fresh and natural ingredients. The menu varies with the day, but most lunch dishes are under $5, and could include the Yowza Burger (a garbanzo patty), barbecued tempeh on a garlic and pepper sub, teriyaki tofu, stuffed cabbage, a spinach-and-carrot casserole with cheddar-cheese dressing, lasagne, and tofu enchiladas. Mikel seems to be known in these parts for his hot and spicy vegetarian chili that he serves with corn bread; "he's never lost a chili contest," claim his friends. All of the bread and rolls, including cinnamon rolls with raisins, are home-baked and delicious. Plan on spending about $10 for a complete dinner, which will include soup or salad, homemade dinner rolls, and the entree. The Oasis serves lunch from 11 a.m. to 3 p.m., dinner from 5 to 9 p.m., Monday to Saturday. Closed Sunday.

The Hanalei area has been woefully short of budget eating places, but the opening of the **Ching Young Village Shopping Center** helped a bit. Now we have a decent Chinese restaurant and several snack shops to choose from. **Foong Wong** is a large, simple restaurant, rather sparsely decorated, but with good, if somewhat bland, Cantonese food: plate lunches run $3.85 to $6, and dishes like char siu, beef with oyster sauce, and chicken with black bean sauce are all under $5. . . .

Papagayo Azul in the old Ching Young building is a little Mexican eatery at which you order at the service window and take your food somewhere to feast upon. Tacos are $2.25; burritos, $3.75; burrito Papagayo (with everything!), $4.75. They even have char-broiled chicken, $4.50 for a half. . . . The **Village Snack and Bakery Shop** has plate lunches like fried chicken and teriyaki beef for $4.25, and is also a popular spot for breakfast, which runs from $1.95 to $3.50. The best treats here are the home-baked pies: guava, lilikoi, chiffon, lemon-cream cheese, at $1.25 a slice. Tofutti too. . . . You can get your pizzas on a homemade whole wheat crust with sesame seeds at **Pizza Pizza**, which really works at making a good pie; they use fresh vegetable toppings and herbs picked from their own garden. It's $1 for a small slice, $6.95 for a small pie, or try their unusual pizzaritto: that's cheese, vegetables, meats, and spices rolled up into a pizza shell and eaten like a burrito, $3.75. Delivery in the area: tel. 826-9494.

The **Hanalei Shell House,** on the main street in Hanalei, is a small restaurant that's long been popular with the locals. It's been in the same family for years, and now the younger generation—Steve and Linda—have taken over and spruced it up so that it looks quite good, with wooden tables, ceiling fans, plenty of greens. The bar up front is always lively. They serve breakfast from 8 to 11 a.m., with several specials, like $2.95 for three eggs, hash browns, toast or muffin. Lunch features half-pound burgers, from $4.50 to $5.95, omelets and quesadillas, from $5 to $6.95. The dinner menu always includes fresh, locally caught fish, sautéed or broiled, market-priced; blackened fish Cajun style was $16.95. Exotic tropical cocktails are available all day, seven days a week, from 8 a.m. till midnight. Dinner is served until 11 p.m., later than any other place in the area.

Hanalei also has a couple of food stands that are fine for quick snacking. You'll usually find Roger Kennedy and his **Tropical Taco** on the main highway in front of the Dolphin Restaurant, where he dishes up gourmet-quality, all-organic burritos, tacos, and the like, all including beans, meat, lettuce, salsa, cheese, and sour cream (vegetarian combos too), a complete lunch for around $3 to $5. So successful has this operation been in the past nine years that Roger's partner, Mike Williams, now runs another Tropical Taco in the Kapaa Shopping Center, on the other side of the island (see above). Take your food over to the shady riverbank just a few steps away and enjoy your "picnic."

The most scenic restaurant in the area? Could well be **Café Hanalei** at the luxurious Princeville Sheraton Hotel, the very model of what a seaside hotel should look like. Café Hanalei has ceilings done in quilt motifs, tile floors, cane chairs, waterfalls flowing down volcanic rocks, a sun-drenched balcony, and glorious views of Hanalei Bay below. Try this for the view and ambience, but only if you don't mind paying a rather high price: at lunch, Greek salad is $7.75, burgers are $8.50, and main courses, $12.50 to $14!

At Kokee

If you're going to go up to Waimea Canyon—and, of course, you should, it's nice to know that you can now tie your visit in with a meal at Kokee Lodge (tel. 335-6061) in Kokee State Park, which has spruced up its dining room and greatly expanded its hours, so that it now serves breakfast and lunch daily, dinner Friday and Saturday nights. This is a simple, rustic dining room with views of mountain and meadow, quite pleasant, where you can get fresh fruit and the usual egg and meat dishes at breakfast, served from 8:30 to 11:30 a.m. Lunch, 11:30 a.m. to 3:30 p.m., is the time for green salad, a fruit bowl, burgers ($3.95 to $4.50), Portuguese bean soup, the local "soul food" ($3.25), or a daily modestly priced special. Dinner is served weekends from 6 to 9 p.m., so after you've watched the sun go down over the canyon, you can relax with a drink and order such dishes as boneless Cornish game hen, kal-bi ribs, teriyaki steak, filet of mahimahi, or vegetarian fettucine, from $8.95 to $9.25. Any time of the day you can enjoy their homemade hot cornbread, quite delicious, served with Kauai honey, $1.50. We love their desserts such as: lilikoi-chiffon and chocolate-buttercream pie, plus whatever special they've baked that day. They serve Lion Coffee (the best), herb as well as regular tea, and cocktails, beer, and wine, too.

Undoubtedly, you'll see the magnificent moa (chickens) of Kokee on the grounds of the lodge. These are jungle fowl, descendants of birds carried to Hawaii centuries ago by the Polynesians in their outrigger canoes. The brightly plumed chickens, protected by the state, survive only here, in the mountains of Kauai; those on the other islands were destroyed by mongoose, which, somehow, never got to Kauai.

3. The Night Scene

IN AND AROUND LIHUE: The center of nighttime activity in Lihue has always been the Kauai Surf Hotel, which, by the time you read this, will have been transformed into the grand and glorious new **Westin Kauai.** Undoubtedly, it will have a full complement of night spots, including a disco. Down the road a bit from town, in the industrial area at Nawiliwili Harbor, is the **Club Jetty,** on the wharf, where things start to jump about 10 p.m. It's live-band entertainment and disco sounds Tuesday through Saturday with D.J. Aunt Betty and bands imported from Honolulu and the mainland. Beer is $2 to $2.50; mixed drinks, $2.50 and up. There's a cover charge every night except Tuesday and Wednesday.

At the Kauai Hilton at Hanamaulu, the disco action takes place at **Gilligan's,** where the goings-on get going around 7 p.m. and things stay busy until 2 a.m. weekdays, 4 a.m. weekends. Gilligan's also offers Monday-night football and a variety of theme evenings.

The best cantina in town is **Rosita's** at Kukui Grove Center, a popular bar and lounge, where you can admire the artwork, listen to local entertainers, and sip Rosita's "world-famous margaritas." You can have them by the pitcherful for $7.50, or by the glass at $3.50 (fruit margaritas are $3.75). Come by during the 4:30 to 6:30 p.m. Happy Hour when there are specials, plus music on Wednesday, Thursday, and Friday. Entertainment on Thursday and Friday nights. The bar is open daily from 11 a.m. to 11 or 12 at night.

Park Place at Harbor Village is the newest disco in town, boasting a huge dance floor, live entertainment, a pulsing sound system, and video, too. The doors open at 8 p.m. and seldom close until 4 a.m. Closed only on Monday.

Watch the papers for news of free shows put on at the **Kukui Grove Center.** They often take place on Friday nights or Saturday mornings, right on the mall. These shows by local entertainers are sometimes every bit as good as those at the high-priced clubs.

EAST KAUAI: You must see the **Coco Palms Hotel** at night. Five miles out of town on Wailua Bay, it's on the site of an ancient coconut grove and lagoon, where Hawaiian royalty once lived. Flaming torches cast eerie shadows on the water, there's much blowing of conch shells and other ritualistic goings-on, with an effect that reassures the visiting movie stars here that they've never left the set. Come around sunset time for a drink at the gorgeous cocktail lounge overlooking a natural lagoon (drinks at the Lagoon Terrace start around $3.50) to catch the impressive and very moving torch-lighting ceremony—a Kauai must.

Come back to Coco Palms around 9 p.m. and you may be able to see their excellent dinner show—free! Of course, if you have dinner here (complete meals from around $15), the show is included. But many people stand at the open sides of the dining room to catch glimpses of the show, and once, friendly hotel people even brought us chairs! Leading island song or dance groups perform every night.

The best **luaus** in Kauai are held at two hotels in this area: daily except Monday at the **Sheraton Coconut Beach Hotel** ($36 for adults, $22 for children 12 and under); and on Tuesday, Wednesday, Thursday, Friday, and Sunday at the **Kauai Resort Hotel** ($34 for adults, $21 for 8-to 11-year olds, $14 for 3-to 7-year-olds). Reservations are suggested: phone 822-3455 at the Sheraton, 245-3931 at the Kauai Resort; both provide free shuttle service from many hotels and condos in the Lihue and Wailua areas.

Only on Sunday, the **Kauai Hilton & Beach Villas** present a new and entertaining show called "Flames of Fantasy," which recounts the history of Hawaii from ancient times to today, with mythical menehune characters—which the kids will love taking part in. Unless you want to spend $36 for adults, $26 for children for the 6:30 p.m. dinner show, come at 7:45 p.m. for the cocktail show:

it's $18 for adults (including one mai tai), $13 for kids 3 to 12 years old. Reservations: tel. 245-8691.

Probably the longest Happy Hour—let's call it a "Happy Day"—takes place at the **Jolly Roger.** From 6:30 a.m. to 7 p.m. every day, standard drinks are available at special prices. Dancing begins around 9:30 p.m. when guitarist Jimmy Limo and his one-man band take the stand with everything from rock 'n' roll to country western.

AT POIPU BEACH: This side of the island is a bit quieter after the sun sets. Undoubtedly the liveliest place is the **Poipu Beach Hotel,** where there's usually a variety band playing for dancing on Friday and Saturday nights; various groups entertain the rest of the week. Drinks are moderately priced at the big Mahina Lounge. . . . It's lovely to walk down to the beach here at night and along the waterfront to the neighboring **Waiohai Hotel.** Its Terrace Restaurant is right out on the beach, overlooking the breaking surf. You can have a drink at the Terrace Bar, or just catch the sounds of dinner music, enjoy the view, and perhaps decide to come back here for a meal the next night (their salad bar is expensive, but one of the best around, and their Sunday champagne brunch is renowned far and wide). . . . Our favorite spot at the Sheraton Kauai is the **Poipo Winery,** a wine bar featuring wines by the glass, bordered by a lagoon filled with exotic Japanese koi fish. There's dancing and entertainment nightly at the **Drum Lounge,** overlooking the ocean. And if you're in Kauai on a Sunday, you'll enjoy Chief Taeza and his Polynesian Revue, along with a buffet feast, starting at 6 p.m. (phone 742-1661 for reservations). . . . The setting for drinks is pure tropical magic at **Plantation Gardens Restaurant,** once the gracious home of a plantation manager.

THE PRINCEVILLE-HANALEI AREA: Tahiti Nui, on Hwy. 56, just before Aku Road and a stone's throw from Hanalei Shell House, has been the place for local color for many years. Sometimes it's incredibly busy, other times rather quiet, but always with a group of locals, and, it seems, many gays, hanging out at the bar. The place has been done up with pareau fabric, Tahitian woodcarvings on the walls, bamboo, and a thatched ceiling. The atmosphere is super-friendly. Jackie Onassis liked it so well that she came here two nights in a row and stayed until closing. The entertainment is impromptu; local entertainers often come in and sing, and owner Louise Marston, a bubbly Tahitian, can usually be persuaded to sing and do the hula. All this, and reasonable prices for drinks too. Beer starts at $1.75. Louise serves dinner too, with a limited menu ($9.95 to $12.95) including items like chicken curry with fresh papaya or pineapple, smoked ribs, or catch of the day, served with rice, bread, and salad. Lunch, served from 11 a.m. to 2:30 p.m., offers dishes like poisson cru (Tahitian raw fish), fish salad, ribs, hamburgers, and fish sandwiches, from $3 up to about $11 for fish of the day. There's a delightful luau Monday, Wednesday, and Friday nights, for around $20. Reservations are a must (tel. 826-6277). This show is so popular that people even call from the mainland for reservations!

Fortune is fickle. We're told that the really "in" crowd in Kauai now hangs out at **Charo's,** a beautiful restaurant and bar on the beach near the Colony Resort in Haena. Haena is about a 15-minute drive from Hanalei, along many winding roads and narrow, one-vehicle-only bridges, so we suggest a "designated driver" if you're going out here to eat, drink, and make merry.

The glamorous new Sheraton Princeville Hotel has a wonderful night spot called the **Ukiyo Bar,** as in the Japanese woodblock prints. Prints adorn the walls, booths are separated by etched glass, and there's live music and/or disco until 2 a.m.

READERS' SELECTIONS ON KAUAI: "We returned with pleasure to the **Green Garden Restaurant** after a visit to Waimea Canyon and had a rewarding experience. I went ahead to get a table while my husband parked, and in so doing he locked our one car key inside. The hostess heard of the problem from me, and while he was trying unsuccessfully to reach AAA, she urged me to get him to 'enjoy his lunch, and one of our boys will open it for you.' And so he did, in about two minutes. Obviously, Green Garden will remain a favorite, and the lilikoi pie is as delicious as ever" [*Authors' Note:* We had exactly the same experience once at Green Garden; these people seem unphased by any problem.] . . . "Whenever I'm in Hawaii, I like to eat as many 'pineapple boats' as possible, but find it increasingly hard to do so. However, I discovered that both **Farrell's** at Coconut Plantation and **Woolworth's** at Kukui Grove Center have excellent ones for under $5. . . . We stayed two weeks at the **Kauai Sands** in a very large room with a quite modest, but certainly adequate kitchenette. With the rental car included, we considered it a very good buy and will undoubtedly return. The room had recently been refurnished; the grounds are well kept; and the personnel helpful and friendly" (Elizabeth Greer, El Cerrito, Calif.).

"We saw the **Polynesian shows** at the Kauai Hilton and at Coco Palms. We paid $18 at the Hilton, but there was no charge at Coco Palms: just the cost of one drink. We thought that was a good bargain, since both shows were similar. . . . The **Islander on the Beach Hotel** on the grounds of Coconut Plantation was delightful, although the rates are not quite budget. There are no phones in the rooms, no elevators in the three-story building, no bar or restaurant, but the Jolly Roger Restaurant is next door, and their prices are moderate, they have a nice atmosphere, and the waitresses are friendly" (Mrs. Marilyn Wade, Bainbridge Island, Wash.). . . . "Your best dinner bargain in the vicinity of Coconut Plantation is **Al & Don's Oceanfront Restaurant** in the Kauai Sands Hotel. The ambience is Polynesian and guests receive personalized service. The menu features a surprisingly extensive variety of dishes for a budget hotel: ham steak Hawaiian, chicken Oriental, mahimahi scampi, beef Hawaiian, leg of New Zealand lamb, gulf shrimp, sirloin, or calamari steak, from $5.85 to $8. And, the price of each entree includes soup or tossed salad, bread, french fries, whipped potatoes or rice; and dessert" (Connie Tonken, Hartford, Conn.). . . . "All the main restaurants in Hanalei are overpriced, so we ate at a sort of diner called **The Black Pot Luau Hut.** Large portions of delicious food, either Chinese or American, are served. The teri-bacon burger was wonderful. Still a bit steep, but prices were better than at other Hanalei eateries. A lot of locals come here" (Maggie L. Berry, Hayes, Va.).

"We spent eight weeks on Kauai. The two of us together spent about $64 a day on accommodations, meals, car rental, inter-island air fare, sightseeing, entertainment, etc.—in short, everything except the bus and air fares from here to Honolulu and return. . . . **Rent-a-Jeep** in Lihue also has some older cars, '82 Datsuns, for example, with a monthly rate of $11 per day including insurance. Some rust, dents, torn upholstery, and missing parts, but they run reasonably well and no one would suspect you of being a visitor, so there would be little likelihood of a break-in. We rented for two months. . . . **Lawai Restaurant,** about ten miles west of Lihue on Hwy. 50, next to the Lawai Post Office, is popular with local families. Hawaiian, Chinese, Japanese, and Korean plates are $3 or $4. . . . The **Rib 'n' Tail** Restaurant in the Kapaa Shopping Center has live music and dancing nightly, until 1:30 a.m. on Friday and Saturday. No cover, drinks from $2. It attracts a generally older crowd of locals and visitors, unlike most of the other dance places. . . . **Star Market,** in the Kukui Grove Shopping Center, Lihue, carries a great variety of fresh and frozen and precooked meats and fish, including octopus and lau lau—pork and fish wrapped in taro and ti leaves and steamed. . . . Buy a small Styrofoam cooler for about $3.29 at **Long's Drugs** to keep your picnic lunch and beverages cool on the hot beach. . . . The Seventh Day Adventist Church, which runs Kahili Mountain Park, also has a summer camp in **Kokee State Park,** consisting of several cabins, one of which has a kitchenette. We rented it for $7 double for six days while we hiked the many trails in the park and in Waimea Canyon" (Jack and Ruth Phillips, Summerland, B.C., Canada). [*Authors' Note:* See text for details on Kahili Mountain Park.] . . . "We stayed at Kokee State Park for several nights. Having camped there in October 1980 in a pick-up camper, we were surprised to find January was more than nippy—and downright cold at night. Fortunately, we had opted for a cabin this trip, and the fireplace was really essential in the evenings. This was a minor complaint on an otherwise great stay—we even got used to those roosters" (John and Eleanor Vick, Longmont, Calif.).

"We found the international buffets at the **Kauai Beach Boy Hotel** the runaway winners at dinner time. We went to three of them, namely, the Mexican, Japanese, and Western, and they were all excellent" (Dr. K.C. Lee, Alberta, Edmonton, Canada). . . . "We were fortunate enough to find an apartment at the **Prince Kuhio** for three nights with Den and Dee Wilson, a most accommodating and charming couple. Our apartment was a dream spot and made it most difficult to leave when we moved on to Oahu. We cannot recommend the Prince Kuhio and the Wilsons highly enough!" (Helen Dyan, Elmwood, Conn.). [*Authors' Note:* Our sentiments exactly.]

"After yearly trips to Hawaii checking out your tips and those of your readers, we have discovered a real jewel to pass on to others. The **Koloa Landing Cottages** in Poipu turned out to be the most pleasant place we've ever stayed in the islands. They are well decorated, sparkling clean, and roomy. The Zeevats—Hans and Sylvia—made sure we saw some unusual sights. They even led us in their truck. Sylvia shared all the fruits grown on their grounds (bananas, limes, lemons, mangoes, etc.). Tell your readers not to miss an experience far removed from the big hotel scene, but close enough to check it out" (Gretchen and Ron Cowan, Huntington Beach, Calif.). . . . "I stayed at the Koloa Landing Cottages and had a great experience. The husband-and-wife owners are extremely helpful and friendly. Hans gave me an informative guided tour of Koloa and Poipu Beach, including a snorkeling lesson. This kind of human touch is something lacking in the mass tourism scene that is Hawaii, despite the great friendliness of most individual Hawaiians" (J. Dennis Harcketts, Falls Church, Va.). [*Authors' Note:* See the text for details.]

"For anyone heading to Kauai after the initial shock of Waikiki, we highly recommend staying in the **Kapaa** area, rather than Lihue-Poipu Beach or Princeville-Hanalei. While Kapaa lacks magnificent beaches, there is good swimming and secluded beaches are accessible down cane-haul roads. Kapaa's location allows easy driving to all Kauai's major attractions, and while there is only one large tourist complex in the area (Coconut Plantation), small shopping plazas dot Rte. 56. A number of moderately priced restaurants with excellent food are right in town or nearby—Ono Family, Kintaro's, and Kountry Kitchen, just to name a few. But Kapaa's greatest asset is its people, whose open friendliness is a much better reflection of Hawaii than the glitter of Honolulu" (Robbie and Alan Kolman, Rensselaerville, N.Y.).

"The **Ahana Motel Apartments** on Akahi Street in Lihue were very basic, but the charm of its proprietors and its location make it luxurious. Our kitchenette apartment came with a large closet, full bath, TV, kitchen with many, many dishes and utensils, and a view of the flowers and banana trees. The manager is quite charming. She spent some time telling me about Japan and what it was like to be Japanese on Hawaii during World War II. The apartments are close to two shopping centers, which have many fine, varied, and reasonable shops, and several nice eateries are close by" (Nancy Goertz, Sandia Park, N. Mex.).

"We stayed at **Polihale State Park** and **Kokee State Park.** One needs permits to camp at any state park. On Kauai, the permits are issued at the State Building in Lihue, or one can write to Division of State Parks, P.O. Box 1671, Lihue, HI 96761. Rangers checked our permits. To stay at **County Campgrounds**, go to the County Building in Lihue. If it is after 5 p.m., one goes to the police station. The county permits are $3 per person per night; the state permits are free, but the office is closed by 3:30 p.m. As for restaurants, I recommend **Denmar's Pancakes** in Lihue (good, cheap breakfasts) and **Tahiti Nui** in Hanalei" (Rebecca Kurtz, Anchorage, Alaska). . . . "Few car-rental agencies are willing to rent to **campers.** Vandalism is scaring the companies off. When applying for a permit, campers should ask how many others are currently camping at each spot, and which have indicated plans to remain there for a bit. There is safety in numbers: don't camp alone" (Frank and Joyce Terwilliger, Swarthmore, Pa.).

"At the **Tip Top Bakery**—which we agree is marvelous!—try 'pipi kaula' with your eggs or pancakes. It is Hawaiian smoked beef, sort of halfway between beef jerky and smoked ham and very lean. . . . You can eat Hawaiian food by going to the local markets, which are generally considerably cheaper than markets in the tourist areas, especially on Kauai. You can get take-out lau lau, lomi-lomi salmon, and of course, poi. Many exotic

Japanese delicacies are readily available, plus more standard things like saimin noodles plus dishes that are very cheap" (Ernest Callenbach, Berkeley, Calif.). . . . "We were delighted with the courteous, efficient service and fine facilities at the **Poipu Beach Hotel,** but swimmers should be warned that the beautiful lagoon at their beach is filled with treacherous rocks and razor-sharp coral just a few feet from the shoreline; three of us received nasty cuts" (Bob and Doris Ryan, Grand Island, N.Y.).

Chapter XII

SEEING KAUAI

1. Lihue
2. The Eastern and Northern Route
3. The Southern and Western Route

COUNT ON AT LEAST three days to see Kauai. After Lihue, the first two should be devoted to separate all-day trips, which between them circle the island: (a) an eastern and northern trip all the way to Hanea and the Na Pali cliffs, and (b) a southern and western trip, whose high points are Waimea Canyon and the magnificent end-of-the-road climax, Kalalau Lookout. To skip either would be unthinkable. The remaining third day is for side excursions, swimming, and going back to all the idyllic little spots you discovered on the first two trips. Even with three there's hardly enough time.

1. Lihue

Starting place for your adventures is Lihue, once a sleepy plantation village that is beginning to look startlingly modern what with shopping centers, supermarkets, and the like. Near the Lihue Shopping Center, you'll note a restoration area; four old concrete homes of German architecture, formerly occupied by Lihue Plantation employees, have been restored and are now known as the **Haleko Shops,** with several interesting shops and restaurants on the grounds. We think a visit to the **Kauai Museum,** 4428 Rice St., adjacent to the shopping center and across from the post office, is well worth your while. Stop in first at the Wilcox Building to examine the changing art, heritage, and cultural exhibits of both Orientalia and Hawaiiana. The **Museum Shop** here is one of our favorites, with its fine collections of South Pacific handcrafts, tapas, baskets, rare Niihau shell leis, Hawaiian books, prints, and missionary dolls. The Rice Building, entered through a covered paved walkway and courtyard, contains the permanent exhibit, "The Story of Kauai," an ecological and geological history complete with photographs, dioramas, and an exciting 20-minute video shot from a helicopter. Be sure to see the Plantation Gallery, a permanent showcase for a collection of splendid Hawaiian quilts, plus koa furniture, china, etc. The museum is open from 9:30 a.m. to 4:30 p.m. Monday through Friday. Closed Saturday and Sunday. Admission is $3 for adults; children under 18 are free when accompanied by an adult.

A few blocks away from the museum, on Hardy Street, stands the **Kauai Regional Library,** a handsome contemporary building, where the latest audiovisual aids, including closed-circuit television, are available. Note Jerome Wallace's impressive abstract batik mural measuring 10 feet high and 27 feet long. Library hours vary with the season but are usually 8 a.m. to 4:30 p.m., plus

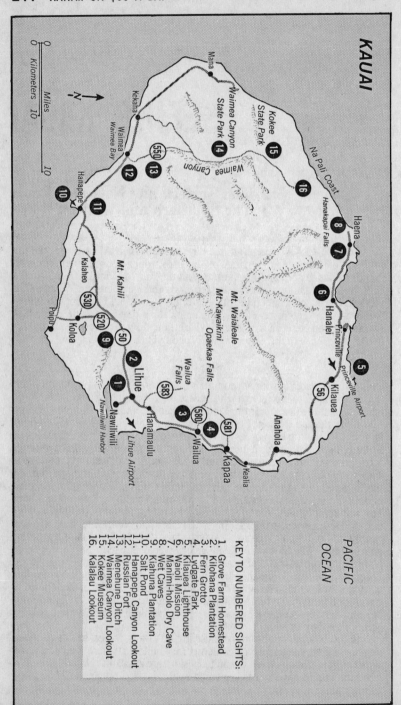

KAUAI

PACIFIC

OCEAN

KEY TO NUMBERED SIGHTS:

1. Grove Farm Homestead
2. Kilohana Plantation
3. Fern Grotto
4. Lydgate Park
5. Kilauea Lighthouse
6. Waioli Mission
7. Manini-holo Dry Cave
8. Wet Caves
9. Kiahuna Plantation
10. Salt Pond
11. Hanapepe Canyon Lookout
12. Russian Fort
13. Menehune Ditch
14. Waimea Canyon Lookout
15. Kokee Museum
16. Kalalau Lookout

some evening hours. Ask about their free programs, which include films, art shows, story hours, and ethnic programs.

At 3016 Umi St., Suite 207, on the second floor of the Lihue Plaza, is the headquarters of the **Hawaii Visitors Bureau** (tel. 245-3971), with information on just about everything, including tips on where to play tennis and golf, hunt, fish, and go camping.

ON THE BEACH: If you follow Rte. H-50 a mile toward the sea from Lihue up until its junction with 51, you'll come to the deep-water port of **Nawiliwili** (where the wiliwili trees once grew), Kauai's largest harbor and the site of a bulk-sugar plant that looks out on **Kalapaki Beach** across the bay. Although it adjoins the grounds of the luxurious Westin Kauai, this is the town beach, and you are welcome to use it. The surf, similar to that at Waikiki, is fairly gentle, with enough long rollers to make surfing or outrigger canoe rides great fun. It's one of the island's best beaches.

LIHUE SHOPPING: Pint-sized Lihue now has the largest of all neighbor-island shopping malls, the $25-million **Kukui Grove Center.** Since it's just four miles from the airport on Rte. 50 (headed toward Poipu), it makes a logical first stop in town to stock up on food and vacation needs. **Star Market** has everything from boogie boards to gourmet take-out foods. At **Sears** you can shop for the whole family, rent a car, survey a good selection of Hawaiian wear and island souvenirs. Such other trusty island familiars as **Long's, Woolworth's, Liberty House, Waldenbooks,** and **J.C. Penney** are here. If you need a good book to read on the beach, don't miss **Rainbow Books,** by far one of the most tasteful bookstores we've come across in a long time. Their selection of books is so appealing that you might be tempted to spend your whole vacation right here. They also have a good selection of children's books, plus T-shirts for the five-to-ten year-old set that read, "Color Your Mind With Books," $5.95. Under the same roof is **Stone's Gallery** for tasteful graphics, ceramics, jewelry, and other fine crafts, most by local artisans. This might be the place for you to buy a print by Pegge Hopper (her portraits of Hawaiian women with haunting faces and abstracted bodies are very popular in the islands; prices start at $12 and run into the hundreds), or a hand-painted T-shirt for $25, or a variety of posters that begin at $10, unframed. Note the hand-woven baskets from the Big Island, the tapa cloth, the photos of Old Hawaii by Boone Morrison. In the center of the store, perched between books and art, sits **Rainbow Coffees,** with wonderful teas and coffees to take home or sip in the store along with light meals and heavenly pastries (See Chapter XI).

See You in China is another of our favorite Kukui Grove boutiques. This gallery and gift shop shows jewelry, totes, tiles, and other crafts by local artists, and beautiful clothing, most of it in cotton, rayon, or silk. Note their "Art to Wear" collection by Jacqueline, from $60. For the kids: adorable, handpainted T-shirts, and children's tote bags—silkscreen on canvas, $16.50. . . . **Butterflies Too?** is a love of a store, with many items that *look* expensive but are not: for example, Christmas tree ornaments in the shape of tutu dolls, locally made and sold year 'round, $4.98; happi coats, made on the island, from $30; locally-made rompers and sundresses for children, $14.95; layette sets hand-crocheted in Kauai, $20; shell paintings by a local father-and-daughter team at $18; matching tiles and coasters designed in Hawaii and hand-painted in Greece, at $8.95 for tiles, $13.98 for a set of six coasters; batik duffle bags at $32; and more. You'll solve many gift problems here.

In addition to attractive kitchenware for the condo crowd, **Great Gourmet** has some terrific food to take home and eat: deli sandwiches, cheeses, pâtés, wines, coffee and teas, plus bread fresh from its own bakery (which smells wonderful!). Depending on the day, you might get onion cottage-cheese, sourdough, raisin or sweet bread, or French baguettes. Great Gourmet also stocks Dr. Tara Flynn's Essential Herbs Plus, a locally-grown and produced product that contains Hawaiian spirulina plus a variety of herbs. Try either "Table Seasoning," "Cooking Seasoning," or both. A chef at one of the major Poipu hotels is using them with great results.

Sally's Creations has created some coral fashion rings and earrings, averaging about $10. . . . Women's fashions can be found at **Deja Vu. . . .** and **Island Fashions and Gifts** has cute clothing for the keikis. . . . **Coral Grotto** shows exquisite jewelry, plus artful coral sculpture by Coralie, from $12. . . . You'll find artful Oriental imports at **House of Teak and Gifts,** cute cards, stuffed animals, and American-style whimsey at **Jenai's Hallmark Shop. . . .** And **General Nutrition Center** runs many specials and is a good place to replenish your vitamin supply—as well as get some fruit or vegetable juice.

The **Kukui Nut Tree Inn** for family-style meals and **Rosita's Mexican Restaurant** for spicy south-of-the-border fare are the big restaurant draws here, but there are about half-a-dozen good snack shops, too (see preceding chapter). Free entertainment is often presented on the mall stage; check the local papers for details. Kukui Grove Center is open weekdays from 9:30 a.m. to 5:30 p.m., on Friday night until 9 p.m., on Sunday from 10 a.m. to 4 p.m.

Physical fitness buffs take note: you don't have to miss your daily workout while you're in Kauai. Next door to the shopping center, at 4370 Kukui Grove St. (tel. 245-7877), is the **Kauai Athletic Club,** where guests may indulge in aerobic classes, weight lifting, racquetball, lap swimming, etc., to their heart's content, at fees of $10 per day single, $18 per couple. It's a beautiful, classy club, and the instructors are excellent. It has reciprocal privileges with many health clubs, maybe yours. (Up on the North Shore, the same people run the **Hanalei Athletic Club** in the Princeville Golf Clubhouse, which has an excellent pool, Nautilus equipment, weights, aerobics, and massage.) Open until 10 p.m. weekdays, 5 p.m. weekends.

Lihue Bargains

Savvy Honolulu shoppers will probably remember the Warehouse Showroom, which offered fabulous values on resort clothing and woodcarvings. Well, Ivy and Gale Gabbard, the people in charge there, closed their Honolulu showroom and moved back home to Kauai, and the bargains are better than ever at their manufacturer's outlet store called **Rainbow Rags,** right in Lihue, at 4303 Rice St., in the Rice Shopping Center. Because this is a "from sewing machine to you" operation, the Gabbards can afford to offer ridiculously low prices, like short muumuus from $12.50, long ones from around $20 and up, as well as aloha shirts from $9.95 to $22.50—all items that would easily cost twice as much elsewhere. Samples and overruns from their own regular and designer's collections are priced at less than wholesale. Everything is first quality, no seconds; and in-house specials change from time to time. As if all that weren't enough, from their 20 years in the wholesale wood business the Gabbards have amassed a huge collection of local and imported woodcarvings, in monkeypod, mango, koa, and milo woods, which they will offer at greatly discounted prices until the supply runs out. A great place to stock up on gifts!

Always a good budget stop for resort fashions in Lihue is the big **Hilo Hattie's Fashion Center** at 3252 Kuhio Hwy. Phone them at 245-3404 and they'll take you out to the factory, where you can buy men's aloha shirts from $18, women's long muumuus from $30, plus monkeypod dishes, macadamia-nut candies, and the like, all at excellent prices. There are always great specials here.

THE OLD HOMESTEAD: A visit to the **Grove Farm Homestead** takes a little advance planning, either by mail or by phoning 245-3202 for reservations. But it's worth the effort, as this is a trip backward in time, to the days of the old Hawaiian sugar plantations. Grove Farm Homestead has been lovingly preserved and still has a lived-in look. The plantation was founded by George N. Wilcox, the son of teachers who arrived with the fifth company of the American Board of Missions sent to Hawaii in the 1830s. (Part of Wilcox's original sugar plantation is now the site of Kukui Grove Center; see above.) His niece, Miss Mabel Wilcox, who was born and lived on the plantation all her life, left her estate as a living museum. The Homestead tour is leisurely, with stops for light refreshment along the way in the big kitchen. The old homes are lovely, furnished with antiques, Oriental rugs, and handsome koa wood furniture; there is an abundance of books, and sheet music is open on the piano. You'll visit the very different servants' quarters too. Tours are held only on Monday, Wednesday, and Thursday, last about two hours, and get under way at 10 a.m. and 1:15 p.m. The cost is $3. Phone at least a week in advance, or write (reservations are accepted up to three months in advance) to Grove Farm Homestead, P.O. Box 1631, Lihue, Kauai, HI 96766.

KILOHANA PLANTATION: The same George Wilcox, founder of Grove Farm Plantation, built his own dream house back in 1935 and called it "Kilohana," which, in Hawaiian, means "not to be surpassed." The Wilcox family lived at the estate for 35 years, during which time it was the setting for much of the cultural and social life of upper-class Kauai. The house was closed in 1970, went through a short incarnation as a school, and has now been painstakingly restored to look just as it did in the 1930's, with many of its actual furnishings and artifacts. Now it is a combination historical house-museum and shopping bazaar, with boutiques taking over the old children's nursery, the family bedrooms, the library, the cloakrooms, and the restored guest cottages on the estate grounds. There is a variety of things you can do at Kilohana, like taking a 20-minute, horse-drawn carriage ride ($5), a guided tour, or a walk through the extensive grounds with their manicured lawns and gardens. You can also view live agricultural exhibits and displays of Hawaiian arts and crafts, and partake of a variety of cultural events. But mostly what you may want to do, in a setting like this, is browse and shop. There's a beautiful collection of shops, none of them inexpensive, but all offering quality in accordance with Kilohana's standard of excellence.

Before you begin your shopping, stop in to have a look at the foyer of the main house, where you'll see two enormous monkeypod calabashes—reputedly the largest in the state of Hawaii. In the olden days, Hawaiian kings stored their feather quilts in such calabashes: later, missionary women used them as "trunks" for patchwork quilts. These, however, are replicas, made to be used in the movie, *Hawaii*.

In the house, be sure to see the shop called **Island Memories;** it's in the fireplace with a library, boasts museum-quality replicas and one-of-a-kind island crafts. We admired the Japanese parasols with designs by noted artist Theo Morrison at $8, the kites, Hawaiian-pillow quilt kits, and the Hawaiian Christmas tree ornaments. . . . The **Hawaiian Collection,** also in the main house, has rare Niihau-shell leis, woodcarvings, a good scrimshaw collection, plus Hawaiian coins, stamps, and monarchy documents. . . . Koa wood toys, collector dolls, and children's gifts from Hawaii, many handmade, can be found at **Tutu's Kiddy Korner,** along with charming children's fashions, and grass skirts for $6. . . . Note the shells and nautical objects, the fine coral jewelry, at **Sea**

Reflections. . . . Folk art from Japan, gift items, antiques, and kimonos represent the Japanese mood at Kilohana at **Half Moon Trading Company.**

On the estate grounds are a clutch of charming little shops. **Handworks of the Pacific** reminds us of the Volcano Art Gallery on the Big Island, showing as it does, the works of some of Hawaii's most talented artists photos by Boone Morrison, Dietrich Varez prints, which we found on T-shirts, exclusive here, at $11. . . . Just about our favorite Kilohana shop is **A Crystal Journey,** which offers "unique gifts from the earth mother." These include natural quartz and amethyst crystals, crystal jewelry, tapes, metaphysical books, and pyramids. It's a good source for information on Kauai's spiritual and holistic community. One of the owners, a lady named Almira, is also involved in selling black pearls, one of the world's rarest gems, at very reasonable prices. You can phone her to discuss it all, toll free 800/521-6333. . . . Next stop might be **Kauai Certified Tropicals,** which specializes in tropical flowering plants and foliage, already certified for shipping. They also have coconuts for $2.50, which you can address and mail back home.

It's nice to tie a visit to Kilohana in with lunch at **Gaylord's,** a courtyard restaurant in the estate house, which has food to match its elegant setting; later you might come back to **The Carriage House** for an evening cookout (see preceding chapter for details).

Kilohana Plantation is located on Hwy. 50, two miles southwest of Lihue, headed towards Poipu. It's on the other side of the road and very close to Kukui Grove Shopping Center. Open daily from 9 a.m. For information, phone 245-7818.

WHALE WATCHING: Kauai waters not only host swimmers and surfers and snorkelers, they also host hundreds of humpback whales who migrate here every winter (December through March) from Alaskan and Arctic waters seeking warm climes in which to mate and breed. How do you get to see these nonpaying guests? Easy! You take one of the whale-watching cruises that have become so popular in Kauai and Maui in recent years. One of the best is run **by Lady Ann Cruises:** two boats, each well designed for picture-taking with a high bow and stern railing, depart twice daily from Lihue for a 2½-hour cruise at a cost of $35 per person. Only 23 passengers are allowed. Bring your cameras, of course, plus comfortable clothes: these whales are playful creatures and enjoy diving, breaching, blowing, maybe even bumping your boat and sending up a spray of water 20 feet high! There are hydrophones on board, so you may get to hear the whales singing! Phone 245-8538 for reservations.

THE SPORTING LIFE: There are plenty of opportunities for hiking, fishing, camping, golf, water sports, and the like on Kauai for those who have the time to stay and enjoy them. Check with the Hawaii Visitors Bureau or write to them at P.O. Box 507, Lihue, HI 96766. Hiking information is available at the Department of Land and Natural Resources, in the State Building in Lihue. For State Forest Reserve trail information, write to the District Forester, Division of Forestry and Wildlife, P.O. Box 1671, Lihue, HI 96766; for State Park information, write to the Park Superintendent, Division of State Parks, P.O. Box 1671, Lihue, HI 96766.

KAUAI ON HORSEBACK: A great way to enjoy the sights of Kauai is on horseback. **High Gates' Ranch** (tel. 822-3182) at Wailua Homesteads in Wailua rents horses for $18 per hour ($9 for children), and offers several guided rides; a special favorite is a four-hour round trip to Keahua Arboretum, stopping for a picnic lunch beside a lovely, clear pond perfect for a swim. (Daredevils can plummet into the water from the rope swing on the mango tree at water's edge.) Cost is $55.

GUIDED TOURS: If you'd prefer to concentrate on the scenery while somebody else does the driving, give a call to a company called **Chandler's Kauai Tours** (tel. 245-9134). We've had excellent reports on this outfit. For tabs of $18 to $20 per person for a half-day trip and $32 to $45 for a full-day excursion, they'll take you, with a small group of others, in a van to tour such spots as Waimea Canyon, Hanalei and Haena, Opaekaa Falls, and Polihale Beach. For those in a hurry, they offer a chance to circle the entire island, seeing both Waimea Canyon on the west coast and Hanalei Bay and Haena on the east, all in one day.

2. The Eastern and Northern Route

Now you're ready for one of the big trips, an excursion around the glorious north and east shores of Kauai. Highway 56, which starts at Kuhio Hwy. in town, takes you the entire length of the tour. The distance is 40 miles each way, and it will take you a full day.

KAPAIA AND HANAMAULU: After you've gone a few miles out of town at Kapaia, you'll find a turnoff to the left to **Wailua Falls,** about four miles inland. Watch for the white fence on the right of the road and listen for the sound of rushing water; soon you'll see the HVB marker. After you've seen them, don't be tempted to drive farther; turn around here and drive back.

Look now, on the left as you're driving to Wailua on Kuhio Hwy. (Rte. 56), for a quaint store called the **Kapaia Stitchery,** especially appealing in that many things in it are made by hand. Owner Julie Yukimura makes items like wrap skirts, kimono tops, pareaus, and aloha shirts, which she sells at low prices. She also asks local craftspeople, especially senior citizens, to make things for her; we found lovely handmade, crocheted shawls and tops, priced from $40 up. Her own 92-year-old grandmother, Mrs. Shima Yukimura, is the master crocheter who does all of the shawls and jackets. Most exciting of all are the patchwork coverlets made of modern Hawaiian fabrics by four local grandmothers. We spied one in the window and guessed that its price was at least $150; we couldn't believe that it was only $70. A darling baby quilt with a pattern of Oriental children was $60. We hope Julie has a few quilts on hand when you're there; we don't need to tell anybody who knows about hand work that they are fantastic buys at the price and each represents weeks of painstaking work. There's a good collection of specially selected Hawaiian print fabrics, from about $5 a yard for cottons. Julie takes orders on Hawaiian quilting cushions; you choose the fabric and pattern and receive an excellent piece of workmanship; price is about $80 to $90. For do-it-yourselfers, there are Hawaiian-quilt pillow kits, handpainted needlepoint designs of local flowers and themes. There's always something new here; last time we saw some geisha-print cushion covers at $35 and Kauai keiki string dolls, which collectors scoop up at just $8.95.

WAILUA: Continuing on Hwy. 56, you'll soon come to the mouth of the **Wailua River** and one of the most historic areas in Hawaii. Here, where the Polynesians first landed, were once seven heiaus, or temple sites, by the sacred (wailua) waters. Just before you get there, you'll come to **Lydgate Park,** on the right, a grassy picnic area directly on the water, in which are the remains of an ancient "City of Refuge." You'll get a better idea of what a City of Refuge actually looked like when you see the restored one at Kona on the Big Island. But the concept here was precisely the same. In the days when the Hawaiians still carried on their polytheistic nature worship, life was bound by a rigid system of kapus, or taboos, violations of which were punishable by death. But if an offender, or a prisoner of war, could run or swim to a City of Refuge, he could be purified and was then allowed to go free. Not too much of the City of Refuge remains, but if you wade out into the river you may discover some ancient carvings on the rocks, once part of the heiau. More practically, **Lydgate Park Beach** is one of the best beaches on Kauai for children. Two natural "pools," created by rocks, make it safe for them to swim and play in the ocean. The snorkeling is lovely, there are stripies and butterfly fish feeding on the rock, the water is clean and clear, and the sand is white. There are rest rooms, showers, and barbecue pits near the beach. Alas, there have been reports of vandalism here.

A relatively new Hawaiian ghost story got started out here. It seems that the old jail across from the Wailua Golf Course (now replaced by a new facility) may have been haunted. Local people tell us that it was once a burial ground and, before that, a battleground. Whatever the reason, the building shook, the lights went on and off by themselves, and strange mumblings were sometimes heard from the top floor. The police really did not like to draw duty there. Seems that once one of Lihue's Finest was so shaken up in the middle of the night that he took all the prisoners, put them in his car, and took them to the police station in Lihue!

The Wailua, one of the two navigable rivers in Hawaii, is also the place where you can rent a tour boat for an idyllic three-mile trip to the fantastically beautiful **Fern Grotto**—an enormous fern-fronted cave under a gentle cascade of water, unapproachable any other way. Personally, we'd love to take this trip in our own private craft and instead of being "entertained," spend the time contemplating the rare tropical trees and flowers that line the bank and pondering on the old Kauai alii whose bones still lie undiscovered in the secret burial caves of the cliffs above. But the tour boats are well run, the captains are entertaining, and the musicians' singing of the "Hawaiian Wedding Song" in the natural amphitheater of the Fern Grotto is a unique experience.

The cost of the 1½-hour boat trips is $8.32 (children, 4- to 12-years-old, half price), and both **Waialeale Boat Tours** and **Smith Motor Boat Service** make the cruises. Their phone numbers are 822-4908 and 822-3467, and you should phone in advance to make a reservation.

You may want to make a little excursion now to visit **Smith's Tropical Paradise,** a 22½-acre botanical garden that features a Japanese garden, a replica of Easter Island, huge tiki heads, a tropical fruit garden, and a small Polynesian village. Adults pay $4, children $2. This is also the site of an excellent luau and Polynesian show; you can see the show alone for around $12, enjoy the whole shebang for around $45. For reservations, call 822-4654 or 822-9599.

At this point on Hwy. 56, a side road called the **King's Highway** (named after the kings who had to be carried uphill in a litter, lest their sacred feet touch the ground) leads to the restored heiau, **Holo-Holo-Ku.** It's so serene here now that it's hard to realize that this was once a site for human sacrifice—where bloodthirsty deeds were done to calm the ancient gods.

Now you move on from Hawaiiana to observe some of the history of the Japanese settlers in Hawaii, recorded in a quaint cemetery just up the wooden stairs to the right of the heiau. If you continue driving along the King's Highway, you'll pass a rice field and soon, **Poliahu Heiau,** now a park that affords you a splendid view of the Wailua River. Next is **Opaekaa Falls,** plunging down from a high cliff (the name, quaintly, means rolling shrimp). At the top of the falls, nestled in a lush green valley is the **Kamokila Hawaiian Village,** where an ancient settlement has been restored. A guided tour here ($5 adults, $1.50 children) is an excellent way to gain an experience of pre-missionary Hawaii. Knowledgeable guides will show you the Oracle Tower (where villagers left gifts for the gods), the warriors' houses, the men's and women's eating houses, the medicine house (landscaped with Hawaiian medicinal plants), the chief's house, living house, sleeping house, and birthing house (in which are actual ancient Hawaiian birthing stones found in the area). You'll see craft and salt-making demonstrations, watch a demonstration of Hawaiian games and then be invited to participate in them. There are taro and banana patches, and a group of friendly pua'a—Hawaiian wild pigs of the type brought to the islands by the very first Hawaiians. A visitor is sure to come away with quite a respectable knowledge of the traditional ways of the Hawaiian people.

Kamokila Hawaiian Village is open Monday through Saturday from 9 a.m. to 4 p.m. For pickup from nearby hotels, phone 822-1192.

When you retrace your path to Hwy. 56, you'll see a little group of buildings on the right, across from the Coco Palms; it's the site of the **Rehabilitation Center Shop,** which features handcrafted coconut and woven lauhala products, made by the disabled, at reasonable prices. Tinkly wood chimes make delightful gifts.

At some point you're going to want to visit **Coco Palms,** perhaps for its splendid evening torch-lighting ceremony. Have a look at some of the attractive shops here; they are more reasonably priced than you might expect. **Treasury,** for one, has many tasteful artifacts like banana-bark paintings, feather jewelry, and hand-crocheted pillow cases. The **Chapel in the Palms,** scene of many a Hawaiian wedding, was originally built by Columbia Pictures for the movie *Sadie Thompson* starring Rita Hayworth, which was filmed here on the grounds.

On the ocean side of the road, at 4-370 Kuhio Hwy., is **Restaurant Kintaro,** where shoppers should make a stop even if they're not planning to eat. In an annex to the restaurant is **D.S. Collection,** a gallery-shop showing paintings, ceramics, glass, and other works by local artists, as well as some handsome imports from Japan: ivory, celadon, Kukeshi dolls, sake, and tea sets. We saw an excellent collection of Hiroshige prints, from $15 to $60. Many good gift ideas here, and prices begin modestly.

Kinipopo Shopping Village, on the ocean side of the road (across from Sizzler), isn't all that big as shopping centers go, but we found a few likeable places here. **Toucans** has women's sportswear in wild, jungly prints; most everything is 100% cotton or other natural fabric. . . . **Bachman's** has the elegant touch—in women's fashion, needlepoint, Niihau shell necklaces, and more. We like their exclusive handpainted canvas tote bags, $28, done by a local artist. Silkscreened T-shirts by Almost Paradise, are attractive, around $40. And we met Jean Ricciardi here, a local woman who hand-crochets custom-made bikinis of 100% cotton, from about $60. Phone her at 826-7308 for details. . . . No, you won't find dolls at **Barbie and Ken's World,** just lots of Hawaiian wear—muumuus, aloha shirts, matching sets for the family—at good prices, and made on Kauai.

The Market Place

Back on the highway now, continue toward the Coconut Plantation hotels and there, near the Islander Inn and the Kauai Beach Boy, you'll find Kauai's prettiest answer to the shopping complex craze: the **Market Place at Coconut Plantation.** It's a handsome setup, with concrete planked walkways, country decor, flowers and shrubs everywhere, and enough diverting shops (over 70 at last count) to keep you busy for an hour or two. We have a few special favorites, like **Waves of One Sea,** with such international gifts as batik table linens from Java, lacquer boxes from Thailand, Fukagawa porcelain from Japan, Russian stone carvings, and the island's largest selection of fans from around the world. Jewelry handmade of peacock and pheasant feathers begins at $13. Note the charming cards by Margaret Leach, watercolors based on old Hawaiian legends and executed so that they have a stylized, petroglyph look, $2 each; her posters, signed, are $25. Serving trays with a design of Hawaiian menu covers from the days of the S.S. *Lurline* are fun items at $15. . . . **Plantation Stitchery** specializes in needlepoints and patterns, and has a few dresses, too. . . . We saw some great sundresses for around $35 at **Batik Boutique. . . . Tahiti Imports** sells beautiful clothing and hand-screened fabrics for very reasonable prices. . . . **Ye Olde Ship Store** is the place for maritime gifts, antiques, and scrimshaw. Handcast solid brassware goes for surprisingly nice prices, and the plaque that reads "On this site in 1897 nothing happened" ($19) appeals to our crazy sense of humor. Antique brass ship keys, circa 1875 to 1925, from Hawaiian and Pacific ships, would make neat little gifts at $2.99 each.

Be sure to visit the exquisite **Kahn Gallery,** where a consistently high level of taste is evident in the selection of paintings, woodcuts, watercolors, pottery, and crafts by Hawaiian artists. Pegge Hopper, George Sumner, Guy Buffet, and Diane Hansen-Young are among their stars. The originals and limited-edition prints by these artists are shown here: posters of their work, among those of other artists, can be found at **The Poster Shop,** on the other side of The Market Place. Also impressive are the Hawaiian baskets and koa wood bowls, and the unusual collection of Niihau shell necklaces, which begin at $30 and go up to $4,500. Small paintings to carry home and limited-edition prints could start as low as $25, although most are in the several-hundred dollar range.

Isle Style lives up to its name, with above-average crafts, accessories, jewelry, like titanium bracelets and earrings, stained glass mirrors, pillows in Hawaiian quilt patterns ($36), and wonderful canvas hats and visors, handpainted in Hawaii and exclusive here, at $41 for the hats, $18 for the visors. Matching bags are $37. . . . **Port of Kauai** is a maritime gallery with a lot of class: ships in bottles, authentic scrimshaw jewelry, and handsome paintings, originals, and graphics, by Robert Lyn Nelson, are featured. . . . Woodchimes are really inexpensive at the **Pottery Tree.** Ceramic chimes run about $13 to $30; shell chimes, $4.75 to $33. Most are handmade and very artful. . . . You can get scrimshaw, 14-karat gold charms, and Niihau leis at **Kauai Gold;** nuts and candies at **Nutcracker Sweet;** and T-shirts with great designs at **Crazy Shirts**—we love the rock 'n' roll cats.

Beautiful jewelry is not inexpensive at **Hudson & Co.,** but they often make special purchases and pass the savings on to the customer: we saw some freshwater rice-pearl necklaces from China at $49. . . . **Coral Grotto** abounds in all kinds of coral, including beautiful black; necklaces go from about $18 to $38 and up. . . . The **Whaler's General Store** is one of those very useful sundry shops, with everything from macadamia-nut brittle to liquor, sandals, shell souvenirs, and drugstore items. . . . Many kinds of coffees are for sale at **Café Espresso,** including chocolate-macadamia nut ($7.50 for half-a-pound) and decaffeinated Hawaiian Kona ($8.75 for half-a-pound). While you're there, have a cappuccino at $2.10, or a homemade Belgian waffle with fresh strawberries or blueberries, whipped cream, and macadamia nuts, $4.95. (These folks are definitely not thinking about calories.) Fudge, too.

If you'd like to fly a kite on a Kauai beach, the people at **High as a Kite and Toy Company** have some beauties for you; they begin at $5 and go up to around $150 (some can be used for decorative art). Huggable plush animals, made on

Kauai, are store exclusives. . . . Men's aloha shirts by Reyn Spooner cannot be beat; they have the best patterns. This local outpost of **Reyn's** also has womens shirts, muumuus, and other sportswear. . . . **Hilo Hattie's** can always be counted on for great bargains in aloha wear. . . . and **Safari Pomare** can outfit both men and women for that trek to Africa or anywhere, with cotton plaids and khakis, just about everything in natural fabrics. . . . We saw some elegant muumuus for kids, as well as many other lovelies, at **Happy Kauaiian**—which also has special selections for queen-sizes, petites, and sells fabrics too. . . . **Coco Resorts Shop** has great things for the whole family. . . . And **Hale Keiki** specializes in tasteful things for the kids: Hawaiian toys, games, souvenirs, dolls, and books, plus a good selection of Hawaiian T-shirts and aloha wear.

The kids will get a kick out of playing with the heavy equipment from the defunct **Kilauea Mill** that has been transformed into sculptural fountains they can control. When they tire of that, they may enjoy running to the top of the high wooden tower to see the beautiful view. And they'll be delighted with the children's hula show presented by the local hula schools every Thursday, Friday, and Saturday at 4 p.m. Be sure to check the Calendars of Events posted at each entrance for additional free daily activities.

Hungry? No problem. The Market Place abounds in snackbars and restaurants offering inexpensive meals, like **Don's Deli** and **Picnic Basket, Waldo's Fried Chicken,** and **J.J.'s Dog House** (see the preceding chapter). And if you want to catch a first-run movie, the **Cinema I** and **II** (Kauai's only air-conditioned movie houses) are right there. The Market Place is open Monday to Saturday from 9 a.m. to 9 p.m., Sundays and holidays to 5 p.m. Free photo-hula shows are held Thursday, Friday, and Saturday at 4 p.m.

KAPAA AND KEALIA: From Hwy. 56, back on the northern drive, you'll soon see a remarkable formation on the left as you enter Kapaa, the **Sleeping Giant**— the subject of another Menehune tall tale. The old fellow, so the story goes, was a kind of Gulliver whom the South Sea Lilliputians inadvertently killed.

On the opposite side of the road, opposite Foodland, look for a little store shaped like a Samoan house and called **Marta's Boat.** Marta Curry, who has four young children of her own, understands the needs of mothers and children and has stocked her place with items both pretty and practical, much of it handmade. Her specialty is 100% cotton (or silk or rayon; she will not carry blends) aloha clothing for children. Cotton batiks for infants and toddlers are especially lovely. She also has a good selection of educational toys, many of which are good for the long plane ride home. For mom, she's got mainland clothes in aloha fabrics—the kinds of things you'll be happy to wear back home too. Japanese antique rayon blouses are $39. Next door is a natural-foods store run by her husband, Ambrose Curry; pick up a cooling bottled fruit drink here, or stock up if you need anything, for it's one of the few-and-far-between health-food shops on the island. If you're lucky, Ambrose will have some hot tamales in corn husks made by a local cook; fillings include chicken, buffalo, or tofu/pumpkin at $1.50. This is a delicious, cheap lunch.

Some of the most beautiful fish in Polynesian waters live in the rocks and reefs around Kauai. The friendly, professional staff at **Sea Sage,** a dive shop at 4-1378 Kuhio Hwy., in Kapaa, can make the introductions for you, via various snorkeling and scuba-diving excursions. They'll rent you snorkeling equipment at $8 for 24 hours, and they run a "snorkel picnic" for $40. A half-day introduction to scuba-diving is $65, including all equipment. There are many other excursions for more experienced snorkelers and scuba-divers, and a full line of snorkeling and scuba equipment is for sale or rent. Reservations should be made in advance: call them at 822-3841 for details.

Continuing on, now, turn half a mile up the hill just before the bridge over Kealia Stream and you'll come to **St. Catherine's Catholic Church,** which boasts murals by leading Hawaiian artists: Jean Charlot, Juliette May Fraser, and Tseng Yu Ho.

Beyond Kealia, watch for the turnoff to **Anahola Beach** for a glimpse of one of those golden, jewel-like beaches that ring the island.

KILAUEA: The first church you'll see as you drive into Kilauea town, **Christ Memorial Episcopal Church,** has only-in-Hawaii architecture. It's made of lava rock. Its windows, executed in England, are of the finest design and workmanship. On the other side of the road you'll soon see **St. Sylvester's Catholic Church** in Kilauea—something new in church architecture. This octagonal "church-in-the-round," constructed of lava and wood, has a beautiful, open feeling. You'll recognize the work of Jean Charlot again, this time in the fresco paintings of the stations of the cross.

Now follow the road for two more miles to **Kilauea Lighthouse** (turn right into Kilauea to Lighthouse Road, which becomes Kilauea Point National Wildlife Refuge). Kilauea Lighthouse, high on a bluff that drops sharply to the sea on three sides, affords a magnificent view of the northern coastline of the island. Birds drift effortlessly in the wind like paper kites sent up by schoolboys; below, the turquoise sea smashes against the black lava cliffs. The historic lighthouse was built in 1913, has an 8-foot-high clam-shaped lens, but is no longer operative (a small light, 30 feet north of the old structure, is the present Kilauea light). The old U.S. Coast Guard Lighthouse Station has been taken over by the U.S. Fish and Wildlife Service. Bird lovers will have a field day here, as the area is frequented by such unique Pacific sea birds as the red-footed booby, the wedge-tailed shearwater, the white-tailed and red-tailed tropic bird, and the Laysan albatross. Whales, spinner dolphins, and Pacific sea green turtles are also seen in the area. Docents at the Visitor Center next door to the lighthouse can answer questions and point out current wildlife activity. Check out the bookstore with its books on Hawaiian natural history. The Kilauea Point Refuge is open daily except Saturday, from noon to 4 p.m.

On the way to Kilauea Lighthouse, you might want to stop at **Old Kilauea Town,** which includes the **Kong Lung Company,** Kauai's oldest plantation general store (1881); Irmalee Pomroy Flowers; the Lighthouse Gallery; an Italian garden restaurant called Casa de Amici; and Kilauea Theater. The buildings are turn-of-the-century plantation, and the atmosphere charming. Kong Lung is very special, with beautiful antiques, tasteful craft items, home accessories, local island wear, and imaginative gift items. Around the bend is **Jacques Bakery,** whose superlative breads and pastries you'll find in many island supermarkets and restaurants. Stop in and treat yourself to some garlic-and-pepper bread right from the ovens.

Continue, now, past **Kalihiwai Bay,** whose sleepy little village was twice destroyed by tidal waves, in 1946 and 1957, a reminder that the much-celebrated mildness of Hawaii is a sometime thing; the violence of nature (or is it the old gods?) is always here, a sleeping beast that can spring to life at any moment.

HANALEI: The glorious views continue. Keep watching for the lookout at **Hanalei Valley,** where you will be treated to one of the special sights of the islands. The floor of Hanalei Valley, which you see below, is almost Asian, with neatly terraced taro patches and the silvery Hanalei River stretching through the dark greens of the mountains. (A sunset visit here is spectacular; plan it for a later trip if you have time.) You may want to drive through the luxury resort development of **Princeville, at Hanalei**—surely a sportsman's idea of paradise—and perhaps have lunch here at **Chuck's Steakhouse** or **The Oasis.** Back on the road, you'll soon come to **Hanalei Beach,** one of the most imposing beaches in the islands, but swimming is safe only in summer months and only at the old boat pier at the river mouth. In winter, beware of high surf and undertow. To get to the beach, turn right at St. William's Catholic Church (another Jean Charlot mural is inside). There's a public pavilion, dressing rooms, and picnic facilities; your fellow bathers will include many island families.

In Hanalei Valley itself, history buffs will want to note the old **Waioli Mission.** The original church, built in 1841, is now used as a community center. More interesting, we think, is the old Mission House, restored in 1921 and full of fascinating furniture, books, and mementos of 19th-century Hawaii. On Tuesday, Thursday, or Saturday, between 9 a.m. and 3 p.m., you can take an absorbing guided tour here, for which there is no admission charge, although donations are welcomed. Plan on 30 to 40 minutes for this excellent tour. For groups of 10 to 20 persons, however, advance reservations are required and can be made by calling Barnes Riznik at 245-3202 or writing to P.O. Box 163, Lihue, Kauai, HI 96766.

We loved the funky old Ching Young General Store that had sat in the middle of Hanalei town forever, so we looked upon its demise and the construction of the new **Ching Young Village Shopping Center** with mixed emotions. The old-time aura is gone, certainly, but this is a pleasant and practical place with a few shops that are worth your time. The most tasteful of these, for us, is **On the Road to Hanalei,** which shows arts and crafts from all over—Bali, China, and many other places, as well as Hawaii. We saw beautiful tie-dyed pareaus, from $25 to $35, tie-dyed shawls at $75, posters by island artists, books, and crystals. . . . **Hanalei Bay Cargo** has lots of sportswear, some very pretty lingerie, and hand-painted silk dresses (for around $95). . . . The people at **Shanora of Kauai** create and design their own island fashions right on the premises and turn out tasteful attire for everyone, including the kids. Pick up one of their useful instruction sheets on how to tie a pareau, maybe buy a pattern and create your own garment. . . . **Spinning Dolphin** has one-of-a-kind designs. . . . **Village Variety** has lots of just that. . . . And **Jen's Casual Wear** is the place for T-shirts, many of them sporting scenes of Kauai's North Shore. Take a little time to browse through the **Native Hawaiian Cultural Center,** a dozen or so shops all owned by native Hawaiians and selling Hawaiian arts and crafts. Craft demonstrations and shows are often held here. Have a look, too, at the **Native Hawaiian Museum,** a small display of Hawaiian historical artifacts.

If you need some fresh produce, vitamins, or natural sandwiches, stop in at **Health and Natural Foods** . . . **Pua & Kawika's Place** can provide you with fresh flowers . . . For a macadamia-nut shave ice at $1.50, visit Lin Cosbey's **Hanalei Freeze** for what well could be "the best shave ice in town." Other practical resources at Ching Young Village include a **Big Save Market;** a Chinese restaurant, **Foong Wong;** and several fast-food operations (see Chapter XI).

Across the road from Ching Young Village, art lovers might want to take a peek at the **Hanalei Wishing Well Art Gallery.** The selection is eclectic—everything from banana-bark art to ceramics, from shells to custom jewelry, drawings, paintings, dresses, and handpainted T-shirts. And they also rent surfboards and sell some pretty good shave ice, too!

Our favorite shop in this area is called **Ola's,** and it's right next door to the Dolphin Restaurant in Hanalei. This is a serenely tasteful environment, stocked with beautiful handmade craft items. Silkscreened purses are $5 and $10; hand-blown oil lamps begin at $34; glass beads by Sarah Young start at $30. There are many boxes from all over the world. And many delights for children, too—toys, books, clothing. A serendipitous spot.

Lumahai Beach is next, and you'll recognize it immediately from pictures appearing in dozens of books, postcards, and magazines. It's probably the most widely photographed beach on the island, and deserves its fame: golden sand, a long tongue of black lava rock stretching to the sea, a background of unearthly blue-green mountain. If the surf is not high, swimming will be safe here. It's a little difficult to find the entrance to the trail down to the beach (not indicated by any signs), but once you do it's easy to get down. If the surf is up, admire the view and continue on.

HAENA: Beyond this point stretches the Haena region, where the shoreline gets dreamier by the mile. You can swim anywhere along here with the local people, but be very careful of surf and undertow in the winter months. Many people consider **Haena Beach Park** one of the best beaches on the island (although we personally prefer to swim at Ke'e, ahead), and you won't go wrong swimming, camping, or picnicking here. Haena is what you always imagined the South Seas would be like—golden curving beaches, coconut palms, and lush foliage, jagged cliffs tumbling down to the sea. Is it any surprise that this spot was chosen as Bali Ha'i for the movie *South Pacific*?

On this drive through the Haena region, watch on the left side of the road for the **Manimi-holo Dry Cave,** which was supposedly dug by the Menehunes to capture an evil spirit that had stolen some fish. This is the area from which the Menehunes were also said to have left Hawaii. A short distance from here, up a small rise, is the first of two **Wet Caves,** the **Waikapalae;** about 200 yards farther on is the second, the **Waikanaloa.** For once, the Menehunes were not responsible—the caves were reputedly dug by Pele in search for fire. Finding fresh water instead, she left in disgust. It's reported that you can swim in these pools (the old Hawaiians used to jump off the ledges into them), but we think you'll do better to wait for the end of the road a few hundred yards ahead and an out-of-this-world beach, **Ke'e.** This is one of those gentle, perfect beaches that's almost impossible to tear yourself away from. As you loll on the sand under the towering mountains, listening to the Pacific, which has quieted down to a ripple beside you, it's not hard to picture this spot when it was the site of a most sacred temple of Laka, the goddess of the hula. Nearby are the remains of a heiau that guarded the sacred hula halau, to which novitiates came from all over the islands to study the dances, meles, and religious traditions of their people. From the cliffs above, specially trained men would throw burning torches into the sea (possibly in connection with temple rites). To your left are the cliffs of the **Na Pali Coast** and the end of your auto trip.

If you'd like to see the spectacularly beautiful Na Pali Coast in detail, however, you have three alternatives: by foot, by boat, and by helicopter. For the first, see the Readers' Suggestions, ahead, for tips on hiking around the cliffs. Of the many boat trips offered, one is quite special. **Na Pali Zodiac** boat expeditions take small groups out in boats similar to those used for shooting the rapids on the Colorado River. (The trip is usually smooth and gentle, but can be as wet and wild as the Colorado River on occasion; a licensed Coast Guard captain is in command.) A full day's expedition costs $85; camper drop-offs are $50 one way to Kalalau, $95 round trip leaving from Hanalei. Morning and afternoon excursions are $55. For information and reservations, contact Na Pali Zodiac, P.O. Box 456, Hanalei, HI 96714 (tel. 826-9371 or, toll free 800/422-7824).

Helicopter Trips: Perhaps the most exciting way of all to see Kauai, to experience the grandeur of its remote and isolated areas, is to take a helicopter flight. These are not inexpensive: prices start at $90 and go up to $200 per person for trips over Waimea Canyon and the Na Pali Coast, into the wilderness areas of Kauai, often swooping down the canyon walls to make stops at pristine beaches.

Early-morning and sunset flights can be the most beautiful of all. A number of companies are now offering tours, and competition can be fierce. Local friends have been praising the trips run by "the new kid on the block," **Menehune Helicopter Tours** (245-7705), a small company that's trying harder just because it's new. They're committed to providing a truly personalized service, and their prices were about $20 lower than the other companies' at the time of this writing. Other popular companies include: **Jack Harter Helicopters** (tel. 245-3774), very highly rated; **Papillon Helicopters,** the largest in the state (tel. 826-6591); **Kauai Helicopters** (tel. 245-7403); **Island Helicopters Kauai** (tel. 245-8588); **South Sea Helicopters** (tel. 245-7781); and **Will Squyres Helicopters** (tel. 245-7541). Photographers are advised to bring plenty of film and a wide-angled lens if possible.

3. The Southern and Western Route

This tour is about as long as the northern one and requires another full day. Since the highpoint is Waimea Canyon, you might check with the forest ranger on duty before leaving (tel. 335-5871) to find out if there's fog over the canyon; if so, it might be preferable to save this trip for another day, if you have one. You may, by the way, want a sweater for the slightly cooler (but not at all unpleasant) 4,000-foot altitude of the Kokee region.

OLD KOLOA TOWN: Most of this drive is along Hwy. 50. Starting from Lihue, note the town of Puhi on your left (where you'll see a mountain formation called "Queen Victoria's Profile"). You may want to stop here to visit the delightful **People's Market,** in a little cluster of restored buildings a mile or two outside of Lihue. You can get a smoothie, perhaps cut-up coconut meat, or a ready-to-eat pineapple, plus all sorts of fresh island flowers and leis at very good prices. Reader Holly McAlpen of Half Moon Bay, California, writes: "I highly recommend that anyone, and especially those trying to save dollars, make this a stop. You will come away with a bag of island delicacies for very little money and maybe an orchid for your hair!"

Continue driving now, until you see Hwy. 52 on your left, which leads you through a spectacular arch of towering eucalpytus trees (popularly called the "Tree Tunnel") and into the little town of **Koloa,** Hawaii's first sugar plantation town, Koloa was established in 1835, and continued through most of the 19th century as a busy seaport and home to a thriving sugar mill. The old plantation town has recently been restored, and now Old Koloa Town is an attractive collection of shops and restaurants, plus a few historic sites like the **Koloa Hotel,** a five-room inn built in 1898 for traveling salesmen from Honolulu, and its authentically restored ofuro or Japanese bathhouse. Note the huge monkeypod tree planted in 1925; it stretches halfway across the road. Shops here are worth a little browsing. One of the nicest is **The Poster Shop,** a sister shop to the one at Coconut Plantation. There's a high level of taste here; cards, prints, posters by Hawaii's leading artists would make fine presents for others or as a gift to yourself. Most posters run about $30. Prices are low. . . . **J. Bianucci** shows a selection of earrings and other island jewelry, using seeds, shells, and other objects in an artful manner. . . . There are always good buys in long muumuus and aloha shirts at **The Koloa Town Country Store,** which seems to have a little bit of everything, including macadamia nuts at low prices. . . . Prices on candies, nuts, island souvenirs, and the like are always low at **The Koloa Town Discount Mart.** . . . **Koloa Klothing for Men** has good selections and fair prices. . . . On Poipu Road, **That Tropical Feeling** has all sorts of marvelous swimwear and coverups. . . . **Hawaiian Kite Company** stocks hundreds of brightly colored kites, ranging in price from $7 to over $100. On clear days with a reasonably brisk breeze, there is usually someone from the shop flying kites in the little park on the main street. . . . **Koloa Town Discount Mart** has take-out snacks and drinks, beach towels, postcards, muumuus, aloha shirts, Tom Selleck posters, all kine stuffs. . . . **Tots, Tees, & Toes** dispenses just what you'd expect—things for kids, T-shirts, sandals, cute hand-screened T-shirts for babies, all fairly priced. . . . **Koloa Jewelry** displays the Maui Divers jewelry, pink and black coral, as well as some very attractive gold charms (sea birds, dolphins, whales), pearls, jades, and corals. And a quite interesting selection of netsuke, too. . . . **Koloa Gold** is yet another jewelry shop, dealing in tasteful gold charms and coral. . . . **Koloa Casuals** has lots of those wonderful dresses with cutwork from Indonesia, as well as shell necklaces, hats, and sunglasses. . . . **Koloa Mill,** a deli and liquor store (mostly the latter) has a great apron that reads: "Dinner will be ready when you hear the smoke alarm go off!"

About the only place in Koloa town that isn't restored to the nines is **Sueoka's,** a wonderful old "mom and pop"–type grocery and sundries shop with crackseeds displayed alongside jellybeans and rubber zoris cheek-by-jowl with Rinso and Cheer. We love it. Just behind and attached to Sueoka's is a little snack bar where you can get a super meat-loaf plate lunch for $2.50, six wonton or a bowl of saimin for $1, plus sandwiches and local-style plate lunches from $2.10 to $3.

Lappert's ice cream fans should know they can get their fix at **Lappert's Aloha Ice Cream;** the day we were there, flavors included blueberry cheesecake, egg nog, pistachio almond, apple strudel, hula pie, and more. (For the best prices on Lappert's, see ahead, under Hanapepe and Waimea.)

Note: Walking tours of Old Koloa Town are offered twice a week. If you're interested, call 742-9773 for details.

POIPU BEACH: With its glorious dry climate, golden sandy beaches, and breathtakingly beautiful surf, this is one of the choice areas of Kauai. From Old Koloa Town, Poipu Road leads you right into the heart of the area. Your first stop here might be at a place rich in both Hawaiian history and horticultural splendor, the **Gardens at Kiahuna Plantation.** As for the history, it was supposedly on this site that Laka, goddess of the hula and sister of Pele, goddess of the volcanoes, trained her initiates. For whatever it's worth, the vibrations are very good, and the gardens are spectacular; many of the monstrous cactus plants look like something out of Middle Earth. There is no charge to walk around the gardens. You can walk from here onto the beautiful grounds of the Sheraton Kauai Hotel. To reach the gardens, drive roughly 14 miles from Lihue on Hwy. 50; then take Hwy. 52 to the Gardens at Kiahuna Plantation.

If you're not surfeited by shopping yet, by all means, drive in to see **Kiahuna Shopping Village** (right off Poipu Road, opposite Kiahuna Plantation), a tasteful selection of island stores, none of them cheap, but all high in quality. One of our favorites is **Tideline Gallery,** where nature provides the inspiration for handsome handcarved ornaments and mirrors of mango wood. An orchid or sunflower carving is $20; mirrors begin at $40. . . . **Elephant Walk** could set you up for an elegant and expensive safari, if you were going; but elephant-hair jewelry is reasonable. . . . **Tutu's Toy House** has darling things for your keikis; we saw tiny happi coats, dresses, Hawaiian dolls, even clothing for teddy bears. . . . You can also outfit the little ones at **Trader's of Kauai,** which has precious stuffed animals and outfits for Hawaiian Cabbage Kids. . . . Marine art by such painters as Robert Nelson and Diane Thanos, ivory scrimshaw by Peter Kinney and Robert Sickles, complement a collection of marine antiquities and artifacts at **The Ship Store Gallery.** . . . **Tropical Shirts** has just that—myriads of original silkscreened T-shirts, some with tropical flowers. . . . **Pomare Fashion** is well known for their Polynesian-style resort wear in strong colors and patterns. We saw striking totes by Laurel Burch, handpainted beach hats from China at just $15 and $18. . . . If you haven't got your **Crazy Shirt** yet, there's a branch of the ubiquitous chain here, too. "Sake Sistah" and "Sushi Bar Kauai" are two of the popular sayings.

Even if you can't afford $300 or $400 for a feather collar, you must, at least, see the work of the island artist called **Bobbi** at **Jewels of Kauai.** Art to wear is Bobbi's stock-in-trade, and her fiber art workshop in Honolulu is considered one of the best anywhere. She fashions extraordinary collars made of feathers, shells, and other natural materials; somehow, when you put them on, you imagine yourself as a royal princess. They are modeled after royal Hawaiian robes and capes, and have a bit of an Egyptian feeling. Collars without feathers begin at $87.50. (We're putting these on our "must have" list as soon as we win the lottery.)

Feeling hungry? **Keoki's Paradise,** one of our favorite Kauai restaurants is right here, and so is **Pizza Bella,** for a light Italian meal (see preceding chapter). You can also satisfy the hungries with a chocolate-chip cookie from **Penny-packer's** (made right here) or a delicious scoop of Lappert's from **Judy Ann's Ice Cream.**

Kiahuna Shopping Village is open from 9 a.m. to 9 p.m. Monday through Saturday, until 6 p.m. Sunday. The children of Leilani's Keiki Hula Halau are featured performers in a free show, the "Twilight Polynesian Revue," presented here Monday and Thursday at 5 p.m.

Now it's time to stop for a swim. **Poipu Beach,** which you'll reach soon after turning left past Plantation Gardens, is one of the best swimming beaches on the island. Youngsters can swim in a shallow little pool; there's rolling surf farther out, and a picnic area and pavilion here too. A word of advice: Don't spend the *entire* day here, as there's plenty to see coming up ahead.

Readers have written to recommend a good diving facility in this area: **Fathom Five,** on Poipu Road, next to Koloa Chevron. They offer snorkeling lessons plus a snorkeling tour for $30, an introductory scuba-dive (no experience necessary) for $60, and a variety of exciting adventures for certified divers, from $40. They'll rent you equipment, and even take photographs of you underwater. All tours are conducted in small, personal groups. Condo-car-diving packages are available. Call them first to make reservations at 742-6991.

Around the corner from the Chevron station, at 3414 Poipu Road, is **Lotus Blossom,** a lovely and reasonably priced flower and gift shop. Orchid sprays were 50¢ each. We found wonderful, whimsical jewelry at good prices, and short Niihau shell necklaces for just $35.

GEYSERS AND GARDENS: Trace your way back now to the fork in the road and this time take the other branch, the one on the right. Continuing past Kuhio Park (on the site of the birthplace of Prince Kuhio), you come to Kukuiula Small Boat Harbor, more familiarly known as **Sampan Harbor.** Be sure to walk out on the wharf for an absolutely gorgeous view; about a mile ahead to the right is **Spouting Horn,** where the water spurts up through several holes in the lava rock, and to your left is an uncannily blue-green Pacific hurtling itself against the black rocks. When you can tear yourself away, have a look at the vendors selling jewelry outside the parking lot; quality is high, prices consistently among the lowest in the islands. A great place to take care of a lot of gift shopping.

Which eelskin wholesale house is the most wholesale? Hard to say, because such outfits abound in the islands (especially in Honolulu). Certainly, one of the biggest and best is **Lee Sand's Wholesale Eelskin Warehouse** at the Hawaiian Trading Post, which you can find right outside of Lawai, on Koloa Road, where Hwy. 50 meets Hwy. 530. Sands, who claims to be the original importer of eelskin from the Orient, sells to major eelskin distributors throughout the country and to such prestigious stores as Bloomingdale's in New York, where you can be certain the prices are much higher than what you find here. We saw lovely handbags from about $60. It is said that eelskin is 150% stronger than leather and becomes softer and more supple with use. (It's the kind of bag you just can't wear out.) As if eelskin were not exotic enough, this warehouse also sells accessories made of lizard, sea snake (snakeskin sneakers were $67), and (ugh!), chicken feet. Novelty items like wooden postcards are also sold here, and there's a welcome Lappert's Ice Cream kiosk just outside.

Just outside of Kalaheo, watch for enchanting **Kukui-O-Lono Park.** The entrance is through a majestic stone gate, just south of Kalaheo. The name means light of the god Lono; at one time kukui-oil torches here provided a beacon for fishermen at sea. Now the place is a public golf course (greens fees are around $5) and a small park, where you can see a Stone Age Hawaiian exhibit and a charming Japanese garden. There are birds everywhere.

Our next stop is again for lovers of gardens, and this is **Olu Pua Gardens,** a quarter-mile west of Kalaheo past the intersection of Hwys. 50 and 54. Olu Pua Gardens consist of 12½ acres that overlook the Pacific Ocean and surround a former plantation house built in 1931. The botanical collections within the estate include the Kau Kau Garden (edible and economic plants), the Hibiscus Garden and Hibiscus-shaped ponds, the Front Lawn (with flowering shade trees), the Jungle (shaded paths among exotic foliage and flowering plants), and the Palm Garden. Olu Pua is open for guided tours only on Monday, Wednesday, and Friday at 9:30 a.m. Admission is $6 for adults, $4 for senior citizens. For reservations and information, phone 332-8182.

You'll have to make reservations and pay $10 in advance to tour the next garden, but nature lovers and photographers will find it eminently worthwhile. This is the **Pacific Tropical Botanical Garden** in Lawai, a 186-acre garden that adjoins 100 acres of the Allerton Gardens, a private estate. To reserve an escorted tour, which is limited to about ten people, phone 332-7361, or write to Reservations Secretary, P.O. Box 340, Lauai, Kauai, HI 96765. Tours are given Monday through Friday at 9 a.m. and 1 p.m. of the Pacific Tropical Botanical Garden and the Allerton Estate. A walking tour exclusively of the Pacific Tropical Botanical Garden is available on Saturdays at 9 a.m. (To drive there, take Rte. 530 from Koloa and turn left on Hailima Rd. Follow Hailima Rd. to the end, past the Dead End sign to the Visitor Center.)

HANAPEPE AND WAIMEA: Another of the wondrous scenic views of Hawaii awaits you as you approach the town of Hanapepe. Stop at the overlook for a glorious vista of **Hanapepe Valley** below, where rice shoots, guava trees, and taro patches cover the fertile floor. Waimea Canyon is off in the distance to the left. Hanapepe, where you ought to stop for lunch at the **Green Garden** (see Chapter XI), is quaint, with old wooden, balconied Chinese shops and an air not unlike that of an Old West town. Just past the Green Garden is a shrine, hallowed among those devoted to great ice cream. This is the factory outlet store for **Lappert's Aloha Ice Cream.** Lappert's has created a bit of a sensation since it was introduced in Kauai a few years ago by an Austrian firm. It's found in all the best restaurants, and its flavors—passion fruit, mango, chocolate macadamia nut, Hula Pie, brownie fudge, fresh fruit sorbets, praline pecan 'n' cream, Kona coffee, just to hint at the possibilities—are without peer. There are two reasons for getting your ice cream here. One, they have the best selection of flavors on the island; and two, since this is the factory outlet, they always have a scoop-of-the-day special for just 75¢ (as opposed to their regular price of $1.25

for a single scoop, $2.25 for a double). Even those who normally don't care much about ice cream become converts after the first swallow.

Just past Hanapepe, off to the left on a side road, there's another HVB marker, labeled "Salt Pond." Follow Rte. H-543 here, take the first right turn past the Veteran's Cemetery, and you'll find yourself at **Salt Pond,** where the calendar seems to have stopped. It looks like a marsh dotted with strange covered walls, and it is here that salt is mined and dried (some of the drying beds in operation date back to the 17th century) as the Hawaiians have been doing it for centuries. You may be lucky and arrive while they are working; members of a local *hui* collect the crystals during the summer months. Then you can head for **Salt Pond Pavilion,** a great swimming and picnicking beach, with safe, calm water. This beach is a good place to recoup your strength for the next big series of sensations coming up at Waimea Canyon.

But first you arrive at the town of **Waimea,** which, like Wailua, is steeped in history. A favorite deep-water harbor in the olden days, it was the center of government before the coming of the white man, and the place where old Captain Cook decided to come ashore. Whalers and trading ships put in here for provisions on their long voyages in the Pacific. It was also here that the first missionaries landed on Kauai, in 1820. And it was on this site that an employee of the Russian Fur Company, Dr. Anton Scheffer, built a fort and equipped himself with a Hawaiian retinue, promising Chief Kaumaualii help in defeating Kamehameha. The latter got wind of the scheme and gave Kaumaualii orders to get his foreign ally out of Hawaii—which he did, pronto. But the ruins of the old fort, a stone wall mostly hidden by weeds, are still here; an HVB marker points the way on your left, before you come to the Waimea River. The fort may one day be restored—already rest rooms and parking facilities have been built, and some of the old stonework is now visible. Until then, however, there's not much else to see here; the interest is mostly historical.

Again on the right, back on the main street of town, after you've passed the Captain Cook Monument, look for the turnoff to the **Menehune Ditch.** Follow the river about 2½ miles, past some Japanese shops, a Buddhist temple, taro patches, rice paddies, and tiny houses; where you come to a narrow bridge swinging across the river, stop and look for a stone wall protruding above the road for a few feet on the left side. This is all that remains visible of the Menehune Ditch, a remarkable engineering accomplishment that brought water to the neighboring fields several miles down from the mountain. The curious stonecutting here has convinced anthropologists that some pre-Polynesian race created the aqueduct. Who else but the Menehunes? They did the whole thing in one night, and were rewarded by the pleased citizens of Waimea with a fantastic feast of shrimps, their favorite food. They later made so much noise celebrating that they woke the birds on Oahu, a hundred miles away. While you're busy creating some legends of your own, you might see some Hawaiian Huck Finns, placidly floating down the river on rafts made of logs tied together, little bothered by either Menehunes or tourists.

The main highway now continues beyond **Kekaha** to the arid countryside around **Mana,** and beyond that to some enormous sand dunes known as the **Barking Sands.** The Kauaians swear they say "woof" when you slide down them, but that's pretty hard to prove. The U.S. Navy has now closed the area, so take the shorter drive to the canyon; you turn off the highway just past Waimea to Rte. H-550. (A possible side trip at this point could be to **Polihale State Park** for a picnic: just continue on Rte. 50, past Mana.)

WAIMEA CANYON: For your first view of the canyon, drive on to the Kaana Ridge, which leads you right to **Kokee Park and Camp,** very different from anything you've seen on Kauai. You're in the midst of bracing mountain country now, with wonderful hiking trails, freshwater streams for trout fishing (rainbow trout season is each August and September) and swimming, wild fruit to pick in season, wild pigs and goats to hunt. The forest ranger here will give you details on trails. You can relax for a few minutes at the **Kokee Museum**, right next to the **Kokee Lodge Restaurant** and **Kokee Camps** (once again, see Chapter XI), where you could spend a long, blissful holiday.

Now the road goes up, quite rugged in parts, through forests of eucalyptus, silver oak, and koa; soon you'll see the white ohia trees with their red blossoms of lehua (you'll see lehua again when you visit Volcanoes National Park in Hawaii). On you go, to the first lookout (and the best) in Waimea Canyon, **Puu Ka Pele.** Park your car and prepare yourself for one of the most spectacular views in all Hawaii. You're standing now at the top of a 3,657-foot gorge, about a mile wide and ten miles long. Millions of years ago this was the scene of a tremendous geologic fault, a great crack in the dome of the island; erosion, streams, and ocean waves cut the cliffs into jagged shapes whose colors change with the sun and the clouds—blue and green in the morning, melting into vermilion, copper, and gold as the sun moves across it and finally sets. The gorge is comparable to the Grand Canyon, smaller than its Arizona sister, but sometimes outdoing her in the violent rainbow of its colors.

Now it's just four miles for a spectacular climax to this trip, the view from the **Kalalau Lookout.** Driving the winding road for these last few miles, you will pass the Kokee tracking station, now world famous for its part in the success of the Apollo II mission to the moon. It was from this site that a laser beam was flashed to reflectors that Neil Armstrong had set up on the lunar surface. At Kalalau, the thick tropical forest suddenly drops 4,000 feet down to the breathtakingly blue sea beyond, where it melts imperceptibly into the horizon. Below, on the knife-like ridges, are the remnants of irrigation ditches, taro patches, and signs of careful cultivation that have been long since abandoned to the elements. Read Jack London's story, "Koolau the Leper" (in *A Hawaiian Reader*), for a fictional rendering of the indomitable Koolau, who hid in the ridges here and, single-handed, held off the Hawaii National Guard in its attempt to get him to the leper colony at Molokai. His heroic wife crossed the dizzyingly narrow ridges hundreds of times in five years to bring food to her husband and son until they both died of the fearful disease and left her to return to her people alone.

This marks the end of your trip; depending on whether you want an early or late view of Waimea Canyon, you might schedule some of the other sights for the return trip. Another possibility is to drive directly to the canyon, arriving there in the morning, to avoid having your views obstructed by clouds, which sometimes form in the afternoon. Then plan your other events—perhaps lunch at the Green Garden, a swim at Poipu Beach—for the return trip in the afternoon.

READERS' SHOPPING AND SIGHTSEEING SELECTIONS: "During our stay on Kauai we met some really nice people who took us to the top of **Sleeping Giant.** Take a jug of water, camera, and a snack and leave early in the morning. The site at the top is beautiful. You hike past waterfalls, through large pine forests that make you think of the North Woods. This is an easy hike; we were a party of all ages, 6 to 65. Go to the intersection at Coco Palms and ask for directions. Even some of the locals don't know about this. . . . For fresh fruits and flowers at extraordinary prices, go to the **Stadium** in Lihue every Friday at 3:30 p.m. All the locals sell their home-grown produce. Where else can you get ten papayas for $1, pineapples at $1.50 each, a bag of tomatoes for 50¢, and flowers of all kinds for only $1 a bunch? The most popular man there is the one who grows Manoa lettuce and sells it for 75¢ a bag. Papayas are of the Waimanalo variety, and you can taste before buying. We had so much fun, went away with six bags of produce (bring your own bags), and spent about $5. . . . Now for the free things. Hike up to **Kokee** and pick plums in season around mid-July; spend a day at the **Kauai Museum** and talk to the curator. Watch for announcements in the papers of the arrival of the four-masted Japanese training ship, **Kauwo Maru,** which comes into the harbor around early July. Everyone comes out to greet them; a nice Hawaiian ceremony. . . . A good place for shelling is at **Salt Pond Beach.** If you climb the rocks around the right side of the beach you will find most unusual shells. . . . The **Flea Market** is a must. Did we get bargains? Island clothing for our luaus, shirts for $1, decorations to bring back, flowers, fantastic buys, and wonderful people" (Clyde, Barbara, Jeff, and Laura Quid, Schaumburg, Ill.).

"Those **Hilo Hattie** people are really helpful. For cosmetic reasons my wife needed a bathing suit with a high front which was almost impossible to find. I mentioned this to one of the store managers and she had one especially made for her. I also noticed that they now have lower prices in their factory showrooms" (Robert L. Fgerstad, Minneapolis, Minn.). . . . "The **D.S. Collection,** next to Restaurant Kintaro, houses some exquisite works of native artists in pottery, jewelry, and paintings. We priced some of the same lithographs in Princeville and found them to be significantly higher. They also have some fine imported Oriental porcelains. This place is definitely worth a splurge—after all, all that money one saves on lodgings has to be spent somewhere! We purchased a beautiful Japanese woodblock print for $32 and an original watercolor, matted and framed in koa wood for $65" (Jan and Mike Cobb, Buffalo Grove, Ill.).

"If you are taking Smith's flat-bottom boat to the **Fern Grotto,** try to get the 11-year-old son (going on 39) of one of the owners as your guide. You'd never believe the professional routine he has and the great jokes that he can tell. Also, the entertainment on the boat trip back was more fun than some of the entertainment we saw in the clubs. . . . Definitely bring a small container of insect repellent. We used it at the Fern Grotto and at our evening luau on the beach. The mosquitos were unbelievable. We were the only ones not slapping and scratching" (Lorice A. Swydan, Worcester, Mass.).

"For travelers who like to read, we found two bargains. First, **Kokee Lodge** has several shelves of books for sale that they call 'Experienced Books.' They have a good selection of fiction and nonfiction and all of the books are hardcover; most are stamped 'Removed from Circulation' from the Hawaii state libraries. They sell these books for $2 to $2.50—a real bargain for people like me who prefer hardcover books over paperbacks. For paperback bargains, try the **Paperback Hut** at the Coconut Plantation Market Place. They sell used paperbacks in the 50¢-and-up price range" (Scott and Marilyn Helmers, Andover, Mass.).

"We would not have stopped at **Jacques Bakery** if it had not been recommended in your book; it looked like a seedy place. But the bag of Danish pastries we bought were the absolute *best* we've ever had. So *light* and delicious! Thanks for your recommendation. . . . Driving north from Lihue on Hwy. 56, look for the sign that reads, 'Papaya Information Center.' This leads to a fruit stand where many tropical fruits are available. We found the papayas, mangoes, bananas, dried fruits, etc., to be the ripest, freshest, most delicious around, all displayed very nicely and reasonably priced" (Priscilla Worthington Cowan, Tracy, Calif.).

"We found some of the best and easiest snorkeling on Kauai was at **Lydgate Beach Park** at the mouth of the Wailua River. The park has a sandy-bottom swimming area entirely enclosed by a man-made rock reef that is home for a great variety of colorful reef fish, including large parrot fish, all of which will eat bread from your hand. Because of the reef, there are no waves" (Jack and Ruth Phillips, Summerland, B.C., Canada). . . . "Unless one is interested in only one tour of the **Pacific Tropical Botanical Gardens** at $10 per person—the tours are not all the same—I suggest a $25 membership. This entitles two people to free tours, access to satellite gardens (one near Haena, Kauai, and another near Hana, Maui), and discounts at the gift shop" (William S. Connell, Durham, N.H.). . . . "I bought a kite at one of the fancy gift shops and then found the exact kite for sale at the **Ben Franklin** store in Eleele for $9.95! Many of the items offered at the fancy tourist shops can be had for much less at **Long's** or **Pay 'N' Save"** (M.H.C., Lawaii, Hawaii). . . . "Readers should check on possible cancellations if they do not have reservations for the **Grove Farm Homestead Tour.** We were called a day after our inquiry" (John and Eleanor Vick, Longmont, Colo.).

"We would like to recommend the **Will Squyres helicopter ride.** Will Squyres was very good, quite calming, professional, and gave an interesting talk with anecdotes. His staff was pleasant, too. What a ride! Inside Mt. Waialeale! Cost: $100 for an hour" (Susan Cassel, Hastings-on-Hudson, N.Y.). . . . "Our helicopter flight to Waimea Canyon with **Papillon Helicopters** was a fabulous experience, well worth the price. They were playing Bach at full volume on the headsets as we swooped in and out of the canyon. Unforgettable!" (Bob Harrison and Hal Goodstein, Provincetown, Mass.). . . . "The best snorkeling we've ever seen—including the Caribbean—was in the little bay directly in front of the Poipu Beach Hotel. The water is a little wavy here, but if you go out in the morning, it is manageable. The fish are absolutely unbelievable. . . . There is a little market of **jewelry vendors** by the Spouting Horn near Poipu Beach almost every day. We picked up some gorgeous coral and shell necklaces of good quality at three for $5!" (Susan and Terry Young, Crystal Lake, Ill.). . . . "The **Kauai Museum** in Lihue was wonderful. We stopped to take a 'quick' look around and left three hours later—and could have stayed longer" (Bart and Lynda Esterly, Capistrano Beach, Calif.).

"We recommend the **Kukuiolono Golf Course** at Kalahao as the best and cheapest golfing anywhere on the islands. And the scenery is beautiful too" (Ken and Dolores Dugan, Boise, Idaho). . . . "Do arrive early at **Waimea Canyon.** At 8:30 a.m. on a Saturday I shared the glorious view with only a family of mountain goats. It was a peaceful and very special moment of my vacation. At noon, when I passed the viewing point on my way out of the area, I counted eight buses in the parking lot! . . . Do take the **Fern Grotto Cruise** in the late afternoon. It's less crowded and more relaxing" (Paulette Getschman, Cudahy, Wis.).

"A **note of caution** to travelers: Our camera bag with camera equipment was stolen from our car, even though it was locked, while we watched the free Polynesian show at the Market Place at Coconut Plantation, which is held on Thursday, Friday, and Saturday afternoons between 4 and 5 p.m. Local police advise that all equipment—even in car trunks—can be a target for theft, since most people enjoy the show and thieves know they won't be returning to the car at that time" (Karolyn Fairbanks, Oroville, Calif.).

"**Yoneji's** on Rice Street in Lihue is a local grocery store that carries a little bit of everything and is favored by the locals—not your usual tourist shop and a place for good buys. . . . Church bazaars not only offer good food at very reasonable prices, but they also present the visitor with an excellent opportunity to mingle with the local people. Plants, fruits, and fresh vegetables were for sale and there was also a rummage sale" (Louise Alberti, Modesto, Calif.).

"After having lived on Kauai almost two years and made a wide acquaintance among the local population, I feel qualified to tell others how to achieve a rewarding stay on the island—much more rewarding than the sterile, 'prepackaged' entertainments offered to tourists. Plan to stay a minimum of two weeks, and find a hotel that caters to the local people. Next day, explore. You can do this without a car, for a while. Find people with similar interests. Do you like to fish? Check with people at Lihue Fishing Supply. Whatever your interests are, there are people here who will enjoy sharing them with you. Photography? Hiking? See the people at the Forest Service in the state building. Ask questions. Be courteous, friendly. Talk to people—and learn to listen and to understand their slightly different way of speech. Away from Lihue there are 'mom-and-pop'-style grocery stores. Go there in preference to supermarkets. Learn to wear local-style clothes and especially footwear. . . . Island people are very easy to get acquainted with. Eye contact, a smile, and almost any attempt to make conversation will suffice to start an acquaintance" (David C. Moore, Phoenix, Ariz.).

"For those who are doing a substantial amount of cooking, we suggest shopping at the **Kukuiula Store** (Jimmy's, to the locals), located on the road between Koloa and Poipu. We comparison-shopped over a several-week period at stores in Lihue and Koloa and found the Kukuiula Store the lowest overall. For liquor, we recommend **City Liquor** on Rice Street in Lihue" (Robin and Bert Brumett, Seattle, Wash.). . . . "**Wailua Falls** in Kauai—near the Fern Grotto area—are the falls you see at the beginning of the 'Fantasy Island' television show. Also, some of it was filmed at Coco Palms, on their beautiful grounds in the coconut grove. . . . The torchlight ceremony at Coco Palms is still the best one to see" (Mrs. Elliot Gray, Cerritos, Calif.).

"We found the best **snorkeling** on Kauai was at the west end of the **Poipu Beach Hotel,** about 15 feet offshore, in two or three feet of water. Ke's Beach was not nearly as good" (Betty and Bud Eldon, Los Altos, Calif.). . . . "Poipu Beach is excellent for snorkeling—and bad for serious ocean swimming because of the volcanic rock on the ocean floor close in. It's easy to bruise and cut yourself because it is shallow for quite a way out" (Jack and Doris Toussaint, no address given). . . . "Please warn people of the coral and rock on the ocean floor of Poipu Beach in front of the Sheraton Hotel. It's very hard to see and several people cut themselves. Fins are a necessity" (Beth and Chris Baines, Chicago, Ill.). . . . "We were somewhat disappointed in the bird life until we got to **Kokee Camp.** We stayed overnight in one of the cabins, had a very active morning bird walk—this was the best birding area we saw—and spent a very informative afternoon in the museum there" (Linda Adair Wasson). . . . "Serious hikers should take along Craig Chisolm's **Hawaiian Hiking Trails** (Touchstone Press, 1976), $5.95, which is carefully researched and has reproductions of relevant topographical maps with the trails drawn in, as well as detailed verbal directions. Several hikes on Kauai are described. We took two and found the book most helpful and accurate" (Dan Keatinge, Santa Monica, Calif.).

"If readers decide to hike on the Kalalau Trail, beware of theft in cars left there. My gas tank had been drained when I got back and I knew of people whose windows had been smashed. . . . Campers and backpackers should be sure to bring all supplies; there are few camping supply stores in Kauai. Campers should be warned that Kauai's camping permits must be purchased in Lihue. I strongly recommend taking a look at the campgrounds before getting a permit" (Linda Haering, Santa Rosa, Calif.). [*Authors' Note:* There have been recent reports of vandalism and rowdyism at Kauai campgrounds.]

"We have just returned from an extensive trip to Kauai and we implore you to inform your readers of the dangers of the **Haena-Kalalau** 11-mile trail. Despite the fact that we are experienced hikers, in good shape, and had thoroughly read all available material on the trail, we were not prepared for some of the narrow ledges along the cliffs. In three or four places between Hanakoa Shack and Kalalau Valley, the trail narrows to one or two feet with a sheer drop of over 1,000 feet to the rocks below. Children and hikers who are not in the best of shape should not venture past Hanakoa. Locals told us that some hikers had been killed along the trail, but we did not confirm this. A good, safe, round-trip hike would be from Haena to Hanakoa Stream (just past Hanakoa Shack). This can be done in one day. Hanakoa Stream runs rapidly, and it is a good place to fill your canteen and cool your feet. Along the 11-mile trail, there are only three places to camp: Hanakapiai Beach, two miles in; Hanakoa Shack area, six miles in; and Kalalaua Beach, 11 miles in. The Hanakoa Shack area is hot, humid, and loaded with mosquitoes. The entire trail takes at least seven hours, and more like ten hours if you rest along the way. Hikers should not be on the trail after dark" (Bob Rose, Ted Januszewski, and Reed Snyder, Oxon Hill, Md.). . . . "We spent two days making day hikes along the **Na Pali Cliffs** trail. It is a fairly easy foot trail extending 11 miles along this most magnificent coastline. Of course, it isn't necessary or even advisable to go the full 11 miles; a two-mile walk to spectacular **Hanakapiai Beach** is really quite negotiable for all but the lame and infirm, providing they have stout footgear. This means heavy-soled tennis or deck shoes or 'desert' boots, and socks. The trail is not difficult, but it is rocky, and slippery in spots. A word of warning about the beaches along the trail. Those who are very modest or upset by nudity should be forewarned: the mode of dress at these beaches is undress. Hanakapiai has a marvelous stream flowing right into the ocean at the beach, so after a swim in the invigorating surf, one can rinse off in cool, fresh water. It is also a good idea to bring a canteen or a cup as the walker will get thirsty. There are a number of little springs that are safe to drink from along the way, but we wouldn't drink from the larger streams without using Halazone tablets" (Joann Leonard, Los Angeles, Calif.). . . . "The **Kalalau Trail** on the Na Pali coast is only for people who are fit and like to hike. We hiked only as far as Hanakapiai Beach. My suggestion: Get a sturdy walking stick or cane when you start out. At the very beginning of the trail, previous hikers had left their sticks as a courtesy" (Thomas M. Nickel, San Diego, Calif.).

"I have read several books on the **Kalalau Trail,** so was unprepared for the conditions of the first two miles to Hanakapiai Beach. It is rated as a hardy family hike, with good shoes recommended. My husband and I are in our 30s and in good shape. We wore proper clothes and hiking boots, and carried our camera and a snack in a fanny pack to free our hands and keep things dry. It had rained for at least four days previous to our hike, off and on, and that may have been part of the problem, but I understand rain is the norm there, so maybe not. Most of the last mile to the beach was downhill on wet, clayey, bare trail. I have never been on anything that slippery. I am not exaggerating when I say it was like walking on ball bearings. We saw people dressed in street shoes and thongs, people carrying videocamera equipment in large metal suitcases, and people with four- and six-year-old children. Under *no* circumstances should they have been on the trail, at least in wet conditions. For us it meant totally muddy clothes, legs, and boots, and an occasional bruise. For them it could have meant injury or worse. Please stress to your readers that although the first two miles of the Kalalau Trail are probably easy when dry, they are treacherous when wet. Even if the trail is dry, it is necessary to cross Hanakapiai Stream to get to the beach. On the day we went, that meant jumping precariously from wet rock to wet rock and scaling a muddy steep hillock on the other side, which is okay for unencumbered adults, but not for small children or adults carrying videocameras or wearing street shoes. . . . Consider buying a **videotape** of Kauai, especially if you're not taking a helicopter trip. There's a choice of formats, and prices run from $39 to $50. Some of the Waldenbooks, like the one at Kukui Grove Shopping Center, play the tapes so you can decide. It's a marvelous keepsake, even more realistic than pictures or slides" (Maggie L. Berry, Hayes, Va.).

"On the north shore of Kauai, from the end of the road at Ke'e Beach, we hiked the two miles into **Hanakapiai Beach** (one hour and 20 minutes each way). A very rough, muddy, and precipitous trail. And when we arrived there—only huge boulders and pounding waves, no sand at all. They say the sand is only there in the summertime. . . . We tried tent camping, but it wasn't very much fun because of the rain, the risk of theft, and the long, dark evenings. Also, a rented car is usually essential because the campgrounds are far from grocery stores. The city/county parks generally were vandalized and offered very poor camping. The few state parks were much better; well equipped and maintained: **Malakahana** on Oahu near Laie and **Polihale** on the west side of Kauai were particularly beautiful. The last five miles to Polihale is through a muddy cane-haul road. . . . "We were glad we took sweaters and rain jackets. During December, January, and February we needed them quite often, especially when it rained at an altitude of 4,000 feet. I could have used a pair of leather hiking boots on some of the rocky, muddy trails. It was 41° Fahrenheit one night at Kokee State Park" (Jack and Ruth Phillips, Summerland, B.C., Canada). . . . "While driving to Kokee, I picked up a young man with a tight necklace who said that he lives in the wild part of Kauai, which he reached by a two-day hike from Kokee Camps. He gets supplies by boat. I asked him if he owned land there, but he said the land didn't belong to anyone. I asked him why he lives there. He said, "Because it's like the Garden of Eden, with fruits and flowers'" (Mark Terry, Honolulu, Hi.).

"We drove on from Kalalau Lookout for about one mile of paved road to the **Puu O'Kila Lookout**, about a third around the canyon rim, from where the view of the ocean far below is completely different. The trail to **Pihea**, along with four other trails, starts from here" (Mrs. Parker Hollingsworth, Pacific Grove, Calif.). . . . "Definitely drive beyond Kalalau Lookout to the **Puu O'Kila Lookout.** This was the most spectacular view of our trip The beauty and silence of the Na Pali Cliffs and coast from this point cannot be described—as we reached the lookout, a rainbow was forming over the cliffs! There's a narrow ridge trail that lets you see the cliffs from many angles—it was easy to walk, but muddy in spots" (Debra J. Tait, Burlington, Mass.).

"**Polihale Beach** is not good for swimming, but it's a marvelous picnic-sketching-walking beach. There are long vistas of white sand, cliffs coming down to the ocean, fire pits, picnic pavilions—and no one there. Camping is allowed farther on. Go past Kekaha on Rte. 50; when 50 goes left at the intersection, turn right on the narrow, paved road. Turn left at the HVB marker that reads 'Polihale Sacred Springs,' and follow the dirt road through the sugarcane field five miles to the beach" (Mrs. J. C. Chognard, Menlo Park, Calif.). . . . "**Polihale Beach** is very beautiful, a nice place for picnics, sunning, or just loafing. But we've been hit by sand fleas every time we visited it. Every year it's a toss-up —do we suffer the bites or forget it all. The beauty of the beach always wins out. There's some nudity at the far end of the beach near the cliffs, but it can be avoided by staying near the main section" (Michael J. Toennessen, Bellingham, Wash.).

"The **Fruit Market** on Hwy. 56 North past Kapaa was the only place, including the grocery store, where we could find guavas. What a treat! They also had coconut meat in baggies. The **People's Market** on Hwy. 50 South put a straw in a coconut for $1 and our boys loved it" (Mr. and Mrs. Steven Benner, Nevada, Mo.). . . . "Catholics visiting Lihue should not miss the 9 a.m. Sunday Mass at the **Immaculate Conception Church,** a mile out of town past the hospital. We heard the most magnificent choir at a folk mass there, consisting of 50 voices, five guitars, two electric guitars, two ukuleles, and an organ,

singing Hawaiian tunes given religious lyrics" (Ray Van Vorse, Maynard, Mass.). . . .
"We rented a VW **camper** that came with a tent for our boys. This is the best way to travel
on Kauai, for you can stay at many of the beautiful beaches and parks, and if the north side
gets rain you can easily drive to the sunny side. We went in winter, and the weather was
often stormy and windy. We met many lovely Hawaiians at the parks and were invited to
join in a local feast and party; it was the highlight of our trip. We loved **Polihale Beach:**
good puka hunting, good wading, and our favorite camping beach—and it's the warmest
one in winter" (Phyllis Montague, San Diego, Calif.).

Chapter XIII

THE ISLAND OF HAWAII

1. Hilo
2. Between Hilo and Kona
3. Kailua-Kona

EVER HEAR OF a tropical island with black beaches, snow-capped mountains, cedar forests, and one of the largest cattle ranches in the world? This is **Hawaii,** twice as large as all the other Hawaiian Islands combined (4,030 square miles), the orchid capital of America, and the residence of Pele, the goddess of volcanoes, who still stages some spectacular eruptions every couple of years. Islanders invariably refer to it as the Big Island, although it is sometimes called the Orchid Island or the Volcano Island; all the names are appropriate and all suggest part of the fascination of this astonishing continent in miniature. To know the 50th state, you must know the island of Hawaii.

Like all the neighbor islands, the Big Island is more expensive for the budget tourist than Oahu; nevertheless, you should be able to stay fairly close to your $50-a-day budget. Your car rental—unless it's split up three or four ways— is your biggest expense here, for driving distances are sizable, especially from one side of the island to the other (about 100 miles).

Hawaii is about 200 miles souteast of Honolulu, and either Hawaiian, Mid Pacific, or Aloha Airlines will take you to **Hilo** on the east or to **Kailua-Kona** on the west in roughly half an hour. You can also fly directly to or from Kona from the West Coast. Which city should you choose as your first stop? We've done it both ways and our considered opinion is that it doesn't make a particle of difference. Let your itinerary and the airline schedules—the ease with which you can make connections to the next island on your agenda—be the determining factor. Hilo, the only real city on the island and the second largest in our 50th state, is the takeoff point for the imposing Volcanoes National Park and the lava-scarred Puna area. Hilo has been experiencing a slump as of late, but it still has its own gentle charm. Kona is fishing and the beach. From either you can drive across the island and see all the sights. We prefer to stay in one hotel in Hilo and one in Kona, but it's possible to make one side of the island your base if you don't mind long drives (please limit your driving to daytime hours for safety!). Read up on the hotels, restaurants, and nightlife in each area in this chapter, the particular sights in the next, and you'll know just where you want to stay and for how long.

U-DRIVES: Most agencies on the Big Island offer a flat rate with unlimited mileage—you buy the gas. You have your choice of the trusty and popular inter-island outfits like **Alamo, Dollar, Budget,** etc., whose main offices are all in Honolulu (see Chapter IV, "Transportation Within Honolulu," for details), or local agencies like **Phillip's U-Drive** (tel. in Hilo, 935-1936; in Kona, 329-1730), whose cars can begin at $17.95 in winter, $14.95 in summer. These prices are for economy, standard-shift cars, mostly Datsuns and Toyotas. Automatics and American cars are higher. You can make advance reservations by writing to any U-Drive company in Hilo but there are usually plenty of cars available (except at the peak tourist seasons), and the budget-minded driver can often do best by some careful on-the-spot shopping.

Keep in mind that the U-Drive business is a highly competitive one here as elsewhere, with rates in constant flux; you may be able to get a flat rate or a better deal than you expected just by asking. Also note that there is, alas, usually a ferrying charge of between $20 and $30 if you rent your car on one side of the island and return it on another, which is what most tourists do, renting in Hilo and returning in Kona, or vice versa.

1. Hilo

ARRIVAL IN HILO: You'll know why it's called the Orchid Island as soon as you arrive at General Lyman Field: rain may be helping those orchids to grow. But don't despair; it's just a "Hawaiian blessing" and probably won't last long. Nobody in Hilo lets a little drizzle interfere with comings and goings. (In winter an occasional rainstorm will hit this part of the island harder than any other.) There's no public transportation into town, so pick up your car or get a cab (about $4) to take you to your hotel.

BUSES: For all practical purposes, you're going to need a car in Hilo, even though there is a city bus system. It's limited; however, the **Hele-On** bus does make two trips a day around town, one early in the morning, one in midafternoon. You can ask for the bus schedule at your hotel or call the MTA at 935-8241 or 961-6722.

The **Mass Transportation Agency** (MTA) also provides island-wide public transportation bus service with buses operating Monday through Saturday, and fares ranging from 75¢ to $5.25 per ride. Bus routes connect Hilo with Kailua-Kona, Waimea, Honokaa, Pahoa, and Volcanoes National Park, among others. Again, call MTA at 935-8241 or 961-6722. Bus schedules are sometimes available at the **State Visitor Information booths** in the airport, and always at the **Hawaii Visitors Bureau** in the Hilo Plaza Building, Suite 104, 180 Kinoole St. (tel. 961-5797). Mrs. Lei Branco is the helpful lady to contact.

HOTELS IN HILO: Every now and then you come across a little hotel where you know you could comfortably settle down for a long, long time. Such a place is the **Dolphin Bay Hotel,** at 333 Iliahi St., Hilo, HI 96720 (tel. 935-1466), in a quiet residential neighborhood of Hilo, that's just a four-block walk to town. The 18-studio unit meanders in and out of a lush tropical garden resplendent with papayas, breadfruits, bananas, and the like; it's the only hotel we know where you are invited to step right outside your room and pick your breakfast! The rooms are modern, quite large, and nicely furnished, with full kitchens and large tub-shower combinations in the bathrooms. The carpeting in the rooms extends into the bathrooms and even up to the front and back doors—yes, most rooms have both. The standard studios, which rent for $25 single, $31 twin, sleep one or two comfortably. The superior studios, usually with a twin and a double bed (plus a built-in Roman-style tub!), are larger and can easily sleep

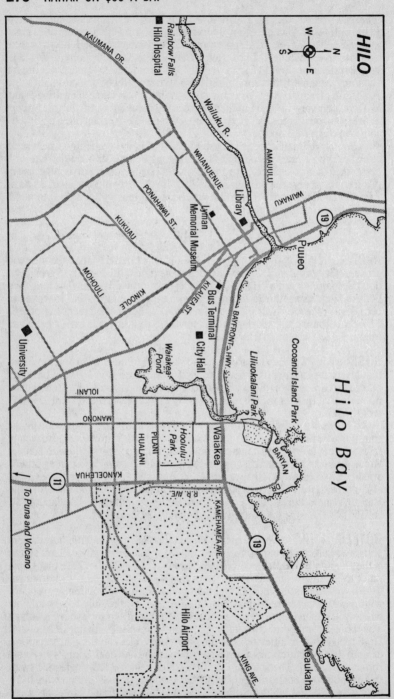

three; these are $31 single, $41 double. There's also a marvelous honeymoon room with an open-beamed ceiling and a large lanai for $39; and some really spacious one- and two-bedroom apartments, perfect for families, are $51 for the one-bedroom, $57 for the two-bedroom, $7 for each extra person. Favorable weekly rates are available. Since the hotel is near Hilo Bay, a cooling breeze keeps the units pleasant all year long. Manager John Alexander dispenses the same kind of warmth and hospitality that have made this one of our best island finds over the years. He and his staff will map out tours, arrange trips, and advise on the best restaurants. Write or phone in advance if you can, since the guests who come back each year—many from Canada and the Midwest—keep this place hopping. Lots of readers' hurrahs for this one, even though there is no pool (see the Readers' Selections, ahead).

Hilo's original budget hotel, the Palm Terrace, which had fallen below our standards in the past, has been under new management for several years now, and offers an acceptable budget alternative for undemanding types. Now it's called the **Lanikai Hotel,** 100 Puueo St., Hilo, HI 96720 (tel. 935-5556). There are just 31 rooms here, about six of which have small refrigerators with hotplates. The hotel has been repainted, carpeted, and good secondhand furniture from the late, lamented Kona Inn has been used for the refurnishing. Rooms are a decent size, with orange or mustard spreads, open closets, showers (but no tubs), no telephone, radio, or TV. It is just above the highway, so there might be some traffic noise. Since the hotel does not require a lease, people looking for a place to live in the area find this a good choice for a month or two. Rates go from $18 to $20 single, $21 to $24 double, daily; $80 to $100 single, $110 to $120 double, weekly; and $208 to $240 single, $250 to $265 double, monthly. The Lanai, an inexpensive local restaurant, is on the premises, as is Kona's, a friendly little lounge.

The **Hilo Hukilau Hotel** (tel. 935-0821), near Hilo Bay, has long been a pleasant place to stay. The local branch of the kamaaina-owned Hukilau Hotels (there are others on Maui) has attractive rooms with lanais, TVs, and phones—rooms that look out either over the freshwater swimming pool or lush tropical gardens. The lobby is decorated with lauhala-weave walls, bamboo, and tapa cloth. Wood fenceposts, Polynesian murals, and tikis permit you to forget the mainland. There's a dining room and cocktail lounge. Singles and doubles are $39 standard, $44 superior, $46 deluxe. An additional person is charged $10. A hotel-and-car package for two persons goes for $49 standard, $54 superior, $56 deluxe, and includes hotel room and a Budget Rent-A-Car. Locals advise of noise from traffic on weekends. The toll-free phone to Hawaii is 800/367-7000, or write to Hukilau Resorts, 2222 Kalakaua Ave., Suite 714, Honolulu, HI 96815.

Uncle Billy's Hilo Bay Hotel, right on the ocean at 87 Banyan Dr. (tel. 935-0861), is a happy place, owned and operated by a Hawaiian family. It's run on "Hawaiian time" and the pace is leisurely; you can feel that pleasant Polynesian paralysis setting in the moment you step into the South Seas lobby, with fishnets and tapa-covered walls to remind you where you are. All rooms have air conditioning and television plus private lanai. The higher priced rooms are huge: two double beds are lost in the room, and the appointments—like a Princess telephone and a broad marble vanity—are elegant. Standard rooms are $44 single, $49 twin; superiors are $49 and $54; deluxe are $54 and $59; and oceanfront are $59 and $64. Kitchenettes are available in superior and deluxe rooms for an additional $10. Room-and-car packages are also available. Standards are $54 and $59; superior are $59 and $64; deluxe are $64 and $69; and oceanfront are $69 and $74. Most rooms face a tropical garden that leads to a path to the swimming pool, next to the ocean on Hilo Bay. Uncle Billy's Restaurant, right in the hotel, is a fun restaurant for food and entertainment (see ahead). For toll-free reservations, call 800/367-5102 direct to Hawaii, or write to 87 Banyan Dr., Hilo, HI 96720.

Worlds away from the pleasantly hokey tourist world of Banyan Drive is the **Hilo Hotel,** at 142 Kinoole St., Hilo, HI 96720 (tel. 961-3733), a businessperson's hotel in the center of town. The outside is very pleasant, with lava-rock walls, a large swimming pool, spacious gardens, and the excellent Fuji Restaurant for Japanese food and drinks, where the locals like to gather. The hotel rooms, all of which have a telephone and bath with stall shower, are clean and adequate, but nothing at all fancy. But the price is okay: standard singles or doubles in the Kalakaua wing at $28. Kona coffee in the morning is complimentary. This is the kind of place where you might find the members of a neighbor-island high school baseball team spending their vacation. At night, it's so pleasant to sit on the rocking chairs on the porch and listen to the tranquil Japanese music piped into the lobby.

When the lush, luxurious Sheraton Waiakea Village Hotel closed a few years ago, there was some question as to what would happen to the property. Now we know, and the answer is good news for the budget tourist. Half of the original ten buildings, containing 144 studio and one- and two-bedroom suites, have been turned into the **Waiakea Villas Hotel,** 400 Hualani St., Hilo, HI, 96720 (tel. 961-2841). The other half are long-term apartment rentals. These handsome Polynesian-style buildings are set amidst 13½ acres of meandering waterways and lagoon in a giant tropical garden. Rooms, which are very large, are handsomely furnished in the island style, and private lanais all overlook either garden or waterways. Each room (except the standard) has a full kitchen, color TV, and air conditioning. There's a swimming pool on the grounds, as well as a restaurant, Springwater Café, and Kay's, a wonderful bakery whose pastries and coffees are perfect for breakfast. Rates for a standard studio, with a king-size bed or two double beds is $27; a superior studio with king or two double beds and kitchen is $32; a deluxe, large studio with king-sized bed is $40; a one-bedroom suite with a king or two doubles is $55; and a honeymoon suite with king is $90. There is a $5 charge for each additional person, $5 for a crib, no charge for children 11 and under if no bed is requested. Rates subject to change.

Another Hilo property that's undergone many a change in the last few years is the **Country Club Apartment Hotel,** 121 Banyan Drive, Hilo, HI 96720 (tel. 935-7171). Formerly the Royal Pacific Travel Lodge, this place mostly rents on a weekly and monthly basis ($133 to $147 weekly, $290 to $360 monthly), but they do have some rooms for transients, and these go, single or double, for just $25 standard without TV, and $27 with TV. A room-and-car package is $38.95. The rooms are quite acceptable for this price, and there is an attractive pool, too, right out on Hilo Bay.

The bed-and-breakfast concept offers an alternative to the hotel scene: rooms and breakfasts in charming private homes throughout the islands. The Big Island is no exception. The local representative of the inter-island group, **Bed & Breakfast Hawaii,** P.O. Box 449, Kapaa, Kauai, HI 96746 (tel. 822-7771), is Mrs. Joan Long, 110 Makani Circle, Hilo, HI 96720 (tel. 959-9736). Rates start at $20 for singles, $30 for doubles. There is a $10 yearly membership fee: with a $2.40 airmail fee for postage, this includes a directory of homes and apartments.

RESTAURANTS IN HILO: Hilo's restaurants do quite well for the budget tourist. By eating where the local people do and avoiding all but a few of the tourist restaurants, you can eat not only cheaply but well. A good place to start is **Ken's House of Pancakes,** right at the intersection of Banyan Drive and Rte. 11. This is a prime budget eating spot: good location, good low prices, good food. Modern pinpoint lighting and bright-red booths or counter seats give you a feeling that you're in competent hands. At breakfast, pancakes start at $1.95, waffles at $2.45. Once you start adding berries to the batter and meat or whatever on the side—the varieties and combinations seem endless—prices go up; but they manage to stay around the $3.45 mark. Good news: Lunches and dinners (which include a tossed green salad, potatoes, and hot roll) are the same price. They begin with filet of mahimahi at $6.50 and move up through such choices as veal cutlet, prawns, fried chicken, to a broiled steak at $7.75. Many local favorites are also offered. Pop by from midnight until 6 a.m. and you'll be treated to an early brunch—all the pancakes, plus imaginative omelets with an international touch, in the $3.75 to $5.75 range. Our kind of place.

Also our kind of place is **Kow's Deli,** in the Kaiko'o Hilo Mall, a brightly modern cafeteria with orange Formica tables, wooden chairs, and murals on the wall. The star here is authentic Chinese food, served deli-cafeteria style. Order one of the $3.35 plate lunches or dinners and you'll get a choice of any two of the nine tasty entrees (roast duck, shoyu chicken, beef broccoli, etc.), plus rice or noodles. Special breakfasts are $2.50, for which you get noodle roll, stewed pork bun (a house specialty), rice cake, hash, and tea or coffee. Kow's stays open until 7:30 p.m., and the prices do not go up. This place caters mostly to local people and is usually thronged with busy shoppers, so you know the values have to be good. Even if you're not eating here, you might want to stop by for some of those luscious Chinese cookies—spice cake, wedding cake, black bean cake—in the window.

Mexican food served in a clean, healthful (there's a health-food store adjoining), and cheery atmosphere is what you'll find at **Norberto's El Café** at 11 Waianuenue Ave. (tel. 961-4941). Local friends swear it's the best Mexican food on the island. Prices are modest: complete dinners run from $8.25 to $9.35, and along with entrees like burritos rancheros, enchiladas grandes, or rellenos tampico (cheese-stuffed fried chilis) come soup, a good green vegetable salad, refried beans, rice, corn chips, and salsa. Vegetarian ingredients can be substituted in any dish; you can even have beans cooked in vegetable oil rather than lard. Try the guacamole to start, the chocolate cream pie to finish. Margaritas can be had by the glass or pitcher. Norberto's serves dinner from 5 to 9:30 p.m. Monday through Saturday. Closed Sunday.

For a true taste of Japan, the place to go is the **Nihon Cultural Center,** newly opened at 123 Lihiwai St. (tel. 969-1133), overlooking Hilo Bay and lovely Liliuokalani Gardens. Authentic to the last detail, the Nihon Cultural Center houses an art gallery, a traditional tea room, an auditorium for cultural events, and at the heart of it all, a restaurant where traditional Japanese chefs ply their art. Of course there is a sushi bar—the menu describes these dainty morsels of fish and rice as "health foods"—and a dining room for regular Japanese meals. Sashimi, tempura, and tonkatsu lunches run $4.50 to $8; beef curry and pork cutlet curry each cost $4. Lunch specials are $5.75 and include two items and accompaniments. The same combination platters are $6.75 at dinner. Dinner specials, from $8.50 to $22, include sukiyayi, a broiled fish meal, a broiled eel meal, and shabu shabu, a fanciful beef dish. Traditional Japanese soup, pickled vegetables, fruits, and rice dishes accompany the meals. A traditional kaiseki full-course dinner runs $15 to $22. Of course there's sake or Japanese beer to wash down your meal, and green tea ice cream for dessert. Lunch is served from 11 a.m. to 2 p.m., dinner from 5 to 9 p.m.; the sushi bar is open from 11 a.m. to 2 p.m. and 5 to 10 p.m. Reservations are advised.

You can relax in a very pretty setting at the **K.K. Tei Restaurant,** 1550 Kamehameha Hwy., between Hilo and the airport (tel. 961-3791). **K.K.** stands for the late K. Kobata, who was Japanese, and the food is mostly Japanese, with some American specialties. Lunch is an especially good buy; our favorites are the complete Japanese ozen lunches, served on a lacquered tray. With your under $6 main course—perhaps tonkatsu or beef teriyaki—come miso soup, rice, pickled vegetables, mukozuke, raw fish or salad, and tea. Seafood salads, sandwiches, and noodle dishes are also available. Dinners are a bit more expensive but still a good buy: beef or chicken sukiyaki on the Japanese menu is about $9. American-style seafood and steak dishes start at around $8. If there are at least six of you, call for reservations to sit in one of the pretty ozashiki rooms; from here you'll see the authentic Japanese rock garden and pool. The bar begins dishing out free pupus from 11 a.m.

There's another K.K. restaurant that you should know about. At 413 Kilauea Ave. (tel. 935-5216), next to the Safeway, is **K.K.'s Place,** a Japanese-American fast-food operation, sparklingly clean, and offering tasty plate lunches —with two entree choices like fried fish, chicken hekka, pork cutlet, and meat cutlet—from $3.50 to $4. Meals are served day or night at the same price. A good place to remember whenever you feel hungry and in a hurry. You'll usually find Mrs. Kobata at the Place, and son Paul at the K.K. Tei.

Reuben's Mexican Food, 336 Kamehameha Ave., across from the waterfront (tel. 961-2552), is a real local hangout. Aside from its shocking-pink color scheme and Mexican murals on the wall, it has little in the way of decor, but it's large (there's plenty of breathing room between the tables), has a big bar, and the food is good. Reuben's is run by Reuben and Sue Villanova (he's from Mexico, she's from Hilo), and his brother, Vicente, who is the chef. Our appetizer of nachos ($2.75) was hot and tasty; so was our chicken sour-cream enchilada combination plate for $5.50. At least 19 combination plates, which include beans and rice, run $5.50 to $7. À la carte orders, like the tasty bean and beef burrito that we enjoyed, with stripped beef, frijoles, chilis, grated cheese, lettuce, and guacamole in a flour tortilla, are around $3.50. You'll find lots of local families here, enjoying the food, the low prices, and the memorable margaritas. Open Monday through Saturday from 11 a.m. to 9 p.m. and closed Sunday; same menu all day.

What brings the Mercedeses and other fancy cars to the modest Puainako Town Center? Although not many tourists know of it, the Chinese population has discovered **Ting-Hao Mandarin Restaurant** (tel. 959-6288) and they come to enjoy the wizardry of Ting Cheng, the master chef, recently of Taiwan, whose repertoire includes some 200 banquet dishes; he cooks Peking, Mandarin, Szechuan, and Cantonese style so there is quite a variety on the menu. Everything we've tried—and we've dined here many times—has been special. Corn eggdrop soup is unusual and subtly flavored; pot stickers, those tasty dumplings that are both steamed and fried (on one side), are a great beginning to your meal. Outstanding main courses in the Mandarin style include shredded pork with fungus and golden egg, shredded pork with garlic sauce (watch out, it's hot!), and the eggplant with garlic sauce, each $4.50. Unusual and delicious, too, are the Kung Pao ika (that's cuttlefish) with spicy paprikas, $6, and the Kung Pao shrimp with spicy paprikas, $7, the minced chicken with lettuce, $8, and the chicken with cashew nuts, $5.50. Most of the entrees are very inexpensive (around $3 to $5), and hearty enough to fill you up for many hours. In fact, we usually find the portions here so generous that we wind up taking containers back to our kitchenette apartment for the next day's lunch. At lunch, between 11 a.m. and 2 p.m. each day, there are four daily specials, served with either egg fu yung, spare ribs, or an egg roll, for $3.25. Vegetarians can enjoy a number of good dishes. Ting-Hao is a large, very clean restaurant, simply decorated, with fans and prints on the wall. Service is helpful and friendly; there's a warm, family feeling here. It is open Monday through Saturday from 11 a.m. to 9 p.m., and on Sunday from 5 to 9 p.m. Puainako Town Center is past the airport, and not far from Prince Kuhio Plaza; the restaurant is near Foodland.

Although it's one of the city's newer dining establishments, **Restaurant Osaka,** 762 Kanoelehua St. (tel. 961-6699), is fast becoming a Hilo tradition, and it's easy to understand why. From the clean, modern decor and cozy family atmosphere to the varied menu, very tasty food, and generous island portions, Restaurant Osaka is simply a very good place to eat. At lunch, you have your choice of sandwiches, American dishes, noodle dishes, and a full Japanese menu of tempuras, teriyakis, ginger pork, chicken or beef tofu, and fried fish, priced from $4.50 to $4.95, all served with soup, rice, tsukemono, and tea. Prices for sushi are the same at lunch and dinner (from $5.25 to $8.25); the nigiri we tried was delicious and artfully served on lacquer trays. Dinner offers similar bargains. Complete meals start at $5.25 for the fried fish prepared in a variety of styles, and go to $7.95 for the beef or chicken sukiyai. They are served with appetizer, soup, pickled vegetables, and tea. Children's combination dinners are $4.75. Be sure to try the exotic desserts: pumpkin mousse, passion fruit, or guava chiffon pie, a bargain at $1.50. If you're in a hurry, the take-out sushi is reasonably priced: $12.50 buys you 34 pieces of a varied selection, great for a picnic or a meal at home.

Restaurant Osaka is open for breakfast, lunch, and dinner, from 7 a.m. to 11 p.m., and the bar, which serves free pupus with drinks, stays open until midnight.

Overlooking the Ice Pond at Reed's Bay is a new restaurant that's quickly become a hit with local people and visitors alike. It's **Harrington's,** 135 Kalanianaole St., near Banyan Drive (tel. 961-4966). There's an atmosphere of casual elegance here in the open-air dining room and lounge, an "up" mood, and delicious food. Plan on this one for a splurge meal, since most entrees—like mahimahi forestière, New York steak, veal or chicken marsala, sautéed scallops, and the like—are in the $10 to $15 range (they are accompanied by rolls, soup, choice of salads and starch). However, there is a way to eat here inexpensively, albeit lightly. Ask to be seated in the lounge rather than the main dining room, and along with your beer or drink you can order from the appetizer and side-dish menu, which means that items like deep-fried calamari strips, mushrooms tempura, etc., ranging from $2.50 to $5.50, will be served cut up, pupu style. You could even have a stuffed potato for $1.25 and a house salad (Caesar or pasta or tossed greens) for $2.25. Be sure to make reservations if you do sit in the dining room, since this is a very, very popular scene. Open nightly from 5:30 p.m.

If you've never tried Korean food, Hilo is a good place to do so. **Koreana Restaurant** in Waiakea Square, 100 Kanoelehua Ave. (tel. 961-4983), offers all of the traditional dishes like kal-bi, ko kee, kim chee stew, seasoned octopus, oxtail soup, mandoo and noodle soup, and prices are reasonable: from about $4 to $7. At either lunch (10 a.m. to 5 p.m.) or dinner (5 to 9 p.m.), your entree will come served with soup, vegetable, rice, and kim chee, giving you a chance to sample a little bit of a lot.

Downtown at 168 Keawe St. is a place the locals like very much: **Restaurant Satsuki** (tel. 935-7880). It's small, very clean, plain, and neat, with a sushi bar on one side, a screen dividing the room. Formica and vinyl chairs and tables. Might as well go with Satsuki's Special Teishoku; $5.95 at lunch, $6.15 at dinner, it includes any two choices of either fried shrimp, shrimp tempura, yakitori, pork teriyaki, teriyaki fish, or butterfish, served up with various side vegetables, plus soup, rice, and tea. Donburi dishes with soup, tsukemono, and tea, are $4.15 to $6.50. Open for breakfast, lunch, and dinner.

Another local place where you can't go wrong is the ten-table **Tomi Zushi,** 68 Mamo St., where $5 to $6 buys you a good Japanese dinner, in the company of lots of local people who are heartily lapping up the food. There is no attempt at decor here: walls are institutional green, and tables are just tables. You come for the food. Here's what the average $5 to $6 buys: a choice of any two main courses like fried shrimp Tokyo style, shrimp tempura, wok sashimi, beef or pork or fish tempura, accompanied by soup, pickled vegetables, rice, and tea. Plate lunches are $3.50. Plan on this when you want to eat quickly, as it's no place to relax and visit. Tomi Zushi closes at 8:30 p.m., and is open every day but Wednesday. Only dinner is served Sunday.

Like to dine at one of the best restaurants in town for just $6.95? You can do so at **Rosey's Boathouse,** 760 Piilani St. (tel. 935-2112), if you pass up the seafood and meat specialties and concentrate instead on the copious salad bar, as we recently did. This is one of the better soup-and-salad bars around, with cottage cheese, sprouts, mixed beans, a good green salad, fresh pineapple spears, etc. Rosey's rates high for atmosphere (panels of rough-hewn wood, crystal chandeliers, black leather booths, subdued nautical decor), service by the friendly young waiters, and very good food. There are well-priced dinners here each night: mahimahi at $8.25, teriyaki chicken and kal-bi at $8.95, and teriyaki steak at $9.95, all including salad and bread. Fresh local fish and sea-food dishes go from $8.25 to $17.95. Specialty of the house is chilled mainland beef, and all broiling is done over a ki'awe charcoal fire. Children's dinners are priced from $3.95 to $5.95. Rosey's is open for dinner only, from 5:30 to 10 p.m. every day; and the bar does not close down until 1 a.m. Entertainment is on Tuesday through Saturday, with a musical mix that goes from jazz to contempo-rary Hawaiian. Vegetable tempura and fettuccine Alfredo are among the exotic pupus served at the bar until midnight. Prices start at $2.50, and portions are generous! Reservations are suggested.

Sun Sun Lau, 1055 Kinoole (tel. 935-2808), is a venerable Hilo institution, very large and nicely decorated (screens make the huge space seem more inti-mate), that has been popular with local families for over 40 years now. A survey by *Gourmet Guide of Hawaii* recently chose it as the Big Island's top Chinese restaurant. Prices are modest. Such delicious house specials as young corn chicken, lemon chicken, stuffed tofu, Peking tofu, and crab rolls run from $4 to $6.50. Lunch specials, which include chop suey, tomato beef, spare ribs, and crisp wonton, are $4.25. While you're here, take a look at the fascinating seed and candy section. Cracked seed, a Chinese specialty, has become popular all over the 50th state and here you see one of the best selections anywhere: salted lemon seed, cherry seed, shredded mango, even something called footballs, which are made out of olives! The handsome gift section also includes canned Chinese food, artful tea pots, and beautifully hand-carved camphor chests from Hong Kong that run from about $28.65 to $395. Sun Sun Lau is open Friday, Saturday, and Sunday until 9 p.m., every other day until 8 p.m. (closed Wednes-day).

Jimmy's Drive Inn, at 362 Kinoole St. (tel. 935-5571), is a popular local place offering some of the best prices in town. The "drive inn" is misleading; you don't eat in your car but at clean chrome tables or at the counter. Japanese meals go from $4.95 to $6.95, and there are daily dinner specials like chicken-katsu, beef stew, fish tempura, breaded scallops, and captain's platter, which go from $5.25 to $6.95, quite a bargain considering that they are accompanied by rice, vegetables, tossed salad, and coffee or iced tea. On the regular menu, there are about half-a-dozen complete dinners and complete seafood dinners priced between $5 and $5.95; and these include such entrees as barbecued steak, liver and bacon, ahi, butterfish, and shrimp tempura, all accompanied by soup or salad, fries or rice, vegetable, bread, and beverage. Open from 8 a.m. to 10 p.m. daily except Sunday.

At Prince Kuhio Shopping Plaza

You'll want to spend some time seeing Hilo's big, new, multimillion-dollar Prince Kuhio Shopping Plaza out on Hwy. 11, and while you're at it, you can have some pretty good meals, too. Best bet is **Kow's Deli & Chinese Restaurant,** a sister to the Kow's at Kaiko'o Hilo Mall, which looks like a cute coffeeshop dressed up with large fans and Chinese prints on the wall. The food is excellent and inexpensive—most dishes are between $3 and $5—and all the favorites are here, like chicken with oyster sauce on crisp noodles, pressed duck with crisp almond sauce, cake noodles, and a large selection of seafood, for which Kow's is especially known; steamed fish with black bean sauce or ginger and onion sauce is priced according to the market. Local people love this one.

Also at Prince Kuhio is a pleasant **Woolworth's Restaurant,** which offers inexpensive meals on the order of roast turkey, crispy fried chicken, tempura shrimp platter, and beef stew, local style, plus sandwiches, burgers, and breakfast and fountain specials. **Arby's,** a member of the popular chain, offers its roast beef sandwiches, plus good breakfast specials. And the sparkling **Boomer's Fountain** has daily hot lunch specials, complete with rice and vegetable. Service is quick and efficient and prices go from $2.75 to $3.50. Ice cream, milk shakes, and other fountain treats are popular here.

Eating at the Hotels

The popular **Hukilau Restaurant** in the Hilo Hukilau Hotel, Banyan Drive, is managing to hold the price line on three good meals a day. They have a lunch special every day at $2.55, which includes entree, salad bar, rice or potato; and at least a dozen à la carte entrees (filet of mahimahi steak, stuffed tomato salad, etc.) are just $2.85 to $5. Dinner features two menus, seafood and regular. Most seafood dinners are priced at either $7.95 or $8.95 for the likes of salmon steak, fresh fried oysters, fresh abalone steak, rainbow trout, soft-shell crab, and fresh fish of the day, all served with soup of the day and salad bar. On the regular dinner menu, entrees go from $6.95 to $9.95 for the likes of calves' liver, prime rib roast, teriyaki steak, and steak and lobster, again accompanied by soup-and-salad bar. Breakfast here is fun, too, especially when you have the pineapple hotcakes or french toast with macadamia nuts. The dining room is pleasant, and the staff has plenty of aloha.

For a traditional Japanese meal—and for an excellent bargain as well—don't miss the **Restaurant Fuji,** in the Hilo Hotel, 142 Kinoole St. (tel. 961-3733). This is one of those gracious, relaxed places where you can really get comfortable; you can sit either at the tempura bar (where you watch your dishes simmer and sizzle), at the comfortably spaced tables in the dining room, or at tables with hibachi grills overlooking the pool. The hotel is owned by Japanese interests and caters to a Japanese clientele, so you can be sure the food is authentic. At lunchtime recently, we sampled the very good butterfish ($6.50), and the barbecued chicken and egg ($5.90) with green salad, soup, vegetables, rice, and tea. There are a number of dinners under $8—yosenabe teishoku for $7.90 and pork ginger teishoku for $7.50, to name two you might want to try.

Meals on the Run

One of the most popular coffeeshops in town is **Dick's** in the Hilo Shopping Center, a lively local place with sporting pennants on the walls. Many of our readers have written to recommend it over the years. On the à la carte dinner menu, you could choose entrees like chicken cutlet, grilled fish filet, teriyaki steak oriental, grilled pork chops, most in the $3.50 to $4.50 range, with New York–cut steak under $6. And along with your main course comes soup or salad, starch, rolls and butter. Lunch features burgers from $1, gourmet sandwiches like pastrami on French bread or steak sandwich for under $3, "lite lunches" (sandwiches plus soup or salad) from $1.65 to $1.85—and homemade pies and cream pies for dessert for under $1! And there are daily lunch specials for $2.35 to $2.40. In addition, there are five weekday lunch and dinner specials under $3. Breakfast is inexpensive, too: you could have a complete breakfast of grilled mahimahi, with toast, and hash-browns or rice, for $1.95. A local friend raves about the fried chicken and the rhubarb pie, but advises that you come early, as only one rhubarb pie is baked each day. Dick's serves all three meals, Monday through Saturday; on Sunday it's breakfast Deli only.

The Kaiko'o Hilo Mall, behind the government buildings, is a boon for hungry, hurried budgeteers. In addition to Kow's Deli (see above), there's **Koji's Bento Shop,** small and cozy with deep-cushioned booths, stained-glass lamps, a pleasant atmosphere. In addition to hamburgers, hot dogs, and several varieties of the island favorite, loco moco, there are many bento lunches to choose from—pork, beef, chicken, shrimp, from $3 to $3.50.

Just across from Kaiko'o Mall, at 804 Kilauea St., you might want to remember **Kawika's** if you're planning a picnic lunch. It's a real deli-type place where you can pick up pastrami, corned beef, turkey, or ham with sides of potato salad, pickles, and the like, at reasonable prices.

Whenever we'd drive by **Café 100,** 969 Kilauea St., we'd notice huge lines of local people at the windows of this popular drive-in. We joined them one day and found out why: it's hard to spend more than $3.50 for a full hot lunch. Fried chicken, beef stew, breaded mahimahi, and teriyaki steak are all served with rice and vegetables. The natives swear by the local favorite, which is reputed to have been invented here: loco moco, a hearty meal of a hamburger patty and fried egg on rice, topped with brown gravy; it's $1.25. They even have loco moco T-shirts! Chili and sandwiches of all kinds start at 85¢. Try their specialties: yummy mahi sandwiches and fresh banana shakes. Good to remember when you're in a hurry and the traveler's checks are running low.

Shibata's, at 264 Keawe St., in the heart of the downtown shopping area, is a popular local spot for breakfast (hotcakes, french toast, each run $1.30) and lunch. Plate lunches like teriyaki steak or baked chicken cost $1.65 to $2.95, and there's a loco moco bowl for $1.30.

McDonald's of Hilo, at the corner of Haili and Ululani Streets, is an enclosed, air-conditioned restaurant, with tables and swivel chairs, hanging plants, and tile floors. . . . You'll find a familiar **Dairy Queen** on Wainuenue Street, just up from Kinoole Street. There's another Dairy Queen on Banyan Drive at the Kamehameha intersection. . . . You can get salads, spaghettis, sandwiches, and, of course, those thick and crusty pizzas at **Pizza Hut,** 233 Kilauea. . . . **Kentucky Fried Chicken** is just one block from Kaiko'o Hilo Mall, at 348 Kinoole St. . . . Within two blocks of each other on Kilauea, you'll find **Wendy's** and **Burger King.**

Although we weren't much taken with the shops at the **Waiakea Kai Shopping Plaza,** 88 Kanoelehua, there is a collection of fast-food places here that could prove useful. Nicest of all is a big, family style **McDonald's,** with Tiffany-type stained-glass dividers, lamps, booths, a cheerful atmosphere, and the usual low prices . . . **Magoo's Pizza** has sandwiches and baked chicken dinners in addition to tasty pizza pies, plus beer, a jukebox, booths, and a moderate-to-high noise level. . . . Not only can you get all kinds of frozen yogurts and toppings at **Ono Yogurt, Meals & Munchies,** but also homemade vegetarian soups, salads, terrific chili, and some pretty good sandwiches like chicken, tuna, pastrami, ham, roast beef, and cheese, from $1.10 to $2.50. And their $2 breakfast specials—quiche, toast, and fruit cup; or croissant, juice, fruit, and coffee—are deservedly becoming very popular. . . . **Robert's Bakery** can supply you with their wonderful Portuguese sweet bread, an island favorite, for $1.80; or two pounds of tasty macadamia-nut or coconut "Cookies from Hawaii" for $8.85, packed ready to carry or mail home.

At **Plaza Crackseed,** not only will you find many varieties of cracked seed sweets and ice cream, but also diet shave ice and nondairy tofu desserts made with such local fruits as mango and guava—great for the calorie conscious.

Local pastry aficionados swear that heaven is a morsel of a macadamia-nut brownie or a fresh fruit tart or a cheese croissant or some other bit of "edible art" that emerges from the ovens of **Kay's Creations,** on the grounds of the Waiakea Villas Hotel, 400 Hualani St., #12. Try one of Kay's European-style wonders (she also does French bread, baguettes, and quiches) with a cup of coffee for an elegant breakfast or snack. Pastries are reasonably priced, from 75¢ to $2.15. One friend swears that Kay's white-chocolate cheesecake is far and away the best thing she has ever tasted!

While you're at Waiakea Villas, stroll down towards the water and you'll find a charming spot for lunch. The **Springwater Cafe & Bar,** in a Polynesian-style building, is a friendly oasis which rates high on atmosphere—polished woods inside and large windows open to the air. Choose from generous deli-style sandwiches with a choice of breads, quiches, soups, salads, homemade chili, and nachos with "the works," $2.25 to $4.95. For a delicious light lunch, try the fresh vegetable plate with seven steamed veggies and hollandaise or peanut curry sauce, $3.95. By night, Springwater's is a place for drinks and entertainment, and the same light menu is served during dinner hours. Open Monday through Saturday until 2 a.m. and Sunday until 2 p.m.

For a yummy natural snack, remember **Hilo Natural Foods,** 306 Kilauea St., the big health-food store in town. Inside, you'll find **Hilo Natural Foods Kitchen,** with table and counter seating, as well as take-out. Daily offerings include mock chicken salad, organic turkey sandwiches, avocado bean burritos or tostadas, homemade soup of the day, plus hot lunch specials. Prices range from $1 to about $4. There are also fresh lemonade, carrot juice, smoothies, and incredibly delicious fruit freezes. Up front they have Kona farms coffee made with spring water. Food is served only on weekdays, from 10 a.m. to 3 p.m. (2 p.m. Saturday), but there are always sandwiches, salads, and other treats in the cooler. Closed Sunday.

Bear's Café, that stylish little place (marble-topped tables, hand-stenciled walls) that adjoins The Most Irresistible Shop in Hilo at 110 Keawe St. (tel. 935-0708) is also proving to be irresistible—so much so that its original menu of a variety of coffees and pastries keeps expanding: now they start the day (at 7 a.m. weekdays, 8 a.m. Saturdays) with breakfast items like papaya with yogurt, souffléd eggs, and "egg busters" (eggs, cheese, and ham on English muffin), and offer deli and vegetarian sandwiches (around $3), salads, hot and cold soups ($1.50 to $2), in addition to the original coffee and pastry menu, until closing at 5 p.m. weekdays, 4 p.m. Saturdays. What fun to sample 12 kinds of coffee drinks, as well as indulge in the likes of chocolate eclairs, coconut macaroons, croissants (plain and cheese), pies, cakes, and quiches, plus Bare Bear's Brownies and Frosted Bear Brownies. You can also buy fresh-roasted coffee beans by the pound to take home. House coffee is 70¢ per cup, and pastries average about $1.95. Bearvo! Closed Sunday.

THE NIGHT SCENE IN HILO: Nightlife is quieter than it used to be in Hilo, with the closing or conversion into condominium apartments of several major hotels. However, there's still enough to keep you busy making the rounds of some of the favorite places.

For an inexpensive, family-style evening in Hilo, try **Uncle Billy's Restaurant** at the Hilo Bay Hotel. The hotel and restaurant are owned and operated by Uncle Billy and his Hawaiian family, and each night at 7:30 there's a free hula show, a totally nonslick, warm-hearted revue. Helpings from the large salad bar are included with dinners. Most meals are priced from $7.95 to $12.95; the menu includes fish catch of the day, island steaks, shrimp, teriyaki chicken, and daily chef's specials. The restaurant has been redecorated in South Seas decor with shells and large grass chandeliers, and is more attractive than ever.

If it's just drinks, music, and maybe dancing you're after, there are several good spots around Hilo. **Harrington's,** 135 Kalanianaole St., has a scenic location overlooking the Ice Pond at Reed's Bay. You can listen to music in the lounge, enjoy reasonably priced appetizers and drinks in a wonderfully romantic setting. . . . It's no cover, no minimum, and Happy Hour prices (from 5 to 7 p.m.) at the **Hoomalimali Bar** of the Naniloa Hotel, with "Naturally" playing from 9 p.m. to closing for listening and dancing on Thursday through Saturday. . . . The plush Hilo Hawaiian Hotel has a **Menehuneland Lounge** with the little people scrambling all over the walls. It's Hawaiian music beginning every night at 5, then contemporary music from 8:30 p.m. to closing; no cover, no minimum, and some of the best prices for beer and house wine in town. Free pupus are served from 4 to 6 p.m. . . . In historic downtown Hilo, on 60 Kaewe St., there's elegant **Roussel's** for cocktails nightly; and on weekends, enjoy jazz, dancing, and theme parties with musical revues, no cover and no minimum in the lounge. Mixed drinks start at $2.50. . . . Delicious pupus are served free with drinks at lively **Springwater's** at the Waiakea Villas Hotel. Entertainment, Wednesday through Saturday, ranges from folk and pop to Hawaiian; mixed drinks are $2 and up. . . . The nicest place for hand-holding and a quiet drink is **Rosey's Boathouse,** 760 Piilani St. Entertainment varies nightly in the intimate lounge, from light rock 'n' roll to traditional Hawaiian music. All drinks are poured with premium liquor, and start at $2. Try the delicious hot pupus served till midnight; portions are hearty. . . . At **Uncle Billy's Lounge** at the Hilo Bay Hotel, mixed drinks start at just $1.55, and a Bird of Paradise, the house special, is $3 from 3 to 6 p.m., when there is often a lounge special like two-for-one wine coolers. . . . There's no entertainment and scarcely any atmosphere at the **Hukilau Hotel** bar, but always a local crowd full of fun, a big TV screen, and drinks at some of the lowest prices in town. . . . When the bars close down, you can get some nourishment over at **Ken's House of Pancakes** (see above), where they serve pancakes and omelets through the wee hours of the morning. . . . For a more substantial meal, choose from the large menu selection at **Mun Cheong Lau Chop Suey Restaurant** on Keawe St. It stays open until 2:30 a.m. on weekdays and 4 a.m. on weekends.

2. Between Hilo and Kona

In our next chapter we'll describe the drive from Hilo to the resort center of Kona, a trip you should take. Right now we'll tell you about some hotels and restaurants at which you might stop en route.

HOTELS AND RESTAURANTS ON THE NORTHERN ROUTE: Forty-four miles north of Hilo on the northern, or Hamakua Coast, route, and not far from the cattle country of the Parker Ranch, is the venerable **Hotel Honokaa Club,** Honokaa, HI 96727 (tel. 775-0533), which has been serving local business people and hunters for over 50 years now. Undemanding types will find the $20 singles, $22 doubles with private bath and TVs acceptable. The hotel's inexpensive restaurant and bar are very popular with the local people. If you're driving through on a weekday, between 11 a.m. and 2 p.m. you can get a big meat-and-cheese hero, with salad bar and beverage, or plate lunches, between $4 and $5.

Just down the main street aways, and situated between several charming boutiques, is **Honokaa Pizza & Subs.** Create your own pizza from $6.25, or choose a hot, stuffed calzone or hot sub sandwich, $2.95 to $3.95. Around back, down a narrow alley, is hidden a "must try!" Sample some of **Donna's** home-made cookies and shortbread (coconut, macadamia nut, or oatmeal) and you'll want to take home a bucket; a half-gallon tub assortment is only $5.50. Yummm! The best cookies we had on the island.

From Honokaa, it's 15 miles on Hwy. 19 to Kamuela (or Waimea), heart of the Parker Ranch cattle kingdom. The best budget place to stay in this delicious-ly cool mountain town is the **Kamuela Inn** (tel. 885-4243), a modest but pleasant place. Most of the 19 rooms have color cable TV, and all have private bath. Singles start at $31; doubles go from $31 to $40; suites (two rooms, bath—some with tub—and kitchen, capable of sleeping four to five) are $45 to $50; junior suites (kitchenette, capable of sleeping three to four) are $45; a rollaway bed is $5 extra. Continental breakfast is free. Scenic grounds (there are "bottle brush" trees with red flowers that really look like bottle brushes) just outside the hotel and a friendly management are pluses here. Write to Kamuela Inn (attn. Bill Kashnig, Manager), P.O. Box 1994, Kamuela, HI 96743. There are restaurants nearby and good swimming 12 miles away at Hapuna Beach Park.

A newer, more spacious and expensive accommodation in this area is **The Parker Ranch Lodge,** a modern 20-unit motor hotel within walking distance of the Parker Ranch Center and all its sightseeing, shopping, and eating facilities. Horseback riding and golf are nearby, some excellent beaches a reasonable drive away. Each room boasts quality furnishings, attractive decor, color TV, and beamed ceiling. From this cool, 2,500-foot elevation you have a view of rolling green meadowlands and mountains. Singles are $39; doubles (king-size bed) are $46; twins (two queen-size beds) go for $53. Reservations advised: The Lodge, P.O. Box 458, Kamuela, HI 96743 (tel. 885-4100).

Waimea Garden Cottage in Waimea has to be one of our very favorite places on the Big Island. This is the perfect rustic retreat, an elegant country cottage where you can live in graceful surroundings, do your own cooking if you wish, spend your time riding or hiking in the mountains, or swimming at Hapu-na Beach or the Mauna Kea Beach Hotel, just eight miles down the road. Bar-bara and Charlie Campbell, a charming local couple, have created the cottage near their own home, incorporating some of the materials found on the site of an old Hawaiian homestead into a striking new architectural design. A small foyer leads down a step or two to the main room, furnished in eucalyptus and other natural woods, with antique furniture, two single beds which can be made into a king, plus a futon, beautiful rugs and wall hangings, and color TV, of course. Not only is the kitchen complete, the refrigerator is filled with freshly picked local fruits and eggs taken from the chickens a few hours before. In fact, you are invited to pick your own limes, bananas, lemons, and oranges and gath-er your own eggs from the chickens right on the grounds! If you are lucky enough to get into this place, you're in for a bargain as well as a treat, since the cottage rents for only $49 nightly, $320 weekly, $1250 monthly (we wish we could stay a month!). There is a two-night minimum stay. Write to Barbara and Charlie Campbell, P.O. Box 563, Kamuela, HI 96743, or phone them at 885-4550.

Ask local people about good restaurants in Waimea, and the first name you hear is usually **Edelweiss,** on Kawaihae Road (tel. 885-6800). So popular has Edelweiss become in its few short years of existence that it was recently rated as the best continental restaurant on the Big Island by the *Gourmet Guide of Hawaii*, topping even the famed dining spots at the Mauna Kea and Mauna Lani Hotels. This is a homey place with a European country feeling, and chef Hans Peter Hager's cuisine does not disappoint. The luncheon specialty of bratwurst and sauerkraut is $4.25; also popular is the Puu Haloa ranch burger at $5, or in a more continental mood, the sautéed chicken breast with champignons and Monterey Jack cheese, $5.50. Several light dinners are offered at $7.75, and the regular dinners are decently priced, $9.75 to $15.75 for the likes of chicken liver omelet, roast duck bigarade, and calves' liver with onions, including soup of the day, salad, vegetable, and beverage. The house specialty of sautéed veal, lamb, beef, and bacon with pfefferlinge (European wild mushrooms) is $15.75 and very tasty. You can start your meal with appetizers like melon prosciutto or escargots, and end with a satisfying Bavarian cream pie or Bavarian cassis (each $2) or simply fresh Kamuela strawberries. Edelweiss serves lunch daily from 11:30 a.m. on, and dinner from 5 p.m. to closing. Closed Monday.

A standby for many years in this area is the **Parker Ranch Broiler** (tel. 885-7366), sitting majestically at the head of the Parker Ranch Visitor Center. Its interior is plush turn-of-the-century saloon vintage. Lunch offers hot sandwiches and dishes from $3.50 to $7.50, with dinner the more elaborate meal. You can eat inexpensively here by having the soup of the day and an excellent salad bar, or the vegetarian platter and soup, for $6.50. Most dinner entrees cost more, from about $12.95 to $17.95, with the most popular item the prime rib paniolo, served with salad, oven-hot bread, and potato, rice, or pasta, at $15.25 for the regular cut, $13.50 for the missionary cut. Lunch offers hot sandwiches and dishes from about $3 to $7.50. Lunch is from 11:30 a.m. to 2 p.m., dinner from 5:30 on.

For a meal on the run in this area, you can join the local families at the **Kamuela Drive-in Deli,** next to the Parker Ranch Center. It's a plain, unpretentious spot where you can eat either in your car or at the indoor tables. The prices are low and the portions big. They open at 5 a.m. for breakfast, when they cook up a storm of hotcakes, and bacon and eggs. But have the Portuguese sausages instead; they're the real thing. The rest of the day they serve sandwiches like roast beef, $1.75 to $1.95 (no doubt from the Parker Ranch); and hot platters like curry or beef stew or teriyaki steak for around $3. The only thing high here is the elevation—almost 3,000 feet.

You can get other quick meals in Waimea at **Masayo's,** across from Edelweiss, a luncheonette with hearty local specialties like curry stew, loco moco, and pigs'-feet soup, from $3 to $4. Or try the **Paniolo Country Inn,** a large, attractive spot with wooden booths and tables; it's a sister restaurant to the popular Paniolo Pizza in Kona (described below), and specializes in hearty ranch-style breakfasts plus tasty pizzas and Mexican dishes. In the Parker Ranch Visitors Center, **Auntie Alice's Pie and Coffee Shop** is cozy for a quick bite.

Prefer a light, natural-food snack? **Rainbow Mountain Natural Foods** (next door to Mike's Printing) has a complete kitchen and health-food store: soups, smoothies, salads, chili, and the like, are made only with natural ingredients and are all inexpensive. Try the soup and cornbread at $1.95, the huge garden salad at $3, or a chapati, burrito, or carrot juice shake. There are sandwiches too, and always daily lunch specials. You take your food to the benches outside.

Want to sample some good Thai food and/or fresh baked goods? Go to **Heritage House Bakery,** located in the Bric-a-Brac Building on Lindsey Road, across from Edelweiss. It's a bright and cheery place with a tempting selection of American and European pies, cakes, pastries, and croissants, either plain or filled (50¢ to $1.50). The Thai menu of curries and noodle dishes is priced at $2.95. Volcano chicken, deep-fried with a tamarind and hot chili sauce, is $3.75.

If you're in a hurry, try the taro puffs or curry puffs; they're filling and only $1. Open for breakfast, lunch, and all-day snacks from 6:30 a.m. to 5 p.m. Closed Sunday.

If you branch off from Waimea for an excursion into the Kohala district, you might want to experience a bit of local color by staying overnight in Hawi at the **Old Hawaii Lodging Company** (tel. 889-5577), where a new management has freshened up the rooms a bit and taken over from the venerable Luke's Hotel. Nothing fancy at this simple local hotel, but then neither are the rates: $17 single, $20 double, $27 triple. There's a $10 surcharge on stays of one night. **Kohala Inn,** right on the premises, offers burgers from $1.50, lunch and dinner specials at $4.25 and T-bone steaks from Parker and Kahua ranches around $8.50. You're at 500 feet in altitude here, so expect warm days and cool nights. Write to Old Hawaii Lodging Company, P.O. Box 521, Kapaa, HI 96755.

A small hotel in this area offers possibilities for a retreat-like vacation. The **Hawaiian Plantation House,** also known as **Aha Hui Hale** (tel. 889-5523), was once a sugar plantation manager's house; now it has been converted into a guest house with just three one-bedroom and one two-bedroom suites, each of which includes a living room, bathroom, and color TV. Guests share the communal dining rooms and kitchen. There's a pool out on the tropical grounds. Rates per suite are from $60 for one or two persons, $8 for each additional occupant. For reservations and information, write to P.O. Box 10, Hawi, HI 96719.

Since the construction of the Queen Kaahumanu Hwy. it is now possible to drive along the seacoast from the Westin Mauna Kea Hotel to the Kona Airport and on to Kona. And it is also possible for those who want to experience the charms of this area to stay in their own luxury apartment just three miles past that glorious resort (and near the Sheraton-Waikoloa) at the **Puako Beach Condominiums,** as isolated a retreat as one could want. These condominiums are deluxe apartments with complete kitchen, large living room, and all the amenities of home, including electric appliances and a color TV; each is furnished differently by its owner. There's a large swimming pool as well as good ocean swimming nearby. Rates for one-, two-, and three-bedroom apartments run from $55 to $59, $80 to $84, and $95 to $99. Weekly and monthly rates on request. Not inexpensive, but a bargain compared to the rates at Mauna Kea! Reservations: Puako Beach Condominiums, 3 Puako Beach Dr., Kamuela, HI 96743 (tel. 882-7711).

HOTELS AND RESTAURANTS ON THE SOUTHERN ROUTE: Driving the

southern route (Hwy. 11) from Hilo to Kona, or vice versa, you have several delightful possibilities if you want to spend the night. First there's the famed and venerable **Volcano House,** right on the brink of Kilauea Crater, where the ancient kahunas (priests) once gathered to make sacrifices to Pele. Standard rooms (in a separate building) are $37 single, $40 double; rooms in the main building are $44 single, $47 double; and deluxe accommodations, with a view of the crater, are $48 and $51; an extra person is charged $10. Where else can you take a bath with live volcanic steam? A breakfast here in the early-morning mountain air, seated at a table near the window where you can gaze right into the volcano as you savor your ono french toast and ohelo-berry preserves, is one of the special treats of Hawaii. Reservations: Volcano House, Hawaii Volcanoes National Park, HI 96718; or phone 967-7321. A new management may be making rate changes.

Any former Boy Scouts or Girl Scouts in the crowd? You might try one of the ten cabins at **Namakani Paio Campground,** in Volcanoes National Park, three miles beyond Volcano House. Designed for those "who desire true outdoor living," they are of Polynesian design, frame construction, and they're furnished with a double bed, two single bunk beds, and your own lanai. You share a common bathhouse with your neighbors. The tab is minimal: about $16 per night for up to four people and linens are included. Write to Volcano House (the concessionaires) at Hawaii Volcanoes National Park, HI 96718, or call them at 967-7321.

You have several interesting choices of atmosphere for lunch on this trip. The traditional lunch stop here has long been **Volcano House** (tel. 967-7321), noted for its lovely buffet—a tempting array of salads, fruits, and main dishes, served with beverage and dessert, in a spectacular setting overlooking Halemaumau Crater. The cost is $8.15 for adults, $5.75 for children. The dining room at Volcano House, named Ka Ohelo, in honor of the sister of Madame Pele, the fire goddess, has been attractively enlarged, so that seating on two levels can provide views for up to 260 people. However, since lunch is a very busy time, what with all the tour buses disgorging hungry passengers, we prefer to come here for a superb and quiet breakfast, served up to 10:30 a.m. Just remember to offer some of the ohelo-berry preserves to Madame Pele first, as a sign of respect. (Ohelo is the fruit from the lehua trees, sacred to Pele; you can also sample it in ohelo-berry pie, served at Volcano House's snackshop.) The dinner menu includes Korean chicken ($6.50), mahimahi ($10.50), and prime rib ($16); and all dishes come with rice, vegetables, salad bar, and coffee or tea.

Two miles south of Volcanoes National Park entrance, watch for the sign that reads "Golf Course," directly across from the Kilauea Military Camp. It will lead you to the **Volcano Golf and Country Club** (tel. 967-7331). Here's where local people take visitors to avoid the Volcano House crowds. The clubhouse, open to the public, has a rustic modern dining room with glass windows, huge ceiling, and wood-burning fireplace. From the windows, you can gaze at Mauna Loa and often sight the rare Hawaiian Nene goose. Complete lunches, including soup, feature home-cooked American, Japanese, and Hawaiian foods, from $2.95 to $6. Lunch is served daily except Monday, from 11 a.m. to 3:30 p.m., breakfast from 7 to 10 a.m. weekdays.

Less polished than the country club, but with all the fun of a real general store and the people who frequent it, is the Volcano Store in Volcano Village. Make your way up to the big ramshackle porch, half of which is given over to the simple tables and chairs of the **Volcano Store Diner** (tel. 967-7210). Nothing fancy about this place, but if the sun (or rain) is beating down on you, you'll be quite cozy at the little indoor café with wooden floor and walls, sunlight slanting in off the roof, and works by local artists on the walls. You place your order up front, then sit down and wait. The food is good and reasonable. Specialty burgers are tasty and so is the mahimahi-on-sweet-bread sandwich at $3.25. You can have plate lunches like stew, chili dog, or fried chicken from $2 to $4.25. Try their shakes too—guava, banana, and papaya are delicious. Open for breakfast and lunch only, at this writing, from 7 a.m. to 4 p.m.

Inside **Volcano Store** you might want to pick up some cone sushi or hardboiled eggs or other munchies to nibble on as you drive along. This is one of the best places to buy orchids and anthuriums, which can be mailed anywhere. To get to Volcano Store, reached before Volcanoes National Park, stay on Highway 11 until Haunani Road; then go straight ahead to the stop sign, and it's right there.

If you can hold out for another hour or so before lunch, continue your drive on the southern route until you come to Punalu'u, home of the famous Black Sands Beach—and of the **Punalu'u Black Sands Restaurant** (tel. 928-8528). In a dramatic indoor-outdoor setting, in full view of the ocean, is a delightful restaurant under the direction of a new and creative young chef. It's great fun to stop here for their buffet lunch, since the chef puts out something like 25 different dishes every day, including hot foods like fish, chicken, kalua pig, ham, or beef, along with lomi lomi salmon, poi, steamed rice or potatoes, many salads, and fresh fruit. All the breads and sweet muffins are made right here, as are the goodies on the dessert tables—such temptations as bread pudding or haupia, macadamia-nut swirls or chocolate pudding. The cost of this feast, which is attractively displayed in a native canoe, is $8.75, $6.75 for children. Salads and sandwiches (about $4.95 to $6.95) are also available on the à la carte menu. If you're in the area at night, come back for a splurgy gourmet dinner (chicken St-Germain, shrimp tempura, pepper steak, etc., from $11.75 to $16.95, $8.75 soup and salad bar), followed by dreamy desserts such as almond amoretto torte or fresh pineapple Romanoff (umm!). The buffet luncheon is served from 10:30 a.m. to 2 p.m. every day, regular lunch until 4 or 5 p.m.

On your way to the Puna area of the Big Island (see "Seeing Hawaii," Chapter XIV), you'll pass through the little town of Keeau. An enjoyable restaurant here is **Mama Lani's,** in the shopping center (tel. 966-7525). Actually, Mama Lani and Papa Lani are a young couple with four active children. They've created a charming Mexican restaurant with a warm feeling and a clean, crisp look: dark-wood tables, white stucco walls, tile floors. Everything is made on the premises. Dinner entrees, served with refried beans and Spanish rice, run from about $6.25 to $6.75 for the likes of tacos, enchiladas, burritos, and chimichangas. Or create your own combination plate for $8.50. Grilled fish served with a fresh green salad is often available, and may also be served Mexican style, with beans and rice. Lower-priced lunch specials are served from 11 a.m. to 4 p.m. Desserts like Kahlua cheesecake and Mexican flan are homemade, and they boast the "best margaritas" around (try the passionfruit!). Of course there's a full bar. Mama Lani's is open Monday to Saturday from 11 a.m. to 9 p.m.

In about ten miles you'll come to another little town, Pahoa, about a 40-minute drive from Hilo. An oldtimer here is the **Pahoa Chop Suey,** a few hundred yards on the Hilo side of Pahoa, which has a clean, tiny (ten-table) eat-in section and a busy take-out window from which issues forth an endless variety of tasty Cantonese Chinese dishes, all from $3.75 to $5. Open Tuesday through Sunday. Right on Government Road, the main street, you'll find the **Pahoa Inn Coffee Shop,** a pleasant place with interesting local art on the walls, which starts serving lunch at 2 p.m. Three dinner specials daily might include fried chicken, meat loaf, or T-bone steak, at $4 to $5.25, and come with potatoes, vegetable, and a salad. Reasonable! No smoking at this one.

Just about halfway between Hilo and Kona you come upon an oasis in the lava flows. This is the beautiful town of Naalehu, the southernmost community in the United States. To us, stopping off here at the **Naalehu Coffeeshop** is one of the highlights of the drive, since it's much more than an eatery, and Roy and Arda Toguchi—the people responsible for the restaurant/gift shop/art gallery in this historic old building—are more than just proprietors. The Toguchis are artists in their own right, and they number the greatest among their friends. You'll see Roy's artistry in his fabulous bonsai garden (which he'll be delighted to show you), in his mural of Mauna Loa behind the counter, and on the handmade menu. The same fresh and delicious foods are available at both lunch and dinner. We've never been disappointed in the fish, the beef cutlet, or the teriyaki beef barbecue. The entrees come with salad, vegetable, bread, rice or potatoes, and the total cost is $7.95; other entrees go to $9.95. Don't miss the homemade banana cake. The sandwiches are good too: the Hawaiian fish-burger, the Farmer John baked ham, oven-baked turkey sandwich, and others are all served with relishes and salad, $3.25 to $4.75. After your meal, check out the art gallery and Menehune Treasure Chest, and browse among the local handcrafts. If it's anytime between September and March, be sure to see the flaming sphere poinsettias blooming out back. If you approach from Naalehu, make your third left when you pass the school; from Kona, turn right when you pass the theater. The coffeeshop is just 100 feet on the left-hand side, across from the shopping center —where, incidentally, Roy's brother runs the **Green Sands Snack Bar,** a little take-out place for plates like chicken hekka, pork tofu, chopped steak, and chili, from about $1.95 to $4.25.

3. Kailua-Kona

The Kona Coast is to the Big Island what Waikiki is to Oahu—the resort area. Unlike Waikiki, though, it still has a small-town charm. Once the playground of the Hawaiian alii, Kona lures deep-sea fishermen (its marlin grounds are the best in the Pacific), families, anyone looking for relaxed, tropical beauty. A handful of hotels offer pretty decent budget rates.

HOTELS: A neat bargain, right in the center of town on Alii Drive, is the **Kona Bay Hotel,** a sister establishment to Uncle Billy's Hilo Bay Hotel, and run by the same family management. Kimo and Jeanne Kimi are the friendly folks in charge here. They have landscaped their newer hotel (formerly the garden wing of the Kona Inn) with bridges and ponds and a Polynesian longhouse restaurant surrounding a large circular swimming pool. The thatched roof over the registration desk and the koa wood tables in the lobby create a warm Hawaiian feeling. All rooms are of comfortable size, smartly done up in green, gold, and brown color schemes, with Polynesian prints on the walls, air conditioning, bathrooms with full tubs and showers, and good-size lanais. Most have a refrigerator, and many have two double beds. And all this comfort is at a realistic price: singles, $44 to $54; doubles, $49 to $59. Add $10 for an extra person, $10 for a studio kitchenette. Car-room-and-breakfast packages are available at good rates, starting at $59 for two. For reservations, phone direct to Hawaii toll free 800/367-5102, or write Kona Bay Hotel, 87 Banyan Dr., Hilo, HI 96720.

If you want more luxury and still a good price, try, also on Alii Drive, the **Kona Islander Inn,** a rambling, plantation-style complex that boasts some of the nicest hotel rooms in the area, plus a pool set in a glorious garden and a barbecue pit out by the pool. All rooms here are identical, but the price is $48 for garden or poolside rooms, $54 for ocean-view rooms. Third and fourth persons in the room are not charged extra. Rooms are beautifully decorated in earth tones, with rich orange carpets; all have two twin beds, plus a queen-size sofa bed, shower (no tub), and a private lanai furnished with a table and two director's chairs. An extra person is charged $7. There's a refrigerator in every unit, and the kitchenette package of hotplate and utensils is available on request. For reservations at Islander Inn, call toll free 800/331-8076, or write to Islander Inn, 75-5776 Kaukini Hwy., Kailua-Kona, HI 96740 (tel. 329-0711).

A good choice, smack in the center of town, is the **Kona Hukilau** (tel. 329-2455), whose sister hotel we've told you about in Hilo. This is a very similar place, with most of the rooms overlooking the large lovely pool. The rooms are smartly furnished, have twin- or king-size beds, air conditioning, and TV, and from many you can see the harbor across the road. Or you may just want to laze on the sundeck, which looks out on Alii Drive and the harbor, and watch the world go by below you. Single or double, standard rooms are $39; superior, $44. An extra person is $10. An economical package plan includes hotel room for two and a Budget Rent-A-Car at rates of $49 standard, $54 superior. For reservations, write Kona Hukilau Hotel, 2222 Kalakaua Ave., Suite 714, Honolulu, HI 96815, or call toll free 800/367-7000.

The same Hukilau management is also in charge at the 240-unit, five-story

Kona Seaside Hotel, (tel. 329-2455). Although it's off the main drag, at the intersection of Kuakini Hwy. (Rte. 11) and Palani Road (Rte. 19), it's just a parking lot away from the shopping and restaurant excitement of Alii Drive. Size is the byword of the Seaside—large rooms, spacious lanais, and an extra-large pool. Blue is the theme of the well-appointed rooms, all of which are equipped with TV, air conditioning, and a switchboard-serviced telephone. Prices are excellent, considering the comfort. Rates are $45 standard, $49 superior, $55 deluxe. For a similar car package as above, add $10 (rates are subject to slight increase). Extra persons are charged $10 each. Write to them at Kona Seaside, 2222 Kalakaua Ave., Suite 714, Honolulu, HI 96815; or call toll free 800/367-7000.

In a garden setting overlooking the ocean, a bit away from the bustle of Alii Drive and very close to the Kona Hilton, is the petite **Kona Tiki Hotel** (tel. 329-1425), a longtime budget favorite in Kona. All the rooms have private oceanfront lanais looking out on the blue-green pounding surf (and it really does pound—noisily—against the sea wall). The ocean is great for fishing and snorkeling; there's a freshwater pool for gentler swimming. So popular has this small, unpretentious hotel been over the years, that its rooms had seen a great deal of use; now they've been nicely spiffed up with new furnishings, including queen-sized beds, ceiling fans, and a small refrigerator in every room, even those without kitchenettes. The low rates are $29, single or double, for a standard room, $33 for a room with a mini-kitchenette, $5 for each extra person; maximum of four in a room (and that's a bit small, except for a very close family). Prices may be subject to change. Friendliness abounds at the Kona Tiki; it's the kind of small, family-owned hotel where guests usually get to know each other. You can help yourself to Kona coffee and doughnuts in the morning. You can drive from here to the center of town in 3 minutes, or walk it in 15 minutes. For reservations, a month in advance usually, two months in advance in busy seasons, write: Manager, Kona Tiki Hotel, P.O. Box 1567, Kailua-Kona, HI 96740. Specify first and second choices on rooms with or without kitchenette; very few kitchenettes are available. Minimum stay is three days.

Condominiums are very big in Kona these days, and surely one of the nicest is the **Sea Village,** an idyllic spot overlooking the ocean just outside of town at 75-6002 Alii Dr. This is a large resort complex, with a tennis court, a swimming pool, and Jacuzzi whirlpool bath on the premises, snorkeling off the rocks in front of the hotel for strong swimmers. Living quarters are outstanding: the apartments are beautifully furnished, ultra-spacious and luxurious, with huge living rooms, one or two bedrooms, shiny modern kitchens fitted with every appliance including dishwashers, washer-dryers, and refrigerators with automatic ice makers. Bathrooms are lovely, and there is ample closet and storage space, weekly maid service, private lanais. Although rates here are higher than our usual budget ones, if you come during off-season (May 1 through December 15), you can get a one-bedroom garden apartment for two persons for just $50; it's big enough to sleep four, at $6 per extra person. A two-bedroom apartment for up to four persons is $66; it can sleep six. Ocean-view apartments go up to $60 and $78; oceanfront apartments run even higher, to $66 and $84; high-season rates add $16 more per unit. There is a discount of 10% on monthly stays. A minimum stay of three nights is required. For reservations, write to the Sea Village Condominium Resort, c/o Paradise Management Corp., Kukui Plaza C-207, 50 S. Beretania St., Honolulu, HI 96813 (tel. 538-7145); or call toll free 800/367-5205.

A few miles farther along Alii Drive is another stunning condominium resort, the 155-room **Kona Bali Kai,** fronting the ocean at 76-6246 Alii Dr. Luxury, comfort, beauty—this place has it all. Rooms are exquisitely and individually furnished, with every convenience—full kitchens, washer-dryers in many units, color TVs, direct-dial phones, daily maid service (unusual in most condominiums), and lanais from which those in the front building can watch the spectacular surf and tireless surfers (other buildings afford views of mighty Mt. Hualalai or lush gardens). Although the surf is too strong here for casual swimmers, a good swimming beach is a mile away, and right at home is a sunning beach amid the coral reef tidal pools, a swimming pool, Jacuzzi, and sauna. There are barbecue grills on the beach, and a Pupu Pantry in the lobby area for essential groceries and sandwiches. Arrangements can be made at the activities desk in the lobby for golf (three miles south), tennis (two miles north), or for a variety of adventures nearby. Considering the quality of this resort, rates are respectable: studio rooms for one or two persons are $55 mountainside of road, $80 oceanside. One-bedroom apartments for one to four persons are $75 mountainside, $95 oceanside; and spectacular two-bedroom, two-bath apartments, which can comfortably sleep up to six people, are $115. Add $10 per unit from December 20 through March 31. For reservations, phone toll free 800/367-6040, or write Kona Bali Kai, 76-6246 Alii Dr., Kailua-Kona, HI 96740 (tel. 329-9381).

Thirteen miles south of Kailua, on Hwy. 11—and 1,400 feet high in the coffee country—is the place where you'll find the most reasonable accommodations in the Kona area, the **H. Manago Hotel** in the village of Captain Cook (tel. 323-2642). But staying here means more than getting a clean, comfortable room for rock-bottom prices; it's a way to get to know the nontourist Hawaii. For the Manago Hotel is part of the history of the Kona coast, a favorite with island people since 1917, when two young Japanese immigrants, Kinzo and Osame Manago, started serving meals in their own house and gave the salesmen and truck drivers who wanted to stay overnight a futon to sleep on. The dining room and hotel grew over the years, and now a third generation of family management has taken over. The older rooms, with community bath, are strictly for nonfussy types: they rent for $15 single, $18 double, $20 triple, $21 quad. Rooms in the newer wing, with private baths and lanais, are modern and comfortable. These rooms are $21, $24, and $27 (single, double, and triple) on the first floor; $22, $25, and $28 on the second floor; and $24, $27, and $30 on the top floor. The gardens that they overlook, incidentally, are tended by 90-year-old Osame Manago, who grows rare orchids and anthuriums in one garden, and fresh vegetables, which are served in the restaurant, in the other. She also creates the hand-knotted patchwork quilts found in some of the rooms. A Japanese-style room, with futons and its own furo (deep hot tub), is dedicated to Kinzo and Osame, and rents for $30 single, $35 double. It's delightfully quiet and cool here throughout the year. The hotel restaurant is a favorite with local people for its home-style Japanese and American cooking; breakfast starts at $3.50, lunch and dinner about $5 to $8.25 (a typical meal is beef or fish with three kinds of vegetables, and beverage). They're known for their pork chops. And incidentally, the three-story frame building looks down the foot of the mountain to Kealekekua Bay, where Captain Cook met his end. Owner Dwight Manago advises reserving about three weeks ahead in season, two weeks other times. Address: P.O. Box 145, Captain Cook, Kona, HI 96704.

There's a new bed-and-breakfast place near Kona, and we've had nothing but good reports on **Pacific Island Bed & Breakfast**, on Melo Melo St. (call for directions), P.O. Box 391025, Kailua-Kona, HI 96739-1025 (tel. 325-1000). Kate Sullivan has redecorated a charming, hillside country house, and each of its four accommodations offers comfortable, nicely furnished rooms, queen-size beds, and ocean views—as well as continental breakfasts in the morning and a cheese and fruit tray in the afternoon. Rates are $40 single, $50 double for the Plumeria Room; $35 single, $45 double for the Pau Hana Room; $50 and $60 for the Palm Lanai, with its own private balcony. The two-bedroom Bali Hai Suite, which has its own kitchen and garden patio, is $85 and $95. Kate is the daughter of screen actor Frank Scully, so don't be surprised to find film people here. The guest house is a few miles outside of town, close to the airport, so a car will be a must if you stay here.

RESTAURANTS: You won't break the budget by eating at the **Spindrifter** on Alii Drive (tel. 329-1344), and you'll be treated to some great views along with the good food; since the rustic building is right on the water, you can watch the crashing sea from your table. Dinner is an attractive package that includes an appealing salad bar and crudités of fresh cauliflower and broccoli (among other items) for dipping, plus hot bread and butter. Salad bar alone is about $6.75. We had enough to eat even before they brought our main courses, teriyaki chicken breasts, and chicken piccata, $12.95 and $13.75. Other seafood and meat entrees run higher, pastas lower. Lunch also features salad, sandwiches, and a few smoked meat specialties. Locals claim Spindrifter's terrific omelets make it the best breakfast place in town. Drinks are special here too, especially during the long, 11 a.m. to 7 p.m. Happy Hour, when mai tais are only $1.50. Valet parking is available.

Every time we dine at the **Ocean View Inn,** just north of the Kona Hukilau on Alii Drive (tel. 329-9988), we realize why it has survived and thrived for so many years while other newer, flashier establishments come and go. This business has been owned by the same family for over half-a-century. It's a big, comfy place, nothing fancy; the view across the road is ocean all the way, the tables are filled with local residents, and the waitresses are oldtimers who know their trade. American and Chinese meals are inexpensive and generous. And it has a wide variety of Chinese vegetarian dishes that are surprisingly delicious. Vegetarians bored with yet another salad bar had best make tracks for this place. Dishes based on vegetarian beef (textured vegetable protein) and tofu run from $2.75 to $3.95; the sweet-and-sour crisp vegetarian wontons rank with the tastiest Chinese food anywhere. Dinners offer good value: they include soup or fruit cup, rice or mashed potato or fries, green salad (with a choice of dressings, including blue cheese), tea and coffee. At a recent meal we dined on broiled ahi (the fish of the day), and for the same $7.50 could have had broiled ono, breaded mahimahi, or butterfish. There are at least 24 other choices between $5.25 and $8.95, including corned beef and cabbage, fried chicken, and roast pork with apple sauce. And there are over 80 Chinese dishes beginning at $3; a Chinese plate dinner is $4.50; roast duck and roast chicken are $4.25 each. Lunch is also a good buy, with many hot plates to choose from, like shoyu chicken or teriyaki steak, from $4.95 to $5.50. These are served with rice or potato, salad, and beverage. Breakfast too, with everything from ham and eggs and french toast to beef stew, saimin, and poi.

So you want to live the good life dining at the **King Kamehameha Hotel** restaurants? For breakfast or lunch, try the pretty Kona Veranda Coffee Shop, which offers many dishes—on the order of Polynesian chicken, mushroom burgers, sandwiches—from $4 to $6. Or have dinner in the atmospheric Moby Dick's between 5:30 and 6:30 p.m., when early eaters can choose "Sunset Selection" entrees beginning at $9.75. On Sunday you can treat yourself to a big-splurge champagne brunch at Moby Dick's from 9 a.m. until 1 p.m.; the enormous buffet table is laden with 12 hot entrees, bountiful salad and fresh fruit selections, an omelet station, as well as a fabulous fresh pastry buffet. And there's live entertainment throughout the brunch.

There's an outpost of Middle Earth right on Alii Drive, across from the Kona Hilton Hotel. It's known as **Tom Bombadil's Food and Drink,** born in the uplands of Kuakini Hwy. and now in a land by the sea. And while murals and decor and names on the menu are mythic (Aragorn pizza, Misty Mountain sandwiches, Smeagol's Fine Fishes), the food is downright substantial, filling, and delicious. Tom Bombadil's is known for its wonderful broasted chicken (the unique taste is a result of its being deep-fried under pressure), about $5.95 for a two-piece dinner; for excellent pizzas, from $3 (small); and for nifty hot or cold sandwiches (ham, roast beef, avocado and cheese, and such), direct from Gold-berry's Pantry, served with potato chips and a kosher pickle, from $4.50 to $8.50 for the huge submarine. There are also neat appetizers like batter-fried zucchini and an antipasto platter that two or three hungry hobbits could share, beautiful salads, spaghetti, and lasagne, and a full line of cocktails, including a spectacular mai tai. Enjoy ocean-view dining from the covered lanai, or relax in the cozy pub area while the friendly Middle Earth people are preparing your picnic. A winner for casual dining, and great for families too. Tom Bombadil's is open daily, serving continuously from 11 a.m. to 10 p.m. All food is available for take-out by phoning 329-1292 or 329-2173.

For the best Mexican food in Kona, the locals are voting for the **Old Kailua Cantina,** on Alii Drive across from the Kailua Pier (tel. 329-TACO). Actually, there's nothing "old" about this place; it's a relatively new establishment, moved into the one-flight-up, over-the-bay digs of a former Japanese restau-rant. But the decor is nautical now, and the food is *muy bueno*. Early diners can enjoy specials like hombre burritos, nachos, taco grande, chile colorado, and Mexican pizza, $3.75 to $6.50, between 4 and 6 p.m. every night. Specialties of the house include a number of dishes at $8.95 or under: enchilada suissa, carni-tas, legumbres picados, chile colorado, served with rice and refried beans, and corn or flour tortillas. Burrito fans have six different choices, from $6.95 to $10.95. Seafood, ribs, and fish of the day are also available. Prices stay pretty much the same at lunch and dinner. There's a big, lively bar (the margaritas with fresh fruit are great), a friendly crowd, and good food every day from 11:30 a.m. to 10:30 p.m.

There's another popular Mexican restaurant, this one "up mauka," where a lot of transplanted mainlanders have followed the Hawaiian rainbow. Close to town, about a five-minute drive out on Kuakini Hwy. in the Sunset Shopping Plaza is **Jose's** (tel. 329-6391), where the Martinez family are in charge. It's a big restaurant, attractively decorated, with Mexican paintings on the wall. Try to sit out on the pretty lanai. The waiters and waitresses are attentive, the margaritas just fine, and the food well priced and well seasoned. You can have several com-bination plates for $7.95 to $9.85 (taco, tostada, beans and rice, etc.), or special-ties like enchiladas suissas (sour cream and chicken enchiladas, beans and rice) at $7.45, or burrito del mar (a delicacy of flour tortillas stuffed with Alaskan king crab meat and garlic butter, topped with cheese and sour cream) at $9.25. Among the appetizers, nachos were delicious, and so was the unusual dessert called capirotada: vanilla ice cream topped with Mexican bread pudding and whipped cream. The Mexican sundae—coffee ice cream topped with coffee li-queur and sprinkled with coconut—is another sweet treat. Jose's is open week-days and Saturday from 11 a.m. to 10 p.m.; on Sunday from 4 to 9 p.m.

A good Mexican restaurant right in town is **Reuben's Mexican Food** (tel. 329-7031), just off Alii Drive on Sarona Road. This is a sister establishment to the one we've told you about in Hilo (see above), and the food is just as deli-cious. *Gourmet Guide of Hawaii* gave this restaurant a "Best Specialty" award. The setting is a little classier—an indoor-outdoor dining area furnished with darkly polished woods. Prices are reasonable: from $5.50 to $7 for lusty combi-nation plates and specialty dishes like crab enchiladas with a mild green chili sauce, chicken flautas, fish grilled with garlic, and chicken marinated and baked in Chef Vincente's special sauce. At lunch, there are about ten specials to choose from at $3.25 to $4.25. Reuben's is open Monday to Saturday from 11 a.m. to 11 p.m., on Sunday from 4 to 11 p.m.

Cousin Kimo's Steak 'n' Seafood Restaurant (tel. 329-1393), on the garden lanai of Uncle Billy's Kona Bay Hotel on Alii Drive, is a popular and pretty spot, owned and operated by a local Hawaiian family. It features the same kind of reasonably priced dinners as the Hilo Bay does; the house specialty is fresh fish caught off Kona daily on their own boats. Four to five varieties of fish are offered, at prices ranging from $9.95 to $11.95. Other choices include roast beef, scampi, huli huli chicken, and New York–cut steaks. Your entree includes as much as you want from the soup and salad bar. There are entertaining free hula shows nightly at 6:30 and 7:30 p.m.; dinner is on from 5:30 to 9 p.m. Remember this place too for delicious breakfasts, with plenty of island fruit and pancakes. There's often a breakfast special for under $3.

Just across the street from Cousin Kimo's, at the Kona Inn Shopping Village, is another of Uncle Billy's ventures, **Hurricane Annie's Garden Terrace Restaurant** (tel. 329-4345), and it's truly a charmer. Picture yourself dining in a lush garden under a gazebo while strains of nostalgic music drift in from the piano bar where Sam (that's right, play it again) keeps a lively and friendly crowd of regulars enchanted night after night. As if atmosphere were not enough, once you've tasted such creative menu selections as Shrimp Diane, blackened filet mignon, catch of the day with a luscious sauce of mango, banana, pineapple, and coconut, or fresh tuna with tomato-basil sauce, you'll vow to return. Pasta dishes, other Italian entrees, ribs, and a good wine list round out the menu. Most entrees are priced from $9.95 to $12.95. Hurricane Annie's is open daily from 11 a.m. to 10:30 p.m., and Sam can be heard six days a week from 6:30 p.m. until closing.

If you're going to have just one splurge meal while you're in Kona, let it be at **Fisherman's Landing,** on the oceanfront of the Kona Shopping Village on Alii Drive (tel. 326-2555). The newest jewel in Uncle Billy's crown, it boasts an idyllic location right on the waterfront, just behind the Kona Inn Shopping Village. Splashing fountains and pools and nautical decorations all set the stage for the grand show put on by the pounding surf smashing up onto the beach. While you're enjoying it all, order a drink and study the menu. Delicious appetizers include steamer clams, fresh sashimi, teriyaki beef skewers, and dragon roll, from $3.95 to $5.50. You can't go wrong with the fresh fish: they are caught from Uncle Billy's own boats on the Kona Coast every day, and at least seven will be served up for dinner that night (you'll see them displayed on the ice sculpture up front), kiawe broiled, and priced from $15.95 to $17.95. Meat lovers can have chicken avocado, veal Oscar, filet mignon, and New York steak, among other choices, from $12.95 to $16.95. And for those who favor Oriental dishes and wok specialties, we can recommend entrees like shrimp tempura, Asian seafood with black bean sauce, chicken macadamia with pineapple lichee, from $12.95 to $15.95. All entrees are accompanied by homemade soup or salad (their Oriental salad is superb) and freshly baked bread from the restaurant's own ovens. Dessert is as outstanding as everything else here, so save room for, say, some zabaglione with fresh fruit, or dream cake, or banana cream pie. Lunch is fun, too, featuring a sandwich-to-order deli, broiler items like teriyaki beef, chicken Hawaiian, salads, etc., from $5 to $7.

Fisherman's Landing is open daily, from 11 a.m. to 2 p.m. for lunch, from 6 to 11 p.m. for dinner. There's music every night, Hawaiian and classical. Reservations are essential.

Amy Fine was one of the founders of Laulima, Honolulu's first natural-foods restaurant, back in the 70s. Laulima is gone now, but Amy is right here in

Kona, presiding over **Amy's Café,** in the North Kona Shopping Center, 75-5629D Kuakini Hwy., at Palani Road (tel. 329-5629). Amy has branched out, however, from serving strictly vegetarian food into what she calls the "New American Diet"—and that means a commitment to providing wholesome food made from natural ingredients, using organically grown produce whenever possible, eschewing preservatives and additives, and even creating some dishes without egg or oil or dairy for those on special dietary regimes. Did we also tell you that the food is also delicious? Lunch, daily from 11 a.m. to 5 p.m., features an excellent fruit and vegetable salad bar, served with vegetarian soup of the day (usually sans oil or dairy), and homemade whole-wheat bread (Amy bakes all her own breads, rolls, and pastries), and is a mighty filler at $6.25, all you can eat. Hot entrees, $2.95 to $6.25, include a vegetarian surprise, lasagne (with garlic bread, salad, and vegetables), tostadas, chili, and catch of the day, market priced. Burgers are a bit different here; they can be vegetarian as well as beef, accompanied by a variety of sauces, and are presented on freshly baked whole wheat buns with tomato, sprouts, pickles, and garnish, $2.95 to $4.95.

Dinner, 5 to 9 p.m. Monday through Saturday, also offers the salad bar at $6.95 and similar entrees as at lunch, with the addition of sirloin steak, a shrimp dish, and "steamed and saucy vegetables," from $7.95 to $11.95. All entrees are complete dinners and include either salad bar or soup, brown rice, fresh steamed vegetables, and homemade bread. Don't even think of skipping dessert here, especially if they have the fresh papaya pie: papaya slices, lightly glazed with orange sauce and coconut, sitting atop an oatmeal crust, add up to perfection. Also memorable: lilikoi cheesecake and a no-egg, no-dairy applesauce cake. Bring your own beer or wine. Amy's is a simple place with about a dozen tables, changing art exhibits on the walls (many for sale), and either classical, Hawaiian, or mellow contemporary sounds in the background.

Doug's Diner, 75-5626 Kuakini Hwy. at Kamehameha Square (tel. 329-9297) is Kona's only 24-hour restaurant. It's decorated in the "fabulous fifties" style, complete with walls dedicated to Marilyn Monroe and James Dean. And yes, a jukebox full of golden oldies in front of a small dance floor, if the urge hits you. Doug's is large and pleasant, with booths, fountain service, and a terrace area for outdoor dining. If you've had one papaya too many and feel luau'd out, this might be the place for you—french fries, malts, chili burgers, old-fashioned hot dogs, BLT's, and grilled cheese. It's also perfect for the kiddies. Actually, Doug's serves full-course dinners with "real" mashed potatoes and all the trimmings, with half-a-dozen entrees—meat loaf, fried or broiled chicken, country-fried steak, roast beef, roast pork, and mahimahi—from $5.50 to $7.95. For desserts, how about a hot fudge sundae or a banana split? The menu goes for 24 hours, and there is a half-priced menu for children. Doug's has a large and yummy breakfast menu which is also served 24 hours; try the banana or macadamia-nut pancakes or the huevos rancheros. Open seven days a week.

For a charming experience of Thai dining, drive over to the industrial area, close to town, and treat yourself to a meal at **Lanai's Siamese Kitchen,** 74-5588A Pawai Place (tel. 326-1222). This is a gracious indoor-outdoor spot (ask to be seated on the lanai), where you can sample authentic Thai cuisine, cooked with fresh and natural ingredients and Oriental spices, at very modest prices. An especially good deal is the $4.95 to $6.95 luncheon when, in addition to a complimentary pupu (have it with your wine or beer), you choose from such main dishes as Lanai Siamese noodles (rice noodles sautéed with pork and shrimp, topped with plum sauce and nuts), chicken curry with cucumber sauce, spicy garlic and pepper sautéed with cabbage. At dinner, you might start with one of the flavorful soups (co co soup is chicken or fish in spiced coconut milk; thom yum is a hot and sour concoction with lemon grass and chicken or seafood), proceed to similar entrees as at lunch ($5.25 to $7.50), or have noodles and fried rice, "adventure dishes" like squid with chili and mint, or crab claw in a pot, all priced from about $5.25 to $8.95. Your dishes can be ordered mild, spicy, or very spicy; we chose the mild and were perfectly contented. No MSG is used. Along with your meal, have some sun tea or homemade lemonade, $1.

Lanai's Siamese Kitchen serves lunch from 11 a.m. to 3 p.m., dinner from 5 to 9 p.m., Monday through Saturday. Closed Sunday. A delight.

There's not much Chinese food available in the Kona area, so **King Yee Lau,** situated atop the Kona Inn Shopping Village on Alii Drive (tel. 329-7100), is very welcome. It's a large and attractive room, open on one side to the ocean view; "Lazy Susan" tables make it easy to sample the goodies. Both Cantonese and Mandarin cuisines are served here, but the house special is called the "Sizzling Hot Platter"; this means that such dishes as pepper-steak, fresh seafood platter, and boneless sautéed chicken are served on hot platters (hear them sizzle and see them smoke), with gravy on the side. They are priced from $8.25 to $10.95. Mongolian beef, lemon chicken, and Kona fresh fish with vegetables of the season are other popular choices. Most dishes are in the $4 to $5 range. Lunch is served from 11 a.m. to 4 p.m., and dinner from 4 to 9:30 p.m., every day. Parking is free.

There are lots of places for quick meals in town. **World Square Shopping Center,** right on Alii Drive, boasts a large picnic area with tables under umbrellas out in the back, near the bus stop. Pick up a tasty snack from any of the fast-food stands and enjoy an inexpensive meal. **Gelato Tropico** is popular for pizzas, salads, and that delicious Italian ice cream in such tropical, un-Italian flavors as papaya or macadamia nut or passion fruit . . . World Square also has its own branch of **Colonel Sanders Kentucky Fried Chicken:** three pieces with all the trimmings, for $3.95.

Mission Taco, a new fast-food Mexican place in Kamehameha Square, is fine for take-out or eating on their lanai. They pride themselves on using "healthy ingredients" in such dishes as their combination and deli plates from $2.99 to $3.99, nachos at 99¢, a Mexi-melt at $2.59, crispy bean burritos at $1.29, and their own tasty Mission potatoes at 94¢.

Fast foods in a lovely atmosphere make **McGurk's Seafood & Sandwiches** a good choice for lunch. Situated on Alii Drive near Hulihee Palace, and decorated in white and blue with nautical accents, McGurk's has both indoors and outdoors tables. You might take-out fish and chips, shrimp and chips (three pieces at $4.25), or sandwiches ($2.25 to $3.65), or stay and have a scallop and chips plate with macadamia-nut coleslaw ($4.15) while enjoying a splendid ocean view. For delivery, between 11 a.m. and 1 p.m., phone 329-8956.

Exotic **Sibu Café,** in Banyan Court on Alii Drive, is a semi-open place where you can sample the mood and food of Indonesia. Blue tile tables, wooden chairs, revolving fans overhead, and Balinese decorations set the scene. Served every day from 11:30 a.m. to 10 p.m. are satés—skewers of marinated meats or vegetables broiled over an open flame, from $5.50 to $5.75. Far Eastern specialties like Balinese chicken, spicy pork, ginger beef, Indian curries, and vegetarian stir-fries are also reasonable ($5.25 to $6.25), and everything is accompanied by either brown or fried rice plus a marinated cucumber-and-onion salad. Combination plates are excellent, and so is their special peanut sauce. They've recently introduced authentic Thai specials served every day. Healthy portions and a great taste for the price. Beer and wine are available. For free delivery in the Kailua area between 11:30 a.m. and 3 p.m., phone 329-1112.

Our award for the most scenic snackshop in Kona has to go to **Harry's Deli** in the Kona Inn Shopping Village. Its eight or nine tables are perched right on the garden and beach, in the kind of setting usually reserved for much fancier establishments. In the middle of a broiling Kona afternoon, this place is c-o-o-l. Harry's offers quite a sophisticated selection of sandwiches—European-style kitchen sandwiches like turkey and avocado with all the trimmings, croissant sandwiches, and stuffed pita pockets, most priced at $3.75. If you're not ready for a meal, just stop by for a sweet and some ocean breezes. You can also pick up sandwiches, fruit, and gourmet goodies to go.

It's not really a restaurant, but **Suzanne's Bake Shop** on Alii Drive, a few doors from Mokuaikaua Church, serves as a breakfast place and snack shop for many people. The doors are open at 5 every morning, and that's when fragrant and flavorful doughnuts, danish, breads, rolls, and other goodies start coming out of the ovens. Danish are 75¢ to $1.10 each, and the caramel/macadamia-nut danish is a special treat. A few chairs and tables outside afford a view of the passing parade and the ocean across the street.

For those who like hearty buffet meals, the **Kona Chuckwagon Buffet,** 75-6082 Alii Drive (tel. 329-2818), about a mile and a half south of town, is a good bet. The breakfast buffet is $3.95, the lunch one is $4.95, dinner, $6.95. Dinner and lunch see at least three meats on the table (perhaps ham, roast beef, barbecued beef ribs, fried chicken), plus chili, potatoes, vegetables, rices, and a soup and salad bar with a selection of 20 items. It's located in the Casa Emdeko condominium.

The lovely **Kona Inn Restaurant** (tel. 329-4425) in the Kona Inn Shopping Mall is a splurge for us at dinner: meals in the $10 to $20 range. But it's such a special spot, with a spectacular view of the bay and some tables perched right at water's edge, that it's worth your while to have lunch here. You can have chowder and salad for $4.95, a vegetable casserole for $6.95, cashew chicken for $7.45, and a host of good sandwiches like hot pastrami with Swiss cheese, french dip, or tuna melt, for $5.45. An inexpensive way to dine with the upper class. Come by for cocktails on the lanai on Tuesday or Thursday for a free hula show.

Keauhou is one of the loveliest areas on the Kona Coast, with its grand resort hotels, historic sites, glorious views of bay and mountains, and now the new Keauhou Shopping Village. Several places offer interesting possibilities for a meal. Although **Mitchell's** (tel. 322-9966), a fine dining restaurant with live music and dancing is a bit too pricey for us at dinner (most entrees from $15 to $20), it's quite reasonable at lunch, and the setting is beautiful. This is an atmospheric spot with bougainvillea tumbling over the lanai, white-and-blue tile floors, bamboo, cane-backed chairs, greenery everywhere. For lunch, you might choose a Keahou club or hot Italiana sandwich at $5.50; quiche and salad served with a glass of champagne at $6.95; an open-faced crab melt at $7.95. Be sure to order a glass of wine with your meal; Mitchell's is known for an extraordinary wine list, very fairly priced, and over 60 wines can be sampled by the glass. Lunch is served from 11 a.m. to 2 p.m. Monday to Saturday; on Sunday from 10 a.m. to 2 p.m., it's an elegant champagne brunch.

Don Drysdale's Two (tel. 322-0070), a sister restaurant to the popular Don Drysdale's Club 53 on the waterfront in Kailua, is another popular gathering spot here, especially with sports fans who will be sitting in the huge, pennant-bedecked bar area, watching their favorite teams on the TV. There are also some very attractive dining areas here, with multicolored linen napkins sparkling on wooden tables with upholstered straw seats. Lunch, served from 11 a.m. to midnight, concentrates mostly on hearty sandwiches; dinner, 5:30 to 11 p.m., offers such specialties as bleu cheese chicken, barbecued pork ribs, prime ribs of beef, tiger prawns in garlic butter, accompanied by soup or salad, vegetables or starch, from $9.95 to $15.75. Fabulous tropical drinks and ice-cream/ liquor drinks are great for sipping out on the lanai; you can have one served in Don Drysdale's Official Baseball Mug and take the mug back home with you, all for $6.50.

You don't have to be a golfer to enjoy a meal at **The Vista,** the attractive restaurant at the Keauhou Golf Course, which does, indeed, have a beautiful vista: its large bay windows overlook the golf course, the Kona Surf Hotel, and the ocean. Regular dinner entrees, which are served with salad or soup, vegetables, rice or potatoes, and roll with butter, include at least five items under $10 (chopped beef steak, breaded tonkatsu, sauteed mahimahi, half-broiled chicken, and beef kebab, $6.95 to $9.75). Seafood and steak specialties go up to $21. Lunch offers soups, salads and sandwiches, plus entrees like New York steak teriyaki, chicken curry, and assorted fried seafood, from $5.75 to $9.75. Free transportation is provided within the Keahuhou resort area. Cocktail service begins at 7 a.m., breakfast is served from 7:30 to 11 a.m., lunch from 11 a.m. to 3 p.m., dinner from 5:30 to 9:30 p.m.

For a change of ambience from the tourist world of Kailua, drive out on Rte. H-11 (one block mauka from the main street of Kailua), a few miles south to **Teshimas's,** at Honalo in coffee-growing country, a very popular place for over 44 years with the local Japanese, Hawaiians, Filipinos, and haoles. You might spot Sen. Dan Inouye there—he always comes in for a meal when he's in Kona. Say hello to Mrs. Teshima—she's a great lady. On our last visit she proudly showed us the report that Teshimas's had won first prize—the Gold Plate Award—for the best Japanese cuisine on the Big Island from the *Gourmet Guide of Hawaii*. You can have a complete teishoku lunch of miso soup, sashimi, sukiyaki, plus various side dishes, served on an attractive black lacquered tray, from $4.50 to $6.25. At dinner, vegetable tempura and shrimp tempura run $5 and $8.75, and there are plenty of dishes like oyako donburi, beef teriyaki, and sashimi from $3.75 to $8, all served with miso soup, tsukemono, rice, and tea. Sashimi is priced according to the market. Breakfast is on from 6:30 to 11 a.m.; lunch, from 11 a.m. to 2 p.m.; dinner, from 5 to 10 p.m.

Take your choice of food and mood at the **Kona Ranch House** (tel. 329-7061), on Hwy. 11, on the corner of Palani and Kuakini. For a splurge, choose the lovely Plantation Lanai, so pretty in wicker and green: dinner features steaks and seafood ranging from $10.50 to $15.95. For a meal that's right within our budget, choose the adjoining Paniolo Room or "family-style" room, open for dinner from 5 to 9 p.m. Best buy in the house is the $8.95 Paniolo Platter: along with the entree, which changes every night (mahimahi, teriyaki steak, barbecued chicken or beef ribs, roast turkey, etc.), comes salad, cornbread, corn on the cob, a choice of rice, fries, baked beans or mashed potatoes, and even a small dessert. Regular menu items like barbecued chicken and steaks are priced around $7.95 to $9.95. Children's menus, burgers, tasty tropical drinks, luscious homemade desserts—Kona Ranch House has all of this, and reasonably priced breakfasts, too. The Kona Ranch House is open every day from 6:30 a.m. to 9 p.m.

The lively **Kona Coast Shopping Center,** near the intersection of Hwys. 11 and 19, offers you a chance to mingle with the local folk at some inexpensive restaurants. There's a branch of the **Sizzler Steak House** national chain here: a big handsome place where steaks are cooked to order and you serve yourself. Prices are always low: fish platter, $4.59; teriyaki steak platter, $6.29; quarter-pound hamburgers, $2.39 or $3.19—served with toast and baked potato, french fries, or rice. There's a pretty good salad bar too, containing egg salad, pasta, taco chips, avocado dip, potato salad, cold tofu cubes, greens, and fresh pineapple—hearty enough for a meal alone, $4.49; with a regular platter, it's $2.59. Open 6 a.m. to 10 p.m. Sunday to Thursday, till midnight on Friday and Saturday. The answer to a hungry family's prayer . . . **Paniolo Country Café** is more than just a pizzeria. Their South of the Border specials—burritos, enchiladas, tostadas, quesadillas, and the like—are priced from $3.50 to $7.50 and *muy bueno*. Sandwiches like the Turkey Tom—sliced turkey smothered with tomato, onion, melted cheeses, and sprouts—are all served on hot rolls with Hawaiian chips; at $4.25 to $5.75, they make a small meal in themselves. Salads are good too, the large ones, at $6.50, can feed two of you if you want to make a whole meal of them. Pizza pies begin at $2.30. Full bar service is available. When you're visiting upcountry in the Waimea region, note their other restaurant, **Paniolo Country Inn** . . . Marcie's Okazuya is a small place specializing in hamburgers and teriburgers; and you can take them outside to the outdoor seating. Prices go from $1.50 to $1.65 . . . **Betty's Chinese Kitchen,** small but sparkling, offers Oriental food in serve-yourself cafeteria style; most dishes are $3.15 for two portions, $3.65 for three, $4.15 for four. Betty also has an interesting selection of dim sum—pork manapua, brown sugar manapua, egg rolls, and Chinese doughnuts, from 25¢ to 65¢ each . . . **Monster Burger** is true to its name: it offers a half-pound Monster Burger at $3, a quarter-pound Mama Monster at $1.85, and a Baby Monster at 65¢. They also have lunch and dinner plates of items like roast beef, boneless chicken fry, mahimahi, from $2.99 to $4.99, including salad and rice or french fries. Breakfast specials at $1.99, too . . . **Kona Deli Seafood,** popular with the local people, sells seafood salads, and meat and cheese sandwiches to go.

On your way to City of Refuge at Honaunau (see Chapter XIV), there are some good places to stop. The **Aloha Café** (tel. 322-3383), in the lobby of the Aloha theater in Kainaliu, has wonderful, healthful food and an unusual atmosphere. The artistically decorated counter-service café is in the lobby of the theater, but it's even more fun to sit out on the terraced lanai that borders the building, especially all the way down near the meadow. The menu features homemade vegetarian soups, veggie salads, eggplant sesame cheese burgers, vegetarian burritos, lots of sandwiches, and even a non-health-food item or two like great char-broiled burgers. Sandwiches run about $4.25 to $4.50. If you get there in time for breakfast, you'll be treated to three-egg omelets, pancakes, and whole-wheat french toast, $3.25 to $5.25. Even if you don't have a meal here, stop in for some of the homemade fresh baked goods. The day we were there it was raspberry linzer tortes. Ono! Their baked goods, sandwiches, and burritos are also served at the World Square Theater in Kailua, and you don't have to pay admission to the theater to get the food. Aloha Café, by the way, seems to be local headquarters for transplanted mainlanders to hang out, so it's always a fun stop. Open every day except Sunday from 8 a.m. to 3:30 p.m. only. Their adjoining health-food and gift store can provide picnic ingredients—sandwiches to go, cheeses, organic fruits (we recently tried organic lichees!) and vegetables. They also offer a large selection of gifts and cards, specializing in children's gifts and books.

Down the street from the Aloha is the quaint **Roaster's Kona Coffee,** with its old-world charm. Coffees, espresso, cappuccino, pastries, and light fare are served in this cafe from 7 a.m. to 5 p.m. daily. You can also buy fresh coffee beans here.

The dining room of the **H. Manago Hotel** in Captain Cook (tel. 323-2642) is the place to catch a slice of local life. This big, family-style restaurant has enjoyed a good reputation for years among the local people, although very few tourists make their way here. Everything is served family style: big plates of rice, salad (macaroni salad is especially good), vegetables, whatever the cook has made that night are brought out and served to everyone at the table, along with such entrees as pork chops, liver, ahi, opelo, ono, mahimahi, or steak; the prices go from about $5.50 to $8.25. The menu is limited and the food is not fancy, but this is a good chance to experience the nontourist life of the Kona Coast. Very pleasant. They serve all three meals, dinner from 5 to 7:30 p.m. week days; to 7 p.m. Friday, Saturday, and Sunday.

Everybody likes the **Canaan Deli** in Kealekekua, across the street from the Bank of Hawaii. It's a New York–type deli started in 1972 by several young Christians with a mission: high-quality food served with aloha. The deli features kosher-style sandwiches using fresh island beef and locally baked breads (hot pastrami and rare roast beef run around $3.75), homemade salads, and Italian specialties. All sandwiches come with a choice of salad and kosher pickle. They even have lox and bagels! Scrambled eggs and omelets are breakfast favorites, with a $1.99 breakfast special from 7 to 9 a.m. And the homemade Italian dinners are fun: accompanied by minestrone soup or salad, and garlic bread, entrees like fettuccine Alfredo, ravioli, spaghetti, and pesto run from $3.25 to $6.95. There's New York–style pizza, too.

If you're ready for a big-splurge meal now, we can't think of a more idyllic place to have it than at **Kona Village,** a glorious hideaway resort on an oasis in the lava flows at Kaupulehu, about 15 miles from Kailua-Kona. The lunchtime buffet, served outdoors in a garden setting at this luxurious Polynesian village, where guests live in private thatched huts, is yours for $18, and so filling that you probably won't want to eat again until the next day. We counted something like 37 dishes on the smörgåsbord. You line up, first, for the cheeses (good bries, cheddars, and the like) and breads, including crisp Armenian lavosh and hot rolls. Then on to the salads, which include raw tuna (sashimi) and hot tuna (delicious). We found nothing overly marinated or mayonnaised, as is so often the case with buffets. Next comes the fruit tray where, pausing among the kiwis and cherries and melons and papayas and such, you could linger indefinitely. But don't stop here: five or six hot dishes might include breaded shrimp, fried rice with bacon, chicken, and sweet-and-sour fish. For dessert, you could have home-baked banana bread and malasadas—as much as you want of everything, of course. Beverages and cocktails are served at your table. Be sure to call in advance for reservations (tel. 325-5555), as only expected guests can get past the guardhouse and gain access to this special Hawaiian place.

THE NIGHT SCENE IN KAILUA-KONA: There's plenty of nighttime entertainment in these parts, even if you don't make it to one of the big luaus, either at the King Kamehameha Hotel or at the exotic Kona Village Resort at Kaupulehu. If you don't mind skipping the pig and poi, you can see a free Polynesian show, "Polynesia Unlimited," at the Nalu Terrace of the sumptuous Kona Surf Resort Tuesday and Friday night for the price of two drinks (they begin at $3.50). Showtime is 7:45. It's worth the drive just to see the Kona Surf anyway. Happy Hour, from 4 to 6 p.m., at the Nalu Terrace features free pupus and drinks beginning at $1.75, and there is always a group playing soft music as the sun sinks into the sea. A free Polynesian show accompanies dinner at 6:30 and 7:30 p.m. nightly at Cousin Kimo's (see above).

You will, of course, want to see a torchlighting ceremony. Happily, there's no charge at all for that. Just take yourself to the beach in front of the **King Kamehameha Hotel** at luau time on a Sunday, Tuesday, or Thursday evening just before sunset and watch the beautiful ceremony, as torches are lit on land and sea, in the shadow of an ancient heiau. Then you might proceed to the **Bill-**

fish Bar, situated around the lovely pool, where there is a variety of musical entertainment every night from 5 to 10 p.m. Happy Hour prices prevail from 5 to 7 p.m.

Bartender's Ocean Breeze is a popular, boozy place, right next to the Kona Hilton tennis courts on Alii Drive. Not only can you get low-priced drinks here—call drinks at $2.75, draft beer and wine coolers at $1.75—but you can also broil your own half-pound Breeze Burger for $3.25 or New York steak for $4.50. Open daily from 10:30 a.m. to 2 a.m.

One of the most atmospheric small lounges in town is the **Spindrifter** on Alii Drive, where the tables and chairs are *that* close to the ocean. Spindrifter has the longest Happy Hour in Kona: from 11 a.m. to 7 p.m. daily, it serves mai tais at $1.50, plus fresh oysters or fresh clams on the half-shell at 85¢ each, in the Oyster Bar and Lounge only. Entertainment every night. . . . Another very popular lounge overlooking the water is **Don Drysdale's Club 53,** where the exotic drinks—like Frozen Baboon, Fuzzy Willie, and Hawaiian Sunset—are unique, and where the pupus—shrimp scampi and deep-fried zucchini—are really special. There are burgers and sandwiches too, to go along with the drinks. . . . At the **Pool Bar** of the Keauhou Beach Hotel, it's Happy Hour between 4 to 6 p.m. every day and all drinks are half price. . . . Happy Hour fans should also note the long Happy Hour—11:30 a.m. to 10 p.m.—at the **Whaler's Bar** in Hurricane Annie's; that's when mai tais, Blue Hawaiis, piña coladas, and chi chis are just $2.50. . . . During the Pau Hana hours, 4 to 6 p.m., draft and domestic beers are $1, and well drinks are $1.50 at **Tom Bombadil's. . . .** From 2:30 to 5:30 p.m., it's Happy Hour at **Paniolo Pizza;** that's where mai tais and chi chis are $2.50, and margaritas and daiquiris, plain or with fruit, are just $1.75. . . . There are many different specials at **Old Kailua Cantina.** On Pau Hana Fridays, 3 to 6 p.m., it's a "Tostada Bar" with free pupus; Monday night sees the football crowd watching the game on two big-screen TVs and enjoying $1 hotdogs and $1.50 nachos. Bloody Mary's are only $1 on Monday between 11:30 a.m. and 3:30 p.m.

If you're in a disco mood, go to romantic **Eclipse**—candles, wooden beams, mirrors, and the disco sound. It's on Kuakini Hwy. across from Foodland. Dinner from 5 to 9 p.m. and disco until 2 a.m. . . . At trendy, atmospheric **Mitchell's** at Keahou, there's dining and dancing to the Big Band sound. At 10 p.m., the bar area comes to life and there's disco dancing to a live rock band until 1:45 a.m. Appetizers and desserts are served until 1 a.m. . . . After the kitchen closes at **Fishermen's Landing,** the terrace area overlooking the ocean is still open for drinks and entertainment. Usually there's a guitarist. A wonderfully romantic spot.

Also highly recommended for that romantic mood is the **Windjammer Bar** at the Kona Hilton, where you can listen to the sound of the surf smashing up against the rocks as you sit out on the patio and watch the Pacific perform. Either the West Hawaiian Revue or the Freitas brothers will be playing Hawaiian music in the Windjammer Lounge. Walking around the big hotels like the Hilton, examining their gardens and lagoons by moonlight and floodlight, is a show in itself.

The bars have closed and you're hungry. Easy. Go to **Doug's Diner** at Kuakini Hwy. for a malt, a burger, or a very, very early breakfast. This place never closes, be it sunlight or moonlight.

READERS' SELECTIONS ON HAWAII: "We discovered that we could get a better deal on hotel accommodations by going through a **travel agent** than by going directly to the hotel. For example, we got a package deal from a travel agent in Kona that included a rental car *and* a room at the beautiful Keahou Beach Hotel, right on the beach near Kona, for only $44 a day. If we had gone directly to the hotel for the room, it would have cost $55 per night, without the car . . . Our favorite place to eat dinner was **Volcano House.** A complete chicken teriyaki dinner was $8.95, and included one of the best soup-and-salad bars available. I thought it an excellent buy, considering the fine food, excellent service, unique location, and pleasant Hawaiian music" (Linda Fox, Soldotna, Alaska). . . . "The **Sea Village** in Kailua-Kona was, without a doubt, the best bargain of our entire three-week trip. It was exquisite and all you said it was and more. Friends of ours stayed there in 1983 and found it exactly the same. They came back raving about what a beautiful place it was" (Mrs. Leone Prozny, Edmonton, Alberta, Canada).

"After much exploring we found that the coffeeshops of the big hotels on the Kona Coast are now catering to customers who want light, inexpensive dinner menus. We would especially like to recommend the coffeeshop at the **Kona Surf** for an excellent dinner, reasonable prices, and good food. This is a lovely garden setting; at sunset, a runner lights the torches. In the same hotel, you can take in the very professional hula show. The 'no cover, no minimum' advertising is quite true; there is no pressure to buy drinks and lots of seating space at tables. A delightful and inexpensive evening. Another pleasant coffeeshop dinner was in the **Kona Hilton,** on the waterfront, with the sunset to look at" (Evelyn and Sid Ramsden, Richmond, B.C., Canada).

"We stayed at a delightful condo in Kona and paid $609 for a week, which included our car. We were sick when we found out another couple there had gone through a **realtor** in Kona instead of a travel agent and were paying $595 for a month. Anyone interested in renting a condo in Kona should contact various realtors there and compare costs. They are much less expensive" (Ruth E. Dishnow, Wasila, Alaska). [*Authors' Note:* Rates in the condo market are extremely changeable. One apartment complex is usually handled by several realtors, each of whom has a block of apartments; or apartments are rented by individual owners. For anyone who has the time, comparison shopping is certainly advisable on a lengthy stay.]

"The new **KTA supermarket** in the Keauhou Shopping Village has a very good deli that prepares generous portions of take-out meals at reasonable prices. These are excellent for picnics, eating on the go, or for an inexpensive meal in your room. By the way, this is one shopping center worth visiting for its parking lot alone. The view up the Kona coast toward Kailua town is superb, and it's a great sunset-watching spot" (Robbie and Alan Kolman, Rensselaerville, N.Y.).

"We run a small Hilo bed-and-breakfast called **Hale O'Makamaka** (House of Friends). We have a very humble home on the slopes of Mauna Kea at the 1,200-foot elevation; the nights are cool. We have an indoor spa (hot tub) that we enjoy, and make available to our overnight guests. Our guest room has a private bath. We have only the one double bed, so discourage travelers with children. Our rate for two people is $27.50; for a single, it's $16.50 per night. We like to have advance reservations whenever possible, but sometimes take spur-of-the-moment guests. Write to Fabian and Nancy Toribio, 2564 Ainaola Dr., Hilo, HI 96720 (tel. 959-9789)" (Nancy Toribio, Hilo, Hi.).

"You may consider **flying standby** to the outer islands and realize considerable savings. We flew to each island on standby, and never had to wait for a flight. Also, note that Hawaiian Airlines flies the biggest planes (727s) between the islands and would have more available seats for this system" (John Sinclair, Louisville, Ky.). . . . "The **King Kamehameha Hotel,** in Kona has so much to offer visitors. The Kona Veranda Coffeeshop had the best hamburger of any—the new Mauna Loa Burger with a fine garnish of onion curls and the best steak fries, adorned with a Vanda orchid. Across the street, **Quinn's**—plain out front but with a pleasant dining area out back—had an outstanding vegetable omelet with mushrooms and a mouth-watering sandwich of fresh avocado, beansprouts, and delicious cheese. In fact, Kona restaurants served the most reasonable and delicious food we had on our trip" (Beth and Bake Baker, Englewood, Fla.).

"Above all else, **Volcano House** must not be missed. Sitting on the rim of Kilauea Crater, it invokes the feeling of a mountain lodge. Volcano House is small and intimate with a friendly staff. It has a wood fireplace in the lobby, but no TVs (who needs them here in this setting!). We live in the mountains of New Mexico, but I have never seen stars like those at Volcano House. Where else but in Hawaii can you stand on a tropical island shivering in the chill below a 10,000-foot-plus mountain with snow in early October" (Nancy Goertz, Sandia Park, N. Mex.).

"We have just returned from Hawaii and want you to know that the **Dolphin Bay**

Hotel in Hilo is the best, cleanest, and most friendly hotel we have stayed at in 12 trips to the islands. Fresh bananas, papayas, and mangoes each day free, and beautiful grounds to surround you, and very reasonable cost, $31 a day with kitchen. We have found that we can see Hawaii without paying a fortune. Thanks for telling us about the little hotels, especially the Dolphin Bay in Hilo and Kona Tiki in Kona. They are like old Hawaii" (Tom and Marg Keall, Surrey, B.C., Canada).

Chapter XIV

SEEING HAWAII

1. Around Hilo
2. Puna and Volcanoes National Park
3. Across Hawaii
4. The Kona Coast

COUNT ON A MINIMUM of four days on the Big Island for relaxed sightseeing: the first day for touring in and around **Hilo;** the second for visiting the **Puna area** and **Hawaii Volcanoes National Park;** the third for driving across the island from Hilo to **Kailua-Kona** on the western coast; and the fourth for exploring the **Kona Coast.** This gives you two nights at a hotel in Hilo and one or more in Kona. You can, of course, add a few more days at either end. It's also possible to arrive at Hilo, drive immediately to the Volcano area for a few hours, and then continue right across the island to Kona, where you can then relax in the sun for as long as you want. Or fly into Kona and reverse the trip, from west to east. The following itinerary will give you the basic information, around which you can do your own improvising.

1. Around Hilo

Most of the residents of Hilo are convinced that this is the world's greatest little city, and they wouldn't consider living anywhere else. The fact that they live—quite literally—between the devil and the deep-blue sea, bothers them not a bit. See those huge mountains that dominate the skyline? The bigger one, Mauna Kea, is an extinct volcano, but her smaller sister, Mauna Loa, is still very much alive.

If you've read Michener's *Hawaii*, you'll remember how the Alii Nui Noelani went to Hilo in 1832 to confront Pele and implore her to halt the fiery lava that came close to destroying the town. Pele has toyed with the idea more than a few times since, as recently as 1935, 1942, and 1984, but she has always spared the city—even without the intervention of priestesses. The citizens are convinced she always will. They feel just as nonchalant about tidal waves—at least they did until 1960. On the May morning when seismic waves hurtled across the Pacific headed for Hawaii, the citizens of Hilo had hours to evacuate; instead, some of them actually went down to the bridge to watch the show. This time the gods were not so kind. Sixty-one people were swept into the waves and a big chunk of waterfront area was wiped out. For several years after, one could see the devastation along the ocean side of Kamehameha Avenue; now there is grass and palm trees. Past Pauahi Street, however, look to your right and see the surprisingly modern architecture of the county and state office buildings. The construction of these buildings caused one of the liveliest controversies in the

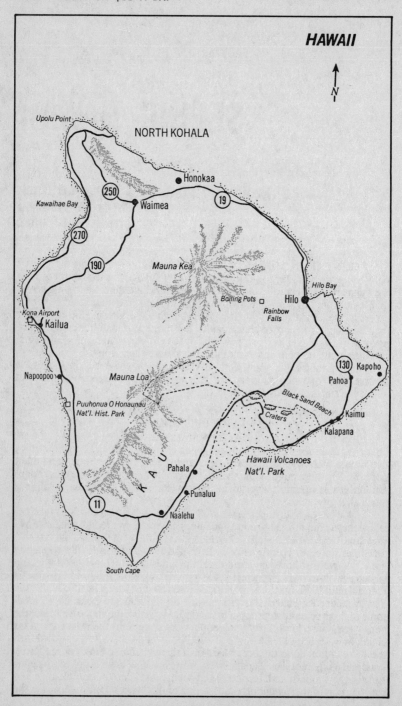

HAWAII

↑
N

Upolu Point

NORTH KOHALA

● Honokaa

250

Kawaihae Bay

19

Waimea

270

190

Mauna Kea

Boiling Pots □   Hilo

Hilo Bay

Rainbow
Falls

Kona Airport

● Kailua

Napoopoo ●

Mauna Loa

130   Kapoho

Pahoa

Puuhonua O Honaunau
Nat'l. Hist. Park

Black Sand Beach

Craters

Kaimu

Kalapana

K A U

Pahala ●

Hawaii Volcanoes
Nat'l. Park

● Punaluu

11

● Naalehu

South Cape

history of the city; the reasoning was to inspire confidence in the devastated bay-side area. The optimists won the day, and Hilo still continues to defy further tsunami activity.

This knowledge impresses itself strongly on the mind of the visitor, making Hilo far more than a make-believe world for tourists. It forms a curious back-drop to the beauty and gentleness of this city arching around a crescent bay (Hilo's name means new moon). Once a whaling port of the Pacific, Hilo is still a seaport, from which raw sugar (note the bulk-sugar plant on the waterfront) and cattle are shipped to the other islands and the mainland. Flowers are big busi-ness too; 132 inches of rainfall a year (most of it at night—but there are plenty of misty mornings too) makes the orchids and anthuriums grow as crabgrass does on suburban lawns elsewhere. Nearly a quarter of million tropical blossoms are sent from Hilo via airplane all over the world.

GARDENS, GARDENS, GARDENS: And here's where our sightseeing tour of Hilo begins, with a visit to one of the most beautiful of its gardens, **Hilo Tropical Gardens.** Follow Hwy. 12 to the eastern strip of town where you'll find the gar-dens at 1477 Kalanianaole Ave., about two miles from the airport. Old-timers will remember this place as Kong's Tropical Gardens; new owners have taken over and the place promises to be better than ever. Paved walkways (accessible to the handicapped) lead you through a tiny jungle of tropical flowers, shrubs and trees, splendid orchids, native Hawaiian plants and herbs, past water lily pools, waterfalls, even a Japanese pond with footbridge and statuary. After you've seen the gardens and used up a little bit of film, stop in at their gift shop of Hawaiian handcrafts made by the people of Hawaii: wood products, photo-graphs, notecards, food items, and of course, flowers. Anything can be shipped home. Free admission. Open daily from 8:30 a.m. to 5:30 p.m. Phone 935-4957 for driving directions.

If you haven't been surfeited by all this, you might also try **Orchids of Ha-waii,** 2801 Kilauea Ave., which allows you to view its nursery and packing oper-ations. Plants, seeds, and cuttings are available to take back with you or ship home without any restrictions. To get there, drive southward on Hwy. 11 and turn right at Palai Street and left onto Kilauea Avenue. You'll see Orchids of Hawaii just after you cross the one-lane bridge on the left. Open weekdays from 8 a.m. to 4 p.m., closed on major holidays. Free admission.

Kulani Flowers Anthurium Farm, about a mile farther on the same road, goes all out for the visitor; a guide escorts you on a tour through the nurseries to see an exotic assortment of anthuriums (including the multicolored "Obakes"), a collection of rare palm-tree and macadamia-nut and papaya orchards as well. Open daily from 9 a.m. to 5 p.m. To reach Kulani Flowers, take Hwy. 11 toward the volcano. Take your second right after the four-mile marker on Mamaki Street, then the first left on Kealakai Street.

Another very pleasant place to visit is **Hirose Nurseries,** 2212 Kaneolehua Ave. They give you free flowers, and you explore the beautiful hothouse and gardens on your own. It's about three miles out of town on Hwy. 11, on the left-hand side of the road, near Kahaopea Street.

On the way back toward town, stay on Manono Street as it crosses Kame-hameha Avenue and continue on the drive along Hilo Bay. Soon you'll spot the **Nihon Japanese Culture Center** which, in addition to serving authentic and ex-cellent Japanese cuisine (see Chapter XIII), has an art gallery, a tea room, and spaces for music, dancing, films, and other entertainments. Check to see if any-thing special is going on. Now there's **Liliuokalani Gardens** coming up on your right, lovely with its Japanese bridges, ponds, plants, and stone lanterns; you can picnic here. It's believed to be the largest such formal Oriental garden and park outside Japan. Look for the authentic Japanese tea ceremony house. Now on your left is **Coconut Island,** a favorite picnic spot for the local people. If you continue around the park, you'll find yourself on Banyan Drive, which takes you past many of the elegant resort hotels in the city. The magnificent trees are labeled in honor of the celebrities who planted them; James A. Farley was one, Amelia Earhart another; Cecil B. De Mille has a tree, and so does Mrs. De Mille. At the end of the drive is **Reed's Bay Park,** a cool picnic spot on the bay.

To see our favorite gardens, however, you'll have to drive in another direction, about three miles south on Hwy. 11 (the road to the volcano) from Hilo Airport, then turn left onto Makalika Street just after Hwy. 11 divides; drive in seven-tenths of a mile (look for the familiar Hawaiian warrior sign for the turnoff), and you'll soon find **Nani Mau Gardens,** a recently developed wonderland of 20 acres full of the fruits and flowers of many lands; orchids are only some of the growing things here. The gardens are a work of love on the part of Mr. Mac Nitahara and his family. The macadamia and coffee trees, the air plants, the incredible varieties of hibiscus, orchids, and ginger are some of the things you'll see. They'll let you smell everything too—from vanilla orchids to fragrant allspice leaves. Mr. Nitahara is working especially hard to grow Hawaiian herbs and to propagate their lore as well—it's fascinating to see and learn about the herb that helps heal broken bones (the noni plant), the one that clears up sinus trouble (olena), the one that cures coughs (ohaloa), and the one that heals cuts (ti leaf). Get Mr. Nitahara to tell you about the herb that cured his father of high blood pressure! When you come back from your tour, which takes about an hour, they bring you a cup of fresh fruit—perhaps papaya, pineapple, bananas, even fresh guava—whatever is in season. You can stay in the gardens as long as you like, to picnic or just relax. Open daily, from 8 a.m. to 5 p.m.; admission is $3.50 for adults, $1.50 for children 7 to 12; below 7, no charge.

Hawaii Tropical Botanical Gardens is unique; it's a wild nature preserve that is being developed to protect the natural beauty of a tropical rain forest. You must drive about five miles from Hilo and make a donation of $6 (tax deductible) to get there, but for serious students of nature and photographers, it's well worth it. The garden's 17 acres are dotted with myriads of waterfalls, meandering streams, a huge variety of tropical plantlife; there's a lake with tropical water lilies and a stretch of rugged ocean coastline. No food is sold here and there are no picnicking facilities. For reservations (advised) and driving directions, phone 964-5233. Open 9 a.m. to 5 p.m. Monday through Saturday, 11 a.m. to 5 p.m. on Sunday.

A HAWAIIAN ZOO AND AN ENVIRONMENTAL CENTER: While you're visiting the gardens in this area, you might also want to take in a charming Hilo attraction: the **Panaewa Equestrian Center and Rain Forest Zoo** complex. It's just outside the city as you drive on Rte. 11; turn right on the Stainback Hwy. and watch for signs on the right to the zoo. This is by no means the big time, as zoos go; it's a small place but with its own special Hawaiian charm. You'll see denizens of the South American rain forest, the rare Hawaiian "nene" (goose), the Hawaiian "pueo" (owl), many brightly plumaged birds, and peacocks roaming the grounds; cutest of all are the monkeys, especially the capuchins, who seem to enjoy the funny humans walking about. Free admission. Open every day from 9 a.m. to 4 p.m.

THE TRAIL OF KAMEHAMEHA: Now it's time for some Kamehameha lore, since the Big Island is where that doughty old warrior was born and where he first started dreaming his dreams of glory and conquest. Continue your journey on Kamehameha Avenue, turn left at Waianuenue Street (Norberto's Restau-

rant is at the corner), and drive three blocks to the modern County Library on the right side. See the two stones out in front? The bigger one, the **Naha Stone**, was Kamehameha's Excalibur. According to Naha legend, only a chief of the royal blood could even budge the gigantic boulder; any warrior strong enough to turn it over would have the strength to conquer and unify all the islands of Hawaii. Kamehameha did the deed, but since the stone weighs at least a ton, no one has, as yet, bothered to repeat it.

HILO'S NATURAL SIGHTS: Best time to see the next sight, **Rainbow Falls**, is early in the morning. Come between 9:15 and 10 a.m., when the sun gets up high enough over the mango trees so that you're apt to see rainbows forming in the mist. But it's pretty at any time, and so are the beautiful yellow flowers growing near the parking lot. You reach the falls by taking Rainbow Drive off Waianuenue Avenue. If you'd also like to see the **Boiling Pots,** deep pools that appear to be boiling as turbulent water flows over the lava bed of the river, continue along Waianuenue about two miles, past some of the nicest homes in Hilo and a huge monkeypod tree, to Peepee Street. From the parking lot you can walk over to the edge and observe the show below. Both Rainbow Falls and the Boiling Pots are part of the **Wailuku River State Park.**

Now we head for the **Kaumana Cave** and a chance to see some of the work of Pele at close range. The cave is a lava tube, created in 1881, when Pele came closer to wiping out Hilo than at any other time. Lava tubes are sometimes formed when lava flows down a ravine or gully; the top and sides cool while the center keeps racing along. Millions of years of volcanic eruptions have left hollow tubes like this all over the islands; in many of them are hidden the bones of the alii, which were always buried in remote, secret places. Of the two tubes here, only the one on the right—whose entrance is an exquisite fern grotto—is safe for exploration. The one on the left is treacherous, and who knows—perhaps the bones of Kamehameha, never discovered, are buried here? To get to the caves, return to the fork at Hwy. 20 and turn right to the other branch of the fork, Kaumana Drive. The cave is about three miles out; an HVB marker indicates the spot.

A CHURCH AND A MUSEUM: On we go, from paganism to Christianity. When you get back to Kamehameha Avenue, watch for Haili Street; turn onto it in a mauka direction (away from the bay and uphill); cross Keawe, Kinoole, and Ululani Streets, and on the left-hand side you'll see **Haili Church.** It's architecture is pure New England, but its fame stems from its great Hawaiian choir. Continuing up Haili Street, you next cross Kapiolani Street, and on the right-hand side you'll find the **Lyman House Memorial Museum Complex** at 176 Haili St. You can visit either the old missionary house and the new $1-million museum addition, or both. The original Lyman House is another of those old mission homes that the grandchildren and great-grandchildren turned into a museum, and this one, originally built in 1839, has now been fully restored and furnished as a home of the 1850–1870 period. Hilo's oldest structure, the white-frame building contains hand-molded New England glass windows, doors made of native koa wood, and the original wide koa floorboards. As you tour the rooms, you'll see how the missionary family lived: the clothes, old four-poster beds, white marble-topped table stands and dressers. The fascinating Hawaiian artifacts and worldwide curios that used to be displayed here have now been transferred to the newly built Lyman Museum building. In this very modern museum, you begin at the Island Heritage Gallery on the first floor where a raised relief map shows routes taken by all the groups that came to Hawaii. Then you can see the artifacts of each group and study their cultures; the Hawaiian exhibit includes a full-size grass house. Stone Age implements, feather leis, etc. Other ethnic exhibits include an intricately hand-carved Taoist shrine brought to Hilo piece by piece in their luggage by early Chinese sugar plantation workers. There are also Japanese, Portuguese, Korean, and Filipino displays.

The second floor also has fascinating exhibits, among them the Earth Heritage Gallery with its display of volcanic eruptions and worldwide mineral collections, one of the finest and most extensive such collections in the Pacific; a large Pacific shell collection, covering many examples of beautiful and rare shells; and Man's Heritage Gallery, containing beautiful collections of old glass, Oriental furniture, screens, and a large collection of Oriental art.

Lyman House is open from 9 a.m. to 4 p.m. Tuesday, Thursday, Friday, and Saturday; closed Wednesday, Sunday, and major holidays. Admission is $3 for adults, $1.50 for children, $2 for seniors.

SHOPPING IN HILO: Shopping is concentrated in three areas here: downtown, where stores and boutiques are housed in quaint wooden buildings; at the Kaiko's Hilo Mall, just behind the County and State Buildings; and out on Hwy. 11, at the new, mega-bucks Prince Kuhio Plaza Shopping Center. Let's start out at **Kaiko'o Hilo Mall,** which has everything from a supermarket to a drugstore to souvenir shops, plus some more sophisticated shops. Have a look at **Book Gallery,** where you can learn a lot about Hawaii; pick up some island cookbooks, books for the keikis back home, or some of the unique Petroglyph Press paperbacks, printed right here in Hilo. . . . **J.C. Penney's** has a branch here and, as usual, value and selections are excellent. . . . There's a **McInerny's** too. . . . **Shiigi Drug** has loads of souvenir items. . . . We like the cheeses, candied herbs, and teas at **Gourmet Hut Hawaii.** (Their take-out sandwiches are really good.) . . . **The Puka** and **The Kiosk,** two gift huts located in the center of the mall, carry better-than-usual merchandise.

Although **Hilo Hattie's Resort Shop** here has prices that are below average for island wear, you can do even better by going directly to **Hilo Hattie's Fashion Center & Factory** at 933 Kanoelehua (tel. 961-3077 for free transportation), on the main highway going out of town, just a few blocks past the airport. Not only can you see the garments being made, but you can get them at a lower price than in the retail shops. It's open seven days a week, from 8:30 a.m. to 5:30 p.m.

Just down the street from the mall, crafts-minded people should stop in at **Hawaii Modelcraft,** located at the Hilo Shopping Center, 1221 Kilauea Ave., right next door to **Maile's Hawaii** (a wonderful source for Hawaiian-made treasures), and **Teddy & Friends.** This is a great hobby store for kids of all ages. The people here freely dispense hospitality and travel tips to visitors along with know-how on local crafts.

Uncle Billy's Polynesian Market Place, at the Hilo Bay Hotel, 87 Banyan Dr., is an enormous clothing-gift-souvenir store, with low prices on just about everything. Some of the clothing is made in their own garment factory. We saw muumuus beginning at about $30.

For health-food buffs, we're happy to report that small Hilo has two big and exciting health-food stores. The older of the duo is **Hilo Natural Foods,** 306 Kilauea St., stocked to the brim with natural foods, herb teas, cheeses, natural vitamins and supplements, honeys, breads, books, plus a Natural Foods Kitchen for snacks and light meals. You'll find plenty here that you'll want to bring back to your kitchenette apartment or nibble on right here at the store.

Then there's **Abundant Life Natural Foods Store,** which occupies the premises of an oldtime pharmacy (and still retains much of that feeling) at 90 Kamehameha Ave. They consider themselves to be one of the state's most complete natural-foods stores, and indeed the selection is fascinating: over 200 varieties of herbs, teas, and spices; fresh, locally grown produce; plus natural vitamins, groceries, and quality skincare products, including suntan oils and lotions with sunscreens. There is also a nice assortment of locally crafted items. You may want to try some of their tropical fruit jams, all made locally with Hawaiian honey. Freshly pressed carrot juice and sandwiches are prepared daily for take-out. And you'll probably find it hard to resist some of their delicious snack items on the way out.

If you'd like to take some anthuriums home with you, be sure to stop at **Anthuriums of Hawaii,** 530 Ainaola Dr., where you can see anthuriums of every color and description (green and red "hula dancer" or "lipstick" anthuriums, for example), and enjoy the friendly hospitality of the owners. They're the kind of people who, simply because we inquired about different varieties of ginger, rushed to our car as we pulled out with a big stalk of fresh ginger to take with us—compliments of the house. They'll pack and ship anthuriums anywhere, and prices are reasonable. Everyone gets two anthuriums and whatever fresh fruit is in season free—just for visiting. The owners ask that you call 959-8717 for directions before you come.

Across the street from the Hawaii Visitors Bureau, at 195 Kinoole St., is **Hale Manu Lauhala Weaving,** which has hats (from $9.50), baskets, placemats, and other weavings made by local craftspeople. . . . A few doors along, at 201 Kinoole, is **Old Town Printers & Stationers,** the retail store of the Petroglyph Press, which has been publishing books on Hawaiiana since 1962. Drop in to browse through their notes and postcards and an outstanding collection of maps. Better yet, walk around the corner to their new retail store at 169 Keawe St. called **Basically Books.** It is a general bookstore with a fine collection of Hawaiiana, plus globes, notecards, tins, and other attractive gift items.

There's an artistic touch to a handful of downtown shops, all of them close to each other on or near Keawe Street. The **Potter's Gallery,** located in the Mamo Mart, 176 Mamo St., shows hand-blown pottery and porcelain done with an Oriental flair. It always has a selection of functional stoneware by Randy Morehouse, plus rotating shows by Big Island artists (Mamo Mart, by the way, mostly of interest to local people, is the only indoor parking lot we've ever seen surrounded by shops!).

We have to agree with owner Sally Mermel that her place at 110 Keawe St. is indeed **The Most Irresistible Shop in Hilo**—at least for people who like a wide variety of items to choose from—everything from great stationery and cards to wood stoves. She has an outstanding collection of 100% cotton Chinese T-shirts; hand-screened by local artists (from $18 to $23), local jams and jellies, a kitchen section with delightful ceramic items (stoneware juicers, colanders) and koa wood utensils (rolling pins and bowls) by island potters and carvers. Sally represents the work of some 40 island artists and craftspeople, so you might see stained-glass mirrors and lamps, watercolors, needlepoint kits, patchwork quilts, hand-screened canvas bags, and the like. Children will love the dollhouse furniture, books, handmade wooden toys, and lots of cute T-shirts. Sally has another store of the same name at the new Prince Kuhio Plaza Shopping Center. And adjoining the original shop is **Bear's Café** (see Chapter XIII), with wonderful coffees, light foods, and desserts, all with a bear theme—Bear Claws, Teddy Bear Pie—and more.

The newly renovated and quite attractive 1922 Pacific Building, which houses The Most Irresistible Shop in Hilo, is also home to several other tasteful boutiques. The **Picture Frame Shop and Gallery** features prints and paintings by local artists like Pegge Hopper, John Thomas, Robert Nelson, and Kim Taylor Reese. They also have some attractive koa-framed mirrors. Prices range from $5 for tiny vases and $6 for hand-thrown mugs, to $75 for large ceramic plates and bowls. . . . A lot of the items at **The Futon Connection** are too big for you to carry home, but do have a look at their hand-painted parasols at $12.95, and beautiful, large paper fans at $24. Balinese hand-carved and hand-painted birds of paradise, banana trees, fish, frogs, and more are moderately priced; and many other unique gift items range from $7 to $35. . . . Don't miss **The Chocolate Bar,** you chocaholics out there; it's famous for its coconut/chocolate sushi—a Hilo original! All candies are homemade, and begin at 25¢ a piece.

Prince Kuhio Shopping Plaza will remind you of Kaahumanu Center on Maui or Kukui Grove on Kauai; it's vast, it cost millions to build (in this case $47.5), it boasts the traditional big department stores like Liberty House and Sears, plus a handful or more of charming little boutiques. **The Most Irresistible Shop in Hilo,** which we've told you about above, has cloned its downtown location (except for Bear's Café) and is now here as well, with the same kind of tasteful merchandise. . . . **Imagination Toys** is an educational toy center, with all kinds of creative playthings. . . . And **Once Upon A Time** is a charmer, full of stuffed animals, whimsical teddy bears, Victorian dolls, funny slippers, and more. . . . **Contempo Casuals** is known for trendy sportswear, beachclothing, disco wear, and creative costume jewelry at reasonable prices. And there's another branch of **The Chocolate Bar** here (see above), with many novelty Hawaiian candies, like chocolate sushi, chocolate aloha greeting cards, and macadamia-nut candies. Chocolate teddy bears at $1 are adorable. **Mrs. Field's Cookies** is here, too, with no less than four kinds of chocolate brownies: double chocolate, nut chip, macadamia nut, and coconut.

There's a good Chinese deli here—**Kow's**—as well as several other restaurants, but keep in mind, that you're about a two-minute drive from the Puainako Town Center, home to **Ting-Hao Mandarin Restaurant,** one of the best in town (see Chapter XIII).

WAILOA CENTER: The building that looks like a volcano, just behind the State Office Building, is actually the **Wailoa Center,** a continuing free exhibit that accents the natural history and culture of the Big Island. Wall niches and free-standing displays are changed every month or two, so you might get to see an exhibit of Hawaiian-born artists, a display of the history and culture of the island, or one on ancient Hawaiian antiques. There's a permanent exhibit on tsunamis (tidal waves); a tsunami monument stands next to the building. The people here are happy to provide information and suggestions for visitors. Services and admission are free. The entrance is on Piopio Street, between the State Office Building and Kamehameha Avenue. It's open Monday through Saturday from 8 a.m. to 4:30 p.m.

TIME FOR A SWIM: Your ramblings have worn you out, your budget hotel doesn't have a pool, and you want a swim. Where do you go? We'd head out on Kalanianaole Avenue, drive three miles to **Onekahakaha Beach Park** or a mile farther to **James Kealoha Park,** where the swimming in the rocky bay is okay if not memorable. But it's pleasant to drive through this Keaukaha area, the most beautiful part of Hilo, to see the exquisite private homes, some with their own tranquil Oriental fish ponds. Picnic and swimming spots continue until the end of the paved road. Watch for the signs pointing to **Richardson's Ocean Park,** the home of an outdoor marine recreation and interpretive center. You can swim, snorkel, fish, and surf in waters that front the center; tour a coastal trail which features coastal plants and brackish water ponds, and/or picnic on the lawn areas. The center contains marine life displays which interpret nearby ocean and coastal environments. Open Monday through Saturday, 8:30 a.m. to 4:30 p.m. Free admission. Phone 935-3830 for details.

If you favor pool swimming, join the local people at the Olympic-size **Kawamoto Pool** (tel. 935-8907) at Kuawa and Kalanikoa Streets, near the Civic Auditorium. Admission is free. Open weekdays from 11 a.m. to 1 p.m. for adults, from 1 to 4 p.m. for everybody: on weekends 10 a.m. to 12 noon for adults and 1 to 4 p.m. for everybody.

2. Puna and Volcanoes National Park

You must not leave the Big Island without paying homage to the goddess Pele. Not to visit her residence at Halemaumau, the firepit crater of Kilauea (this is the smaller volcano nestled along the southeastern slope of Mauna Loa), would be unthinkable. If Pele is entertaining, you're in for one of the world's great natural spectacles; if not, just a look at a volcano and what it can do will be a big experience.

Although everybody goes to the volcano, a lot of tourists miss one of the most fascinating places of all: the Puna region east of the volcano, where you get a feeling of what a volcanic eruption means, not as a geologic curiosity, but in terms of the farms and stores and orchards and graveyards and cucumber patches that got in its way. We'll also show you how you can continue right on to Volcanoes National Park—feasible if you get started early, as you'll be covering quite a bit of territory. It's easier, though, to break this up into two separate day trips.

THE DRIVE TO PUNA: This outing begins on Volcano Hwy., Hwy. 11, which branches off from Kamehameha Avenue southward past the airport. About six miles out of town, you'll come to a possible stop, the **Mauna Loa Macadamia Nut Corporation,** the world's leading grower, processor, and marketer of macadamia nuts. Macadamias—Luther Burbank called them "the perfect nut," and they taste better than peanuts—are a big crop for the islands. On the drive from the highway to the Visitor Center (past roads with names like Butter Candy Trail or Macadamia Road), you'll see hundreds of thousands of macadamia trees planted in this area. From an observation gallery you can see the processing and packing operation, and observe colorful displays on history and horticulture. You can also take a mini Nature Walk through a macadamia-nut grove with papaya, monkeypod, and banana trees. Open daily from 9 a.m. to 5 p.m.

At **Keaau,** you may want to turn left off Volcano Hwy. and drive through town until you find Hwy. 13 and Keaau, an old, rather rundown plantation town that is now home to many artists and craftspeople. Across from the shopping center is our favorite Keeau stop, **Keeau Natural Foods and Bakery,** since it's here that you can stock up on guilt-free temptations, like chocolate-almond cheesecake and chocolate/macadamia-nut cookies, made only with organic flours and no sugar. There were plans for opening a bakery café soon. Prices on a variety of items are reasonable here, and they have Seva Foundation (the worldwide relief organization) T-shirts for $1. Next door, **Puna Buds** sells Hawaiian flowers and plants and ships them to the mainland at low prices. Also interesting are the prints of famous artist Dietrich Varez at $9 and $15.

Back on the road now, **Pahoa** is about ten miles farther along; here you'll enter the area that received the brunt of the 1955 eruption of Kilauea. This had been peaceful farm country for a hundred years, dotted with papaya orchards, sugarcane fields, coffee farms, pasture lands. Then a rift in the mountain opened and the lava fountains began to spout eratic cauldrons that here turned a farm into ashes, there left a gravestone or an old building untouched. You'll see cinder cones along the road and tiny craters still steaming. The most spectacular —and chilling—scenery comes later.

You might note that there are usually **local vendors** in downtown Pahoa selling anthuriums, puka products, papayas, and the like—all at very reasonable prices. Look for the one selling six papayas for $1. Don't be lazy: get out of your car and stock up! Nowhere else can you beat these prices. Other worthwhile stops are **Pahoa Natural Groceries** (if you need any) and the **Little Mermaid,** which features handmade clothes, fabrics, and beautiful jewelry at very inexpensive prices.

Follow the signs now to Kalapana, which brings you to one of the most incredible beaches in the world; the black-sand beach at **Kaimu.** The unexpected color effects are the results of explosions of black lava hitting the sea. Graceful palm trees make the picture idyllic, but don't try swimming here, for the currents are treacherous. Continue on a short way to the right to **Harry K. Brown Park,** which ought to be a model for builders of seaside parks. The whole place looks like something out of *Alice in Wonderland,* with tables and enormous mushrooms of chairs carved out of lava rock; the lichen moss beginning to grow on them gives them a light-gray patina. There's a reconstructed heiau platform, and more practical things like a saltwater swimming and wading pool, rest rooms, cooking facilities, and showers. See those funny-looking trees that look as if they're resting on stilts? Those are the pandanus trees, one of the special glories of the islands.

A bit down the road, you'll pass the **Star of the Sea Painted Church,** one of the two painted churches on the island. Since the ancient Hawaiians were accustomed to outdoor worship of their pagan gods, the murals on the walls of these little churches were designed to create an outdoorsy feeling. (You'll see the other, much older, painted church just off the road to Honaunau, when you explore the Kona coast on the other side of the island.)

You could continue about five miles beyond this point to the **Queen's Bath,** a natural pond where the royal queens supposedly bathed *au naturel,* and where commoners peeped on pain of death. And there you will see that the latest lava flow along Kilauea's eastern rift zone has crossed Hwy. 130, stopping just before the Queen's Bath and detouring slightly, and then flowing down to the sea. Forty-nine lava flows, one as recently as late 1986, comprise an eruption which has been going on since 1983. Check a new map for road conditions when you arrive.

Continue on a few more miles to the **Wahaula Visitor Center.** This tasteful Hawaiian museum on the site of an ancient heiau is the beginning of the coastal section of Hawaii Volcanoes National Park. The heiau has been stabilized and is worth visiting (tel. 965-8936). (Incidentally, just east of the Visitor Center is the Royal Gardens subdivision, which has been undergoing heavy damage since eruptions of Kilauea began in 1983.) Here you're going to have to make a choice. You can continue on this road, past the ancient Hawaiian village of Kamoamoa and on to Puu Loa, where hikers rave about the trail along a vast field of petroglyphs. Now you're on the Chain of Craters Road, which connects with the Crater Rim Drive. Crater Rim Drive circles the summit caldera of Kilauea Volcano, the park's primary attraction.

Let's assume, however, that you will take the Chain of Craters Road in the reverse direction from park headquarters, on another trip. For today, you might turn around and retrace your path to Rte. H-137, toward Kapoho and a fantastic 15-mile trip across one of the most exciting coastlines in Hawaii. From the red rollercoaster of a road, you'll see where the tropical jungle alternates with black rivers of lava that laid waste miles of earth before they reached their violent end in the steaming Pacific. The sea pounds relentlessly on the black lava rocks, eventually to grind them into more black sand; on the land the jungle creeps back slowly, reclaiming the land for itself and breaking it down into what will one day again be red earth. This is how the islands of Hawaii—and many of the earth's surfaces—were formed, and no textbook description will ever leave such a vivid picture in your mind.

There's another visitors' attraction in this area: **Kalani Honua** is a cultural and arts educational farm and health spa, offering classes, special events, and performances; theater groups perform here. For information, phone 961-3529.

En route, there are two good spots for picnicking, fishing, or hiking (no swimming): **McKenzie State Park** near Opihikao and **Isaac Hale Park** at Pohoiki. If you continue in the direction of Pahoa on Hwy. 32, you'll reach **Kapoho,** a Hawaiian Pompeii that was buried under spectacular lava flows in 1960. The day-by-day fight to keep the village from being overwhelmed by the lava flow and pumice cinders from the new cinder cone (which now overlooks the sad remains of Kapoho) was one of the most dramatic episodes in recent Hawaiian history. A cinder cone on the concrete floor is all that remains now of Nakamura's Store, and nearby, a desolate lighthouse stands inland from the new coastline created by the lava flow. A few miles farther on, just before Pahoa, you'll pass **Lava Tree State Park.** An old lava flow encircled the trees here, and they were eventually burned out, but the lava trunk molds remain, surrealistic witness to the whims of Pele.

You'll note that you've now described a triangle almost back to Pahoa; from here it's Rte. 130 back to Keaau, and then home to Hilo.

THE VOLCANO: It's more exciting than ever to visit the volcano, because for several years there has been a great deal of activity in Mauna Ulu, Pauahi Crater, and others. These new eruptions on the flanks of Kilauea were big enough to spurt enormous fountains of fire 1,800 feet up above the crater's rim. In 1984 both Kilauea and Mauna Loa were active at the same time, the first time this has happened since 1868. Lava flows came dangerously close to the city of Hilo. And just why has Pele been acting so uppity lately? Could it be that she's been angered by the prospecting for geothermal sources that has been going on in the Campbell Estate lands, where much of the recent activity occurred? Some conservationists and local people are saying so, and another Pele myth may be forming. Be that as it may, you're going to want to see what's happening. You can call the park rangers at 967-7311 before you start for news of the latest eruptions and viewing conditions. Call 967-7977 anytime for recorded information on eruptions. But whether or not anything is happening, the volcano trip is a must.

Your excursion to the volcano will start on Hwy. 11 out of Hilo, just as the Puna trip did, but this time you stay on that road all the way to **Hawaii Volcanoes National Park.** It's a drive of about 30 miles. Be sure to take a warm sweater; the air gets refreshingly cool 4,000 feet up at Kilauea Crater.

A possible stop for flower fanciers—and for lovers of local color—is **Volcano Store,** in tiny Volcano Village, reached just before you get to the park (on Hwy. 11, make a right at Haunani Road directly to the store). Half of the porch, as we've told you in the previous chapter, is devoted to the Volcano Country Kitchen; the other half is the place where local people go to scoop up reasonably priced sprays of orchids from late November through early May (a spray of about 18 orchids sells for $3.75 to $5.50). We've seen tiny anthuriums for about $1.75 a dozen, calla lilies for $2 a dozen, and long-lasting cymbidium (volcanic cinder blossoms) and others, all for tiny prices. The store will pack and ship anywhere.

Once you reach the park area, signs will direct you to the headquarters building, which should be your first stop. Entrance is $2 per person, or $5 per car. Check with the very helpful park rangers here for directions to the current eruption—if any. You may have to do some hiking over lava beds to see the show, but it's well worth it. (Bring heavy shoes.) And do note that sulfurous fumes are dangerous to those with respiratory problems and can be pretty repulsive even to those without; you may want a clothespin for your nose. It's possible, however, that you'll be able to drive right to an eruption, as we once did; simply get out of your car, and watch one of the most awesome shows on earth. The reason, by the way, that it is safe to watch a volcano like Kilauea erupt is that it produces lava that flows along the surface; Mount St. Helens volcano in Washington state and most others in the world, by contrast, produce steam and ashes that explode into the air.

The park rangers can also supply you with a driving map and information on hiking trails. You can learn a little bit about volcanology at the **Visitor Center,** and you should try not to miss the terrific color films of the latest eruptions; the show goes on every hour on the hour from 9 a.m. until 4 p.m. The most popular display case here always seems to be the one of letters of people who took rocks from the volcano—despite being warned never to do so—hit a spell of bad luck, and sent them back. Many of the letters ask forgiveness of Madame Pele. For example: "My friends are no longer in my life, I am divorced, I've lost my business, my property is being foreclosed. Pele is angry about something. . . . I took the rock. . . . Pele is a very busy woman and surely she would not miss a handful of stones from the firepit. Right? Wrong!" Amazingly enough, this display is changed every three months with more letters and more rocks making their way back to Hawaii.

Now that you know not to break any Hawaiian kapus by taking lava rocks back home, walk a few doors from park headquarters to the **Volcano Art Center.** Here, in the 1877 original Volcano House Hotel, a nonprofit group shows the work of over 200 artists and craftspeople, most of them from the Big Island. Bowls and sculptures of native Hawaiian woods and fine arts reflective of Hawaii are for sale, as well as posters, and many small items that would make distinctive gifts: Bill Irwin's koa cheese boards ($35) or chopsticks ($12), or Barbara Irwin's herbal hot pads, for example, which give off the scent of cinnamon and clove when a dish is placed on them ($10). Have a look at Be Wright's knockout "swimwear jewelry," beginning at $12 for bracelets. There are excellent fine and performing arts programs for long-term visitors, as well as concerts and special events. During the month of December, Christmas is celebrated with a blazing fire, hot apple cider, holiday music, and Santa Claus, too. Write P.O. Box 189, Volcano, HI 96785, or call 967-7511 for more information. Always a worthwhile stop.

The Volcano Art Center is also the place to pick up a "Tales of Old Hawaii" self-guiding tour tape to accompany you on your explorations of the volcano. Created and narrated by Dr. Russ Apple, a noted authority on Hawaiian history, it affords an insight into the natural history, legends, and lore of the area. Three tapes are already available: *Chain of Craters, Crater Rim Drive,* and *Hilo to Volcano;* eventually, Dr. Apple will cover all the major roads of the Big Island. Rental of the tape and a tape deck is $10. Tapes can also be picked up and/or returned at the Lyman House Museum and the Hilo Hawaiian Hotel back in Hilo.

Just across the road is **Volcano House,** which we've described in Chapter XIII. Situated as it is on the rim of the crater, it's also a great spot for sunset watching—best done from the cocktail lounge where the bartenders, volcanologists all, have whipped up something called "Pele's Delight," a combination of rum and lilikoi that manages to be pink at the bottom, fiery orange at the top. Eruption movies are shown in the lobby every night at 8:30 and 9 p.m. And it's so cozy just to sit here for a few minutes in front of the fireplace, where the fire, so it is said, has been burning continuously for over 100 years.

But enough of these man-made frills. It's nature you came here to see. There are some simple nature trails that begin right in back of Volcano House, and we urge you to take at least one. The upland air is fragrant, the vegetation glorious, the views spectacular. The silvery trees that look something like gnarled birches are ohia, and their red pompom blossoms are lehua, the flower of the Big Island, sacred to Pele. (It's rumored that if you pick one, it will rain before you arrive home.) That's the big bald dome of **Mauna Loa** towering 10,000 feet above you into the heavens; you're on **Kilauea,** which rises on its southeastern slopes. Pele hangs out in Halemaumau, the firepit of this enormous, 2½-mile-long crater.

To see the important views, you merely take the 11-mile circle road in either direction around the rim of Kilauea Crater. The rangers' map is easy to follow. We'll begin our trip around this wonderland of rain forests and volcanic desert at the **Sulfur Banks,** just west of park headquarters. The banks have that familiar rotten-egg odor. Farther along the road you'll see eerie wisps of steam coming out of some fissures, but don't be alarmed—they've been puffing along for centuries. You can stop to enjoy a hot blast from the steam jets, a natural underground "sauna."

Just beyond the Kilauea Military Rest Camp, there's a road that swings off to the right and across the highway that brought you here; if you follow this side path, you'll come upon an interesting clump of tree molds, formed in the same freakish way as the ones at Puna. The 100-acre **Bird Park** (Kipuka Pualu) is here too, a sweet spot for a picnic or a nature ramble through many rare trees; but you'll have to be sharp to spot the birds chirping away above your head.

Driving back to the rim of the crater road, turn right and continue the journey into the weird world ahead. You'll get your first view of Halemaumau, that awesome firepit 3,000 feet wide and 300 to 400 feet deep, from the lookout at the **Volcano Observatory,** and a better view a few miles beyond. For a more intimate glimpse of Halemaumau, the three-mile (one-way) hike through a hushed forest to the eerie heart of the volcano is recommended. The walk, a tough one, starts at Volcano House; be sure to get the descriptive pamphlet at headquarters to guide you. Or you can simply drive along the well-marked Crater Rim Road to **Halemaumau Overlook.** When Halemaumau decides to act up, everyone from here to the Philippines seems to descend on the area; whole families sit bundled in their cars all night long watching the awesome fireworks. Nobody can say when Pele will blow her top again. It is still local custom to appease her, but now that human sacrifice is out of fashion, she is reputed to accept bottles of gin!

The drive now takes you to the area hit by the 1959 eruption of Kilauea Iki (Little Kilauea; all the volcanoes have little sisters here). A boardwalk has been set up over the cinder ash here; and a walk along this **Devastation Trail** will take you past the twisted ghosts of white trees felled by the lava. At the end of the trail you can look down into the **Kilauea Iki Crater.** (This walk takes about 15 minutes, so to conserve energy you might send one member of your party back to the parking lot to bring the car around to the lookout area at the end of the walk.) A favorite four-mile hike around the crater's edge begins here.

The forest takes over at **Thurston Lava Tube** a few miles farther on, and a magnificent prehistoric fern forest it is. The lava tube shaded by this little grotto is another of those volcanic curiosities, even more spectacular than the one you saw in Hilo.

What else you see on the road will, of course, depend on what Madame Pele has been up to. Again, be sure to check with the rangers to see that you haven't missed anything.

Note: If you haven't made the trip to Puna outlined above, you might wish to take Chain of Craters Road all the way to the Wahaula Visitors Center on the coast, then take Rte. 130 to the black-sand beach at Kaimu, then directly on this road to Pahoa (or for a more scenic trip, take Rte. 137, the coastal road to Pahoa), then home to Hilo on 130.

HUNTING AND CAMPING IN THE VOLCANO AREA: If you're brave enough to tackle Mauna Loa (the largest mountain in the world, more than 32,000 feet from sea floor to summit—18,000 of them below sea level), make your requests for information and permits for overnight trips to the superintendent, Hawaii Volcanoes National Park, Hawaii. The area is under the jurisdiction of the federal government and is administered by the National Park Service, U.S. Department of the Interior. There is an overnight camping area at the **Namakani Paio Campground,** two miles from Volcano House. Ten cabins, nicely furnished, with beds and cooking utensils, each sleep four people, at about $16 per night (more details in Chapter XIII).

In addition, Hawaii Volcanoes National Park manages three drive-in campgrounds on a first-come, first-served basis at no charge: these are the above-mentioned Namakani Paio on Hwy. 11, 2½ miles west of park headquarters, with eating shelters, fireplaces, water, and rest rooms; Kipuka Nene, on Hilina Pali Road, 11½ miles south of park headquarters, with eating shelters, fireplaces, water, and pit toilets; and Kamoamoa, one mile west of the Wahaula Heiau Visitor Center, with eating shelters, fireplaces, pit toilets, and water at a nearby area. You cannot reserve sites in these campgrounds in advance. There is no camping fee and no permits are required. However, your stay is limited to no more than seven days in any one campground.

Backpackers who wish to camp in the Volcano area must register at the Kilauea Visitor Center or the Wahaula Visitor Center before beginning their trip (shelters and cabins are managed on a first-come, first-served basis at no charge). They may use the two Mauna Loa Trail Cabins (one at Red Hill at an elevation of 10,000 feet, ten miles from the end of the Mauna Loa Strip Road, and another on the southwest side of Mokuaweoweo, the summit caldera, at an elevation of 13,250 feet, each with bunks but no mattresses) or the Pepeiao Cabin, another patrol cabin on the Ka'u Desert Trail at Kipuka Pepeiao.

Oddly enough, Mauna Loa's sister, **Mauna Kea,** belongs to the state, and is administered by the State Department of Land and Natural Resources, which is responsible for the maintenance of the camping facilities on the mountain. This is great hunting country, and not a few of the sportsmen use bow and arrow. Mammal game consists of wild pigs and sheep; the birds are pheasant, chukar partridge, and quail. For all the details on seasons and licenses, write to Conservation Resources, 75 Aupuni St., Hilo, HI 96720.

Slightly higher up the mountain, in the saddle at 6,500 feet, **Pohakuloa** is the base camp for recreational activities in the Mauna Kea area. It has seven housekeeping cabins that sleep up to six each, rates from $10 for one person to $30 for six people. Again, these are completely furnished and equipped, from bedding and dishes to an electric range and refrigerator. Also available are two immense barracks, each containing four units, each with eight beds—just great for a huge family or a U.N. convention. Prices range from $8 for one to $2 per person for 64 persons. One huge mess hall with a restaurant-size kitchen is shared by both buildings. You can write to the Department of Land and Natural Resources, Division of State Parks, P.O. Box 936 (75 Aupuni St.), Hilo, HI 96721 (tel. 961-7200).

For additional information on camping around the Big Island, details on current conditions of parks, fees, etc., contact the County Department of Parks and Recreation, 25 Aupuni St., Hilo, HI 96720. Remember that summers and holidays get booked far in advance.

3. Across Hawaii
There are three possible routes across the Big Island from Hilo to the Kona coast.

THE CHOICES: (1) If you're continuing on from the volcano, simply follow the excellent Hwy. 11 another 90 miles. You pass through the Ka'u Lava Desert (where an explosion of Kilauea in 1790 routed an army of Kamehameha's chief enemy, Keoua) and can stop off at Punalu'u to see the black-sand beach. You hit the pretty little village of Naalehu before encountering mile on mile of lava flows, until you get to the other side of Mauna Loa and the welcoming Kona coast.

(2) If you're starting from Hilo, however, and have already been to the volcano, it's impractical to take this 126-mile route, when you can reach Kona directly in 96 miles, and sample in-between terrain so varied that Hawaii seems more like a small continent than a large island. We're referring to the drive along the majestic Hamakua Coast, through the rolling pasture lands of the Parker Ranch, and then around Mauna Kea and Hualalai Volcano to Kona.

(3) An alternative route for the first 50 miles of this trip crosses over the saddle between Mauna Loa and Mauna Kea, giving you wild, unforgettable views of both—but also a not-so-comfortable ride. Car-rental companies prohibit driving on this Saddle Road—Hwy. 20 out of Hilo—mostly because help is so far away. If your car breaks down, the tow charge is enormous, not to mention your being stranded in the wilderness! Not recommended.

(The drive in the opposite direction, from Kona to Hilo, is described briefly at the end of this section.)

THE HAMAKUA COAST DRIVE: The drive we prefer—and the one that we'll explore in depth—starts from Hilo on Hwy. 19, paralleling Kamehameha Ave. along the waterfront and heading for the northern shore of the island and the Hamakua coast. This is sugar-plantation country, miles of cane stretching inland to the valleys (the produce eventually goes to the bulk-sugar plant in Hilo and then to the mainland), the coastline a jagged edge curving around the sea, broken up by gorges and streams tumbling down from the snow-capped heights of Mauna Kea. The views from the modern and speedy Hwy. 19 are good, but if you really want to soak up the scenery, get off now and then on the old road that winds through the gullies and goes to the sea.

Ten miles out of Hilo, at Honomu, the HVB marker indicates the way to **Akaka Falls.** Four miles inland on a country road, you'll find not only the falls—perhaps the most beautiful in the islands, plunging dizzily 420 feet into a mountain pool—but also a breathtakingly beautiful bit of tropical forest turned into a park, lush and fragrant with wild ginger, ancient ferns, glorious tropical trees and flowers. It's a rhapsodic spot, very difficult to leave. Console yourself, then, with a brief stop at the **Honomu Plantation Store** in Honomu, a general store with a little bit of everything—groceries, liquor, Hawaiian woodcarvings, souvenirs—at good prices. Sandwiches at the snackbar are very reasonable, and the free samples of sugarcane and fresh macadamia nuts are quite tasty.

The little town of **Laupahoehoe**—you can drive down to it from the highway—is a "leaf of lava" jutting into the Pacific, its local park another idyllic spot for a picnic. But it's also a grim reminder of the savagery of nature that is always possible in Hawaii; a skeleton of a school building still stands where 20 children and their teachers were swept away into the sea by the 1946 tidal wave.

If you have time for a little hiking and nature study now, watch for the signs leading to **Kalopa:** this is a 100-acre Native Forest State Park containing trees, shrubs, and ferns indigenous to pre-Polynesian Hawaii, with trails through the ohia rain forest and many spectacular views—a nice spot for a picnic. Cabins are available for rental here, through the County Department of Parks and Recreation.

Thirty miles past Akaka Falls you reach **Honokaa,** second-largest city of the Big Island, the site of the **Hawaiian Holiday Macadamia Nut Factory,** where you can view the plant and visit the retail store, which features a mind-boggling array of 200 macadamia-nut products. A macadamia-nut festival is held here in late August. Follow the warrior signs to the "Macadamia Nut Capital of the World." Open daily 9 a.m. to 6 p.m. On your way down the hill to the factory, you might want to stop in at **Kamaiina Woods;** handcrafted wooden products are available, and prices begin at just $3. Closed Sunday. Back on the main street, stop by, if you have time, at **Rice's of Hawaii,** to browse and "talk story." Clocks, curios, carvings, old weapons, antique furniture, and genuine Hawaiian artifacts abound in this unusual store. Ask owner Jim Rice about local myths. Open in the afternoons.

Honokaa is best known as the takeoff point to pastoral **Waipio Valley.** This side trip from your cross-island route takes you eight miles from Honokaa, branching off to the right on Rte. H-240. The best way to explore this spectacular valley (where 7,000 full-blooded Hawaiians lived less than 100 years ago; today there are fewer than 10, plus a few hippie families) is by the **Waipio Valley Shuttle,** a 1½-hour Land Rover tour starting and ending at the Waipio Valley Lookout (a pleasant spot for a picnic with a view). The tour takes you down into the valley, through taro fields, a $200,000 Ti House, the Lalakea fish pond, a black-sand beach, and the dramatic Hiilawe Falls (the water drops 1,200 feet here when it's running). Believe it or not, there is also a hotel in the valley where, if you've made advance reservations with owner **Tom Araki,** you may be able to spend the night. It has all of five rooms and one bath, and has absolutely no truck with such modern amenities as hot water, telephones, restaurants, or even electricity. A friend of ours, a very successful businesswoman in Honolulu, swears she'd rather spend her vacations here, in remote Waipio Valley, than anywhere else. For reservations, write to Tom Araki, at 25 Malana Pl., Hilo, HI 96720. As for the Land Rover trip, the cost is $15 for adults, $5 for children 2 to 12. Trips leave daily on the hour from 8 a.m. to 4 p.m. Make reservations by calling 775-7121 in Kukuihaele. We continue to have excellent reports on Allan Shattuck and Brian Nelson, the talented people who run this service.

Whether or not you go down into Waipio Valley, you should pay a visit to **Waipio Woodworks,** snuggled in the sleepy town of Kukuihaele, which overlooks the valley (turn at the sign that reads "Kukuihaele 1 mile"). Here, at Waipio Woodworks, local craftspeople and artisans display some incredible island wood products, which begin at low figures and go up. Don't be shy: ask to see Joe, out back; he's the owner and resident craftsman, and a very friendly person. His three sons help him with the woodwork, and the family takes much pride and puts a lot of aloha into their work. Open every day, 9 a.m. to 5 p.m.

The Parker Ranch

On the next leg of your trip you'll begin to see why Hawaii is so often called a continent in miniature. West of Honokaa, winding inland on Hwy. 19, the sugar plantations of the tropics give way to mountain forests of cedar and eucalyptus as you climb up the slopes of Mauna Kea toward a vast prairie of rangelands and the plateau of Kamuela (also known as Waimea) and the 225,000-acre **Parker Ranch,** one of the largest cattle ranches in the United States under single ownership.

King Kamehameha started the whole thing, quite inadvertently, when he accepted a few longhorn cattle as a gift from the English explorer Capt. George Vancouver. They multiplied and ran wild until a young seaman from Newton, Massachusetts, John Parker, tamed them and started his ranch. The Parker family still owns it today, and many of the current generation of paniolos are descendants of the original Hawaiian cowboys. Parker Ranch is the biggest, but certainly not the only one; ranching is a way of life on the Big Island.

For years, visitors have wanted to tour the Parker Ranch, but it was so vast that this was impossible. A few years ago the ranch came up with a solution, and the **Parker Ranch Visitor Center** was opened. It's well worth an hour or so of your time to look around. The show starts with a 15-minute narrated audiovisual presentation in the Thelma Parker Theater that describes the history and present-day workings of the ranch. Then you move on to the John Palmer Parker Museum, examining artifacts and mementos from the Parker Ranch and from Hawaiian history, plus a collection of trophies and mementos of Duke Kahanamoku, Hawaii's great swimmer and Olympic athlete. You can visit the Parker Ranch Museum anytime between 9:30 a.m. and 3:30 p.m. Monday to Saturday. Admission is $2.25 for adults, $1.25 for active-duty military personnel and those between 12 and 18, 75¢ for those 7 to 11; 6 and under, free. Prices subject to change.

Shopping and Sightseeing in Waimea

The Parker Ranch Visitor Center sits in the **Parker Ranch Shopping Center,** a good place to start a shopping excursion in this bright little mountain town. At the **Paddock Shop,** adjacent to the Visitor Center, you can buy locally handcrafted gifts and mementos: Parker Ranch T-shirts and caps, belt buckles, lauhala hats, plus unusual items such as handmade pheasant- and peacock-feather hatbands, from about $30. . . . Of all the many treasures at **Setay,** a jewelry shop a few doors away, the ones we covet most are the "Swinger Rings," which revolve continuously on tiny roller bearings. Not inexpensive (they start at $415 and go up into the thousands), but foolproof conversation-starters. . . . Have a look at **Up Country Down Under,** where you can find shearling sheepskins from New Zealand. . . . **Ragamuffin's** has some adorable children's clothing. . . . **Alfred Shaheen** and **Reyn's,** well-known island shops, have outposts here, too. . . . **Big Island Natural Foods** may be just the ticket if you're in need of chakra T-shirts or organic chickens. . . . **The Wine Seller** offers wine, cheeses, nice sandwiches, and a few tables where you can relax with some croissants and coffee. . . . **Kamuela Delights** serves colossal ice cream cones in a variety of flavors and toppings.

Back on the main road through the center of town, we never miss a stop at the **Waimea General Store,** a tasteful bazaar with a highly sophisticated potpourri of merchandise: distinctive handcrafts—koa-wood bracelets, toys, stamp boxes, eggs, many by Le Tas de Bois—kitchen gadgets, toys and games, handmade baby quilts, men's clothing, distinctive ceramics (note their "Morris Platters"). Fans of the artist Guy Buffet, who does wonderful, whimsical paintings of Old Hawaii, can find the Guy Buffet Calendar and cards here.

If you're an art collector, or simply appreciate beautiful work, stop in at **Waimea Design Center,** next door to the General Store. There's an extraordinary collection of works by local artists here, in batik, fiber, paintings, and watercolor. When you come into your fortune, come back to furnish your home with exquisite originals of handmade koa furniture by Martin & MacArthur: dining tables, roll-top desks, hand-turned wooden bowls, and much more.

The **Kamuela Country Living Store,** 64-1040 Mamalahoa Hwy. (Hwy. 19), is another local favorite. Browse among their very large selection of books on Hawaiiana (as well as cookbooks and children's books), select some teas, jams, or coffees for gifting, and note their complete line of gourmet and regular kitchenware. They also carry sheepskin products from New Zealand, perfect for this cool ranching country.

Pure Orchid is a specialty food store on Hwy. 19, at the New Fukushima Store. If you're staying for a while, sign up for an Oriental cooking class; if not, pick up some local produce and browse through intriguing cookbooks like *Breadfruit, Bread and Papaya Pie, Recipes of Micronesia and the Outer Pacific.*

Waimea Sand Box, an old favorite here, is on the second floor of the Kamuela Plaza building, at the 56½-mile marker (that's a half mile from the Parker Ranch Center on the opposite side of the street). Unusual paperweights, featuring black and green sand with shells and rocks embedded in them, would make fine mementos of the Big Island. And so would Clark Maddock's watercolors and lithographs and Elizabeth Frutiger's delicate banana-bark artworks, which use no paint and range in size from postcard ($6) to 12 by 16 inches.

Your last stop in this area could well be the **Kamuela Museum** (tel. 885-4724), the largest private museum in Hawaii, founded and owned by Albert K. Solomon, Sr., and Harriet M. Solomon, great-great-granddaughter of John Palmer Parker, the founder of Parker Ranch. You'll see ancient and royal Hawaiian artifacts (many of which were formerly in Iolani Palace in Honolulu) alongside European and Oriental objets d'art, plus cultural objects brought to the islands by various ethnic groups in the 19th century. A charmer. The museum is at the junction of Rtes. 19 and 250; open daily, including holidays, from 8 a.m. to 5 p.m.; $2.50 admission for adults, $1 for children under 12.

And if all this browsing has knocked the wind out of your sails, a side trip to the **Espresso Veranda** in the Spencer House on Hwy. 19, may be just the thing. Refresh yourself in this open-air garden setting, sip your cappuccino and try some of the delightful pastry selections. Open seven days a week.

The Lively Arts

Waimea, by the way, is something of a cultural center for the Big Island. While you're here, you may be lucky enough to catch performances by such groups as the Peking Acrobats, the Honolulu Symphony, or the Morea Dance Theatre at the 500-seat **Kahilu Theatre and Town Hall,** just across from the Parker Ranch Visitor Center. It's a handsome facility (a gift by Parker Ranch to the community) for professional touring productions and contemporary films. For ticket information, phone 885-6017.

A SIDE TRIP FROM KAMUELA: From the cool green oasis of Kamuela, you can make another side excursion, 22 miles to the little town of **Hawi,** on the northernmost tip of the Big Island. The drive is along Rte. 25, winding uphill through the slopes of the Kohala Mountains, and the sights are unforgettable— the Pacific on your left, looking like a blue-velvet lake lost in misty horizons; the shimmering, unearthly peaks of Mauna Kea, Mauna Loa, and Hualalei, their slopes a jumble of wildflowers, twisted fences of tree branches, and giant cactus. Your destination, **Hawi,** is an end-of-the-world spot, recommended for those who like to be far away from the nagging complexities of civilization. There's Old Hawaii Lodging Co., an inexpensive hotel, and a more expensive inn called Aha Hui Hale (see Chapter XIII), but that's about as much truck as they'll have with any newfangled amenities.

Hawi's riches—and those of its neighboring **Kohala district**—are in its memories. The great Kamehameha was born in this area, and if you travel east a few miles to **Kapaau,** you'll see a statue of the local hero that looks amazingly like the one you saw in Honolulu. Actually, this one is the original; it was made in Florence, lost at sea, and then found after another just like it had been fashioned for the capital. On your way back, take Rte. 270 out of Hawi and stop in at **Lapakahi State Historical Park,** a restored native Hawaiian village by the sea. The trip to this North Kohala area is thrilling, but remember that you've got to come down the road again (Hwy. 270), which links up to Hwy. 19 and the Kona coast), adding a total of 44 miles to your cross-island trip.

You have two routes to choose from now, as you head across the island from Waimea. Route 90 takes you along the mountain road entering **Waikoloa Village,** a residential community with stables, guided trail rides, tennis, and golf (Waikoloa Stables information, tel. 883-9335; golf, 883-9621). Six miles from the village and you're on Hwy. 19 and at the entrance to the **Sheraton Royal Waikoloa Hotel,** a luxury resort nestled against ancient fish ponds. **Anae'hoomalu Bay,** a splendid crescent-shaped white-sand beach is great for swimming and snorkeling; public facilities and picnic tables are provided at no charge. If you have time, take a guided tour along the restored petroglyph trails, a quick jaunt along the King's Pathway, or a tour of the varied eating and drinking spots here. Just five miles north of the Sheraton, on Rte. 19, you'll approach the entrance of the **Mauna Lani Bay Hotel;** to our way of thinking, it is one of the most purely beautiful resorts anywhere, especially in its landscaping and gardens and the massive indoor waterfall in the Grand Atrium. Golfers rave about the Francis Ii Brown golf course here, an 18-hole championship course carved out of barren lava. Sunday offers a plentiful buffet lunch (phone 885-6622 for current prices and reservations). You can then continue along the coastal road, Queen Kaahuumanu Hwy. (Rte. 19), until you reach Kailua-Kona. Or you can leave Waimea on Rte. 19, and drive about 12 miles to the deep-water port of **Kawaihae,** where you descend through prairie land, cows grazing, and ocean vistas all about you, until you're suddenly in sultry tropics. On the road above the harbor is **Puukohola,** a well-preserved heiau and historical park that figures importantly in the history of the islands. It was here that Kaahumanu, the sweetheart-queen of the great Kamehameha, after his death began the breakdown of the dread kapu (taboo) system by the startling act of eating in public with men (previously, such an act would have been punished by death). But the place is better remembered for a bloody deed that should forever disencumber you of notions that Stone Age warfare was all good clean fighting. Remember Keoua, Kamehameha's biggest rival, the one who lost an army at K'au? Kamehameha had decided to dedicate this heiau to the war god Kukailimoku, and invited Keoua to a supposed peace parley in the new temple. Instead, he had him speared as he approached the land and sacrificed to the god. Then he was free to unify Hawaii and the other islands.

After digesting this gory bit of history, you deserve a change of pace. A mile and a half back, on a right fork just past Samuel Spencer Park, is the much-touted **Westin Mauna Kea,** one of the in places for the beautiful people. The architecture and landscaping are elegantly imaginative, the rooms nestling along the brow of a hill overlooking the crystal waters of Mauna Kea Beach below. You can wander a little about the public areas of this seaside caravanserai, perhaps bumping into a celebrity or two en route to the golf course. Note the magnificent plantings, the authentic Hawaiian quilts, and the splendid art collection, which ranges from Oriental bronzes and a gigantic 7th-century Indian buddha to primitive masks and woodcarvings from New Guinea. After many years the beach has been opened to the public (but only ten parking spaces provided!), and you can also join the leisure class at lunch: a lovely, splurge buffet runs under $20. (Considering that there are hot dishes like stuffed Cornish hen and beef Wellington among the dazzling array of fresh fruits, salads, cheeses, hors d'oeuvres, home-baked breads, and scrumptious desserts, it's worth the money.) The Sunday buffet brunch is reported to be even more spectacular! Not far away are two public beaches where you might want to stop for a picnic: **Samuel Spencer Park** (popular with campers and sometimes a bit un-kempt) and, about three miles farther south, the more spacious **Hapuna Beach** (watch, however, for signs indicating possible dangerous tides and rip currents). Continue on Rte. 19 through the lava desert, with the possibility, on clear days, of glorious views of all the volcanoes of Hawaii and perhaps of Haleakala on Maui too. Lava flows from Mauna Loa and Hualahai mark the eerie landscape, punctuating the miles until you emerge at last into the verdant world of the Kona coast.

(*Note:* We're sorry to have to issue this caveat, but we've been told that rowdies sometimes hide in the bushes near these beaches, wait for tourists to dutifully put their valuables in the trunks of their cars, and then proceed to pick the locks while the tourists are out on the beach. If you're going to put anything in your trunk, do so a few miles before you reach your destination.)

FROM KONA TO HILO: If you've arrived at Kona first, you drive across the island to Hilo on Hwy. 11, through the K'au Desert and miles and miles of lava flows, desolate enough to be reminiscent of Dore's engravings. But before the landscape turns bleak, there's plenty of magnificent scenery. Should you make the drive in November or December, you'll see unbelievably beautiful poinset-tias, riot upon riot of red color. For a swim, you might try **Hookena Beach Park,** 22 miles from Kailua. It's a long drive down the road to an almost-deserted, lovely sandy beach. **Manuka State Park,** farther on, with its arboretum of ex-traordinary plants and trees, is a good spot to stretch your legs and perhaps have a picnic lunch. The approach to the little village of **Waiohinu** is marvelously sce-nic, and the village itself, once a small farming center, is one of the quaintest on the Big Island. Have a look at the monkeypod tree planted by Mark Twain, and a few miles farther on you can make a side trip (about a mile and a half off the highway) to the black-sand beach at **Punaluu.** Another favorite jaunt is the 12-mile drive off the highway outside Naalehu down to **Ka Lae** (South Point). Local people fish here on this wild shore of cliffs and surf, the southernmost point in the United States. Now you approach the desolate K'au region where Pele obligingly destroyed an army of Keoua, Kamehameha's archenemy, in 1790; the footprints of the victims can be seen under glass. The landscape is moon-like, and we don't mean that only poetically; space scientists are studying the lava fields of the Big Island in the belief that actual conditions on the moon may be similar. The lava flows lead you to Kilauea, Hawaii Volcanoes National Park, and on to Hilo.

4. The Kona Coast

A man we know in Kona, a refugee from the Bronx, swears he will never go back home. "I've found my bit of paradise right here, and I'm staying!" A lot of other people have waxed ecstatic about Kona, the vacation resort of Hawai-ian royalty ever since the word got out that the sun shines here about 344 days a year. (Kona winds, that nasty stuff they get in Honolulu, should be properly called southerly winds, say the Konaites.) It's such a deliciously lazy spot that you may be very contented doing nothing at all in Kona. Of course, looking at the surf as it smashes along the black lava coast, noting the brilliant varieties of bougainvillea, the plumeria, the jasmine tumbling about everywhere, and laz-ing on the beach can keep you pretty busy. But we suggest that you take a day off from these labors and have a look at the sights. (You'll need wheels, but if you haven't rented a car, a scooter might do. **Rent-Scootah** at the Kona Lighthouse, 75516 Palanika, tel. 329-3250, for one, can fix you up with a Honda moped at rates starting at $10 for two hours.) Kona is an important historic center; within the space of a few miles, Captain Cook met his end, the New England missionaries got their start, and Kamehameha enjoyed his golden age.

The tiny village of **Kailua-Kona** is the resort center, modern enough to be comfortable, but still unspoiled. Ami Gay, the very helpful lady at the Hawaii Visitors Bureau office, in the Kona Plaza Shopping Arcade, can help you with all sorts of practical information. There's a U.S. Post Office in the General Store at the Kona Shopping Village, across the street.

TOURING THE TOWN: There's only one street, Alii Drive, running down the length of Kailua, so you won't get lost. Start up at the King Kamehameha Hotel, in the northern end of town, at the site of the monarch's heiau, which has been restored. There are tasteful museum-caliber displays highlighting Hawaiian history throughout the lobby and various free activities: ethnobotanical, historical, and "hula experience" tours are held several times a week. Enquire at the hotel for a schedule. Just about 150 years ago, Kamehameha ruled the Hawaiian Islands from a grass-roofed palace on this very site (Lahaina became the next capital; Honolulu did not become the capital until 1820). The old king died here in 1819, only a year before the first missionaries arrived from Boston, bringing with them the purposeful Protestant ethic that would effectively end the Polynesian era in Hawaii.

They were responsible for the **Mokuaikaua Church,** standing on the mauka side of Alii Drive, a handsome coral and lava structure that is the oldest church in Hawaii, built in 1838. Note the sanctuary inside; its architecture is New England, but it is made of two Hawaiian woods, koa and ohia. Across from it, on the ocean side of the street, is **Hulihee Palace,** until 1916 a vacation home for Hawaiian royalty. Now it's a museum, full of Hawaiian furniture and effects, as well as more primitive curiosities like Kamehameha's exercise stone (it weighs about 180 pounds, so maybe that story about the Naha Stone isn't so crazy after all). Check out the charming little gift shop; it has an especially nice selection of native woods (handsome koa wood dinner plates are $35), plus books and jewelry. Profits go to the Daughters of Hawaii. The museum is open from 9 a.m. to 4 p.m. daily; closed federal holidays. Admission is $4 for adults, $1 for students 12 to 18, 50¢ for children under 12.

On the oceanfront at Kona Inn, **Uncle Billy's Grass Village** was just getting under way at the time of our last visit. You know Uncle Billy—his family runs the Kona Bay Hotel, Cousin Kimo's Seafood and Steak Restaurant, Fisherman's Landing, and Hurricane Annie's. Local students plus some from Samoa are building four grass shacks, or *hales*, to be the scene of demonstrations of the old Hawaiian crafts, which will also be sold here. An estimable project.

KONA "UP MAUKA": The shore road extends for about six more miles, but we're going to leave it temporarily, taking a left at Hualalai Street and heading out of town on Hwy. 11 (the mauka road). Kona "up mauka" is far removed from the tourist scene at Kailua. It is, for one thing, the place where Kona coffee, that dark, rich brew you've seen all over the islands, is grown. Hawaii is the only state in the union that has a commercial coffee crop. There are no big plantations, only small farms where everybody in the family pitches in to bring in the crop. Watch the road for the shiny green leaves of the coffee bushes with little clusters of red berries at harvest time. There are small cattle ranches here too, although they're not visible from the road. You'll see the local folk at places like the H. Manago Hotel in Captain Cook.

The drive is a beautiful one, winding through the cool mountain slopes, with fruit trees and showers of blossoms all around. If you're in the mood for a little offbeat shopping here, there are several possibilities. In Holualoa, **Pineapple Patch** offers quilting kits with free one-day instruction on Hawaiian quilting. . . . The locals swear by **Kimura's Fabrics** in Kainaliu Village; some say Mrs. Kimura has the best collection of fabrics in the islands. Hawaiian and Japanese prints are specialties, and prices are reasonable. . . . Look for the **Aloha Theater and Café** in Kainaliu now, and perhaps stop in for a tempting pastry or snack (see the preceding chapter). . . . Next door is the **Aloha Village Store,** where you'll find cards, baskets, toys, gourmet items, plus healthy snacks and vitamins. . . . Across from it is **Blue Ginger Gallery,** which offers glass art, ceramics, jewelry, and handpainted silks. . . . **Paradise Found Boutique** is the place for unique clothing, like beautiful cut lacework garments from Indonesia, as well as sought-after antique aloha shirts. Gift items by local artisans as well as Oriental imports too. They have another shop down in Kailua town. . . . **Sterling Thimble** has Hawaiian quilts, straw hats, and custom dresses.

Next stop for shoppers should be the **Grass Shack** in Kealekekua, a real grass shack with bananas growing out front—a longtime favorite in these parts. The inside is laden with tasteful and authentic Hawaiian and South Pacific handcrafts, including one of the largest collections in the islands of locally made wood items. They also have original watercolors of local fish and birds at $7.95, original "Grass Shack" tiles at $45, adorable "tutu" magnets made of macadamia nuts and dried flowers at $2.95—even a collection of antique postcards of Hawaii from the 1930s and '40s at 75¢ each. Burmese jade is sold at the most competitive prices around. The nice people here will give you a native flower and some coffee beans for planting as you leave; within three to four weeks (the time it takes for the seed to germinate) you're on your way to having your own potted coffee plant.

After about 12 miles from the beginning, the road winds gently down the slopes of the mountain (watch for the HVB marker), past the **Captain Cook Coffee Mill,** the only remaining mill still in operation, through the lush tropical village of Napoopoo on to **Kealakekua Bay.** Visitors are welcome at the mill.

Art lovers should definitely plan a stop in Captain Cook to visit the **Mauna Loa Gallery.** Owner Sarah Ishihara represents the work of the renowned artist Jean Charlot, as well as that of some 65 other artists and craftspeople, mostly from the Big Island, working in a variety of media. There's a gift section, too, specializing in unique and unusual items at reasonable prices, all created by island artists. You might pick up a koa mirror (from $14), some creatively designed jewelry (from $10), or a variety of exquisite handmade cards and papers. Everything is in impeccable taste. Open Monday to Friday from 9 a.m. to 5 p.m., or by appointment (tel. 323-3662).

Note: If you have a spare weekend and are looking for something creative to do, you can do it here: take a workshop in basketry, collage, Japanese woodblock prints, papermaking, fiber arts, gyotaku (fishprinting), etc. Call 323-3662 for details.

A monument to Captain Cook is visible across the bay, erected at a spot near where he was killed in 1779. It was here that Cook and his men pulled into the Kona coast a year after their first landing on Kauai, were again treated as gods—and wore out their welcome. When their ship was damaged in a storm and they returned to Kealakekua a second time, the men got into a fight with the natives and Cook was killed trying to break it up. You can't see the monument up close unless you approach it from the water. There's a **"Captain Cook Cruise"** that leaves Kailua wharf daily; it gives you a good look at the monument and lets you swim and snorkel in the bay. It's a good way to combine a suntan and a history lesson for $17.30 for adults, $8.65 for children 2 to 12, plus tax (tel. 329-6411).

There are two plaques you can see on the Napoopoo shore: one commemorates the first Christian funeral in the islands; the other is in honor of the remarkable Opukahaia, a young Hawaiian boy who swam out to a ship in 1808, got himself a job as cabin boy, converted to Christianity, and convinced the missionaries that they were needed here in the pagan, ignorant Sandwich Islands. Right near the shrines are a very few jewelry stands that offer good buys in clothing and necklaces of local seeds and kukui-nut leis.

THE KONA SHORE: Continuing along the shore road now to Honaunau, you'll pass **Keei Battlefield,** a lava-scarred stretch where Kamehameha started winning wars. In the tiny fishing village of **Kei,** there's a beach with good swimming.

But the best is yet to come: Honaunau and **Pu'uhonua o Honaunau National Historical Park.** This ancient, partially restored Pu'uhonua still has about it the air of sanctuary for which it was built over 400 years ago. In the days when many chieftains ruled in the islands, each territory had a spot designated as a place of refuge to which kapu breakers, war refugees, and defeated warriors could escape; here they could be cleansed of their offenses and return, purified, to their tribes. (There is another such place on the island of Kauai, near Lydgate Park, but this one is far better preserved.) The heiau, **Hale-o-Keawe,** the temple of the purifying priests, has been reconstructed (it was in such temples that the bones of the high chiefs of Kona—which had mana, or spiritual power—were kept), and so have the tall ki'i built for the god Lono. After you've driven into the park and left your car in the parking lot (an improvement over the old days when the only way to get here was to run, or, if one came from the north, to swim, since the feet of commoners were not fit to tread on the Royal Grounds on the north side of the place of refuge), we suggest you take in one of the orientation talks given daily at 10, 10:30, and 11 a.m., and at 2:30, 3, and 3:30 p.m., in the spacious amphitheater staffed by the National Park Service, which administers this facility. Besides explaining the concept of refuge, the park ranger also talks about the plants and trees of the area. Then you're free to have a swim (but sunbathing is not allowed), a picnic, go snorkeling or fishing—or just absorb the peace on your own. Or you can tour the area by yourself with a self-guiding leaflet. "Cultural demonstrators" are usually on hand, carving woods, pounding poi, and performing other such ancient Hawaiian tasks. Canoes, fishnets, and traps are on display, and often are being used outside the huts. Entrance fee is $1.

There's one more curious sight in Honaunau, which you reach by turning north on a side road as you go back up the highway. This is **St. Benedict's Church,** which everybody calls the "Painted Church." The Catholic missionaries, more adaptable than their Protestant predecessors, created biblical murals that gave a feeling of spaciousness to the tiny church, presumably so that the congregation would have more of a feeling of the out-of-doors—to which pagan nature worship had accustomed them.

Between Pu'uhonua o Honaunau and the Painted Church, you might want to stop in at **Barry's Nut Farm,** which not only sells macadamia nuts reasonably ($5 buys three pounds in the shell), but also offers self-guided tours of a lovely five-acre botanical garden, with some 1,000 varieties of plants and flowers. The gift shop features items made by local artists (note the koa wood cribbage boards at $24.95), and they have a very pleasant restaurant offering moderately priced soups, salads, sandwiches, and nut treats—plus delicious, prize-winning homemade desserts on the order of freshly baked macadamia-nut chocolate cake. And they have the best macadamia-nut brittle anywhere! They're on Hwy. 160, open daily (tel. 325-9930).

Nearby, at the junction of Middle Keei Road with Hwy. 11 in Honaunau, is the **Kona Coast Macadamia Nut Company,** where you can get good prices on air-dried macadamias made up into luscious chocolates; irregular chocolate-covered nuts may run as low as six for 70¢, and you can often buy a pound of nuts—edible rejects—for $1. The sign reads "Buy at your own risk"; we did, and they were slightly burnt-tasting, but not bad. Open daily (tel. 328-8141).

Back on Hwy. 11 and headed toward Kailua now, you continue for about 11 miles until you come to a turnoff to the left that brings you back to the shore at Keauhou Bay. Before you descend, though, you might want to stop off to have a look at the handsome **Keauhou Shopping Village,** where you could have a drink or a meal at the ever-so-pleasant Mitchell's or Don Drysdale's Two (see Chapter XIII). There are some attractive small shops here, like the **Keauhou Village Book Shop,** where, in addition to a vast array of books, we found wonderful old postcards reading, "Aloha from Waikiki, 1935"; **Futon Connection of Kona,** with many varieties of floor seating, exquisite cards; **Possible Dreams,** with prints, gift items, silk flowers; **Small World,** with a large selection of both clothing and toys for children. At **The Showcase Gallery** you're likely to see an exhibit by such leading island painters and craftspeople as Herb Kane, Jane Chow, John Thomas, among others. Among the small treasures here, we found feather pendants beginning at $10, prints and serigraphs from $15 to $150.

Drive down to the shore now to explore the grounds and public areas of the fabulous **Kona Surf Hotel.** The Oriental and Polynesian art objects scattered about, the glorious use of natural materials, the 14½ acres and 30,000 plants on the property make it a sightseeing stop in its own right. Complimentary garden tours are given Monday, Wednesday, and Friday at 9 a.m., but you're welcome to come on your own and have a look. Opposite the Keauhou Beach Hotel in this area is **Kona Gardens.** If you're in Kona on a Wednesday, Thursday, or Saturday morning, this is a "must" stop. Between 8 a.m. and 3 p.m., there's a colorful flea market; 75 to 125 vendors sell everything from apples to antiques, from crafts to clothing, and a great time is had by all. Local friends praise it highly. There is no admission fee for buyers.

Continuing back to Kailua now, the old vies with the new for attention everywhere. To your left is a modern small-boat harbor; to your right, faintly visible on the mountain slopes are the remains of a rocky royal slide down which the alii of Hawaii once scooted into the water below. Coming into sight soon is Kahaluu Beach Park, and your sightseeing labors are over.

THE LAZY LIFE: Now you can concentrate on the important business of Kona, sun-worshiping. **Kahaluu Beach Park** is a fine place for swimming, snorkeling, and picnicking. There's a pretty lagoon, the swimming is safe, and the sand, once a fine white, is now salt-and-pepper, thanks to an ancient lava flow that came pounding across it. But we are partial to **White Sands Beach** (sometimes called "Disappearing Beach," since the high surf occasionally removes and then returns the sand), a gorgeous, if tiny, spot. Palm trees arch across the sand, the surf is a Mediterranean blue, and the brilliant reds, yellows, and purples of tropical blossoms are everywhere. Be careful, though, when the surf is rough. Back in Kailua, you can swim in front of the luxurious King Kamehameha Hotel; the beach here is a public one, something that old King Kam would probably have approved of. The water is very gentle, safe for kids.

THE SPORTING SCENE: There is, of course, no dearth of sporting activities in Kona. Deep-sea fishermen consider Kona their favorite place in the world. Deep-sea fishermen must also be rather affluent, since they think nothing of calling **Roy Gay** (tel. 329-6041) and having him arrange a fishing boat charter at about $350 a half day, $450 a full day. Split two or three ways, it's considered a bargain! Meanwhile, us ordinary folk can view the catch. The morning weigh-in of the giants is from noon to 1 p.m., the afternoon one from 4 to 5 p.m., at the pier in front of the King Kamehameha Hotel.

A number of our readers have written over the years to recommend an idyllic snorkeling adventure aboard the *Kamanu,* a 36-foot catamaran run by **Kamanu Charters** (formerly Pacific Sail and Snorkel; tel. 329-2021 for reservations, or write to P.O. Box 2021, Kailua-Kona, HI 96745). The great thing about this trip is that it's just as simple for nonswimmers as it is for Red Cross lifeguards, since those who wish to may enter the water in an inner tube. Jay Lambert, who runs the tours, claims that snorkeling is even easier than swimming, requiring little exertion or water knowledge. And everybody likes to hand-feed the many varieties of small tropical reef fish abounding in the crystalline waters where the boat drops anchor. Those who only want to sail without getting wet are welcome too. One of our readers, Marty Iabis of Prospect, Illinois, wrote us: "The cruise was organized by two very congenial fellows who make each trip cozy and informal, unlike the mass atmosphere most tourists have to put up with —this was on a first-name basis and only 10 to 15 persons aboard. My husband and I found it to be one of our most memorable experiences on the island!" You receive free transportation by van to the boat, then sail to an isolated reef; equipment, professional instruction, and even a glass of guava juice or beer and wine and some freshly cut pineapple are provided, all at $28 for adults, $16 for children 12 and under (free for toddlers under 2). Jay also runs exclusive sunset/ cocktail sails.

Golf? That's easy too. The place to play is at the beautiful **Keauhou Kona Course,** six miles south of Kona; make arrangements at your hotel. If it's tennis you're after, try the free public court at the **Kailua Playground** near the Kona Sunset Hotel, or the four courts at the Old Airport Tennis Court. Courts are also available at nominal cost at the Hotel King Kamehameha, the Keauhou Beach Hotel, the Kona Hilton Beach and Tennis Resort, and the Kona Surf Hotel.

Those who would like to hike through the Big Island's beautiful trails are advised not to hike on their own, but to consult local hiking clubs and try to join one of their excursions. If no group hikes are scheduled, they can advise you on where you can hike safely. Two Big Island clubs to contact are **Kona Hiking Club** (tel. 325-6638) and **Hiking Club of Hilo,** Moku Loa Group (tel. 966-7579).

If you can afford a fee of about $60 for an all-day trip, you can have a great adventure with **Paradise Safaris,** a group that takes very small groups (five people) on custom-designed, all-day explorations to such destinations as the top of Mauna Kea, down into Waipio Valley, and to the Green Sand Beach at South Point. Special trips can be arranged for astronomy, natural history, birdwatching, archeology, photography, and hiking enthusiasts. Delicious Hawaiian-style meals are grilled over a fire and served picnic style. For information, phone Paradise Safaris at 329-9282, or write in advance to P.O. Box A-D, Kailua-Kona, HI 96745. Arrangements for this trip can also be made with Kona Charter Shippers Association (tel. 329-3600).

This is great country for those who like to ride. Ten minutes away from Kailua-Kona are the slopes of Hualalei, where you can ride at elevations of from 1,500 to 3,000 feet, through beautiful pasture lands, courtesy of **Waiono Meadows.** Rates are $15 per person per hour, $28 per person for a two-hour ride. They'll provide free transportation to the slopes as well as arrange special breakfast, picnic, fishing, and sunset-dinner rides. Call them at 329-0888 for information.

Note: for complete listings of Big Island sports facilities, stop in at the office of the Hawaii Visitors Bureau.

CRUISES—DAY AND NIGHT: A variety of cruises run by **Capt. Bean** are a venerable institution on the Kona Coast. They offer that something for everyone, and prices are reasonable. For reservations, tel. 329-2955.

The two-hour glass-bottom boat ride is a bargain at $7 for adults, $3.50 for children under 12. Enjoy the underwater marine life and hula dancing as well. Boats depart at 9 and 11 a.m.

For the more adventurous, Capt. Bean offers a one-hour snorkeling safari aboard the 75-foot *Keana;* it's $10 for adults, $5 for children under 12. Boats depart every day at 1:30 p.m., and equipment is included in that price.

Want to go native? Well, the captain has a half-day Kealekekua Bay cruise in an authentic Polynesian war canoe, and it's the largest glass-bottom boat in Hawaii. Learn the history of the Kona coast, swim or snorkel in the clear blue waters, enjoy a light lunch with the crew, and sing along to the old songs and dances of Hawaii, all for $18 for adults, $9 for those under 12. The boat departs at 8:30 a.m.

Let's not forget romance. Capt. Bean's three-hour sunset or moonlight cruise is a truly fun-tastic experience with an open bar, all you can eat, and a troupe of authentic Polynesian dancers. For several hours, these 25 young people will regale you with an unparalleled display of energy and enthusiasm as they dance the dances of the Pacific islands. Before you know it, you're dancing, too! Adults only, $32. Departure times at 5:15 and 8:15 p.m.

All boats depart from the Kailua Pier near the King Kamehameha Hotel.

SHOPPING IN KONA: The Kona shopping scene has blossomed like everything else in this bubbling resort town. At last count, there must have been something like 100 stores and shops, some in quaint arcades, some in small centers and hotels, others just there, all on or just off Alii Drive.

A good place to begin might be the shopping arcade in the **Hotel King Kamehameha. Island Togs** has some tasteful women's clothes, and prices are quite reasonable. We've always had good luck here. . . . Say hello to the real live mynah bird who lives in a cage at the **Mynah Bird.** He says "aloha" and a few other things while you're busy viewing a collection of lovely fabrics. The shop will do custom work and alterations. . . . **Gifts for All Seasons** is crammed with tasteful items: Hawaiian-style Christmas ornaments; hand-woven bamboo baskets from the Philippines; wonderful missionary, Hawaiian, and visitor dolls in soft sculpture; beautiful fans; banana-bark paintings starting at $6. Their crocheted pillowcovers—lined, washable, and with zippers, handmade in the Philippines—are a very popular item at $7.95. And the manager, Ruth Mace, promises she will also do personal shopping via mail: phone her at 329-2911, ext. 10, or write to her at 75-5660 Palani Rd., # D1, Kailua-Kona, HI 96740.

Proceed to the **Seaside Mall** across from the King Kam, to the **Butterfly Boutique,** where they'll show you shorts, skirts, and sarongs in subdued Hawaiian prints. Plenty of bikinis, one-piece bathing suits, and a large selection of dresses. There's always a sale rack. . . . A sign on the door of **Island Silversmith** reads "We only look expensive," and they're right. A good-looking sterling-silver tiki on a chain was just $18. . . . Handpainted tops by Hans Jutte, very practical and comfortable, were $22.50 at **Bubi Sportswear;** great short caftans, one size, were $33. . . . The **Muumuu Factory to You** has lots of good dresses at low prices.

In the **Akona Kai Mall,** art lovers should check out the **Akona Kai Gallery,** which shows beautiful work by Hawaiian artists. You may not want to spend $300 to $400 for brass sculptures by such Hawaiian names as Benjamin Rasquinio and Craig Fuller, but small wall sculptures start under $100 and there are charming coffee mugs for $12. Small sand paintings begin at $3.

Whatever else you do, don't miss the **Kona Arts & Crafts Gallery,** across from the sea wall in this area of Alii Drive. It's one of the few places that deal solely in *genuine* Hawaiian crafts: their woodcarvings, for example, are made only of native woods such as milo, ohio, or koa; monkeypod is not used, because it is not indigenous to Hawaii. Prices can go way up for the works of fine art here, but there are many small treasures too: colored sand magnets from $1.50, banana-bark paintings, notecards of native materials, bookmarks made from the flowers of Hawaii, limu art (limu is an edible seaweed) from $7.95 to $45. Do note their chime collection: they bear the imprints of native ferns grown on volcanic soil, pressed into the lava, and then fired, and have a worldwide reputation; from $12.95. The shop also carries genuine hula instruments (made of gourds with seeds), and much more. Owners Fred and Sally Nannestad are knowledgeable about their collection and take time to explain the intricacies of these native arts. Very worthwhile.

If you haven't brought the right walking shoes with you (doesn't it always happen?), stop in and see Dan and Pat Werking at the **Sandal Basket** on Alii Drive. They have a very large selection for both men and women, the prices are excellent, and the service first-rate. No wonder this shop has been here for over 24 years!

Cross the street now to the ocean side where you'll find another big shopping arcade: **Kona Inn Shopping Village,** with more than 50 shops and a bevy of restaurants (both **Fisherman's Landing** and **Kona Inn,** directly on the waterfront, are top-notch). An old favorite here is **The Shellery** (which also has another store across the street in World Square and one at the King Kamehameha). The selection of freshwater and cultured pearls here is truly outstanding, as are their offerings of ivory, coral, lapis, jade of the finest quality, and precious stones. They have inexpensive gift items too, like gold-plated shell pendants for as little as $1.50 each, and many fine specimen shells. Kids will love the 360-gallon aquarium with its amazing fish. . . . If black, pink, or gold coral jewelry is what you're after, visit the **Original Maui Divers,** an island tradition. . . . Distinctive Hawaiian tiles, all hand-painted on koa wood (from $25), can be found at **The Treasury.** . . . **Eastern Treasures of Kona** offers shirts with Japanese prints, plus handpainted woodcarvings of fish and butterflies, about $20. . . . Boys' and girls' Hawaiian clothing is priced reasonably at **Kona Inn Children's Wear,** whose selections go from infants through young teens. . . . A few doors down, the same people run **Fare Tahiti Fabrics,** a fabric shop with Hawaiian and Tahitian prints in cotton, polyesters, and the new rayon "silkies." Prices are reasonable, from $4 per yard. Note too the beautiful silkscreen-printed Alfred Shaheen panels at competitive prices. Hawaiian patterns are also available. . . . The **Kona Gold Mine** specializes in those 14-karat solid-gold pineapple charms that everyone seems to like so much. Prices begin at $10 and go way up, but they often run 50% discount sales. . . . If calories are irrelevant, pick up some coconut shortbread or macadamia-nut cookies at **Mrs. Barry's Kona Cookies.** One of our readers, Charles Rabin of New York, writes that "These cookies were one of the many reasons I regretted departing Kona!". . . . We found stylish modern and vintage fashions for women at **Flamingo's,** and classy items for men at **Flamingo's for Men.** . . . The **Wild Orchid** specializes in women's swimsuits and clothing; and at **Noa Noa,** you can come away with a different look. Indonesian clothing, hand-painted cotton batiks, jewelry, and sandals, plus Indonesian artifacts.

Have an ice cream or snack on a breezy lanai overlooking the ocean at **Harry's Deli,** or sip some espresso or cappuccino and munch on a pastry at **Kona Kai Farms Coffee House.** . . . Running out of things to read? Help is at hand in the **Middle Earth Book Shoppe,** across Alii Drive and one flight up in the **Kona**

Plaza Shopping Arcade, stocked with a good selection of maps and charts as well as books. . . . Downstairs in this same arcade is **Coral Factory,** a huge place with every kind of coral imaginable, and many good gift items at reasonable prices. We also like **Marlin Casuals** in this same arcade; it always offers very tasteful resort wear at competitive prices. . . . **Paradise Found,** next to Suzanne's Bakery, specializes in resort wear that is elegant and casual at the same time; prices are good.

Near the intersection of Hwys. 11 and 190 is the **Kona Coast Shopping Center.** Here, the old Taniguchi's, razed when the King Kamehameha Hotel was rebuilt, has been relocated in a modern supermarket setting and renamed **KTA.** The store is slick and modern now, with none of its pretourist local character, but it's still a good place to stock up on food for your kitchenette apartment. It also might pay to join the local folks at places like **Pay 'n' Save,** a huge drugstore with very low prices for film and other items, and **Kona Health Ways,** with a large selection of herbs, roots, teas, spices, and some fresh produce.

If candy is your passion, be sure to visit the **Kailua Candy Company** at 74-552C Kaiwi St., in the industrial area, a few blocks from Alii Drive (take your first right after the intersection of Hwys. 11 and 190). You'll be taken on a tour of the kitchen and given lots of free samples of chocolates and dry-roasted macadamia nuts. It will be hard to resist buying some to take home with you, even though the average price is $14 a pound, for these are handmade and hand-packed candies, made with real butter, no preservatives, and a great deal of pride by the family who operates the business. They call them the best tasting candies in Hawaii, and you might just agree. Their newest treats: "Tropical Truffles."

As long as you're in the industrial area, you might as well stop in at a local favorite, **Pot Belli Delli,** to pick up some of their New York–style deli sandwiches (about $2 to $4) and you'll be all set for a picnic down the road at the old airport beach. Call in for special or large orders by 10 a.m. for a noontime pickup (tel. 329-9454).

A BIG ISLAND CALENDAR: Can't decide when to come to the Big Island? Here's a list of some events that may help you make your plans. April is the time for the **Merrie Monarch Festival,** including competitions, workshops, and mini-performances at Wailoa Center, lots of free shows at the tennis stadium, and more hula than you can shake a hip at. . . . May Day is **Lei Day:** there's usually lei making in the hotel lobbies. . . . A major event for local artists is the **Big Island Spring Arts Festival,** held in May or June. A wonderful chance to see the best of island arts. . . . **July 4** is a big time for community gatherings: rodeos in Waimea and Naalehu, rough-water swims in Hapuna, and an anniversary celebration for Pu'uhonua o Honaunau in Kona, showing off old Hawaiian crafts in a cultural festival. . . . Also in July is the **International Festival of the Pacific** in Hilo, including free Shakespeare in the Park performances, parades, dances, and displays of the multiethnic peoples of Hawaii. . . . **Bon Dances** are big events in both July and August. . . . In late July or August, sportsmen from all over gather for the **Billfish Tournament** in Kona. . . . The **Honokaa MacNut Festival,** featuring unusual races with macadamia-nut bags, nut balls for a golf tournament, and more, is held in late August. . . . **Aloha Week** festivities in October are special on the Big Island: the opening ceremony is at Halemaumau with dance performances and offerings to Pele. . . . The **Kona Coffee Festival** is held in mid-October.

Note: If you'd like a reminder of all the major sports events in the islands—from the Windsurfing Regatta in January to the Kona Stampede in March to the Ironman Triathalon World Championship in August to the Honolulu Marathon in December, pick up a copy of the Hawaii Visitors Bureau's beautiful new sports calendar, fully illustrated, for $2 at any HVB office.

READERS' SIGHTSEEING AND SHOPPING SUGGESTIONS ON THE BIG ISLAND: "The best thing to see in Hilo is **Hilo** itself. We are talking 'the real Hawaii' here. It doesn't look as if it has changed much in the last 80 years. And a local real estate salesman told me, 'I hope Hilo never changes.' Several barber shops offer haircuts at $3. Prices of real estate are very low in Hilo and in Puna, but jobs are scarce and wages are low. I was told that some people living in Puna pay $25 a month to ride vans to work in the big hotels in South Kohala. They can sleep in the vans" (Mark Terry, Alameda, Calif.). . . . "The visit to **Waipio Valley,** via Waipio Valley Shuttle, was one of the high points of our visit. Scenically it is overwhelming in its beauty, and the historical insights provided by our driver, who was raised there, enhanced our enjoyment. There is another spot that, in a way, complements Waipio Valley. It is the **Pololu Overlook** at the end of the road going east from Hawi, on the north Kohala coast of the island. Not as grand as Waipio, but still very scenic; it is the western boundary of these Hawaii sea cliffs, while Waipio is pretty much the eastern one" (William S. Connell, Durham, N.H.).

"We wanted to tell you about the fishing charter we had in Kona. We made last minute plans to go fishing and couldn't find a charter boat to take us. My husband asked the locals and they recommended a local fisherman by the name of **Francis Pe'a** (tel. 322-9139). We called and met him and he took the men out fishing for the day for $70 each. They were gone for six hours and had a great time. They said he handles the boat very professionally and very safely. One of the men caught a 28 lb. ono (king mackerel) and Francis tried very hard for them to catch tuna. Especially nice was Francis' invitation to dinner featuring ono, of course. He called his wife from the boat and they invited us when they came on shore. We shared a delightful fish dinner and wonderful company with Francis and his family. A wonderful chance to experience Hawaiian hospitality and cooking" (Paul and Marie Asiaf, Plymouth, Mass.).

"Please tell your readers that for anyone traveling alone, Hawaii is perfect. Many places and people, I feel, gave me preferential treatment *because* I was alone. They seemed to go out of their way to see that I had a good time. Two places that are an example are **Orchids of Hawaii** and **Hale Manu Lauhal Weaving.** I spent a long time in both places just enjoying the good conversation" (Patricia Kelly, Pascagola, Mo.). . . . "We highly recommend **Kamanu Catamaran Cruises** (formerly Pacific Sail and Snorkel). Jay Lambert is a great catamaran captain. The snorkeling was super, and fruit and juices awaited us on the boat afterwards. Jay will even pick you up at your hotel. A highlight of our trip! . . . We hopped aboard **Captain Bean's glass-bottom boat** and had a great morning watching colorful fish along the coastline. While on board we were treated to a hula show, free juices, Hawaiian music, and a 'general hula class.' They will even dress you up in native costume for pictures. I advise those prone to motion sickness to take Dramamine beforehand. I'm usually not prone, but they stop the boat to watch the fish and the waves then take over" (Patti Connor, Arlington, Mass.).

"In my opinion, the best shop in all of the Hawaiian Islands is the **Volcano Art Center** on the Big Island, which sits next door to Volcanoes National Park headquarters and across the road from the current Volcano House. This art center, housed in the original Volcano House built in 1877, contains handcrafted items of the finest quality from island artisans. Beautiful koa, mango, milo, and other native wood bowls, boxes, and cutting boards, may be purchased, as well as feather leis, ivory jewelry, petroglyph notecards and postcards, among others. They will package and mail any item purchased there" (Teresa M. Zent, Taneytown, Md.). . . . "A United Airlines employee at Kahului gave me this helpful tip. If your plane stops in Hilo en route home, buy flowers at the airport—fresher and cheaper. I bought a beautiful orchid, carnation, and plumeria lei, and orchid plants were $1 to $2 less than at other flower stands elsewhere. The saleswomen were extremely helpful and cordial" (Elizabeth C. Greer, El Cerrito, Calif.).

"**Parasailing** is available at the Kona wharf area. The day my daughter 'flew,' participants included both sexes, aged 21 to 75—that's right, 75, a woman—who enjoyed the flight at the end of a 300-foot tow rope. Usually the driver of the towboat can start you off and land you dry on their launching raft anchored out from shore—but wear a bathing suit just in case you get dunked. Parasailing is also available at Lahaina, Maui, but is more expensive" (Janet Bryan, Stockbridge, Ga.). . . . "One can drive on a paved road to the

11,200-foot level on **Mauna Loa** from the Saddle Road side. One can also drive on a paved road to the 9,000-foot level on **Mauna Kea,** and from there to the summit. It is a very reasonable dirt road that could be done in a standard automobile, although signs state one must have a four-wheel-drive. The views from the top of Mauna Kea at 13,800 feet are quite unique and well worth the visit. Beware of headaches as one ascends from sea level to over 13,000 feet. . . . About two miles north of Kailua on Rte. 19 is **Honokohau Beach,** a nude beach. Turn left for the beach. Park by the boat harbor and walk north about one-third of a mile through the bushes. It is quite safe and a very natural feeling to swim nude. One feels the way the old Hawaiians must have felt, before the Puritans arrived" (Daniel Zak, Portland, Ore.).

"We snorkeled at Hanauma Bay in Oahu, and Poipu Beach and K'ee Beach in Kauai, but we found the best snorkeling by far to be at **Kahalou Beach Park** in Hawaii, about three miles south of Kona. One day I took out some bread and when I let some pieces go, we had hundreds of fish within reaching distance of us. This definitely was a highlight of our entire trip" (Richard Marks, Lodi, Calif.).

"One of the big athletic events in the islands is the **Triathalon.** It's said to be the single most grueling athletic contest in the world; it's much harder to be a participant in this than in the Olympics. Over 600 brave souls entered the contest twice last year. Briefly, it is a 2½ mile swim, then a 117-mile bike race, then about a 50-mile run with no resting in between. It starts about 8 a.m., and many do not finish until the wee hours. . . . There's an interesting **Fourth of July Rodeo** in Waimea. Instead of the typical bucking broncos you would expect from a mainland rodeo, they have hilarious 'wild cow milking,' and also relay races on horseback. . . . Kailua Kona's annual **Billfish Tournament** in July features a parade bearing floats and entries from countries like Samoa, Fiji, and New Zealand" (Barbara King, Kailua-Kona, Hi.).

"John Alexander, the delightful host at the **Dolphin Bay** in Hilo, gave us a helpful hint that we want to pass on. He told us to buy our flowers at an inexpensive place, such as a grocery store or small florist, obtain a carton, and pack them carefully with shredded, wet newspapers, covered with plastic, to keep them moist. We did this, and carried them on the plane with us. I am writing this over a week later and they are still in good shape. I have four dozen anthuriums and six birds of paradise to give to my friends, and all for just a little over $15" (Mrs. Dean James, Celina, Ohio).

"For those who enjoy snorkeling, we would like to recommend a lagoon only five miles south of Kailua-Kona at milepost 5. **Kahaluu Beach Park** has picnic tables, showers, rest rooms, and a beautiful large lagoon from one to three feet deep. Part of the lagoon is closed from the sea by a row of rocks. According to the local groundskeeper, the Menehunes were to create a fish pond in trade for some land. Since the Hawaiian who bargained with the Menehunes had second thoughts about the deal, he would crow like a rooster from a coconut tree every morning at 3 a.m. The Menehunes, who worked by night, thought morning was approaching, so they stopped work, never completing the fish pond. All types of fish are present in this lagoon, including a few Crown of Thorns" (Charles Kinney, Hayward, Calif.). . . . "When visiting the **petroglyphs at Puako,** be sure to take along some material suitable for making rubbings. Burlap and wax crayon (seen in the Lyman Museum) were very effective. There are two sites; the second one, about a quarter mile past the first, has a much wider variety of carvings" (Patricia Scruggs, Chino, Calif.). . . . "The **K.T.A. Supermarket** had great prices on macadamia nuts: I paid $2.09 for a five-ounce can on sale" (Martha F. Battenfeld, Brighton, Mass.). [*Authors' Note:* This is a family-owned supermarket, with two branches in Kona, two more in Hilo. They have good sales all the time.]

"We took a nice side trip to Pololu Valley Lookout on the northern tip in the **Kohala** district. After viewing the beautiful valley we stopped about three miles back down the road from the lookout on Hwy. 27 at **Keokea Park,** which had a lovely view, picnic tables, outdoor showers, and a little sea pool. There is a sign off Hwy. 27; you can drive in from the road about one mile" (Mr. and Mrs. Donald Plumlee, Santa Clara, Calif.). . . . "We found canvas shoes much more desirable than sandals when we visited **Volcanoes National Park** and the Pu'uhonua o Honaunau at Kona; the volcanic pebbles are difficult to walk on and get between your toes, and the canvas shoes give you a firm footing. Since we were in Hawaii in November and December we did have rain, and my washable canvas shoes were not ruined by the red mud I encountered several times or the deluge of rain we had to paddle through in Hilo" (Mrs. Jack Morgan, Vacaville, Calif.).

"The **fishing pier** across from Liliuokalani Gardens Park has a very interesting fish auction at 7:30 a.m. weekday mornings, when the boat operators sell to licensed fish markets. The auction takes only a few minutes, and visitors may ask questions. In Kona, the weighing in of marlins and tuna is very interesting and starts at about 4 p.m." (Mrs. Charles H. Gould, Seattle, Wash.). . . . "It is interesting to drive up the 13-mile road on the slope of **Mauna Loa** for the view. From there the trail leads to the summit. On this ride in the morning at 7 a.m., I saw plenty of wild pigs and wild goats. Before Waiohini, it is worthwhile to drive nine miles down to the left to the **South Point** (Ka Lae), the southernmost point of the U.S. There is a lighthouse and steep cliffs. The fishermen have to tow the fish over the cliffs from their boats" (Prof. Dr. W. K. Brauers, Berchem-Antwerp, Belgium).

Chapter XV

THE ISLAND OF MAUI

1. Hotels
2. Restaurants
3. The Night Scene

EVEN THOUGH SHE LIVES two blocks away from highly celebrated Waikiki Beach, a woman we know in Honolulu regularly spends her vacations in Maui. The reason? To go to the beach! In addition, however, to possessing some of the world's most marvelous beaches, this second-largest island in the Hawaiian archipelago boasts one of the great natural wonders of the planet: Haleakala, the world's largest dormant volcano. Add to all this a string of gorgeous little jungle valleys where the modern world seems incredibly remote, a picturesque whaling town kicking its heels after a long sleep in the South Seas sun, and a wonderfully hospitable local citizenry intent on convincing you that Maui no ka oi—Maui is the greatest. You just might end up agreeing.

Maui has been going through the throes of enormous expansion. But while new hotels and condominium apartments have been and are being built at a formidable rate, the island still manages to retain a graceful, unhurried feeling. The laws here are stricter, and nowhere on Maui has there been such wanton destruction of natural beauty as there has been in Waikiki.

Although most of the new condominium apartments are in the luxury category, some are fine for us. But even with these additions to the hotel scene, a room in Maui is probably going to be more expensive than one in Waikiki. Meals, however, are reasonable, and there are plenty of opportunities to do your own cooking. Again, your biggest expense will be car rentals or guided tours, your only alternative on an island with very limited transportation. A bus service and an oldtime tourist train run between the Lahaina and Kaanapali areas, and there's another bus service between Wailea, Kihei, and Lahaina, connecting eastern and western Maui, but that's about the extent of it.

CHOOSING A BASE: Maui is small enough so that you can logically make your headquarters at one hotel and take off each day for various sightseeing and beach excursions: to **Haleakala,** to the historic old whaling town of **Lahaina,** and to remote, romantic **Hana.**

The **Wailuku-Kahului** area, closest to the airport, is centrally located for sightseeing excursions but lacks a really good beach. The best beach area close

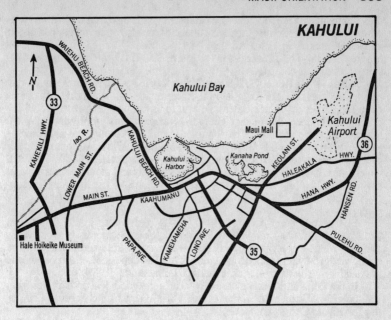

to Kahului is **Kihei** (about a 15-minute drive) and this also enjoys a central location. The liveliest and most beautiful area, to our taste, is the **Lahaina-Kaanapali-Napili** region, about 40 miles from Kahului. All of these places work as a base; the only place on the island that is inconvenient as a base if you want to move around is **Hana**; you might want to plan an overnight stay there as the drive each way is a long one, although most people do it on a one-day trip.

ARRIVAL IN KAHULUI: Your plane will land at the very modern and airy Kahului Airport. The terminal is located in the seven-mile-wide valley that binds together the two great volcanic masses of Maui—the West Maui Mountains and Haleakala on the east—and accounts for the name Valley Isle. You're just a few miles here from modern Kahului and graceful old Wailuku, neighbor towns competing peacefully for the title of largest city. From the airport, you'll have to take a taxi to your hotel, unless you're going to rent a car. If you need assistance, stop by the state information kiosk at the airport. The **Maui Visitors Bureau** is a short drive from the airport, at 172 Alamaha St., Suite 100, in the industrial area. They have an extensive supply of visitor information (tel. 871-8691 for driving directions).

If you're going to be staying in West Maui, you can save some driving time by flying directly to the new Kapalua-West Maui Airport on smaller planes from the fleets of Hawaiian and Mid Pacific airlines. (Mid Pacific uses Reeves aircraft of the type flown for many years by Royal Hawaiian Air Service, which recently closed passenger service to West Maui.)

U-DRIVES: As in all the neighbor islands the major low-cost, all-island car rental companies are represented in Maui. **Alamo, National, Budget, Tropical,** etc., all have representatives here. The best place to make your reservations with these companies is in Honolulu (see Chapter IV, "Transportation Within Honolulu," for details). Some of the local agencies can also offer you good deals, at either flat rates or time plus mileage. At **Trans Maui U-Drive** (tel. 877-5222, or toll free 800/367-5228) charges start as low as $19.95 flat rate for either a stick-shift or automatic compact.

Atlas U-Drive (tel. 877-7208, or toll free 800/367-5238) requires a three-day minimum. Their charge for a late-model compact with standard shift ranges from $18.95 per day, three-day minimum, to as low as $12.95 per day, 30-day minimum, flat rate, no mileage charge. All sizes of cars are available. A $50 advance deposit is required. They'll provide prompt and courteous airport service. Write them at P.O. Box 126, Puunene, Maui, HI 96784. We continue to get excellent reports on **V.I.P. Car Rentals** (tel. 877-2054, or toll free 800/367-6080), which offers flat rates of $16.95 per day, plus weekly and monthly rates at great savings. The helpful owners, Carol and Ron Williams, advise that they will supply readers of this book with a 10% discount. They also say that rates may change, so please call early.

El Cheap-O Rent-A-Car (tel. 877-5851) rents older model Toyotas at $16.45 a day (three-day minimum), $95 a week, or $295 a month. Newer models and four-wheel-drives are also available. Reservations are suggested and will be acknowledged by return mail upon receipt of a $50 deposit. Free airport shuttle is available. Write them at P.O. Box 1065, Puunene, HI 96874.

In the Lahaina-Kaanapali area, you can get a good deal on flat rates from **Rainbow**, 741 Wainee St., Lahaina (tel. 661-8734), which charges $14.50 per day for Toyota Corolla compacts.

1. Hotels

IN KAHULUI-WAILUKU: Kahului has a string of four hotels within minutes of the airport and across the road from three very attractive shopping centers dotted with inexpensive restaurants. The beach here, however, is rocky and can be fairly rough. With the development of a very good beach area in Kihei, just 15 minutes away, these hotels have become largely the place for local business travelers and for very large tour groups, since Kahului does offer a central location for touring all of Maui. If you choose to stay here, your best bets are the Maui Hukilau and its sister hotel, the Maui Seaside. At the pleasingly Polynesian-style **Maui Hukilau,** standard singles and twins are $44; superior, $49; deluxe, $53. Add another $10 to $15 and you have the use of a Budget Rent-A-Car compact automatic, free mileage. Like another wing of the Maui Hukilau (same swimming pool, same restaurants, etc., and under the same management) is the newer **Maui Seaside,** with large, light, tastefully furnished rooms, all boasting air conditioning, color TV, refrigerator (but no cooking facilities), and two double beds. There are no lanais, but most of the rooms have lovely views of mountain, sea, or garden. Standard singles and twins are $49; superior, $55, deluxe, $60. Kitchenette apartments are $65, and a Junior Suite with refrigerator, sleeping four, is $75. Again, add another $10 to $15 for the use of a Budget Rent-A-Car automatic compact, free mileage. For reservations at both the Maui Hukilau and the Maui Seaside, write to Sands, Seaside, and Hukilau Resorts, 2222 Kalakaua Ave., Suite 714, Honolulu, HI 96815, or phone toll free 800/367-7000.

If you're planning to stay in the area for quite a while and need an apartment, check out **Puuone Gardens Apartments** at 471 Liholiho St. (tel. 244-5240) in Wailuku.

IN KIHEI-WAILEA: The closest beach area to Kahului (about 15 minutes away) is the Kihei-Wailea section of Maui—a windswept stretch of sea and sand, with miles and miles of unspoiled ocean beach, the waves lapping at your feet, air warm and dry, and the mighty volcano of Haleakala and its changing cloud colors to gaze at from the shore. It's blessed with the least rain and best weather in all of Maui. Full-scale tourist development began here not so long ago, and the area has blossomed mightily since then, with scores of condominiums, plus new restaurants and small shopping centers opening to keep pace. There are three luxury-class hotels in Wailea, the Hotel Inter-Continental, the Stouffer Wailea Beach Hotel, and the Maui Prince. Beaches here can be rather windy in the afternoon (get your swims in the morning and save sightseeing for later). Despite its beauty, the Kihei-Wailea region remains less glamorous and exciting, at least for us, than the Lahaina-Kaanapali region (see ahead), but if you like a quiet vacation, you'll do well at any of the places described below.

When a hotel has a very large return clientele—as much as 75% year after year—you know it's doing something right. Such is the case with **Nani Kai Hale,** at the very entrance to the Kihei area, blessed with a location on an excellent swimming beach, nice accommodations, and the ministrations of managers Jeanne and Larry Forsyth, who do a lot to create that oldtime aloha spirit. Guests receive a pineapple in their room on arrival, are invited to a coffee-and-doughnuts party at the beach on Saturday morning, and sometimes to a hukilau run by the native Filipino family who live next door (a hukilau, once common but now quite rare on the islands, is a 700-foot fishing net pulled in by hand). There's always a congenial group around the pool or out on the sandy beach; swimming is excellent, but snorkeling is limited. The apartments are condominium, and decor varies with the individual owners, but all are attractively furnished, have either queen or twin beds, good sofa beds in the living rooms, well-equipped kitchens, private lanais; most do not have telephones. In summer, a three-day minimum is required. Rates begin at $28 for a room and bath only (no kitchen or lanai). A studio is $40; a one-bedroom, two-bath apartment with ocean view is $50; a one-bedroom, two-bath apartment beachfront is $60. For four people, a two-bedroom, two-bath apartment is $75. During the winter, December 16 to April 15, rates are $35, $55, $70, $85, and $100, and a seven-day minimum is required. An extra person is charged $7 in summer, $9 in winter; children under five stay free. For reservations, write Nani Kai Hale, 73 No, Kihei Rd., Kihei, Maui, HI 96753, or call toll free 800/367-3705. The local phone is 879-6032.

Two former readers of this book, Milt and Eileen Preston, started traveling to the islands a few years ago and then decided to settle there. Now they have their own place in Kihei, and will give you a warm welcome at the **Sunseeker Resort,** across a tiny road from Kihei Beach. There are just half a dozen studios, plus one- and two-bedroom apartments here, and although the studios are not lavish, they are nicely furnished with a cheerful color scheme, original artwork, color TV, upholstered furniture on the lanais, cross-ventilation, and a full kitchen. These go for some of the best prices in the Kihei area: The studios are $35, single or double. The one-bedroom apartments, with a couch in the living room that opens to a double bed, require a stay of three days. They rent for $45, single or double ($6 for each extra person); the two-bedroom apartments are $70 for four people. These rates apply from May 1 to October 31; add $6 the rest of the year. The Prestons will provide you with free barbecue equipment. For reservations, write them at P.O. Box 276, Kihei, Maui, HI 96753 (tel. 879-1261).

Close by, the **Nona Lani** consists of eight individual cottages, each standing alone in a grassy tree-filled area. The cottages afford an ocean view, and there is a beach for swimming and walking 20 yards away. Delightfully furnished and decorated, with rich wood panels and thick carpets, they feature a living room, full bedroom (with a queen-size bed), kitchen, bath, color TV, and an open lanai with dining table. Since there are two beds in the living room, a family of four could be comfortable here. From April 17 to December (when there is a four-night minimum), rates are $49 for two; from December to April 16 (when there is a seven-night minimum), prices are $65 for two. For reservations, write to Dave and Nona Kong, 455 S. Kihei Rd., Kihei, Maui, HI 96753 (tel. 879-2497).

Both these places are near the beach at the stop where the 1792 arrival of Capt. George Vancouver is commemorated by an HVB marker and a Thunderbird totem carved by the Nootka Indians on Vancouver Island.

The **Lihi Kai Cottages and Apartments** have been a staple in the Kihei area for many years. The complex of 25 one-bedroom cottages and apartment units is set in a garden and looks out over a protected bay and small-boat landing. Although the furnishings here are showing their age (black-and-white TV, twin beds, pay phone outside, etc.) and may seem a bit spartan compared to the newer, more lush condominiums elsewhere, the rooms are acceptable, each with wall-to-wall carpeting, kitchen, and a private lanai with floral landscaping. Kalama Park, a lovely, uncrowded swimming beach, is right at hand. Mrs. Jeanette DiMeo, the owner-manager truly goes out of her way to help her guests. Lihi Kai is especially popular with long-term residents, but transients are welcome. However, Mrs. DiMeo asks that you book reservations as far in advance as possible, especially during the period from November 1 to March 31, because so many guests keep coming back year after year. Daily rates are $40 a couple for a minimum of three days, $8 for an extra person. During the low season—April to December—daily rates are the same, but weekly rates of $210 and monthly rates of $525 are available. Write to Lihi Kai Cottages and Apartments, 2121 Iliili Rd., RR 1, Kihei, Maui, HI 96753 (tel. 879-2335). (See the Readers' Selections, ahead, for comments on Lihi Kai.)

We've always shied away from high-rise condominiums, but after we visited **Kahale Makai Resort (Village by the Sea)**, we were convinced that, in this case at least, bigger also means better. The two five-story buildings house some 168 units, and some have been superbly decorated by their owners. All have full kitchen, laundry, central air conditioning, and color TV. The two buildings, right on the ocean, are separated by a well-tended lawn on which there is a pool and putting green, Jacuzzi, barbecues. Also available are saunas and shuffleboard; tennis courts and golf are nearby. An in-house convenience shop makes housekeeping easy in case you've forgotten something at the supermarket in Kihei, or in Kahului, 15 minutes away. As with most condominiums, several rental agents handle units here, but the one offering the most reasonably priced units is Village Rentals, Azeka's Place, P.O. Box 1471, Kihei, Maui, HI 96753, which can also be reached toll free at 800/367-5634. Studios for one or two persons go from $35 a night during the off-season (April 15 to December 15), and from $45 the rest of the year. One-bedroom units begin at $40 off-season, $55 in; two-bedroom units at $65 a night off-season, $90 in; and two-bedroom deluxe oceanfront apartments for four people begin at $68 a night off-season, $85 in.

Kahale Makai Resort is right on the ocean, but you may want to walk a bit to a good swimming beach, as this one tends to be a bit rocky.

Can't choose between the tennis courts and the beach? **Leinaala Oceanfront Condominiums** makes life easy for you, since this cozy little complex of 25 apartments is sandwiched on both sides by public tennis courts and faces on a beautiful beach. And after your game, you can cool off in the freshwater swimming pool if you choose. All of these one- and two-bedroom apartments are nicely and individually furnished and all have complete kitchen facilities. Off-season (May 1 through December 15) rates are $65 for the one-bedroom unit, $80 for the two-bedroom. In winter the one-bedrooms are $75 and the two-bedrooms are $90. An extra person is charged $10. There's a five-night minimum stay in winter, four nights in summer. For reservations, write the managers, Norm and Nancy Sanders, Leinaala Oceanfront Condominiums, 998 S. Kihei Rd., Kihei, Maui HI 96753 (tel. 879-2235).

The traditional big hotel in this area is the casually relaxed **Maui Lu,** a collection of low-rise, Polynesian-style buildings on 30 acres of tropical grounds, complete with a large Maui-shaped swimming pool, sandy beach, tennis courts, and a spirit of "ohana" or "family" that gives a stay here the feeling of an older, more gracious Hawaii. The rooms are modestly priced by the standards of the larger hotels, especially when one considers that all have those handy conveniences, refrigerator and coffee maker, as well as phone, color TV, and air conditioning. Furnishings are attractive. Many units offer kitchenettes and some even have full kitchens. For those not cooking in, the Hale Kope Coffee Shop serves breakfast, and the Long House serves excellent dinners. From December 19 through April 15, standard rooms, single or double, run $83; superior, $93; deluxe, $103. From April 15 to December 19, prices go down considerably, to $68, $78, and $93. An extra person is $10; no charge for children under 18 sharing a room with their parents and using existing bedding. Inquire about hotel-and-car packages. For reservations, write Aston Hotels and Resorts, 2255 Kuhio Ave., Honolulu, HI 96815, or phone toll free 800/367-5124 from the mainland, 800/592-3351 from the islands. Maui Lu is at 575 S. Kihei Rd., Kihei, Maui, HI 96753, and the local number is 879-5881 (call collect from Canada).

On the beach at Kihei, the **Menehune Shores,** offers family accommodations in a big, beautiful condominium complex. You could almost stay here and not want to leave the grounds—there's the ocean, a conventional swimming pool, and the "Royal Fishpond," a protected stone and reef formation built by the ancient Hawaiians, right on the premises, as well as Idini's, specializing in seafood and Italian dishes. There's a whale-watching platform on the roof garden. All apartments face the ocean, are individually decorated, and have a full electric kitchen, with refrigerator-freezer and washer-dryer. The one-bedroom/one-bath units rent at $65 for two, $75 for three. Two-bedroom apartments with two baths are $75 for two, $5 more for each additional person, up to $95 for six people. Three-bedroom units with two baths cost $100 for five, $110 for six. From April 6 to December 15 there's a 20% discount. Across the road are studios that rent for $35 a day all year round. For reservations, write Kihei Kona Rentals, P.O. Box 556, Kihei, Maui, HI 96753 (tel. 879-5828).

We'd have to call **Luana Kai,** 940 S. Kihei Rd., one of the nicest condos in the Kihei area. This low-rise complex is gracefully situated on eight acres of beautifully landscaped grounds, and wherever you look from its 113 rooms, you'll see garden or ocean views. Step from your room—well, almost—to the ocean or swimming pool, heated whirlpool, saunas, tennis courts, putting green, barbecue area; everything is close at hand. Best of all, there's a peaceful feeling here. Inside, carved wooden doors lead to one-, two-, and three-bedroom luxuriously furnished apartments in light woods, all with full electric kitchens, telephones, TVs, lanais, and every comfort for vacation living. During the long off-season, from April 20 to December 15, one-bedroom garden apartments for up to two persons are $80; two-bedroom garden apartments for up to four, $95; three-bedroom garden apartments for up to six, $135. During high season, the rates are $100, $120, and $170. One-bedroom ocean apartments are $90, two-bedroom ocean apartments are $110 during off-season; in high season, rates go up to $110 and $135. Weekly rates are also available. An extra person is charged $8; children under 12 stay free; minimum stay is three nights. For reservations, call toll free 800/367-7042 from the mainland, 800/426-8328 from Canada. The local phone is 531-7595. You may also write to Hawaiian Islands Resorts, P.O. Box 212, Honolulu, HI 96810.

A unique hotel in this area—or in any area, for that matter—is the **Mana Kai Maui Condominium Hotel**, 13 years old, 98 rooms big, and offering a combination of condominium apartments and regular hotel rooms in a lively, upbeat setting. Situated on a beautiful crescent of beach (it's known as one of the best snorkeling beaches around), with a pool, an airy, open restaurant, and all sorts of activities going on, it offers a lot under one roof. If you're watching the budget, stick to their hotel rooms; these are small bedrooms with either a king-size bed or twin beds under a king-size spread; louvered closet door, telephone, color TV, and an attractive bathroom with a large vanity sink. Breakfast in the restaurant—for one or two people—is included in the daily rate of $57.50; add $10 and you can have the use of a car with unlimited mileage. All in all, a very attractive package. If you want to splurge, take one of their one-bedroom apartments at $103 or a two-bedroom for four people at $124; again, $10 more gives you a car. For reservations call toll free from the mainland and Canada, 800/525-2025. Or write Mana Kai Maui Condominium Hotel, 2960 S. Kihei Rd., Kihei, Maui, HI 96753 (tel. 879-1561). Readers of this book will be granted a 10% discount.

Although it's across the street from the ocean, all units are oceanfront at **Shores of Maui**, an attractive, two-level condo complex of one- and two-bedroom apartments. Snorkeling is good right across the street, and there's a sandy swimming beach just a block away. You can relax in the good-size swimming pool, soak in the spa, play a little tennis, enjoy a barbecue here. Apartments are nicely and individually decorated, all with dishwasher, washer-dryer, TV, and summer rates, May 1 to December 19, are quite modest: $45 per day for a one-bedroom/one-bath unit, $270 weekly; $60 per day for a two-bedroom/two-bath unit, $360) weekly. The one-bedroom units can sleep up to four; the two-bedroom unit, up to six. It's $7 per night for each extra guest. In winter, the one-bedrooms are $60 daily, $360 weekly, and the two-bedrooms are $75 daily, $450) weekly. For reservations, write to Shores of Maui, 2075 S. Kihei Rd., Kihei, Maui, HI 96753, or phone toll free 800/367-8002. The local phone is 879-9140.

AT MAALAEA BAY: Down by the small boat harbor at Maalaea Bay, a few miles from Kihei, is a wonderful beach area, and perched here, at Maalaea Village, is a small group of condominiums. **Hono Kai Resort,** one of the most reasonably priced of the lot, would make an ideal place for a family vacation (minimum stay is five days). You can swim in front of your door or at the public beach 50 yards away—or try your luck with surf at the harbor, which, according to some of the locals, is "the fastest surf in the world." All units are on the ocean side of the street and have at least one or two bedrooms, and all are nicely furnished. Shoji doors separate the living room and bedroom; the two-bedroom units all have lofts. There are full kitchens, including dishwashers, cable TV with HBO on request, even use of boogie boards and surfboards free. There's a swimming pool, washers and dryers on every floor, and two good restaurants—Buzz's Steak House and The Waterfront, nearby. We've had several good reports from our readers about this place and about managers Jim and Jeanne McJannet, who also manage two adjoining properties: **Makani A Kai** and **Kanai A Nalu.** Rates at Hono Kai, slightly lower than at the others, average around $45 for the one-bedroom garden view, $55 for the one-bedroom ocean view, and $50 for the one-bedroom oceanfront during the summer; during the winter the rates go up about $5. Ask to see if they still have summer specials. For reservations, write Hono Kai Resort, RR 1, Box 389, Maalaea Village, Maui, HI 96793, or phone toll free 800/367-6084. The local phone is 244-7012.

IN LAHAINA, KAANAPALI, AND ON NAPILI BAY: The area surrounding the historic old whaling town of Lahaina, about 30 miles from Kahului, might be a good place to move on to after a day or two in the Kahului or Kihei areas; or it could serve as a base of operations for your entire stay in Maui. In the heart of it all, out on the wharf overlooking the harbor, is the **Pioneer Inn,** an island landmark and a historic sight in its own right. For years, kamaiinas, tourists, movie stars, sailors, and beachcombers sat out on the big lanai in front, wondering what was happening back in civilization. Well, Lahaina is very civilized now, but the old hotel is still there, quaint and colorful, and the old rooms, clean but not at all fancy, are a good buy for Lahaina. Those in the mauka building are air-conditioned, have private bath and lanai, and go for $36 single, $39 double for an outside room; $39 and $42 for a courtyard room; $52 single or double for a superior room; an extra person is $10, a child under five is $5. Most rooms have a queen-size bed plus a twin. Fun for adventurous types. And the food is still good. The Harpooner's Lanai serves breakfast and lunch (and more potent stuff all day), and at night it's broil-your-own steak around the patio. The Pioneer Inn is at 658 Wharf St., Lahaina, Maui 96761 (tel. 661-3636). Honolulu phone: 949-4121, weekdays.

Without a car, almost any vacation on Maui is difficult. But lack of wheels will not be a hindrance to anyone who chooses to stay at the **Maui Islander**, a hotel that affords peace and privacy (its units are spread out over nine acres of tropical grounds) while providing proximity to everything you could want in the area: it's a three-block walk to a sandy swimming beach, a two-block stroll to the activities of Lahaina Harbor, a block away from the shops and restaurants of Front Street, two blocks to the supermarket, and a short bus ride to the resort life at Kaanapali Beach. You can be picked up at the airport and taken to the Maui Islander at a nominal cost. And the hotel-condo itself is lovely: the 372 units are simply but very nicely decorated in island style with light woods, tile bathroom, color TV, telephone, tidy kitchen (except in the hotel rooms). Right at home is a swimming pool, a barbecue and picnic area, and a tennis court that is lit at night. Guests can consult the staff at the activities desk for advice on planning their days, and partake of free lessons—in hula, lei making, scuba-diving. And the price for all this comfort and convenience is not bad: $69 for two people in a hotel room, $82 for up to three people in a studio, $95 for up to four people in a one-bedroom suite. (Rates are subject to change.) For reservations, phone toll free 800/367-5226, or write to Maui Islander, 660 Wainee St., Lahaina, Maui, HI 96761. The local phone is 667-9766.

Slightly more expensive and very attractive is **Lahaina Shores,** overlooking Lahaina Harbor. It's composed of 200 units, all with complete electric kitchen including utensils, wall-to-wall carpeting, air conditioning, and lanais offering ocean or mountain views. The seven-story building, a charming example of Victorian architecture, is very much in keeping with the rest of old Lahaina—a welcome contrast to the burgeoning concrete high-rises flourishing all over the rest of the island. A swimming pool with adjacent heated therapeutic Jacuzzi sits ocean side, just off the huge, airy lobby. A mountain-view studio is priced at $82, an ocean front room is $94, single or double. In the luxury category are one-bedroom units at $112 ocean-view, $129 oceanfront, single or double. Penthouses go to $144 for a mountain-view and $162 for oceanfront rooms. (Prices subject to change.) No charge for children under six; additional persons, $9. You can swim in front of the hotel, play tennis across the street. For reservations, phone toll free 800/367-7042, or write to Lahaina Shores, 475 Front St., Lahaina, HI 96761. The local phone is 661-3309.

True budget-minded folks will find the **Lahainaluna Hotel,** an 18-room wooden building of uncertain but venerable age, acceptable if not at all glamorous. Rooms are small, furnished with cheap but serviceable furniture; some are air-conditioned, all have their own bathroom (shower, no tub), and black-and-white TV. For $30 you get a single or double room with a lanai, two single beds, and a mountain or ocean view; $25 or $23 gets you an inside room without a view, but quieter; half of these rooms have double beds. There's a $7 charge for each extra person, a two-day minimum stay, and no maid service for stays of three days or less. The location is right in the midst of the busy Lahaina shopping-nightlife-restaurant scene; during the Christmas-New Year's holidays, confirmed reservations must be made two months in advance. Write to Lahainaluna Hotel, 127 Lahainaluna Rd., Lahaina, Maui, HI 96761 (tel. 661-0577). There is no parking space at the hotel.

A few miles outside of Lahaina, on Maui's exquisite west coast, you approach the Kaanapali-Napili region, one of Hawaii's most desirable vacation areas, blessed with miles of gorgeous beach and stunningly blue skies, with the famed Royal Kaanapali Golf Courses thrown in for good measure. The luxury hotels here are way beyond our budget, but just in case you're wondering which of the hotels has the lowest prices, it's the **Kaanapali Beach Hotel.** There are a number of standard rooms that go from around $120, single or double, $15 for each extra person. (Rates are subject to change.) The rooms are large and well decorated, and have TVs, refrigerators, and private lanais facing into a garden. The Kaanapali Beach has a spacious open feeling, with its huge garden, a whale of a swimming pool (yes, it's in the shape of a whale), a beautiful ocean beach right next to the rock formation (which makes it good for snorkeling) on which the neighboring Sheraton Maui sits, and all the comforts of the luxury life. Certainly worth a splurge—if your pocketbook is up to it. The Kaanapali Beach aims to be "the most Hawaiian of the hotels," and its gracious staff and unusually sensitive management live up to that ideal. Reservations: Amfac Resorts Hawaii, P.O. Box 8520, Honolulu, HI 96830 (tel. toll free 800/227-4700, or 661-0011 in Maui).

For families with lots of kids, or for two couples traveling together, an apartment at the **Maui Sands** is ideal. Imagine an enormous living room (about the size of two average hotel rooms put together), beautifully decorated, with two small but comfortable bedrooms, twin beds in each, a full electric kitchen, tropical ceiling fans, color TV, a view of gardens or ocean from your private lanai, and enough space for six people to stretch out in—for a cost of $108 (garden-view) to $131 (oceanfront) per day for four and $7 for each additional body. You'd expect to pay twice as much for anything comparable at the luxury resorts. This attractive hotel, just past the Kaanapali gold coast area, also has one-bedroom apartments at $83 or $100 double; and apartments close to the road (for heavy sleepers) at $67 for the one-bedroom, $94 for the two-bedroom. (Rates are subject to a slight increase.) There is a four-day minimum most of the year, longer at the peak of the winter season. Since the Maui Sands was built when it was feasible to buy large lots of land, there is plenty of it to spare; the grounds are abloom with lovely trees and plantings, there's a comfortable swimming pool and sunning area (free coffee is served there in the morning), a big laundry area, and oh, that wonderful beach! At sunset, it's pure enchantment as you watch the sun seeming to sink right between the islands of Molokai and Lanai off in the distance. A coral reef forms a natural ocean pool, and that white sand stretches off for miles in the distance; you could walk all the way to the Kaanapali strip if you had a mind to. The hotel is completely refurbished, including new furniture. Managers Kay and Adele Kunisawa are cordial hosts, and some weekends they provide Hawaiian entertainment and free mixers for a cocktail party. Off-season, April 15 to December 15, there's a 10% discount for a stay of seven days or more, a 20% discount for 30 days. Readers continue to praise this one. Write to Maui Sands, 3559 Honoapiilani Rd., Lahaina, Maui, HI 96761. The toll-free reservation number is 800/367-5037 and the local number is 669-4811.

The same Maui Sands management is in charge at the select units at **Papakea,** right next door, and these little homes are even more luxurious. Creature comforts include two pools, two Swedish saunas, two tennis courts, shuffleboard, barbecues, putting green, and picnic areas. Of course it's all on the beach. During the summer season (April 15 to December 15), a group of three can stay in a garden studio for $91, a group of four in a one-bedroom for $119. Phone the same toll-free number—800/367-5037—anytime between 8 a.m. and 5 p.m. Hawaii time to make reservations.

You'll have to walk across the street to get to the beach from **Honokowai Palms,** but that little extra effort pays off well. Over the years, we've had consistently good reports from people who've stayed at this complex of spacious one- and two-bedroom apartments. These are older apartments, not as luxuriously furnished as some of the newer condos, but very good value for the money. One-bedroom apartments for two people, with ocean view and lanai, are $55; with neither view nor lanai, $50. Two-bedroom apartments for two people, without ocean view or lanai, are $55. The one-bedroom apartments can accommodate four, the two-bedroom apartments can hold six; each additional person is charged $6 daily. There's a large pool to dunk in, barbecue area, and ample all-electric kitchens to make cooking easy. The management is friendly and helpful; there's a warm, cozy feeling here. A three-day minimum stay is required, and so is a $100 deposit. For advance reservations, phone toll free 800/843-1633 or write to Honokowai Palms, 3666 Lower Honoapiilani Hwy., Lahaina, Maui, HI 96761 (tel. 669-6130 in Maui).

Oceanside along this same stretch of Lower Honoapiilani Rd. in this beautiful West Maui area is the graceful **Hale Kai,** whose 40 condominium apartments look out on flowering gardens, a park, and a good-sized pool that fronts on the ocean beach. Each is decorated differently and each has a different view: Manager Patty Saunders reports that some guests come back year after year for the ocean view, others for the quiet park-side units. Rooms on the upper levels have handsome cathedral ceilings. All are furnished nicely with electric kitchens, TV, private lanais. One-bedroom apartments for two persons go for a daily rate of $75, a weekly rate of $420 to $450. Two-bedroom apartments for four persons average $100 daily, $600 to $650 weekly. An additional person is charged $8 a day. Minimum stay is three nights, except for Christmas, when it is two weeks. No credit cards are accepted. For reservations, write to Hale Kai, 3691 Lower Honoapiilani Rd., Lahaina, Maui, HI 96761 or call 669-6333.

The condominium units, all oceanfront, at **Noelani,** in the Kahana area, are beautifully furnished, and the view from your oceanfront lanai—of Molokai Island, blue seas, and tropical gardens—is even more beautiful. There are two freshwater swimming pools at seaside, good snorkeling right in front, and a wide sandy beach adjacent to the property. Managers John and Donna Lorenz host mai-tai parties at poolside several times a month so that guests can get to know one another. The studios, which rent for $65, are furnished in Pacific decor, with dressing room, bath, and kitchen. The one-bedroom units at $85 have their own dishwasher and washer-dryer. There is an extra-person charge of $5. Two- and even three-bedroom apartments are available, and so are weekly and monthly rates; three-day minimum stay. Write Noelani, 4095 Honoapiilani Rd., Lahaina, Maui, HI 96761 (tel. 669-8374). The toll-free number from the mainland and Alaska is 800/367-6030.

Every time we have a look at the **Pohailani Maui,** it grows a little bit more. The original eight-unit complex now has 29 units at the water's edge, plus another 85 two-bedroom duplex apartments on the mountainside. Two tennis courts, two pools, and other facilities are spread out over eight acres—not to mention a stretch of sandy beach, perfect for gentle ocean swimming. Each of the seaside units is spacious, attractively furnished in studio style (with such touches as big, old-fashioned ceiling fans), and boasts large kitchenette, color TV, private phone, plus a lanai that is perfectly enormous. Low-season rates, April 16 to December 16, are $50 for two in a studio, $60 for a deluxe studio, $70 for the two-bedroom town houses. High-season rates, December 16 to April 16, are $60, $80, and $90. There is a three-night minimum stay (14 nights from December 20 to January 5), and a three-night deposit necessary to confirm reservations. For reservations, contact Rainbow Reservations, P.O. Box 11453, Lahaina, Maui, HI 96761, or phone toll free 800/367-6092 (tel. 667-7858 locally). The hotel's phone is 669-5464.

The **Mahina Surf** is a fine place to settle in for real at-home living. We inspected the units on our last visit and found them to be not only charming and attractively furnished, but well priced for the area: from April 15 to December 15, it's $70 per night (minimum stay of three nights), $465 a week; during the high season, December 15 to April 15, it's $80 per night, $532 per week. These rates are for two people in a one-bedroom unit with complete kitchen and accessories, color TV, telephone, and an ocean view. These units can actually sleep four: each extra person is charged $8 per night. Two–bedroom units are available for an extra $15 per day, and two-bedroom/two-bath units for an additional $20. Sizes of the apartments vary, but all are little "homes"; the cutest are those with a loft area upstairs that serves as a second bedroom, and these are big enough to sleep six. The 56-unit complex is situated on a rocky strip of ocean, and snorkeling is fine, but there is no sandy beach; there is, however, a big pool as compensation. Write to Mahina Surf, 4057 Lower Honoapiilani Rd., Lahaina, Maui, HI 96761 (tel. 669-6068 or toll free 800/367-6086). Inquire about their excellent deals on car rentals.

Now you're approaching Napili Bay, a gorgeous little stretch of sea and sand where not very long ago the breadfruit, papaya, and lichee trees ran helter-skelter to the sea. For us, this area is the end of the rainbow, and we don't mean the one likely to be arching across the sugarcane fields, as you approach: the setting is perfect, and the swimming, from a gentle reef-protected beach, among the best in the islands. Here you'll find the **Mauian Hotel,** with 44 attractive studio apartments big enough for four, each with private lanai, all-electric kitchen, one queen and one trundle bed (that opens into two), and all the conveniences of home. From April 15 to December 15, doubles are $70 garden-view, $75 ocean-view, and $90 oceanfront; in high season, it's $80, $85 and $100. For those capable of tearing themselves away from the idyllic beach, there's shuffleboard and a freshwater swimming pool (a big laundry and ironing area too). Write to Mauian Hotel, 5441 Honoapiilani Rd., Lahaina, Maui, HI 96761 (tel. 669-6205). Toll-free reservations: 800/367-5034.

One of the very nicest places in this area is the **Napili Surf Beach Resort,** which has 54 soundproof luxury units perched on the tip of Napili Bay, on a particularly lovely curve of beach. Each of these units is completely equipped for easy housekeeping, and has color TV and handsome furniture; the private lanais overlook the pool, garden, or ocean. You'll have to spend your hard-earned splurge money: $81 double for the studios, $109 for the huge one-bedroom units. But wait—managers Bob and Marge Putt also have newer garden units, at $71 double. These 18 off-beach studios, called Napili Puamala (garden of flowers) are small but super-neat and functionally designed; they come with color TV, radio with digital clocks (something rather rare in hotels), full kitchens, dishwashers, the works. There may be a special summer rate for these units. All these units overlook the pool. No matter where you stay, though, it's fun to get together with the other guests out on the lawn in the evenings when Bob and Marge often bring in entertainment. It may be a well-known island group like the No Ka Oi Four or just some friends or guests who like to sit around with a guitar and sing the old songs. In such a gracious setting, with such warmly hospitable people in charge, the coconut palms swaying in the evening wind and the sea lapping gently at your feet, it's hard to remember what you were planning to worry about. Write to Napili Surf, Napili Bay, Maui, HI 96761 (tel. 669-8002). An advance deposit is required.

If snorkeling is your passion, you're going to be very happy at **Honokeana Cove,** a lovely resort condominium located directly on a private, rocky cove where the snorkeling is tops. Swimmers need walk only about five minutes to a gentle sandy beach. Each of the condo's 38 units is close to the water and the pool oceanside; the grounds are also ideal for whale-spotting. We were told that a whale once gave birth at the entrance to the cove! When you're not busy watching whales, snorkeling, or admiring the grounds with its beautiful trees—we spotted a 160-year-old Kamani nut (or false almond) tree—you can be enjoying the view from your lanai and the comforts of your apartment, each individually owned and decorated. Rates can go up quite a bit here for the larger apartments and town houses; your best bets are the one-bedroom apartment for two people at $80 and the two-bedroom unit for four people at $108. An extra person is charged $9, regardless of age; minimum stay is five nights. No credit cards are accepted. The management is cordial, arranging a pupu party every Friday to bring the guests together. For reservations, write Honokeana Cove Resort Condominiums, 5255 Lower Honoapiilani Rd., Lahaina, Maui, HI 96761 or phone toll free 800/327-4947. From Canada, call collect: 800/669-6441.

Napili Shores, at 5315 Honapiilani Hwy., is a condominium on Napili Bay with a number of accommodations as hotel units. It is a delightful low-rise group of buildings with its own sundries store and an attractive Thai restaurant, Orient Express, on the premises. When you watch the sunset from the pool deck, you'd swear you could reach out and touch Molokai. From April 1 to December 19, studios are priced at $99, $110, and $121 double for garden area, ocean-view, and oceanfront respectively. There's a charge of $8 for an extra person, a maximum of three persons in the studios. Winter rates are $116, $127, and $138. The one-bedroom apartments, with a maximum of four persons, are $121 and $138 for garden area and $132 and $149 for ocean-view. Niceties include full kitchen, telephone, color TV, laundry, two freshwater pools (one with Jacuzzi), shuffleboard, croquet, and, of course, that idyllic Napili Beach bay. Free snorkeling lessons are given every Thursday, mai-tai parties are held on Friday, and breakfast is served in the Gazebo every morning. Write Napili Shores, 5315 Honoapiilani Hwy., Lahaina, HI 96761, or phone toll free 800/367-6046. The local phone is 669-8061.

Not a hotel, not a condo, but a country inn in the European manner is what the **Coconut Inn** calls itself. Just five minutes away from Kapalua, and sharing the glorious views and scenery of that lush resort, Coconut Inn is a two-story, 41-unit retreat on a hill overlooking Napili Bay. The inn is situated mauka—on the mountain side of the road—which means that you have to cross the street to get to the beach. But that is scarcely a hardship, especially since that location can help you realize substantial savings in this pricey western Maui area: rates of

$60 for a studio for two, $70 for a one-bedroom unit for three, and $75 for a loft big enough to sleep four; an additional person is charged $7.50. All the units are pretty, attractively decorated in the island style, not large, but comfortable enough, and with fully equipped kitchen and bath with both tub and shower. All have color TV, direct-dial phone, and twin or king-size beds. The different buildings on several ground levels are set in a beautiful tropical garden that shelters a pool, a hot tub, and a special "quiet area" surrounding a small pond and brook. You're welcome to cut flowers from the garden to brighten your room, or herbs from the tubs in the garden to brighten your cooking. Resident managers Laurie Ott and Paul Levesque are eager to please. And as if all this weren't enough, a continental breakfast of freshly baked breads, island fruit, and brewed Kona coffee is included in the price of your room. A lovely, moderately priced choice and very welcome. For reservations, write Coconut Inn, P.O. Box 10517, Napili, Maui, HI 96761, or phone toll free 800/367-8006. In Hawaii, call 669-5712.

IN HANA: Since Hana is one of the more remote, untouched areas in Maui (in all Hawaii, in fact), you might well want to spend a few days here just relaxing and being utterly away from civilization. But you'll have to look hard for reasonably priced accommodations, as there are very few places, and their rates are climbing every year. If you write well in advance (or happen to be lucky), you may be able to get a room.

The most inexpensive accommodations in Hana are available courtesy of the Division of State Parks. These are the housekeeping cabins in **Waianapanapa State Park,** a few trails away from a black-sand beach. The attractive bungalows are snuggled among the pandanus trees, some overlooking the ocean, and are supplied with bedding, towels, cooking utensils, dishes, electricity, and plenty of hot water. The only fly in the ointment may be mosquitoes: a reader who spent a hot August week here advised taking insect spray and repellent. Each two-room cabin has its own lanai, can sleep six persons, and rents for $5 to $10 per person a night, depending on the number of occupants. Rates may change soon. The maximum stay is five nights. For reservations, write to Division of State Parks, P.O. Box 1049, Wailuku, Maui, HI 96793 (tel. 244-4354).

For deluxe studio and one-bedroom apartments where you can prepare your own meals (almost a necessity in Hana, where there are very few eating places), the **Hana Kai-Maui Resort Condominiums** are a fine choice. The rates for the studios are $75 double, $6 for each additional person (no charge for children under 2). These studios, maximum of three persons, include a bath with bath-shower combination, dressing vanity, well-equipped kitchen, and private lanai—a spacious open room where you can enjoy the ocean just a few feet away. The two- and three-story buildings are scattered over a fairly wide area. One-bedroom apartments are $90 double, and can sleep up to five. (Rates are subject to change.) One ocean front building has a barbecue lanai for everyone to use. The beach is stony, black, and better for surfers than swimmers, but there is a mountain pool on the grounds. For reservations, write Hana Kai-Maui, P.O. Box 38, Hana, Maui, HI 96713 (tel. 248-8426).

Mrs. Alfreda Worst, the owner of **Heavenly Hana Inn,** has created a miniature Oriental garden-like atmosphere in her four units, each of which has two bedrooms, a light-cooking facility, TV, a dining area, bath, screened lanai, and its own private entrance. The inn is small but charming, and the inside door of each unit leads to the lobby and lounge. Outside, leading to the street, is a winding walkway through a screened Japanese gateway guarded by stone lions, symbols of good fortune. Rates are $75 double, $85 triple, $95 quad. An additional person is charged $8. Mrs. Worst also has two separate rental units away from the Inn: a small beach cottage on Hana Bay for one to four adults, at $70 to $90 per night, and a two-bedroom family cottage in town overlooking the ocean and Kauiki Hill, for families of up to seven. The latter, called Li'l Barn-by-Sea, rents for $60 to $100. Write to Mrs. Worst at P.O. Box 146, Hana, Maui, HI 96713 (tel. 248-8442).

Hana Bay Vacation Rentals started out eight years ago with Hana Bayview and Kauiki Cabin, both known to readers of this book. Now managers Stan and Suzanne Collins have branched out and are renting nine properties scattered throughout the Hana area, with a wide variety of locations, including on the beach, in and out of town, plus some in very secluded and private places. They offer apartments, cabins, and homes, with either one, two, or three bedrooms, with ocean and mountain views. All are fully equipped with the essentials for comfortable vacation living. They can accommodate as few as one, as many as 15 in a group, at prices ranging from $50 to $200 per night for two people, plus $10 to $20 for each additional person. Each cabin and home is private, and all have a full kitchen, and they even have cable TV. A half-million-dollar home sleeps six, at rates of $200 per night, three-day minimum. Stan and Suzanne can also arrange car rentals in Hana if you decide to fly direct; they will have you picked up at the airport. For reservations or more information, write or phone Hana Bay Vacation Rentals, P.O. Box 318, Hana, Maui, HI 96713 (tel. 248-7727).

Located conveniently close to Hana Bay and the stores are the **Aloha Cottages.** Each redwood cottage has two bedrooms (queen-size bed in one and twin beds in the other), a living room, complete kitchen, and bathroom. Each has a view of Hana Bay. The recently built cottages are well ventilated, comfortably furnished, and clean. All necessities are provided, including daily maid service. Rates are: $45 to $55 for two and $8 each additional person. Write to Mrs. F. Nakamura, P.O. Box 205, Hana, Maui, HI 96713 (tel. 248-8420). *Note:* See the Readers' Selections at the end of this chapter for several rave reviews for the Aloha Cottages.

2. Restaurants

IN KAHULUI: If you like buffet meals as much as we do, then you should know about the Rainbow buffet lunch served in the pretty main dining room and pool terrace of the **Maui Beach Hotel.** It's on daily from 11 a.m. to 2 p.m., and it's a real winner at $7.45 for all you can eat, $5.45 for kids. Local people like it because it includes many Oriental dishes not usually seen on buffet meals: we ourselves are partial to the tsukemono (pickled vegetable salad) and kamaboku (fishcakes). Also there for the taking—and still more taking—are those delicious Kula onions, Maui potato chips, lots of greens, sunflower seeds, rice, hot breads, three hot entrees daily (perhaps fried chicken, spaghetti and meatballs, beef stew), and rich desserts like chocolate pudding and cakes baked daily by the hotel's own bakery shop.

In and around the big shopping centers across the way from the hotels—the Kahului Shopping Center, the Maui Mall, and the Kaahumanu Shopping Center—are several places that are fine for a modest meal. The **Maui Mall** is fairly bursting with inexpensive places to eat. Sir Wilfred's Coffee, Tea, Tobacco, known for the best selection of pipes and cigars in Hawaii, has enlarged its popular espresso bar; now it's **Sir Wilfred's Caffè,** and while it still has something like two dozen espresso and cappuccino creations at modest prices ($1 to $2), it also serves breakfasts and light lunches, soups, home-baked croissants, Maui champagne, and fine wines by the glass at good prices. Decorated with island woods and featuring paintings by local artists, it's a very attractive and inviting spot: prices are low, and the quality of the food, atmosphere, and service is high. You can try their breakfast special of steamed eggs (steamed with "hot air" from the espresso machine, so that they are light and fluffy with no fats or oils being used), served on a whole-wheat croissant at $2.80 any time of the day. The chef's talents are shown to good advantage in his flavorful tarragon chicken salad, the Wailea pea salad (peas, celery, nuts, bacon, and sour cream) and in the unusual Boboli pizza. Also good are the lox and bagels and brie or other cheeses with French bread—all from $1.50 to $5. And the cappuccino comes in flavors—chocolate, coconut, almond, licorice, mint, orange, or maple —take your choice. A breakfast Happy Hour, 8:30 to 11 a.m., will cure morning-after blues with Bloody Marys at $1.25. And there's entertainment Friday evening until 9 p.m. Definitely the top choice at Maui Mall. Look for their new place at The Cannery in Lahaina.

If your taste runs to pizza and grog, and a dimly lit, Tiffany-shaded atmosphere with good sounds on the stereo is just your thing, visit **Applegate's Pizza Factory** at Maui Mall. There's often an all-you-can eat spaghetti special at $3.99, and live disco most nights. Pizzas run from $5.20 for small pies, and there are also plenty of burgers, from $4. Baskets of fried chicken or shrimp are around $6.95; and you can get salads and delicious sandwiches from $3.95 to $6.50. Dinner items go from $7.50 to $15.95, and include New York–cut steak. There's wine, beer, and drinks for those of age, and "Under Eighteen Drinks" like "Snoopy" and "Charlie Brown" (fruit-juice combinations) are available for the younger set to sip along with their supper.

Still hungry? **Restaurant Matsu** at Maui Mall is a sparkling clean little Japanese place for tasty sushi, noodles, fish, and luncheon or dinner plates ($3.20 to $4.20), with good Bento (take-out) specialties as well. Next door to it is **Siu's Chinese Kitchen,** with American-Chinese breakfasts, family-style Chinese dinners, and fast-food Chinese lunches, from 11 a.m. to 5 p.m. A lunch plate with three choices is $2.95, a tasty house noodles special, $3.95.

The homemade, super-rich ice creams at **Dave's Ice Cream** in Maui Mall are really good: so good, in fact, that *People* magazine recently voted Dave's coconut-and-macadamia-nut flavor as one of the top five exotic ice creams in the United States. Try it, or cast your vote for green tea, lichee, mango, or other far-out flavors. They're also at the Wharf in Lahaina.

Our personal favorite in the Kaahumanu Shopping Center is **Idini's Liquor and Deli** (the liquor store is in the back, the deli part in front). Flowered tablecloths and lots of plants and paintings set a relaxed mood for big Italian sandwiches, hot corned beef and veggie sandwiches, croissant sandwiches, most from $2.95 to $5.95. Homemade soups are $1.95 to $3.75. We like the $4.95 salad bar and the French bakery products—mushroom and spinach quiches, croissants, even New York–style cheesecake. Every night there's an Italian dinner special—it could be homemade lasagne, fettuccine, veal parmigiana, or chicken cacciatore—for $6.95 to $7.95, including salad bar. Beverages are both alcoholic and non-alcoholic—wine, beers, cocktails, espressos. Owner Bob Idini is planning to bring his successful concept to other islands soon. A pleasant stop.

You'll always find **Ma-Chan's Okazu-Ya** in the Kaahumanu Shopping Center packed; it's known for its local-style foods, low prices, quick service, and tasty meals. No matter what time of day you fancy having breakfast or lunch or dinner, anywhere from 6 in the morning until 8 or 9 in the evening (until 3 p.m. Sundays), you can get it here. Miso soup with salted cabbage, omelets with meat, loco mocos, hearty sandwiches, and lunch/dinner plates of teriyaki, spareribs, beef cutlet, roast beef, mahimahi, and the like ($3.25 to $6.25, the latter for New York steak) are available whenever. For dessert, try shave ice with ice cream and aduki beans, an island treat, 95¢. Note their take-out delicatessen for a huge variety of local ethnic foods; great for eating at one of the benches in the mall or for a picnic meal.

A local Japanese friend put us on to a special find for all you sushi lovers out there. He suggests you go to the Bento (take-out) section at **Shirokaya's,** the Japanese department store in Kaahumanu Center, order an assortment of sushi for about $3.95 to $4.95, and have yourself a picnic. The food—including futomakki, tekkamaki, and chirashi—is scrumptious (other Japanese dishes are also available), and the price about half of what it would cost to have sushi in a restaurant.

Like to read with your meal? Or play Scrabble? Or listen to classical music? Make your way to Maui's favorite coffeehouse, **The Artful Dodger's Feed 'n' Read,** at 55 Kaahumanu Ave., in the Old Kahului Store. There's an extensive selection of new and used books here (see the next chapter), and a limited, but tasty food menu: quiches, pizzas, salads, and sandwiches from The Bakery in Lahaina (see ahead), all under $4; and a variety of coffee drinks (cappuccino, caffe latte, café mocha, etc.) from 75¢ to $1.85. In the same mini-mall is a new branch of the old Kihei standby, Gaspare's Place and Pizza (see ahead, under Kihei Restaurants), serving good sandwiches, pizzas, and hot entrees; modest prices.

Those who have developed a taste for Hawaiian food should head for Puunene Avenue, on the other side of the Kahului Shopping Center, and join the local folks at the **Aloha Restaurant.** The place is quite plain, and you're apt to be the only tourists there, but it's air-conditioned and comfortable, and the menu offers more than a dozen dinners, from $3.50 (for omelets, rice, and salad), none more than $7.50. You can have a dinner of kalua pig, lomi salmon, and poi (all traditional luau ingredients), or make up your own, from a large list of à la carte dishes. It's fun to come on a Sunday, between 11 a.m. and 9:30 p.m., when there's a Hawaiian buffet, $8.95 for adults, $5 for children. Inexpensive American meals ($3.50 to $5) and sandwiches, too, and plenty of beer and harder drinks at the bar are reasonably priced. Lunch hours are 11 a.m. until 2 p.m., dinner from 5 until 9 p.m. daily.

Maui has long needed a quality, local fast-food Mexican restaurant, and **Taco Lei Maui,** 100 Kamehameha Ave. (near Safeway), is definitely it. It's spacious and pretty, with plenty of window seats, and each tile table has an orchid plant. The secret ingredients here are the Maui beef, the Maui-grown lettuce, tomatoes, and onions, and the tortillas made on Maui. Put them all together and you get great burritos, tacos, nachos, salads, and combination plates, from $1.19 to $3.49, the latter price for the tasty taco salad ólei. Our favorites here are the nacho plates at $3.29, more than ample for one and big enough for two nottoo-hungry eaters to share. Draft beer is available by the glass and pitcher; there is also wine by the glass and margaritas. A good family choice, offering the kind of value you associate with restaurants charging much more. There is a smaller location in Kaahumanu Center.

Attractive, moderately priced Chinese restaurants are hard to find on Maui, so praise be for **Ming Yuen** at 162 Alamaha St., in the Kahului Light Industrial Park, off Hwy. 380. The food here just gets better all the time, and the service, by many long-time employees, provides a "family feeling." The specials here are authentic Cantonese and the spicier Szechuan cuisine. We always like to start off with crispy wonton and Chinese spring rolls, $3.95 and $4.75. The menu here offers a very wide choice of entrees, like Mongolian beef, lemon chicken, mu shu pork (a personal favorite), and Hunan beef, all about $5.50 to $8.50. Should you prefer something spicier, choose the hot Szechuan eggplant, $6.25, one of their excellent vegetarian dishes. The desserts here are a little different: we like the Mandarin mousse and cheesecake, Ming Yuen serves lunch all day, beginning at 11:30 a.m.; dinner is on from 5 to 9 p.m. seven days a week. Reservations requested (tel. 871-7787).

IN WAILUKU: Local-style food served in hearty portions, at old-fashioned prices, and in gracious surroundings: that's the combination that made **Chums,** 1900 Main St. (tel. 871-7787), a favorite right from the start. The same family that runs Ming Yuen have put their creativity to work here and come up with another winner, so pretty with koa-wood booths, many plants, and old, classic posters on the walls, a great place for "chums" to hang out. And the food is delicious, from the homemade oxtail soup with grated ginger, two scoops of rice and Chinese parsley, practically a meal in itself ($4.25); to the burgers and sandwiches ($3.50 to $4.75); the Hawaiian-special plate meals (around $5); and the broiler specialties ($5.75 to $6.95). Every day the chef comes up with a few delicious specialties: perhaps poached mahimahi with white wine and mushroom sauce, plus rice or macaroni salad, and veggies at $5.50; a filet mignon and snow crab leg combination with the same accompaniments, at $7.50; broiled ono with garden vegetables, and lemon herb butter, plus accompaniments, for $6.50. As you can see, prices like this went out of style years ago! Chums opens at 6:30 a.m. for hearty breakfasts served until 11 a.m., (french toast made of Portuguese sweet bread stuffed with fruit jam, fried rice and egg, Hawaiian chop steak are favorites), and then serves the regular menu all day long to 11 p.m., to midnight weekends.

Lunch at **Naokee's Restaurant,** at 1792 Main St. (tel. 244-9444), is a longtime budget tradition in Wailuku. Naokee's is a modern, attractive three-level restaurant, with steakhouse decor, a bar, table service, and a very cozy feeling about it. At night, most steak and fish dinners begin at $8.75 and go up, but lunch is another story, and that's where we come in. That's when just about everything on the menu goes for $5 and under—and that includes broiled filet of fish, sirloin butt, Korean barbecue, and chopped steak, all served with rice, vegetables, and a little kim chee on the side. The dinner prices are not bad, considering that everything is served with rice, soup, salad, a basket of delicious garlic bread, and beverage, and that there are a few entrees in the lower price categories—but you can't beat lunch. There's also a special New York–cut steak served lunch or dinnertime for $6.95. Naokee's is just past the bridge on the right, as you head for Wailuku from Kahului. Lunch is from 11 a.m. to 2 p.m., dinner from 5:30 to 9 or 9:30 p.m. every day.

Local people put us on to **Archie's,** at 1440 Lower Main St. (tel. 244-9401), and we're glad they did. It's a Japanese restaurant, with just a touch of the Orient in the fans lining the walls; otherwise, it's plain but pleasant enough, with orange booths and green chairs, Formica-wooden tables, and wood paneling. Dinners are a real bargain: along with the soup, pickled vegetables, rice, and tea that are mandatory for any Japanese meal, come such main courses as chicken tofu, fish nitsuke, teryaki chicken, and shrimp tempura, from $4 to $8. Very popular at both lunch and dinner—for around $4—is the nabeyaki udon: that's vegetables, chicken, fishcakes, and shrimp tempura. And also at lunchtime, the tempura udon at $4.20 is big enough to make a meal one. Open Monday to Saturday from 10:30 a.m. to 2 p.m. and 5 to 8:30 p.m. Closed Sunday.

Not far from Archie's, at 1063 E. Lower Main St. (tel. 242-9630), is another Japanese restaurant, **Tokyo Tei,** that's also a big favorite with the local people. Again, the atmosphere is simple and pleasant, the quality of the food high, and the prices easy to take. Lunch and dinner meals include rice, miso soup, and pickled vegetables along with such entrees as teryaki pork, beef sukiyaki, and sashimi, all priced between $4.25 and $7.50. You'll know why the restaurant is famous for its tempura dishes once you bite into the shrimp tempura—five large, flavorful shrimp, served with rice and soup, along with the traditional Japanese accompaniments. And their teishoko combination plates, $6.50 to $8, are very popular. This is a nice place for families, as children are treated graciously here. Lunch is served form 11 a.m. to 1:30 p.m., when there are a number of specials from $3.75 to $4.50; dinner is from 5 to 8:30 p.m.

PAIA AND ENVIRONS: Paia is one of our favorite little towns—full of seekers from everywhere who've found the natural lifestyle they were looking for in these Hawaiian uplands. Since the area is only a 15-minute drive from Kahului, at the beginning of the road to Hana and just past the cutoff to Rte. 37 (the Haleakala Hwy.), a visit to the restaurants here can be worked into almost any itinerary.

Our favorite place in Paia—at 89 Hana Hwy.—is **Dillon's Restaurant** (tel. 579-9113), which calls itself "a tropical hideaway," and that's just what it is. The bamboo walls, tropical decor, outdoor garden, and orchid paintings on the wall are all the art and craft of Casimir (Charles Powell), an island painter; the inspired menu is the work of his wife, Nancy Powell. The Powells are transplanted New Yorkers who have brought a touch of both sophistication and hominess to their restaurant, and the local people and visitors have responded enthusiastically. Travelers on their way to Hana often stop by between 7 and 8 a.m. for the eggs Benedict special at $4.95 ($7.95 other times), french toast with Kahlúa, or those great fresh banana pancakes with compote syrup. The kitchen and bar are open every day for breakfast, lunch, and dinner, with a continuous pupu menu available until closing. There is always a wonderful quiche with salad, a superb frittata (an open-faced vegetable omelet topped with hollandaise), the "best burgers you ever ate" (could well be, with fresh Maui onion, crispy french fries, kosher dill pickle), and the Coral and Jade sandwich (veggies, onion, avocado, and cheese on whole-wheat bread), which comes with french fries and a slice of orange; all are reasonably priced, and portions are very large. New England–style clam chowder, made from scratch, is a welcome treat out here in mid-Pacific. For a more extensive meal, you might have a mahimahi lunch at $8.95 or a complete mahimahi dinner at $13.95; dinners include a choice of soup or salad, fresh garden vegetables, rice or fries, and hot french bread. Dillon's house pasta is a caloric wonder: artichoke, spinach, and semolina homemade pasta generously sautéed in butter, mushrooms, fresh cream, garlic, basil, and parmesan cheese, $11.95 for the complete dinner. There's New York steak, too, and steak and pasta combinations. Also very popular is the "Lite Dining" meal, which includes meat or vegetarian lasagne, and "really Italian" spaghetti with meatballs, $7.95. Desserts are a must: Nancy brought her recipe for New York–style cheesecake and offers a blue-ribbon chocolate layer cake, too. Dillon's is a homey place, homey enough, Nancy advises to make whatever you want. Everything is cooked to order here, so sit back and sip one of the fresh tropical fruit drinks of the day, while your meal is being prepared; the last time we were there it was passion-fruit daiquiri! This food is worth waiting for.

If you need a picnic lunch for your trip to Haleakala or Hana, the place to stock up is **Pic-nics** on Baldwin Avenue right in Paia (you'll recognize it by a bright orange-and-yellow awning), a cheerful, clean, Formica-table-and-benches place, which is known all over the area for its sandwiches: especially the spinach-nut burgers, served on whole-wheat sesame buns, and piled high with lettuce, tomato, sprouts, and dressing; they are $3.35 and terrific. They also serve a filet of mahimahi for just $4.35. Everything is delicious, since they use, as much as possible, only freshly grown local produce and organically raised island beef. The very popular excursion lunches include sandwiches, Maui potato chips, salads, seasonal fruits, homemade cookies and desserts, plus many other basket stuffers, and begin at $6.95. No need to call ahead: your order will be prepared quickly. Pic-nics also features cappuccino, freshly baked breakfast pastries, and fruit pies for breakfast while you're waiting for your order. Great. Open daily from 7:30 a.m. to 6:30 p.m.

EN ROUTE TO HALEAKALA: Since there is no food to be had in Haleakala National Park, you might want to eat on your way to—or from—the crater. Two places in Pukalani, about halfway between Kahului and the park entrance, do very nicely. Your best bet for an inexpensive snack is **Bullock's of Hawaii,** a snack shop where you get delicious hamburgers, cheeseburgers, "moonburgers" (a meal in themselves), from $1.75 to $3.25. Be sure to try the sensational shakes, a combination of nectars, juices, and ice cream; we loved the guava, but they also have pineapple, mocha, and coffee, each $2.50. Full breakfasts, complete with coffee, juice, toast, rice, and upcountry jumbo eggs delivered fresh daily, range from $2.75 to $5.95, for steak and eggs. Open daily from 7:30 a.m. to 9:30 p.m.

For a special treat after the high of the volcano, come gradually down to earth with dinner at **Kula Lodge** (tel. 878-1535), on the slopes of Haleakala in the delightful mountain town of Kula. This is a charming country inn, where you can gather around the fireplace for cocktails and watch the sun go down over the mountains. You might have soup or Caesar salad to begin, perhaps escargots or stuffed potato skins; then on to such main courses as the chef's pasta of the week, fresh fish of the day, sesame chicken, or shrimp scampi; most dishes run between $9.50 and $13.95, and are served with vegetables, potato, or rice of the day. Our favorite dessert here: fresh strawberries dipped in chocolate with Grand Marnier, $4.50, perfect accompanied by one of the house's imaginative espresso drinks, with or without alcohol. There are also daily lunch specials, sandwiches, and breakfasts too. Kula Lodge serves dinner Friday, Saturday, and Sunday from 5:30 to 9 p.m., lunch daily until 3 p.m., breakfast from 7 to 11:30 a.m.

Another enjoyable place to eat is in nearby Makawao, a few miles off your route to Haleakala, but worth making a little detour for; turn right at Pukalani. Our favorite restaurant in this quaint little cowboy town is **Polli's Cantina,** a cute little place at 1202 Makawao Ave. (tel. 572-7808), at the corner of Olinda Street, which specializes in "cold beer and hot food." The decor is Mexican, the clientele is local, the music is loud, and the food is very tasty. Taco salad is $5.50; cheese enchiladas, $3; a bowl of chili, $4. Fresh fish, steak, and lobster are available, too. We love their desserts, especially the buñuelos: Mexican pastries topped with vanilla ice cream, drizzled hot pure maple syrup, and cinnamon, $3.50. *Muy bueno!* Polli's is open daily from 11:30 a.m. to midnight, with live entertainment on Thursday, Friday, and Saturday evenings, and on Sunday afternoons; Happy Hour is from 2:30 to 5:30 p.m.; and Sunday brunch is on from 10:30 a.m. to 2 p.m. There's another great Polli's—Polli's on the Beach—in the Kihei area (see below).

If you'd just like to pick up some sandwiches or snacks, check out the attractive deli section of the **Rodeo General Store** at 3661 Baldwin Ave., which receives early-morning bakery deliveries of plain and stuffed fresh croissants. Sandwiches start around $3.50; there is also teri chicken. The store is known for a great selection of wine at very reasonable prices.

IN KIHEI AND WAILEA: Remember the name **Azeka's Place:** this lively shopping center is a good spot for budget watchers to get a good meal in Kihei. In addition to pancakes, omelets, waffles, burgers, and such, the **International**

House of Pancakes offers some 20 dinner specialties from $5.95 to $10.95—and these include breast of chicken parmigiana, country-fried steak, roast pork, London broil, and delicious spit-roasted chicken. The price of the entree includes green salad or soup of the day, natural-cut fried or other potatoes, steamed vegetables, and dinner rolls with whipped butter. And dinner, lunch, or breakfast is available anytime this place is open, which means from Sunday through Thursday, 6 a.m. to midnight, Friday and Saturday 6 a.m. to 2 a.m. The high-ceilinged dining room has comfortable booths and a pleasant atmosphere.

Barbecue buffs will have a good time at **Sailmaker's Barbecue Rib House,** in the same Azeka Place shopping center (tel. 879-4446). Baby back pork ribs, beef ribs and chicken, featured in a number of styles (sweet and sour, Cajun, Texas, Chinese) are priced from $6.95 to $7.95 at lunch, from $10.95 to $14.95 at dinner. At dinner, salad bar or soup, vegetable, and corn bread come along with the tasty entrees. Budget lunch specials are offered every day for either $3.95 or $4.95 (such as teriyaki burger, beef stir fry, tuna-melt sandwich), and well-priced Early Bird specials from 4 to 6 p.m. nightly; $6.95 to $7.95 for the likes of hickory-smoked chicken, New York steak, mahimahi and veggie stir fry, or Hawaiian chicken. And there are some imaginative pupus to begin with, like seafood-stuffed mushrooms, lemon-marinated shrimp, sashimi, potato skins ($4.25 to $5.95); lots of ice-cream desserts; and a full list of imported beers, coffees, and alcoholic ice-cream drinks. Sailmaker's serves breakfast from 7 to 11:30 a.m., lunch from 11:30 a.m. to 5 p.m., dinner from 5 to 11 p.m. The cocktail lounge is open all day and evening.

Tucked away in a corner of Azeka's Place is the new **Island Deli,** where a sign proclaims: "Confucius say, 'Man with hungry belly must eat at Deli'." Well, you won't be hungry for long if you join the local folks at this bright and tidy little place. There's an all-you-can eat soup and salad bar that looks fresh and inviting, at $4.95, and a variety of meat sandwiches, from $3.15 to $4.25, generously laden with cheese, tomatoes, lettuce or sprouts, onion, chips, celery, carrot sticks, and pickles, on a choice of good breads. We especially like their specialty sandwiches (have one on either bread or a croissant), like lox and bagel or island chicken salad, made with cheese, pineapple, and walnuts, $4.15 to $4.95. Open from 7 a.m. to 9 p.m. every day.

Old Maui hands will remember **La Familia,** a name synonymous with Mexican food for over ten years in Wailuku. La Familia Wailuku has closed now, but in its place have sprouted two new La Familias—one in Kihei and another at Kaanapali Beach. The Kihei La Familia, in Kai Nani Village at Kamaole Beach Park (tel. 879-8824), is one of the happiest spots in Kihei; once the 2 to 6 p.m. Happy Hour gets under way and they start pouring those frosty margaritas for $1.25, the large, circular tiled bar and its lanai look to be the "in" place in town for a smart young set. Dinner service starts at 4 p.m. and continues to 10 p.m. Come around sunset time and you're in for a special treat: the dining room is glassed in on three sides, affording a splendid view of the ocean. You might even catch a view of humpback whales. Mexican specialties are reasonably priced, from $6.99 to $8.95 for such dishes as steak ranchero, Judy's sour cream enchiladas, crab tostada, and chimichangas. Combination plates are $8.95. Steak and seafood entrees go from $9.95 to $12.95. Desserts include a delectable mud pie (cookie crust topped with ice cream, fudge sauce, and whipped cream). Beverages include imported Mexican and domestic beers, 32-ounce margaritas, and "Maui Wowies." La Familia is open every day and serves cocktails until midnight. Every Aloha Friday, Frosty Margaritas are 99¢ from 2 to 6 p.m. and again, from 10 p.m. to midnight.

In the same Kai Nani Village, **Kihei Prime Rib House** (tel. 879-1954) has long been an island favorite. It's a bit high for our budget, but arrive early—

between 5 and 6:30 p.m.—and enjoy their Early Bird special: prime rib dinner or fresh island fish at $9.95. Their salad bar, included with all dinners, uses only locally grown fruits and vegetables, and can be enjoyed alone at $8.95. Ocean-view dining and the work of internationally known artists on the walls adds to the warmth and charm.

You may remember Polli's Mexican Restaurant from upcountry Maka-wao; you'll be even happier to find the same good food and good drinks here in a perfectly wonderful location at Kihei, at the Kealia Beach Center, 101 N. Kihei Rd., at the entrance to Kihei (tel. 879-5275). **Polli's on the Beach** has tall, beamed ceilings, wooden tables, straw chairs, tile floor, plants, and piñatas; best of all is its huge dining lanai with umbrellaed tables that juts right out over the beach, so that you feel *that* close to the water. What a spot for sunset watching, whale watching, people watching, or just sitting in perfect contentment as you sip your margaritas and munch on delicious Mexican food with an island flair! Everything is made from scratch each day by Polli, who combines fresh Maui ingredients with spices and chiles from her family in Arizona. The *entremesas* (appetizers) are a bit unusual here: Mexican pizza and an invention called baked bajas—that's potato shells filled with taco, bean, or cheese dips at $5, and a great way to start a meal. Most combination plates are $7.50 to $8.50 (there are tofu enchiladas for vegetarian types); à la carte entrees average about $3 to $4. Try the house dressing with your salad; it's an unusual blend of cashews and garlic. Steak, lobster, and fresh fish are also featured, at higher prices. Los niños can have their own plates at $5. Good desserts include buñuelos and amaretto cheesecake. Polli's is open every day, serving lunch between 9:30 a.m. and 2:30 p.m., dinner from 5 to 10 p.m., drinks throughout the day. Happy Hour is on from 2:30 p.m. to 5 p.m., and there's Sunday brunch, from 10:30 a.m. to 5 p.m. Come by on a Thursday, Friday, Saturday, or Sunday night and enjoy some live entertainment, too.

Gaspare's Place and Pizza, in the Island Surf Building at 1993 S. Kihei Rd. (tel. 879-8881), always has something special for the budget diner. Until 11 a.m. there are breakfast specials: two eggs, toast, and jelly for $1.25, two eggs plus various meats for $2.25. Then at lunchtime, from 11 a.m. to 2 p.m., daily specials and lighter portions of the dinner entrees, served with a salad. Plate lunches are available from 11 a.m. to 4 p.m. Dinner offers such Italian favorites as spaghetti, fettuccine, lasagne, and broasted chicken, all served with salad bar and garlic bread, from $6.50 to $8.25. There are always good pizza pies (made from an old family recipe), and sandwiches served hot from the oven, with french fries: submarines, meatballs, burgers, vegetarian submarines, most under $5. There are both booths and tables here, a cocktail lounge and bar, and a casual mood. Open Tuesday through Saturday until midnight. Note that there's a newer Gaspare's in the Old Kahului Store in Kahului town, a historic Kahului building converted into a mini-shopping complex, about three minutes from the airport at 55 Kaahumanu Ave. The menu is the same at both locations, and both offer free delivery to hotels and condos.

You'll enjoy the Italian café atmosphere at **Rainbow Pasta & Pizza** in the Rainbow Mall at 2439 S. Kihei Rd. (tel. 879-0080)—and the food is *delicioso* too. Prices are reasonable. In addition to excellent pizzas (from $6.95, regular), they have tasty specialties like calzone (both meat-filled and vegetarian), pizza, potato skins, a salad bar, and pastas, in a create-your-own pasta format in which you choose both noodles and sauce, all priced from $3.25 to $11.95. From 11 a.m. to 3 p.m., there is a $4.95 luncheon special; and from 5 to 9 p.m., there is a nightly dinner special at $7.95, featuring Italian dishes. Happy Hour is from 2 to 5 p.m. daily. Open every day from 11 a.m. to midnight.

People appreciate good value when they see it, and that's why **Kihei Seas,** upstairs at the same Rainbow Mall, 2439 S. Kihei Rd. (tel. 879-5600), is kept busy every night. The food is top quality, the atmosphere is pleasant and cozy if not spectacular, and value for the dollar is very good. It's especially good if you come for one of the Early Bird specials served from 5 to 7 p.m.; along with a turn or two at the fabulous, 44-item salad bar, you get stuffed baked potato or Polynesian rice and freshly baked rolls and butter to go with your entree of prime rib, catch of the day, chicken tempura, petite New York steak, or top sirloin and lobster tail, $8.75 to $9.95. If you come for the Twilight Diners special, served from 5 to 10 p.m., you'll still be doing well, with sirloin and lobster tail, fisherman's platter, or sweet-and-sour shrimp, with all of the above accompaniments, at $11.95. In fact, you can't go wrong here anytime: the regular menu tends mostly to seafood and steak, with such house specialties as prime ribs, bouillabaisse, and lobster tempura; most entrees are around $10.95 to $13.95. Dinner is served every night from 5 to 10 p.m., and there's entertainment and dancing nightly. Reservations advised.

Wailea, just beyond the Kihei area, is wealthy condo country, and the home of three stunning hotels, the Maui Inter-Continental Wailea, the Stouffer Wailea Beach Resort, and the Maui Prince. You might want to have a meal at the Lanai Terrace at the Maui Inter-Continental Wailea; it's a beautiful oceanfront room with panoramic views of the Pacific and nearby islands. Best buys are the Sunset Special—a complete prime rib dinner for $11.50 and the Early Bird Specials for $10 and under, based on whatever ingredients the Executive Chef finds at a reasonable price for the best quality. Both are served between 5 and 6 p.m. There's also an attractive luncheon buffet every day between 11:30 a.m. and 2:30 p.m., for $10.25.

When we get rich, we're going to have all our meals at Raffles at the Stouffer Wailea Beach Resort. Definitely. Until that happy day, however, it's fun to play rich by having a "Big Splurge" Sunday Champagne Brunch in this lovely dining room, six-time winner of the coveted Travel Holiday Award. Brunch is priced at $21.50 for adults, $10.75 for children under 12, and is considered to be the most elaborate Sunday Champagne Brunch on Maui, which is perhaps a bit of an understatement. Consider just a few of the delights on the table: omelets made to order, eggs Benedict, gravlox marinated in dill sauce, lox and bagels, sushi, rack of lamb, prime roast beef, homemade breads and rolls, teriyaki beef with vegetables, crab salad in avocado, shrimp salad in artichoke hearts, several pastas, oriental vegetable salad, green salads of arugula, raddicio, and spinach, and the world's most incredible pancake dish: Pancakes Romanoff—thin pancakes layered with fresh raspberry puree, topped with meringue, with strawberry sauce for ladling! As if all this weren't enough, there's an absolutely staggering dessert table, laden with chocolate-mousse pies, macadamia-nut pies, cheese cakes, blueberry strudels, huge containers of ice cream—well, you get the idea. You can come for this feast as early as 9 a.m. and stay until 2 p.m., if you like, or any portion in between. Of course, the glasses of champagne and the cups of steaming coffee are bottomless. Reservations are a must: 879-4900.

Any day of the week—but especially on Wednesday at noon when there's an SRO fashion show by Judges Beyond the Reef—it's fun to come back to the Wailea Beach Resort for a light meal at the **Maui Onion.** This semi-open poolside spot is a little high for our budget (salads and sandwiches around $7 and $8), but do, at least, try their specialty: Maui Onion Rings. They take those famous sweet Kula onions (grown only on the slopes of Haleakala), dunk them in a rich egg batter, dust them with oriental "Panko" tempura flour and deep fry them crisp and golden, $3.75 and a treat. Maui Onion serves only between 11 a.m. and 6 p.m. daily.

Remember **Ed and Don's** at the Wailea Shopping Center for a pleasant snack or lunch in this area: they have gourmet sandwiches of pastrami, turkey, curried chicken salad, ham, etc., from $2.85 to $4.25, and lots of good ice creams. Open from 9:30 a.m. to 4 p.m. only.

IN LAHAINA: Lahaina's restaurants reflect its easy, relaxed approach to living. The food is not gourmet, but the **Harpooner's Lanai** of the Pioneer Inn is always fun. At one of the pretty tables on the terrace across from the boat landing, you might order a sandwich lunch—mahimahi burger, Reuben on Russian rye, or teriyaki steak, from $4.65 to $5.50—all served with potato salad or french fries. A big bowl of seafood chowder is $1.95. Lunch is served only until 2:30 p.m. For breakfast, you get pineapple or guava juice, toast with butter and jelly, and all the coffee you desire for $1.95, wiki wiki. Your fellow diners are likely to include local people, the boating set, tourists, and perhaps a lone beachcomber.

For dinner at the Pioneer Inn you move onto the **South Seas Patio** (tel. 661-3636) for a broil-your-own steak, ground beef, or mahimahi treat on the open grill. The price of your entree, from $6.95 to $14.95, includes all you can eat at the salad bar and baked barbecued beans. The **Snug Harbor Restaurant** here has four complete dinners—eggplant and zucchini, deep-fried chicken, rib bones, and pork chops, from $7.95 to $10.95, including salad bar, baked beans, vegetable, rice or potatoes, plus fresh catch of the day and other higher-priced entrees.

You'll think you've stepped back to the 50s, or even the 40s, when you eat at **Happy Days, Café of Yesterday,** in the Lahaina Marketplace (tel. 667-6994). And well you might have. The place looks like an old-fashioned malt shop, complete with a soda fountain behind the counter, seven seats at the counter itself where you could order a malted or a cherry Coke or a hot fudge sundae, and a large dining room open to the air on both sides. Old movie posters (remember Gary Cooper in *Friendly Persuasion?*), antique sheet music, advertising slogans, record albums of Elvis, and such memorabilia provide the decor. And the food is the same as they used to serve at the corner malt shop way back when; they specialize in burgers, hash browns, hot dogs—but with a difference. The difference is that they emphasize quality, grinding all their own meat, baking their own hot-dog and hamburger buns and bread for sandwiches. Breakfast, served from 7 to 11 a.m., features biscuits and gravy (an old midwest tradition) at $1.65; terrific old-fashioned (not Belgian) waffles baked with fresh buttermilk every morning ($2.95); three-egg ranch omelets ($3.95 to $5.95), made the way the Toddle House Coffee Shops used to make those "Humpty Dumpty" omelets back in the 30s. Then there's lunch and dinner, served continuously from 11 a.m. to 10 p.m., when you can have burgers from $3.95, hot dogs from $2.50, hearty sandwiches, homemade soups, good salads, homemade chicken pot pie ($4.75), and yummy hashed brown potatoes. Everything is made from scratch, including the flaky crust of the all-American apple pie (they also have Kentucky pecan and macadamia-nut and blackberry pies—ummm!). The low prices, the mood, and the good, fresh food, have made Happy Days just as popular with locals as with tourists; both have been keeping it humming since the doors first opened in mid-1986. Looks like Californians Ken and Donna Blasingham, who've been dreaming about opening a place like this for a number of years, have come up with a winner.

Everybody seems to like **Longhi's,** 888 Front St. (tel. 667-2288), an on-the-sidewalk, across-from-the-ocean café where the Italian-accented specialties are fresh and luscious, the mood convivial (lots of plants, koa tables, backgammon tables, a lively bar, and friendly service), and the desserts—and sunsets—something to write home about. Sit upstairs or downstairs—the rooms are similar, but there's an even better ocean view upstairs. Owner Bob Longhi goes to

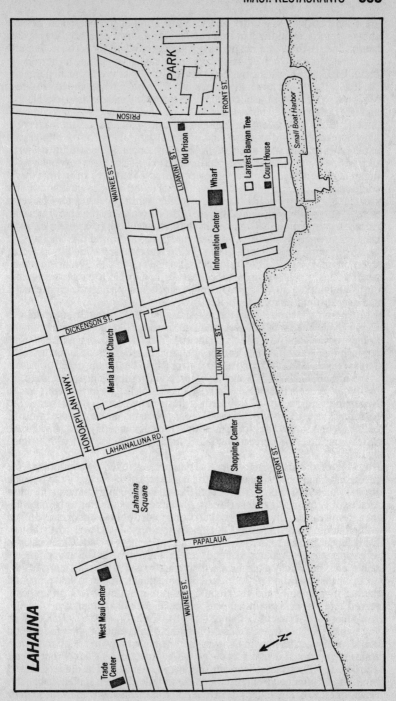

great lengths (like New York and Italy) to bring in the finest and freshest cheeses, produce, and Italian cold cuts, makes his own pastas, bakes his own breads and pastries, and maintains a gourmet standard throughout. Because everything depends on freshness, the menu is always verbal: the night we were there, linguine with a delicious pesto sauce was $10, as was eggplant parmigiana. It was $14 for shrimps and scallops, $15 for pasta scampi, and $19 for fresh Maui fish. It's easy for the bill to climb here since the entrees are served alone, and side dishes can add up (salad at $3.50, vegetables, etc.), so our recommendation is either to go all out and consider this a big splurge, or tell the waiter how much money you want to spend, and let him plan the menu for you. It's wise to eat lightly and save your strength, in fact, for Longhi's otherworldly desserts; they've become something of a legend around town, since there have been 1,000 different ones in the restaurant's nine-year history. You never know what they'll come up with, but you might sample, as five of us did, an incredible strawberry shortcake, a superb macadamia-nut pie (better than any pecan pie we had ever tasted), an unusual chocolate cake pie (chocolate cake between pie crusts with custard between the layers), a mouthwatering mango-topped cheesecake, and a cooling strawberry mousse. All desserts are priced at $4, and they are huge, so be sure to bring a friend to help you. There's an extensive wine list, including selections that you can order by the glass. Longhi's opens at 7:30 a.m. for breakfast (frittatas, omelets, homemade coffeecake, and strudel), and serves continuously till about 10 p.m. or later. On Friday and Saturday nights there's live music and dancing until 1 a.m.

Around the corner from the restaurant, at 930 Wainee St., next door to Kaiser Clinic, is **Longhi's Pizzeria and Delicatessen,** offering deli favorites in the Longhi's style: good hot and cold sandwiches at about $4.50, pizzas from $7 for a ten-inch individual pie, and Longhi's delicious pastries, breads, and desserts. Tables outside come and go; plan on this for a take-out for the beach or picnic.

Mr. Sub, long one of Honolulu's most popular submarine shops, is repeating its quality act in Lahaina. It's at 129 Lahainaluna Rd. (near Front St., next to Nagamine Camera), with wonderfully fresh ingredients, good sesame-seed rolls, quick service, and low prices. This one is takeout only, so choose from one of 27 different sandwiches (or create your own combination), and head for the beach or a picnic. Prices are around $2.50 for a half, under $5 for a whole. Open daily.

One of the most atmospheric restaurants in Lahaina, overlooking the ocean and handsomely done in South Seas beachcomber style, is the **Lahaina Broiler** (tel. 661-3111), just opposite the Lahaina Shopping Center at the intersection of Front and Papalua Streets. Dinner entrees are apt to be high (although you can usually get chicken curry or breaded pork chops or char-broiled ground sirloin from $7.95 to $9), but lunch is inexpensive and well worth the tab. Daily lunch specials for between $5.75 and $6.25 might include Cajun chicken or shrimp, sautéed scallops, seafood Creole, and the mahimahi almond sherry sandwich is practically a meal in itself, at market price. Breakfast starts at 7:30 a.m., lunch is on from 11:30 a.m. to 2:30 p.m., dinner from 6 to 9:30 p.m., and the bar swings until midnight. Should you run into a huge tour group being served here, as occasionally happens, better come back another day.

Moose McGillycuddy's Pub & Café, 844 Front St. (tel. 667-7758), which you may remember from Waikiki, offers the same brand of good food, good booze, and good fun here in Lahaina. It's one flight up, with a big bar, a lively atmosphere, and some tables set out on the lanai overlooking busy Front Street. The Moose is known as a "bargain" in pricey Lahaina, and its dinners, served from 5 p.m., offer good value: entrees like teriyaki chicken, stuffed mahimahi, New York steak, range in price from $7.50 to $11.95, and come with soup or salad, baked potato or rice or fries, and hot bread. Then there are other favorites like the giant taco salad at $6.50, Mexican specialties like sizzling beef or chicken fajitas at $7.95, a variety of burgers like the University Burger ("highly ranked bacon and intelligent cheddar"), from $3.95 to $6.95. Three-egg omelets are served with fresh fruit and Texas toast, up until 5 p.m. Looking for something different in a sandwich? How about grilled mahimahi filet with banana, on whole wheat, for around $6.25. The Moose's hot 'n' juicy pizzas (from $6.95 small) are good; so are salads and munchies like hot potato skins and deep-fried zucchini. Margaritas and daiquiris are the big booze selections here, along with coffee drinks, Hawaiian exotics, and way-out house specialties. The Moose's breakfast specials are considered the best deals in Lahaina: the Early Bird, served from 7:30 to 9:30 a.m., $2.29 for two eggs, bacon, toast, and orange juice; and the Beggar's Banquet, $2.89 for three eggs any style, with potatoes or rice, Texas toast, and fresh fruit garnish. Open from 6:30 a.m. until late, late.

Downstairs from the Moose, in the same Mariner's Alley arcade, a few sidewalk tables outside, an espresso machine within, and a sparkling, tile-floor atmosphere will make you think you're in Italy—well, at least you're at **Marco's Gelato d'Italia Ristorante,** 844 Front St. (tel. 661-8877), which has gained a reputation for some of the best Italian food on Maui. From noon to 2:30 p.m., you can have a light lunch here, which might consist of a tasty Italian salad (spinach, pasta, antipasto), from $4.50 to $5.25; specialties like grilled chicken and fish and pastas, $5.75 to $8.50; or tempting calzone (Italian turnovers). We're partial to Marco's special, which is filled with prosciutto, ricotta, mozzarella, and mushrooms, $6.50. Dinner, served from 5:30 to 10 p.m. seven days, offers some meat and seafood dishes in the $11.50 to $18 range, but there are excellent pastas from $8.25 to $10.50, and those delicious calzone, now $8.25. Both lunch and dinner specials are usually offered. There's a full bar, wine and beer are at the ready, and so is cappuccino. And don't miss the gelato, that lovely low-fat Italian ice cream: gelato and sorbetto are made fresh on the premises, and truly delicious. This is quality food at a fair price for expensive Lahaina. A local friend swears it's the best food on Front Street!

Fujiyama, in the Lahaina Shopping Center (tel. 667-6207), is our favorite Japanese restaurant in the Lahaina area. It's not fancy, but it's clean and cozy and definitely has atmosphere. And it's known for the best sushi bar on Maui. For an exotic appetizer, try the ikura oroshiae—that's grated radish topped with salmon roe! We like the chicken yakitori, barbecued chicken on a stick, and the kani sunomono—that's crab with cucumber. The combination dinner of various teriyakis and shrimp tempura, served with soup, salad, vegetables, rice, and tea, is a winner at $10. For two or more and a tab of $14.25 each, you can have dinner cooked right at table by a lovely waitress; choose from the likes of sukiyaki, shabu shabu (all beef), or yosenabe (sea food), served with all of the above accompaniments. Or try the sushi/sashimi platters, priced between $5.75 and $7.75. Fujiyama is open for lunch, weekdays only, from 11 a.m. to 1:30 p.m., and for dinner from 5 p.m. on. The sushi bar is open at both meals.

Haute cuisine with an island accent—that's what you'll get at **Gerard's** in the Lahaina Market Place, corner of Front St. and Lahainaluna Rd. (tel. 661-8938), where Chef Gerard Reversade has built a formidable reputation for himself in a few short years. Diners come from all over Maui for a special meal here because they know they're getting the freshest and finest of ingredients. Gerard changes the menu every day according to market availability, and the preparation is impeccable. Dinner is expensive (entrees $22 to $24), but splurge just a bit at lunch for a memorable experience. You might start with a cup of cream of spinach soup at $2.50, have a main course like mussels sauce poulette, ono sauteed with Grenoblaise, a spinach-and-cheese omelette, or veal liver with apples and onions, from $6.50 to $9.50. The wine list is extensive and fairly priced: a glass of house wine or champagne is only $3.50. Treat yourself to a delectable item from the pastry tray. The restaurant is charming and petite, with just a dozen or so tables, in a semi-open courtyard facing the street. Each time we eat at Gerard's we marvel again at his genius. For those who really care about food, an experience not to be missed.

Gerard serves lunch every day except Sunday, from 11:30 a.m. to 2:30 p.m., and dinner every night from 6 to 9:30 p.m. Reservations are imperative at dinner, but usually not necessary at lunch.

The **Lahaina Tree House Bar and Seafood Restaurant,** smack in the midst of the Lahaina Market Place (tel. 667-9224), has come up with a real innovation: you can sample and share seafood all day long here, putting together a meal from a wide variety of shrimp, oyster, clam, mussels, scallop entrees, plus seafood and fish soups; most items are priced from $5 to $8. Inexpensive daytime specialties include a soft-shell crab sandwich on sourdough bread, with Creole mustard and onions at $5.95, and macadamia-nut breaded fish spears for $6.95. Our samplers gave high marks to their Caesar salad and seafood chowder, each $5.95, and, for dessert, to a light and fluffy chiffon cake called Lemon Luv, $2.50. They also offer full dinner service, with catch of the day items a bit beyond budget, but pasta at $8.95, and garlic shrimp and oysters at $9.95. The restaurant really is in a gigantic tree, with red and blue buntings on the ceiling, simple wooden tables, and a relaxed, open feeling. It's open from 10 a.m. to 10 p.m., serving lunch all day; dinner starts at 6 p.m.

Not only does **The Wharf,** a nifty shopping complex at 658 Front St., have some of the most tasteful boutiques in the area, it also has a good supply of quick-service restaurants. For breakfast or lunch al fresco, **Lani's Pancake Cottage** (tel. 661-0955) is the place to go. The indoor area with its counters and booths is pleasant enough, but they also serve on a large umbrellaed terrace. Breakfast is on until closing, so anytime is fine for banana or strawberry pancakes ($3 and $3.95) or the omelet to end all omelets: the Chef's Mess Omelet, made of five eggs and filled with the likes of Ortega chili and cheese, bell peppers, Swiss cheese, etc.—$12 for two of you, $14 for three. Their tuna melt sandwich—grilled tuna and cheese with a small green salad—makes a good lunch at $3.85, and so do such fanciful entrees as a chili relleno burger (meat plus cheese and chilis on sourdough, dipped in egg batter with relleno sauce—not bad!) or more usual items like a bowl of chili or honey-dipped fried chicken, from $3.45 to $5.75. Beer and wine are available. Open 6:30 a.m. to 3:30 p.m. only.

Next door to Lani's, sharing the same outdoor terrace area, is **Mama's Original Maui Pizza** (tel. 667-2531), where you can get pizza by the slice for $1.35 and partake of the salad bar ($4.95), or stuff yourself at the all-you-can-eat buffet of pizza, spaghetti, garlic bread, salad bar, and fruit for dessert—$5.95 at lunch, $8.95 at dinner. Free delivery from Lahaina to Kapalua. Lunch from 11 a.m., dinner from 5 p.m.

We like the motto of **Skippers Seafood 'n Chowder House,** up in the front area of The Wharf: "Get good seafood without getting soaked." They're quite right: you're too far from the ocean to worry about the salt spray, and the prices are very good. Call this one a medium-fast-food operation: you place and pay for your order at the cashier's, then proceed to sit either indoors at booths or outdoors under umbrellaed tables in the very pretty patio bar (tropical mixed drinks are excellent here). The servers will bring the food to your table. All of the fish is deep-fried and served with fries or rice, plus cole slaw. You have a choice of cod and mahimahi: one piece of fish is $2.99; two pieces are $3.99; three pieces, $4.99. There's fried chicken in a basket too, chicken and fish combo, family meals, a children's menu, New England clam chowder, a salad bar (one serving at $2.99, all-you-can-eat at $4.99), carrot and chocolate cakes for dessert, and wine and beer. All in all, a safe and scenic harbor for a family meal.

Tucked away in a cozy corner on the first floor of The Wharf is **Sang Thai Cuisine,** which offers a peaceful atmosphere, authentic Thai dishes, and modest prices at both lunch and dinner. À la carte specialties like Thai ginger beef, Evil Prince, lemon beef or chicken, and sweet-and-sour pork, are only $5.95 to $7.95. There are noodle dishes, salads, spicy soups, good seafood choices and for vegetarians, a veritable bonanza: a dozen dishes, all from $4.50 to $4.95. Sang Thai serves lunch and dinner every day from 11 a.m. to 10 p.m.

For those who savor the bookish life, the most charming place at the Wharf will have to be **The Whaler's Bookstore and Coffee House.** Here, in a shady corner at the top of the Wharf, people are sitting quietly on the patio engaged in such pursuits as reading or writing letters—all the while munching on light snacks like quiches ($2.25) and sipping some wonderful coffees, English teas, hot Ghirardelli chocolate, iced cappuccino, and the like. Drinks are 75¢ to $1.95, and there are good homemade cookies, cakes, and pastries to accompany them. You can also buy Kona coffee by the pound—and books, of course, to give you something to do out on the patio.

Stick to the pasta and chicken dishes on the low side of the menu, and you can have a very reasonable and atmospheric meal at **Bettino's,** at Whaler's Market Place, 505 Front St. (tel. 661-8810). Bettino's is tucked away in the rear of this little shopping complex, affording you a view from its lanai of the oceanfront at Lahaina Harbor. The menu is mostly Italian, and the food is good. Along with your orders of, say, fettuccine Alfredo or marinara, chicken breast parmesan, or broiled breast of chicken, all from $8.50 to $10.95, you'll get soup or salad, fresh vegetables, rice or pasta or fries, and rolls. Fish and steak dishes are higher. Lunch is moderately priced, and specials include mahimahi, fish and chips, and Maui-style ribs, from $5.50 to $7.95, plus a goodly array of burgers and hot sandwiches. It's a nice place, too, for breakfast: omelets and pancakes. Bettino's serves breakfast from 7 a.m. to 2 p.m. (full bar service starts at 8 a.m.), lunch from 11 a.m. to 2 p.m., and dinner from 5 p.m. to closing. Open every day. *Note:* It's easy to park here, just across the street.

Lahaina Square (just behind Lahaina Shopping Center) is a good place for hungry budgeteers to note. Here you'll find **Amilio's Delicatessen,** which has good sandwiches, some with an Italian flair, to take out or eat here; the price range goes from $2.95 for tuna or cheese, to $4.40 for Amilio's special of many meats and cheeses. There's apt to be a special offer, like one sandwich at 99¢ when you buy another deli sandwich at full price. There's a choice of good breads, deli meats, and cheese if you wish to make your own sandwiches. Open most days from 9 a.m. to 1 p.m., until 9 p.m. on Friday, on Sunday from 10 a.m. to 4 p.m.

Stacks of kiawe wood and Hawaiian ranch decor set an upcountry mood, but here we are in tropical Lahaina, at **Chris' Smokehouse BBQ** in Lahaina Square (tel. 667-2111). The baby back pork ribs and kiawe chicken are good and tasty—they're marinated overnight in barbecue sauce, then smoked over kiawe wood and broiled over kiawe charcoal to give them a very special flavor. There are five complete dinners on the menu under $10—and that means that along with your four-rib rack of baby back pork ribs, smoked sausage links, half a smoked kiawe chicken, char-broiled boneless breast of chicken, or three smoked beef ribs, you also get freshly baked cornbread muffins with honey-macadamia-nut butter, cole slaw, and two choices among ranch-style baked beans, sweet potato fritter, homemade steak fries, or steamed rice. Higher-priced dinner entrees include various combination plates, New York strip steak, and charcoal-broiled fresh fish, about $11 to $14. À la carte dishes run from about $2 to $10. Come at lunchtime and you can sample Chris's tasty smoked meats in open-face sandwiches with barbecue sauce at $4.50 to $5.50, served with coleslaw, cottage cheese, or steak fries. Or, you can have their "Cheeseburger in Paradise" special, 5 ozs. of fresh ground beef with real cheddar cheese and all the fixings, for $1.95. You're given a plain, white paper placemat and crayons for doodling while you're having a drink and waiting for your meal. Our Häagen-Dazs hula pie was a bit of a disappointment at $3, so next time we'll try the giant chocolate-chip cookie at $1. Chris's serves dinner every night from 5:30 to 10 p.m., lunch Monday to Saturday from 11:30 a.m. to 2:30 p.m.; Happy Hour is 2:30 to 5 p.m.

Christine's Family Restaurant at Lahaina Square (tel. 661-4156) is just the place to bring a hungry family; they'll eat heartily and well, and there won't be a big dent in the budget. It's very popular with the local people for its home-style cooking. Readers have written to praise their breakfasts: you get two eggs, your choice of meat, either hash-browns or two scoops of rice, plus toast, for about $4.85. Lunch features lots of burgers and meat sandwiches around $4, plus plate lunches—beef teriyaki, roast pork, ham steak, and the like—in the $4.85 to $5 range. At dinner, served from 4:30 to 9:30 p.m., prices run from $4.95 to $9.75 for dishes like chicken cutlet, beef teriyaki, tonkatsu (deep-fried breaded pork, an island favorite), top sirloin, and lemon chicken. Along with the main course come rice or potato, tossed green salad or soup. There's nothing fancy about Christine's, but it is large and comfortable, with a smaller counter up front, and booths and tables in the back, a large sunset painting on the wall. It's open Monday to Thursday from 6 a.m. to 9:30 p.m., on Friday and Saturday 24 hours.

More family choices in the same Lahaina Square include a familiar **Jack in the Box,** as well as a **Baskin-Robbins,** and a large **Denny's.**

The local people have given a warm reception to **Thai Chef,** a cute little restaurant in the Lahaina Shopping Center (tel. 667-2814), offering Thai specialties in a pleasant setting: Thai decorations on the walls, lacy curtains, white tablecloths under glass. Tell the waiter if you want your food mild, medium, or hot, so he can help you choose from among salads, soups (we like the chicken soup simmered in coconut milk with ginger at $6.95), a variety of curries, noodles, and such specialty dishes as stuffed chicken wings or fried crab legs with bean sauce. Vegetarians have a complete menu of their own: appetizers, soups, noodles, and main dishes. It's all reasonable: most dishes are priced at $4.95 or $5.95, a few going up higher to $7.25. Open Monday to Saturday from 11 a.m. to 3 p.m. and from 5 to 10 p.m. Closed Sunday.

Just past the railroad depot on Honoapiilani Hwy. you'll spot a familiar building: it's a **Pizza Hut,** the home of those thick, crusty pizzas with the chewy, cheesy taste. This attractive spot, with its red curtains at the window, cozy booths and tables, attracts a large family crowd, since both pizza and pasta are filling, tasty, and inexpensive. If you come between 11 a.m. to 2 p.m. Monday through Saturday, they'll guarantee that your personal pan pizza ($2.25 for the supreme, $1.99 for the pepperoni) will be ready in five minutes, or the next one's on them. As for the regular pies, create your own with any two ingredients chosen from the scores available at $6.60 small, $10.20 medium, $13.20 large. Beer and wine by the glass and the pitcher. Open from 11 a.m. to midnight; no lunch on Sunday.

At the edge of town, Kaanapali side, is **Naokee's Too,** 1307 Front St., which has been offering one of the best deals anywhere on a one-pound New York steak: with salad, rice, and vegetable, it's $6.95. Naokee's is a very plain little luncheonette right on the ocean, but the food is excellent. For $3.95 you can get such selections as Korean barbecue, beef stew, roast pork, roast beef, hamburger steak, and fried chicken, along with rice and salad. Neighborhood kids like to come here to play Pac-Man. A good place for "local color."

Next to the train depot (the Lahaina-Kaanapali Railroad) at 991 Limahina Pl. is a "Maui secret."

Many of the fine restaurants in town get their bread and pastries from **The Bakery.** It's a popular spot, crowded with locals who come early in the morning for the best croissants around, brioches, pain au lait, hot from the oven. Butter bread, $1.25, and cheese butter bread, $1.95, is their specialty. They also offer gourmet-quality deli items and sandwiches to go (on the order of cheese broccoli or smoked pork loin and cheese). Worth stopping by just to inhale the aromas! *Note:* Local friends advise that their prices on California wines, Maui champagne, and imported champagne too, are so good that they should be kept a secret!

BARGAINS AT KAANAPALI BEACH: The strip of luxury hotels along Kaanapali Beach boasts a goodly share of luxury restaurants, but just a few where the budget diner can relax. So it's good news that the **Moana Terrace** of the beautiful new Maui Marriott Resort offers a Sundowner Dinner, served only between 5 and 6:30 p.m. Three or four entrees—perhaps beef, mahimahi, or teriyaki—are featured each night. All entrees come with soup or salad, dessert, and beverage. The price is $11.95. Some other time, when you're ready for a little splurge, come back to the Moana Terrace for the spectacular buffet served between 5 and 9 p.m., one of the best on the island. There's a different theme every night: Wednesday and Sunday, it's a prime rib buffet; Monday and Friday, it's a Hawaiian feast; Tuesday, Thursday, and Saturday, a seafood buffet. The tables are laden with more dishes than you could eat in a week, and the dessert selection alone is mind-boggling. The price is $16.95 for adults, $6.95 for children under 10. The room is exquisite, open to the sea, furnished with airy wicker: plants abound (tel. 667-1200 for reservations).

There's another popularly priced eating spot at the hotels: the **Kaanapali Beach Hotel Koffee Shop.** Breakfast begins at 7 a.m., lunch at 11 a.m., and dinner at 5 p.m. Be sure to check the luncheon specials, perhaps pot roast, barbecued ribs, beef stew, or roast chicken, plus hot and cold sandwiches, $3.95 to $5.95. At dinner you can have hot platters such as roast turkey, fried shrimp, breaded veal cutlet or New York–cut steak, from $4.95 to $6.95, plus a nightly dinner special at the same price, which includes entree, vegetable, potatoes or rice, rolls and butter. Service is cafeteria-style, and since the coffeeshop is at the entrance side of the hotel, you can walk right in after parking your car, without having to go through the hotel lobby.

We've already told you about La Familia in Kihei (see above). **La Familia Kaanapali** (tel. 667-7902) serves the same delicious menu of moderately priced Mexican food specialties and good drinks, but has its own distinct *muy simpático* atmosphere—it's at the entrance to the Kaanapali Resort area, across from the Hyatt Regency Maui, overlooking the 18th hole of the Royal Kaanapali Golf Course. The huge lanai is great for drinks, especially during the 4 to 6 p.m. Happy Hour, when frosty margaritas are only 99¢, and other drinks are similarly discounted. Interesting specials are offered for dinner every night: perhaps fresh fish, scampi, steaks, from $12.95. Good service, a relaxing atmosphere. La Familia Kaanapali serves breakfast, lunch, and dinner every day from 11:30 a.m. to 10 p.m.

AT WHALER'S VILLAGE: There's a salty but slick flavor to the handsome complex of shops and museum attractions at Maui's Whaler's Village, and you

can be sure that oldtime seamen never had food as good as you'll find in the village's restaurants. From the green umbrellas over the outdoor tables to the fully stocked deli case and banners inside, the flavor of **Ricco's Old World Delicatessen,** on the lower level of Whaler's Village, is definitely Italiano. Their sandwiches, generous and tasty, are served on French roll, deli rye, or whole wheat, with lettuce, tomato, Maui onion, Italian dressing, and pickle: you might have lean corned beef, picnic ham, rare roast beef, turkey breast, or veggie, at $3.85 Mama size, $4.25 Papa size; oven-toasted specialties, like Ricco's Italian combo, deli club, and the "Kula Kraut" Reuben, are all one size, $4.85. Ricco's pizzas are fun too (try the Aegean with feta cheese and Italian sausage, or the Hawaiian with pineapple and ham) for something different. Pasta dishes, $6.95 to $7.95, include an excellent veggie lasagne, and a regular one too. Salads, homemade cannolis, cheesecake and carrot cake for dessert, and a big selection of ice-cold beers, wines by the glass, carafe or bottle, add to the enjoyment. A fun place, good for a quick and tasty meal. Open daily from 11 a.m. to 10 p.m.

The **Rusty Harpoon** (tel. 661-3123) has been a Whaler's Village standby for many years: it's been totally renovated now, with a handsome interior (green colors, beautiful woods, a view of the ocean as well as the kitchen from every table), and a new menu concept: "nouvelle California-Maui cuisine." And it's still known for excellent value for the dollar. Come for the Early Bird specials, nightly between 5 and 6 p.m., and for $10, you can have dishes like chicken marsala, bay shrimp linguine, prime ribs, or fresh fish of the day, including fresh vegetables and rice pilaf or pasta. Most regular dinner entrees range from $9.95 to $13.95, and that includes chicken picatta, stir-fried chicken, lemon barbecue chicken, fettuccine primavera, or four-cheese lasagne. Five fresh fish dishes are offered every night. Rusty's still has its famous half-pound, bun-less burgers at $7.50 and $7.75, and there are some super salads—shrimp Louie, chicken walnut, fresh fruit, three-salad taster—from $7.50 to $8.95. Appetizers have an international flavor, from fried mozzarella to kal-bi to pizzas to nachos and sashimi and sushi. Rusty's uses only fresh local produce, rolls its own sushi, and makes its own pastas and wonderful fresh island desserts. Of course those famous fresh-fruit daiquiris (how about banana, pineapple, or peach?) are still there and still called the "finest in the Western world." There's a full bar, a lively crowd, lots of fun. Rusty's serves breakfast from 8 to 11 a.m., lunch from 11:30 a.m. to 3 p.m., dinner from 5 to 10 p.m. There's an Early Bird menu from 5 to 6 p.m., and from 3 to 5 p.m., its "Beer and Burger"—a half-pound burger and draft beer from $5.25. And, oh yes, that sunset over the ocean is terrific!

Is **Chico's Cantina** (tel. 667-2777) the best Mexican restaurant in Maui? Our local friends rave about this place, and we can see why. It's got a great tropical atmosphere, open-air yet protected from the elements, with white adobe walls, colorful Mexican hangings, heavy wooden furniture; the service is friendly; the food is both imaginative and delicious, and served in generous portions; and the price is right. Combination plates, for example, which include rice and beans, are $6.95 to $8.95. House specials, accompanied by soup or salad, are mostly $8.50 to $8.95, and that includes arroz con pollo and specialties from many areas of Mexico, like chicken mole, or eldorado Veracruz (mahimahi sautéed with vegetables and a spicy sauce in the style of Veracruz). Start your meal with appetizers like ceviche and mini-chimichangas, end with flan or "el hula pie." The taco bar is fun, and so is the cocktail lounge, comfortable enough for families and serving nachos for just $1. Chico's Cantina has a large seating capacity, and even waiting is comfortable. A *simpático* choice. Lunch is on from 11:30 a.m. to 2:30 p.m., dinner from 5 to 10:30 p.m., cocktails from 11:30 a.m., and the Taco Bar is open from 11:30 a.m. to midnight.

Sunset can be spectacular at Whaler's Village, so praise be that **Leilani's on** the Beach (tel. 661-4495), a handsome, multilevel restaurant that affords a view of the ocean, has an excellent Sunset Special every night between 5 and 6 p.m.; that's when you can get a complete dinner for $8.95, with soup, salad, and such entrees as fish, chicken, or teriyaki brochette. Regular meals, from about $10 to $20, fit best into our splurge category. But you can sample a light menu of delicious appetizers and soups downstairs in the PuPu bar. Open daily, 4 p.m. to midnight.

Yami's Soft Frozen Yogurt, with a few outside tables to sit at on the lower level of Whaler's Village is fine for a quick bite. Relax with one of their yogurt shakes like the Queen's Quencher, yogurt plus lemon and coconut, $1.95; or snack on a papaya stuffed with yogurt and topped with fruit, $2.65; or try one of their good sandwiches—tuna, avocado, raw milk cheese, and egg salad—served on cracked-wheat bread with tomato and alfalfa sprouts, for $2.95. Their cheesecake frozen yogurt is a winner.

The only restaurant we know of with its own pool, right on a glorious beach, is **El Crabcatcher** at Whaler's Village. This is a glamorous place, with dinner too pricey for us, but you can make do at lunch with sandwiches starting at $5.95. Sit at an outside table, relax, have a drink and pupus, and enjoy a swim in the pool or ocean.

We've had good letters over the years about the **Kahana Keyes Restaurant,** in the Valley Isle Condominium at Kahana, three miles north of the Kaanapali Beach Resort (tel. 669-8071). People like it because it has one of the best salad bars in the area, as well as an excellent Early Bird special for $8.95, including the salad bar; the entree changes nightly, and might be barbecued chicken, lobster tail, prime rib, even New York–cut steak. The regular menu features seafoods, steaks, and lobster, with prices from about $10 to $20. There's live entertainment and dancing. Dinner is on from 5:30 to 10 every night.

AT KAPALUA: We hardly expected to find a moderately priced eating place in the posh pastures of Kapalua Bay Resort, but find one we did. The **Market Café,** at the Kapalua Shops, is a small restaurant with the flavor of a European sidewalk café and with the flavor too of cheeses and wines (over 400 to choose from), espressos and cappuccinos, imported beers (we counted about 30), luscious ice-cream drinks, rich desserts, and a variety of inexpensive items served throughout the day, like deli sandwiches at $5.95, burgers at $4.50, soups and salads. Dinner, served from 5 p.m. on, has a number of entrees under $10, such as chicken parmesan, teriyaki chicken brochettes, calves liver and onions, lasagne, and spaghetti. Mud pie, strudel, pecan or macadamia-nut pie, and carrot cake are special dessert treats. From 9 to 11 a.m. Monday to Saturday, until 1 p.m. Sunday, there is a variety of egg dishes, omelets, and pancakes to choose from; those cooked with fresh fruit are especially good. Open daily.

There's no natural foods restaurant in Lahaina at this moment, but the local health-food store, **Healthy's Down to Earth Natural Foods** at 136 Dickenson St. (tel. 667-2855), does have salads, sandwiches, soup of the day, smoothies, and hot food to go. Entrees like lasagne and enchiladas run from $3.10 to $4.25. It's open daily from 10 a.m. to 9 p.m., until 7 p.m. Sunday.

IN HANA: There are very few public restaurants in Hana, but the ones that do exist are lovely. Take yourself to the glorious **Hotel Hana-Maui,** newly redone, and more *luxe* than ever, perhaps to splurge on its sumptuous à la carte luncheon, served from 11:30 a.m. to 2 p.m. Specialties include delicious seafood caught fresh in Hana waters. Picnic fixings are available from the Hana Ranch

Store. The newly remodeled and more casual Hana Ranch Restaurant, a bit away from the hotel in the Hana Ranch complex, has a good buffet, plus salads, sandwiches, and hot entrees; plan on spending between $4.75 and $8 for lunch, served from 11 a.m. to 4 p.m.

For a more reasonable lunch (or breakfast) in Hana, the place is **Tutu's,** which has been holding forth at Hana Bay for many years. Tutu's packs an excellent picnic lunch, and also has local-style plate lunches for under $5, plus very good fresh fruit salads, green salads, sandwiches, ice cream, and frozen bananas dipped in chocolate! You can call them at 248-8224 to order your picnic lunch.

3. The Night Scene

IN KAHULUI: Nightlife is relatively quiet in this area. Your best bet, as usual, is in the big hotels. On Friday and Saturday from 9:30 p.m. you can catch the sounds of the Sakuras in the East West Dining Room of the **Maui Palms Hotel** (dress code). . . . At the Red Dragon Disco of the **Maui Beach,** the mood is more mod than Hawaiian: DJ Eric Valdez keeps the crowds happy three nights a week: Thursday from 10 p.m. to 1:30 a.m., Friday and Saturday until 2 a.m. . . . You can also disco over at **Applegate's Pizza** in Maui Mall most nights of the week. . . . **Idini's,** in the Kaahumanu Shopping Center, stays open until 11 p.m., and has a full bar and a very varied beer selection. . . . In the Maui Mall, **Sir Wilfred's Caffè** is a relaxing and inexpensive spot. In the late afternoon, up until closing at 6:30 p.m., beer is $1.25 to $1.75, bar drinks $1.75. All drinks are poured from a premium well. Live entertainment Friday evening til 9 p.m.; Hawaiian and jazz. . . . Check the shopping centers for free Polynesian shows, presented several times a week. Maui Mall, for one, sometimes presents top revues from Honolulu clubs—free.

IN LAHAINA: Lahaina at night is the place for the drinking set, with no shortage of swinging bars. For a start you might try the **Harpooner's Lanai** at the Pioneer Inn; salty atmosphere and moderate prices. A must for sunset watching and "characters." . . . A sophisticated crowd gathers at **Longhi's** on Friday and Saturday nights for dancing to live music (until 1:30 a.m.). . . . The **Whale's Tale Restaurant** on Front Street always attracts a lively crowd. Beer from $2.25, plus good burgers and sandwiches under $5. . . . **Moose McGillycuddy's Pub & Café** offers $1 off on all drinks, ice cream drinks, wine, draft and bottled beer—and on all pupus, too—during its 3 to 6 p.m. Happy Hour. In case you can't wait that long, there's an Early Happy Hour from 11 a.m. to 3 p.m. with the same prices.

IN KIHEI AND WAILEA: The place to dance in the Kihei area is at the Kihei Seas Restaurant at the top of the Rainbow Mall, where pianist Dennis Manawaiti and guitarist Miles Yoshida keep the crowds happy with "oldies but goodies." Then, from 11 p.m. on to the wee hours, it's video disco.

You can take your choice of luaus in this area: famed island entertainer Jesse Nakaoka presents **Luau Polynesia,** one of the best shows in the islands, at 145 S. Kihei Rd. (tel. 879-7227 for reservations) on Wednesday and Friday at 5 p.m. The price is $35 for adults, $20 for children under 12 (free under 3). . . . There's another super luau at the **Maui Lu Resort** on Saturday at $32 for adults, $19 for children (reservations: 879-5858). . . . If it's Wednesday, it must be the luau at **Stouffer Wailea Beach Resort,** held in a beachfront garden setting at 6 p.m. The "Hawaiian Hula Revue" is the featured entertainment. Adults pay $38, children under 12, $21 (for reservations, phone 879-4900). . . . *Note:*

Check local listings when you arrive: prices, days, and entertainers change frequently.

At the same Stouffer Wailea Beach Resort, the **Lost Horizon** nightclub offers live entertainment nightly except Sunday and Monday. Sounds range from contemporary to '20s and '50s music, rock, country, and Hawaiian. No cover charge (reservations not taken). A Hawaiian trio plays at the Sunset Terrace from 5:30 to 8:30 p.m. Monday through Saturday.

AT KAANAPALI BEACH: More fun and games await you at the big beach hotels at Kaanapali. One of the greatest shows in town takes place every night at the **Sheraton Maui,** and it costs absolutely nothing to be in the audience. As the sun begins to set over the water, torches are lit all the way to the point. A native Hawaiian boy stands atop Black Rock (that eerie perch from which the souls of the dead were supposed to depart to the other world), throws his leis into the water, and then looks down some 20 feet or so to the waiting ocean below. The crowd—on the beach, lining the lobby floors—holds its breath. He plunges in, surfaces, and the evening festivities are under way.

If you need something to steady your nerves after that spectacle, make your way to the nautically decorated **Barkentine Bar.** The ship models, volcanic rock floor-to-ceiling columns, and the tables with compass designs are all unusual and handsome, but somehow we never notice anything except the view; from the crest of this black lava cliff overlooking the sea it's a spectacular one, a must for us collectors of Hawaiian sunsets.

Choosing among all the luau and dinner shows in the Kaanapali area can be difficult: all of them are good, none is inexpensive (most run about $36).

The Royal Lahaina Luau at the **Royal Lahaina Resort** is considered one of the best; it's presented nightly at 5:30 p.m., costs $36 for adults, $18 for children 12 and under (tel. 661-3611 for reservations). . . . *Drums of the Pacific* at the **Hyatt Regency Maui** is one of the few to offer a cocktail show: the $22 tab includes a mai tai and a souvenir lei, tax, tip, and a chance to see a spectacular production of Pacific dancing (Samoan slap dances, Tahitian drum dances and shimmies, spear and knife dances, fire dances, etc.). The dinner show is $36 for adults, $30 for children 5 to 12, free under 5. Call Hyatt at 667-7474 for reservations.

For us, just walking around the Hyatt is another kind of show: its displays of Oriental art, gracefully situated throughout the public areas, are worthy of any fine museum. Be sure to stroll the grounds, too, of its exquisite next-door neighbor, the **Marriott Resort.** Stop to sit in the lobby and you can enjoy the sounds of music, usually a jazz pianist, coming from the open Lobby Bar. For something a bit more organized, try the **Banana Moon** nightclub here, where disco is usually the order of the night, from 8 p.m. to 2 a.m. The two-level club allows you to dance and/or talk. . . . An attractive older crowd enjoys the good pupus, good conversation, live music, (and comfortable seating as well), at **Marriott's Makai Bar.**

READERS' HOTEL AND RESTAURANT SELECTIONS ON MAUI: "**Swan Court** in the Hyatt Regency at Kaanapali is by far the most delightful place for 'the big splurge.' The restaurant is open to a pond/garden setting with black and white swans gliding by, service is very attentive, and food is excellent. Most entrees are in the $20 to $28 range, and there is a huge dessert buffet at dinner. Breakfast is also served here, buffet style. Swan Court accepts reservations until 4 p.m. at 667-7474, ext. 59, and after 4 p.m. at ext. 3309. However, hotel guests have first priority on reservations between 7 and 9, so it's easier for 'outsiders' to get reservations between 6 and 7 or after 9 p.m. . . . **La Bretagne** off Front Street serves very good French food in a charming garden atmosphere and takes reservations at 661-8966. . . . In Lahaina, our favorite was the **Oceanhouse,** right on the harbor at 831

Front St. (661-3359), which serves breakfast, lunch, and dinner. We especially enjoyed dinners with fresh seafood. The catch of the day prepared Créole style was excellent, as were both the blackened fish and steak. No reservations accepted. . . . We figured out how to beat the system at the **Chart House,** which serves a terrific dinner, but never takes reservations. Put your name down on their list and then go shopping in Lahaina; they'll let you know when to be back. . . . We have stayed at **Kahana Village** five times. The units are very spacious and well appointed. When two couples share a two-bedroom unit, the rate is quite reasonable in today's world, or if three couples share a three-bedroom unit. Kahana Village also attracts families and, unless you are terribly fond of children, should be avoided during school holiday periods" (Bob Harrison and Hal Goodstein, Province-town, Mass.). [*Authors' Note:* Kahana Village is a beautiful oceanfront resort located on a sandy beach. Off-season rates for two-bedroom apartments are $115 to $135 ocean-view, $140 to $160 oceanfront; three-bedroom apartments are $140 to $160 ocean-view, $165 to $185 oceanfront. Address: 4531 Honoapiilani Rd., Lahaina, Maui, HI 96761. Call toll free 800/824-3065.]

"The best salad bar on Maui, by far, is at a new restaurant/inn called **Mark Edison** in Iao Valley. It has several seafood items on the bar, plus many international dishes. And it is just $6.95! This is quite amazing, considering how much mediocre food we found at higher prices" (Pat McCallum, Bethesda, Maryland). . . . "The most fantastic eating ex-perience of our lives was on Maui, in Lahaina, to be exact. On the corner of Front and Hotel Streets is **Swenson's Ice Cream Parlor,** which serves a concoction called the Walk-away Waffle Sundae. Start with a sweet waffle cone (made on the premises while you watch), and add your choice of ice cream—a huge scoopful. The turtle-chocolate-caramel ice cream was fantastic, and the chocolate macadamia nut was worth the 25¢ extra. Then the topping of your choice: our choice was hot fudge. Next come chopped macadamia nuts, then whipped cream, followed by chocolate sprinkles topped off with a cherry. It's served in a paper cone, to catch the drips, and with a spoon. This is one of the best treats you will ever eat. We liked it so much that we went back to Lahaina on our last day just to have this for our lunch. After this, ice cream will never be the same. Do yourself a favor and try it on your next trip!" (Barbara Hackel, Decatur, Ill.). [*Authors' Note:* We watched people eating these on our last trip, but we didn't have the nerve.]

"We went to Maui in November via Mid Pacific Air. We stayed at the **Maui Sands,** and it is everything you said it was and more. Our favorite restaurant in Lahaina was **Kimo's,** a splurge, but the food, service and view were fantastic. We tried the Rainbow Buffet at the **Maui Beach Hotel** on our last day. It was all there for the taking, and did we ever take! Among the four of us, I think we managed to try everything. This is the best place to sample Oriental dishes" (Don and Donna Hammons, Mesquite, Tex.). . . . "After some very windy days in Kihei (not typical we were told), we moved on to the **Papakea Beach Resort** in Kaanapali for the remainder of our stay. It was everything we dreamed a vacation would be! Our one-bedroom unit with a huge sleeping loft (really a two-bedroom) cost us $94.50 a day, but we never regretted spending it. Papakea is a vision of loveliness everywhere you look. The grounds are meticulously tended and filled with beautiful plantings. Other bonuses were two putting greens, two pools, two Jacuzzis, 'swimmercize' classes each morning, tennis clinics, and a rum-punch party by the pool with entertainment on Friday. This is a quiet, family-oriented resort, yet very close to the abundant restaurants, supermarkets, and shops of Kaanapali" (Frances S. Kielt, West Hartford, Conn.). [*Authors' Note:* Current rates would be about $119. Call toll free 800/367-5037 for information.]

"We spent 13 nights at **Honokawai Palms,** and received a 10% discount—if we had stayed 30 nights we would have gotten a 25% discount. Its location, between Kaanapali and Napili/Kapalua, gives you the best of both worlds, a luxury environment at a budget price. You have access to the best beaches and resort hotels on Maui, but stay at an inex-pensive (for Hawaii) apartment. We are hoping to return to Maui and the Honokawai Palms. As you suggested, we used Mid Pacific for our flight from Oahu to Maui. Our Sen-ior Citizen tickets cost $32.50 each" (Owen and Betty Babcok, Interlaken, N.Y.) [*Au-thors' Note:* See text for details on Honokawai Palms.]

"The overall price increase was more obvious on Maui than elsewhere, but we found the new **Denny's** in Lahaina Square to be a treat. The decor is like no other Denny's seen by us across the country: lovely fans in motion, live plants on each table and in the rest-room, along with attractive, framed prints and a decorated, vaulted ceiling. And I found a delicious pineapple boat served with a choice of bread or crackers for under $5. What an unexpected treat" (Elizabeth Greer, El Cerrito, Calif.).

"We have three vacation rentals near **Hookipa Beach Park,** an exciting area due to the phenomenal growth of windsurfing. They are the best locations for serious windsurfers. From The Cove, 5 Kaiholo Place, you can walk 500 yards to Mama's Beach with your windsurfing equipment. This is a complete Hawaiian-style beach house, fully equipped, with three bedrooms, two full baths, color TV, phone, garage, washer-dryer, weekly maid service. It rents for $150 a night. We have another three-bedroom home at 616 Hana Hwy., across the street from a cute little beach and a short drive to windsurfing at Hookipa, which also sleeps six to eight and rents for $125. Our third place is at 618 Hana Hwy: we have a three-bedroom, two-bathroom, and kitchen apartment upstairs for $180 a night, and a one-bedroom, bath, and kitchen unit downstairs for $75 a night. A three-day minimum stay is required. For information, write or call Tim and JoAnne Gardner, #5 Kaihold Place, Paia, Maui, HI 96790 (tel. 808/878-2127)" (Tim Gardner, Paia, Hi.).

"**The Bakery** in Lahaina, on the same street as the Lahaina-Kaanapali Railroad depot, has delicious blueberry or cinnamon-apple muffins for 70¢. They are so huge you could make a meal of one of them. Their sticky buns, encrusted with pecans, go perfectly with a cup of fresh Kona coffee" (Deanne M. Miltoma, Sacramento, Calif.). [*Authors' Note:* Agreed. See text for details.] . . . "People should take quarters with them for the **Pay and Park** lots in Lahaina. It costs $2 for all day and is self-pay (quarters only). It was impossible to find a merchant who would give us $2 change in quarters. . . . **Safeway,** behind Maui Mall in Kahului, had the best food prices on the entire island. Very clean, lots of fresh produce, a bakery, a deli. . . . We highly recommend **Napili Point Condos.** Clean, spacious, well-equipped, lovely grounds—and what an incredible view" (Ted and April Ziegenbusch, La Palma, Calif.).

"We loved the **Nona Lani Cottages.** When my wife mentioned to Mr. Kong that Oahu had been rather disappointing in regard to fruit—especially since in New York we can buy any type 24 hours a day—he immediately gave us a tour of the luscious garden and picked tamborines (a cross between an orange and a tangerine), cherry guavas (another fruit we didn't know of before), as well as regular guavas and lemons, which he allowed us to pick any time we felt like eating some. It was great. The atmosphere of the cottage was also just right and the location perfect—although the sound of the highway was a little bit disturbing at first, but soon absorbed by the sound of the breaking waves" (Isabel and Horst Cerni, New York, N.Y.). . . . "We were just so pleased with our accommodations at the **Lihi Kai Cottages** and the helpful ways in which both Jeanette and Joe DiMeo go about making your stay perfect. . . . Our apartment was immaculate. . . . Our three weeks with the DiMeos will always be a special memory" (Louis and Margaret Sedivy, Los Gatos, Calif.).

"We thought you might like to know of a bed-and-breakfast in Haiku called **Haiku-leana.** We enjoyed the many personal touches during our stay, enhanced by its owners' creative and artistic use of antiques, collectibles, and Hawaiian flowers—baskets of protea in the living room and bedrooms, orchids in the bathroom! Our hosts shared their favorite lesser-known Maui spots. Each breakfast brought different Hawaiian fruits and tea specialties and Mac Nut Coffee! All this on a quiet, restful acre of ground made the price reasonable ($50 double, $40 single) and our last evenings on the islands memorable! Write to Clark and Denise Champion, 69 Haiku Rd., Haiku, HI 96708" (Miriam Foster, Urbana, Ill.). . . . "We were totally delighted with **Shores of Maui** in the Kihei area. We were greeted by a very pleasant resident manager who led us to our beautiful apartment. It was not only beautifully decorated, but equipped beyond what we expected. Microwave oven, even a cooler for picnic lunches. A lovely lanai for breakfast and dinner overlooking the pool area. Everyone was in agreement that Shores of Maui had everything, including a central location for sightseeing. At $55 per night—unbelievable!" (Mrs. Donald Phillips, Drexel Hill, Pa.). [See text for details on Shores of Maui.]

"We highly recommend the **Napili Bay,** close to Kaanapali Beach and Lahaina. These are studio apartments with one queen-size bed and two singles and kitchen; they are reasonably priced. We had clean, fresh linens each day, including beach towels; the rooms are not air-conditioned, but have adjustable shutters so you can feel the incredibly refreshing trade winds and hear the ocean at night. It cost us $50 for groceries for two people for a week and we ate well. Efficiencies are great! The owners were like grandparents to us, extremely friendly and accommodating" (Francine Schept, White Plains,

N.Y.). [*Authors' Note:* Napili Bay's address is 33 Hui Dr., Lahaina, Maui, HI 96761 (tel. 669-6044).]

"The **Aloha Cottages** that you mention in Hana are wonderful. When we arrived, Mr. Nakamura gave us a basket of local fruits. He immediately suggested some good places to see in the area. He is also the barber in Hana, and I got a good haircut for $3.50 and learned all about Hana from him: he has lived here 30 years. The Nakamuras have built another cottage and may expand to a third. We highly recommend it. Be sure to ask Mr. Nakamura how to get to the secluded *red sand* beach in Hana" (Peter Sinclaire, New Britain, Conn.). . . . "I want to thank you for listing Mr. Nakamura's Aloha Cottages at Hana. We had not even unpacked before he shinnied up a papaya tree and plucked the ripe fruit for our pleasure. We stayed in his larger cottage and can hardly express the feeling. It is large, and as the old saying goes, 'you could eat off the floors'—and I really mean it. The furnishings are spare, but it is one of the most peaceful places we have ever stayed. One could easily stay a week instead of just overnight" (Bart and Lynda Esterly, Capistrano Beach, Calif.). . . . "We stayed one night at the **Hana Kai Resort Apartments** in Hana, a real tropical hideaway. We did cook our own steak in the barbecue, with several other couples. We wish we had planned to stay there longer" (Peter and Mary Tannen, Albuquerque, N. Mex.).

"I called **Maui Sands** on their toll-free number (tel. 800/367-5037) because their rates were among the best in the Kaanapali area. And I thought I'd ask them if they had a discount rate for clergy. As it turned out, they gave me a 20% discount. Other clergy would, I'm sure, be glad to know this" (Rev. Bob Waliszewski, no address given). . . . "We discovered why **condos** are so much cheaper than hotels; their services are meager. Maid service is usually every other day. It is harder to obtain touring advice and assistance than in a full-service hotel. We recommend that first-timers stick to hotels, unless they have their trip very well planned" (Jeff and Chris Jacobsen, Rinton, Wash.). . . . "Your readers may be interested in hearing about the cabin at **Poli Poli Springs State Park,** on the slopes of Haleakala at 6,472 feet. The cabin is in a heavily wooded camping area—there are even redwoods—and the view, of central and western Maui, as well as Molokai and Lanai, is outstanding. The park is crisscrossed with miles of hiking trails, some of which lead to Haleakala Crater. The cabin has three bedrooms and will sleep up to ten. There is some furniture, a wood heating stove, a gas cooking range, complete cooking utensils, and bedding. There is no electricity. For information and reservations, write or call the State Department of Land and Natural Resources, Division of State Parks, P.O. Box 1049, Wailuku, Maui, HI 96793 (tel. 244-4354)" (Roberta Rosen, Long Beach, Calif.).

Chapter XVI

SEEING MAUI

1. Kahului-Wailuku and Kihei-Wailea
2. Haleakala, the House of the Sun
3. The Road to Hana
4. Lahaina
5. Kaanapali and Kapalua

THREE DAYS is the absolute minimum for savoring the varied charms of Maui, figuring one day in the **Kahului-Wailuku** and **Kihei-Wailea** areas, and **Haleakala,** another at **Lahaina** and **Kaanapali** in western Maui, and a third day for the trip to and from **Hana.** And this is going at a pretty rugged pace. If you can manage a few more days, we strongly urge you to do so. It's so pleasant to relax here after you've seen the sights. *Note:* Excellent maps are available in the *Maui Drive Guide,* which your car-rental company will give you free.

1. Kahului-Wailuku and Kihei-Wailea

THE KAHULUI AREA: **Kahului** is too new to have any historic sights, but it's considered a good example by city planners of what a model city should be. You can spend a pleasant hour or so browsing through its shopping centers. Maui's biggest shopping complex, **Kaahaumanu Shopping Center,** opened a few years back, and a better name for it might be Ala Moana No. 2. Like its Honolulu counterpart, it has **Sears** at one end, **Liberty House** at the other, and that fascinating Japanese department store, **Shirokiya,** in between. Most of the 50-odd stores here are geared to local residents, but there are a few places catering to gift buyers. Our favorite of these is **Nani Pacifica Center for Performing Plants,** which abounds with gift items of high artistic quality, reasonably priced. We saw Maui potpourris, a beautiful collection of Hawaiian flowers in silk—anthuriums, protea, hibiscus, bird of paradise, and more. They also have Maui's largest collection of miniatures for dollhouses and collectors, porcelain collector dolls made on Maui, handpainted wood jewelry, windchimes and locally made Christmas tree ornaments—not to mention their certified Hawaiian cuttings, bulbs and plants. One of those places it's hard to tear yourself away from. . . . Also on a high level is **Maui's Best,** a new store which features crafts and candy made on Maui. Lovely craft items include potpourris, trivets, pillow kits, Christmas tree ornaments, children's clothing, great handpainted T-shirts, sweatshirts silkscreened with Japanese prints, bamboo vases, all reasonably priced. . . . As for the candy, it's **Island Princess Candies:** be sure to sample their chocolate-covered Kona coffee beans, their double-dipped macadamia nuts with two kinds of chocolate, and their cooling sherbet drops. Super!. . . . You can get island and Oriental prints by the yard, well priced, at **Sew Special,** which also has some wall hangings that would make neat gifts. . . . Kids and hobbyists will enjoy **Kan-Bee Toy,** a very large shop with good values. . . . **Toda's** has all kinds of souvenirs, plus Japanese dolls. . . . Need new shoes? Women can color-coordinate and design a shoe and have it custom-made for them in 15 to 20 minutes at **Sassy Straps,** which has an amusing idea. You choose a sole and a pattern, the widths and colors of the straps, and they put it all together for you. Cost, from about $20 to $35. They also have terrific unisex slippers by Sensi which contour to your feet, locally made baby booties exclusive here, from $10 to $15, and exotic foot jewelry. . . . You might find some sake cups to take home with you, or charming Hakata dolls, at **Shirokiya,** which also has those wonderful sushi take-out lunches we've told you about in the preceding chapter. . . . In case you haven't sampled crackseeds yet, **Camellia Seeds** is the place; or you can munch on freshly baked cookies at **David's Cookies,** on ice cream at **Baskin Robbins,** or on gourmet franks at **Orange Julius. Idini's** and **Ma-Chan's Okazu-Ya** plus several other places (see Chapter XV), are fine for meals.

It's also fun to visit the **Maui Mall,** a busy scene with its frequent sidewalk sales. Have a look at the Petroglyph Garden. The petroglyphs are carved into boulders, and are representative of ancient ones. Prof. Edward Stasack, noted authority on petroglyphs, supervised the work. You're invited to make rubbings of them if you wish: all you need is cotton fabric and a big felt-tipped marker. . . . You can get some good buys in muumuus and aloha shirts too, at **Island Muumuu Works.** This is a wholesale outlet for Hilda of Hawaii (there are several stores in Honolulu), and most of the beautiful, first-quality muumuus are just $37.50. Lace muumuus are $55; aloha shirts (we spotted some neat ones in a whale motif) are $16. What a treat! Island Muumuu Works has recently opened

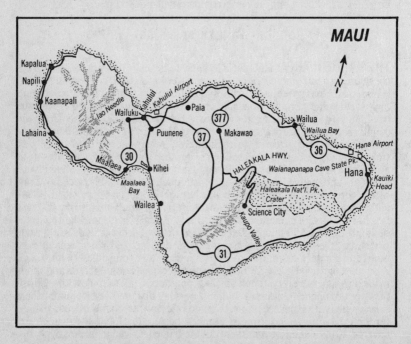

in a new store in Lahaina at 180 Dickenson Square. . . . Children's clothing is very special at **Baby's Choice,** which also carries bedding, cribs, and furniture in addition to darling items like tiny happi coats for little girls. . . . Sportswear is quite tasteful at **Wow! Swimwear** and **Allison's Place.** . . . **JR's Music Shop** has some very good selections. . . . **Long's Drugs** offers some of the best values for souvenirs and sundry items. . . . And you can stock up on groceries at **Star Super Market,** where the locals shop; if you're going to be cooking in your kitchenette apartment, it pays to stop here after getting off the plane before driving on to the more expensive resort areas. . . . You can pick up a T-shirt that reads "Eat, Drink and Be Maui" at the **T-Shirt Factory.** . . . **Roy's Photo Center** has probably the most complete supply of camera accessories and films on Maui. . . . If you're into macramé, stop in at **The Knot Hole.** Not only do they carry macramé supplies and give classes, but they also have Hawaiian Christmas ornaments and cute little protea dolls, made on Maui, at $14.95. . . . **Sir Wilfred's Coffee, Tea, Tobacco Shop** has more than its name implies; in addition to a great selection of pipes, cigars, tobacco, and coffee beans, it also has gourmet gifts (how about a jar of macadamia-nut butter or a bag of Makawao mint tea) and gadgets, plus an espresso bar, a full bar, and a delightful menu of light foods at Sir Wilfred's Caffè. . . . Stop in at **Waldenbooks** if you've run out of reading material, and at **Maui Natural Foods** for anything and everything in the health-food line; it is the most complete store of its kind in the area.

Woolworth's has an inexpensive coffeeshop here, **Dave's** is great for exotic ice-cream flavors, and the **Pizza Factory** has pizza and pizzazz. Free entertainment is held here often; check the local papers for announcements.

Finished with all that shopping? You deserve a rest, some coffee, and some cultural sustenance as well. Do as we do, and pay a visit to **The Artful Dodger's Feed 'n' Read,** a wonderful bookstore-coffeehouse in the Old Kahului Store at 55 Kaahumanu Ave., right near the airport, a historic old building recently converted into a mini-shopping mall (tel. 871-2677). The only problem is, you might want to spend all day here. There are acres of used books and records and magazines to browse through (we spotted old copies of *The Mother Earth News, Psychology Today,* sections on Eastern Religion, Asian Studies), as well as good selections of current titles. Then there are divine coffees and pastries and sandwiches to choose from, courtesy of The Bakery in Lahaina (which we've told you about in the preceding chapter). And then there are the changing art shows, the varied cultural events, the entertainment—which could be anything from a poetry reading to a jazz recital to a concert on the Celtic harp, almost all of it free or at nominal charge. You might get involved in a game of Scrabble or backgammon, watch a chess tournament in progress, read the papers, or just hang out. Advice: get their calendar, and plan to come back. This is one of our favorite Maui discoveries. Closed Sunday

Another good stop on anybody's itinerary is at **Airport Flower & Fruit,** 460 Dairy Rd. (first stop sign from the airport on Rte. 38). Visit this one just before you get on the plane to leave Maui, or better still, phone the owner, a delightful lady named Mrs. Sally Anne Goodness (honest!) at 871-7056, tell her what flowers and fruits and other goodies you want to take home with you, and she will have everything ready, efficiently boxed and certified for export. All you do is carry it on the plane. Her prices are surprisingly low, her range of products wide —anything from sweet Maui onions to pineapples to candies to mustards to cut flowers and orchid plants—and her service most helpful. We also spotted small gift items here at prices lower than elsewhere, as well as beautiful leis at $4.95 (at the airport, similar ones were going for $7.95 to $9.95). When you're thinking about Christmas presents, remember that Sally Anne welcomes mail orders too: Airport Flower & Fruit, P.O. Box 3046, Kahului, Maui, HI 96732.

Kahului also boasts the only deep-water harbor in Maui, a bulk-sugar loading plant, the cannery of the Maui Pineapple Company, and the Hawaiian Commercial and Sugar Company, the driving force behind the town's development (most of the homes belong to plantation workers). Out near the airport, at the **Kanaha Pond Waterfowl Sanctuary** you can see where migratory birds from our northwest mainland take their winter vacations.

Close to the Kahului Airport is an attraction for those interested in exotic jewelry. This is **Flora Hawaii,** a company that transforms fresh orchids, other flowers, and leaves into lasting pieces of jewelry and wall decor through the electroplating process: some are finished in gold plate, others preserved in their natural color and shape. Visitors are invited to tour the factory showroom from 9 a.m. to 4 p.m. weekdays; free pineapple juice is served. Flora Hawaii is located two minutes from the airport, just between the intersection of Hwy. 38 with Hwy. 36 and 35 (tel. 877-7958).

THE WAILUKU AREA: Historic old Wailuku, the commercial and professional center and the seat of Maui County (which also includes Molokai and Lanai), is quite different from Kahului—even though it's right next door. Drive westward along Kaahaumanu Avenue out of Kahului about three miles; you'll pass the Maui Professional Building at High Street on the right, and then, about one block farther on to the left on Iao Road, you'll reach the **Maui Historical Society Museum.** These buildings, on beautiful shaded grounds, once housed in the Wailuku Female Seminary (where young females could be kept safely "away from the contaminating influences of heathen society") and the home of Mr. Edward Bailey, the seminary instructor. Today they are full of fascinating bits of Hawaiiana, from ancient petroglyphs and necklaces of human hair worn by the alii of Maui to missionary patchwork quilts and furnishings. Dating back to 1833–1850, the building itself was completely restored in 1974–1975, and is an excellent example of Hawaiian craftsmanship and Yankee ingenuity. This smaller building, once the dining room of the school and later Mr. Bailey's studio, has been restored as a gallery of his paintings of Maui in the late 1800s. The museum is open daily from 10 a.m. to 4:30 p.m. A donation of $2 for adults is appreciated.

Just off Kaahaumanu Avenue, across from the Wailuku War Memorial on Kanaloa Street, you may want to make a stop at the **Maui Zoological and Botanical Garden.** Beautifully and lovingly maintained, the Botanical Garden contains an abundance of native Hawaiian plants, many of which can no longer be seen anywhere else. At the very front of the garden is the Maui Zoo, a new little zoo that has been stocked largely by its big sister, Honolulu Zoo. The majority of the collection consists of lovable farm animals—we like the noisy feral sheep or "hipa" as they're called here; there are also some very happy monkeys and a few tropical birds, notably peafowl and parrots. Admission is free.

Now, if you need to stock up on local produce, natural foods, vitamins, and the like, you can do so at bargain prices at **Healthy's Down to Earth** at 1910 Vineyard St. Local folks praise their daily lunch special, which includes a salad, for $3.95. Closed Sunday.

Not far from Wailuku, in the sugar plantation village of Waikapu, you can sightsee, shop, eat, and have an educational experience—all under one roof (or better yet, one sky) at **Maui Tropical Plantation.** Designed as a showplace and marketplace for the tropical agriculture of the islands, Maui Tropical Plantation does offer free admission to its official agricultural pavilions and exhibits. But you will probably want to hop aboard the Tropical Express ($5 for adults, $3 for kids) for a half-hour tour that traverses some 50 acres planted in bananas, papayas, coffee, pineapple, macadamia nuts, sugarcane, and other crops. The tour operates between 9:30 a.m. and 4 p.m., with departures every half hour, and a 15-minute free hula show during peak hours. Then you'll want to visit the Tropical Market, with a huge variety of flowers, fresh produce, and gifts (mailing service is available). And you might end up at the Tropical Restaurant for a nice luncheon buffet, or at the Snack Bar for some sandwiches, fruit and vegetable salads, and tempting desserts. There's a Sunset Bar-B-Que Monday and Wednesday, 5:30 and 8:30 p.m., $38 for adults, $28 for children. All in all, a very pleasant family-type excursion that could occupy a good part of the morning or afternoon. Maui Tropical Plantation is on Honoapiilani Hwy. at Waikapu, open daily 9 a.m. to 5 p.m. (tel. 244-7643). Inquire about shuttle-bus service from Lahaina and Kaanapali.

Back to sightseeing: Continue on now in the direction of Iao Valley, and about two miles from Wailuku, on the right, you'll note a sign reading **"Black Gorge President Kennedy Profile."** The jagged mountain cliff ahead of you, which does bear a resemblance to JFK's profile, has been there for centuries, but not until relatively recently, of course, did people begin to notice its timely significance. In another mile you'll come to **Iao Valley,** a wildly beautiful gorge dominated by the **Iao Needle,** 2,250 feet of green-covered lava rock reaching straight up into the sky. In this dramatic setting, Kamehameha won the battle that was to give him the island of Maui; the local warriors, accustomed to spears and javelins, were no match for Kamehameha's forces supplied with cannon by two English sailors. The carnage was so intense that the waters of Iao Stream were dammed up by the bodies of the conquered, giving the stream its present name: Kepaniwai, damming of the waters. Now all is tranquil here, save for the shouts of happy keikis wading through the pools at **Kepaniwai Park,** where present-day Mauians love to go for a picnic or a swim. Beautifully landscaped gardens with Oriental pagodas, swimming, and wading pools provide a palatial playground in this crisp mountain valley.

KIHEI-WAILEA: If you're staying in Kahului, Kihei is your nearest beach, about a 15-minute drive, via Rte. 38 and then Rte. 35 right to Kihei. Both Kamaole Beach and Kalama Park are fine, but the beach is public everywhere, and you can swim where you like. Look for **Azeka's Place,** a lively shopping center on the ocean side of the road, and browse among a collection of tasteful shops. Our special favorite here is **Alchemists' Garden,** a store with an old-world look: we loved their cards, china, porcelain jewelry from Italy, oils and perfumes from Egypt (oils are sold at $2 a dram), and "gold by the inch," from 75¢ an inch, which they'll make up into necklaces and bracelets. Note Laurel Birch's quite stunning enamel jewelry, from about $16 to $80 for earrings and necklaces. They have a good selection of Christmas tree ornaments too. . . . Another highly tasteful boutique is **Rainbow Connection,** which, in addition to its many condo decorative items, has a unique jewelry collection: we admired the handmade, hand-painted porcelain jewelry (from $25 to $90), the earrings and necklaces made of Hawaiian volcanic glass (from $12 to $45), the brass shell items, and jewelry and hand-carved wooden mirrors from Bali. . . . Browse through a good selection of books at **Silversword Bookstore,** pick up some beachwear at **Leilani** or **Tropical Traders.**

You may want to stop in at **Vagabond,** where you can not only rent a surfboard, but also stock up on bags, tank shirts, and all kinds of necessities for the beachcomber's lifestyle. . . . **Wow Swimwear** has something for "everybody." . . . **Maui Dive Shop** can outfit you for scuba or snorkeling and take you on a tour. . . . **O'Rourke's Tourist Trap** is a good place to get any necessities you forgot to pack, as well as postcards, monkeypod souvenirs, and the like. . . . **Lobster & Roses** has pretty clothes, gauzy dresses and tops, and those tiny High

Voltage bikinis. . . . **Liberty House** has its usual excellent selections. . . . **Pingo's Yardarm** features muumuus and aloha shirts in tapa and palaka prints, and makes clothes to order, at good prices. . . . And **Ben Franklin** has a little bit of everything.

Note: Check the local papers for news of the Swap Meet and Flea Market usually held on Saturday in the courtyard of St. Theresa's Church, near Azeka's Place on Kihei Road. Many local artisans take part. We saw some beautiful hand-painted blouses here for $17; the next day, we spotted them in a gift shop for $35! Hours are 7 a.m. to 3 p.m. Farmer's Markets are often held Tuesday and Friday on the grounds of the Suda Store.

In the Kealia Beach Center at 101 N. Kiehi Rd. (underneath Polli's on the Beach restaurant), **La Pré Shell and Gift Shop** has some attractive jewelry at reasonable prices. Our $9 shell necklace—which we'd seen elsewhere for several dollars more—was a hit!

On the ocean side of the street, at 1770 S. Kihei Rd., is the **Gallery Makai, a** distinctive small gallery that represents such well-known artists as Guy Buffet, Pegge Hopper, Richard Nelson, and Shige Yamada. And if a visit here whets your appetite for art, continue on to the **Stouffer Wailea Beach Resort** and have a look at the splendid artworks in the public areas, noting especially Ruthadell Anderson's weavings adjacent to the front desk, Nancy Clark's banners in the Palm Court, Tom Van Sant's concrete intaglio work on the Wailea Terrace, and his superb mural in the main lobby, an impressionistic colored-paper collage of a volcanic eruption and the streams of lava cascading down the mountains into the sea. Quite a stunner.

The Wailea Shopping Village in this area is also of interest to art lovers. **Elephant Walk,** a shop and a gallery, has a superb selection of posters by such noted island artists as Diane Hansen-Young and Kim Taylor Reece, from about $35. It also has fine examples of feather work and pottery. Other tasteful shops here include **Alexia Natural Fashions** (natural-fabric clothing for women), and **Sea and Shell,** which has nicer-than-usual island gifts, with a good selection of windchimes.

Drive a little further on and you can explore the **Makena Resort Maui Prince Hotel,** very modern and elegantly understated. Two waterfalls run down into the central courtyard and lead to the Japanese rock garden. You may want to stop in at the Café Kiowai on the garden level for a $4 dessert (like tropical soufflé with kiwi and papaya slices) and a $2 cup of coffee.

2. Haleakala, the House of the Sun

Any schoolchild on Maui can tell you the story of the demi-god Maui, the good-natured Polynesian Prometheus, who gave man fire, lifted the Hawaiian Islands out of the sea on his fishhook, and trapped the sun in its lair until it agreed to move more slowly around the earth—so that his mother could have more time to dry her tapa before night came! And where did this last, most splendid achievement take place? Why, right at **Haleakala,** 10,023 feet up in the sky, just about the closest any Stone Age person—or god—ever got to the sun.

With or without benefit of legends, Haleakala is an awesome place. The world's largest dormant volcano (its last eruption occurred two centuries ago), its 33-mile-long, 24-mile-wide, 10,000-foot-high dimensions make Vesuvius seem like a mud puddle. Even more spectacular is the size of the volcano's crater: 7½ miles long, 2½ miles wide, big enough to swallow a modern metropolis or two within its moon-like desert. Haleakala is one of the great scenic wonders of Hawaii.

TO THE SUMMIT: Plan on at least three hours for the Haleakala excursion (37 miles from the airport each way) and bring a warm sweater or jacket with you (it gets surprisingly cold and windy two miles up). We feel it's best to get an early start on this trip, since there's less likelihood of clouds early in the day. You might call the park headquarters (tel. 572-7749) to check on cloud, road, and weather conditions before you start out. There's no place to eat once you enter **Haleakala National Park,** but you might pack a picnic lunch and stop at Hosmer's Grove on the lower slopes. You can have a very good breakfast, or get sandwiches or a snack at **Bullock's of Hawaii,** in Pukalani, about halfway between Kahului and the park. You might also stop off at the **Pukalani Superette,** a real upcountry store, where you can get mangos for about half of what they cost in town, plus delicious homemade sushi and lumpia, and local Japanese and Filipino delicacies. The drive starts in Kahului on Rte. H-32; head eastward to Haleakala Hwy. (Rte. H-36), on which you turn right. Shortly after Rte. H-36 swings left, it's intersected on the right by Rte. H-37, which takes you to Rte. H-377, the Upper Kula Road, where you head up into a cool forest of flowers, cactus, and eucalyptus.

Among the most striking flowers that bloom in this mountain soil are protea, and you may have noticed that protea are becoming a new commercial crop for Maui. If you'd like to see them growing in their natural habitat and perhaps buy some to take home or have shipped, stop at one of the protea farms that dot these Maui uplands. **Sunrise Protea Farm,** for one, is located on Hwy. 378, two miles from Hwy. 377 (at the 4,000-foot elevation). You can walk through the garden (from mid-June to September, the dormant season for protea, there probably won't be much to see), have a look at their crafts center, perhaps buy an "introductory bouquet" for under $20.

Now watch for the turnoff to Rte. H-378 to the left, Haleakala Crater Road, a snaky two-lane highway curving through the clouds. You'll see cattle and horses on the pasture lands of Haleakala Ranch as you climb the slopes of the volcano. At 6,700 feet, you reach the entrance to Haleakala National Park. You'll then see **Hosmer's Grove** on the left, a scenic place to picnic (or camp) among rare trees and plants. Temperate tree seedlings from around the world have been planted here, along a half-mile trail of native shrubs and trees that are home for a variety of birds; you may see a pueo (short-eared owl) or a ringnecked pheasant. Stop at park headquarters a mile ahead at 7,030 feet, where the friendly and knowledgeable rangers will give you maps, instructions, directions for hiking the trails, and camping permits. Admission to the park is $1 per person or $3 per car. The choicest way to see Haleakala is to go into the crater on foot or horseback, but you must check with the rangers before you do.

Now you're ready for the ascent on this South Seas Everest, to the **Haleakala Observatory Visitors Center,** two miles up on the edge of the crater. Inside the octagonal observatory, you learn that the early Hawaiians used the crater as a highway across eastern Maui, camping in its caves and building rock shelters. The last eruption from the crater was prehistoric, although there was an eruption from the flanks of Haleakala just 200 years ago, and very likely the volcano will erupt again; it is dormant, not extinct. But the most thrilling show is what lies beyond the glass: a dark kaleidoscope of clouds and colors and light played against what might well be the deserts of the moon. On a clear day you can see over a hundred miles to the horizon, your field of vision encompassing 30,000 square miles of the Pacific; from this altitude, the volcano's vast cones look like so many sand dunes. Their rust-like colors change as the day grows old. At sunrise the crater is in shadow; it seems to give birth to the sun. From midday to sunset the play of sun and shadow is more subtle, and sunset, according to some, is the most muted and lovely of all. One of the easiest ways to get a spirited controversy going among Mauians is to ask whether sunset or sunrise is more superlative at Haleakala; suffice it to say that both are considered among the great natural sights of the world.

The summit of Haleakala is a half mile beyond at **Red Hill,** atop a cinder cone 10,023 feet high. Nearby, there's a satellite-tracking station and a **Science City** complex (the clear air here in mid-Pacific permits research that could be done nowhere else), which you reach via the Skyline Drive.

On the way down from Haleakala, you should stop for some different—and spectacular—views of the crater at **Kalahaku** and **Leleiwi** lookouts. (Because of safety hazards, you cannot stop at these places on the drive uphill.) At Kalahaku, you view the vast crater on one side; on the other you'll spot western Maui and your first silverswords (unless you've seen some on the Big Island). The silversword is a botanical rarity, a plant that will grow only on lava rock, at the highest altitudes. These curious, oversize cousins of the sunflower have sword-like leaves, and when they're ready to blossom (between June and October) they shoot up a stalk the size of a man. The whole thing turns into a tower of pink and lavender flowers, blooms once, and dies, scattering its seeds into the cinders to begin the phenomenon all over again. At the next lookout, Leleiwi, you may, with great luck, get to see the rather spooky specter of the Brocken; the sun must be strong at your back with misty clouds overhead in order for you to see your own shadow in the rainbow-mist of the crater. It doesn't happen often, but when it does, it is unforgettable; a ranger told us that he has seen it many times, and with as many as seven rainbows!

Coming down from the heights of Haleakala, it's pleasant to stop on the lower slopes at **Sunrise Market,** near the beginning of Crater Road. Take out your personal or business card and tack it up along with the thousands of others that dot these walls: people like this friendly place so much they like to leave a memento here. You can have a free sample of fresh papaya, buy some sandwiches or local fruits, get a cup of coffee, a slice of banana cake, or even some pineapple/macadamia-nut fudge from the Maui Fudge Kitchen. Prices are low on a variety of items: we spotted a magnificent poster of Haleakala Crater for $9 that was selling for $15 elsewhere. They also sell protea bouquets and dried protea products. And if you like, you may stroll and take photos on their carnation farm.

CAMPING AND RIDING IN HALEAKALA: Hiking buffs take note: you can spend a magnificent two or three days in Haleakala for spectacularly low prices. At Haleakala there are three dormitory cabins, each sleeping 12, for overnight lodging. The cabins have running water, wood-burning stoves, and cooking and eating utensils. All you need bring is food, water, a sleeping bag, and matches! The three form a sort of triangle in the crater, and you can go from one to the other on your exploration. **Kapalaoa Cabin** is at the middle of the southern end of the crater, **Paliku Cabin** is northeast of Kapalaoa at the eastern tip, and **Holua Cabin** is northwest of Paliku across at the western tip of the crater. Write to the Superintendent, Haleakala National Park, P.O. Box 369, Makawao, Maui, HI 96768, to make reservations for use of the cabins. Give the details of your proposed trip, the number in your party, dates of the stay, and names of the specific cabins you wish to use each night. The price is minimal: $5 per person per night, $2.50 for children 12 and under, with a minimum of $15 per night, plus a $15 key deposit. There is an additional charge of $2.50 per person for firewood. Cabins may be occupied for no more than three consecutive nights, with a maximum of two nights' stay in any one cabin. So popular are these cabins that assignments for each month are chosen by lottery 60 days prior to the beginning of the month. In other words, if you want a reservation sometime in the month of July, be sure your request is received before May 1.

We should note that these cabins—and these trails—are for experienced hikers in good physical condition: the Park Service warns that "wilderness travel is arduous; the elevation and exertion required to return from the crater floor place excessive physical demands upon the body. Pits, cliffs, caves, and associated sharp rocks are dangerous."

If you'd like to ride down into the crater, get in touch with the people at **Pony Express Tours,** who offer half-day rides, down to the crater floor and back up, lunch included, at $80 per person. No experience is needed. A full-day ride, nicknamed "heavy duty," is for rugged types only, explores the crater floor extensively, and costs $120 per person. Gentler one- and two-hour rides are also offered at Haleakala Ranch, on the beautiful lower slopes of the mountain, for $20 and $40. For all trips, you must wear long pants and closed-toe shoes. Contact Pony Express Tours, P.O. Box 507, Makawao, Maui, HI 96768 or phone 667-2202. You can also reach them through any of the Activity Desks in Lahaina and Kaanapali.

Did you know that you can coast downhill on a bicycle, all the way from the 10,000-foot summit of Haleakala to sea level below? You must be a skilled rider and in good physical condition, and it helps if your nerves are in good shape. Several outfits offer these tours; our local correspondent, who lived to tell the tale, claims that **Cruiser Bob's Haleakala Downhill** offers the best experience. They have both a sunrise trip (departure at 3 a.m.), which includes a continental breakfast and champagne brunch, and a day trip, which departs at a more civilized 8 a.m., and includes continental breakfast and a picnic lunch halfway down the slopes. Riders of all ages are welcomed, but there is a five-foot minimum height requirement. The price is approximately $80, and may vary slightly from season to season. For reservations, phone 667-7717. A neat family adventure.

MAKAWAO:

On your way back down from Haleakala, it's easy to make a visit to Makawao, Maui's very own cowboy town, the scene every Fourth of July of the famed Makawao Rodeo. Turn right at Pukalani for just a few miles and you'll find yourself on the main street of what looks like something out of the Old West. This is a good place to stop off for a snack; local people swear by the fried doughnuts on a stick at **Komoda's General Store**—as well as by their great macadamia-nut cookies and cream puffs. You can get various espressos and coffees, light dishes like bagels and cream cheese, waffles and tofu enchiladas at cute little **Zambala's,** a one-flight-up café on Baldwin Avenue, perhaps pick up some sandwiches at the **Rodeo General Store** (see preceding chapter), or splurge on dinner at the **Makawao Steak and Fish House** at 3612 Baldwin Ave., which has long been popular in these parts. Local shops sell everything from ranch supplies to lovely clothing to island arts.

Unless you're planning to stop at **Paia** on the way to Hana (see below), we recommend that you do so now. Instead of taking the road back to Pukalani, just take Baldwin Avenue a few miles into Paia, where you can shop for gifts and antiques and hobnob with the local people before heading back home.

HAWAIIAN VINEYARDS:

An unusual side trip you might want to take on your way back from Haleakala is to the **Tedeschi Vineyards,** on Hwy. 37 in the beautiful Maui upcountry at the Ulupalakua Ranch, not far from the town of Kula. The vineyard welcomes you for a free, self-guided tour daily, from 10 a.m. to 5 p.m. After experimenting with 140 different varieties of grape, Emil Tedeschi found the one he was after. The result is Maui Carnelian champagne, so delicious, and a great buy at around $18 in stores. His first wine, Maui Blanc, a light pineapple wine, is also very popular in the islands. The latest release is a red table wine, Maui Nouveau, in the Beaujolais style. The bottling area was once a dairy, the aging cellar is in the basement of the old jail, and you attend your wine-tasting session in the jail proper. After your tour, you can buy Maui wine T-shirts or gold-dipped grape blossoms as mementos (tel. 878-6058).

3. The Road to Hana

Ten thousand feet down from the moon canyons of Haleakala, curving around the base of the old volcano, is a world light-years away, a place of such tropical lushness and splendor that it conjures up the word "primeval." This is remote Hana and the curving road leading to it—a road carved under the fringe of the lava cliffs, plunging down on one side to the sea, emerging on the other from overhanging jungle watered by the thousand streams of Haleakala.

In all of Hana, there are just a few dozen modestly priced hotel rooms. (The town's chief industry is the exquisite Hana Maui Hotel, which caters to wealthy travelers only.) If you can reserve one of these (see the preceding chapter), it would be worth your while to stay overnight; otherwise, you'll have to do Hana in a one-day trip. Count on two to three hours each way, more if you want to savor the magnificent scenery. And be sure to check with the Highway Department about road conditions before you take off. If the weather has been wet, you could get stuck in landslides or mud. If it's raining heavily, forget the Hana trip altogether. Parts of the road are easily washed away, and it may take hours for you to be rescued (which happened one year to friends of ours). There's always tomorrow, or the next visit to Maui.

Even though extensive highway repaving has made it much easier to drive the Hana road, it is still rugged and winding. There are plenty who love it as well as some who think that, despite the glory of the scenery, it's just not worth the effort. A picnic lunch is essential, unless you want to eat at the expensive Hana Maui or one of the little snackshops on the road or in Hana. Besides, you'll be traveling through the kind of country for which picnics surely were originally invented.

Hana glories in its remoteness. Rumor has it that a road is not being built because the local people like to keep Hana the way it is—difficult to get to. The current road was not completed until 1927, and by that time, the Hasegawa General Store had already been in business 15 years and a hotel was already operating there. Hana's lush isolation attracted the late aviator and environmentalist Charles Lindbergh, who spent his vacations in Hana and is now buried there.

Because of its remoteness, Hana has been slow in accepting change. Throughout its history it has assimilated new cultures, new religions, and new institutions, but Hana has not become part of them; rather, they have become a part of Hana.

STARTING IN PAIA: Start eastward on Rte. H-32 in Kahului or Wailuku and switch (right) to H-36. You may want to stop at **Dillon's Restaurant** on the Hana Hwy., or **Pic-nics** on Baldwin Avenue in Paia, to pick up a picnic lunch (see Chapter XV), or take some time now, or on the return trip, to browse some of the antique, decorator, and gift shops that have sprung up in this unspoiled, upcountry community. Be sure to visit the **Maui Crafts Guild** at 43 Hana Hwy., a cooperative gallery showing outstanding work by local craftspeople. The two-story gallery carries a variety of crafts, ranging from bamboo (directly from the bamboo groves of Maui) to silk batik fashions and gift items. Prices can go way up for some of the furniture, wall sculptures, stained glass, but there are many items at small prices too: we recently spotted printed tablecloths at $18, Raku pottery at $17, lauhala ornaments at $5.

The nice thing about shopping in Paia is that it is a local, not a tourist, area.

Rents are not as high as in Lahaina or Kihei, so shopkeepers can afford to give you lovely things at good prices. One of the nicest of the local shops is **Tropical Emporium** at 104 Hana Hwy., where Veronica Popejoy specializes in natural fabrics (cottons, raw silks, rayons), shows "marbled" fabrics worked into tops and dresses, and has lots of cutwork and embroidered items. Best of all, she will coordinate a "look" for you that will work back home, too. . . . Another popular shop in this little cluster (they're all on either side of, or across the road from Dillon's Restaurant on Hana Hwy.) is **Jaggers,** 100 Hana Hwy., where you'll find handpainted, mostly made on Maui clothing. They also have men's trunks, T-shirts, and aloha shirts with a windsurfing theme. . . . **Rhonda's,** 76 Hana Hwy., is the place for handmade Hawaiian quilts, quilt pillow kits, and patterns. If you'd like to learn quilting yourself and have the time, inquire about their Saturday morning classes. Rhonda's also has handcrafted dolls, antiques, and children's clothing. . . . A small sawmill in nearby Haiku supplies the beautiful woodcrafts that you can see at **Exotic Maui Woods,** 85 Hana Hwy. We've seen a mango-wood nene goose at $30, dolphins and whales of koa wood at $110. Baskets begin at $10. . . . **Summerhouse,** 124 Hana Hwy., is an old favorite here. Their specialties are casual island wear in natural fibers, Oriental imports, and a swimsuit collection extraordinaire. . . . At the **Paia Art Center,** 120 Hana Hwy., the outstanding shop is **Rona Gale's Design Studio and Boutique.** Nothing here is inexpensive, but her collection is truly unique. We saw island designs by local artists handpainted on raw silk dresses and tops, plus other works by Maui artists in lesser-priced cottons. Nifty reversible cotton sweatshirts, designed here and made in India, were $60. . . . **Trade Winds Natural Foods** has whole-wheat croissants, bagels, muffins, and other munchies, in addition to the usual health-food line. . . . And the **Paia General Store** has everything a general store should have—including, because this is Maui, those wonderful macadamia-nut brownies and chocolate-chip macadamia nuts. Resist, if you can, and continue on your trip.

Before you get back on the road to Hana, however, you might want to make a short detour in Paia to **Hookipa County Beach Park,** otherwise known as "windsurfing capital of the world." Windsurfing, or sailboarding as it is also known, is an enormously popular new sport (it was introduced as an exhibition sport at the Los Angeles Summer Olympics in 1984), and nowhere are conditions better for it than right here on the northern shore of Maui. It's fun to watch the windsurfers anytime, and if there happens to be a competition going on (make local inquiries), you're in for a special treat.

Now it's back on the road to Hana. The highway runs straight and easy, through cane fields, until you get to Pauwela. Here's where the road becomes an Amalfi Drive of the Pacific; the view is spectacular, but keep your eye on the curves. The variety of vegetation is enough to drive a botanist—or photographer—wild. Waterfalls, pools, green gulches beckon at every turn. You'll be tempted to stop and explore a hundred times, but keep going, at least until you get to **Kaumahina Park,** where you might consider picnicking high on the cliff, looking down at the black-sand beach of Honomanu Bay below, watching the local folk fish and swim.

Believe it or not, from here on the scenery gets even better. From the road, you can look down on the wet taro patches and the peaceful villages of **Keanae** and **Wailua,** to which a short side trip, to see the old Catholic church built of lava rock and cemented with coral, is eminently worthwhile. It seems that this coral was strewn ashore after an unusual storm in the 1860s, providing the villagers with the necessary material to construct their church. To commemorate this miracle, they constructed the **Miracle of Fatima Shrine,** which you will see on the Wailua Bay Road, at the 18-mile marker (turn left at the road sign).

Not far from the shrine is **Uncle Harry's Fruit Stand and Living Museum,** which, in the two or three years that it's been open, has become one of the most popular spots on the Hana Road. And with good reason: not only can you pick up locally grown fruit, get a sandwich, and buy a souvenir, but you can also get to know the native Hawaiian family who runs the place, and who makes all of the crafts—rare wood tiki carvings, hand-carved wooden bowls of native woods, delightful Hawaiian Christmas ornaments, Hawaiian shell jewelry, and more. "Uncle Harry" Mitchell, his son, Harry Jr., and his daughter-in-law, Joanne, abound with aloha. Their little stand is on their home property; you're welcome to take pictures of the fruit trees, flowers, and lush greenery. They often give free samples of fruits, breads, coconut huskings; maps and visitor information—as well as rest rooms—are available. And they sell and ship fruit and gift packages everywhere. Refreshing.

In a little while, you get another vista of Keanae from Koolau Lookout. In the other direction you look through a gap in the cliff over into **Haleakala.** A little farther on is **Puaa Kaa Park,** another made-in-heaven picnic spot. The flowers are gorgeous here, and so are the two natural pools, each with its own waterfall. You might have a swim here before you continue. On you go, past grazing lands and tiny villages, to **Waianapanapa Cave,** another possible side excursion. This lava tube filled with water is the place where a jealous Stone Age Othello was said to have slain his Desdemona. Every April, the water is supposed to turn blood-red in remembrance. Near the cave is a black-sand beach (not always safe for swimming), another great place for a picnic. Just before reaching Hana, you arrive at **Helani Gardens,** a five-acre tropical botanical garden, through which you may take a self-guided tour.

They also have restrooms and a picnic area. Admission is $2 for adults, $1 for children.

HANA: Your first vision of heavenly Hana may be a letdown, if the black-sand beach is not as neat as it should be. But you can explore the views, watch how the other half lives over at the big hotel, or make a few historical pilgrimages.

Not a little history was made at Hana. The Big Three—Captain Cook, the Protestant missionaries, and the vacationing Hawaiian royalty—were all here. You can even follow the road to a historic Stone Age delivery room near the cinder cone of **Kauiki Head,** where Kamehameha's favorite wife, Kaahaumana, was born (there's a plaque near the lighthouse). Or you can just walk around the town for a while and soak up the atmosphere. A must on your list of sights should be the **Hasagawa General Store** where, it is reported, you can get anything and everything your heart desires (just like at Alice's Restaurant) in one tiny shack. A song was written about the place some years ago, and it has not changed in spite of all the hullabaloo. As for practical matters, the store has clothing, books, film, wine, and sporting goods, but because of the scarcity of restaurants in Hana, the food department—plenty of local fruit, some vegetables, mostly sausage meats, and some staples—will be of most interest to you. And you may not be able to resist—as we couldn't—the bumper stickers that read: "Fight Smog—Buy Horses, Hasagawa General Store" or "We visited Hasagawa General Store—far from Waikiki."

A visit to the **Hana Cultural Center** in the middle of town will fill you in with a bit of the history and background of this quaint town. Opened in 1983, the Cultural Center got most of its collection from local residents, and it's full of wonderful old photographs, Hawaiian quilts (note the unusual Hawaiian flag quilt dating from the 1920s), plenty of memorabilia from the 30s and 40s, as well as old artifacts and tools, and rare shells. Admission is free; the center is open Monday to Saturday, 11 a.m. to 4 p.m. (tel. 248-8622).

Hana's best beach, **Hamoa,** is at the Hotel Hana-Maui, but you can also swim at the public beach on Hana Bay, at the black-sand beach at Waianapanapa State Park, and at the "red-sand" beach (ask locals how to get there). Most visitors drive about ten miles past Hana on to Kipahulu, an unspoiled extension of Haleakala National Park and **Ohe'o Gulch** (formerly, but incorrectly, known as the Seven Sacred Pools), a gorgeous little spot for a swim. Here the pools drop into one another and then into the sea. But it's a roller-coaster ride on a rough, narrow road filled with potholes, and again, unless you dote on this kind of driving, it may not be worth your nerves.

En route to Ohe'o Gulch, you'll pass **Wailua Gulch** and a splendid double fall cascading down the slopes of Haleakala. Nearby is a memorial to Helio, one of the island's first Catholics, a formidable proselytizer and converter. A tribute to his work stands nearby—the *Virgin of the Roadside,* a marble statue made in Italy and draped every day with the fragrant flower leis of the Hawaiians. The good road runs out a little farther on at Kipahulu, so it's back along the northern route, retracing your way past jungle and sea to home base.

Now for the fourth of your day-long trips:

4. Lahaina

If Haleakala and Hana are nature's showplaces on Maui, Lahaina is man's. It was there that some of the most dramatic and colorful history of Hawaii was made: a hundred years ago Lahaina was the whaling capital of the Pacific, the cultural center of the Hawaiian Islands (and for a time its capital), and the scene of an often violent power struggle between missionaries and sailors for—quite literally—the bodies and souls of the Hawaiians.

Your trip to Lahaina and the western Maui coast happily combines history with some of the most beautiful scenery in the islands. Take your bathing suit and skip the picnic lunch, since there are plenty of places en route where you can eat. Since there's no paved road completely circling the western tip of Maui, we'll take the road as far as Honokahua, and return by driving back along the same road to Kahului—a route that is more interesting and comfortable than the drive on the unpaved portion between Honokahua and Waihee on the northern shore. The trip begins on Hwy. 32, which you follow through Wailuku to Hwy. 30 (High Street), where you turn left. At Maalaea the road swings right at the sea and continues along the base of the West Maui Mountains, along a wild stretch of cliffs pounded by angry seas, until it reaches Lahaina, 22 miles from Kahului.

THE SIGHTS OF LAHAINA: Lahaina today is a comfortable plantation town, with pretty little cottages, a cannery, sugar mill, and acres of cane and pineapple stretching to the base of the misty western Maui hills. It has for some years been in the process of a restoration that will cover the 150 years or so during which Lahaina rose from the Stone Age to statehood—from the reign of King Kamehameha I to the annexation of Hawaii by the United States. Re-created will be the days when Lahaina was the capital of the Hawaiian monarchy (before the king, in 1843, moved the palace to Honolulu, where there was a better harbor); the coming of the missionaries; the whaling period; and the beginning of the sugar industry. The restoration is being lovingly and authentically carried out by the Lahaina Restoration Foundation, a devoted group of local citizens and county and state interests. The project is proceeding at caterpillar-like speed, but there are enough historic landmarks around to keep you busy.

Begin your exploration out on the old pier in the center of town, where you can gaze at the famed **Lahaina Roads;** from the 1820s to the 1860s this was the favorite Pacific anchorage of the American whaling fleet. Over on your left are the soft greens of Lanai, to the north the peaks of Molokai, on the south the gentle slopes of Kahoolawe. During the winter and early spring, you may get to see some nonpaying tourists sporting about in the water; these are the sperm whales that migrate from their Aleutian homes to spawn in the warmer waters off Lahaina.

For the whalers, this place was practical as well as beautiful; they were safe here in a protected harbor, they could come or go on any wind, there was plenty of fresh water at the local spring, plenty of island fruits, fowl, and potatoes. And there were also Hawaiian women, who, in the old hospitable way of the South Seas, made the sailors feel welcome by swimming out to the ships, and staying a while. To the missionaries, this was the abomination of abominations, and it was on this score that violent battles were fought. More than once, sailors ran through the streets setting houses on fire, rioting, beating up anyone who got in their way, even cannonading the mission house. You can see the evidence of those days at **Hale Paaho,** the old stone prison (on Prison Street, off Main), where sailors were frequent guests while the forays lasted.

Across the street from the waterfront, you'll see the **Pioneer Inn,** which may look oddly familiar—it's been the set for many a South Seas movie saga. Back in 1901 (it has since been tastefully renovated and enlarged) it was quite the place, the scene of arrival and departure parties for the elegant passengers of the Inter-Island Steamship Company, whose vessels sailed out of Lahaina. And since it was too difficult to make the hot trek to central Maui immediately, arriving passengers usually spent the night here. Walk in and have a look around: note the lovely stained-glass window one flight up from the entrance to the **Harpooner's Lanai** and the grandfather's clock at the foot. The lanai itself is a wonderful place to waste a few years of your life while soaking up the atmosphere.

Across Wharf Street from the hotel, a little to the north of the lighthouse, is the site of a palace used by Kamehameha in 1801, when he was busy collecting taxes on Maui and the adjoining islands. And across from that, where the Lahaina Branch Library now stands, is another spot dear to the lovers of the Hawaiian monarchy, the royal taro patch where Kamehameha III betook his sacred person to demonstrate the dignity of labor.

The huge banyan tree just south of the Pioneer Inn covers two-thirds of an acre; it's the favorite hotel for the town's noisy mynah bird population. In the front of the tree is the **Court House,** a post office, and police station, the post office part of which has been functioning since 1859. Between the Court House and the Pioneer Inn, you'll see the first completed project of the Lahaina Restoration, the **Fort Wall.** It's built on the site of the original fort, but since rebuilding the whole fort would have destroyed the famed banyan tree, the authorities decided to reconstruct the wall instead, as a ruin—a ruin that never existed.

Now that you've seen how the whalers lived, let's see how their arch opponents, the missionaries, fared. Walk one block mauka of the waterfront to Front Street and the **Baldwin Home**—so typical, with its up- and downstairs verandas, of New England in Polynesia. The old house, built in the late 1830s with walls of coral and stone, served as a home for the Rev. Dwight Baldwin, a physician and community leader as well as a missionary (and incidentally, the founder of a dynasty; the Baldwins are still an important family in Maui). Thanks to the Lahaina Restoration Foundation, the house has been faithfully restored; you can examine Dr. Baldwin's medical kit (the instruments look like something out of a Frankenstein film), kitchen utensils, and china closets, old photographs and books, the family's furniture and mementos, all the little touches of missionary life 100 and more years ago. Open daily. Admission is $2 for adults and free for children accompanied by their parents for a personally guided tour.

The Restoration Foundation also operates the floating museum ship *Carthaginian,* moored opposite the Pioneer Inn. Its "World of the Whale" exhibit features a series of colorful multimedia displays on whaling, whales, and the sea life of Hawaii. Maui's own humpback whale, which comes to these waters each winter to mate and calve, gets special treatment through videotape presentations made on the spot by the National Geographic Society, the New York Zoological Society, and others. The ship has been restored as a 19th-century brig and is open daily from 9 a.m. to 4:30 p.m. Admission is $2 for adults, free for children with their parents. (If you visit between January and May, when the whales are "in town," be sure to drop by the Whale Report Center at the *Carthaginian* berth where sightings pour in by phone and radio, and you can add your personal observations to the scientific data being compiled.)

Head now for Wainee Street (to the right of Lahainaluna Road); here, where the recently built **Waiola Church** now stands, is the site of Wainee, the first mission church in Lahaina, to which the Reverend Baldwin came as pastor in 1835. The old cemetery is fascinating. Buried among the graves of the missionary families are some of the most important members of the Kamehameha dynasty, including no fewer than two wives of Old King Kam: Queen Keoupuolani, his highest born wife, and Queen Kalakaua.

Outside of Lahaina proper, opposite Wahikuli State Park, is the **Lahaina Civic Center,** an auditorium and gym, with a dramatic mosaic by one of Maui's most famous artists, Tadashi Sato.

Five miles east of Lahaina, on the highway headed toward Kahului, are the well-preserved **Olowalu Petroglyphs.** Two to three hundred years old, these rock carvings depicted the occupations—fishing, canoe-paddling, weaving, etc.—of the early Hawaiians. Unfortunately, they are rather difficult to get to.

On the other side of Lahaina, on the road leading toward Kaanapali, is another historical spot, the **Royal Coconut Grove of Mala.** Mala, one of the wives of Kamehameha, brought the trees from Oahu over a century ago. They are now being replaced by local citizens as part of the restoration.

For collectors of Orientalia, it would be unthinkable to leave Lahaina without a visit to the **Japanese Cultural Park** of the Lahaina Jodo Mission. In a beautiful spot perched above the water is a 3½-ton statue of Amitabha Buddha, erected to commemorate the centennial anniversary of Japanese immigration in Hawaii. You can meditate here as long as you wish, strike the huge temple bell, and perhaps leave a small donation in the offertory (there is no admission charge). *Note:* It's easy to miss this place. As you drive along Front Street, look for the big sign that reads "Jesus Coming Soon." Then turn makai on Ala Moana Street and you'll find the Buddha.

If you want to continue your sightseeing out in the Kaanapali resort area now, there are two ways to go, in addition to driving your own car. The first is the Shoreline bus, which connects Lahaina and Kaanapali for $1.50, leaving Lahaina from the Shopping Center every hour and half hour most of the day. It's more fun, however (and also more expensive: $7.50 round trip, $4.50 one way, half fare for children), to hop the oldtimey **Lahaina-Kaanapali & Pacific Railroad,** a reconstructed, turn-of-the-century sugarcane train for the 12-mile round trip between Lahaina and Kaanapali. You'll be entertained with songs and stories en route by a singing conductor, and kids will get a kick out of the hoot of the locomotive's whistle. The railroad terminal is on Honoapiilani Hwy., one block north of Papalaua Street; the bus service from the Pioneer Inn, Boat Harbor, Shopping Center, etc., to the terminal is free. Before or after the trip, you might want to check out the stand at the station that sells fresh coconuts, chilled for eating and drinking, $2, plus fresh-trimmed sugar cane, $1.75.

Note: Shoreline Transportation also provides service from Lahaina to Maaleaa, Kihei, and Wailea, linking western and eastern Maui. For schedules and fees, phone 661-3827.

SHOPPING IN LAHAINA: We must confess: the thing we love to do most in Lahaina is shop. While the reconstruction of the historical sights is proceeding slowly, Lahaina (and Whaler's Village at Kaanapali Beach, see below) is fast emerging as one of the best shopping areas in the islands, second only to Honolulu. On each one of our visits there are new and exciting shops, boutiques, galleries to visit. Perhaps it's the influence of the young people and other newcomers moving into the area; they keep everything constantly stimulating and alive.

First, let's get your car parked. Finding a spot on the street is not easy, although it's often possible on Front Street, on the ocean side. Also try the Lahaina Shopping Center, the area behind the Wharf Shopping Center, at the corner of Front and Prisons Streets and at the corner of Front and Shaw Streets. If that doesn't work, however, drive in to one of the commercial parking lots like the one behind Baldwin House, at the corner of Luakini and Dickinsen Streets: charges are reasonable. Across from the parking lot is a place where you can get fresh island produce to take home, and in front of that is a stand selling ice-cold coconut juice for $1.50.

Cool and refreshed now, let's start our wanderings, perhaps at **Apparels of Pauline,** 697 Front St., a shop a bit different from most others in Hawaii. The emphasis here is on good-quality, handmade clothing at reasonable prices. Most of the artwork for their unique handpainted pieces—blouses, T-shirts, dresses, hats, handbags, and so on—is done on Maui. Their Balinese shirts and sundresses, batiked by hand, are another plus, and so is their collection of Indonesian handicrafts—mirror frames, curio cabinets, and wooden papaya, coconut, and banana trees. Handpainted T-shirts average $30; Japanese kimonos $40, batik sundresses, $59.

Not too many places like the **South Seas Trading Post** at 851 Front St. are left in Lahaina, places where the owners still search out and find authentic South Seas and Oriental treasures. Although there are many collector's items here—primitive art from New Guinea, bronzes and buddhas from Thailand, precious jades from China—most of the items are surprisingly affordable: consider, for example, one-of-a-kind jewelry designs using antique pieces, $25 to $75; freshwater pearl necklaces with precious gemstones, from $18; hundred-year-old porcelain spoons from China, at $10; Christmas ornaments in the shape of whales, $3.50—and much more. . . . **The Whaler, Ltd.,** at 866 Front St., is just about the only honest-and-true nautical shop in the old whaling port of Lahaina. They have lanterns that run on oil, brass lamps and hooks in various shapes, scrimshaw and ivory carvings, whaling prints and boxes, carvings of whales and whalers, and more.

Central to the Lahaina shopping scene is **The Wharf,** 658 Front St., a stunning three-story arcade built around a giant tree, with a fountain and a stage on the lower level, a glass elevator, a number of attractive eating places, and dozens of shops reflecting high quality and taste. Soft contemporary music plays throughout the complex as you shop. Here you'll find places like **Ocean Magic,** which has casual wear plus beautiful hand-embroidered tablecloths from China, eel-skin wallets, and other treasures. . . . **Alberta's Gazebo** no longer has a real gazebo, but it does have some knockout imported clothing; we loved the appliquéd jackets from the Phillipines. Alberta creates necklaces from a collection of extraordinary beads: 200- to 800-year-old African trading bead necklaces (from $50 to $60) and 2,000-year-old Inca and Aztec beads (up to $200). Local shell necklaces, bracelets, and earrings begin at just $1.50. . . . We've always liked the fashions—in good taste and well priced—at **Luana's Originals.** Much of the clothing—for both men and women—is made here on Maui. . . . The people at **Nature's Emporium** are doing such good work that you really ought to buy something here. They're Maui headquarters for Greenpeace, and carry a large selection of Greenpeace and Earthtrust products—artwork, posters, jewelry, T-shirts, many gift items at moderate prices.

Hawaii Arts and Crafts is a must stop. It's a showcase for work by island artists in many media: we admired the woven baskets, the blown glass, the Raku pottery, the Hawaiian volcanic glass, and ceramic jewelry. Treeshell (fungi) necklaces are about $32, and cute little made-on-Maui ceramic whales are under $10.

Have you always wanted a genuine Panama hat? The **Maui Mad Hatter** has them, plus scads of other chapeaux—every known type of hat weave, including Maui Iauhala, for men, women, and children. Proprietor Shell Hansen, who invites visitors to his factory in Paia, claims, "If you've got the head, I've got the hat!" . . . Children can be outfitted with island clothes at **Little Polynesians,** and they'll love the hand-carved toys and the stuffed animals at **Geppetto's Workshop.**

We've already told you about the restaurants at The Wharf, but if all you want is a cookie to nibble on, or perhaps a coffee drink to go with it, try the delicious homemade goodies at **Whaler's Book Store,** a combination bookstore and European café, where you can sip your cappuccino in un-Lahaina-like peace. We often find stunning local books of art and photography and Hawaiiana here that are not readily available elsewhere: especially lovely is a new book called *The Hula,* by Jerry Harper. Check the papers for news of frequent entertainments at The Wharf; shops stay open late, so a visit here can be a good evening's activity.

Some of Hawaii's leading artists show their works at the **Lahaina Gallery,** 117 Lahainaluna Rd. Stop in to see some of our favorites: mystical Chinese landscapes by David Lee, charming Hawaiian primitives by Guy Buffet. The same artists show in three sister galleries, **Casay Gallery** at the Wharf, **Kapalua Gallery** in the Kapalua Shops at the Kapalua Bay Hotel, and **Gallery Kaanapali** at Whaler's Village. Be sure to see the exciting selection of posters and limited edition prints at the **Nagamine Poster Gallery** at 143 Lahainaluna Rd. Pegge Hopper, Robert Nelson, Guy Buffet, and David Lee are among the island artists represented.

If you happened to miss **Island Muumuu Works** in the Maui Mall, make up for that now by going to their new branch in Lahaina, at 180 Dickensen St., in Dickensen Square. Almost all the muumuus at this outlet store for the famous Hilda of Hawaii manufacturer are just $37.50, and their styles are truly flattering (we always note how many Maui women are wearing them each year). Men's aloha shirts, too, plus some attractive haku leis, all at low prices.

Once it was a pineapple cannery. Now the heavy equipment and the factory workers are gone, and in their place are a supermarket, a drugstore, scads of boutiques and restaurants, and plenty of tourists. Lahaina's newest shopping center, and its first enclosed, air-conditioned one, **The Cannery,** was just opening at 910 Honoapiilani Hwy. at the time of our last visit. It's a boon to people staying out this way, since the **Safeway Supermarket** stays open round the clock, and **Long's Drugs** fills a variety of needs. There is ample parking. As for the smaller shops, they are branches of favorite islands stores, like **Reyn's** for tasteful men's casual wear; **Alexia Natural Fashion** for stylish women's clothing in linen, cotton, and other natural fabrics; **Blue Ginger Designs,** where everything is made of handblocked batik fabrics; and **Super Whale,** which always has wonderful children's clothing. **Sir Wilfred's Coffee, Tea & Tobacco,** one of our favorites from Maui Mall is here; so, too, is **Pappoule's** for Greek food and pastries, and **Marie Callender's,** an outpost of the Oahu favorite known for its wonderful pot pies.

You can hardly miss the ads for **Hilo Hattie's Fashion Center** at 1000 Limahana Pl., in the industrial area near the sugarcane train. Hilo Hattie's provides free bus service from the courthouse at Lahaina Harbor seven times daily, and once you're there, they'll give you free leis, refreshments, and take you on a factory tour. You can choose from some 10,000 garments at good prices. Phone 661-8457 for information. While you're in the industrial area, have a look around too at some of the outlet stores. There's a **Coral and Gifts** outlet, and a **Lobster and Roses** sportswear outlet. Merchandise varies from day to day, but value can be excellent.

5. Kaanapali and Kapalua

Head out of Lahaina now for a bit of sightseeing at some glamorous hotels, shopping, and swimming. Your first stop should be at the splendid **Hyatt Regency Maui,** where you can have a look at the $80-million, 20-acre complex, lush with waterfalls, gardens, tropical birds, an acre-long swimming pool with its own bar in a lava cavern, an atrium lobby surrounding a 70-foot-tall banyan tree, and an elegant shopping arcade that rivals Rodeo Drive. A walk here is like touring a park-botanical garden and an indoor-outdoor museum of priceless Oriental art. This aesthetic and architectural tour-de-force offers gorgeous vistas wherever you look. You might want to pause and have a drink at the Weeping Banyan Bar beside a lagoon—and please don't throw crumbs at the penguins! Note too the unusual ceilings in the shops—there is one in stained glass—and perhaps pick up a trinket at a place like **Elephant Walk,** where prices go way up for safari exotica, but are relatively down-to-earth for elephant-hair jewelry.

By all means, pay a visit to the **Maui Marriott Resort** on Kaanapali Drive, next to the Hyatt Regency. This is an example of modern hotel architecture and landscaping at its best, especially beautiful at night, when lights, flowers, and tropic moon over the ocean create dazzling effects.

Your next stop should definitely be the new **Westin Maui Resort** (still under construction at the time of this writing), another gorgeous pleasure palace by the sea, with two million dollar's worth of artwork gracing the public areas and gardens, a spectacular, multi-level swimming pool complex fed by waterfalls and bridges (even bigger than the giant pool at the Hyatt Regency), and swans gliding just a few feet from the registration desk.

As you continue driving, you may want to stop at the **Sheraton Maui Hotel,** which sits atop **Black Rock,** the perch from which the souls of the dead Hawaiians were said to leap into the spirit world beyond. The majestic hotel, not in the least bit haunted, is worth having a look at, especially for the 360-degree view from the top, a sweeping panorama of ocean, islands, and mountains. The tasteful Polynesian formal lobby is on the top floor; you've got to take the elevators down to everything else, including Kaanapali Beach.

By the way, beaches are public in Hawaii, so you can swim at any of the hotel beaches you like. If you stop for a swim at the graciously Hawaiian **Kaanapali Beach Hotel,** a longtime favorite in this area, you're likely to run into a gentleman by the name of Richard Miano out at the beach shack. You'll recognize him by two fancy macaws, Molokai Joe and Foxy Lady, perched on his shoulders. These brilliantly-colored birds are quite tame and will be happy to perch on *your* shoulder, too, while Richards snaps your picture, and then turns it into a postcard to mail to envious friends back home. (We love the inscription on the inside: "Wish you were here! Having a great time in Hawaii. But since you can't be here—send money!") It's $3 for the first card, then $2 each for ten or more, delivered to your hotel.

WHALER'S VILLAGE: The main shopping attraction out here is Whaler's Village, recently done over and now bigger and better than ever. The one- and two-story buildings are of uniform design and materials, authentic reproductions of the type of buildings that the New England missionaries constructed in Lahaina between 1830 and 1890. First, pay a visit to the **Whaler's Village Museum** (on the third floor of Building G), study its absorbing collection of whaling memorabilia, and perhaps see the whaling film shown every half hour in the museum's theater. After you've boned up on history and soaked in some gorgeous views, you can concentrate on the serious business of shopping, and there's plenty to concentrate on.

One-of-a-kind, rare, unusual—these are words to describe the very special offerings at **Sea & Shell,** one of our favorites here. Everyone connected with this place seems to be talented; many of the employees paint cards and watercolors, create belts, and hair jewels; owners Mike and Madeleine Abrams do all the beautiful mountings and mirrors, and offer unique jewelry by local artisans. Prices begin as low as $3 for hand-carved napkin rings from Bali; wonderful "bird bags" in the shapes of swans, flamingos, and toucans are $32, and a conversation piece anywhere. . . . **Ka Honu Gift Gallery** is a delight, with lots of Hawaiian handmade works: dolls, ceramics, bowls of milo and koa wood, and Christmas ornaments that would look great on the tree back home. . . . If money were no object, we'd simply buy out all the fabulous Gayle Pope designs shown at **Silk Kaanapali, Ltd.** In addition to handpainted and unusually tailored clothing, the shop carries striking bags and other accessories, starting at about $30. . . . **Foreign Intrigue** is another mecca for beautiful women's clothing. . . . If you've forgotten your sunglasses, pick up a pair at **Eyecatcher Sunglasses.** The selection is huge and distinctive, albeit pricey. . . . Scrimshaw collectors should head straight for the **Lahaina Scrimshaw Factory,** where there's an impressive selection of quality art executed by over 45 different scrimshaw artists, most of them residents of Maui. There's a prize antique collection as well, with prices going up into the thousands. Do-it-yourself scrimshaw kits are available too, from $4.95 to $15.95. Since the people here are fervent "Save the Whale" supporters, they will continue to create fine-quality scrimshaw on nonendangered fossil walrus ivory. They've become so popular that they've opened an additional store in Lahaina, at 718 Front St., and a third at the Maui Marriott Resort. . . . Everything offered for sale at **Blue Ginger Designs** is made of batik, and that includes fabrics by the yard, and clothing for women, men, and children, as well as home furnishings. Blue Ginger, by the way, is the name of the native spice that grows wild in Singapore. (There's another shop at **The Cannery** in Lahaina.) . . . **Lahaina Printsellers** has some fascinating antique maps and prints that would look great on those walls back home. . . . Don't miss **Super Whale Children's Boutique** if you have your own kids with you or some back home to buy presents for. They have one of the best selections of Hawaiian-made children's clothing we've seen in the islands, including handpainted, appliquéd, and embroidered outfits for infants, an extensive swimwear selection and matching muumuus and aloha shirts. The size range goes from infants to 14 for girls, to size 20 for boys. Styles are unique and prices fair: bikinis from $12.50, short muus from $9, and shirts from $12.

We've already told you about some of the nifty restaurants at Whaler's

Village—**Rusty Harpoon, Ming Court, Leilani's on the Beach, Chico's Cantina** (see the preceding chapter).

THAR SHE BLOWS! From mid-December until the end of April, some 400 celebrities arrive in Maui, and everybody wants to see them. It's estimated that approximately 400 North Pacific humpback whales migrate 3,000 miles from their home in Alaska to mate and bear their young in the warm waters off Hawaii. You can probably spot a few whales from the beach or your lanai, but it's also fun to take one of the whale-watching excursion boats that leave daily from Maui harbors. All of the cruises are good, but we like to support the ones run by the **Pacific Whale Foundation;** when you travel with them, you're in the company of expert research scientists, and proceeds benefit the foundation's research and conservation efforts to save the endangered humpback whale. Cruises depart daily from Maalaea Harbor, last 2½ hours, and cost $20 for adults, $10 for children under 12. Be sure to bring your cameras for some spectacular shots. Call the Whale Hotline at 879-8811 or Maui Discoveries at 667-5358 for more information.

TO KAPALUA AND THE NEARBY BEACHES: One of the nicest things about the Hawaiian islands is that all beaches—even those at the fanciest hotels—are open to the public. As you stroll by the beachfront hotels (the Sheraton Maui, the Royal Lahaina, the Kaanapali Beach, the Marriott, the Westin Maui, the Hyatt Regency), you can stop by for a snack or a drink and treat yourself to a swim. Kaanapali Beach is superb, and we can personally recommend the swimming at both the Royal Lahaina and the Sheraton. The swimming is also good right behind Whaler's Village. Should you happen to pass this area during sugarcane harvest time, the hotels overlooking the sea may look like huge haunted palaces, uncannily spooky through the dense smoke.

On to more practical matters: **Honokawai Beach Park** is another good place for a picnic or a swim. If you're a shelling nut, get out your bucket and trek along the Kaanapali beaches, which are also good for more ambitious sports like skindiving and spearfishing. A mile or two past this is Kapalua where you should definitely stop to see the **Kapalua Bay Hotel,** the ultimate luxury resort. You probably won't want to book a room here (doubles start about $150), but take time out to explore the grounds and to visit **The Shops at Kapalua,** one of the most serenely tasteful of island marketplaces. **Auntie Nani** (of the Super Whale family) is here, and can outfit young teens as well as children. **Distant Drums,** "a cultural art gallery," showcases art, handcrafts, and jewelry from Bali, New Guinea, Asian and South Pacific shores, much of it museum quality. But there are some charming low-priced items, too, like bracelets handmade in Hawaii from woods indigenous to the islands, laminated and lacquered so you can wear them in the water, from $15 to $30; straw baskets from Sri Lanka at $15; handmade earrings from Bali, starting at $18. Enormously popular are their handcarved, handpainted tropical fish, the kind you see when you're out snorkeling in Maui waters: they go from $5.50 to $38, small to large, and are made in Sri Lanka. Ask about their Hawaiian quilts and pillows.

Have a sandwich and an espresso now, at the European-style **Market Café** (see Chapter XV), which also purveys a multitude of baskets, antique copperware, cheeses, and deli items. Or in the precincts of the hotel itself, join the leisure class at one of the best buffet lunches in the islands. That's the **Mayfair Buffet,** served in the hotel's graceful dining room every day between noon and 2:30 p.m., a feast of such lavish and delicious proportions that it is well worth the roughly $15 tariff. Or more simply, wander out to the **Bay Club.** Here you can have a medium-priced lunch, a drink, or simply walk out to see the breath-taking views, with blue sea at every vista. **Fleming Beach** is fine for swimming and snorkeling. Let the peace and beauty stay in your memory as you turn around and go back the way you came—the road continuing around the island is a poor one—driving the 32 miles back to Kahului.

Note: Despite any information you may receive locally, nude sunbathing is definitely against the law in the state of Hawaii.

HIKE MAUI:
So you want to get off the beaten path, away from the tourist routine, and explore the backcountry, the mountains, the jungles, and waterfalls and rain forests, perhaps even trek into the crater of mighty Haleakala, on foot. The best way we know to do all this is to team up with an amazing gentleman named Ken Schmitt, a professional nature guide and much more. Schmitt has lived in Maui for seven years, most of the time in the open, sleeping under the stars, living on wild fruits and vegetables on the jungle paths. He is a scholar, an explorer, an expert in the natural history and geology of Maui, and in the ancient legends and wisdom of Hawaii. He leads very small groups, or individuals, on a variety of 50 different hikes, which range from easy walks to arduous treks, and cost anywhere from $50 per person for a half-day tropical-valley hike to $85 for an excursion into Haleakala (children are about half-price). Personalized trips concentrating on special interests can be arranged. We've had ecstatic reports on these hikes.

We asked Ken what he might suggest for our budget-conscious readers: "Take one or two of my day hikes to find out everything necessary to enjoy camping or backpacking on Maui. Then you can live for free, fishing and eating wild fruit, taro, and sweet potatoes. Of course not everyone wants to live this way, but it can be done, and I will show you how. Each of my excursions is a workshop in natural history and environmental knowledge. In one day I can teach people as much as they could learn in weeks of research, including the following: locating safe and beautiful places to camp; selecting an itinerary appropriate to current weather conditions and personal interests and abilities; finding trailheads and following the trails; what fruit is in season and where to find it in the wilderness; where to rent equipment and what is needed; possible hazards in the environment and how to cope with them; how to get around without a car; where to buy inexpensive groceries, including farms that sell their own fresh fruit and vegetables. The emphasis of my programs is enhancing our connection with our natural environment and teaching the skills that we need to feel comfortable in Hawaii."

Sounds great to us. You can write in advance to Ken Schmitt at Hike Maui, P.O. Box 10506, Lahaina, HI 96761, or phone him when you arrive, at 879-5270.

READERS' SIGHTSEEING AND SHOPPING SUGGESTIONS ON MAUI: "On Maui we found a new service that I would recommend highly to anybody planning to take the road to Hana. 'Hana Cassette Guide' is available for $20 from Craig at the Dairy Rd. Chevron station on Rte. 380, before Rte. 36. Craig is a local photographer and is currently renting out of his van parked at the service station. (He may have permanent space by the time you are there; check the local sightseeing guides for his ad, or call 572-0550.) Craig narrates the tape himself and he is a joy to listen to. He is well-versed in local lore, legends, and facts about the 54 bridges, the uncountable waterfalls, and scenic views. We took the tape player out of the car whenever we stopped and the people around were interested in hearing the comments. Also included is a picture book of the wildflowers and a souvenir map. We consider this our 'Best Buy' on our trip to Maui" (Dennis N. Benson, Uniontown, Ohio). . . . "Your readers may want to know about **Tom Barefoot's Cashback Tours** (tel. 661-

8889). You can book any and all of your activities through them and get an immediate 10% cash back at time of purchase" (Pat McCallum, Bethesda, Md.).

"We certainly endorse your recommendation to visit **O'Rourke's Tourist Trap;** the shops do have outstanding bargains in all kinds of souvenirs, including T-shirts and Polynesian instruments. They also are very willing to handle special orders. . . . **Tropical Blossoms of Maui** in Paia is a "hole in the wall" full of inexpensive souvenirs. . . . The Lindbergh family has requested that local tourist information services not reveal the location of Charles Lindbergh's grave; it seems that some tourists have taken to removing portions of the grave stones as souvenirs!. . . . While Maui has many scenic beaches, there aren't many easily accessible from hardtop roads that are consistently suitable for novice snorkelers. In calm conditions, several of the west side beaches are acceptable. But when swells or windy conditions exist, your choices rapidly dwindle. One very notable exception is **Black Rock Cove** at Kaanapali. This sheltered cove has clear water and scores of colorful, small fish. If you are staying outside of this immediate area, just park in the Whaler's Village lot, walk to the beach, and head north about a quarter-mile; the cove is just below the Sheraton Maui Hotel. Tourists should also be advised that the many boat services that offer snorkeling excursions to Molokini Island are subject to weather effects; if conditions at Molokini are choppy, they will go instead to some alternate site (but this generally won't be announced until you're well underway)" (Dale Knutsen, Ridgecrest, Calif.).

"The ride to Hana was most enjoyable without the worry of driving. We went with **Trans Hawaiian Tours** and enjoyed the bumps, curves, waterfalls, and breathtaking and hair-raising views. Jeff, our guide and driver of the van, was most enthusiastic about the road and even showed us a few somersaults and high dives at the sacred pools. On the return trip, he brought us to a beautiful lava formation in the ocean at a dead end road somewhere between Wailua and Haiku" (Lorice A. Swydan, Worcester, Mass.). . . . "We discovered protea flowers, a variety of beautiful blossoms that grow on the slopes of Haleakala; they are the native flower of South Africa, and grow only there, in Australia, in Southern California, and now in the volcanic soil of Maui. The place to get them is at the **Hawaii Protea Cooperative** on Kula Hwy. 377, on the grounds of Kula Lodge. Prices for these fabulous flowers, which can be dried and last a very long time, go from 90¢ to $9 a blossom. You can also order flowers by mail. Send them $30, and they will send you whatever is currently in blossom—much cheaper than buying similar flower arrangements at home. Their address is Hawaii Protea Cooperative, P.O. Box 68, Kula, Maui, HI 96790" (Bob Harrison and Hal Goodstein, Provincetown, Mass.).

"We drove to **Hana** from Kahului airport in two hours. The road is much improved over the way it was on our trip four years ago. Readers should be cautioned that Hana is now under siege by tourists, and it is not unusual to see hundreds of cars, tour vans, and small tour buses on the road. The section of highway below Hana to the Seven Sacred Pools is narrow, bumpy, and full of traffic. Even so, the trip is well worth the effort" (Joe D. Kinard, Gree, S.C.).

"Ask Paul Gomez—or maybe anyone who is there—at the **Information Tourist Booth** in front of The Wharf in Lahaina for specialized personal tourist trips. They are always coming up with new things to show tourists. One day he took us to a windsurfing competition at Hookipa Beach; another time he arranged for three of us to hike into the interior with a native Hawaiian guide" (Rue Drew, New York, N.Y.). . . . "We took advantage of riding at the **Rainbow Ranch,** near Kaanapali Beach. A variety of riding tours is available at all levels of experience for reasonable prices. Good quality horses and great guides" (Patti Connor, Arlington, Mass.).

"For those who enjoy island artists, but don't have the hundreds of dollars needed to purchase an original David Lee or Robert Lyn Nelson painting, I suggest a stop at the **Nagamine Poster and Photo Gallery,** 135 Lahainaluna Rd. They carry poster-size reproductions of works by these and other artists at affordable prices. For example, I bought a Nelson poster for $35. Even better is the **Village Gallery,** at their main location just mauka of Baldwin House in downtown Lahaina and the **Village Gallery at the Cannery,** also on Front Street. The Gallery carries works by many excellent local artists not found in the more commercial galleries: this is a good place to see the great variety of ways in which island artists interpret their surroundings. There is a wide range of sizes, styles, media (including wood), and prices. I noticed prints by Dietrich Varez (whose work adorns the lobby of Volcano House, on the Big Island) for only $15. (There is, however, a better selection of Varez's works at the Volcano Art Center.) In short, the Village Gallery is a good place to sample the local art scene. . . . Although the road to Hana is no worse (barring washouts) than many mountain roads in my native West Virginia, I recommend letting someone else drive so you're free to watch the scenery. We thoroughly enjoyed the drive-in, fly-out tour by **Holo Holo Maui Tours.** The flight back to Kaanapali gave us an interesting new view of the terrain we had traversed so slowly earlier that day. Tours are also available in which they drive both ways" (Brent Warner, Charleston, W. Va.).

"Our most enjoyable **snorkeling** spot was near the rocks below the Maui Sheraton. The area is so beautiful, and public walkways lead right to the beach. Our daughter loved it here because she didn't have to go out too far to snorkel, and the water was calm, so we could lay across an air mattress to see the fish. This is a perfect way for youngsters or beginning swimmers to view the underwater world. It was also fun watching the windsurfers and natives diving off the cliffs." (Julie Martin, Huntington Beach, Calif.).

"Maui has some 150-odd miles of coastline with some superb beaches. But if you're bored with sun and sand, try something different—say, a **hike into Maui's backcountry,** and enjoy some of the pristine beauty seldom seen by the average tourist. Pick up the book *Hiking Maui,* by Robert Smith (Wilderness Trail Guide Series, $4.95); it's splendid reading. It also covers a large variety of hikes, complete with maps, difficulty ratings, where to obtain permission if needed, with a sensitive, no-nonsense approach to hiking. Our favorites: the Iao Stream (no. 16) or, for the more history minded, the King's Highway (no. 15) in La Perouse Bay" (J. A. Drouin, Edmonton, Alberta, Canada).

"We have our own snorkeling equipment and enjoy seeking the less-crowded spots. If you drive on the road that goes past Kihei and Wailea, south of Wailea the road continues to Makena. At the end of the road is a massive lava flow that forms **La Perouse Bay,** which is now an official sanctuary for over 90 species of exotic reef fish. We were the only ones snorkeling there. A word of caution: It is quite rocky, so be sure to wear something on your feet" (Mr. and Mrs. Dennis W. Randall, Seattle, Wash.). . . . "The whale-watching cruises are expensive (around $20) for what you see. By law, they can only go within 300 yards of a whale. You can see the **whales** romping just as well from La Familia lanai on Kamoole Beach II, and drink $1.25 margaritas as well. The whales are most active when the wind blows in the late afternoon" (Mary Popovitch, Calgary, Alberta, Canada).

"You should warn people about the highway to Lahaina and Kaanapali. **Highway 30** is two-lane and very heavily traveled. There are lots of slow-moving trucks and it is almost impossible to pass. If you aren't staying at one of the hotels in that area and plan to drive there for dinner from Central Maui or Kihei, allow plenty of time. At night, watch out for the drunks. Driving that road at night is not a fun experience. . . . We thoroughly enjoyed **Haleakala.** It is fantastic. However, for those who want to stop at the various lookouts, particularly the area near the silversword plants, be sure and have some insect repellent. We were pestered by some of the meanest flies we have ever seen. They love faces and bare legs. You mention insect repellent, but it was for Hana. We saw only one mosquito on our trip to Hana" (Don and Nancy Gossard, Bellevue, Wash.). [*Authors' Note:* In the tropics, mosquitos come (and thankfully, go), depending on seasons and changing climatic conditions. Our advice: Always have your insect repellent handy in country areas.]

"It's becoming very popular to get up early to catch **sunrise on Haleakala.** The total experience of leaving the hotel at about 3 a.m., driving up the mountain in pitch blackness, meeting other people with the same crazy idea, then slowly waiting for the sun to rise over the crater is absolutely breathtaking. At that hour, however, a sweater, jacket, and blanket *may* suffice for only some. It was cold! Bring breakfast/lunch and enjoy amid other sun/nature worshipers or on your own" (Francine Schept, White Plains, N.Y.). . . . "On the early-morning drive to **Haleakala Crater** for sunrise it took me an hour and ten minutes from Kahului, and I am a cautious driver. It was freezing at the Visitors Center— about 45 degrees in late August—so I would suggest gloves, especially for photographers; my 'shutter finger' was stiff from the cold! First light—30 to 40 minutes before sunrise—is as lovely as the sunrise and should not be missed. On the way down, I was the only person to stop at Leleiwi Lookout, sharing it with a park ranger for two hours; I think the view from the lookout is superior to the one at the Visitors Center" (Martha F. Battenfeld, Brighton, Mass.). . . . "For calm and shallow **snorkeling,** pull off Hwy. 30, south of Olowalu General Store. This is not a park, just a shallow beach. So good, they give beginner scuba lessons here" (Vic and Bev Suzuki, Thornhill, Ontario, Canada).

"Our four nights at **Waianapanapana Park** were at our No. 1 idyllic spot. Hana was having a week-long Aloha Week festival. We went to a real Hawaiian luau with great performers for $6; the previous night the ladies of the village gave a real hula show at the village soccer field—free. October is a great time to go to Hana, as there are very few guests. Try the red-sand beach for snorkeling at **Hana Park,** near the old frame school house, now a library, and follow the trail down a meadow, around a cliff, to a secluded beach behind a natural lava breakwall. Caution: Young couples still swim in the buff here! For golf in Maui, go to **Wailuku Golf Course:** 18 holes, most overlooking the ocean. A real fun place!" (Richard Welse, Westfield Center, Ohio).

"The book *Hiking Hawaii* by Robert Smith (Wilderness Press: Berkeley, 1977) is excellent. It has lots of hikes from family outings to those that are very tough going. . . . One of the nicest waterfalls and swimming holes is located exactly 2.8 miles toward Hana from the Seven Sacred Pools at a bridge. It was still going even when lots of others were dry" (Dr. Michael Baron, San Francisco, Calif.). . . . "We found the prettiest part of Maui to be that short section of Hwy. 30 that goes past the **Napili Bay** area: towering cliffs, crashing waves, lush valleys. Few tourists seem to drive up here because they know the road ends. We packed a picnic dinner and ate it in total isolation on a cliff overlooking the water. It was one of the best moments of our honeymoon" (Sue and Terry Young, Crystal Lake, Ill.). . . . "The road past **Nakalele Point to Kapuna** marked 'impassable' on most tourist maps is definitely just that! The trip is 14 miles, not 5 as stated in most brochures, and a total disaster. We ventured a couple of miles on the road ourselves and had to turn around when the road became too narrow for our car. However, a couple we were traveling with covered the entire 14 miles, and it took them several hours, which they say were harrowing at best. The scenery is not any more spectacular than you can find on other island roads and the driving is so nerve-wracking it is unlikely you will be able to spare any time to view the scenery anyway. The road to Hana is described as treacherous in some brochures, but it is no comparison to this road—save yourself some time and nerves and just don't bother with this route" (Mr. and Mrs. Wes Alton, Edmonton, Alberta, Canada).

"We found the **municipal beach** between Lahaina and the hotel beach complex great! Protected and much less surfy than in front of our hotel" (Mrs. Morris Finck, Shaker Heights, Ohio). . . . "The best snorkeling beach on Maui (we discovered it ourselves and it was later pointed out to us by islanders) is **Honolua Bay** on the north end of the island near the end of Hwy. 30. Overnight camping permits should be obtained from the Maui Pineapple Company in Lahaina, but we did not have one and had no problems" (Sandra Johnson, Santa Paula, Calif.). . . . "South of Kihei is **Kamaole Park,** which is actually three beaches. Each is calm, sandy-bottomed, and almost deserted on weekdays. On this and a previous visit we saw a whale frolicking just offshore" (Bob and Doris Ryan, Grand Island, N.Y.).

"**Camping** is still inexpensive. On Maui, you pay for County Park, Hookipa, and Baldwin Park, $3 per adult and 50¢ per child. State parks are free. For County Park permits: War Memorial Gym (next to Baldwin High School), Kaahumanu Avenue, Wailuku, Maui, HI 96793. Office hours are 7:45 a.m. to 4:30 p.m. Monday to Friday. For State Park permits: State Office Building, Wailuku" (Frank Bogard, Pasadena, Calif.). . . . "Taking the road to Hana, we stopped at the **arboretum,** which is on the main road just before the turnoff to the rock and coral church mentioned in the book. This was the highlight of our Hana trip, as the gardens were beautiful with the exotic trees and plants clearly labeled for the haoles. There are about two miles of path to hike (all level), it's free, and would make a lovely place for a picnic—there are some picnic tables available" (Barbara L. Mueller, Tucson, Ariz.). . . . "The best snorkeling we found was at the southern edge of the **Kaanapali Airport.** The water was clear and safe for children, the coral plentiful and well below the surface, and the variety of fish amazing. Even beginning snorkelers will enjoy this beach, which is reached by turning in at the last Kaanapali sign going north, then walking about 50 yards down to the beach" (Nick Howell, Camp Springs, Md.).

"I'd like to pass on some information I learned the hard way. I mentioned to a clerk in a market that I was planning to drive to Hana the next day. He said, 'If it's raining when you get halfway, turn back, or you can get stuck out there.' I assumed he was being overly cautious. It sprinkled off and on as we drove to Hana, but it's a long trip and we didn't want to waste our day. The sun was shining as we visited the Seven Sacred Pools, and water rushed from the very top pool to the ocean. On our way back, cloudy but no rain, we were stopped in a line of about 30 cars, trapped by a landslide on a narrow, cliff-hugging road. Rescue crews had been called, but it took two hours with men, shovels, and a bulldozer to clear the road so we could get by. It could have been a tragedy, and we learned to take seriously what the Hawaiians say. They know best!" (Mrs. Donald B. Newton, Saratoga, Calif.).

Chapter XVII

THE ISLAND OF MOLOKAI

1. Island Hotels
2. Island Restaurants
3. The Night Scene
4. Shopping
5. Seeing the Sights

WHAT'S THE MOST HAWAIIAN of the Hawaiian islands? If you're thinking in terms of the Hawaii of 50 years ago—the Hawaii before high-rises and shopping centers, before billboards and commercialism, then it might well be the little island of Molokai. The closest of the Neighbor Islands to Oahu, 261-square-mile Molokai remains the least developed and most sparsely populated of the major Hawaiian islands. Its resident population, only about 6,000, has the highest percentage of people with native Hawaiian ancestry anywhere in the islands (with the exception, of course, of privately-owned Niihau). The environment is rural and the lifestyle traditional. Imagine a place with no buildings over three stories high, no elevators, no traffic lights (let alone freeways!), no movie theaters, no fast food or supermarket chains. Instead, think of great natural beauty, vast uncrowded spaces, and ideal conditions for golfing, hunting, riding, windsurfing, big-game fishing, boating (swimming is not ideal here, since the beaches can be beautiful but the water rough), and leading the lazy life in an unspoiled setting. If that's the kind of relaxed Hawaii you're thinking about, then you should definitely visit Molokai.

Molokai sometimes gets overflow visitors from better-known tourist destinations, people who didn't even know what or where Molokai was. Yet once they start to unwind here, they find they like it, and come back again. Kamaainas have been in the know about Molokai for a long time: it's a favorite weekend spot for family holidays.

In the past, Molokai was known mostly for its treatment center for Hansen's disease—leprosy—at Kalaupapa, and as a pineapple plantation island. And somehow, the tidal wave of progress that has swept the islands since statehood has left Molokai behind; it appears, at first glance, like a midwestern town in the Depression '30s. Yet there's a down-homeness and a realness here that most people find appealing, and a genuine friendliness among the locals. Artists and craftspeople, seeking a last refuge from overpriced civilization, are beginning to settle here. In some parts of the island there is a sense of tranquility that is almost palpable. And Molokai is changing. Although the pineapple industry is being phased out and many of the local people are experiencing hard economic times, luxury facilities for visitors are on the rise. Before Molokai changes too much, come see what rural Hawaii is still like. A visit to Molokai can be a rewarding experience, especially since you won't have to break the bank to do it: prices here are still somewhat lower than elsewhere in the state.

GETTING THERE: Molokai is 20 air minutes from Honolulu, 15 minutes from Maui. It is easily reached via **Hawaiian Airlines,** which runs 50-seat DH-7 aircraft into Hoolehua Airport on a frequent schedule. A cluster of commuter airlines, which run tiny planes (anywhere from five- to nine-seaters), also call at Molokai: these are **Air Molokai, Princeville Airways,** and **Reeves Air.** Prices can be quite low, especially on weekdays (about $30 roundtrip, Honolulu to Molokai), and flying low on one of these small planes can be quite thrilling, as we discovered on a recent Air Molokai flight. Molokai lies between the islands of Oahu and Maui (it can easily be seen from western Maui) and is, in fact, part of Maui County. Route it on your way to or from either Maui or Honolulu. A one day trip is quite feasible.

DESTINATION MOLOKAI: Molokai is serious about putting out the welcome mat for visitors and, to that end, has set up the Destination Molokai Association to promote tourism. If you phone their toll-free number, they'll send you a comprehensive brochure listing hotels, resort condominiums, tour companies, auto rental companies, restaurants, visitor activities, and airlines serving the island, as well as individual brochures put out by these firms. From continental U.S., as well as Alaska, Puerto Rico, and the Virgin Islands, phone toll free 800/843-5978; from Canada, phone toll free 800/423-8733, ext. 447. If you're already in the islands, phone 567-6255.

MOLOKAI, PAST AND PRESENT: Although Molokai is known as "The Friendly Isle," that friendliness has really not been tested yet, as far as mass tourism goes. You might easily be the only mainland visitor on the few minutes' flight from Oahu or Maui, and your fellow passengers will more than likely be island people visiting relatives, or plantation people arriving on business.

The Friendly Isle was once known as the Lonely Isle. The power of Molokai's kahuna priests was feared throughout the other islands. Warring island kings kept a respectable distance from Molokai until, in 1790, Kamehameha the Great came to negotiate for the hand of the queen, Molokai's high chieftess, Keoupuolani. Five years later he returned with an army to conquer Molokai on his drive for Oahu and dominion over all of Hawaii.

Today Molokai presents a tranquil scene, a Polynesian island untouched and unspoiled. A thickly forested backcountry populated with axis deer, pheasant, turkey, and other wild game makes life exciting for the hunter. For those of you who just like to look and sightsee, there is magnificent Halawa Valley with its healing pool at the foot of Moaula Falls; the less rugged Palaau Park with its Phallic Rock; Kalaupapa Lookout and Kalaupapa itself, an isolated peninsula, refuge for the victims of the once-dreaded leprosy, which today you can visit on a guided tour. But more about that later.

You won't have to rough it on Molokai. The few hotel facilities are excellent, the roads are for the most part quite good, and you'll be able to get whatever comforts and supplies you need—from rental cars to color movie film. The drinking water is as pure as you'll find anywhere in the world, and the restaurants, most located in the three major hotels on the island, serve very good meals.

One word of advice: Go directly to your hotel from the airport and get comfortable and adjusted to Molokai before visiting its nearby principal town, Kaunakakai. This sleepy village, made famous by the song "Cock-eyed Major," is best appreciated once you're in the Molokai mood. Especially after Waikiki.

To get a little head start on your sightseeing, you might note that, between the airport and town, on the ocean side of the road is Kapuaiwa, one of the last surviving royal coconut groves in the Hawaiian islands, planted in the latter part of the 19th century. It was planted in honor of Kamehameha V and given his pet name. Opposite the grove is Church Row, a lineup of tiny rustic churches.

U-DRIVES: You're going to need a car if you want to explore Molokai on your own, and it won't be difficult to get one, since Molokai now has local outlets of four major all-island rental companies: **Tropical Rent-A-Car, Dollar Rent-A-Car** (previously Molokai Island U-Drive), **Budget Rent-A-Car,** and **Avis.** (See Chapter IV for details on all-island rentals.) And they're all right at the airport. Tropical has a base rate of $25.95 for a compact stick shift, $27.95 for a compact automatic four-door sedan, $29.95 for a compact wagon, and $33.95 for a medium-sized car. The local number is 567-6118. For toll-free reservations and information, call 800/367-5140.

We continue to get good reports on Avis, and drove Avis on a recent trip. Rates are about $38 a day for a four-door automatic; during the off-season, cars run from about $24 to $31. Avis is the only company renting four-wheel drive cars, the kind necessary for some rough, jungly roads. Inquire about prices for these. The local number is 533-3866; the toll-free reservation number is 800/331-1212.

Dollar Rent-A-Car offers compacts starting at $27.95 and full-size cars for $44.95. The local number is 567-6156; the toll-free reservation number is 800/367-5006.

Budget Rent-A-Car would not quote rates to us, but they are generally competitive. For toll-free reservations and information, phone 800/527-0700.

1. Island Hotels

Molokai at this moment has a grand total of seven hotels and condos—and that's more than twice what they had a few years ago! Since there are so few, we'll give you the details on all of them; they're not all budget, but they all offer good quality for the money.

The drive from Hoolehua Airport to the town of Kaunakakai takes about ten minutes, across what seems to be typical western grazing land. About a quarter mile from the town, following Rte. 45 along the beach, you'll see the **Pau Hana Inn,** the best choice in town for us budgeteers, the most local and the most laid-back. Pau Hana is a relaxed, cottage-type hotel with about 40 units, some in the garden, others facing the ocean or pool. Rates start at $25 single or double for small, extremely plain but clean budget rooms, with two twin beds and shower, in the longhouse. They go to $32 double for standard rooms in the cottages, with twin beds and bath; nothing fancy, but adequate, especially considering the natural beauty all around you. For $52 (poolside) and $62 (ocean-front), you get the newer and larger superior units, most with two queen-size beds, spacious lanais, tub-shower combinations, and more expensive furnishings. Superior studios with two double beds and kitchenette are $62; deluxe oceanfront suites are $92. An extra person is charged $10; crib charge is also $10. A swimming pool compensates for the rather poor ocean beach. The oceanfront dining room is open for three reasonably priced meals a day. Write to Pau Hana Inn, P.O. Box 546, Kaunakakai, Molokai, HI 96748, or call toll free, 800/367-8047, ext. MKK; from Canada, call 800/663-1118. The local phone

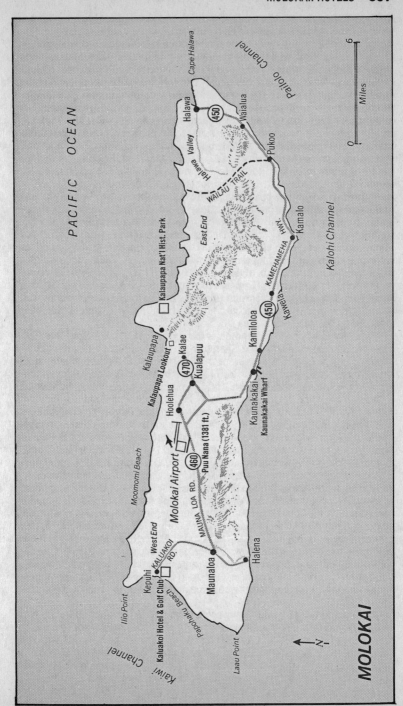

MOLOKAI

←N

PACIFIC OCEAN

Cape Halawa

Pailolo Channel

Halawa

450

Waialua

Pukoo

WAILAU TRAIL

Kamalo

Halawa Valley

East End

KAMEHAMEHA HWY.

Kalohi Channel

Kalaupapa Nat'l Hist. Park

Kawela

450

Kamiloloa

Kalaupapa

Kalaupapa Lookout

Kalae

470 Kualapuu

Kaunakakai

Kaunakakai Wharf

Hoolehua

Molokai Airport ✈

460

Puu Nana (1381 ft.)

Moomomi Beach

MAUNA LOA RD.

Halena

West End

Maunaloa

Kepuhi

KALUAKOI RD.

Kaluakoi Hotel & Golf Club

Papohaku Beach

Ilio Point

Kaiwi Channel

Laau Point

Miles

0   6

is 553-5342. Pau Hana is now affiliated with Aston Hotels and Resorts in Honolulu, and has been refurbished to be cozier than ever.

The prices are just a bit higher at **Hotel Molokai,** a modern Polynesian village that maintains the aura of the gracious past. In separate three-unit cottages are lovely rustic bedrooms with baths and all the modern-day comforts, including wall-to-wall carpeting and deliciously comfortable basket swings out on the furnished lanais. There's a swimming pool (the waterfront here is a shallow lagoon behind the reef, popular for snorkeling but not good for swimming), a comfortable open lobby, and an excellent dining room where the "family" (staff) entertains their guests at dinner nightly. Although this is an oceanfront hotel, the waves break a quarter mile out, leaving the lagoon tranquil and still, with only a lapping sound to lull you to sleep. (*Note:* light sleepers may want to ask for a room away from the restaurant area.) Now for the rates: standard rooms, single or double, are $42; superior (garden floor) rooms are $52; deluxe accommodations on the upper floor, with lanai, go for $62 to $72. Only deluxe rooms can accommodate one or two extra persons, $10 per person. Crib charge is $10. In conjunction with Air Molokai and Avis, the hotel often runs a "2-nighter for 2" special deal, which includes round-trip air fare from Honolulu or Maui, two days at the hotel, and the use of a rented car for two days, at prices beginning at $99 per person, based on double occupancy. The nice thing about this is that the return portion of the trip can be used to continue in the direction you're going—that is, from Honolulu to Molokai to Maui, or vice versa. Let's hope this package is available when you're there. For toll-free reservations, call 800/367-5124, ext. MKK. The local address is P.O. Box 546, Kaunakakai, Molokai, HI 96748. The local phone is 553-5374.

The grandest of Molokai hotels is the sparkling **Kaluakoi Hotel and Golf Club** (which started life as the Sheraton-Molokai), a luxury resort situated about 15 miles from the airport next to the glorious, three-mile stretch of almost-deserted Kepuhi Beach. The 292 rooms in two-story cottages (overlooking ocean or golf course) all are beautifully appointed (some have high-beamed ceilings) with wood, rattan furnishings, and vibrant Polynesian colors. All rooms have a refrigerator and half of them—the deluxe ones—have a wet bar as well. Besides the beautiful ocean (often not safe for swimming), there's a handsome free-form swimming pool with a black bottom (which keeps the water warm), bar service at poolside, the championship 18-hole Kaluakoi Golf Course (a golfing friend tells us that at night deer come out to drink at the water hazards!), four lighted tennis courts and a tennis pro, all sorts of shops and services, and the Ohia Lodge and Paniolo Broiler for excellent meals. As we sipped a cool drink by the pool recently, one of the guests smiled at us and said: "I think I'll never leave." We could understand that feeling; it's like being at one of the beach hotels at Kaanapali in Maui, but with nothing else around. It's luxury all the way here, and that includes the rates too: $79, single or double, for garden-view; $89 for deluxe garden-view; $99 for partial ocean-view; $100 for ocean-view. One-bedroom, ocean-view luxury suites for up to four people are $125; one-bedroom, ocean-view cottages, for up to four, are $150. For reservations, phone Colony Hotels and Resorts toll free at 800/367-6046. The local phone is 552-2555.

If you want to settle into your own apartment in this area, there are two excellent condo choices: Paniolo Hale and Ke Nani Kai, both of which are part of the larger Kaluakoi Resort, a 6,700 acre development which also includes the Kaluakoi Hotel and Golf Club and the beautiful, three-mile long, Papohauu Beach. Next door to the Kaluakoi Hotel, on Kepuhi Beach, **Paniolo Hale** is adjacent to the golf course (in fact, one must cross the fairway to get to the beach). Wild deer and turkeys are frequently seen on the grounds. There is a swimming pool and a paddle tennis court, and guests receive a reduced rate when golfing at Kaluakoi. The Kaluakoi Hotel also offers its four lighted tennis courts to Paniolo Hale guests for a nominal fee. This is a luxury condominium complex. Best buys here are the one-bedroom/two-bath units, at $95 for up to four persons. Studios rent for $75 for two, and two-bedroom-two-bath units go for $115 for up to four persons, with a maximum of six; extra persons over four in a unit are charged $8. Car-and-condo packages are also available: $95 for the studio for one to two persons, $110 for the one-bedroom for one to four persons, and $120 for the two-bedroom for one to six persons. There are also ocean-view units. Hot tubs are available on the lanais of all two-bedroom units for an additional charge. All the apartments have full kitchen, TV, telephone, and attractive island furnishings. Each unit has its own screened lanai (a touch of old Hawaii), which you walk right onto from your room, without going through a door. Minimum stay is three nights. The nearest restaurant is the Kaluakoi Hotel, about one block away along the sea wall, and the nearest grocery store five miles away (it closes at 5 p.m. and all day on Sunday). We continue to receive good reports on this one. For reservations, phone toll free 800/367-2984. From Canada and Hawaii call collect 808/552-2731 for reservations, or write to Paniolo Hale, P.O. Box 146, Maunaloa, Molokai, HI 96770.

There's an air of tranquility about **Ke Nani Kai** that makes you feel this is the kind of place where you could stay for weeks and simply unwind, never missing civilization a bit. Located at the entrance to the Kaluakoi Hotel (actually between the 8th and 17th fairways of the golf course), this is a superb condominium resort, with some 55 units available to the general public. One- and two-bedroom apartments are handsomely and individually furnished, with very large living rooms, cable color TV, bedrooms with sliding doors, lanais affording splendid views, superbly equipped kitchens, washer and dryer in every unit. On the grounds are an enormous swimming pool (with a shower in the shape of a tiki god), two tennis courts, a whirlpool spa; the beach is just a short walk away. Hanging flowers cover the trellises of the units. For all this comfort and luxury, rates are quite reasonable. A one-bedroom apartment with garden view is $75 for up to four guests; with ocean view, $85. A two-bedroom garden-view unit is $95 for one to six people; with ocean view, $105. Cribs are available for $7 per night. Minimum stay is two nights. All rates are subject to change. The address of Ke Nani Kai is Maunaloa, Molokai, HI 96770 (tel. 552-2761). For toll-free reservations, phone 800/367-7040.

Molokai's two other condominium complexes are a bit older, and more reasonably priced. **Molokai Shores** is located just a mile from Kaunakakai, between the Pau Hana Inn and the Hotel Molokai. The three-story, 102-unit oceanfront apartment building has very pleasant one-bedroom/one-bath and two-bedroom/two-bath units, all with ocean views, color TV, well-equipped kitchens, and private lanais overlooking tropical lawns. Picnic tables, barbecue units, and a putting green make outdoor life pleasant, and there's a pool for swimming (the beach is not particularly good here). The one-bedroom units rent at $68 daily for two people, and most can accommodate four ($8 for each additional person per night); and the two-bedroom/two-bath units are $90 for two, and can accommodate six. A minimum stay of two nights is required. For reservations, write Molokai Shores, Star Route, Kaunakaki, Molokai, HI 96748 (tel. 553-5954).

The east shore of Molokai is a newer area for tourist development, and it's quite lovely, a good base of operations for some nice swimming beaches and excursions to Halawa Valley. Nestled against the East Molokai mountains is **Wavecrest Resort,** with tennis courts, a swimming pool, and all the amenities necessary for at-home resort living. There's not much of a beach, but it's okay for fishing. The 126 one- and two-bedroom condominium apartments are all smartly furnished with fully equipped electric kitchen and color TV. From your private lanai you can see Maui, right across the water. One-bedroom apartments run $46 to $56 for two people; two-bedroom units are $66 to $76 for up to four persons. From December 20 to April 20, add $5 per night. For reservations, call toll free 800/367-2980. The local phone is 558-8101.

In this same area, just past the 16-mile marker at Pukoo, is **Swenson's Bed and Breakfast.** Here's a perfect retreat for those who really want to get away from it all. Diane and Larry Swenson, whose house fronts on a sandy swimming beach, are renting a fully equipped beachfront cottage with living room, kitchen, bedroom and bath, which can sleep four people. The rate is $50 per night for two, $66 per night for four; there is a two-night minimum stay. The rate includes continental breakfast: coffee, juice, fresh fruit, and Swedish pastries. Within walking distance is Pukoo Lagoon, and from your window, views of Maui, Lanai, and the ocean. Write to Diane and Larry Swenson, Star Route 279, Kaunakakai, Molokai, HI 96748, or phone 558-8394.

Two other Molokai families are currently offering bed-and-breakfast accommodations in the same area. Marian and Herb Mueh, in Kamalo, have a separate cottage; Nadine and Dick Williams in Kawela have a rental unit in their house. Both have two-day minimums and charge between $45 and $65 a day for fully equipped apartment units and continental breakfast. For information, phone the Muehs at 558-8236 and the Williams at 553-3838.

2. Island Restaurants

There aren't many restaurants to choose from in the only business district on Molokai, on Ala Malama in Kaunakakai. Local friends advise that you keep your eyes peeled (especially on Tuesday and Friday) for Christita Reyes, a Filipino lady who parks her bright-blue station wagon in town around lunchtime and sells local delicacies from the back of the wagon. All dishes are cooked in a certified kitchen, and you can usually get shoyu or teriyaki chicken, vegetable tempura, coconut candy on a stick, and other goodies, at very reasonable prices. Another local lady also sells food from her station wagon, this one an older model but also painted a shiny blue. Her lunches too are both affordable and delicious. **Molokai Buyers,** a natural-foods cooperative at the west end of town, has a juice-bar operation called The Oasis (Monday through Friday, 10 a.m. to 2 p.m.), where, in addition to freshly squeezed juice, tropical fruit smoothies, and the like, you can get sandwiches (the whole multi-grain bread is baked fresh in Hawaii, the organic lettuce and greens are grown on Molokai) of avocado, mock tuna, hummus, and the like; hot and cold nachos; whole-wheat burritos with vegetarian ingredients; tempeh burger plate lunches, hot tofu pita sandwiches, and salads for lunch, all for under $3.50. **Kanemitsu Bakery** on Ala Malama has delicious breakfasts, served from 5:30 until 11:30 a.m., and takeout lunch food as well—plus its famous and flavorful Molokai French bread (a great gift item, by the way, for friends in Honolulu). They also bake excellent cheese and onion breads and even sell fresh fish—if the fishermen bring them in that day. This humble bakery actually turns out up to 1,900 loaves a day, and will deliver bread to the airport in cartons. It opens at 5:30 a.m., and is closed on Tuesdays.

For a sit-down meal in Kaunakakai, you have three pretty good possibilities: a Chinese restaurant quaintly called Hop Inn, Mid-Nite Inn, and a local Filipino place, Oviedo's. Don't let the dreary outside appearance of **Hop Inn** put you off; just about every building in town shows its age, and inside you'll find a clean place and good Chinese cooking. The à la carte dishes are reasonable:

we spent $5.25 for shrimp chop suey, $3.95 for lemon chicken. Watch for Hop Inn on the left as you drive up Ala Malama Street from Kam Hwy.

We don't know why they call it **Mid-Nite Inn,** since it's never open at midnight: 5:30 a.m. (they get up early on Molokai) to 1:30 p.m. and 5 to 9 p.m. are more like it at this venerable local establishment, with tables, booths, and tasty, inexpensive food. Owner Art Kikukawa and his sons are super-friendly, and you know they've got to be nice people if they're offering delicious fresh fish dinners, fried and served with rice and kim chee, for all of $3.95 to $5.25! The highest price on the menu is $10.75, for steak, while most regular dishes like fried chicken with fries, fried aku, shrimp, or corned beef and cabbage go for $3 to $4.75. You're welcome to bring your own bottle of wine: they'll gladly uncork it and provide glasses at no charge. Breakfast is also available at good old-fashioned prices like $1.25 for hotcakes and coffee. (For a solution to the name mystery, see the Readers' Selections, at the end of this chapter.) Open daily, except for Sunday dinner.

To sample Filipino food, sit down for lunch or get a take-out plate at **Oviedo's,** a simple, home-style restaurant on the main street in Kaunakakai. Oviedo's is open from 10 a.m. to 7 p.m. every day, and features such Filipino specialties as pork adobo (adobo is a kind of stew), tripe stew, and beef stew, $5.50 for a lunch or dinner plate.

If you're driving the long 25 miles out to Halawa Valley, there's a **Neighborhood Store** some 16 miles out on Rte. 45, your last stop for provisions. In addition to picking up home-grown bananas and papayas, as well as cold drinks and ice cream, you can also have snacks at their new fast-food counter: fish, chicken and turkey burgers, saimin, fried noodles, stew and rice, shoyu chicken, chili, hot dogs, and the like, as well as occasional specials like chicken and papaya soup, are all reasonably priced.

Now for the best restaurants on Molokai—starting at the three major hotels. They can rise into the slightly splurgy category but are well worth it. The Hotel Molokai's restaurant is superb. Its name, **Holo Holo Kai** (tel. 553-5347), means to sail in the sea—appropriate, since the restaurant is right on the edge of the ocean and open to its charms. It's easy to imagine you're off in Tahiti or some other South Seas isle (you are) as you enjoy the peaceful Pacific mood. You can stay right within our budget here if you choose one of the à la carte selections like pasta primavera, baked cod, or beef and vegetable with steamed rice, served with dinner salad, all around $7. Or have the all-you-want soup-and-salad buffet (the fruits and vegetables are fresh from the garden), which includes that wonderful Molokai French bread, for around $6.50. Add a few more dollars, and you can have the soup-and-salad buffet, plus rice or fries or mashed potatoes, plus fresh island vegetables (beans or carrots grown on Molokai), and entrees such as mahimahi, teriyaki chicken breast, shrimp tempura, top sirloin or teriyaki steak, for around $8.50 to $14. Beef stew, a local favorite, is served with rice or poi, and elicited from one of our readers, Jack Lindberg of San José, California, the comment that "it is a bottomless bowl of hearty munching: it approaches my Irish mother's blend—ummm!" Fresh catch of the day (at market price) is a dinner specialty, and there are weekend steak specials. Lunch features a daily special at $5.50, the soup-and-salad buffet, and a variety of salads and sandwiches. Entertainment by singer-guitarist Kimo Paleka accompanies dinner, served daily from 6 to 9 p.m., on Thursday, Friday, and Saturday night. Lunch is served from 11:30 a.m. to 1:30 p.m. Box lunches, around $5, are, to our appetite, big enough for two.

Now here's a special tip for those of you who are going to be in Molokai only for one day. Take an early morning flight out from Honolulu or Maui, and go directly from the airport to the Hotel Molokai, where breakfast is served up until 10:30 a.m. Treat yourself to either of their famous breakfast specialties—Holo Holo Kai french toast—which is Molokai bread in a banana-egg batter, with a choice of meats—or our personal favorite, papaya pancakes—this is hot cakes dipped in a special papaya batter, topped with crushed macadamia nuts, plus a choice of breakfast meats. Each of these treats is $4.50. Now, after your coffee, you're set for a day of exploring Molokai.

The mood is different at the **Pau Hana Inn Restaurant** (tel. 553-5342); you dine indoors in a big rustic dining room with a tremendous fireplace. Doors open to the outside, where a seaside café provides evening dancing and entertainment. Dinner is well priced, with most entrees—like catch of the day, honey-dipped chicken, barbecued beef short ribs, New York strip steak—in the $7.50 to $12.50 range. Specialty of the house is prime ribs, a 10 ozs. cut for $11.95. The price of the entrée includes a salad bar, a hot vegetable, fries or rice or mashed potatoes, Molokai bread and butter, and a beverage. Not a bad deal at all! At lunch their daily specials around $5, like spaghetti with garlic bread and salad, fried chicken, plus sandwiches, from about $3.50 to $4.75. While you're here, be sure you walk out to see the enormous banyan tree (it's a Bengalese banyan, also known as an East Indian fig tree), which has been standing sentinel over the ocean here for almost a hundred years.

Pau Hana Inn Restaurant is generally open from 6:30 to 10:30 a.m., 11 a.m. to 1:30 p.m., and again from 6 to 8:30 p.m., but it's all "Hawaiian time."

The most expensive of the hotel dining rooms is the glamorous **Ohia Lodge** of the Kaluakoi Hotel, (tel. 552-2555), a South Seas spot overlooking the water, where there's music for dancing every night. Many of the local people feel the dining room is the best on Molokai. Be prepared to spend from $10.40 to $28 for a variety of fish and seafood entrees, including prawns and lobster thermidor, plus prime ribs, filet mignon, veal marsala, vegetarian delight, and pasta dishes. With your entree, always beautifully prepared, come salad bar and vegetables. Lunch is more reasonably priced; there are specials like vegetarian platters and curries, Mexican fiesta, quiche florentine, as well as a variety of salads, burgers, and hot and cold sandwiches (how about salmon mousse and avocado?), from $5.10 to $9.60.

For a real budget meal in this area, dine with the islanders at **Jo Jo's Café** (tel. 552-2803), not far from the Kaluakoi Resort; it's in Maunaloa, in the tavern section of the old Pooh's Restaurant. Owner Jo Jo Espaniola and her son-in-law, Perry Buchalter, create a charming atmosphere. The old antique bar is still here. The menu is the same all day, and the prices are low for the likes of chopped steak, breaded fresh tuna, fried akule, butterfish, Korean ribs, from $3.50 to $7. Fresh fish and island specials change daily. You can have a hamburger for $1.25 ($1.50 deluxe), cheeseburger for $1.50 ($2 deluxe), a super teriyaki steak sandwich for $1.65, plus hot dogs, saimin, and salad. Try one of their fresh island homemade toppings on an ice cream sundae, or have a piece of pie—all of 80¢—for dessert. Funky and fun. Open daily, except Saturday, from 11 a.m. to 7:30 p.m.

Should you be driving through the little town of Kualapuu, you can stop off for some Filipino food at **Rabang's** (tel. 567-6616), a homey little place that specializes in various types of adobos (stews), with a variety of Filipino sauces and spices to season them. Mixed plates, containing a meat or chicken dish, starch, and vegetables, are $5. Rabang's is open every day, from 10 a.m. to 7 p.m.

3. The Night Scene

Nightlife on Molokai, as we travelers know it, is almost all in the major hotels. A dance band plays every night at the **Ohia Lodge** of the Kaluakoi Hotel. You might want to try a Molokai Mule (it has a kick!) in the cocktail lounge; it's

$6.75, and you take home the mug. . . . The bar at the **Hotel Molokai** is a pleasant place to be, since it's in between the pool area and the open-at-the-sides dining room; so you can have a drink and watch the entertainment by Kim O Paleka on Thursday, Friday, and Saturday night. During the 11 a.m. to 6 p.m. Happy Hour, beer is $1 to $2.50, drinks run $1 to $3.50. At the **Pau Hana Inn** a musical group plays until 1 a.m. on Friday and Saturday in the huge seaside cocktail garden, and there's dinner music Sunday through Thursday from 6:30 to 9 p.m. During Happy Hour—4 to 6 p.m.—beer is $1.50; standard drinks, $2.50; call drinks, $3 and $3.75.

In general, one might say that night life on Molokai is impromptu. It all depends on when local people feel like doing things (people here are not apt to let work interfere with their lives!). But check the local papers; there may be a hula show or even a luau at the Pau Hana Inn when you're in town.

4. Shopping

Molokai is perhaps the only place in the islands that is *not* heaven for shopping buffs—so much so, that many locals go off-island (they'll fly to Honolulu on one of the little commuter planes) to do their shopping—and that includes even grocery shopping.

The local supermarkets, grocery shops, and liquor stores on Ala Malama, the main street of Kaunakakai, and a general store here and there in the country just about do it. Perhaps the most artistic spot in town is **Molokai Gallery** on Ala Malama. Not only does Jeanne Holtby specialize in the work of local artists and craftspeople—you're apt to find original Molokai glassware and mugs, carvings, paintings, coconut and lauhala weavings—but she also carries original silkscreen casual wear for men, women, and children, plus some wonderful T-shirts in original designs. Prices are quite reasonable for the quality. Open every day.

To stock up on organic local produce—papayas, bananas, avocados, sprouts, etc.—try **Molokai Buyers** (next door to the laundromat), which sells the usual natural-food store fare plus other items at the lowest possible prices. They also have an excellent juice bar/restaurant called The Oasis. Pick up a sandwich or get some Cosmic Cabbage or Maui Onion Salsa, a local delicacy. For the best selection of books on the island, try **Port of Call,** also on Ala Malama on the second floor over the bank. Their strength is in Hawaiiana and paperbacks, and they also have a big selection of Hawaiian tapes and records—and a unisex hairstyling salon as well. To learn where the fish are biting, and to get fishing, diving, and camping gear, plus boogie boards, T-shirts, and ice, the place to go is **Molokai Fish and Dive,** also on Ala Malama. But they're more than just a dive shop. They have a huge selection of T-shirts designed and printed for them and sold exclusively here. You can shop late, until 10:30 p.m. every day at **Wine and Spirits Unlimited,** for groceries, meats, even T-shirts. **Imamura's** on Ala Malama has a little bit of everything, and is lots of fun to poke around in.

Our favorite Molokai shopping is out in **Maunaloa** (not far from the Kaluakoi Resort). Once a thriving plantation town, Maunaloa has been declining since Dole closed shop in 1975; however, young artisans are seeking it out and showing their wares here. We should tell you at the start that this is the most laid-back "shopping area" we've ever come across, with shops staying open more or less as inspiration moves the owners, who often seem to be out fishing or surfing or visiting Honolulu. However, one owner who's always on hand and happy to greet visitors, is Jonathan Socher of the **Big Wind Kite Factory.** Jonathan and his wife Daphne not only create some beautiful, high-flying kites (which are sold in many neighbor island shops, as well as in Fiji), but they even offer free flying lessons with modern 80-mph "aerobatic kites." It's also fun to take a mini-tour of their mini-factory, where they demonstrate the techniques of kite making. Their most popular items are pineapple windsox and mini-kites at $12.95, and rainbow-spinning windsox at $15 to $35. Note Daphne's newest limited-edition hula-girl kite—"it dances"—at $38. Also popular are their kite kits for kids, to color, cut out, and fly, at $12.95. A great browsing spot, open every day.

Adjacent to the Kite Factory, Jonathan has created **Plantation Gallery,** which shows the work of several island artisans. One is the **Tao Woodcarver** (Bill Decker) who creates beautiful hand-carved bowls and boxes of rare Hawaiian woods; large items, like desks and sculpture, are available on commission. You'll probably find Butch Tabanao and his deerhorn jewelry, hair combs (from $12), and cribbage boards (around $30) made from the axis deer of Molokai—unless the surf is up. The gallery/shop is decorated with orchid plants and an aquarium, and there's a garden outside. On our last visit we also spotted Hawaiian quilt pillow-case kits at $25, Rainbow Gecko T-shirts at $10.95, Big Wind Kite Factory T-shirts at $10, and even "Worn Again" Hawaiian aloha shirts, $9.95. Note the collection of cards and prints by such island artists as Jerry Buum, Sarah Selnick, Janet Holaday, John Thomas, and Herb Kane. A collection of Hawaiiana books is planned. While you're here, inquire about Hawaiian-smoke kiawe chips to use in place of hickory chips, for real island-flavored barbecuing.

The **Molokai Red Dirt Shirt Shop** is next door, with original Molokai-designed T-shirts and sportswear. We saw handsome handpainted coverups at $30 and $40. . . . You'll find hand-wrought rings, charms, bracelets, and "petroglyph" pendants in 14-karat gold at **Molokai Mountain Jewelry**—that is, unless goldsmith Ed O'Neal is out on the golf course; his "official hour," we were told, is noon to 1 p.m. on Thursday.

Across the road from this little cluster of shops are several little cottages. In one of them, Lori Cavanaugh, the owner of **Dolly Hale** (that's pronounced "holly" and means house) creates charming handcrafted dolls, priced from around $7.50 to $20. Angel dolls are made of coconut fiber with macadamia-nut heads, then decorated with shells, dried flowers, seeds, and ti leaves, that have been collected locally. One-of-a-kind, these are a must for the doll or Christmas-tree ornament collector. No regular hours here; let's hope she'll be open when you're there.

Hotel shopping is limited in Molokai, but do stop in at **Jo's of Molokai** in the Hotel Molokai, where Jo and Bob Johnson have been offering fashions and crafts by Molokai artists and others for many years. We've found some nice things here over the years, and prices are usually lower than they are on the other islands.

5. Seeing the Sights

Sightseeing on Molokai requires a bit more determination on the part of the visitor than it does on the other islands. A great deal of the island, including its best beaches, belongs to private ranches. A visit to the island's most spectacular scenic spot, Halawa Valley, involves some rugged driving and an hour's hike. To reach Kalaupapa, the major point of interest on the island, you either have to fly, hike, or ride a mule down a steep pali. But if you're willing to put up with a few obstacles, you might find sightseeing on Molokai among the most rewarding adventures of your trip to Hawaii. Sightseeing tours and local guides are especially helpful on this island.

PURDY'S NUT FARM: We don't know of any other macadamia farm in Hawaii where the owner will greet you personally and take you on a tour of his orchards. But a visit to Purdy's All Natural Macadamia Nut Farm, the only working macadamia-nut grove on the island, is different. Owner Tuddie Purdy conducts a very good tour, and not only does he tell you all you ever wanted to know about macadamia nuts, but he also shows you a variety of Hawaiian fruits and flowers. Most fun of all, you get to crack some macadamia nuts and try them raw. Then you'll be given some fruit and macadamia-blossom honey to taste, plus samples of their toasted macadamia nuts, which are remarkably light, surprisingly non-oily—and absolutely delicious. They'll give you the recipe for their Ono Toasted Macadamia Nuts, and you can also buy them right on the spot. The farm is located on one-and-a-half acres in Hoolehua Hawaiian Homesteads, and open every day from 9 a.m. to 1 p.m., or by appointment: phone 567-6601 daytime, 567-6495 in the evening. It's not far from the airport, but it's best to ask for driving directions there. If you're in Molokai for a one-day trip, this could be a fun way to start the day.

THE TRIP TO HALAWA VALLEY: For a beautiful day on Molokai, get up early, have your hotel pack you a picnic box lunch (or put one together from the supermarkets in town), hop into your car, and head for Halawa Valley. The trip is just about 25 miles from Kaunakakai along Kamehameha IV Hwy., but it will probably take you two hours to get there, since the last part of the driving is rough going. This is Molokai's southeastern coast, dotted with ancient heiaus, old fish ponds (some of which are used for scientific studies), and many coastal churches built by Father Damien and others. You won't be able to see the heiaus unless you get permission to go on private property, but you can stop in at **St. Joseph's Catholic Church** in Kamalo. The church, and the lovely statue outside, were designed and built by Father Damien, who was a skilled carpenter. A little further on is Father Damien's **Lady of Sorrows Church,** where you'll see a statue of Damien in a pavilion near the church. As you drive by the Kamalo mountains, watch for rainbows and double rainbows—they're not uncommon here. When you get to Mapulehu, at Mile 15½, look on the right for a sign to the **Mapulehu Mango Patch,** the largest mango patch in Hawaii, with over 2,000 mango trees of many varieties, plus a coconut grove. You can stop to pick up some tropical fruits here, as well as mango and other fruit juices at a little stand fronting the ocean. (Snorkeling tours and equipment are also available.) Your next little side trip could be to **Pukoo Lagoon,** for a swim or picnic. After you spot the Neighborhood Store on your left, look for a dirt road on the right. Drive down it, being wary of pot holes and mud puddles, until you see the pavilion of the Manae Canoe Club. Then drive right out to the lagoon or the sandy beach. From here you can see Maui, only nine miles away. This, and the beach farther along the road at Waialua, are typical of many secluded little beach coves along this coast. They're unmarked and difficult to find, so best to ask local people for directions.

About 20 miles out, past Pauwalu, the broad country road begins to narrow, and soon you're on a one-lane road where the sharp turns force the car to practically creep along while the scenery becomes more beautiful every minute. Then you begin to climb up, up, through the ranchlands of **Puu O Hoku Ranch,** from which a narrow road takes you into the Halawa Valley. We hope you do make it into the valley, because this is veritably a tropical paradise, a remote Shangri-La that one may find difficult to believe still exists. Once a populous area, it was swept by a tidal wave in 1946 and largely deserted. You can explore the valley (a few people still live here), have a swim in the bay, or make a roughly two-hour hike to the valley's most spectacular point, **Moaula Falls.** (You'll probably need mosquito repellent.) The rewards are a picnic or a swim at the base of a waterfall that plunges relentlessly down from dizzying heights. The water is cold and delicious, but according to Molokai legend, it is only safe to swim here if the ti leaf that you throw in floats. If it should sink, you'll have to make your own decision. Remember to make this trip in the morning, since, after a hike back to your car, you'll have to drive another two hours or so back to your hotel. *Note:* Since so many people have difficulty finding the falls, we refer you to Mr. and Mrs. Wayne Ditmer's letter in the Readers' Selections, ahead.

KALAUPAPA LOOKOUT: Even if you don't get to Kalaupapa itself, you should pay a visit to the Kalaupapa Lookout in Palaau Park. It's an easy trip on very good roads, about ten miles from Kaunakakai on Hwy. 46. After you make your right on 47 and begin to climb to Upper Molokai, the air becomes fragrant with eucalyptus and pine. Park your car at **Palaau State Park,** a well-maintained and popular camping and picnicking spot for the local people. A short walk through towering cypress and pine and suddenly you're high, high up, looking down immense cliffs to the Kalaupapa peninsula below. From the lookout, you can see the world's tallest seacliffs, 3,300 ft. high at Umilehi Point. A series of six informative plaques tell the Kalaupapa story, but official descriptions seem superfluous. Just standing here, gazing down at the peninsula below, you are caught up in some of the tremendous sorrow of those who lived their lives of exile at Kalaupapa.

There is another trail, this one a bit longer (and steeply uphill some of the way) that leads to the **Phallic Rock.** According to legend, barren women who made offerings to the rock and spent the night here would then become capable of bearing children. Supposedly, an unfaithful husband of one of the minor goddesses was transformed into this rock and his mana still remains there.

While you're pondering this story (wrongdoers were often turned into stone in Hawaiian mythology), get back into your car and drive down the hill. A right turn on Rte. 48 will take you through the little town of Kualapuu, where a Del Monte pineapple plantation is being phased out, and where diversified agriculture is a growing industry (Molokai is now the state's leading producer of watermelon). Turn left on Puupeelua Avenue and you arrive back at the airport road.

If you're in the mood for traveling, continue west on Rte. 460 past the airport, and you're on Maunaloa Road, which goes ten miles to the old Dole pineapple village to Maunaloa, about 1,300 feet high with its unusual little crafts shops (see above).

MOLOKAI RANCH WILDLIFE PARK: Yes, you can go on a safari of sorts in Molokai, a camera safari to see some 500 African and Asian animals that live on the grounds of the 1,500-acre wildlife preserve known as Molokai Ranch Wildlife Park. These are rare and endangered species, primarily antelope. The cost of the hour-and-a-half tour is $12 for adults, $6 for children, and arrangements can be made at the Kaluakoi Hotel Travel Desk, or by phoning Rare Adventures at 567-6088. We get good readers' comments on this one.

THE SPORTING LIFE: You'd like to live the sporting life on Molokai? It can be easily arranged, whether your wish is to go windsurfing, sailing, whale-watching, fishing, or even for a helicopter ride. As for windsurfing, it's a full-fledged island craze, and some say Molokai is the best place of all to do it (it's even rumored that in-the-know Maui windsurfers are seeking Molokai out for even better wind and water). Newcomers to the sport should contact George Peabody of **Windsurfing Molokai** (tel. 588-8253), who will take you by the hand

and give you private lessons in shallow, protected waters off the southeast coast of Molokai. Then you're ready for the channel between Molokai and Maui, considered one of the best windsurfing areas in the world. Private lessons for all levels of ability cost about $25; unguided windsurfing, from about $15 (for beginners only) to $35. George can also arrange boat excursions to Lanai, Maui, or north shore points. Windsurfing Molokai is located on the coast highway (Kamehameha IV Hwy.), ocean side, just past the Wavecrest Resort (Star Route Box 179). Phone in advance for reservations and directions.

Deep-sea fishermen who want to try their luck with marlin, mahimahi, shark, tuna, ono, and other big-game fish found off Molokai waters have several good choices here. The **Noio Fishing & Trading Co.,** P.O. Box 551, Kaunakakai, Molokai, HI 96748 (tel. 558-8910), can take you out on their 41-foot sport fishing boat, *Noio,* for a full-day or half-day trip, of tournament quality fishing. If you can share a charter, the cost should not be out of line. They also run charters for whale watching, snorkeling, and inter-island trips. **Alele II Charters,** P.O. Box 121, Kaunakakai, Molokai, HI 96748 (tel. 558-8266) is also recommended for deep-sea fishing and whale watching, and they too, sail from Kaunakakai Harbor.

If you love to sail, consider the 50-foot yacht *Rodonis,* docked at Kaunakakai Wharf (tel. 553-3311), which takes no more than six people at a time on its sailing charters. They'll take you out for sail training or to see the whales ($47), put you on a sunset Happy Hour cruise (pupus and beverages for about $36 per person), or on a one-day snorkeling cruise to Lanai for $89 per person.

The boat cruises run by **Hokupaa Ocean Adventures** (tel. 558-8195) are a bit different, since they depart from Halawa Valley and tour Molokai's north coast, cruising beneath the world's highest sea cliff. The four-hour cruise aboard their 25-foot twin diesel-engine cabin cruiser, *Mahealani,* costs $50 per person. At scenic spots along the way they stop for bottom fishing and snorkeling.

For an incredible view of Molokai from the air, climb aboard a **Royal Helicopter** chopper (tel. 567-6733). Scenic tours of the north coast, in which you will fly close to the highest waterfall in the state of Hawaii (Kahiwa, 1,750-feet high), swoop into deep jungle vales, and get a bird's eye view of Kalaupapa at a cost of $75 per person for a half-hour jaunt. If you can afford the $150 tab, their circle-island trip is one you will never forget. In addition to seeing the north coast, you're treated to a spectacular view of the ancient Hawaiian fishponds literally scalloped on the south coast of Molokai.

To explore Molokai's beautiful countryside on horseback, you have only to get in touch with the people at **Hawaiian Horsemanship Unlimited,** P.O. Box 94, Kualapuu, Molokai, HI 96757 (tel. 567-6635). They lead half-day and full-day trail rides in the Kalae area, at rates of $50 and $75. This is for experienced riders only: Western or English saddles are provided; a riding helmet is suggested.

All of these excursions and adventures can be arranged at hotel travel desks. The Kaluakoi Hotel, for one, has a full-scale travel desk that can be very helpful.

Note: When you participate in active sports, you do so at your own risk. Some of the companies listed above may or may not carry insurance. You may wish to make inquiries when you make your plans.

BEACHCOMBING: Papohaku Beach, on Molokai's western shore, part of Kaluakoi Resort, is the largest white sand beach in the Hawaiian islands, almost three miles long. It's the ideal spot for a beach picnic, but not—alas—for ocean swimming, since the water here is usually quite rough in winter. During summer, waters are generally calm. There's access at Papohaku Beach Park, which

has picnic grounds, barbecues, showers, a pavilion with restrooms and changing area, plus parking. Camping is also available.

THE TRIP TO KALAUPAPA SETTLEMENT: Even some of those who have never been to Hawaii have heard about Father Damien and what he did for the destitute lepers on Molokai about a century ago. Kalaupapa is where he performed his labors, and it is still in operation as a center for the treatment of leprosy—which is now politely called "Hansen's disease." Some 100 patients and former patients are still left on Kalaupapa, and to visit them—and their island home—is an extraordinary experience. It is not, however, a trip we advise everyone to make. It is not for those who get nervous just thinking about diseases (although leprosy has been arrested by modern drugs and is presumably not contagious), and it is definitely not for those with idle curiosity. The people of Kalaupapa do not wish to be patronized. It is for those with genuine interest and concern, for those who would like to meet some of the most gentle and remarkable people in the islands. Getting to their beautifully but tragically isolated home takes a bit of doing, and the emotions the trip can raise have been overwhelming to more than one visitor. We can promise only one thing: it is a special kind of experience, and one not easily forgotten.

There are a couple of ways to get to Kalaupapa. The one that's the most exciting is the famous mule trip run by **Rare Adventures/Molokai Mule Ride.** Mule riders should be between 16 and 70 years of age and weigh no more than 225 pounds. We might add that only those who are accustomed to riding should attempt this one, although many nonriders do take the trip. It's an unforgettable experience as the mule descends a spectacular, steep switchback trail 1600 feet below the towering cliffs at Kalae into Kalaupapa. You are met at the peninsula, given a tour and a picnic lunch, and then returned to the trail for the ride to the top at 2 p.m. Cost is $65, plus tax. Call the travel desk at Kaluakoi Hotel (tel. 552-2662) or the stables (tel. 567-6088). You can make reservations in advance by writing to Rare Adventures, Ltd., P.O. Box 200, Kualapuu, HI 96757.

It's more economical, of course, to hike down the trail; it's a scenic 3⅛-mile cliff walk that should take about an hour and a half. It's safe for most hikers; the hike *up* the pali, however, is arduous, so best to fly back. You must be at Kalae Stables by 8:30 a.m., since all hikers must go down before the mules do. **Rare Adventures "Molokai Hike-In"** costs $25 and includes a pass to enter Kalaupapa Peninsula, a picnic lunch, and the ground tour of the settlement. Call the above number in advance. *Note:* Rare Adventures now has a new toll-free number: from the mainland, 800/843-5978; from Oahu, 537-1845.

There is, of course, an easier way to get to Kalaupapa, the one we personally favor, and that's by air. Call Richard Marks' **Damien Molokai Tours** at 567-6171 (the only tour service operated by former patients who know Kalaupapa from the inside out) and they will arrange for you to fly in from upper Molokai via a nine-passenger shuttle flight for $24 round trip. Keep in mind that you cannot walk past the gate at the top of the cliff trail or around the peninsula without a permit, according to Health Department rules (Damien Molokai Tours will handle all permits). Minors under 16 are not allowed at Kalaupapa. Bring some lunch, as there are no stores or restaurants open to visitors at Kalaupapa. Yes, you may bring your camera and binoculars. To make advance reservations for the tour, you can phone 567-6171, or write Damien Molokai Tours, Box 1, Kalaupapa, Molokai, HI 96742. The full, four-hour grand tour costs $16 per person. What you'll see on that tour—the early settlement of **Kalawao** where Father Damien's church remains, the cemetery where he was buried before his remains were returned to Belgium, the grave of **Mother Marianne,** the healing springs of

Siloama, the **Kauhako Crater,** and a glorious view of Molokai's towering mountains—is just the beginning. (Both Father Damien and Mother Marianne, by the way, are candidates for canonization by the Roman Catholic Church.) All the tour guides are ex-patients, people who can give you a look at Kalaupapa off the record. It is a magnificent sight—a testimony to the patients who took barren lands and turned them into Eden, a testimony to the medical pioneers and missionaries who preserved so many lives; and yet it is a strangely paradoxical place. Despite the fact that many of the inhabitants live in cozy little houses and spend much of their time gardening and watching TV, Kalaupapa is one of the most silent places on earth. There are no children on Kalaupapa. Only a small minority of the residents have their spouses living with them; when pregnancy occurs, the expectant mother is usually flown from the island for the delivery, where she either remains to raise her child without its father or chooses to return to Kalaupapa alone. And this is the deepest of sorrow of all the sorrows of Kalaupapa.

There is another sorrow of Kalaupapa—the fear that, since there are so few patients left and since all of them have been cured or at least "arrested"—that Kalaupapa will one day soon give way to the gods of progress. The state government once talked about phasing out the patients at Kalaupapa and eventually turning the area into another giant tourist facility. Although the former patients may be physically able to return to society, it is hard for them to imagine a society in which their disfigurement—many are fingerless, toeless, scarred—would not, indeed, turn them into the social lepers of biblical days. Most are silent about this, a few are vocal and protesting. As wards of the state, they have little voice in determining their own future. Happily, their dream has come true: under legislation recently passed by Congress, Kalaupapa will be left as it is until the last of the residents has died. It is now known as Kalaupapa National Historic Park. The remaining residents, most in their 50's and 60's, like to joke about themselves as an "endangered species." But all of them now live here by choice. What was once a veritable prison has now become a sanctuary.

Like so many visitors who come to Kalaupapa, you may want to stay here a few days to really get to know the people. But it is almost impossible; except for family members and "officials having business in the Settlement," overnight stays have not been permitted. However, we have been informed that Damien Tours may have overnight accommodations available for selected groups or couples—not for mule-train passengers. Inquire to see if these are available.

READERS' SELECTIONS ON MOLOKAI: "The paved road to **Halawa Valley** ends at a natural parking area and turnaround where you should look for a blue Datsun 'pickup' with snack items for sale (chips, soda, shave ice, bananas, fresh pineapples). Mr. and Mrs. Dudoit, the vendors, told us that they're here daily from 8 or 9 a.m. to 6:30 p.m. However, local residents warned us that Mr. Dudoit's first love is fishing and that he works on 'Hawaiian time' (which means whenever he feels like it). . . . Our favorite gift item was the raw keawe honey produced by the **Molokai Honey Company** and available at most of the grocery stores in Kaunakakai. It, and Molokai bread from **Kanemitsu Bakery,** are also available at **Kepuhi Sundries** in the Kaluakoi Hotel, but at higher prices. . . . Be sure to try the fresh fish at Mid-Nite Inn. As a resident of Hawaii (Honolulu), I assure you that the akule and mullet (fish) served there is authentically 'island style' and very delicious" (June Honda, Honolulu, Hi.). . . . "The **Mid-Nite Inn** is as good as you said. We had a steak dinner, an ahu dinner, a side order of kim chee, Coke, coffee, and one dessert—*all* delicious—for a total of $14.04. We're going back tonight" (Pam Corwin, Olympia, Wash.)

"You can get to **Kalaupapa** by foot, on a mule, or by air. We chose air and were glad we did. We had four fascinating hours with **Richard Marks,** a fine guide. By mule the stay is only one-and-a-half hours, not nearly enough. We understand the mule trip is not all that safe, especially for us seniors. We saw some mule riders as they returned, and they looked pooped. Also, it is cheaper by air, $24 fare and $16 for the tour; it is over $50 by mule" (William S. Connell, Durham, N.H.). . . . "Our tour with Richard Marks was one of the most informative, inspiring tours we've ever taken. I would go again in a minute, only this time I would take a battery-operated tape recorder and tape what Marks had to say. What a remarkable man he is!" (Marymae H. Seaman, Lakewood, Colo.). . . . "We stayed at the **Molokai Shores Condos.** Of all the places we had stayed in the islands, this was the most pleasant. Every room has a view of the ocean. The rooms are very homey and comfortable. We found a great secluded beach with excellent snorkeling at a public beach park on the southeast end of the island. It also had barbecue grills and picnic tables. Above all, the residents really are friendly" (M.H.C., Lawai, Hi.).

"Readers should be warned that on the road going two miles northwest of Hoolehua, the two-lane paved road gets to the top of a hill and ends with an eight-inch drop and goes right into a one-lane dirt road. There is no warning as to the dead end, and there is even a painted strip in the middle of the road about 20 feet from the end. We were going about 50 mph in the rain and went off the end right into a huge, deep puddle of water and were fortunate to get out without being stuck" (Kenneth Kendall, Omaha, Nebr.).

"The **Molokai Ranch Wildlife Safari** is a great tour. The animals come right up to your van—fantastic. You can sign up for horseback riding at the Kaluakoi Hotel, even if you are not staying there. We were picked up for our ride by H. 'Nobu' Shimizu, who took us on a personal tour of the island after our horseback ride. He showed us the true aloha spirit" (Nancy Grant, South Easton, Mass.).

"Molokai is no place for swimming. Heavy surf along the north and western shores during winter months makes the beaches unswimmable except for experienced surfers. Residents claim that swimming is unsafe even in summer because of undertow and rip-tides. The local swim team has to practice off the wharf in Kaunakakai, as there is no other real swimming area. The best beach we found is **Kawakili**, the public beach on the west coast. It's spectacular, still has lots of sand, and extends back into a wooded area. Camping is permitted there weekends. Of course, swimming conditions are not good in winter (locals tell us they are better in summer), but there is a saltwater pond that seeps in behind the beach, which is clear and quiet—ideal for children and sometimes deep enough for a swim. To reach this beach, however, you must look for a small sign on the north side of the highway at about mile 12½ that says 'Beach,' and drive the narrow dirt road for about *seven miles!* Snorkeling enthusiasts coming to Molokai should also be prepared for the fact that there really isn't any of note. You can get out to the reef from the Jay Cee beach on the south shore at about mile 20 if the tide is not too low. There is also a good spot at a tiny piece of beach just over the rocks to the east of Jay Cee, where a channel through the rocks takes you to deeper water and some nice coral heads. The current there, however, is very strong." (Judy Rosen, Alexandria, Va.).

"Visit the **Big Wind Kite Factory** in Maunaloa. The charming, hospitable owners are also technical giants when it comes to explaining the aerodynamics of various styles of kites. These are not the remembered paper-and-stick creations of long ago, but modern, jet-age wonders. With kites imported from all over the world, the shop is a delight, even if just to browse. If you are fortunate, the owner may take out his 'triple-decker' stunt kites and bedazzle you with dives and twists as the kites rattle crisply in the breeze. Beware, though—it is tough not to buy at least two! . . . It is still possible to be the 'only one' on a beach in Hawaii. Take a stroll along three-mile **Popohaku Beach,** just south of the Kalua-koi Hotel. Most of the water farther along is free of coral and slopes gently to wave level— good for body surfing, but the undertow may be dangerous, so 'know your water.' Snorkel toward the east end, past the 19-mile marker at a pretty little park. Lots of coral. Very shallow, lots of interesting fish. Great for poor swimmers since it is only waist deep way out" (Jack Lindberg, San José, Calif.).

"Molokai was the highlight of our ten-day trip to Hawaii. We enjoyed the **Hotel Molokai.** The hotel gift shop, **Jo's of Molokai,** has beautiful, inexpensive clothes and souve-nirs. The hotel employees were all friendly and helpful. . . . We enjoyed shopping at **Takes,** a variety store on the main street in Kaunakakai. After returning our Datsun sta-tion wagon to **Avis,** their employee drove several miles out of her way to show us some sights we had missed. Molokai is indeed 'the friendly isle'" (Marion Montgomery, St. Paul, Minn.).

"I advise your readers to forget their budget when visiting Molokai, for if bound to the budget they would not have the experience of visiting **Kalaupapa.** I flew to the settlement on Polynesian Airways for $24. The Damien Tour costs $16. The returns from the investment will continue, for the experience was filled with love, sensitivity, and affection for a special group of proud people who ask for nothing but their dignity. I suggest that your readers read *Holy Man* by Gavin Daws, published by Harper & Row, prior to their trip. It will give them a broader insight and background" (A. Willet, Jr., Redwood City, Calif.). . . . "We found out why they call it **Mid-Nite Inn** in vol. 160, no. 2, the August 1981 issue of *National Geographic* in an excellent article, 'Molokai.' I quote: 'Art Kikukawa's restaurant, the Mid-Nite Inn, began as modestly as the bakery—with a saimin stand his mother opened. Four nights a week, departing travelers would eat the zesty noodle dish while waiting until midnight to board the inter-island steamer. Hence the name' " (Marceile Gresch, Waukesha, Wis.).

"I went **snorkeling** just south of the Kaluakoi Hotel by the golf course after 5 p.m. The water was not clear enough to see the vivid colors of the fish (which I had remembered from prior snorkeling at Hanauma Bay on Oahu), but I wanted to give it a try anyhow. What I had not counted on, however, was the unpredictable currents near the large rocks. I barely avoided being swept into them, and/or out to sea. In discussion with the locals later, I learned that such experiences are not uncommon there. A safer area would be about 20 to 22 miles east of town on the route to Halawa Valley. I rented full snorkel gear at **Molokai Fish and Dive** in downtown Kaunakakai (tel. 553-5926)" (Mr. and Mrs. Ronald Sandberg, Pleasanton, Calif.).

"If you are leaving Molokai to go back to the mainland, there is no agriculture inspector there. Consequently, you must check all your luggage to Honolulu, pick it up there and take it to the agriculture inspectors, then to your airline back to the mainland. This is a real chore as both Aloha and Hawaiian Air are miles from the main terminal and a porter costs $4 and a taxi about the same, to say nothing of the walk you have to put in! In other words, if you're doing Molokai, don't do it last before you return" (Howard S. Walker, Sequim, Wash.). . . . "We found it very difficult to locate the trail to **Moaula Falls,** and could never have done it without the help of some of the local people. The hike was definitely worthwhile, however. I made the walk down into the **Kalaupapa Settlement.** The trail is a little over three miles long, and descends about 1,600 feet over 26 switchbacks. It is a difficult, rocky trail, but if you are in good hiking condition, you will find it well worthwhile. Coming up took a little longer, but wasn't as difficult as I had imagined, when going down. The tour through the area was a fascinating experience" (Rev. H. W. Schneider, Church of St. John the Apostle, Minot, N. Dak.).

"To get to **Moaula Falls** you must go up the dirt road in front of the small green church on the left side of the river as you face the falls. The small parking lot across from the church is the best place to leave your car. As you go up the road, stay on the main road until it ends; you go by several houses on the way. A trail takes over where the road ends. Go up this trail *only* about 100 yards and you will come to a row of rocks across the trail. Turn to the right here and follow the trail down to the stream. You have to cross *both* forks of the stream here. When you get to the other side, find a trail that goes up the hill perpendicular to the stream. (When you cross a mud flat, you will see an orange mark on a tree. Here, go right through some heavy grass. When you leave the grass, look behind you as you go up the trail. If you see some more orange marks, you know you are on the trail.) Shortly you come upon a major trail that has been blocked off to the right. Turn left and now follow the white plastic pipe and white arrows marking the trail to the falls for a spectacular hike and view of the falls and the pool below. The trail by the houses and through their fields on the right side has been closed off" (Mr. and Mrs. Wayne Ditmer, Mott, N. Dak.). . . . The trail of **Moaula Falls** is not well marked and is difficult to find. My suggestion is this: the walker's trail and the horse's trail are one and the same for most of the way. When starting out, cross both forks of the stream and keep a sharp watch for hoof prints. When you find the hoof prints, you will know you are going the right way. In **Halawa Valley,** a local resident has set up a parking lot on his property. He will watch your car for a small fee" (Thomas M. Nickel, San Diego, Calif.). . . . "We were thankful to 'Johnny of the Valley' for information on how to find Moaula Falls. This incredibly interesting man who is a 'kahuna' seems to look after the park grounds. He is a philosopher and a man to be respected both for his knowledge and spirit. Perhaps other readers might meet him and be inspired by his stories" (Gwenyth Phillips, Wolfville, N.S., Canada).

And so this 23rd edition of *Hawaii on $50 a Day* is *pau*. As every writer knows, no travel book is holy writ; establishments go out of business, owners change, prices go up, quality improves or falls off. Don't become angry with establishments if their prices are higher than those quoted as we went to press; inflation is a fact of life. The book is brought up-to-date every year; be sure you are reading the latest edition available. And we will be grateful to all readers who give us their up-to-the-minute reports on the places mentioned in the book. If you've discovered something new—a hotel, a restaurant, a shop, a beach— we hope you'll share it with us and with readers of future editions of this book. Send your suggestions, comments, criticisms to us, Faye Hammel and Sylvan Levey, c/o Frommer Books, One Gulf + Western Plaza, 15th floor, New York, NY 10023. We regret that we cannot personally answer the many hundreds of letters we receive each year. You can be certain, however, that your letter is carefully noted and appreciated, and that your input is very important to us. Please note that we reserve the right to make minor editorial changes for the sake of clarity and brevity.

And now you're ready to strike out on your own, to sample for yourself the charms of what Mark Twain called "the loveliest fleet of islands anchored in any ocean." Ahead of you lies the newest, and most unique, of the United States.

Aloha!

A HAWAIIAN VOCABULARY

From AA to Wikiwiki

AS WE POINTED OUT in the introduction, there are just 12 letters in the Hawaiian alphabet: the five vowels—*a, e, i, o, u,*—and seven consonants—*h, k, l, m, n, p, w*. Every syllable ends in a vowel, every vowel is pronounced, and the accent is almost always on the next-to-the-last syllable, as it is in Spanish. Consonants receive their English sounds, but vowels get the Latin pronunciation: *a* as in farm, *e* as in they, *i* as in machine, *o* as in cold, and *u* as in tutor. Note also that when a *w* comes before the final vowel in a word, it is given the "v" sound, as in Hawaii. Purists say Ha-vye-ee for Hawaii, but most people call it Ha-wye-ee.

The following glossary will give you a pretty good idea of what the Hawaiian language sounds like. No one, of course, expects you to go around spouting phrases like "Holo ehia keia?" to ask what time it is, but a familiarity with the most important words is what distinguishes the kamaainas from the malihinis.

aa	rough lava
ai (eye)	eat
aikane (eye-kah-nay)	friend, as in "Aloha, aikane"
akamai (ah-kah-my)	smart
ala (al-lah)	road, as in Ala Moana (ocean road)
alii (ah-lee-ee)	noblemen, the old royalty of Hawaii
aloha (ah-low-hah)	welcome, farewell, love
aole (ah-oh-lay)	no
auwe (ow-way)	alas! woe!
Ewa (ehvah)	in the direction of Ewa, a town on Oahu "Drive Ewa five blocks."
hala (hah-lah)	the pandanus tree, the leaves of which are used for weaving

halakahiki
  (hah-lah-kah-hee-kee)   pineapple
hale (hah-lay)   house
hana (hah-nah)   to work
haole (how-lay)   Caucasian, white
haolekane
  (how-lay-kah-nay)   white man
haolewahine
  (how-lay-wah-hee-nay)   white woman
hapa (hah-pah)   a small part, a half
hapai (hah-pie)   pregnant, originally "to carry"

hauoli (how-oh-lee)   happiness
heiau (hey-ee-au)   ancient temple
hele (hey-lay)   to go, to walk
hiamoe (hee-ah-mow-ay)   to sleep
hilahila (hee-lah-hee-lah)   ashamed
holo (ho-low)   to run
holoholo (ho-low-ho-low)   to have fun, to relax
holoku (ho-low-koo)   formal dress with train
holomuu (ho-low-moo)   a cross between a holoku and a muumuu, long and without a train

honi (ho-nee)   to kiss, as in "Honi kaua wikiwiki!" ("Kiss me quick!")

hoomalimali
  (ho-oh-mah-lee-mah-lee)   to flatter
huhu (hoo-hoo)   angry
hui (hoo-ee)   a club, an assembly
hukilau (hoo-kee-lau)   a fishing festival
hula (hoo-lah)   a dance, to dance
imu (ee-moo)   underground oven lined with hot rocks, used for cooking the luau pig

ipo (ee-po)   sweetheart
ka (kah)   the
kai (kye)   sea
kala (kah-lah)   money
kalua (kah-loo-ah)   to bake underground
kamaaina
  (kah-mah-eye-nah)   oldtimer
kane (kah-nay)   man

kapa (kah-pah) — tapa, a bark cloth
kapakahi (kah-pah-kah-hee) — crooked
kapu (kah-poo) — forbidden, keep out
kaukau (kow-kow) — food
keiki (kay-kee) — child
kokua (ko-koo-ah) — help, cooperation
kona (ko-nah) — south
la (lah) — sun, light, day
lanai (lah-nye) — porch
lani (lah-nee) — heaven, sky
lauhala (lau-hah-lah) — leaf of the hala or pandanus tree

lei (lay) — garland
lolo (low-low) — stupid
lomilomi
  (low-mee-low-mee) — massage
luau (loo-au) — feast
mahalo (mah-hah-low) — thank you
ma'i ka'i (mah-ee kah-ee) — good, fine
makai (mah-key) — toward the sea
malihini (mah-lee-hee-nee) — stranger, newcomer
manawahi
  (mah-nah-wah-hee) — free
mauka (mau-kah) — toward the mountains
mele (may-lay) — song, chant
menehune
  (may-nay-hoo-nay) — a mysterious race who inhabited the islands before the Polynesians. Mythology claims they were pygmies.

muumuu (moo-oo-moo-oo) — loose dress, Hawaiian version of missionaries' "Mother Hubbards"

nani (nah-nee) — lovely
niu (nee-oo) — coconut
nui (noo-ee) — big, as in "mahalo nui" ("big thanks")

ono (oh-no) — sweet taste, delicious
opu (oh-poo) — belly
paakiki (pah-ah-kee-kee) — stubborn
pali (pah-lee) — precipice
paniolo (pah-nee-oh-low) — Hawaiian cowboy

pau (pow)	finished
pilikia (pee-lee-kee-ah)	trouble
poi (poy)	crushed taro root
puka (poo-kah)	hole
punee (poo-nay-ay)	couch
pupu (poo-poo)	hors d'oeuvre
pupule (poo-poo-lay)	crazy
ua (oo-ah)	rain
waha (wah-hah)	speech, mouth
wahine (wah-hee-nay)	female, woman, girl
wai (why)	fresh water
wikiwiki (wee-kee-wee-kee)	to hurry

Phrases

Be careful	**Malama pono** (mah-lah-mah po-no)
Bottoms up	**Okole maluna** (oh-ko-lay mah-loo-nah)
Come and eat	**Hele mai ai** (hey-lay-my-eye)
Come here	**Hele mai** (hey-lay my)
Come in and sit down	**Komo mai e noho iho** (ko-mo my ayno-ho-ee-ho)
For love	**No ke aloha** (no kay ah-low-hah)
Go away	**Hele aku oe** (hey-lay ah-koo oh-ay)
Good evening	**Aloha ahiahi** (ah-low-hah ah-hee-ah-hee)
Good morning	**Aloha kakahiaka** (ah-low-hah kah-kah-hee-ah-kah)
Greatest love to you	**Aloha nui oe** (ah-low-hah noo-ee oh-ay)
Happy birthday	**Hauoli la hanau** (hah-oo-oh-lee lah hah-nah-oo)
Happy New Year	**Hauoli Makahiki Hou** (hah-oo-oh-lee mah-kah-hee-kee ho-oo)

Here's to your happiness	**Hauoli maoli eo** (hah-oo-oh-lee mah-oh-lee oh-ay)
How are you?	**Pehea oe?** (pay-hay-ah oh-ay)
I am fine	**Ma'i ka'i** (mah-ee kah-ee)
I am sorry	**Ua kaumaha au** (oo-ah cow-mah-hah ow)
I have enough	**Ua lawa au** (oo-ah lah-wah ow)
I love you	**Aloha wau ia oe** (ah-low-hah vow ee-ah oh-ay)
It isn't so	**Aole pela** (ah-oh-lay pay-lah)
Let's go	**E hele kaua** (au hey-lay cow-ah)
Many thanks	**Mahalo nui loa** (mah-hah-low noo-ee low-ah)
Merry Christmas	**Mele Kalikimaka** (may-lay kah-lee-kee-mah-kah)
Much love	**Aloha nui loa** (ah-low-hah noo-ee low-ah)
No trouble	**Aole pilikia** (ah-oh-lay pee-lee-kee-ah)
What is your name?	**Owai kau inoa?** (oh-why kah-oo ee-no-ah)

AND THEN THERE'S PIDGIN: Despite the earnest efforts of educators to stamp it out, pidgin, that code language of the islands, continues its not-so-underground existence. The Chinese developed it in their first contacts with English-speaking people, but you'll hear it spoken today by all the racial groups, from haoles to Hawaiians. Beachboys, cab drivers, university students, a few who don't know better and a lot who do, all occasionally descend into pidgin. Although its subtleties are unintelligible to the newcomer (that's part of the idea), you'll be able to pick up a few words: *wasamala, wasetime, lesgo, da kine.*

You'll hear all kinds of theories about the indestructibility of pidgin. Some sociological types feel it's a subtle form of rebellion by the dispossessed Hawaiian, not unlike the jargon of mainland blacks. The psychological types call it more of an adolescent code, a desire for teenagers to have their own language. Others say it's just plain bad English. Take your choice, whatever *da kine* reason, pidgin is "in" in Hawaii.

· *Note:* After you've been in the islands a bit, get yourself a copy of Peppo's *Pidgin to Da Max.* It's one of Hawaii's most popular humor-cartoon books (over 130,000 copies in print), available in any book store, and an absolute hoot! We reprint the "Word of Caution to the Non-local: If you don't already speak pidgin, you might need some help from local friends to understand this book. Remember: *Pidgin to Da Max* is not a tourist guide to pidgin. So don't try to speak it after reading this book. You'll just get into trouble." We agree. Don't try to speak pidgin. Just read the book—maybe on the plane trip back home—and try to keep yourself from rolling in the aisles. It's $4.95, published by Bess Press, Honolulu. There is in fact, a whole series of Peppo's Pidgin books now, another one of which is *Fax to Da Max,* which lists "Everything You Never Knew You Wanted to Know About Hawaii," plus lots of "useless fax," too. Another howler.

NOW, SAVE MONEY ON ALL YOUR TRAVELS!
Join Arthur Frommer's $25-A-Day Travel Club™

Saving money while traveling is never a simple matter, which is why, over 25 years ago, the **$25-A-Day Travel Club** was formed. Actually, the idea came from readers of the Arthur Frommer Publications who felt that such an organization could bring financial benefits, continuing travel information, and a sense of community to economy-minded travelers all over the world.

In keeping with the money-saving concept, the annual membership fee is low—$18 (U.S. residents) or $20 U.S. (Canadian, Mexican, and foreign residents)—and is immediately exceeded by the value of your benefits which include:

(1) The latest edition of any TWO of the books listed on the following pages.

(2) An annual subscription to an 8-page quarterly newspaper *The Wonderful World of Budget Travel* which keeps you up-to-date on fastbreaking developments in low-cost travel in all parts of the world—bringing you the kind of information you'd have to pay over $25 a year to obtain elsewhere. This consumer-conscious publication also includes the following columns:

Hospitality Exchange—members all over the world who are willing to provide hospitality to other members as they pass through their home cities.

Share-a-Trip—requests from members for travel companions who can share costs and help avoid the burdensome single supplement.

Readers Ask . . . Readers Reply—travel questions from members to which other members reply with authentic firsthand information.

(3) A copy of *Arthur Frommer's Guide to New York*.

(4) Your personal membership card which entitles you to purchase through the Club all Arthur Frommer Publications for a third to a half off their regular retail prices during the term of your membership.

So why not join this hardy band of international budgeteers NOW and participate in its exchange of information and hospitality? Simply send $18 (U.S. residents) or $20 U.S. (Canadian, Mexican, and other foreign residents) along with your name and address to: $25-A-Day Travel Club, Inc., Gulf + Western Building, One Gulf + Western Plaza, New York, NY 10023. Remember to specify which *two* of the books in section (1) above you wish to receive in your initial package of member's benefits. Or tear out the next page, check off any two of the books listed on either side, and send it to us with your membership fee.

Date_____

**FROMMER BOOKS
PRENTICE HALL PRESS
ONE GULF + WESTERN PLAZA
NEW YORK, NY 10023**

Friends:

Please send me the books checked below:

FROMMER'S $-A-DAY GUIDES™

(In-depth guides to sightseeing and low-cost tourist accommodations and facilities.)

☐ Europe on $25 a Day $12.95
☐ Australia on $25 a Day $10.95
☐ Eastern Europe on $25 a Day $10.95
☐ England on $35 a Day.............. $10.95
☐ Greece on $25 a Day............... $10.95
☐ Hawaii on $50 a Day............... $10.95
☐ India on $15 & $25 a Day........... $9.95
☐ Ireland on $30 a Day............... $10.95
☐ Israel on $30 & $35 a Day $10.95
☐ Mexico on $20 a Day $10.95

☐ New Zealand on $25 a Day $10.95
☐ New York on $45 a Day............. $9.95
☐ Scandinavia on $50 a Day........... $10.95
☐ Scotland and Wales on $35 a Day..... $10.95
☐ South America on $30 a Day $10.95
☐ Spain and Morocco (plus the Canary
   Is.) on $40 a Day $10.95
☐ Turkey on $25 a Day $10.95
☐ Washington, D.C., on $40 a Day $10.95

FROMMER'S DOLLARWISE GUIDES™

(Guides to sightseeing and tourist accommodations and facilities from budget to deluxe, with emphasis on the medium-priced.)

☐ Alaska $12.95
☐ Austria & Hungary $11.95
☐ Belgium, Holland, Luxembourg $11.95
☐ Egypt............................. $11.95
☐ England & Scotland $11.95
☐ France............................ $11.95
☐ Germany.......................... $11.95
☐ Italy.............................. $11.95
☐ Japan & Hong Kong $12.95
☐ Portugal (incl. Madeira & the Azores) . $11.95
☐ South Pacific...................... $12.95
☐ Switzerland & Liechtenstein $11.95
☐ Bermuda & The Bahamas............ $10.95
☐ Canada $12.95
☐ Caribbean $12.95

☐ Cruises (incl. Alaska, Carib, Mex,
   Hawaii, Panama, Canada, & US) $12.95
☐ California & Las Vegas $11.95
☐ Florida........................... $10.95
☐ Mid-Atlantic States $12.95
☐ New England...................... $11.95
☐ New York State $11.95
☐ Northwest........................ $11.95
☐ Skiing in Europe $12.95
☐ Skiing USA—East $10.95
☐ Skiing USA—West $10.95
☐ Southeast & New Orleans............ $11.95
☐ Southwest........................ $11.95
☐ Texas............................ $11.95

TURN PAGE FOR ADDITIONAL BOOKS AND ORDER FORM.

It's 2 am.
It's far from home.
It's more than
a tummyache.

**American Express Cardmembers can get
emergency medical and legal referrals, worldwide.
Simply by calling Global Assist.℠**

What if it really is more than a tummyache?
What if your back goes out? What if you get into a
legal fix?

Call Global Assist – a new emergency referral
service for the exclusive use of American Express
Cardmembers. Just call. Toll-free. 24 hours a day.
Every day. Virtually anywhere in the world.

Your call helps find a doctor, lawyer, dentist,
optician, chiropractor, nurse, pharmacist, or an
interpreter.

All this costs nothing, except for the medical
and legal bills you would normally expect to pay.

Global Assist. One more reason to have the American Express®
Card. Or, to get one.

 For an application,
call 1-800-THE-CARD.

Don't leave home without it.®